# A Critical Companion to Old Norse Literary Genre

# Studies in Old Norse Literature

Print ISSN 2514-0701
Online ISSN 2514-071X

*Series Editors*
Professor Sif Rikhardsdottir
Professor Carolyne Larrington

*Studies in Old Norse Literature* aims to provide a forum for monographs and collections engaging with the literature produced in medieval Scandinavia, one of the largest surviving bodies of medieval European literature. The series investigates poetry and prose alongside translated, religious and learned material; although the primary focus is on Old Norse-Icelandic literature, studies which make comparison with other medieval literatures or which take a broadly interdisciplinary approach by addressing the historical and archaeological contexts of literary texts are also welcomed. It offers opportunities to publish a wide range of books, whether cutting-edge, theoretically informed writing, provocative revisionist approaches to established conceptualizations, or strong, traditional studies of previously neglected aspects of the field. The series will enable researchers to communicate their findings both beyond and within the academic community of medievalists, highlighting the growing interest in Old Norse-Icelandic literary culture.

Proposals or queries should be sent in the first instance to the editors or to the publisher, at the addresses given below.

Professor Sif Rikhardsdottir, University of Iceland, sifr@hi.is

Professor Carolyne Larrington, St John's College, Oxford University, carolyne.larrington@sjc.ox.ac.uk

Boydell & Brewer, editorial@boydellandbrewer.com

Previous volumes in the series are listed at the end of the volume.

# A CRITICAL COMPANION TO OLD NORSE LITERARY GENRE

Edited by
*Massimiliano Bampi*
*Carolyne Larrington*
*Sif Rikhardsdottir*

D. S. BREWER

© Contributors 2020

*All Rights Reserved.* Except as permitted under current legislation
no part of this work may be photocopied, stored in a retrieval system,
published, performed in public, adapted, broadcast,
transmitted, recorded or reproduced in any form or by any means,
without the prior permission of the copyright owner

First published 2020
D. S. Brewer, Cambridge
Paperback edition 2026

ISBN 978 1 84384 564 5 hardback
ISBN 978 1 84384 765 6 paperback

D. S. Brewer is an imprint of Boydell & Brewer Ltd
and of Boydell & Brewer Inc.
website: www.boydellandbrewer.com

Our Authorised Representative for product safety in the EU is
Easy Access System Europe - Mustamäe tee 50, 10621 Tallinn, Estonia,
gpsr.requests@easproject.com

A catalogue record for this book is available
from the British Library

The publisher has no responsibility for the continued existence or
accuracy of URLs for external or third-party internet websites referred to in
this book, and does not guarantee that any content on such websites is, or
will remain, accurate or appropriate

# CONTENTS

| | |
|---|---|
| List of Figures | vii |
| List of Contributors | ix |
| Acknowledgements | xi |
| List of Abbreviations | xiii |

Introduction
 *Massimiliano Bampi and Sif Rikhardsdottir* … 1

## I THEORY

Genre
 *Massimiliano Bampi* … 15
Hybridity
 *Sif Rikhardsdottir* … 31
Terminology
 *Lukas Rösli* … 47
Form
 *Mikael Males* … 61
Orality, Textuality and Performance
 *Judy Quinn* … 73
Manuscripts and Codicology
 *Jóhanna Katrín Friðriksdóttir* … 89

## II THEMES

The Body Politic
 *Hans Jacob Orning* … 115
Geography
 *Dale Kedwards* … 127
Time and Space
 *Torfi H. Tulinius* … 145
Memory
 *Pernille Hermann* … 161
The Human Condition
 *Stefanie Gropper* … 177
God(s)
 *Carolyne Larrington* … 193
Wisdom
 *Brittany Schorn* … 211

## III GENRE IN FOCUS

Skaldic Poetry – A Case Study: The Poetry of Torf-Einarr
Rǫgnvaldsson of Orkney
    *Erin Michelle Goeres*      229
Eddic Poetry – A Case Study: *Sólarljóð*
    *Carolyne Larrington*      245
Þættir – A Case Study: *Stjörnu-Odda draumr*
    *Elizabeth Ashman Rowe*      259
Íslendingasǫgur – A Case Study: *Vatnsdœla saga*
    *Russell Poole*      271
Byskupasögur and *heilagra manna sögur* – A Case Study
    *Kevin J. Wanner*      283
Romance – A Case Study
    *Jürg Glauser*      299

Annotated Taxonomy of Genres      313
Select Timeline      323

*Works Cited*      325
*Index*      359

# LIST OF FIGURES

Figure 1: A fragment of *Laxdæla saga*. AM 162 D 2 fol., c. 1250–1300. 1r. By permission of the Árni Magnússon Institute for Icelandic Studies.     93

Figure 2: A page from *Brennu-Njáls saga* in Þormóðsbók. AM 162 B δ fol., c. 1290–1310. 13v. By permission of the Árni Magnússon Institute for Icelandic Studies.     94

Figure 3: The beginning of *Bandamannasaga* in Möðruvallabók. AM 132 fol., mid-fourteenth century. 114r. By permission of the Árni Magnússon Institute for Icelandic Studies.     97

Figure 4: A page from *Þórðar saga hreðu* in the so-called, Pseudo-Vatnshyrna, a fragmentary manuscript. AM 564 a 4$^{to}$, ca. 1400. 3r By permission of the Árni Magnússon Institute for Icelandic Studies.     98

Figure 5: A page from *Lokrur*, late medieval *rímur*, in Staðarhólsbók. AM 604 g 4$^{to}$, mid-sixteenth century. 18r. By permission of the Árni Magnússon Institute for Icelandic Studies.     104

Figure 6: A page from *Lokasenna*, an eddic poem, in the Codex Regius of eddic poetry. GKS 2365 4$^{to}$, c. 1270. 15r. By permission of the Árni Magnússon Institute for Icelandic Studies.     105

Chart 1: Sagas categorized by degree of Contingency versus Contrivance
(Chapter 18)     290

The editors, contributors and publisher are grateful to all the institutions and persons listed for permission to reproduce the materials in which they hold copyright. Every effort has been made to trace the copyright holders; apologies are offered for any omission, and the publisher will be pleased to add any necessary acknowledgement in subsequent editions.

# CONTRIBUTORS

MASSIMILIANO BAMPI is Associate Professor of Germanic Philology at Ca' Foscari University of Venice.

JÓHANNA KATRÍN FRIÐRIKSDÓTTIR has been a Lecturer at Yale University. She currently holds a post at the National Library in Oslo

JÜRG GLAUSER is emeritus Professor of Nordic Philology at the University of Zürich and the University of Basel.

ERIN MICHELLE GOERES is Associate Professor of Old Norse Language and Literature and Head of the Department of Scandinavian Studies, University College, London.

STEFANIE GROPPER is Professor of Scandinavian Studies at the University of Tübingen.

PERNILLE HERMANN is Associate Professor of Scandinavian Languages and Literature at Aarhus University.

DALE KEDWARDS is a postdoctoral researcher at the Vigdís Finnbogadóttir Institute at the University of Iceland, the National Museum of Iceland and the Museum of National History at Frederiksborg Castle, funded by the Carlsberg Foundation.

CAROLYNE LARRINGTON is Professor of Medieval European Literature at Oxford University and Official Fellow in Medieval English Literature at St John's College, Oxford.

MIKAEL MALES is Associate Professor of Old Norse Philology at the University of Oslo.

HANS JACOB ORNING is Professor of Medieval History at Department of Archaeology, Conservation and History at the University of Oslo.

RUSSELL POOLE is Distinguished University Professor emeritus of English at the University of Western Ontario.

JUDY QUINN is Reader in Old Norse Literature in the Department of Anglo-Saxon, Norse and Celtic at Cambridge University.

SIF RIKHARDSDOTTIR is Professor of Comparative Literature at the University of Iceland and Vice-Chair of the Institute for Research in Literature and Visual Arts.

*Contributors*

LUKAS RÖSLI is Junior Professor of Scandinavian Languages and Literature/ Medieval Studies at the Department of Northern European Studies at the Humboldt-Universität zu Berlin.

ELIZABETH ASHMAN ROWE is Reader in Scandinavian History in the Department of Anglo-Saxon, Norse and Celtic at the University of Cambridge.

BRITTANY SCHORN is a Research Associate in the Department of Anglo-Saxon, Norse and Celtic at the University of Cambridge

TORFI H. TULINIUS is Professor of Medieval Icelandic Studies at the School of Humanities of the University of Iceland.

KEVIN J. WANNER is Professor of Comparative Religion and an affiliated faculty member of the Medieval Institute at Western Michigan University.

# ACKNOWLEDGEMENTS

Various people and institutions have played an important role in bringing this project to fruition. The editors wish to thank Caroline Palmer and Boydell and Brewer for their enthusiasm for this Critical Companion from the moment the project was mooted up to and after publication, and the colleague who acted as anonymous reader for the proposal and final version. Particular thanks to Sarah Thomas and Bonnie McGill for their eagle-eyed work at the copy-editing and proof-reading stages. We would also like to thank the contributors who not only wrote their chapters in a timely way, but also took part in a lively and informative workshop held at Ca' Foscari University in Venice in the spring of 2018, supported by the Swedish Riksbanken Foundation. Further thanks must go to Ca' Foscari University for other financial support, St John's College, University of Oxford for funding and hosting an editorial meeting and the University of Iceland for granting a sabbatical to one of the editors. We are also grateful to Felix Taylor for his useful editorial work and his compilation of the Bibliography and to Íris Ríkharðsdóttir who took the photo for the cover image and the design team at Boydell and Brewer for their lovely design. We extend our warmest thanks to the Árni Magnússon Institute for Icelandic Studies for the permission to utilise images of manuscripts in their holding in the volume and to the National and University Library of Iceland for the permission to utilise an image of the title page of the manuscript Lbs 203 fol. on the book cover.

# ABBREVIATIONS

| | |
|---|---|
| *ANF* | *Arkiv för nordisk filologi* |
| *ÍF* | Íslenzk fornrit |
| *JEGP* | *Journal of English and Germanic Philology* |
| *OED* | *Oxford English Dictionary* |
| *SS* | *Scandinavian Studies* |
| *SBVS* | *Saga-Book of the Viking Society* |
| *SkP* | *Skaldic Poetry of the Middle Ages* |
| *VMS* | *Viking and Medieval Scandinavia* |

# Introduction
*Massimiliano Bampi and Sif Rikhardsdottir*

Literary works from all time periods are read, studied and classified by way of generic definitions that are either more or less explicitly codified within the culture to which they belong or must be (re)constructed *a posteriori*. In either case, the importance of the notion of genre – understood both as a set of formal and stylistic conventions for composing all kinds of literature and as a hermeneutic instrument for analysing literary works and their semantic potential – is hardly disputable. Defining the relevant genre of a literary work is indeed the starting point of any critical work, whether aimed at historical contextualisation or the critical analysis of its stylistic aspects or narrative structures. The relevance of the question of genre goes far beyond what may at first appear mainly as a nominalistic modern preoccupation, for it has a bearing on how modern readers approach literary works and seek to interpret them as historically determined artefacts. The study of Old Norse literature is of course no exception. The broad corpus of texts that have been preserved to our day in an astonishingly large number of medieval and post-medieval manuscripts is quite varied and heterogeneous in terms of style, structure, content and mode, thus bearing witness to the vitality and richness of Old Norse literary expression throughout the medieval period.

The problem of the definition of genre has inevitably attracted sporadic attention from the very beginning of philological and literary studies in the nineteenth century, when the first editions of Old Norse works were made available. Over the last forty years, though, there has been renewed interest within Old Norse scholarship in studying genres in medieval Icelandic literature, especially with regard to the classification of sagas. Much scholarly effort has indeed been expended on discussing whether it is appropriate to categorise the surviving saga corpus using a taxonomy established in the nineteenth and twentieth centuries. Although some genre names, i.e. *riddarasögur* (chivalric sagas) and *konungasögur* (kings' sagas), are attested in the Middle Ages, the current labels are largely modern constructs. Scholarly opinions about genre classification fall broadly into two major categories: on the one side are those who accept the current taxonomy as a modern categorical convenience, and on the other those who argue that the classification system is too rigid and that it therefore provides a misleading foundation for the understanding of the highly diverse forms and structures of saga literature and, indeed, of other kinds of Old Norse-Icelandic texts.

However, this debate seems now to have reached a dead end. The current stalemate is mainly determined by the fact that research on genre has been conducted by individual scholars investigating disparate aspects of the saga corpus and thus focusing almost exclusively on the literary implications of generic definitions. Even more importantly, the dominant interest in the saga corpus has somewhat overshadowed other relevant aspects of the issue of genre classification. The interaction of prose with poetry, the functions of different poetic modes and subgenres, the sustainability of the eddic/skaldic distinction in poetry, the range of genres made available through the assimilation of European and learned models and the implications of integrating Old Swedish and Old Danish texts into genre study are indeed only some of the major questions that still await systematic analysis. To this end, this volume seeks to approach the question of genre in Old Norse literature from a variety of perspectives that incorporate, or at least draw attention to, some of the abovementioned research questions. The study of how literary genres arise, interact and intersect with one another across time contributes to a better understanding of the development not only of the literary system but also of the complex dynamics operating within society as it changed over time. Most importantly, the development of vernacular literature in medieval Scandinavia is influenced by, and interacted with, the literatures and languages of the rest of Europe; the native genre system adapted, mutated and subdivided in response to the new influences.

The impressive investment of resources in the recording of texts attested by the number of manuscripts preserving literary works of different kinds clearly indicates that literature played a major role in medieval Icelandic society, both as a source of entertainment and as a tool meant to serve a variety of different purposes. With the introduction of Christianity, in the early eleventh century, the technology of writing using the Latin alphabet provided medieval Icelanders with a powerful instrument for committing texts to parchment, thus bringing about a major change in the modes of transmission of knowledge across space and time. The same holds true for the Nordic region at large. Writing became by far the most important way of spreading and perpetuating literary works and the various forms of knowledge that they conveyed. Nevertheless, oral transmission and oral composition continued to play a central role. For example, oral traditions influenced the written texts produced by literate people. Moreover, even if a work existed in written form, it was most typically recited orally before an audience.[1] Indeed, lit-

1   For further information on orality and the performative aspect of medieval textuality see Chapter 5 in this volume.

eracy was by and large restricted to a small section of society. In Iceland, a diffuse range of chieftains' farms, monasteries and episcopal seats were the cultural centres at which the elite was educated, works were composed and manuscripts were produced. The heterogeneity of these centres of learning, which served both secular and religious aims and interests, fostered the composition and dissemination of literary works of various kinds, both in verse and prose. As Preben Meulengracht Sørensen points out,

> [a] large proportion of manuscript codices were written at the initiative of private individuals and were the product of the large farms, where they were read aloud to the members of the household, which included men, women and children, the head of the household and his wife, servants and guests, the learned and the laity.[2]

In Norway, Denmark and Sweden, conditions differed slightly by virtue of the existence of the royal and aristocratic courts and associated courtly culture. These provided a venue for the production and dissemination of literary material, particularly in the thirteenth, fourteenth and fifteenth centuries.[3] Norway and Iceland were indeed closely aligned in the commissioning, writing and production of textual materials – until the early fifteenth century at least – due to linguistic and cultural affinities. Denmark and Sweden, on the other hand, developed their own literature in the vernacular (East Norse) at a later stage. This later literary development is directly correlated with the strengthening of the royal courts and aristocratic associations across the region in the fourteenth and fifteenth centuries.

Across both the West and the East Nordic region then, literature was largely experienced and enjoyed as part of a social ritual that was meant to create political or social cohesion through entertainment and/ or literary propaganda. Additionally, literary production and promotion contributed towards shaping a shared identity within the community by using texts as means of cultivating a common view of the present based on a shared view of the past – whether monastic, royal or in terms of local political affairs and conflicts. As generators of cultural memory, the various genres were thus used as tools to construct an image of the past, and consequently they engendered a polyphonic discourse on the relationship between the present, as the time of writing, and the segments of the historical continuum prior to it. Literary genres were also

2   Preben Meulengracht Sørensen, 'Social Institutions and Belief Systems of Medieval Iceland (c. 870–1400) and their Relations to Literary Production', in *Old Icelandic Literature and Society*, ed. Margaret Clunies Ross, Cambridge Studies in Medieval Literature 42 (Cambridge, 2000), pp. 8–29, at p. 25.
3   For a discussion of the political context that shaped literary production, particularly in Norway, see Chapter 7 in this volume.

bearers of ideology and mirrors of social preoccupations, and as such they projected the world-view and the anxieties of the social groups that promoted the production of literature and who also used it to legitimise their positions in the social arena and their ambitions to power. Therefore, the study of genre that this volume aims to promote represents an avenue of research that can provide wide-ranging insights into the functioning of literature within society and the role of social dynamics in the development of the Old Norse literary system throughout the medieval period.

This socio-political aspect of genre research is no less applicable to the later stages of literary reception and circulation and to modern consumption and promotion of particular literary genres. It is an uncontroversial fact that some genres – especially within the saga corpus – became canonised during the course of the twentieth century, primarily as a consequence of an ideologically oriented view of their respective aesthetic and cultural values. Even within the most praised and acclaimed genres (e.g. *Íslendingasögur* or the sagas of Icelanders), some texts have long been considered as a sort of gold standard against which the quality of other works, attributed to the same genre – as well as other related genres as a matter of fact - should be measured and assessed. As is widely known, this led to a hierarchisation of genres and works in the twentieth century that has resulted in some genres being marginalised and neglected. For example, the *fornaldarsögur* (legendary sagas) and the *riddarasögur* were dismissed as symptomatic of the decline of Old Icelandic saga literature after the golden age. For similar reasons, any kind of literary work produced in the fourteenth and fifteenth centuries has attracted far less attention than the monuments representing, according to this view, the heyday of Icelandic literary craftmanship, i.e. the time prior to the annexation of Iceland to Norway in the years 1262–64.

Some of the distorted views arguing for this kind of retrospective hierarchisation are by now largely dismissed as inappropriate and misleading; they have given way to a descriptive rather than a prescriptive approach and a more balanced attitude in recent scholarship. Yet the tendency towards considering some genres, or their later developments, as less interesting is still present. Thus, for example, the younger sagas of Icelanders (such as *Finnboga saga ramma* and *Bárðar saga Snæfellsáss*), hybrid texts combining different generic repertoires (such as *Kjalnesinga saga* and *Kirialax saga*), or the *rímur* (rhymed verse) frequently remain on the margins of the discourse on literary genres and their role in late medieval Icelandic society. What all these examples have in common, however, is that they are the product of the growing complexity, in terms of generic options, of the Old Norse literary system. The combination of sources and various generic forms within a single work can only be understood as a result of a conscious play with conventions.

*Introduction*

While the critical concept of genre is a modern invention, medieval Norse authors and audiences seem nevertheless to have been well aware of many of the generic distinctions or qualifications that their modern counterparts have used to categorise and classify works into particular groups depending on their form, style, content, functionality, themes, or various other denominators. Certain tropes, styles, or topics would have dictated how new works would have been formulated and the audience in turn would have understood that those qualities determined what they were to expect. Those parameters thus sustain what later become known as generic categories, although such categories are always posterior to the literary creations themselves and seek to classify a vague and often undetermined process that is usually much more flexible and non-conformist than the system itself tends to be.

The assembly of generically affiliated work into manuscript compilations suggests that Norse patrons, collectors, or scribes would have considered such works to be related, whether due to their form, their functionality, or their narrative content. The noted manuscript Möðruvallabók, AM 132 fol., features a collection of the so-called *Íslendingasögur* revealing that whoever compiled the manuscript considered the texts to be interrelated or to belong together by virtue of their content, stylistic features, or narrative goal.[4] Yet, as Jóhanna Katrín Friðriksdóttir points out in her chapter, such compilations are largely outnumbered by others that are generically variable. In fact, many medieval manuscripts seem deliberately compiled to feature generic versatility, not for the sake of generic variety, but precisely because they include different materials that have different functions, both within the compilations and presumably for their patrons. Manuscript compilations such as AM 471 4$^{to}$ in the Árni Magnússon Institute for Icelandic Studies contains a collection of *Íslendingasögur*, the so-called *fornaldarsögur* and indigenous romances. Others preserve collections that seem arranged with a specific purpose or goal in mind, such as AM 226 fol. from the mid-fourteenth century which presents a collection of historical materials stemming from the Old Testament (*Stjórn*) along with translations from Latin historiography featuring the Exodus, classical Roman history, the stories of the Jews and of Alexander the Great.

Many of the later compilations of medieval materials comprise an assortment of narratives that are combined by virtue of their functionality (or their derivative function for later audiences and readers), such as the late seventeenth-century JS 27 fol. in the National and University Library in Iceland. This features a collection of translated and indigenous romances

---

4   Admittedly, the manuscript in its present form is likely to have been bound together later than it was written. Yet the uniform layout of the quires may suggest that they formed part of a collection, whether or not intended for a single manuscript (see further in Chapter 6 and Michael Chesnutt, 'On the Structure, Format, and Preservation of Möðruvallabók', *Gripla* 21 (2010), 147–67).

and *fornaldarsögur* collected specifically for their narrative content and for the intended rationale of *skemmtunnar* (entertainment) for its recipients.⁵ Some are even more explicit in their objectives. The early eighteenth-century JS 8 fol. purports to be a

> Thesaurus historicus eður sagnafésjóður útlenskra þjóða forkunnar fróðlegur ... þeim til skemmtunar og fróðleiks er þess háttar fornar sögur heyra vilja
>
> [a historical thesaurus or a collection of stories from foreign nations of great interest ... for entertainment and information for those that are interested in hearing such old tales].⁶

The manuscript evidence thus suggests that while generic categories are modern inventions, medieval authors and compilers had a notion of generic classifications – although these would most likely have differed from our current ones.

The appearance of some of the currently used generic classifications in medieval manuscripts indicates that, at the very least, those specific generic classifications were already in existence and indicate the acceptance of and utilisation of such categories to classify works. As Lukas Rösli notes in his chapter on terminology, the generic term 'konunga sögur' can already be found in an early fourteenth-century manuscript, Holm perg 7 4$^{to}$ in the Stockholm Royal Library, although its usage might simply imply a qualification of the content, i.e. 'sagas of kings' and thus indicate a method of classification based on content rather than necessarily an established generic categorisation.⁷ The same can be said to apply to the term *riddarasögur*. Yet even so, their usage in the Middle Ages does suggest that medieval scribes or collectors were aware of or made use of such distinctions, although they may have been more fluid than they are today and certainly would have been less systematised in terms of their classificatory purposes. Moreover, they may merely have been indicative of a propensity to group together materials based on their presumed content (as per stories of kings or stories of knights), whereas content is only one of many generic markers of modern-day genre theory.

The term *háttr* (mode), attested in the *Prose Edda*, suggests again a generic, or semi-generic, qualification, this time based on form.⁸ The

---

5  JS 27 fol. in the National and University Library of Iceland, title page.
6  JS 8 fol. in the National and University Library of Iceland, title page. According to the title page the manuscript is supposed to have been written by Bjarni Pétursson at Skarð in Skarðströnd in 1729.
7  See also Massimiliano Bampi, 'Genre', in *The Routledge Research Companion to the Medieval Icelandic Sagas*, ed. Ármann Jakobsson and Sverrir Jakobsson (London and New York, 2017), pp. 4–14, at pp. 5–6.
8  See Margaret Clunies Ross, who considers the Old Norse term *háttr* to refer

usage in the *Prose Edda* would seem to indicate a division into various different metrical forms, thereby indicating a fundamental separation between prose and poetry, with the latter qualified by different *hættir* (modes or verse-forms). Unlike the previously discussed terms that seem to focus on content as classificatory indicators, *háttr* thus signals an awareness of and attention to the form of literary or poetic creations and the clear stipulations that dictated the form and shape of the various poetical modes available to Old Norse authors. Such formal qualifications distinguish medieval Norse poetic modes from prose, which seems to have been significantly more pliable in terms of generic fluidity and hybridity. The translations of Chrétien de Troyes' rhyming eight-syllable couplets into prose form in the mid-thirteenth century suggests that the particular *háttr* of Chrétien's romances may not have been relevant to its translator or the audience for which they were intended, thereby shifting the focus from the particular mode or form back to its content or the text's presumed functionality.[9]

Admittedly, the existing metrical forms were singularly unsuited to the long line couplets of Chrétien. Yet, as Geoffrey Chaucer's translations from French and Italian into novel Middle English metrical forms reveal, authors were well capable of adapting and modifying metrical forms to create alternative or new modes of conveying their material. Within the larger Nordic context, the three translations known as *Eufemiavisor* provide another example. Unlike the Old Norse prose translations, the *Eufemiavisor* are composed in *knittelvers*, a metrical form imported from Germany and consisting of rhymed couplets with four-stressed syllables per line. The *knittelvers* gives evidence for a multimodal transmission, i.e. the transition from Chrétien's octosyllabic couplets into Old Norse prose form and then into the East Norse verse-form (in turn based on a German model) or, alternatively, from Old French verse directly into a different metrical form in Old Swedish.[10] This shift between modes signals a malleable approach to generic forms, where modern generic classificatory categories are secondary to the material's specific functionality; this in turn dictated both form and classification into content-oriented groups or manuscript collections.

In this volume we will be using mode to indicate the division into metrical forms and prose. We will therefore be referring to the skaldic mode, for instance, whereas the *Íslendingasögur* would qualify as a genre.

---

specifically to verse-form or metre in *Skáldskaparmál: Snorri Sturluson's ars poetica and Medieval Theories of Language*, The Viking Collection 4 (Odense, 1987), p. 22. See also Kristján Árnason, 'Um *Háttatal* Snorra Sturlusonar: Bragform og braglýsing', *Gripla* 17 (2006), 75–125, at pp. 82–83, and the chapter on 'Form' in this volume.

9  For further information see Chapter 2 on hybridity.
10  The *knittelvers* remained in vogue in the post-medieval period, appearing for instance in the plays of Henrik Ibsen and the works of August Strindberg.

Texts written in prosimetrum can thus fall into various generic categories, while they exhibit also both modes, i.e. prose and verse. While we utilise existing generic categories – as well as the qualifier of 'genre' itself – there is no intention to argue for the validity of such categories or for categorisation in general. The point of the volume is to interrogate the term 'genre', its applicability to Nordic literary materials, its usefulness, its inherent complexities and the relevance of both medieval and modern generic classifications to our understanding of the Old Norse literary heritage. As stated above, given the fact that scholars habitually utilise generic categories in discussions of Old Norse literary production (and in literary criticism generally speaking, whether medieval or modern) – frequently with a caveat regarding their adaptability or legitimacy – the book is intended to engage with the concept of genre as it relates to Old Norse literature in a more in-depth, nuanced and multi-focused way.

The various chapters exhibit the often tangled and contradictory attitude towards genre as a concept. The variety of approaches signals the complexity of generic classifications and the problematic bridging of the gap between medieval literary productivity and modern literary consumption. As stated earlier, latter-day canonisation of certain generic groupings (and the canonisation of certain texts as prototypical of certain generic groupings) based on historically determined ideological systems, political aspirations or standardised curricula in the educational system, have distorted our perception of Norse literary history. This volume makes no effort to address the validity of such historicised predilections for specific genres or categorisations, rather it seeks to foreground the various factors at play in generic classifications and what these may tell us about Old Norse literature.

This book therefore does not seek to offer a coherent theory of genre as such. Rather, each chapter aims to explore the common theme from a given perspective. The chapters differ in terms of how inclusive (or exclusive) they are in their approaches, what meets the criteria of a genre or a subgenre, and in their perception and definition of generic qualifications or determinants. Certain terms reappear throughout the volume: the term 'generic marker' signals the traits or characteristics that can be (and are) used to define a certain genre. The expression 'generic repertoire' indicates the assortment of features that authors would have drawn on (or could have drawn on) to situate their work within a particular generic context, whether intentionally or unintentionally. The term 'chronotope' derives from Mikhail Bakhtin and is intended to signal spatial and temporal indicators – a major factor in Old Norse generic categorisations.[11] Finally, 'hybridity' intimates the fluidity of generic qualifiers as they are moulded, adapted or shifted in the process of literary creation. Genres are

---

11 See Torfi H. Tulinius's discussion of the chronotope in Chapter 9.

## Introduction

neither stable nor predetermined. Generic realisation is always a process that includes initially a certain degree of creativity combined, first, with an unrealised sense of generic parameters and subsequently, at least in some cases, a conscious notion of genre. By the time the generic framework has become established, many literary works being created under the auspices of the genre in question will already be defying those parameters, thereby shifting (and sometimes eradicating) the generic markers or repertoires; this process results in the creation of hybrid works or, in certain cases, in the formation of novel genres or subgenres.

The volume is divided into three sections: Theory, Themes, and Genre in Focus. The first section, Theory, approaches the critical concept of genre from multiple perspectives, addressing the validity of the term as a historicised critical concept and offering some means of theorising 'genre' within Old Norse studies. The second section, Themes, takes a different approach to genre, using as its starting point the generic markers and repertoires that often define Old Norse literary genres. The section presents topics or themes that are cross-generic, yet whose treatment can be said to demonstrate generic conformity or specificity. The third section, Genre in Focus, presents case-studies of several of the conventional Norse genres, such as eddic poetry, *Íslendingasögur*, and romance. The chapters here present focused case-studies of either a specific genre, or selected works within that genre with the intention of qualifying generic categorisations and their validity, showcasing generic deviation, or exploring how hybrid works can help us understand Old Norse literary production and history. The aim is to illustrate the complexities and intricacies of generic determinants and classifications.

The volume opens with Massimiliano Bampi's chapter on 'Genre', which presents the theoretical background of genre studies. The chapter gives an overview of the term's critical history, both within and beyond Norse studies, and seeks to contextualise and theorise the term as a useful tool for discussing and classifying Old Norse literary production. The second chapter follows on by looking more closely at the complexities of generic conformity. Sif Rikhardsdottir proposes 'hybridity' as a useful term to consider genre as a continually morphing, qualifying structure that authors use to engage with the audience and the audience in turn uses to decipher and give meaning to the work by situating it in a particular generic context that comes with pre-established meanings and scripts. In the third chapter Lukas Rösli tackles the terminology, exploring the historicity of the term 'genre' and the associated generic categories in the extant Old Norse manuscript corpus, drawing attention to the anachronistic view of some generic terminology, such as *fornaldarsögur*. Mikael Males in turn addresses form in the fourth chapter, exploring how form shaped, and shapes, our perception of generic categorisation and conformity. The chapter is focused on medieval deliberation about form and how these relate to medieval textual taxonomies and subsequently to modern perceptions of genre. Judy Quinn moves from form to mode, considering the ways in which orality, textuality and performativity impact on and dictate generic affiliations and relevance in the fifth chapter. The final chapter in the section focuses on manuscripts and codicology. In this chapter Jóhanna Katrín Friðriksdóttir investigates how far the manuscript corpus provides evidence of generic perceptions by their medieval compilers and how codicological analysis can influence our understanding of generic affiliations.

The first chapter in the second section, Themes, situates literary production and its associated generic properties in a socio-historical context. Hans Jacob Orning expands on how socio-political structures impact on the development of literary genres or the institution of a generic body of literature, while simultaneously discussing how the concept of genre can illuminate political processes. The second two chapters tackle in turn geography and time and space. Dale Kedwards explores the function of geography or place as a generic marker and the intrinsic nuances associated with geographical localisation and generic classification. Torfi H. Tulinius on the other hand examines the chronotopes of time and space and how these determine (or not) generic affiliations and how these can best be modulated. Pernille Hermann focuses on 'memory' in her chapter; in particular how genres can be considered as sites or repositories of cultural memory. In Chapter 11 Stefanie Gropper explores what constitutes the human condition. She ranges widely across familial relations, conflicts and death, focusing specifically on emotion as a viable domain for accessing and mediating the human condition and the implications that emotion studies may have for genre theory.[12] Carolyne Larrington's chapter on God(s) discusses how deities and their associated ideological and religious systems partake in generic formation and/or generic stability. As with many of the other themes explored across the volume, a work's religious context can be said to dictate the generic framework, while the generic context in turn affects the way in which such religious symbols are conveyed. In the final chapter in the section Brittany Schorn explores the concept of 'wisdom', tracing the dual meaning of wisdom as an ideological concept on the one hand, i.e. as knowledge, and as a genre on the other; one that is focused specifically on preserving and conveying different kinds of knowledge.

The final chapters in the third section, Genre in Focus, each tackle a specific text or group of texts that belongs to a certain genre and the associated literary evidence for it. Erin Goeres and Carolyne Larrington each address the two major poetical modes, eddic and skaldic poetry. Goeres

---

12 For the discussion of emotion as generic marker see also Chapter 2.

discusses the poetry of Torf-Einarr Rǫgnvaldsson of Orkney as a prototypical example of skaldic battle-poetry. Her study focuses on the complexities of generic conformity, not the least when considering the prominence of particular generic markers, such as content or form, and the fact that manuscript or literary context may shift such earlier generic functionalities or determinants. Larrington in turn explores generic (or eddic) hybridity as evidenced in the poem *Sólarljóð*, a thirteenth-century poem composed in the eddic mode. Her analysis suggests that the poem actively compelled the audience to engage with its generic markers in a creative manner that foregrounds the function of the poem's hybrid character for its meaning-production. Elizabeth Ashman Rowe focuses on *Stjörnu-Odda draumr* as an example of the unstable and ill-definable genre of *þættir* (short narratives), to explore generic categorisations and the validity of such categorisations more broadly. Chapter 17 tackles the best known of the Old Norse genres, the *Íslendingasögur*. Russell Poole offers a case study of *Vatnsdœla saga* as a generically transgressive text, expanding on how such transgressions can in fact contribute to our understanding of the saga genre overall. In Chapter 18 Kevin Wanner explores the *byskupasögur* (sagas of bishops) and *heilagra manna sögur* (saints' lives), suggesting that we should reconsider how these texts have hitherto been classified and hence understood. In the final chapter Jürg Glauser takes on the prodigious genre of romance, exploring its generic affinities and complexities.

Finally, the Annotated Taxonomy which follows the three sections is intended to offer a selective overview of the major generic categories currently in use in Old Norse studies along with a short descriptive summary. The taxonomy is intended to be neither prescriptive nor definitive, instead it has been conceived to assist the reader in negotiating the various generic categories and classifications that are conventionally used in Old Norse studies, in contrast to the Companion itself, in which the intention indeed is precisely to debate the validity, nuances and qualifications of those categories.

Overall the volume seeks to engage with the concept of genre as a critical tool, to query the usefulness and validity of the current generic categories and to explore their functionality when it comes to analysing some of the main topos and themes of the Old Norse literary heritage. It is by no means exhaustive, yet it nevertheless spans a broad range of literary works produced in the medieval period in Scandinavia, from the early mythological poems to the later texts, shaped by the trans-European conventions of the romance. It features discussions of some of the better-known Icelandic sagas, such as *Egils saga Skalla-Grímssonar* and *Laxdæla saga*, as well as lesser-known works such as the poetry of Torf-Einarr Rǫgnvaldsson of Orkney, or the little-known *þáttr* (short narrative) *Stjörnu-Odda draumr*. Its geographic range extends across Scandinavia, with an inevitable focus on Iceland as the centre for manuscript production and

*Introduction*

literary perpetuation in the thirteenth and fourteenth centuries and beyond. In addition to providing a heuristic definition of genre – at the same time illustrating the implications of our limited knowledge of generic functionality in medieval literatures in the vernacular – the volume seeks to map Old Norse literary genres, their interactions, delineations, fusions and hybridity, while simultaneously seeking to question the historical, philological and literary justifications of such generic systems. Featuring both theoretical and thematic approaches – and hence probing interconnections between generic determination and socio-political conditions, codicological context, religious (or proto-religious) functionality or literary intentionality – it explores both medieval perceptions of the literary artworks being created and copied as well as the post-medieval perception of those works as cultural artefacts.

# I
# THEORY

# Genre
*Massimiliano Bampi*

> In modern literary theory, few concepts have proved more problematic and unstable than that of genre. Having functioned since Aristotle as a basic assumption of Western literary discourse, shaping critical theory and creative practice for more than two thousand years, the notion of genre is one whose meaning, validity and purpose have been repeatedly questioned in the last two hundred.[1]

These opening lines in David Duff's anthology of seminal works on genre contain *in nuce* some of the main problems that the definition and use of genre as a major theoretical and methodological instrument in modern literary criticism poses for scholars. The very instability of this concept is closely tied to the heterogeneity of critical standpoints from which it has been approached over the course of the last two centuries: either to define and delimit it, or to decree its utter inutility, or even to castigate genre's pernicious nature as the negation of the author's freedom in the creative process.

The broad divergence of opinions that can be discerned in the history of the changing fortunes of genre as a literary category in modern criticism is best viewed against the background of the shift of theoretical paradigms and frameworks that characterise the development of Western literary discourse in increasing measure during the course of the twentieth century. In principle, though, it is safe to assert that any reflection on genre was, and still is, undertaken as a part of a broader investigation of the very nature of literature and the limits of literary activity.[2]

Broadly speaking, modern genre theory can be described as developing around a polarisation of critical stances, corresponding to two major approaches: either normative or descriptive. The normative approach is based on a prescriptive principle and is usually traced back to the traditional tripar-

---

1 David Duff, *Modern Genre Theory*, Longman Critical Readers (Harlow, 2001), p. 1.
2 See Alastair Fowler, *Kinds of Literature: An Introduction to the Theory of Genres and Modes* (Oxford, 1982), pp. 1–19. For a brief introduction to the development of genre studies from the early eighteenth century onwards see Duff, *Modern Genre Theory*, pp. 3–19. See also Kevin S. Whetter, *Understanding Genre and Medieval Romance* (Aldershot and Burlington, 2008), pp. 9–33.

tite system of epic, lyric and drama, derived from Aristostle's and Plato's works. The descriptive stance is ultimately rooted in Russian Formalism and aims to study literary genres as historically contingent artistic configurations, thus avoiding any kind of evaluation based on the degree of adherence of works to a formalised set of predetermined generic features.[3]

If the critical perspective is broadened to include the discourse on genre in medieval literatures, the difficulties that are inherent in the reconstruction of the cultural coordinates of the production and reception of literature in the Middle Ages inevitably enhances the degree of uncertainty. It must be noted here that most genre theory actually hardly ever considers medieval literary production, although a few remarkable exceptions will be mentioned in the following sections. Furthermore, theoretical engagement with medieval genre appears to have diminished considerably after the 1990s. In more recent times, though, a renewed interest can be discerned, mostly in the form of the application of previous theoretical contributions to specific literary traditions.[4]

In what follows I intend to illustrate and discuss the notion of genre and its definition(s) from a theoretical viewpoint, drawing special attention to the implications that any definitional attempt has for our understanding and interpretation of literary works from the Middle Ages. The core issues that this chapter will deal with thus concern two primary domains: the criteria employed to define genre in scholarship on medieval literatures – quite often in conjunction with genre studies in other research fields – and the question of generic borders.

## Defining Genre and its Functions

The fact that medieval genres are not self-evident categories might appear to be a truism. However, although a great deal has been written about various medieval vernacular genres from many perspectives, in literary histories and indeed in most scholarship the very notion of genre has largely been left undefined and its meaning, therefore, is usually taken for granted. The difficulties that meet scholars who engage in this definitional endeavour must be viewed, at least partly, as a consequence of the very

---

3   One of the lingering misapprehensions about Russian Formalism is in fact that it was not interested in literary history and was therefore not concerned with the historical development of literary forms and genres. This view really misrepresents the essence of the theoretical discourse promoted by Russian formalists, as demonstrated, for example, by the works of Tynjanov and Ejchenbaum. For an introduction to Russian Formalism see Peter Steiner, 'Russian Formalism', in *The Cambridge History of Literary Criticism. From Formalism to Poststructuralism*, ed. Raman Selden (Cambridge, 1995), pp. 11–32.
4   Whetter, *Understanding Genre*; William D. Paden, *Medieval Lyric: Genres in Historical Context* (Urbana and Chicago, 2000); Elaine Treharne, *Writing Gender and Genre in Medieval Literature: Approaches to Old and Middle English Texts* (Woodbridge, 2002).

## Genre

nature of medieval vernacular textual production, where a comprehensive codification of generic rules is rather the exception than the norm.

Given the uncertainty surrounding the very existence of generic awareness, as understood in modern genre criticism, clues to the existence of generic distinctions as understood by medieval authors, scribes and publics are usually sought in lexical evidence and in the materiality of manuscript transmission. The existence of medieval terminology to describe writings that appear as discrete vernacular literary kinds, and the preservation of texts belonging to the same genre, or closely related ones, in the shape of manuscript compilations, seem to point in this direction.[5] Yet this kind of evidence is not unproblematic. In the case of manuscript compilations, the fact that texts appear to have been arranged according to a perception of generic affinity has generally not been considered strong evidence for generic awareness. Furthermore, contemporary medieval generic labels pose problems for scholars as they are not used in a consistent way throughout the preserved literary corpus. Some terms are indeed fairly wide-ranging (e.g. *roman/roumance*, *saga*) and are, quite naturally, subject to change of usage across time.[6] More generally, precise generic terminology seems to be linked to the existence of critical discourse and is often to be found in conjunction with retrospective efforts to classify texts rather than in medieval sources. Therefore, where no such critical discourse has developed, generic labels tend to be far from consistent, and their semantic opacity has undoubtedly offered no real help in the interpretive effort.[7] Where no generic terminology is evidenced in medieval texts, a modern one must be coined. This is the case with most terms currently used to classify sagas into a set of groupings. The critical discourse on saga genres for the last forty years is a good ex-

---

5    Keith Busby, 'Narrative Genres', in *The Cambridge Companion to Medieval French Literature*, ed. Simon Gaunt and Sarah Kay (Cambridge, 2008), pp. 139-52, at p. 147; Norman W. Ingham, 'Genre-Theory and Old Russian Literature', *The Slavic and East European Journal* 31:2 (1987), 234-45, at p. 237. For Old Norse literature see especially Stephen A. Mitchell, *Heroic Sagas and Ballads* (Ithaca, 1994), pp. 21-22.

6    See Busby, 'Narrative Genres', p. 140. On the limited reliability of medieval generic terms see also Tony Davenport, *Medieval Narrative: An Introduction* (Oxford, 2004), p. 25 with reference to Middle English generic terminology, and Klaus Grubmüller, 'Gattungskonstitution im Mittelalter', in *Mittelalterliche Literatur und Kunst im Spannungsfeld von Hof und Kloster*, ed. Nigel F. Palmer and Hans-Jochen Schiewer (Tübingen, 1999), pp. 193-210 as regards genre definition in medieval German literature.

7    See, for example, Simon Gaunt, 'Romance and Other Genres', in *The Cambridge Companion to Medieval Romance*, ed. Roberta Kruger (Cambridge, 2000), pp. 45-49. On the question of vernacular genre terminology in general see Barbara Frank, 'Innensicht und "Außensicht": Zur Analyse mittelalterlicher volkssprachlicher Gattungsbezeichnungen', in *Gattungen mittelalterlicher Schriftlichkeit*, ed. Barbara Frank, Thomas Haye and Doris Torphinke, ScriptOralia 99 (Tübingen, 1997), pp. 117-36.

ample of how slippery the ground becomes as soon as we try to account for generic heterogeneity using modern constructs; these at first sight appear to work more as instruments of classificatory convenience than as tools for the interpretation of Old Norse-Icelandic literature.[8]

Whether working with generic labels attested in medieval texts or with labels created *a posteriori*, though, a reconstructive effort is necessary in order to study how various literary forms arise and interact with each other, both synchronically and diachronically. The results of such reconstruction can be quite different inasmuch as it is clear that the perspective from which we analyse texts in search of generic distinctions will very much steer the interpretive process as a whole. Adopting a prescriptive stance inevitably leads to rigid categorisations in order to qualify a limited number of texts within them, thus excluding all other texts that do not seem to comply with the formal and content requirements (often rather vaguely) associated with that genre, as the debate about saga genres, for example, has clearly shown.[9] Generally, it is safe to assert that this kind of normative attitude, together with die-hard misapprehensions about classical discussion of genre (notably by Aristotle and Plato), have shaped our modern way of looking at medieval texts from a generic perspective. However, since medieval literary culture does not seem to have assigned importance to the enumeration and formalisation of distinctive features that constitute a genre, applying the criterion of generic homogeneity to our object of study proves misleading.[10] Furthermore, the adoption of a prescriptive approach fails to acknowledge the importance of the audience's contribution to shaping the creative process of literary works.

A more fruitful way of looking at texts in terms of generic distinctions and affiliations is to view genres as means of a communication strategy employing a varying combination of rhetorical and literary instruments to address a certain public.[11] Genres primarily have a twofold function: a

---

8   Massimiliano Bampi, 'Genre', in *The Routledge Research Companion to the Medieval Icelandic Sagas*, ed. Ármann Jakobsson and Sverrir Jakobsson (London and New York, 2015), pp. 4–14, at pp. 4–7.
9   Bampi, 'Genre', pp. 4–7. See also 'Interrogating Genre in the *Fornaldarsögur*: Round-Table Discussion', ed. Judy Quinn, *VMS* 2 (2006), 276–96.
10  One notable exception is, for example, the late fourteenth-century French treatise *L'Art de dictier*, written by Eustache Deschamps. See Alfred Hiatt, 'Genre without System', in *Middle English*, ed. Paul Strohm, Oxford Twenty-First Century Approaches to Literature (Oxford, 2007), pp. 277–94, at p. 279.
11  Wilhelm Voßkamp speaks of 'historisch bedingte Kommunikations- und Vermittlungsformen' (historically determined forms of communication and mediation); 'Gattungen', in *Literaturwissenschaft: Eine Einführung*, ed. Helmut Brackert and Jörn Stückrath (Reinbek, 1992), pp. 253–69, at p. 256). Alastair Fowler points out that 'genre theory concernes communication and intepretation' and firmly denies that 'the main value of genre is classificatory' (Fowler, *Kinds of Literature*, p. 37). Still, genre classification is undoubtedly used as a starting point in most literary studies.

compositional and a hermeneutic one. The first concerns the creative process itself and defines how authors used generic repertoires to compose a literary text. Recent scholarship on medieval vernacular genres has shown that – more often than our modern expectations lead us to believe – literary invention was based on compositional principles that combine repertoires of conventions associated with a range of genres in ways that are largely unpredictable and not reducible to a predefined set of features.[12] This is the main reason why it is difficult to define medieval texts according to (modern) generic criteria: many texts do indeed seem to defy generic distinction as envisaged in modern scholarship because, consciously or not, we tend to posit homogeneity as one of the fundamental features of generic groupings. In other words, the ascription of a literary work to a certain genre tends to be established on the basis of the presence, in that work, of all the features that are associated with that genre, as mentioned above with regard to saga literature. This kind of approach turns the relationship between theory and empirical observation upside down: instead of using theory to analyse and interpret the data derived from empirical observation, it is superimposed upon textual evidence, forcing the data into a normative framework. It follows that any kind of approach based on the assumption that medieval literary genres are defined by a homogeneous and closed set of properties is doomed to disregard the specificities of most medieval literary production in the vernacular.

The second function of genre is to provide guidance in the interpretive process to the audiences they were, and still are, meant to address. This second function, therefore, is strictly linked to a social and ideological dimension, involving recipients in various periods, both within the medieval world and beyond it. This implies that the same genre can acquire a different meaning throughout history, depending on the context in which it is used. What happened, for example, when a text was extracted from its original manuscript context and transplanted into a new one? Did generic perception change against various backgrounds (whether historical, social or ideological) across time?

The connection between genre and society is highlighted in a number of studies that have marked, in various ways, the theoretical debate during the second half of the twentieth century. Although such studies deal with a variety of epochs of literary production and human communication, they share an interest in viewing generic distinctions as part of a broader investigation of the interplay between social structures and societal changes and the role of literary expression over time.

In his influential essay 'Magical Narratives: On the Dialectical Use of Genre Criticism', the American critic Fredric Jameson describes genres

---

12   Tzvetan Todorov, for example, defines genre as 'a configuration of literary properties, an inventory of options' (quoted from Whetter, *Understanding Genre*, p. 10).

'as literary institutions, or social contracts between a writer and a specific public, whose function is to specify the proper use of a particular cultural artifact'.[13] Similar statements can be found in the field of medieval studies. Walter Ingham, for example, defines literary kind as 'a social convention – a category in the mind of a historical community of writers and readers, whether they conceptualize it or not (the practice of a convention and the articulation of it are different activities).'[14] In the same vein, according to Simon Gaunt

> genres are inherently ideological constructs; the formal and structural features of a text do not produce aesthetic effects that can be divorced from content and thereby from ideology, but on the contrary they signal participation in a discursive framework that implies a world-view with a heavy ideological investment.[15]

Another thought-provoking perspective on genre, albeit not from within medieval scholarship, is provided by several studies by Carolyn Miller. One of the most relevant consequences of her investigation of genre as social action is that 'if genres are phenomenological categories of symbolic interaction, we can posit that they help structure the socio-symbolic world in relevant and informative ways.'[16] It follows, therefore, that genres, as literary categories used to construct a dialogue with their audiences, do not only mirror society (or parts of it) but also contribute to shaping and manipulating it.

All the aforementioned critical standpoints emphasise the collective value of genres, understood primarily as instruments of communication and social interaction, and provide a perspective from which the definition of medieval genres may be fruitfully reconsidered. In order for a certain genre to be interpreted properly, it must be acknowledged and recognised through its distinctive features by its consumers. Broadly speaking, genres can be said to be defined by thematic, structural and functional criteria. How one can precisely identify such criteria, though, is without a doubt one of the most challenging aspects of genre studies. As with any retrospective analysis, the identification of marking traits must be based on their frequency and distribution within the corpus of literary works under scrutiny. The choice of which aspects of a body of works

---

13 Frederic Jameson, *The Political Unconscious: Narrative as a Socially Symbolic Act* (London, 1981), p. 92. On the application of Jameson's definition to medieval literature see Ardis Butterfield, 'Medieval Genres and Genre Theory', *Paragraph* 13:2 (1990), 184–201, at p. 187.
14 Ingham, 'Genre-Theory', p. 236. See also Barbro Söderberg, 'Saga och bulla: fornsvenska genrebeteckningar och medeltida skriftmiljöer', *ANF* 109 (1994), 141–72, especially at p. 143.
15 Gaunt, 'Romance and Other Genres', p. 46.
16 Carolyn Miller, 'Genre Innovation: Evolution, Emergence, or Something Else?', *Journal of Media Innovations* 3:2 (2016), 4–19, at p. 13.

should be taken as criteria for genre definition inevitably determines both how works are grouped together and how, based on this, we understand them as historical products. This is quite clearly exemplified by the different taxonomies of saga literature that result from Sigurður Nordal's classification as opposed to the current grouping customarily employed in saga studies.[17] Whereas the first is based on the relationship between the supposed time of the saga's composition and the time at which the events recounted are said to have taken place, the second is determined by the subject matter treated in the saga and the sagas' internal chronology.[18]

According to Fowler, the range of features that constitute a generic repertoire includes, for example, representational aspects, structure, size, scale as well as systems of values, setting and groups of characters.[19] Among such features, Fowler includes the reader's task, thus drawing attention also to the interpretive aspect of genre definition. In the same vein, Ingham speaks of implied functions attached to literary kinds. The reconstruction of such functions is certainly a task fraught with difficulties as it is heavily dependent on the kind of information available, or reconstructable, regarding each genre's context of use.

In the case of Old Norse literature, the definition of generic features has proved of great importance especially in the case of saga genres. Whereas Old Norse poetic genres tend to be, by nature, more formalised, and hence their features more easily retrievable from the extant corpus, prose genres seem indeed by and large to defy generic classification. As I have suggested elsewhere, although temporal and geographical settings appear to be the most important generic markers for saga genres, as they seem to trigger the selection of a set of representational features of a specific fictional world to which they are linked, other criteria (such as the communicative intent) must be in concord in order to distinguish sagas set in the same time frame.[20]

The role and function of genres in medieval society are also at the very heart of Hans Robert Jauss's seminal work; this still today is an indispensable point of reference for the study of medieval literary genres. His notion of horizon of expectations (*Erwartungshorizont*) foregrounds the importance of the interaction between the text and its intended audience:

> This horizon of the expectable is constituted for the reader from out of a tradition or series of previously known works, and from a specific attitude, mediated by one (or more) genre and dissolved

17 Sigurður Nordal, 'Sagalitteraturen', in *Litteraturhistoria B: Litteraturhistorie: Norge og Island*, ed. Sigurður Nordal (Stockholm, 1953), pp. 180–273, at pp. 180–82.
18 Bampi, 'Genre', pp. 4–6.
19 See Fowler, *Kinds of Literature*, pp. 62–64.
20 Bampi, 'Genre', pp. 7–9.

through new works. Just as there is no act of verbal communication that is not related to a general, socially or situationally conditioned norm or convention, it is also unimaginable that a literary work set itself into an informational vacuum, without indicating a specific situation of understanding. To this extent, every work belongs to a genre – whereby I mean neither more nor less than that for each work a preconstituted horizon of expectations must be ready at hand (...) to orient the reader's (public's) understanding and to enable a qualifying reception.[21]

Although Jauss's theoretical approach has met with criticism for a variety of reasons, it nevertheless proves useful in drawing attention to the importance of viewing each single work as part of a broader network of texts.[22] The emphasis on audience understanding of the relational aspects of texts within the literary corpus can be said to be relevant to the process of literary creation too. Authors – as well as copyists and 'rewriters' – were no doubt subject to the influence of previous works. It would indeed be misleading to think of the creative process as not being based on a knowledge of works that were already part of the literary system, and the same may be said to hold true even for contemporaneous texts. The network of intertextual references that can be detected throughout the whole corpus of medieval literature – including textual production in Old Norse – bears witness to this fact. Accordingly, it would be thoroughly unhistorical to assume that authors (as well as scribes) did not follow compositional conventions, rather than formalised rules and norms, determined by their knowledge of other works. It is safe to assume, then, that it was by way of such conventions that the audience could recognise a work's generic affiliation, which in turn provided the key to understand the communicative intention contained in the text.

## Generic Borders and Generic Hybridity

Jauss's theoretical work on medieval literary genres has also provided a definition of genres that points to their nature as groups or historical families, rather than classes. As such, according to Jauss, they can only be 'historically determined, delimited, and described'.[23] In addition to advocating the adoption of a descriptive stance, this definition foregrounds the historicity and mutability of genres over time. Furthermore, describing them as families highlights the role of heterogeneity as a constitutive aspect of genre formation and development. The texts ascribed to a given genre do not

---

21 Hans Robert Jauss, *Toward an Aesthetic of Reception*, transl. Timothy Bahti (Minneapolis, 1982), p. 79.
22 See, for example, Butterfield, 'Medieval Genres', especially at pp. 185–86; Whetter, *Understanding Genre*, p. 17.
23 Jauss, *Toward an Aesthetic*, pp. 79–80.

therefore have to display all the features that are associated with it, as every text is a constellation of both traditional and innovative traits, variously combined by the writer (whether the 'original' author or those responsible for later copying).

If seen from this perspective, genres will not be considered as immutable and self-contained entities, defined by clear-cut borders. Rather, they are viewed as literary categories marked by varying forms of combination of generic repertoires. The architecture of each text, as well as its internal disposition of the material, is thus the result of specific choices that, from a retrospective viewpoint, may be held to be indicative of a certain communicative intention.

Empirical observation across medieval literary traditions shows that there are variously sized areas of overlap between genres, in which one generic repertoire runs into another to give shape to a hybrid text.[24] Such fluidity is the result of genres being permeable and subject to modifications, derived both from the interplay involving literary kinds and from developments within the social structure of a given culture, as will be shown below.

A comparative scrutiny of how genres are structured in medieval literary traditions leads us to observe that, rather than being characterised by homogeneity, they are best described as multimodal categories. More precisely, they appear to be characterised by a varying degree of multimodality.[25] This has been observed, for example, for saga literature, especially by Margaret Clunies Ross.[26] The study of the forms of multimodality within the Old Norse literary space would not only enhance our knowledge of how the compositional process came about. It would also help to explain better why varying degrees of multimodality and generic intermingling can be observed, synchronically as well as diachronically. A question that is indeed seldom asked with regard to the heterogeneity of literary texts (especially but not exclusively with regard to saga genres) is whether the combination of features from various generic repertoires had a communicative purpose: how did generic heterogeneity and generic hybridisation contribute towards enhancing and widening the expressive range of a literary genre?

---

24 It should be noted here that the term 'hybridity' is used in this context to refer to the combination of definable repertoires that are generally used to give shape to different fictional worlds. Therefore, it should not be taken to imply that such categories are 'pure' as they are themselves to be viewed as the result of combining heterogeneous elements. See further Chapter 2 in this volume.
25 On the distinction between mode (understood as a linguistic category, specifying the means of enunciation such as, by way of example, narration and dramatic imitation) and genre see Gérard Genette, *The Architext: An Introduction*, trans. J. Lewin (Berkeley, 1982), especially at pp. 60–72 (reprinted in Duff, *Modern Genre Theory*, pp. 210–18).
26 Margaret Clunies Ross, *The Cambridge Introduction to the Old Norse-Icelandic Saga* (Cambridge, 2010), p. 70.

If heterogeneity is acknowledged as one of the constitutive elements of genre formation, as suggested by Jauss, then investigating the scale and the forms that generic intermingling takes is one of the most interesting questions in genre studies. Mapping how different generic repertoires are combined within a common framework (whether prose or poetry) and seeking to figure out the expressive value attached to the various configurations of generic intermingling is indeed a key task for future research in this avenue of investigation. The results of such an analytical endeavour would no doubt enhance our knowledge of how literary composition functioned, also in conjunction with audience expectations. Why, for example, were generic features associated with the *Íslendingasögur* and the *fornaldarsögur* combined in such texts as *Víglundar saga* or *Finnboga saga ramma*? In which ways did this form of hybridisation contribute to articulating a more nuanced discourse about the representation of the past? If the social value of genres as categories of literary expression is assumed, any change in the way a given fictional world (whether in prose or verse) is constructed and mediated requires some form of negotiation with its public; it must have been able to enjoy the text, in whatever form it was delivered, and to correctly interpret the intended communicative import.

Thus none of these questions should be seen as pertaining merely to the literary domain. Although it is surely true that they are primarily associated with the process of literary creativity, they also reflect dynamics that operate at the intersection of the literary system with the other systems that constitute culture. In other words, what happens within the borders of the literary domain is determined not only by the mechanisms that regulate the interplay between various genres and modes (synchronically as well as diachronically) but also by that domain's interaction with other systems such as the social, the political and the religious ones, to name only the most relevant.

## Literature as a System

All the questions outlined so far may best be viewed from the perspective of the relational aspects determining the rise and development of genres. As literary categories, genres evolve in response to shifts and changes that affect, in various ways and to different degrees, the overall structure of a cultural system across time. From a theoretical point of view, the ideas expressed by some of the most prominent representatives of Russian Formalism (most notably Tynjanov and Ejchenbaum) and further elaborated by Itamar Even-Zohar in his polysystem theory provide the tenets that have recently been employed, albeit not yet to their full potential, in an increasing number of studies devoted to Old

Norse literary genres.[27] Like Jauss's model, polysystem theory is ultimately rooted in Russian Formalism (and Czech poststructuralism).[28] The basic assumption on which its whole theoretical architecture rests is that semiotic phenomena – such as culture, language, literature and society – can be more adequately understood if regarded as systems 'rather than as a conglomerate of disparate elements'.[29] Literature and literary genres come thus to be viewed as elements that partly depend on the mechanisms that govern the functioning of society and the various forms taken by the interaction between both individuals and groups. Furthermore, genres constitute a hierarchical system in which literary kinds occupy either a central or a peripheral position; this may change over time in response to a variety of factors, as will be shown below.

Considering literary facts from a systemic perspective relies on the assumption, discussed above, that genres are meant to serve a communicative purpose and were thus employed as part of social life. Such purposes would of course have been of various types and be liable to change across time. Broadly speaking, while religious genres had a clearly edifying aim, secular kinds would have fulfilled both entertainment and more clearly ideological functions. All this should be seen in conjunction with the dynamics operating at other levels within the cultural system: for example, societal changes that produced a rearrangement of the hierarchical structure would likely have called for a restructuring of the mutual relations between genres in terms of social relevance. New elites would have supported and encouraged the production and dissemination of literary genres that mirrored their world-view and which could therefore be used as an instrument to legitimise their aspiration to power in the social arena. A case in point is the development of the Old Icelandic literary system after the end of the Commonwealth period, in which, as far as we can judge from manuscript transmission, textual production appears to have privileged such genres as the *fornaldarsögur*

---

27  In addition to Bampi, 'Genre', see, for example, Massimiliano Bampi, 'Literary Activity and Power Struggle: Some Observations on the Medieval Icelandic Polysystem after the Sturlungaöld', in *Textual Production and Status Contests in Rising and Unstable Societies*, ed. Massimiliano Bampi and Marina Buzzoni (Venice, 2013), pp. 59–70, and Siân Grønlie, *The Saint and the Saga Hero: Hagiography and Early Icelandic Literature*, Studies in Old Norse Literature 2 (Cambridge, 2017).
28  Itamar Even-Zohar, 'Polysystem Theory', *Poetics Today* 11:1 (1990), 9–94. For a short introduction see Mark Shuttleworth, 'Polysystem Theory', in *Routledge Encyclopedia of Translation Studies*, ed. Mona Baker and Kirsten Malmkjær (London, 1998), pp. 176–79. Another relevant contribution to understanding literature (and genres) as a system within a broader systemic structure has been made by Erich Köhler, especially in his 'Gattungssystem und Gesellschaftssystem', in *Zum mittelalterlichen Literaturbegriff*, ed. Barbara Haupt (Darmstadt, 1985), pp. 111–29. Like Jauss's arguments, Köhler's theoretical work is rooted in Russian Formalism.
29  Even-Zohar, 'Polysystem Studies', p. 9.

and the indigenous *riddarasögur*. Seen from the viewpoint of polysystem theory, these genres came to occupy a central position in the system, thus exerting an influence over both the composition of new works belonging to such genres as the *Íslendingasögur*, which had previously been more prominent, and the copying of earlier sagas: these then acquired new stylistic traits as they were copied. The rise to prominence of *fornaldarsögur* and *riddarasögur* is linked to changes that occur within the social system of late medieval Iceland; new families were aspiring to prominent positions, quite likely in competition with individuals who could trace their origins back to the ruling elite from the Commonwealth period. It is thus hardly a coincidence that works belonging to a genre like the indigenous *riddarasögur*, one which is not constructed around the same genealogical principle that informs most saga genres, feature prominently in manuscripts owned by members of new families, especially from the West Fjords. Around the same time that both *fornaldarsögur* and *riddarasögur* were becoming increasingly prominent in the Old Norse literary system, new investment both in the creation of new *Íslendingasögur* – showing traits generally characteristic of the generic repertoires of the more fantastic genres – and in the copying of older ones is attested. This might indicate that members of the old elites continued to attach importance to the production and dissemination of literary works as an instrument of both ideological identification and social competition. In other words, then, movements within the literary systems in terms of the hierarchical arrangement of genres appear to mirror dynamics that obtained between social groups of various origins aspiring to prominent positions.[30]

The increasing degree of generic intermingling displayed in sagas written in the late medieval period, especially in the fourteenth and fifteenth centuries, is best understood against the background of the dynamic interplay between literary production and social change briefly sketched above. Rather than offering evidence for the indefinability of genre distinctions, the growing complexity of texts in terms of combination of generic options is rather to be seen as a sign of the enhanced complexity of the literary system; this was mainly a consequence of a process of generic cross-fertilisation.

Such developments are certainly not confined to the production of prose genres. Poetic genres are indeed subject to change and modification over time, as are their mutual relationships and those with prose genres. The major changes that affected Icelandic society and culture (such as, for example, the conversion to Christianity and the annexation to the Norwegian crown) were mirrored in the changing role of poetic genres in social life. A case in point is the development of skaldic eulogies. Whereas some of its subgenres were adapted to

---

30 See Bampi, 'Literary Activity and Power Struggle'.

accommodate the social and religious changes that occurred in Scandinavia from the ninth to the thirteenth century, others became extinct and new types of panegyrics emerged and took on important functions in society.[31]

However, if genres ceased to be productive, it does not necessarily mean that they no longer had a place in social life. For example, from the late twelfth century mythological narrative poems and genealogical poems were employed in the service of the Icelandic aristocracy.

Generally, the Icelandic elites played a decisive role in breathing new life into, amongst others, traditional poetic genres that had been employed to celebrate the deeds of kings and earls in the time prior to the conversion to Christianity. The use of panegyrics, for example, was part of a strategy of political self-promotion on the part of those oligarchic families – most notably the *Sturlungar* – who were contending for power during the course of the late twelfth and the first half of the thirteenth centuries. Icelandic chieftains did indeed begin to identify themselves with the European nobility in the late twelfth, and especially in the thirteenth centuries and thus they invested in the composition of eulogies to immortalise their deeds and achievements.[32] An early thirteenth-century renewal of interest in skaldic verse coincided with the composition of *Íslendingasögur* and *konungasögur*, in which verse sequences were used primarily to corroborate historical events.[33] It is thus safe to assert that a revitalisation of skaldic poetry – especially in the form of royal encomia intended for an Icelandic audience – resulted from the social elites' ideological effort to promote themselves in the struggle for political power, one that made use of various expressive modes (prose and verse genres).

From a diachronic perspective, fourteenth-century developments observed in the domain of poetic genres provide further evidence in support of the view, propounded here, that a polysystemic perspective in studying literary genres can enhance our understanding of how literature functioned as part of social life. By the middle of the century, a new hierarchy of poetic genres had established itself as a consequence of changes affecting the whole literary system. It is indeed by this date that the new genre of *rímur* is thought to have begun to emerge as the leading genre in the poetic landscape, thus undermining the position of other poetic genres, most

---

31 Kari Ellen Gade, 'Poetry and its Changing Importance in Medieval Icelandic Culture', in *Old Icelandic Literature and Society*, ed. Margaret Clunies Ross, Cambridge Studies in Medieval Literature 42 (Cambridge, 2000), pp. 61–95 at pp. 71–72.
32 See Guðrún Nordal, *Tools of Literacy. The Role of Skaldic Verse in Icelandic Textual Culture of the Twelfth and Thirteenth Centuries* (Toronto, 2001), especially at pp. 130–38.
33 Gade, 'Poetry and its Changing Importance', p. 87.

notably skaldic poetry.[34] Although the genesis of the new *rímur*-genre is somewhat obscure, it is clear that it owes much to saga literature on the one hand and to continental verse narratives on the other.[35] In both form and diction, though, *rímur* were also influenced by eddic and especially skaldic poetry. The narrative material derives from both indigenous and foreign sources (e.g. saga, romance, religious literature). The *rímur*-genre thus clearly illustrates the dynamics at play within the literary system: traditional expressive forms alongside models of foreign origin are used to give shape to narratives that were mainly rooted in prose genres. *Rímur* are thus a clear example of how hybridisation of different modes can produce a new genre. What still remains to be investigated is the relationship between this new genre and the other literary kinds still being produced in the fourteenth and fifteenth centuries, when this new form began to establish itself. Were *rímur* and narrative prose genres (mainly sagas), for example, meant to address different needs in the social life of Icelanders in the last centuries of the medieval period? Were certain generic traits of *rímur* (e.g. in terms of narrative motifs) used to adapt already established genres such as *Íslendingasögur* and *riddarasögur* to new communicative needs? As scholarship on both verse and prose genres has so far tended to focus on literary production in the twelfth and thirteenth centuries, the margins of Icelandic literary chronology should receive more critical attention; their inclusion in a broader discourse on the rise and development of literary genres would enable us to learn more about how new forms respond to new needs in terms of communication.

## Conclusion

In terms of generic definition, the Old Norse literary corpus that has come down to us undoubtedly poses a number of problems for scholars. The semantic opacity of genre terminology as found in medieval sources, together with the overall lack of normative and classificatory discourse on genres, especially in prose, makes the identification of generic markers and generic borders an endeavour full of pitfalls. Nevertheless, if we abandon any attempt at investigating compositional complexity in search of generic distinctions this would fail to contribute to our understanding of how medieval literary production functioned, in the Northern world as well as in the rest of Europe. Normative approaches to medieval genre are necessarily doomed to confuse and mislead the observer as they are based on assumptions that do not seem to fit the study of literary pro-

---

34 Margaret Clunies Ross, *A History of Old Norse Poetry and Poetics* (Cambridge, 2005), p. 206.
35 On *rímur* see *Íslensk bókmenntasaga*, ed. Böðvar Guðmundsson, Sverrir Tómasson and Torfi Tulinius (Reykjavík, 1993), pp. 322–50, and Vésteinn Ólason, 'Old Icelandic Poetry', in *A History of Icelandic Literature*, ed. Daisy Neijman, Histories of Scandinavian Literature (Lincoln, 2006), pp. 55–59.

duction in the Middle Ages. Adopting a descriptive stance, based on the assumption that literary kinds are historically contingent instruments of communication and are marked by varying degrees of heterogeneity, enables us to view the rise and development of genres as a semiotically complex process; each text both mirrors already established compositional conventions and contributes to expanding the genre's expressive range, either by adding new features or highlighting elements that may appear as secondary in other texts. The systematic identification of such compositional conventions is a task to be taken on by future research in Old Norse studies.

Theoretical suggestions as provided, for example, by Russian Formalism and especially by polysystem theory, along with the adoption of a comparative view embracing other medieval literatures, will provide scholars with a useful perspective from which to approach genre in Old Norse literature. That literary facts are best viewed as being partly correlated with dynamics operating outside the literary system, as part of a broader system of complex interrelations, provides the starting point for any investigation of the rise and development of genres in the cultural space of the medieval North. The mechanisms that seem to regulate how genres change over time are indeed derived partly from the interplay between genres, according to their hierarchical position. They also derive partly from the operational dynamics in other systems constituting culture, in particular the social dynamics. Genres' changing nature and role is thus best investigated against the background of societal and political changes, in both synchrony and diachrony.

Adopting a systemic approach enables us to understand that both the growing complexity of literary texts, in terms of the combination of various generic repertoires, and the change in the genre hierarchy in the late medieval Old Norse literary system (i.e. in the fourteenth and fifteenth centuries) are two interrelated aspects of the development of literary forms as means of social communication and social action. Judging by the textual and manuscript evidence, the reconfiguration of the late medieval Icelandic literary system, in terms of generic complexity and the hierarchical relationships between genres and modes, produced increasing mobility of generic traits. This, in turn, had a bearing on the suitability of literary texts to mirror certain communicative intentions. Texts that show a higher degree of generic complexity should thus not be regarded as the product of literary creativity *per se*. Rather, they may have been specifically shaped in order to articulate a more nuanced discourse on, say, the representation of the past and its relationship to the present, whether in sagas or in poetry.

The mutability and permeability of genres results from intra- and intergeneric dynamics as well as influence exerted by other systems, but this may also be seen as a sign of their vitality. Through their openness to some forms of transformation, certain genres did indeed manage to retain their social value as a major manifestation of changing interactions between individuals and groups; meanwhile others died out. Variation and change are thus two key concepts for questions about how genres are formed and, beyond the contingency of their origins, how they develop across time.

# Hybridity
*Sif Rikhardsdottir*

Genre as a concept is perhaps one of the more systematically referenced or used critical tool in literary studies. Yet it is very rarely defined. Despite the fact that most literary critics resort to it in one way or another to define their topics or to delineate their arguments, there does not seem to be any general consensus on what genre actually is, how it should be defined and what the generic categories we use actually entail. We usually refer to generic categories dismissively, as simply a gesture of modern pragmatism or as useful (on the basis that they are generally accepted) categorisations to outline our critical arguments. Most critical theory on genre comes from modern literary studies and the applicability of modern genre theory to medieval literatures adds a secondary layer of complexity when it comes to critical discussion on genre and medieval literature.[1]

This chapter addresses genre from the perspective of generic hybridity. It delineates briefly the relevant critical theorising of genre and its anachronistic complexity, suggesting 'hybridity' as a useful concept for approaching generic frameworks for medieval literatures. It then stages hybridity as an umbrella concept that encompasses the shifting nature of generic affiliation, particularly when it comes to translation or transmission of material (both linguistically speaking and in terms of form). Evidence of generic conversions in transmission calls attention to the generic stipulations that govern the creation and appreciation of literary works. Such evidence can in turn assist in understanding how generic markers were understood by medieval authors and audiences and in what way we can successfully utilise them to approach medieval literatures. Ultimately, the chapter suggests emotion as a mode – undeniably one of many – of formulating a theory of genre that encompasses both the creative process itself, i.e. the medieval context of literary production, and our under-

---

1   For a discussion about the applicability of modern genre theory to medieval literature see for instance Ardis Butterfield, 'Medieval Genres and Modern Genre Theory', *Paragraph* 13:2 (1990), 184–201. See also discussions of genres in medieval literature in a special double issue of *Exemplaria* 27:1–2 (2015) on *Theorizing Early English Genre*, ed. Shannon Gayk and Ingrid Nelson; Keith Busby, 'Narrative Genres', in *Cambridge Companion to Medieval French Literature*, ed. Simon Gaunt and Sarah Kay (Cambridge, 2008), pp. 139–52; and Simon Gaunt, 'Genres in Motion: Reading the *Grundriss* 40 Years On', *Medioevo Romanzo* 27 (2013), 24–43. For a discussion of 'genre' as a critical concept more broadly or the critical history of the theory of genres see Chapter 1 in this volume and works cited there.

standing today of the place those works have in literary history and the role they might have played in formulating such histories.

## Generic Verisimilitude and Hybridity

Fredric Jameson notes that the conception of literary history is by necessity preceded by a perception of genre.[2] Indeed, the categorisation of literature into corpora with varying different functions, aesthetic principles and affective impacts itself has a critical history, going as far back as Aristotle and quite possibly further. Moreover, while genre theory tends to be associated with modernity, the Latin scholarly tradition gives evidence that medieval authors and audiences were well aware of generic delineations and functionalities and that these in turn may have been indoctrinated through the Latin curriculum where certain genres served particular rhetorical or ecclesiastical purposes.[3] Generic identification is admittedly always a process in flux that is itself impacted by the shifting modalities of generic representations, both in terms of the works generally conceived to belong to a particular genre and our understanding of that particular genre. Yet, as Jean-Marie Schaeffer points out, generic parameters are restricted by the mandates of communication in the sense that literature is always in some sense an interpersonal communication.[4] Thus communicative acts require a basic comprehension of the underlying code of the communication, in this case the generic framework and markers, to be successful.

From a modern perspective the basic function of genre is organising, categorising and shaping our expectations, our way of thinking and our perceptions of a particular work. One can assume the same applies to the creative process itself, i.e. how an author gives shape to a fictional world by making use of the available generic repertoires. John Frow indeed points out that genres 'create effects of reality and truth, authority and plausibility, which are central to the different ways the world is understood', calling attention to the function of generic borders in terms of ordering and framing knowledge and our perception of reality, whether actual or imaginary.[5] Generic hybridity therefore in some sense reshapes those perceived borders, creating new impressions, new perceptions and potentially making us reconceive what we had previously assumed as given. By proposing the concept of hybridity I do not mean to sug-

---

2   Fredric Jameson, *The Political Unconscious: Narrative as a Socially Symbolic Act* (London, 1981), p. 107.
3   For an overview of genre theory in Greek and Latin literature see Joseph Farrell, 'Classical Genre in Theory and Praxis', *New Literary History* 34:3 (2003), 383–408.
4   Jean-Marie Schaeffer, *Qu'est-ce qu'un genre littéraire?* Poétique (Paris, 1989), p. 80.
5   John Frow, *Genre*, 2nd edn, The New Critical Idiom (London and New York, 2015), p. 2.

gest a status quo of generic stability against which one can judge variant versions. Rather the intent is to signal that an author always and unavoidably conceives of a work against a canvas of pre-existing works.[6] These works provide generic borders that modulate the way in which the new work addresses those borders (by adhering to them or deliberately crossing them). The generic corpus is then reformulated through the inclusion of the new work. The newly formed work therefore reshapes the same generic borders and frameworks that influenced its shaping as the work itself becomes part of the pre-existing generic canvas, subtly modifying it, re-shaping it, or negating it.

Ralph O'Connor's warning about the teleological functionality of generic labelling and hence the notion of hybridity as a deviation from a norm that implies a pre-existing or normative generic purity is therefore duly noted.[7] Any discussion of genre (or generic hybridity) is bound to fall prey to the normative functionality of such stipulations. Yet, one can presume that medieval authors and audiences were aware, even if only implicitly, of generic markers (although these may obviously deviate from our own terminologies and categorisations) since one can indeed identify corpora of texts that reveal similar structures, styles, and behavioural or ideological representations. This would suggest that authors were formulating their works according to some general principles (whether consciously or unconsciously) and that these principles played a part in dictating or shaping the tone of the discourse, character representation and the narrative setting. Genre is thus at the very least a useful guide to identifying and discussing texts' narrative purposes and functionalities. Similarly, the concept of hybridity – freed from its normative function of pre-set generic standards that the hybrid text combines or transgresses – is useful in signalling literary defiance, experimentation, or the destabilisation of an ideological content or aesthetic intent.

As a matter of fact, hybridity might indeed be argued to constitute a form of literary creativity that may have resulted in what we now consider some of the masterpieces of their respective genres. The expansion of the existing generic limitations or frameworks, resulting in the disarticulation of pre-existing standards and conventions, may, ironically, have formalised the genre for latter-day readers in its 'perfected' form, al-

---

6   In some sense this replicates Hans Robert Jauss's theorising of a 'horizon of expectations', whereby the focus is however on the reader's pre-existing expectations when encountering any given work rather than that of the author (see *Toward an Aesthetic of Reception*, trans. Timothy Bahti (Minneapolis, 1982)). Those 'horizons' apply, nevertheless, equally to the author as they do to the reader. Jauss's theoretical approach of reader reception can therefore be said to underlie some the discussion here in terms of the framework of pre-existing expectations and their perpetual renewal.
7   Ralph O'Connor in 'Interrogating Genre in the *Fornaldarsögur*: Round-Table Discussion', *VMS* 2 (2006), 291–93, at p. 291.

though the initial impulse may indeed have been one of generic resistance and reformulation. Tison Pugh argues that hybridity – or more specifically the bringing together of two separate genres whether in confrontation or through incorporation – can serve to negate or destabilise the generic boundaries that frame each genre, thereby creating an avenue for dissent, subversiveness, or playfulness.[8] He utilises genre as means of teasing out the subtle ways in which heteronormativity is undermined in Geoffrey Chaucer's *Canterbury Tales*. According to Pugh, the choice of romance instead of a fabliau as a generic form for the Wife of Bath's tale undermines audience expectations of generic preferences and social conventions. Those generic expectations (and their subsequent destabilisation) create, according to Pugh, a space in which heteronormative power structures can be deconstructed. Whatever one may think of the Wife of Bath's autonomy or lack thereof, Chaucer's play on genre parameters and the critical attention that has been paid to the supposed incongruity of her choice of a tale suggest that active authorial engagement with the generic framework within which he or she is working may provide a means for addressing or conveying subversive narrative messages.

While in the case of the 'The Wife of Bath's Tale', the 'queering' takes place through a (supposedly) intentional confrontation or destabilisation of the audience's generic expectations of the female tale-teller, hybridity allows for a similar sort of destabilisation and reformulation of literary expectations. It creates a space where such normative structures, whether gendered, political, or aesthetic, can be deconstructed. Indeed Tzvetan Todorov claimed already in the 1970s that all major works transgress the pre-existing generic rules and that it is precisely this transgression that makes them great.[9] Perhaps literary greatness can be found in the concurrent perfection of a generic form and its destabilisation, or perhaps more accurately in the fact that great works expand or refute the generic boundaries that they simultaneously perfect. *Brennu-Njáls saga* is certainly an example of this phenomenon, even though it is not a hybrid in the conventional sense of the word.

## Multimodalities and Generic Permanence

Turning to Old Norse literary hybrids, evidence of generic hybridity abounds across more or less all Norse genres, although the most formally predefined genres, including for instance the skaldic mode and its subgenres, are likely to exhibit less generic flexibility then some of the prose genres. The round-table discussion of the generic denominator of *fornaldarsögur* (the legendary sagas) that took place in Denmark in 2005

---

8   Tison Pugh, 'Queering Genres, Battering Males: The Wife of Bath's Narrative Violence', *Journal of Narrative Theory* 33:2 (2003), 115–42.
9   Tzvetan Todorov, *The Poetics of Prose*, trans. Richard Howard (Ithaca, 1992, orig. 1977), p. 43.

and Durham in 2006 exemplifies the multiple different approaches Norse scholars have taken to the topic of genre, from the earlier debates between Joseph Harris, Lars Lönnroth and Theodore M. Andersson in *Scandinavian Studies* in 1975 until this day.[10] The suggested approaches range from insisting on the use of medieval terminologies and taxonomies to a reconsideration of the existing generic markers by focusing instead on alternative approaches, such as themes, character types, rhetorical figures or other means of categorisation. Others have advocated simply accepting the modern categorisations as useful (albeit faulty) classifications. The assumption here is that while medieval authors and audiences in Scandinavia may not necessarily have had an established taxonomy of vernacular genres (whether or not these would have reflected the modern ones), they would nevertheless have been aware of generic modalities and would have adopted (consciously or unconsciously) these when formulating their own works. These modalities would, however, have been more fluid than our more rigid modern categorisations might indicate and their local adaptation more autonomous. Obviously generic categorisations are *ex post facto* attributions or efforts to delineate evidence of adherence to certain principles that are apparent in the texts themselves. The *konungasögur* (kings' sagas), for instance, are identified based on certain principles or standards that reflect their function and their authorial intent, although this basic representative structure and functionality does not preclude a certain amount of space for creative manoeuvring.

Discussion of Old Norse genres has tended to focus on the validity of the generic categories that have become conventionalised in critical discourse on Old Norse literature. These categories in many ways frame our perception of the Norse literary heritage, yet their formulations are frequently fairly arbitrary, or based on external factors that dictate the valuation of a particular genre at the cost of another, at times for political rather than aesthetic purposes. The *Íslendingasögur*, or the sagas of Icelanders, are grouped together on the basis that they feature either the settlement of Iceland and/or later descendants of the earlier settlers. The same can be said of the *fornaldarsögur* and the *riddarasögur* (romances); the former genre is defined by the time and space of its action in the manner of the Bakhtinian chronotope, despite the fact that many of them defy the normative parameters of the genre in style, ideology, or plot structure.[11] The latter is defined by its presumed focus on the world and

---

10 The roundtable discussions were later collated and published in the essay 'Interrogating Genre in the *Fornaldarsögur*', ed. Judy Quinn; Lars Lönnroth, 'The Concept of Genre in Saga Literature', *SS* 47:4 (1975), 419–26; Joseph Harris, 'Genre in Saga Literature: A Squib', *SS* 47:4 (1975), 427–36, and Theodore M. Andersson, 'Splitting the Saga', *SS* 47:4 (1975), 437–41.
11 According to Bakhtin's theory of the chronotope different literary genres would

adventures of knights beyond Nordic borders. The rise and demise of the various Old Norse genres through literary history indeed showcases the socio-political (as well as the cultural-aesthetic) forces at stake in the construction of both literary history and generic canonicity.

Elizabeth Ashman Rowe has queried the appropriateness of the categorisation of the *fornaldarsögur* exclusively on the basis of their setting. She draws on Alastair Fowler's theory to suggest that generic identity comprises multiple other factors, including subject, value, mood and many others.[12] Moreover, both generic affiliations and the genres themselves change over time and so many of the so-called *fornaldarsögur* have attributes that signal the historical development of the genre and its crossings (and fusion) with other generic forms, creating either subgenres or hybrid texts. The early *Yngvars saga víðfǫrla* deviates for instance from the conventional *fornaldarsaga* setting inasmuch as it is not set in a legendary or pre-historic past, but rather in the recent past (early eleventh century), a time more commonly featured in tales of the settlement (*Íslendingasögur*).[13] Moreover, the text conflates historical facts (habitually associated with the *konungasögur* and *Íslendingasögur*) with fantastic elements, customarily attributed to the legendary sagas. Carl Phelpstead, along with Ralph O'Connor, has argued that modern perceptions of a division between historicity vs. fantasy (one of the conventional factors for the generic distinction of the *fornaldarsögur*) discount the creative aspect of historical writing in the Middle Ages.[14] Hence he suggests that generic parameters should be expanded to include texts like *Yngvars saga*, that hover on the borders

---

    display diverse configurations of time and space thereby distinguishing them from each other. For further information on the Bakhtinian chronotope see Mikhail M. Bakhtin, *The Dialogic Imagination: Four Essays*, trans. Caryl Emerson and Michael Holquist (Austin, 1981), pp. 84–258 and Torfi H. Tulinius's chapter in this volume.

12  Elizabeth Ashman Rowe in 'Interrogating Genre in the *Fornaldarsögur*', ed. Judy Quinn, 284–86, at pp. 284–85 and Alastair Fowler, *Kinds of Literature: An Introduction to the Theory of Genres and Modes* (Oxford, 1982). See also Rowe, 'Generic Hybrids: Norwegian "Family" Sagas and Icelandic "Mythic-Heroic" Sagas', SS 65:4 (1993), 539–54.

13  The saga is generally assumed to have been composed around 1200, making it one of the earlier examples of saga writing in Iceland; a time when the generic parameters of oral tales and early writing are assuming their form. See also Torfi H. Tulinius, *The Matter of the North: The Rise of Literary Fiction in Thirteenth-Century Iceland*, trans Randi C. Eldevik (Odense, 2002) and Margaret Clunies Ross, *A History of Old Norse Poetry and Poetics* (Cambridge, 2005), particularly pp. 29–68.

14  Carl Phelpstead, 'Adventure-Time in *Yngvars saga víðfǫrla*', in *Fornaldarsagaerne: Myter og virkelighed. Studier i de oldislandske fornaldarsögur Norðurlanda*, ed. Agnete Ney, Ármann Jakobsson and Annette Lassen (København, 2009), pp. 361–78, at p. 332 and Ralph O'Connor, 'Truth and Lies in the *fornaldarsögur*: The Prologue to *Göngu-Hrólfs saga*', in *Fornaldarsagaerne: Myter og virkelighed*, ed. Agnete Ney, Ármann Jakobsson and Annette Lassen, pp. 361–78.

of the fantastic and the historical, in the corpus of the *fornaldarsögur*. Gottskálk Jensson, however, suggests that this deviation (or generic indeterminacy) may be the result of a generic development of the *fornaldarsögur* from Latin works such as Saxo Grammaticus' *Gesta Danorum*, intimating that the generic form of the *fornaldarsögur* is itself a hybrid.[15]

Philip Lavender instead takes on a late example of a *fornaldarsaga*, *Illuga saga Griðarfóstra*, exploring the intertextual relations of the various versions of the legend (both prose and verse) as well as the associated crossing of generic and modal boundaries of the material, i.e. from prose into verse and vice versa.[16] According to Lavender the plot structure of the saga belongs to the generic realm of the *fornaldarsaga*, yet the narrative content can be found in the various generic (and modal) forms available to medieval and post-medieval authors, including *Íslendingasaga*, *riddarasaga* and *rímur* (rhymed verse). This suggests that generic hybridity may be evidenced not only through the merger of two generic forms, but, more specifically, through the formal (or modal) reconfigurations of a particular story or narrative material. This in turn would imply that content is not a reliable generic marker, unless alternative criteria are used to delineate the particular generic or modal representational form of the narrative material.

Theodore M. Andersson has indeed suggested an alternative mode to the categorisation of saga writing that is based not on their subject matter, but rather on their mode of writing.[17] He argues that there were already certain modes in place in thirteenth-century Iceland for composing or telling a story; a biographical mode (the kings' sagas and bishops' sagas and some of the *Íslendingasögur*), a regional or chronicle mode (i.e. the contemporary *Íslendingasaga* and some family sagas like *Laxdæla saga*) and a feud or conflict saga mode (most *Íslendingasögur* would fall in this category). If Andersson is right here, this would suggest that generic frameworks were already in place at the beginning of saga writing and that authors were not only aware of them, but that they drew on such established narrative forms or modes to give their material its shape. Andersson himself concedes that a single text may cross those modal boundaries, incorporating

---

15 Gottskálk Jensson, 'Were the Earliest *fornaldarsögur* Written in Latin?' in *Fornaldarsagerne*, ed. Agnete Ney, Ármann Jakobsson and Annette Lassen, pp. 79–91. For a discussion of the hybrid character of early saga writing more generally see Alison Finlay, 'Jómsvíkinga Saga and Genre', *Scripta Islandica* 65 (2014), 63–79.
16 Philip Lavender, '*Illuga saga* as *fornaldarsaga*, *riddarasaga* and *Íslendingasaga*: Generic Fluidity in the Late Development of Sagas and Rímur', in *The Legendary Legacy: Transmission and Reception of the* Fornaldarsögur Norðurlanda, ed. Matthew Driscoll et al., Studies in Northern Civilization 24 (Odense, 2018), pp. 187–214.
17 Theodore M. Andersson, *The Growth of the Medieval Icelandic Sagas (1180–1280)* (Ithaca and London, 2006).

patterns from two (or more) forms, suggesting that generic awareness and, more importantly, a sense of generic hybridity was already in place at the beginning of Old Norse literary writing. Jürg Glauser makes similar arguments (although not specifically with respect to genre) by foregrounding an awareness of form and medium in the early stages of the development of literacy and writing in Norway and Iceland.[18] According to Glauser, this awareness signals a consciousness of literariness, which, by association, would imply a cognisance of related generic representational forms.

The emphasis in this chapter remains, as it does in Andersson's work, on *innovation* as the force that shaped not only the genres as we know them, but that was at the same time the source of their deconstruction and ultimate displacement. As with the *fornaldarsögur*, one of the genres that shows a great capacity for flexibility in its generic framework is the Norse romance. The romance is particularly interesting as it is an adapted (or imported) genre. The mode of its transmission and perpetuation can thus provide valuable information about the medieval perceptions of generic markers and affiliations. Once genres traverse linguistic (and cultural) boundaries, do they retain those generic identities or are their generic identities somehow inherent to their original linguistic realisation? Are generic markers in some sense dictated by linguistic (as well as cultural) temperament or disposition and what does that mean in terms of hybridity? The fact that dissimilar genres in Old French, with radically different styles, poetical forms and functionality, were translated into what would become the generic form of Norse prose romance, reveals that their original generic affiliations were of less significance then their narrative content or their presumed ideological function.

Given that proficiency in the metrical principles that dictated the formal design of early Old Norse poetry was valued highly as a craft indicates that Norse authors and audiences were well aware of and appreciated poetic form.[19] Yet, the metrical configurations of the translated material seem to have been fairly inconsequential in its transmission since the ten-syllable assonanced form of the *chansons de geste*, the octosyllabic *lais* of Marie de France and the rhymed couplets of Chrétien de Troyes' romances were translated indiscriminately into prose.[20] Similarly, the often radically

---

18 Jürg Glauser, 'Staging the Text: On the Development of a Consciousness of Writing in the Norwegian and Icelandic Literature of the Middle Ages', in *Along the Oral-Written Continuum: Types of Texts, Relations and their Implications*, ed. Slávica Rankovic (with Leidulf Melve and Else Mundal), Utrecht Studies in Medieval Literacy 20 (Turnhout, 2010), pp. 311–34.
19 See Heather O'Donoghue, *Skaldic Verse and the Poetics of Saga Narrative* (Oxford, 2005) and Guðrún Nordal, *Tools of Literacy: The Role of Skaldic Verse in Icelandic Textual Culture in the Twelfth and Thirteenth Centuries* (Toronto, 2000). For a discussion of form as a generic marker see Chapter 4 in this volume.
20 It should be noted here that the *chansons de geste*, the *lais* and the courtly romance obviously showed greater variety in metrical structures and exhibit themselves

different ideological functionality of these works and the associated socio-political contexts out of which they arose is disregarded as the narrative content is appropriated for its newly formulated function within the Norse context. The stories of Charlemagne, the tales of King Arthur and his knights and the playful short narratives contained in Marie de France's *lais* are reformulated into prose narrative accounts that in turn became the generic premise for what was to become the indigenous Norse romance.[21]

While it is thus the content and perhaps the prestige or presumed ideological context of the French material that dictates the transmission and reclassification of the material into its modified generic form of the Norse romance, the indigenous development of the genre refutes this pseudo-ideological motivation. In its place, the native romance focused its attention on the structural (episodic) formulation, the setting and the literary motifs. The genre of the so-called indigenous (or native) Norse romance shows, as a matter of fact, very little relation to its courtly predecessor. Instead it reveals the modulation of generic affiliation, not on the level of individual literary works, but on the scale of the conception of the genre itself. Hybridity is generally taken to signal the hybridisation of an estab-

---

evidence of hybridity and generic shifts as time passed. Later *chansons de geste* were frequently composed in mono-rhyme stanzas, often with twelve-syllabic lines. Similarly, while the courtly romances translated in thirteenth-century Norway were (most likely) in verse, French authors had by the thirteenth century begun to compose romance in prose, which eventually became the dominant form in French as well. Moreover, the French traditions of both the *chansons de geste* and the romances show evidence of hybridity that defies the notion of generic stability of the material on which the Norse authors were drawing (see for instance Melissa Furrow, *Expectations of Romance: The Reception of a Genre in Medieval England* (Cambridge, 2009); and Marianne Ailes, 'What's in a Name? Anglo-Norman Romances or *chansons de geste*', in *Medieval Romance, Medieval Contexts*, ed. Rhiannon Purdie and Michael Cichon, Studies in Medieval Romance (Cambridge, 2011), pp. 61–75). Yet, the fact that the metrical constraints of the translated material were largely ignored in their transmission nevertheless remains. It is of some interest in this context that a similar indifference with respect to form and generic markers can be observed in the transmission of French material in medieval Flanders, suggesting that the authors and translators had different concerns in their choice of materials and the mode of its deliverance, or, alternatively, that such generic formalities were deliberately ignored or hybridised (see Marjolein Hogenbirk, 'The "I-Word" and Genre: Merging Epic and Romance in the *Roman van Walewein*', in *'Li premerains verse': Essays in Honor of Keith Busby*, ed. Catherine M. Jones and Logan E. Whalen (Amsterdam and New York, 2011), pp. 157–70).

21 Admittedly the Norse version of the *lais*, the *Strengleikar* collection, differs somewhat here as it maintains the particular generic parameter of the *lais*, i.e. their narrative succinctness and brevity. Such narrative economy and conciseness in format would, of course, have been familiar to the audience accustomed to the narrative arrangement of the *þáttr* (short narrative episode), although the thematic approach, content and tonality of the *þættir* differ rather significantly from both the *lais* and their Norse representations.

lished generic form, evidenced in works that show affinities with at least two established and defined genres. Alternatively, hybrids can be said to indicate a deviation from a particular generic standard, thereby intimating the establishment of a 'new' (or a hybrid) generic form through 'external' influences on one or more of its generic factors or markers. The evidence of the transmission of the French courtly material and its reformulation into an indigenous generic form reveals on the other hand hybridity as generic modulation across not only time and space, but moreover as a form of reconception and mediation of generic identity.

The concept of hybridity and multi-modalities in transmission takes us directly back to the Old Norse prosimetric form, i.e. the combination of prose and verse in many of the sagas. The apparent modal distinction there (and its associated generic implications) is so obvious that it generally requires no mention or elaboration. It is unmistakable when there is a shift from the prose narrative to a versified interpolation, whether eddic or skaldic. Similarly, the þættir signal a formal breach with the saga form that nevertheless echoes its main generic markers – its primary deviation being in length. Yet, such shifts raise questions of generic conformity. And the shift – so noticeable as not to require self-conscious comment – calls attention to form and to the function of generic markers in shifting authorial and/or audience positioning.[22] Are these signalled and understood through vocal positioning, through rhythmical or versified means, through metaphoric content, through language use and choices, or a combination of the above? And why would it matter?

Can one assume that since the shift from a prose account to a verse recital within a single text or performance is so apparent that it needs no distinction or clarification? Yet, such generic structures remain the main framework for interpretation, both for basic semantic interpretation of the language used and the more literary one that seeks to decipher metaphoric connotations, allusions, structural and aesthetic correlations and subtle insinuations. Utilising the same interpretative approach to the skaldic verse as to the prose narrative would ultimately fail, as skaldic verse – by virtue of its form and metaphorical intricacies – requires a different set of tools; tools that the author and audiences must be familiar with in order to be able to engage successfully with the material. This navigation through multimodal and multigeneric materials requires a shifting of the interpretative framework and expectations. More importantly, the prose context directly impacts the way in which embedded verses are understood and vice versa, suggesting that hybridity was indeed an essential feature of the

---

22 For a discussion of the use of prosimetrum as means of generic distinction in Old Norse literature see for instance Helen F. Leslie-Jacobsen, 'Genre and the Prosimetra of the Old Icelandic *fornaldarsögur*', in *Genre – Text – Interpretation: Multidisciplinary Perspectives on Folklore and Beyond*, ed. Kaarina Koski and Frog, with Ulla Savolainen, Studia Fennica, Folklorica 22 (Helsinki, 2016), pp. 251–75.

prosimetrum text, and, moreover, that authors and audiences were both aware of this and ready to adjust their interpretative stance with each generic (or modal) shift.

What I mean to draw attention to here is the fact, so obvious as to be potentially overlooked, that the generic framework dictates precisely how the audience approaches literary material. This framework is, however, continually shifting as each reading or hearing repositions the framework anew, subtly shifting it, modifying or adapting its parameters to guide the audience in deciphering its conformities and its deviations as part of a generic game in which both authors and audiences partake. Such frameworks are intrinsic to the mediation of literary meaning and critical in literary engagement as they dictate how readers and audiences are to understand the narrative material. Moreover, as many have suggested before, they are shaped by multiple factors, including style, linguistic choices, setting, plot structure and, ultimately, the emotional valence of a text. The fact that 'Sonatorrek' in *Egils saga Skalla-Grímssonar* provides a means for an emotional outlet that the prose narrative (as a generic form) patently represses reveals that generic markers have a literary functionality in terms of the way in which action, gestures and words are staged and how we are to interpret their staging.

## Emotion as Generic Marker

The suggestion that emotion can function as a generic marker does not solve the dilemma of generic categorisations, but it offers a means of shifting attention from purely structural, stylistic, or thematic focuses to consider how the more immaterial aspects of narratives or texts shape our perception of them and their potential generic affiliations. Such immaterial aspects could include tonality, vocality and affective aspects. Generic debate iterates the observation that hybrid texts show affinities with multiple (two or more) generic categories, but those affinities are often quite vague and difficult to describe. *Sigurðar saga þǫgla* is categorised as a *riddarasaga* due to its setting, thereby separating it from the *fornaldarsögur* (set in the ancient North) and the *Íslendingasögur* (dealing with Icelanders). Its thematic content moreover defines it as belonging to the subgenre of the *meykónga sögur* (maiden king romances), or bridal-quest romance as Marianne E. Kalinke has defined it.[23] Yet, linguistically speaking there is a tonality to the syntactical structure that in many ways is more reminiscent of the language of the *Íslendingasögur* than the romances, particularly the translated ones. Moreover, this variation in tonality is reflected in a certain ethos or behavioural code of the characters that similarly adheres to cer-

---

23 Marianne E. Kalinke, *Bridal-Quest Romance in Medieval Iceland*, Islandica 46 (Ithaca, 1990). Kalinke qualifies the maiden-king romance as a uniquely Icelandic manifestation of the larger European convention of the bridal-quest romance (itself a sub-type of the larger more heterogeneous genre of romance).

tain principles that are reminiscent of those of the *Íslendingasögur*.

While such codes can be said to reflect normative behavioural conventions, they are also (at least partially) generic. Emotional gestures, words and behaviour serve an interpersonal communicative function that is both historically and culturally contingent and so to a certain extent can be said to reflect the cultural conventions of any given community.[24] Once such emotional behaviour becomes part of a textual fabric or narrative agenda the associated emotive gestures and performances assume a literary functionality. They become *literary* motifs that serve a narrative function and as such form part of the textual matrix that comprises the generic identity of a text. Such codes (or emotive scripts) can be described as affective signposts intended to generate certain emotional responses in an audience, or, alternatively, they can be defined as literary signals that serve as signals to guide the audience in the interpretation of events.[25]

The *hvǫt* (whetting) would be an example of the textual staging of emotion for the sake of generating an affective response in the internal (fictive) audience, capitulating to the emotion-inducing (or emotion-framed) socio-political system of honour, value and familial obligations. The pseudo-emotional performance of the *hvǫt* functions simultaneously, however, as a literary signpost to the audience presaging the pending dramatic events of vengeance and deaths, building narrative anticipation and pleasure. Hildigunnr's *hvǫt*-lament in *Brennu-Njáls saga* is a prime example.[26] These emotion-based behavioural codes thus function as literary signals to the reader and thereby serve as key generic indicators. The emotive performance of the *hvǫt* has, for instance, no place in the romance as the socio-cultural context of the honour-code system no longer applies to its particular fictive realm. Hence, its associated affective and performative functions position the reader with respect to the ideological context within which he or she is to interpret the narrative material. The emotive coding of romance draws on entirely different literary and ideological functionalities and so its associated vocabulary and gestural and behavioural conventions reflect this different literary positioning, guiding the reader in how to interpret the material. Shifts in emotional behaviour can therefore cause the destabilisation of generic parameters as audience's expectations of their literary (or aesthetic) function are modified to accommodate their new or alternate functionality. Such shifts thus signal generic hybridity or multimodality

---

24 See for instance Barbara H. Rosenwein, *Emotional Communities in the Early Middle Ages* (Ithaca, 2006).

25 See Sif Rikhardsdottir, *Emotion in Old Norse Literature: Translations, Voices, Contexts*, Studies in Old Norse Literature 1 (Cambridge, 2017), particularly pp. 25–32.

26 See for instance the discussion in Carol Clover, 'Hildigunnr's Lament', in *Cold Counsel: Women in Old Norse Literature and Mythology: A Collection of Essays*, ed. Sarah M. Anderson and Karen Swenson (New York and London, 2002), pp. 15–54.

and may indicate the demise of a genre as a new hybrid one is formulated. It may also indicate the conscious manipulation of such generic parameters to undermine their ideological premise (as is the case with parody, for instance) or to destabilise their literary, ideological, or political premise through the manipulation of the audience's generic expectations.

The presumed subgenre of the maiden king romance mentioned above is indeed ideal for showcasing such multi-modalities in generic affiliations. There are only a handful of stories that are conventionally assumed to belong to the genre (or the sub-group of the romance as a genre) and these reveal an unusual plasticity in generic adherence. Their categorisation is based on thematic content, more specifically on the particular topos of the maiden-king and her would-be suitors. Yet, the stories traditionally categorised under the maiden-king topos not only belong to two separate generic groupings, i.e. the *riddarasaga* and the *fornaldarsaga*, but moreover show traits of multiple other medieval genres or textual conventions.[27] *Sigurðar saga þǫgla* draws on the stylistic and syntactical conventions of the *Íslendingasögur* and the narrative conventions of *fornaldarsögur* to convey its narrative. *Mírmanns saga* reveals, on the other hand, substantially different ethical or ideological traits. The story exhibits traces of hagiographical impulses, both in form and in a narrative focus on inner obligations, emotion and faith. Its language indeed exposes a multimodality that seems almost topographically dictated. The tonality shifts from displaying Norse-oriented qualities at the outset to the more chivalric-oriented linguistic choices as the setting moves further south. In this sense it affirms its affinity to the Norse romance as a geographically contingent generic form. Finally, *Viktors saga ok Blávus* is so convoluted as to suggest that it may have been intended as a semi-parodic form of the romance convention and/or of its sub-generic form of the maiden king romance.

Geraldine Barnes' suggestion that the authors of the indigenous romances knew each other and might have been writing specifically for each other seems plausible in this context and might explain the pronounced generic hybridity of many of the indigenous romances.[28] If the authors

27 Marianne Kalinke and others have categorised the romances *Dínus saga drambláta, Gibbons saga, Clári saga, Mágus saga jarls, Nitida saga, Partalopa saga, Sigrgarðs saga frækna, Sigurðar saga þǫgla* and *Viktors saga ok Blávus* and the legendary sagas *Hrólfs saga Gautrekssonar* and *Hrólfs saga kraka* as belonging to the maiden king topos (Kalinke, Bridal-Quest Romance and Jóhanna Katrín Friðriksdóttir, Women in Old Norse Literature: Bodies, Words, and Power, The New Middle Ages (New York, 2013), pp. 107–34). Others have excluded the two legendary sagas on the basis that these do not exhibit the maiden king topos as a full-fledged motif dictating the story thread, although the concept of a reluctant bride is certainly in place in the earlier legendary sagas (Sif Rikhardsdottir, 'Meykóngahefðin í riddarasögum: Hugmyndafræðileg átök um kynhlutverk og þjóðfélagsstöðu', Skírnir 184 (2010), 410–33).

28 Geraldine Barnes, *The Bookish Riddarasögur: Writing Romance in Late Mediaeval Iceland* (Odense, 2014).

were indeed writing within the confines of a particular generic convention with the knowledge that their audiences would have been aware of those generic parameters and delighted in the recognition of the generic playfulness of the material then these multi-modalities might have been intentional. Even if one cannot assume such literary proficiency on part of the audience of the *riddarasögur* at large (they were after all tremendously popular and read widely), even an unskilled audience would be able to sense and recognise some intertextual ploys and generic instabilities or parodic tendencies. The purpose would thus have been to engage the audience in a literary game of multi-valence and variance in generic formalities.

## Conclusion

It is possible that generic hybridisation is a 'natural' development of generic parameters across time, i.e. that a genre has a lifespan that moves from its early establishment (through social conditions, narrative developments, literary and/or aesthetic evolution and stylistic and linguistic preferences) to a sort of 'peak'. This hypothetical generic climax is then followed by either a dissolution, as the generic framework ceases to be applicable, or hybridisation, as authors begin to experiment with its generic markers, expanding generic borders and obfuscating formerly clear generic affiliations. Evidence of hybridisation in the so-called post-classical *Íslendingasögur* – evidence that has, in fact, often been used to demarcate them from the so-called 'classical' sagas – recurs in the fourteenth-century indigenous romance. No longer arising out of a courtly context, the Icelandic romance has adopted the magical reality of the courtly romance, its stage and its setting (Europe and the world at large). Yet, its linguistic representation, its narrative concerns and its ideological mentalities range widely across the generic discourses available to fourteenth-century authors. As a generic form, the Norse romance itself can thus be classified as a hybrid.

Generic hybridity therefore reveals both an affirmation of generic parameters and their simultaneous negation. These can indicate the demise of a particular genre, whether for socio-political reasons (when a particular literary convention, established on the grounds of a particular socio-cultural premise that no longer applies, fades away), or for aesthetic or literary historical reasons (through shifts in tastes and aesthetic preferences). Such generic prevalence may frequently be random, in the sense that particular conventions survive through their incorporation into the canon, while others die away. And many texts refute any generic categorisations, remaining idiosyncratic evidence of a literary creativity that both defies previous generic stipulations, but which nevertheless does not lead to the establishment of new generic conventions. Dante's *Divina Commedia* may be an example of such a text, despite the fact that it professes to place itself squarely in the Aristotelian generic division between comedy and tragedy, while simultaneously (and consciously) refuting the very parameters that its presumed categorisation would suggest it sought to follow.

The concept of generic hybridity raises the question of the stability of generic parameters, i.e. whether such stability can actually exist. Hybridity can be defined or interpreted as a mode of identifying a process of transformation, the blurred outlines of a generic category. In some sense it can be argued that any new text is a hybrid in the sense that it is always springs out of pre-existing literature, but nevertheless in some respects must break free from the constraints imposed by previous forms as a new invention. Hybridity in some sense can be said to be the domain where literature (as a whole) finds its form, its literary shape and its mode of delivery, largely following certain typologies, yet reformulating them to suit each work anew, thereby simultaneously affirming and transforming those categories. The fact that generic forms emerge and vanish suggests that they are historically and culturally contingent, providing literary means for addressing societal concerns, political conditions or artistic desires and preferences. Generic hybridity thus may provide a method for authors to break free from literary conventions in order to mediate new literary concerns or address alternative or novel cultural circumstances or linguistic realities. This means that generic frameworks may indeed provide necessary, perhaps even crucial, conditions for constantly reformulating narrative techniques: a canvas on which the author is able to recast his or her material in a new light, through new techniques or with new emphases.

Ultimately, the rejection of previous generic forms often signals an authorial assertion of creative value; a negation or refusal of literary conventionality that may nevertheless have been a necessary prelude to the new work. Geoffrey Chaucer's playful incorporation of pre-existing Middle English literary forms in *The Canterbury Tales* in some sense can be said to hybridise the relevant generic forms, thereby changing the audience perception of their functionality. Miguel de Cervantes' *Don Quixote* can only be understood when cast against the previous conventions of the chivalric romance. Its parodic elements only remain comprehensible if the audience appreciates and understands the generic framework out of which the parody is constructed. Similarly, Halldór Laxness' *Gerpla* can be said to both endorse and ridicule the saga form as a memorial of the past and as a national heritage, thereby affirming its generic identity while simultaneously subverting the very identity it claims to authenticate.

# Terminology
*Lukas Rösli*

The scholarly motivation to classify the vast amount of Old Norse-Icelandic texts into different literary genres is perfectly understandable, as classifications ensure systematisation and thus comparability within certain segments of the established system. This motivation is based on the common opinion that Old Norse-Icelandic literature is and always has been accepted as being inherently heterogeneous. Such an opinion can, of course, be affected by at least two different fundamental premises. One would be that the literary texts themselves reflect some sort of self-referential classification or even, perhaps, a kind of genre awareness which is to be understood as an inherent aspect of the literature in question. The other would be that recipients or audiences recognise certain recurring structures, which are often treated as if they are historically stable and invariable, such as media or modes, patterns or schemes within the texts in question; this would then allow the audience to separate these texts into what we call literary genres and label these literary texts using the respective terminology.

This chapter does not aim to critique the use of a genre taxonomy, but rather to question the significance of applicability of today's academic genre terminology as a way of understanding Old Norse-Icelandic literature in a medieval and early modern text culture. The present genre terminology is useful as a way to systematise literature and to place narratives in some form of a comparable schema, but, just as any systematisation, it simplifies both the historico-cultural dimensions of Old Norse-Icelandic literature and its changeability during the transmission of narratives. Furthermore, the present genre terminology, which is used in the study of Old Norse-Icelandic literature to label certain narratives, is based on more or less arbitrary features establishing and defining rather strict boundaries of genres, as I will show later in this chapter.

The aim of this chapter is thus twofold: first, I will discuss the usefulness of today's terminology of genre in Old Norse-Icelandic literature, secondly, I will propose some directions for a more historical approach concerning the terminology of genre in Old Norse-Icelandic literature.

## Genre Terminology in Old Norse-Icelandic Literature

First, it is advisable to clearly define the ways in which the terminology in question relates to the literary research subject. The most obvious way of thinking about Old Norse-Icelandic and its genre terminology would be to understand it in the literal sense, and thus try to find positive evidence of an Old Norse-Icelandic word which might be translated as 'genre' or which at least connotes a semantically defined terminology to describe 'a category of literary composition', which might be the simplest way of defining genre.¹ The problem with such an attempt is that there is no specific term or word in the Old Norse-Icelandic language to describe the literary concept of what we consider as genre today. In other words, where modern mainland-Scandinavian languages and English use the French loan-word genre and modern Icelandic manages with the compound bókmenntagrein to describe the French term genre and its concept, Old Norse-Icelandic has never had a semantically defined terminology to refer to anything like a 'category of literary compositions or genre'. The absence of a linguistically distinct and descriptive terminology for the concept of genre in the vernacular seems to be common to all Scandinavian languages, both in their medieval variations and in their modern national manifestations.² Due to this absence of an Old Norse term for genre one has to find an alternative approach to the analysis of Old Norse-Icelandic literature and the question of a genre terminology.³

---

1   Such a working definition of the term 'genre' is, of course, rather simple. Keeping in mind that standard reference books such as *A Companion to Old Norse-Icelandic Literature and Culture*, ed. Rory McTurk, Blackwell Companions to Literature and Culture 31 (Oxford and Malden, 2005) or *Medieval Scandinavia: An Encyclopaedia*, ed. Phillip Pulsiano and Kirsten Wolf (New York, 1993) make extensive use of the word genre without ever defining its meaning, the suggested working definition might be sufficient for the purpose of discussing the existence of an equivalent in the Old Norse language. For a comprehensive overview of the semantic contents of the word, its different levels of meaning and the scholarly concepts behind the word genre see: John Frow, *Genre*, The New Critical Idiom (Abingdon, 2006). In contrast to such a broad definition of the terminology of genre and its concept see: Harald Fricke, *Norm und Abweichung: Eine Philosophie der Literatur* (München, 1981). Fricke's distinction between 'Gattung' (genus), 'Textsorte' (text type), and 'Genre' (genre) was very influential in German language genre theory (*ibid.*, pp. 135–38). According to Fricke, 'Gattung' is a generic term that refers to a classification of different literary groups, while 'Textsorte' is a systematically rendered defining argument in literary studies, classifying text-types based on their synchronic language norms and their period of origin. Fricke's 'Genre', on the other hand, refers to a historically limited literary institution, including previous texts and even non-literary documents. Therefore, the 'Genre' is a subset of all the texts of a certain 'Textsorte', if these texts have been institutionalised in the literature of a certain historical period.
2   The same absence applies partially to German, which uses both the German word 'Gattung' (genus) and the loan word 'genre'. On the discussion of when the literary term 'genre' entered the English language see: René Wellek and Austin Warren, *Theory of Literature* (New York, 1949), p. 338, n. 8.
3   According to Algirdas Julien Greimas's discourse on the analytical theory of the existence of a semantic universe, the absence – as a term in the category of absence/presence – is one of those terms articulating the semiotic mode of existence of the objects of knowledge. As such, the absence of a term in a

## Terminology

The lack of a specific genre terminology in the Old Norse-Icelandic corpus is in direct contrast with the medieval Latin literary traditions, in which – at least since the birth of scholasticism – there has been an overall systematic distinction between *genus* and *species*, being just the first two of the five *predicable* (followed by *differentia*, *proprium*, and *accidens*) used in scholastic logic used to establish a classification of a possible relation between the predicate and its subject.[4] The systematic distinction was reflected in the shortened scholastic formula *genus proximum et differentia specifica* (roughly translated as 'the closest genus and the specific difference'),[5] based on antique Aristotelian taxonomy. This distinction was used to hierarchically distinguish every generic term and its respective narrowed terms, and not only as a way of distinguishing between literary genres. In a more specifically literary context Isidore of Seville discussed the basic distinction between *prosa* and *carmina* (*Etymologiæ*, book I, chapter 38) and between *facta* and *ficta* (*Etymologiæ*, book I, chapter 40).[6] The definitions of these distinctions could of course be traced back to the Roman-Latin and classical Greek treatises on literary theory and rhetoric, when *poesis* (or poetry, being the art of imitation or *mimesis*) and *logos* (or speech, being the factual counterpart of *mimesis*) were distinguished as the main genres, subdivided into different *genera*, as for example *drama*, *lyric*, and *epic*.[7] These genre-specific classifications from Aristotle's *Poetics* were, however, later made accessible through Francesco Robortello's annotated edition of the *Poetics* from 1548 and were popular among European scholars.[8]

---

semiotic system has still to be understood as a form of 'existing in absence' on the pragmatic axis of what Saussure defined as *langage*. Therefore, the absent term or word is still virtually in existance as part of the cognitive dimension of the *langage*. Thus, the fact that there is no generic terminology describing the concept of genre in Old Norse-Icelandic language cannot be regarded as evidence for the nonexistence of a distinction between different literary genres in Old Norse-Icelandic literature, if literary products are accepted as being a discursive praxis using a self-referential system of semiotics. On Greimas's definition of 'absence' cf. the lemma *absence* in Algirdas Julien Greimas and Joseph Courtés, *Sémiotique: Dictionnaire Raisonné de la Théorie de Langage* (Paris, 1979), p. 1.

4   See also Martin Grabmann, *Die Geschichte der scholastischen Methode*, 2. vols, *Die scholastische Methode im 12. und beginnenden 13. Jahrhundert* (Graz, 1957), pp. 103–124.

5   Ulrich Ernst, 'Gattungstheorie im Mittelalter', in *Handbuch Gattungstheorie*, ed. Rüdiger Zymner (Stuttgart and Weimar, 2010), pp. 201–02.

6   For the respective chapters see: *Isidori Hispalensis episcopi Etymologiarum sive Originum libri XX*, ed. Wallace Martin Lindsay, 2 vols (Oxford, 1911), no page numbers provided in the edition.

7   Stefan Freund, 'Gattungstheorie in der Antike', in *Handbuch Gattungstheorie*, ed. Rüdiger Zymner, pp. 199–200.

8   Francesco Robortello, *In librum Aristotelis De arte poetica explications* (Firenze, 1548).

As I will show later, the modern genre terminology used to classify Old Norse-Icelandic literary works is mainly based on scholarly taxonomies from nineteenth- and twentieth-century literary studies – with the apparent exception of some medieval compilations, frequently considered be accounted for by an awareness of literary genre distinctions. It is often suggested that the Icelandic scribal community or at least some scribes in the Middle Ages were aware of genre distinctions, as some manuscripts look like compilations based on these distinctions, such as the famous Möðruvallabók, AM 132 fol., (containing what we today call *Íslendingasögur*) or AM 152 fol. (containing *riddarasögur* and *fornaldarsögur*).[9] There are at least two objections against such an evaluation of these manuscripts: first, as it is mainly based on contemporary genre definitions and distinctions, which are just applied to and allegedly reconfirmed by these manuscripts, the risk exists that this leads to a circular argument. Second, most of the sagas transmitted in the beforementioned compilations are also included in other manuscripts containing a wide range of different 'genres'. Hence, these evaluations are without any doubt very significant and important in terms of single manuscript studies, but they do not provide enough self-referential informative value concerning generally applicable literary distinctions one could base the distinctions of literary genres upon. As a consequence, we should clearly distinguish between potential genre terminology in Old Norse-Icelandic literature, which refers to a terminology to be detected only in Old Norse-Icelandic literary texts, and a terminology deduced from a systematisation based on theoretical and methodological implications from modern studies in Old Norse-Icelandic literature.

## Genre Terminology

As has been previously discussed, there is no generic medieval Old Norse-Icelandic terminology referring to categories of literary compositions comparable to the term *genre*. These classifications are sometimes called *genres*, but it is more common to repeat a terminology traditionally used in the study of Old Norse-Icelandic literature without actually discussing the problematic nature of these supposed generic terms.[10] The

9   For a thorough discussion of Möðruvallabók see Claudia Müller, *Erzähltes Wissen: Die Isländersagas in der Möðruvallabók (AM 132 fol.)*, Texte und Untersuchungen zur Germanistik und Skandinavistik 47 (Frankfurt am Main, 2001); for a discussion of AM 152 fol. see: Jóhanna Katrín Friðriksdóttir, 'Ideology and Identity in Late Medieval Northwest Iceland: A Study of AM 152 fol.', *Gripla* 25 (2014), 87–128 and her chapter in this volume.

10  In a very informative article Massimiliano Bampi discusses the problem of such traditionally used terminologies on the basis of Old Norse-Icelandic sagas: Massimiliano Bampi, 'Genre', in *The Routledge Research Companion to the Medieval Icelandic Sagas*, ed. Ármann Jakobsson and Sverrir Jakobsson, (London and New York, 2017), pp. 4–14.

overall problem with the terminology used to describe some sort of generic systematisation is that 'the very notion of genre has been largely left undefined in previous research'.[11] Despite the fact that the genre terminology traditionally used in the study of Old Norse-Icelandic literature is built upon self-created epistemological auxiliary concepts which reflect arbitrary structural criteria, most often lacking actual text or rather manuscript based evidence, scholars assume that their genre concepts are both self-evident and contain historical and socio-cultural significance and stability with regard to the transmission of the literature in question. Bampi reflects upon the problem of such an assumed self-evidence of the genre terminology and its concepts, and he concludes: 'the risk that is inherent in the lack of a shared definition of the object of study is quite obvious; it can indeed not be taken for granted that all scholars have the same definition in mind.'[12] Bampi's justified criticism of an undefined genre terminology in the study of Old Norse-Icelandic literature can be taken further, because the individual use of genre concepts and genre terminologies by scholars implicitly contradicts the idea of the genre in its traditional sense, as such heterogeneous use undermines direct comparability. Furthermore, the existence of such different concepts of *genres* derived from individual catalogues of criteria or based on various theories and methodologies suggests that at least some of these genres are built upon anachronistic or even ahistorical assumptions, even if scholars treat these genres as historically stable entities.[13]

In our analysis, the first question should be: what is Old Norse-Icelandic literature anyway? As this is not the place to start a fundamental discussion about the nature of the term *literature* I will simply refer to what contemporary companions define as Old Norse-Icelandic literature, as these books give us a first indication of a classification of the literature in question into genres.[14] In *Eddas and Sagas: Iceland's Medieval Lit-*

---

11 Bampi, 'Genre', p. 7.
12 *Ibid.*
13 For a brief but informative overview over the most influential theoretical approaches and the academic discussion of genre in Old Norse-Icelandic saga literature see Bampi, 'Genre', pp. 4–7. Good insight into the discussion on structural theories and methods as tools to analyse genres and their terminology in saga literature can be found in SS 47:4 (1975), where Lars Lönnroth ('The Concept of Genre in Saga Literature', pp. 419–26) argues in favour of a less rigid concept of genre. In the same issue Joseph Harris ('Genre in the Saga Literature: A Squib', pp. 427–36) defends the status quo, while introducing Ben-Amos' concepts of 'ethnic genres', genre labels contemporary with the period in which a certain literary text was produced, and 'analytic categories', modern scholarly distinctions which, according to Harris, should be disclosed and marked as such by scholars. Theodore M. Anderson ('Splitting the Sagas', SS 47:4 (1975), 437–41) argues in favour of a very detailed structuralist catalogue of distinct stylistic similarities to justify the genre nuclei.
14 In the case of the studies of Old Norse-Icelandic literature the question of what

*erature* Jónas Kristjánsson presents in the table of contents the following overview of the literature he discusses in the book: eddic poetry, skaldic poetry, learned literature (including early laws, genealogies and historiography, as well as foreign scholarly literature), hagiography, kings' sagas, contemporary sagas, sagas of Icelanders, *Íslendinga þættir*, sagas of chivalry, heroic sagas, Jónsbók, and new forms (including ballads, *rímur*, religious verses, and secular poetry).[15] This sequence of genre terminologies seems to structure the described literature in chronological order, based on the supposed time of (oral) origin, as one can assume from the chapter 'The major periods'.[16] Several literary distinctions are recognised, the first being the division into poetry and sagas, which are subdivided and individually labelled, such as eddic and skaldic poetry or kings' sagas and heroic sagas; another distinction separates these specified genres of poetry and sagas from unmarked literary genres such as hagiography and other literary forms. In Carol Clover and John Lindow's *Old Norse-Icelandic Literature. A Critical Guide,* the table of contents lists fewer items: mythology and mythography, eddic poetry, skaldic poetry, kings' sagas, Icelandic family sagas, and Norse romances.[17] In the preface the authors state that their intention was to publish a '[...] serviceable guide to the major genres (or categories, in the case of mythology and mythography) of Old Norse-Icelandic literature [...]'.[18] This statement implicitly distinguishes the presented genres from all other genres in Old Norse-Icelandic literature, which are consequently featured as minor genres. This establishes a sort of hierarchy between the discussed genres and those genres omitted from the book. Besides the differentiation of mythology and mythography as distinct 'categories' there are two primary genre

---

Old Norse-Icelandic literature is, has not, to my knowledge and in contrast to the studies of English, French or German literary studies, ever been discussed in a theoretical way. To enable a thorough discussion of *genre* in Old Norse-Icelandic literature it is fundamentally important to define the concept of *literature* and its limits in the first place. It is all the more surprising that we are able to discuss and analyse *literature* without previously defining our main research subject, and that it is possible for us to divide such an undefined corpus into different groups and subgroups called *genres*. The two presented companions are chosen on the basis of their availability. These two books should by no means be understood to typify the introductory literature, handbooks or companions in the field, and neither did I choose these examples to criticise their approach toward Old Norse-Icelandic literature or their specific classification of this literature into different genres. To obtain more meaningful results one would have to include more standard reference books, including scholarly works on the history of literature from the present and at least the last two centuries.

15 Jónas Kristjánsson, *Eddas and Sagas: Iceland's Medieval Literature*, trans. Peter Foote (Reykjavík, 1997), at pp. 5–6.
16 *Ibid.*, pp. 21–24.
17 *Old Norse-Icelandic Literature: A Critical Guide*, ed. Carol J. Clover and John Lindow (Toronto, Buffalo and London, 2005), see p. 3 for table of contents.
18 *Ibid.*, p. 3.

distinctions (poetry and sagas) with two or three respective subdivisions (eddic and skaldic as the distinctive markers for poetry, and kings', Icelandic family, and Norse romance as markers for the saga subgenres). Furthermore, in Clover and Lindow's guide the terminology used for the different saga genres is not only presented in English but also in Old Norse, according to their standard terminology used in the study of Old Norse-Icelandic literature: the English designations kings' sagas, Icelandic family sagas, and Norse romances are rendered as *konungasögur*, *Íslendingasögur*, and *riddarasögur* respectively. There are further differences when we compare the genre terminology of these two books. The terminology used to refer to one of the poetic subgenres is either *eddaic* or *eddic*, while *Íslendingasögur* are called sagas of Icelanders or Icelandic family sagas, and the term *riddarasögur* is translated as sagas of chivalry or Norse romance; all of these terms connote different meanings and give the impression of an arbitrary use of the respective terminology.[19] Moreover, not only is the terminology used in a rather arbitrary way but so also are the concepts of genre employed in these two books to systematise and categorise Old Norse-Icelandic literature. These are based on very different approaches and a variety of criteria is used to classify these literary texts such as: media (*saga* or prose vs. skaldic or verse), modes (*eddic* vs. *skaldic*), subcategories built upon a variety of features such as narrative styles, textual contents, motifs, timeframes, settings or even the birthplace of the main character (*Íslendingasögur*, *riddarasögur*, or *konungasögur*).[20] The length of a narrative (*saga* vs. *þáttr*), the question of historicity (*Íslendingasögur* as quasi-historical accounts vs. *Íslendingasögur* as a narrated creation of the past), or the alleged level of foreignness of a narrative (translated *riddarasögur* vs. indigenous or Icelandic *riddarasögur*).[21]

---

19 On the problem of *eddic* or *eddaic* being a scholarly rather than a generic term to distinguish this mode in poetry from the skaldic mode, see Margaret Clunies Ross, 'The Transmission and Preservation of Eddic Poetry', in *A Handbook to Eddic Poetry: Myths and Legends of Early Scandinavia*, ed. Carolyne Larrington, Judy Quinn and Brittany Schorn (Cambridge, 2016) pp. 12–32; or Terry Gunnell, 'Eddic Poetry', in *A Companion to Old Norse-Icelandic Literature and Culture*, ed. Rory McTurk, Blackwell Companion to Literature and Culture 31 (Oxford and Malden, 2005), pp. 82–100.

20 For a good introduction to the eddic modes and genres see: Brittany Schorn, 'Eddic Modes and Genres', in *A Handbook to Eddic Poetry: Myths and Legends of Early Scandinavia*, ed. Larrington, Quinn and Schorn, pp. 231–51; a short but good overview over the modes, genres and subgenres of skaldic verses is Chapter 3 (pp. 40–68) in Margaret Clunies Ross, *A History of Old Norse Poetry and Poetics*, (Cambridge, 2005). For a very influential structuralist discussion of different saga genres see Kurt Schier, *Sagaliteratur* (Stuttgart, 1970).

21 For a traditional definition of a *þáttr* (pl. *þættir*) being a short story see Jónas Kristjánsson, *Eddas and Sagas*, pp. 299–301. For a more critical evaluation of the terminology see Stefanie Würth, *Elemente des Erzählens: Die þættir der Flateyjarbók*,

The genre terminology used in the study of Old Norse-Icelandic literature is thus an arbitrary social or scholarly convention, rather than based on the actual self-designation and self-conception of the literature in question. There are, of course, some notable exceptions that contribute to the basis of every argument supporting the existence of 'literary genres in Old Norse-Icelandic literature'; terms such as *konungasögur* and *riddarasögur* are subgroups within saga literature, which are attested by medieval manuscripts.[22] The evidence for a word does not prove our modern understanding of the word as part of a systematic and retrospectively imposed genre structure to be correct. The question is whether these endocentric compounds that include the head word *saga* (noun f. sg.), which can be translated as 1) 'what is said, statement'; 2) 'tale, story, history'; 3) 'the events which gave rise to the story'; or 4) 'tale, report', actually connote the idea of a literary genre at all if used to refer to a literary medium, or if they simply refer to a story with a certain main topic, expressed in the modifier of the compound, which can be either totally fictitious or historical.[23]

---

Beiträge zur nordischen Philologie 20 (Basel, 1991); and for a good introduction to recent scholarship on this topic see Elizabeth Ashman Rowe and Joseph Harris, 'Short Prose Narrative (*þáttr*)', in *A Companion to Old Norse-Icelandic Literature and Culture*, ed. McTurk, pp. 462–78. On historicity and constructed memory see Jürg Glauser, 'Sagas of the Icelanders (*Íslendinga sögur*) and *þættir* as the Literary Representation of a New Social Space', trans. John Clifton-Everest, in *Old Icelandic Literature and Society*, ed. Margaret Clunies Ross, Cambridge Studies in Medieval Literature 42 (Cambridge, 2002), pp. 203–20. For a thorough discussion of the dichotomy with respect to the *riddarasögur* see Marianne Kalinke, 'Norse Romance (*Riddarasögur*)', in *Old Norse-Icelandic Literature: A Critical Guide*, ed. Clover and Lindow, pp. 316–63.

22 The fact that there are only very few such terms to be found in medieval Old Norse-Icelandic manuscripts designating what often is thought of as being a genre terminology triggered a common idiom: 'While the term *konungasögur* and *riddarasögur* are attested in manuscripts from the Middle Ages, we do not find any occurrence of, for example, the terms *fornaldarsögur* or *Íslendingasögur* in medieval sources.' (Bampi, 'Genre', pp. 5–6) or: 'Unlike many of the standard saga genre designations – *Íslendingasögur, konungasögur, riddarasögur,* etc. – which are actually attested in the medieval literature, the term *fornaldarsaga* is a modern coinage, [...].' (Matthew Driscoll, 'Introduction: The Transmission and Reception of the *fornaldarsögur Norðurlanda*', in *The Legendary Legacy: Transmission and Reception of the Fornaldarsögur Norðurlanda*, ed. Matthew Driscoll et al., The Viking Collection 24 (Odense, 2018), pp. 9–17, at p. 9). The compound *konunga sögum* (dative pl.) is for the first time attested in a manuscript Holm perg 7 4$^{to}$, dated to 1300–25, and the compound *riddara sögur* (nominative/accusative pl.) in AM dipl isl fasc V 18, dated to 1396. However, Driscoll is wrong in assuming an existence of the compound *Íslendingasögur* or its singular *Íslendingasaga* as some form of literary genre designation before the seventeenth century. For a discussion of the historicity of the genre term *Íslendingasögur* see Lukas Rösli, 'Paratextual References to the Genre Term *Íslendinga sögur* in Old Norse-Icelandic Manuscripts', *Opuscula* 17 / *Bibliotheca Arnamagnæana* 52 (2019), 151–67.

23 Cf. the lemma *saga* in: Geir T. Zoëga, *A Concise Dictionary of Old Icelandic* (Oxford,

During the discussion on genre terminology at the symposium on *Literary Genre in Old Norse-Icelandic Literature* it was suggested, with reference to its use in the *Prose Edda*, that the Old Norse term *háttr* (pl. *hættir*) had some significance with relation to genre.[24] The word *háttr* has semantic polyvalence ranging from 'mode of life', 'habit', or 'custom', to 'mode' or 'way of doing things', to 'metre'.[25] Margaret Clunies Ross has suggested that in a literary context *háttr* is understood as referring to verse-form, mode or metre.[26] In her article on 'Eddic modes and genres', Brittany Schorn takes up Hans Robert Jauss's argument that 'mode of writing' is contained within a poet or author's genre-related choices during composition, and the 'horizon of expectation' is the frame which helps audiences to understand and interpret the literary material.[27] By applying Jauss's theories on 'Rezeptionsästhetik' (reader-response criticism) to the eddic corpus in this way, Schorn avoids the problems that correlate with ahistorical genre concepts. Schorn states that eddic modes, and also genres, are thus not strictly defined, and that 'the elusiveness of eddic genre is thus more a strength than a weakness' for the Old Norse-Icelandic eddic literary corpus.[28]

## Re-Evaluating Genre Terminology in Old Norse-Icelandic Literature

Given that the present diversity of genre categories is only partially based on intrinsic features of Old Norse-Icelandic literary texts, the genre terminology in question is mainly dependent on the respective normative approaches used by scholars, as well as on the process of ed-

---

1967, orig. 1910), p. 346. In relation to the literary medium *saga*, Schier adds the quality of textualisation to his definition: Schier, *Sagaliteratur*, pp. 1–2.

24 The editors of this volume held a symposium in the spring of 2018 at Ca'Foscari University, Venice, at which most of the contributors presented and discussed the various chapter topics in preparation for this volume. The term *háttr* is used in the section of the *Prose Edda* called *Skáldskaparmál* to define the two categories in which poetry is divided: '*Mál ok hættir*' (Snorri Sturluson, *Edda: Skáldskaparmál, 1. Introduction, Text, and Notes*, ed. Anthony Faulkes (London, 2005), p. 5), which can be translated as 'Language and verse-forms' (Snorri Sturluson, *Edda*, trans. Anthony Faulkes (London, 2004), p. 64). Furthermore, the section of the *Prose Edda* called *Háttatal* is based on the same concept of *háttr* being a verse-form, see Snorri Sturluson, *Edda – Háttatal*, ed. Anthony Faulkes (London, 1999).

25 For even more ways of translating the word *háttr* see Zoëga, *A Concise Dictionary of Old Icelandic*, p. 188.

26 Margaret Clunies Ross, *Skáldskaparmál: Snorri Sturluson's ars poetica and Medieval Theories of Language*, The Viking Collection 4 (Odense, 1987), p. 22, or, *The Fourth Grammatical Treatise*, ed. Margaret Clunies Ross and Jonas Wellendorf (London, 2014), p. 154.

27 Schorn, 'Eddic Modes and Genres', and Hans Robert Jauss, *Literaturgeschichte als Provokation der Literaturwissenschaft* (Konstanz, 1967).

28 Ibid., p. 250.

iting and thus also of canonisation.[29] The structuring influence of genre designations is in fact very closely linked to modern editorial work and the construction of the canon. The most obvious example for such editorial influence on genre terminology is C. C. Rafn's edition of the *Fornaldar Sögur Nordrlanda*.[30] Rafn created the whole genre of *fornaldarsögur* simply by grouping a certain sort of story together and calling all the different narratives by this invented name, accepted by scholars rather uncritically.[31] One of the best examples of the canonisation of an established genre, on the other hand, is the text series known as *Íslenzk fornrit*, which authorises or at least reconfirms the different modern subgenres within Old Norse-Icelandic literature, when grouping and publishing narratives according to certain labels.[32]

So various problems remain with the current use of genre terminology: 1) most genre terminology is based on modern classifications and does not reflect self-referential taxonomies derived from the respective narratives – attested in medieval text witnesses – but are rather arbitrary social or scholarly convention; 2) the classifications used to group texts and narratives into genres are very heterogeneous, although simultaneously rather rigid, and the imposed binary structures from which the genres are constructed are not designed to take account of the hybridity of certain narratives (see Rikhardsdottir, this volume); 3) current genre terminology claims to describe a diachronic situation and some sort of history or chronology of literature,[33] but it is in fact often based on

---

29 According to Preben Meulengracht Sørensen, only the literary medium of sagas and the modes of skaldic poetry and of mythological poems from the Poetic Edda are to be understood as genuine Old Norse-Icelandic literature: Preben Meulengracht Sørensen, 'Social Institutions and Belief Systems of Medieval Iceland (c. 870–1400) and their Relations to Literary Production', trans. Margaret Clunies Ross, in *Old Icelandic Literature and Society*, pp. 8–29.

30 Carl Christian Rafn, *Fornaldar Sögur Nordrlanda. Eptir Gömlum Handritum*, 3 vols. (København, 1829–30).

31 For a discussion of the *fornaldarsögur* see: Torfi H. Tulinius, 'Sagas of Icelandic Prehistory (*fornaldarsögur*)', in *A Companion to Old Norse-Icelandic Literature and Culture*, ed. McTurk, pp. 447–61. The nationalistic impetus of the translation of *fornaldarsögur* is worth noticing, as this so-called genre terminology is most often translated as 'heroic sagas' or 'legendary sagas', and one of the genre criteria is based on the fact, that the diegetic level of these stories most often takes place outside of Iceland and in a time before the colonisation of Iceland.

32 For a catalogue of all available editions of *Íslenzk fornrit* see: https://www.yumpu.com/en/document/view/20064206/islenzk-fornrit [accessed: 09.04.2020].

33 Such a diachronic perspective, in which saga narratives are embedded in a chronological sequence of development, becomes very clear in Kurt Schier's *Sagaliteratur*, among others, or also in sentences such as '[w]hereas the family sagas are a thirteenth-century phenomenon, the productive period of king's saga writing falls in the century ca. 1130 [...] to ca. 1230 [...].', see Theodore M. Andersson, 'Kings' Sagas (*Konungasögur*)', in *Old Norse-Icelandic Literature*.

particular cases studies describing synchronous patterns derived from modern critical editions;[34] 4) the most critical problem is that in many cases scholarship pretends that this genre terminology was immanent in medieval and early modern Old Norse-Icelandic literature, and that current genre terminology reflects a medieval perception of the texts in question.

This chapter does not seek to provide an overall solution for all of the problems mentioned. Nevertheless, I would like to suggest some ideas for future research into the development and possible replacement of these terminologies. These suggestions should by no means be viewed in a hierarchical order, but rather as different approaches which could be combined in various ways. First, scholars of Old Norse-Icelandic literature should be aware of the canonisation effect of some current editorial series. To a large extent, modern editions do not represent historically transmitted text versions, but rather newly created narratives based on both the previously criticised genre classifications and on the contemporary text layout practices and customs of modern book design. A good example from the poetic canon of Old Norse-Icelandic literature is the manuscript GKS 2365 4$^{to}$, better known as Codex Regius of the Poetic Edda. This is already generically labelled as containing eddic poems in its modern designation, despite the fact that the actual manuscript does not indicate a title for the collected poems.[35] Nevertheless, modern editions present the texts in GKS 2365 4$^{to}$ as examples of a particular mode, named 'eddic'.[36] Furthermore, these critical editions not only predetermine our generic understanding of the text, but they also add editorial comments

---

*A Critical Guide*, p. 197. The approach that can be discerned in such category formations that genres can be classified according to certain historical periods is based on dating assumptions that have already been criticised several times, see for example Margaret Clunies Ross, *The Cambridge Introduction to The Old Norse-Icelandic Saga* (Cambridge, 2010), pp. 27–30.

34 The problem arising from the combination of dating narratives, which are usually based on questionable hypotheses, and the genre affiliations ascribed to them in modern editions, was discussed by Vésteinn Ólason using the example of the genre known as *Íslendingasögur*, see Vésteinn Ólason, 'Family Sagas', in *A Companion to Old Norse-Icelandic Literature and Culture*, ed. McTurk, pp. 101–18. The influence that the questionable dating of narratives has on Old Norse-Icelandic literary history was shown by Jürg Glauser in a widely acclaimed article, see Jürg Glauser, 'What is Dated, and Why? Saga Dating in the History of Old Norse-Icelandic Literature', in *Dating the Sagas. Reviews and Revisions*, ed. Else Mundal (København, 2013), pp. 9–30.

35 For a good overview over the problematic preservation and transmission of so-called 'eddic' poetry, see Clunies Ross, 'The Transmission and Preservation of Eddic Poetry', pp. 12–32.

36 The most often used editions in recent scholarship are probably *Eddukvæði*, ed. Jónas Kristjánsson and Vésteinn Ólason, 2 vols (Reykjavík, 2014) or *Edda. Die Lieder des Codex Regius nebst verwandten Denkmälern. 1. Text*, ed. Gustav Neckel, 5. revised ed. Hans Kuhn (Heidelberg, 1983 [1914]).

and other features of modern printed books, expand or resolve abbreviations and interpret illegible passages. Modern editions also superimpose a verse layout in their typography, and divide up the text using titles which sometimes are not present in the actual manuscripts. Instead of using editions to make a scholarly statement about Old Norse-Icelandic literature, we instead have the possibility of using actual manuscripts, both in their material and digitised forms.[37] Editions are no longer necessary tools which scholars must use to verify theories about Old Norse-Icelandic literature. By using actual manuscript evidence, we may be able to make more accurate assertions about the specific genre of a narrative written down in a specific period. In the case of GKS 2365 4$^{to}$ we could redefine our understanding of the poems and their supposed generic ascriptions.[38] Moreover, an analysis of the textual transmission of these poems would reveal the fact that an 'eddic' genre attribution did not come into effect before the early modern period. The same is true for most of the genres into which we divide Old Norse-Icelandic literature.[39] We should thus ask why we have such a strong urge to assign the medieval versions of some texts to certain genres, if we cannot be sure the genres existed in the respective scribal milieu, or at least if they were not evidenced materially in the manuscripts themselves.

Furthermore, taking manuscripts more fully into account offers scholars the possibility of analysing certain textual features, for example paratexts, which might allow them to identify self-referential patterns in texts, indicating both the self-perception of a text and the external perspective of scribes and readers regarding its genre affiliations at a certain time.[40] Some paratexts, such as titles, can be interpreted as indicators of self-referential attribution to a certain grouping of literary texts; these could hint at genre distinction and even to a demonstrable historical genre terminology. Theories of mediality would help us to understand the reciprocal relationship between the written text or narrative, its fixed structure or the materiality of a given textualisation, and the role of mediation in the construction of genre

---

37 The largest online database providing access to the most important collections of Old Norse-Icelandic manuscripts is: www.handrit.org.
38 See Larrington's chapter on 'God(s)' in this volume.
39 For an exemplary study on this topic, see Rösli, 'Paratextual References'.
40 For a standard introduction to the narratological theory and concept of paratext see: Gérard Genette, *Paratexts. Thresholds of Interpretation*, trans. Jane E. Lewin (Cambridge, 1997). For a short case study on paratextuality, memory, and new philology in Old Norse-Icelandic literary studies, see: Lukas Rösli, 'Manuscripts', in *Handbook of Pre-Modern Nordic Memory Studies. Interdisciplinary Approaches*, vol. 1, ed. Jürg Glauser, Pernille Hermann, and Stephen A. Mitchell (Berlin and Boston, 2018), pp. 406–13; for a thorough case study, see Lukas Rösli, 'From *Schedæ Ara Prests Fróða* to *Íslendingabók* – When an Intradiegetic Text Becomes Reality', in *The Meaning of Media. Medieval Scandinavian Text Culture from Epigraphy to Typography*, ed. Anna Catharina Horn and Karl G. Johansson, Modes of Modification 1 (Berlin and Boston, forthcoming 2020).

distinctions.[41] By analysing different stages of textual memories, we might then be able to revaluate why a text or narrative was considered to belong to a certain genre, and why it was labelled with a specific terminology at a certain time.

## Conclusion

This chapter has raised many questions about the usefulness and historical accuracy of our current genre terminology in both Old Norse-Icelandic literature and its studies. To answer some of these questions, I have argued that it is crucial to return to the manuscript evidence and start examining the different textualisations of literary works from the Middle Ages right up to the very last manuscripts from the early twentieth century. Contemporary theories will prove useful in providing new tools to answer the questions raised above, as will historical classifications and the sharing of knowledge with other fields of study, both historical and contemporary. This will be as challenging for renowned scholars as it will be for future researchers, because it will challenge us to rethink the ways in which (we believe) we know how to pigeonhole every narrative and every text group according to its designated genre. It will, however, be a tremendous opportunity for our field of research if we would at least start to make more transparent the ideological concepts underlying the respective genre terminologies we apply to a text or narrative when discussing and analysing Old Norse-Icelandic literature.

---

41 For theories of mediality from a historical perspective see *RE:writing. Medial Perspectives on Textual Culture in the Icelandic Middle Ages*, ed. Kate Heslop and Jürg Glauser, Medienwandel – Medienwechsel – Medienwissen 29 (Zürich, 2018).

# Form
*Mikael Males*

In Old Norse scholarship it is common to define some genres based partially on form and this is true not only of poetry, where metrical form served as a generic definer until the modern era, but also of prose and prosimetra. The *þættir* (short narratives) are by definition short prose narratives and the kings' sagas and sagas of Icelanders often feature skaldic prosimetrum, whereas the legendary sagas may feature eddic prosimetrum. While translated genres and genres derived from them (hagiography, homilies, translated and indigenous courtly literature) do not make use of prosimetrum, they are characterised by stylistic features, such as alliterative pairs. In native genres, that is genres that have (at least to some extent) grown organically out of earlier traditions, one may point to formal features such as parataxis. The genres mentioned so far are distinguished by content, such as the geographical scope or time of action, or by background (indigenous or translated), or by function (religious or secular). Form is therefore only one of several possible generic markers, but since it often figures in scholarly discussions of Old Norse literature, it may be worthwhile to consider whether its relative prominence in the modern discourse corresponds to perceptions expressed in medieval sources.

This chapter analyses explicit medieval discussions of form, focusing on when they occur and how they may relate to a medieval textual taxonomy. When developing a modern taxonomy of medieval literature, it is advisable to consider whether such categorisations correspond to medieval perceptions or not.[1] The answer to that question may provide information regarding how likely it is that authors consciously employed certain features and how they might expect the audience to react when genre conventions are subverted. In this chapter I will suggest that if we wish to reconstruct that taxonomy, the concepts of *discipline* and *tradition* may in some instances be more useful than our own perceptions of genres.

The *locus classicus* for the discussion of early saga form is the report in *Þorgils saga ok Hafliða* about the entertainment given at a wedding at Reykjahólar in 1119.[2] There, we hear, two sagas were told and what ap-

---

1  See for instance Rösli's chapter in this volume.
2  See, for instance *Poetry in Fornaldarsögur*, *SkP* 8, ed. Margaret Clunies Ross (Turnhout, 2017), pp. lviii–lix, and Joseph Harris, 'The Prosimetrum of Icelandic Saga and Some Relatives', in *Prosimetrum: Crosscultural Perspectives on Narrative in Prose and Verse*, ed. Joseph Harris and Karl Reichl (Cambridge, 1997), pp.

pears to be their prosimetrical form is mentioned. Since the passage has been so important to the modern discussion of the topic, I give it in full. The saga account probably dates to the first half of the thirteenth century or somewhat later.³ It is thus at about a hundred years' remove from the events, and possibly more. It reads:

> Frá því er nǫkkut sagt, er þótti lítit til koma, hverir þar skemtu eða hverju skemt var. Þat er í frásǫgn haft, er nú mæla margir í móti ok látaz ekki vitat hafa, því at margir ganga duldir hins sanna ok hyggja þat satt, er skrǫkvat er, en þat logit, sem satt er: Hrólfr frá Skálmarnesi sagði sǫgu frá Hrǫngviði víkingi ok frá Óláfi liðsmannakonungi ok haugbroti Þráins ok Hrómundi Gripssyni, ok margar vísur með. En þessari sǫgu var skemt Sverri konungi, ok kallaði hann slíkar lygisǫgur skemtiligstar; ok þó kunna menn at telja ættir sínar til Hrómundar Gripssonar. Þessa sǫgu hafði Hrólfr sjálfr saman setta. Ingimundr prestr sagði sǫgu Orms Barreyjarskálds ok vísur margar ok flokk góðan við enda sǫgunnar, er Ingimundr hafði ortan, ok hafa þá⁴ margir fróðir menn þessa sǫgu fyrir satt.⁵

[Even though this was thought of as of minor importance, who entertained there and with what they entertained has been related. What is told in the report is now disputed by many, who claim that they have heard [lit. 'known'] of nothing of the sort, since many are ignorant of the truth and think that to be true which has been made up and that to be mendacious which is true: Hrólfr from Skálmarnes recited a saga about Hrǫngviðr the Viking and about Óláfr king-of-warriors and the breaking of the cairn of Þráinn and Hrómundr Gripsson, and many stanzas with it.⁶ King Sverrir was entertained with this saga and he said that such lying tales were the most amusing ones; and yet people can trace their ancestry to Hrómundr Gripsson. Hrólfr had composed this saga himself. The priest Ingimundr recited the saga

---

134–35; for a more recent discussion of the passage and further references, see Ralph O'Connor, 'History or Fiction? Truth-Claims and Defensive Narrators in Icelandic Romance-Sagas', *Mediaeval Scandinavia* 15 (2005), 133–39.

3   See Peter Foote, 'Notes on the Prepositions *of* and *um(b)* in Old Icelandic and Old Norwegian', *Studia Islandica* 14 (1955), 41–83, at p. 68; Peter Foote, '*Sagnaskemtan*: Reykjahólar 1119', in *Aurvandilstá*, ed. Michael Barnes, Hans Bekker-Nielsen and Gerd Wolfgang Weber (Odense, 1984), pp. 65–83, at p. 79.
4   *þá*: *þó* Br, *því* V.
5   '*Sturlunga saga' efter membranen Króksfjarðarbók udfyldt efter Reykjarfjarðarbók*, ed. Kristian Kålund, 2 vols (København, 1906–11), vol.1, p. 22.
6   Even though the verb *segja* literally means 'to say', Hermann Pálsson notes that '*segja sǫgu*' generally means to read aloud from a written text (*Sagnaskemmtun Íslendinga* (Reykjavík, 1962), p. 52). This agrees well with the note that Hrolfr had 'composed' (*saman setta*) the saga himself, a calque on Latin *componere*, which also typically refers to written composition.

of Ormr Barreyjarskáld and many stanzas and a good poem which Ingimundr had composed at the end of the saga, and many wise men hold this saga to be true.]⁷

The author strongly insists on the truthfulness of his account, and the passage has often been taken as an indication of the existence of prosimetrical sagas in 1119.⁸ Both of the sagas mentioned are now lost, but a *rímur*-poem (rhymed verse) about Hrómundr Gripsson has been preserved.⁹ It is clear from the poem that the saga would have been a *fornaldarsaga* (legendary saga) and thus, in all likelihood, any poetry connected to it would have been eddic. There are no traces whatsoever of the saga about Ormr Barreyjarskáld (a poet from the island of Barra in the Hebrides), but some *dróttkvætt* (skaldic) poetry by him has been preserved in *Skáldskaparmál*.¹⁰ Ormr's dates are not known, but he is likely to have lived in the tenth or eleventh century. The poetry recited by Ingimundr in connection with the saga would in all likelihood have been skaldic. Ormr's Hebridean nickname suggests that the action takes place in a skaldic 'sagas-of-Icelanders' time and setting (tenth to early eleventh century) rather than in an eddic '*fornaldarsögur*' time and setting (that is, before the settlement of Iceland); all his preserved poetry is skaldic.¹¹

First of all, it is important to consider what form the author of the passage is actually envisaging. The expression 'ok vísur margar ok flokk góðan við enda sǫgunnar' (and many stanzas and a good poem at the end of the saga) is ambiguous, since it is not clear whether 'at the end of the saga' refers only to the poem (*flokkr*), or to the stanzas (*vísur*) as well as the poem. If the phrase refers to both, the saga is not represented as prosimetrical, but rather as a kind of *opus geminatum* with all the poetry at the end, something for which we have no real analogues in the preserved corpus.¹² If it refers only to the *flokkr*, however, we are dealing with a prosimetrical saga with a long poem at the end, and we do have some examples of this.¹³ The semantics of *vísur* and *flokkr* may be of help here. The singular *vísa* refers to a stanza, without further specification. The plural *vísur*, however, is generally synonymous with *flokkr* (poem without refrain). Illustrative examples include: 'hann orti [...] flokk þann, er Nesjavísur eru kallaðar' (he

7  My translation. Translations are mine unless otherwise stated.
8  See also discussion in Chapter 5 in this volume.
9  See Ursula Brown, 'The Saga of Hrómund Gripsson and Þorgilssaga', SBVS 13 (1947–48), 51–77.
10 See Guðrún Nordal, *Tools of Literacy: The Role of Skaldic Verse in Icelandic Textual Culture of the Twelfth and Thirteenth Centuries* (Toronto, 2001), p. 283.
11 See also Torfi H. Tulinius's chapter in this volume for a discussion of chronotopes as generic markers.
12 *Hákonar saga góða* in *Heimskringla* and some manuscript versions of *Egils saga*, *Ǫrvar-Odds saga* and Arngrímr Brandsson's *Guðmundar saga* give a substantial amount of poetry at the end, but these sagas are also prosimetrical in themselves.
13 See previous note.

composed the *flokkr* that is called *Nesjavísur*); 'Einarr orti um Grégóríúm Dagsson flokk þann, er kallaðar eru *Elfarvísur*' (Einarr composed the *flokkr* that is called *Elfarvísur* about Grégóríús Dagsson).[14]

*Vísur* can also refer to a number of stanzas composed in response to a given occasion, but again, the semantics remain very close to those of *flokkr*. This can, however, hardly be what *vísur* means here, because if it were, there would be no obvious distinction between *vísur* and *flokkr*, and there would have been no point in mentioning both. The difference may be one of authorship: the *vísur* were attributed to the protagonists of the saga whereas the *flokkr* was Ingimundr's own composition (*ortan* 'composed' correlates only with *flokk*). If so, one would expect that the *vísur* would form part of a prosimetrum, since at the end of sagas, we find long poems, not single stanzas by the protagonists. The alternative is to assume that the author is indeed referring to a lost type of saga of a peculiar *opus geminatum* type. To posit such a form *e silentio* when the passage may easily be read in conformity with known forms seems unwarranted, however.

Furthermore, there are good reasons to doubt that the memory of obsolete saga forms would have been preserved for very long. Discussions about the diachronic development of form seem generally to have been restricted to poetic forms rather than the forms of prose or prosimetra. In the famous source-critical evaluations in the prologues to *Heimskringla* and the *Separate Saga of Saint Óláfr*, for instance, discussions of historical veracity regard content, not form, except in one place in the prologue to the *Separate Saga* when poetic form becomes a relevant factor for the preservation of knowledge: 'Þau orð er í kveðskap standa, eru in sǫmu sem í fyrstu váru, ef rétt er kveðit ...' (The words that are found in poetry are the same as they were in the beginning, if the poetry is performed properly).[15] At that point, the author treats poetry and poetry alone, not some combination of poetry and other material. Although many saga authors exhibit an elaborate prose style, references to and between sagas mention content, not form.

The overall differences in the Icelandic treatment of sagas and poetry thus suggest that these authors did not so much conceptualise the sagas in terms of form as in terms of content. It is therefore unlikely that they would have attempted to trace the evolution of saga form and, consequently, that the author of the passage in *Þorgils saga* is describing an obsolete saga form. Rather, he has in mind a prosimetrical saga of the kind found in the preserved corpus. This is supported by the reference to the

---

14 'Saga Óláfs konungs hins helga'. *Den store saga om Olav den hellige efter pergamenthåndskrift i Kungliga Biblioteket i Stockholm nr. 2 4to med varianter fra andre håndskrifter*, ed. Oscar Albert Johnsen and Jón Helgason, 2 vols (Oslo, 1941), p. 91; *Heimskringla*, ed. Bjarni Aðalbjarnarson, 3 vols, ÍF 26–28 (Reykjavík, 1941–51), vol. 3, p. 359.
15 *Heimskringla*, ed. Bjarni Aðalbjarnarson, 2, p. 422 (cf. 1, pp. 3–5).

saga about Hrómundr, where the wording 'many stanzas with it' appears to suggest a prosimetrical form.

If the sagas in question had roughly the form one might expect at the time, this begs the question of why the author focuses on form at all. Other authors did not, but does this imply that saga form was simply an idiosyncratic obsession of this author? I do not believe so. There are several indications in this passage that he shared one fundamental concern with his contemporaries, namely that of historical reliability, and poetry enters this picture. The author focuses on the relation between fact and fiction on two levels: regarding the events at the wedding and regarding the content of sagas. He stresses the identities of the those providing entertainment at the wedding and which sagas were told. He also focuses on authorship: Hrólfr is the author of a saga, whereas Ingimundr had composed a *flokkr*. The author talks about 'lying tales', which nonetheless appear to contain some truth, whereas *Orms saga* is apparently 'true'. All of these claims can be understood as dealing with the veracity of historical events or genealogical information relating to the wedding and the sagas: these men entertained at the wedding and were the authors of these sagas; the content of these sagas therefore relate to historical events and genealogy in a particular way.

In the text, Sverrir is cited as representing the kind of listener who does not believe in some sagas, whereas the author and 'wise men' belong to the other group, noting that the sagas are either partially or entirely true. Scholars agree that this passage was composed sometime during the first half of the thirteenth century or slightly later, and during this period poetry was often used to authenticate historical narrative. This circumstance, in tandem with the consistent focus on truth in the passage, suggests that the repeated mention of stanzas is intended to eliminate the reader's doubts regarding the veracity of the sagas. If the author meant to focus on saga form, this would make him the sole person who does so among medieval Icelandic authors, but if his focus was on historical veracity, then he fully shared the interests of his contemporaries. The tenor of the passage, the focus on historicity in other authors and the use of poetry in the period all suggest that the mention of stanzas is meant to encourage belief in the historical value of the sagas. In sum, this unique testimony to the early development of saga form is not about form at all, it is about historical veracity.

Apart from this passage, very few authors comment on the form of a prose or prosimetrical text. *Elucidarius*, for instance, notes that its text is a dialogue between a pupil and his master, but the framing device is taken over from the Latin source.[16] In general, saga authors express a preoccupation with the content of prose and prosimetrical texts, but not with

---

16 *'Elucidarius' in Old Norse Translation*, ed. Evelyn Scherabon Firchow and Karen Grimstad (Reykjavík, 1989), p. 6.

their form. Such discussions centred on poetry, not sagas. Apart from the passage in *Þorgils saga ok Hafliða*, the fullest description of the form of a prose or prosimetrical work is found in the rubric to Snorri's *Edda* in Codex Upsaliensis DG 11 (MS U):

> Bók þessi heitir Edda. Hana hefir saman setta Snorri Sturluson eptir þeim hætti sem hér er skipat. Er fyrst frá ásum ok Ymi, þar næst skáldskaparmál ok heiti margra hluta, síðast háttatal er Snorri hefir ort um Hákon konung ok Skúla hertuga.[17]

> [This book is called Edda. Snorri Sturluson has compiled it in the way it is ordered here: It first has [the story] of the æsir and Ymir, thereafter poetic diction and poetic synonyms for many things, and finally the metrical list that Snorri has composed about King Hákon and Duke Skúli.]

This description of the contents and order of a work is so rare that it begs the question of why it is found in MS U. This rubric seems to be composed by the scribe, rather than taken over from an exemplar.[18] This means that it can be dated to the beginning of the fourteenth century, and to judge by the manuscript AM 748 1b 4$^{to}$, other copyists had at that time begun to undertake drastic revisions of Snorri's *Edda*, retaining only *Skáldskaparmál* in truncated form. The rubric may constitute a reaction against such adaptations, or it may simply be due to the fact that the constituent sections of Snorri's *Edda* treat very different topics: myth, skaldic diction and metre. Either way, in so far as the presentation of its contents and their order may be seen as a description of its form, this is due to very particular circumstances relating to a unique kind of composite text.

In general, discussions about form and content are kept apart in Old Norse literature, and form belongs to the field of poetry, whereas content belongs to either prose or poetry. Even the reference to the prosimetrical form in *Þorgils saga ok Hafliða* seems not really to be about form, but about the historical veracity of the sagas. Form is here only a means to an end, namely authenticating a truthful historical account. Furthermore, the words 'and many stanzas with it' pertain only to the poetry, there is no mention of the prosimetrical form of the performance as a whole. The prologue to the *Separate Saga* treats the historical reliability of the poetry's content, not its form, and this appears to have been the aim of the

---

17 *The Uppsala 'Edda'*, ed. Heimir Pálsson and trans. Anthony Faulkes (London, 2012), p. 6.
18 The rubric in MS U appears to be modelled on that of *Háttatal*, which in turn was taken over from another exemplar than that of the rest of the *Edda*. This shows that the rubric quoted above was composed for MS U (see further Mikael Males, *The Poetic Genesis of Old Icelandic Literature*, Ergänzungsbände zum Reallexikon der Germanischen Altertumskunde 113 (Berlin, 2020), pp. 116–18).

author of the passage in *Þorgils saga ok Hafliða* as well. These texts seem to present us with a view of saga narrative as units of content, transmitted through tradition and being more or less trustworthy. This implies a relative lack of an individualising stamp on the sagas – they belong to tradition rather than to individual authors – and this accords well with the anonymity typical of historical sagas.

Form and individuality, by contrast, went hand in hand. Most eddic poetry, where the simple metre still allows a focus on content rather than on form, is anonymous, but the daunting formal complexity of skaldic poetry was coupled with a fierce authorial individualism. The authorship of skaldic poetry is typically known, skalds competed to paraphrase each other's poems, and they avoided using the same expressions to such an extent that the vast majority of kennings are only found once in the entire corpus. Skaldic poetry is in one sense extremely bound by tradition, with its strong conventions regarding both metre and diction, harking back to the ninth century, and yet this is where we find notions most akin to modern perceptions of authorship. A skaldic poem has both authorship and formal integrity and these characteristics seem to be interrelated. These are features which modern research often connects to written culture, whereas anonymity and formal flux is seen as typical of oral literature, but in Old Norse literature, it is the branch of literature with the strongest oral tradition which evinces them. This suggests that the distinction between narratives about the past, which belong to everyone and in which form is largely irrelevant, and complex poetry, which belongs to its author and where form is its defining characteristic, has a long pedigree.

## Discipline

During the Old Norse literary flowering of *c*. 1150–1350, another theoretical distinction between texts entered the picture, namely to which *discipline* they belonged. The study of poetry had its place within *grammatica*, whereas historiography did not belong to any intellectual discipline in particular. Grammatical studies in practice also covered what we would think of as rhetoric, not least since no proper rhetorical texts appear to have reached Iceland. This disciplinary affiliation gave poetry a place in the curriculum and thus an institutional underpinning which historiography lacked, and if the prestige of traditional poetry gradually diminished at the royal courts, its study found a new elite context at the schools of monasteries, cathedrals and major churches.

*Háttalykill* (1140s) is a list of metres, which bears witness to a new systematic way of studying vernacular poetry. Slightly later, an anonymous author composed a treatise on kennings – *Litla Skálda* (late twelfth–early thirteenth century) – and this text was used by Snorri in his comprehensive overview of mythology, diction and metre. The main manuscript of eddic poetry, GKS 2365 4$^{to}$ (c. 1270), in turn, appears to have been compiled as a companion volume to Snorri's text, and the second most important witness to mythological eddic poetry, AM 748 1a 4$^{to}$ (c. 1300–25), is a sister volume to *Skáldskaparmál* and the so-called *Third Grammatical Treatise*.[19] It is not clear whether these texts were actually used in a formalised way in schools, but they clearly belonged to the grammatical discourse. Up to and including Snorri's *Edda*, this vernacular variety of *grammatica* was relatively pragmatic and adapted to the peculiar characteristics of skaldic poetry, but with Snorri's nephew Óláfr, that situation changed. When translating Donatus's Latin treatise *Barbarismus* into Icelandic, Óláfr appropriated the authority of a work that was not particularly well suited to skaldic poetry. For that reason, the *Third Grammatical Treatise* is certainly a less useful text than Snorri's *Edda* for the study of skaldic poetry, but it has the advantage of being the most authoritative text on the topics of linguistic vices, virtues, and 'rhetorical' figures and tropes. The incorporation of skaldic poetry into grammatical studies was now complete.

Óláfr's treatment of the figures *parhomoeon* and *paronomasia* is instructive in illustrating how Óláfr went about his construction of skaldic *grammatica*. In Donatus's example of paronomasia, the key words are *amentium/amantium*, differing only in one letter/phoneme.[20] Óláfr's example is 'heldr vill hilmir | herja en erja' (the ruler prefers | warfare to ploughing), where *herja* and *erja* also differ only in one letter.[21] *Hendingar*, however, are contained in one syllable only, and the end-rhymes that do occur are optional and rare. Óláfr has thus masked the difference between the two traditions by choosing an atypical example.[22]

Óláfr treats *parhomoeon* (in the *Third Grammatical Treatise* called *paranomeon*) in a similar way. Donatus's example is from Ennius: 'O Tite tute Tati tibi tanta, tyranne, tulisti' (Oh tyrant Titus Tatius, you drew such great [outrages] upon yourself).[23] This example differs from Old Norse alliteration inasmuch as both medial and initial consonants play a role in it. Óláfr opts for initial alliteration only, and thus for the single most fundamental feature of Old Norse poetry. His example is 'sterkum stilli | styrjar væni' (to the powerful ruler | eager for battle). He comments:

> Þessi figúra er mjǫk hǫfð í málsnilldarlist er rethorica heitir ok er

---

19 See Males, *The Poetic Genesis*, pp. 165–66.
20 *Donat et la tradition de l'enseignement grammatical. Étude sur l''Ars Donati' et sa diffusion (iv$^e$–ix$^e$ siècle) et édition critique*, ed. Louis Holtz (Paris, 1981), p. 665.
21 *Den tredje og fjærde grammatiske avhandling i Snorres Edda tilligemed de grammatiske avhandlingers prolog og to andre tillæg*, ed. Björn M. Ólsen. Skrifter 12 (København, 1884), p. 96.
22 See *Den tredje og fjærde grammatiske avhandling*, ed. Björn M. Ólsen, pp. 195, 208.
23 *Donat et la tradition de l'enseignement grammatical*, ed. Holtz, p. 665.

hon upphaf til kveðandi þeirrar er saman heldr norrœnum skáldskap, svá sem naglar halda skipi saman, er smiðr gerir, ok ferr sundrlaust ella borð frá borði – svá heldr ok þessi figúra saman kveðandi í skáldskap með stǫfum þeim er stuðlar heita ok hǫfuðstafir. Hin fyrri figúra gerir fegrð með hljóðsgreinum í skáldskap, svá sem felling skipsborða. En þó eru fastir viðir saman, þeir sem negldir eru, at eigi sé vel feldir, sem kveðandi helz í hendingarlausum háttum.[24]

[This figure [parhomoeon] is common in the art of eloquence which is called rhetoric, and it is the origin of the scansion which holds Norse poetry together, just as nails hold a ship which a carpenter makes together, and the planks will otherwise fall apart – just so does this figure hold scansion together in poetry with the letters that are called props and main letters [i.e. auxiliary and main alliterating staves]. The former figure [paronomasia] creates beauty by phonetic distinctions in poetry, just as the seams of planks. But if the pieces of wood have been nailed, they will stick together even though the seams have not been well executed, just as scansion is retained in metres without *hendingar*.]

The passage begins with the only mention of rhetoric in Old Norse literature, and it does so in the context of discussing the phonological characteristics of skaldic poetry. Óláfr thereby appropriates not only the authority of Latin *grammatica* by adapting Donatus to skaldic poetry, but also that of *rhetorica*, the other discipline treating the quality of linguistic expression. In fact, his claim seems to be based on some knowledge of the Irish *retoiric* – semi-metrical, alliterative passages of text – rather than of the Latin discipline, which does not fit his description.[25] He is clearly aware of the existence of *rhetorica*, and his knowledge of how the Irish had appropriated its name for alliterative verse allowed him to do the same. It is as if the Nordic peoples had had rhetoric all along, but just needed to be made aware of the fundamental similarity of the Latin and the Norse tradition through Óláfr's learned pen. He also chose to incorporate the two figures that are most applicable to skaldic metrics into a coherent comparison with ship building, and so to draw attention to how they have pride of place among the figures. The simile does not appear to have any Latin antecedents, but Óláfr seems to have construed it based on the ship imagery that is so common in skaldic poetry itself. The *Third Grammatical Treatise* is of particular interest because it is very clear what Óláfr is doing: he adapts the most important texts of the gram-

---

24 *Den tredje og fjærde grammatiske avhandling*, ed. Björn M. Ólsen, pp. 96–97.
25 *Electronic Dictionary of the Irish Language*, s.v. *retoiric*: http://www.dil.ie/ (consulted on 7 October 2018).

matical curriculum to skaldic poetry and he appropriates the authority of the largely unknown but certainly respectable discipline of rhetoric for skaldic poetry. In this regard, he goes much further than the authors of *Háttalykill*, *Litla Skálda*, and Snorri's *Edda*, who were more pragmatic and traditional. Nonetheless, they also composed texts that would not have been produced if a new way of studying texts had not been introduced with Latin learning. With the arrival of the grammatical discipline, Old Norse poetry found a place where it might belong from the perspective of Latin textual taxonomy, and that place was the most fundamental discipline for all learned endeavours. The precondition for its inclusion was its primary concern with form. By contrast, there was no traditional counterpart to dialectic, the third element of the trivium (grammar, rhetoric and dialectic), nor was there a comparable disciplinary home for historiography, although Latin literature had a strong historiographical tradition.

## Conclusion

This analysis allows us to draw some conclusions. Saga literature in general seems not to have been regarded as defined by form, but by content. This is not to say that there were no agreed conventions for which form was seen as appropriate to a given type of content, but these remained implicit. Poetry, by contrast, was strongly defined by form, both with regard to metre and to diction: Old Icelandic poetics had no concept that exactly corresponded to metre. The closest equivalent, generally translated as 'metre', is *háttr*, meaning 'mode' or 'way'. As Kristján Árnason has argued, this designation was largely based on the context and function of a given form ('the court way', 'the old way', 'the Greenland way', etc.).[26] On a formal level, the term *háttr* could encompass all systematically recurrent features, such as line length, catalexis, rhyme and even diction. The concept of *háttr* was retained within skaldic *grammatica*, even though it was at odds with the Latin definition of metre.

Form was what defined poetry, and it was also all-important for its perceived functions. Because of these formal restrictions, poetry could be used in a grammatical setting and it could serve as a vernacular counterpart to Latin school literature. These functions were primarily predicated on the educational system as it was practised, that is without the separate study of rhetoric. As we have seen, however, Óláfr could draw on the perceived authority of the discipline of rhetoric, even though this discipline was not part of the vernacular curriculum.

Of course, we need not restrict our analyses of medieval texts to investigating how medieval intellectuals understood and classified them;

---

26 Kristján Árnason, 'Um *Háttatal* Snorra Sturlusonar. Bragform og braglýsing', *Gripla* 17 (2006), 75–125, at pp. 82–83.

yet at the same time an awareness of medieval taxonomies is a necessary tool in order to avoid anachronism. In this chapter, I have focused on only one parameter, namely form, and only on medieval perceptions of it in order to ensure a clear analysis. I have also drawn attention to the disciplinary home of the study of literary form – *grammatica*, the most fundamental of all disciplines – and the implications of this disciplinary affiliation for the development of Old Icelandic literature.

# Orality, Textuality and Performance
*Judy Quinn*

Among the many kinds of literary texts that have been preserved from medieval Iceland, only a very few could be said to bear a close relation to the texts of actual performances. Homilies might be one example, where the written text was transmitted with the clear objective of forming the basis of a performed sermon. Liturgical texts similarly played a role in the performance of the Christian ritual, within an institutional context where conformity with centralised conventions was intrinsic to both performance and transmission. Other kinds of works indubitably bear some kind of relation to performance but the relation is more oblique, especially in transmission contexts outside of a formal institutional environment like that of the Church. The practice of socially undermining someone while lauding oneself or one's allies through the composition of a memorable stanza or two seems to have been an abiding facet of political interaction in medieval Iceland, and such compositions were most probably transmitted by those party to the political interaction or in sympathy with those whose reputations the verse promoted. The more formal (and usually commissioned) praise-poem, as the modern generic term suggests, must have relied on public declamation for its cultural force in promoting reputations. These performances, or a simulacrum of them, are often captured in saga prosimetrum, where one genre – the saga – quotes other genres – the poetic quip, or a stanza excerpted from a praise-poem. The resultant prosimetric shifts in the narrative are a significant characteristic of the saga genre and repeatedly draw attention to the re-performance of oral compositions within a literary text.

The effects created by the insertion of poetic performances into prose narration are worth investigating in more detail since it is a characteristic common to most of the types of texts belonging to the broad genre of the medieval Icelandic saga. Indeed the restaging of poetry that was composed in the past (or was purported to have been) functions as an important token of authenticity for most saga narratives about the past. Among the generic expectations which accrued as the literary genre of the saga developed, it seems to have been implicit that the narrator was familiar with oral traditions relating to the plot material, including poetry by and about the main figures in the saga. (While not every extant saga text preserves quotations of poetry, most do).[1] By demonstrating their knowledge of this kind of poetry – either through quotation or mention of its existence – narrators established their credibility as purveyors of verbatim reportage. To some extent, the authenticating effect of poetic quotation might be regarded as permeating the narrative as a whole, even enhancing the verisimilitude of reported speech which makes up such a high proportion of saga prose.

In his work on the cultural organisation of experience, the sociologist Erving Goffman used the term 'keying' to describe

> the set of conventions by which a given activity, one already meaningful in terms of some primary framework, is transformed into something patterned on this activity but seen by the participants to be something quite else.[2]

This notion has been adapted by the genre theorist John Frow to indicate 'a shift in transcription of a behaviour from a primary usage to a secondary usage', a description that neatly fits with the circumstances of saga narrators quoting poetry by figures in their narratives.[3] The harking back to a melody already heard but now played in a different key is a productive analogy, borrowed from music theory, which can usefully be applied to textual studies. In its reiteration, the melody is recognisable but not identical to its first introduction in a musical composition; similarly, the verse quoted in saga prosimetrum harks back to its live performance in the past but is shifted from that context and restaged as textual performance by the saga narrator. Within the saga text, the transition is signalled not only by an *inquit* identifying the quoted speaker but also by a shift in rhythm and sound patterning which characterises the poetic voice. Moreover, poetic quotation within a saga generally represents a performance that is kept deliberately short, constrained, it seems, by the generic expectations inherent in the form of saga prosimetrum from its earliest textualisation in the late twelfth century in works such as *Ágrip*.[4] Invoking another analogy from another medium – this time video art – we might describe poetic quotation within saga prosimetrum as functioning somewhat like 'clips' of earlier videos which are spliced into a later work.

---

1   For a survey of the density of poetic quotation in different sub-genres of the medieval Icelandic saga, see Joseph Harris, 'The Prosimetrum of Icelandic Saga and Some Relatives', in *Prosimetrum: Cross-Cultural Perspectives on Narrative in Prose and Verse*, ed. Joseph Harris and Karl Reichl (Cambridge, 1997), pp. 131–63.
2   Erving Goffman, *Frame Analysis: An Essay on the Organisation of Experience* (New York, 1974), pp. 43–44.
3   John Frow, *Genre*, 2nd edn (London, 2015), p. 171.
4   In later compilations of *konungasögur* (sagas of kings) such as *Heimskringla* or *Morkinskinna*, where the density of quotation is much higher than in *Ágrip*, the tendency is nonetheless still towards single-stanza quotation.

While we have a fairly large corpus of extant Old Norse praise-poetry, the entities we might refer to as poems are in fact almost entirely reconstructed from fragments preserved as piecemeal quotations within kings' sagas or poetic treatises, a consequence of this literary taste for short quotations.[5] That taste is accompanied by an apparent disinclination to record the texts of whole poems, at least of entire secular political poems by named poets (that is, the corpus usually designated skaldic praise-poetry) – although collections of anonymous traditional poems (the corpus of so-called eddic poems) were recorded during the thirteenth century. For whatever reason, different kinds of poetry appear to have been treated differently during the period when oral traditions were being textualised in medieval Iceland. Nonetheless, we can reasonably assume that in oral transmission both kinds of poems would have been performed as complete entities as well as, perhaps, as snatches of one or two stanzas framed by prose.[6] In those few instances where an entire secular skaldic poem has been recorded in writing, the circumstances are unusual.[7] Yet it is reasonable to assume that the original audiences of both sagas and poetic treatises would once have known, from oral transmission, not just the fragments that were quoted but in many cases the whole works from which they were drawn.[8]

As a consequence of this, a bifurcation in the projected audience of a prosimetric work needs to be acknowledged: the audience at the time of writing who could probably call to mind more of the work from which a quoted stanza was taken, and the audience of the written prosimetric text who, increasingly – across time and space – would be less likely to have experienced the whole work in performance. I am assuming that our main focus in this volume is necessarily on a modern international audience of Old Norse texts, rather than a posited audience contemporary with the time of writing – though the latter will inevitably flutter through our thinking as we try to deduce things like the horizons of expectations they may have brought to a work.[9] For the audiences contemporary with the writing of

---

5  On the preservation of skaldic poetry and the necessity of reconstructing whole poems from quoted stanzas, see Margaret Clunies Ross *et al.*, 'General Introduction', *Poetry from the Kings' Sagas 1: From Mythical Times to c. 1035*, SkP 1 (Turnhout, 2012), pp. xxxix–xliv.

6  On the possible form of oral prosimetrum, see Stephen Mitchell, *Heroic Sagas and Ballads* (Ithaca, 1991), pp. 67ff; Harris, 'The Prosimetrum of Icelandic Saga'; and Heather O'Donoghue, *Skaldic Verse and the Poetics of Saga Narrative* (Oxford, 2005), pp. 14–15.

7  See Judy Quinn, '"Ok er þetta upphaf": First Stanza Quotation in Old Norse Prosimetrum', *Alvíssmál* 7 (1997), 61–80.

8  For a description of the significant amount of poetry preserved within poetic treatises produced in medieval Iceland, see Kari Ellen Gade's 'Introduction' to *Poetry from Treatises on Poetics*, SkP 3 (Turnhout, 2017), pp. lxxxiii–cxlix.

9  For a discussion of the concept of the horizon of expectations, see Hans Robert Jauss, 'Literary History as a Challenge to Literary Theory', *New Literary History* 2 (1970), 7–37.

saga prosimetrum, the performances of orally transmitted works would have provided a significant but for us unknowable dimension to their appreciation of the prosimetric work and its generic characteristics. For a modern audience, reading rather than hearing saga prosimetrum, there is of course the possibility of an accompanying textual staging of reconstituted poetic works through scholarly editions, accessible in a separate volume or possibly as an appendix to a particular edition, which could be consulted or remembered while reading or pondering saga prosimetrum. This scholarly staging of a reconstituted text, though, is crucially different from the performance of a poetic work in the memories of audience members familiar with it as a socially vibrant performance. Even for the most dedicated and scholarly reader of saga prosimetrum, or for someone steeped in poetic re-enactment, the experience of reading saga prosimetrum nowadays is going to be different from what we can postulate the experience might have been like at the time the saga was first made written text. For most modern readers of saga prosimetrum, moreover, quotations of poetry are frequently viewed as something of a distraction because of our own appetite – generically conditioned by the other kinds of texts we read – for forward-moving prose.

There is therefore a significant difference in scale between the snatches of poetry that decorate saga prosimetrum and the works that we can hypothesise saga narrators drew on. The saga narrating the feud between two twelfth-century chieftains, Þorgils Oddason and Hafliði Másson is a good illustration of this, providing us with a snapshot of the kinds of poetry apparently being composed in a particular milieu in the early twelfth century and the kinds of performances that were happening at the time.[10] More importantly, the saga provides us with evidence of the poetry the saga narrator knew about but did not quote, as well as the poetry that made the cut for inclusion in the saga. It is a puzzling selection and it goes to the heart of what is one of the crucial characteristics of saga prosimetrum: the selection and staging of quoted verse. As orally composed poetry was textualised within the emergent literary genre of the saga, the evidence of this and other sagas suggests that narrators could choose from an array of quotation techniques that soon became conventions of the genre: they might stage the declamation of stanzas as a dramatic interaction between speakers; they might elide the original performance context of a stanza by using it to close their prose account of an episode, or

---

10 The saga forms part of the compilation known as *Sturlunga saga*, and is partially preserved in two fourteenth-century manuscripts: Króksfjarðarbók and Reykjarfjarðarbók. As the text of the saga is fragmentary in both, later paper manuscripts preserving copies of the medieval work have been drawn on by editors. See Ursula Brown's 'Introduction' to her edition, *Þorgils saga ok Hafliða* (Oxford, 1952), pp. lii–lxii, for a discussion of the manuscripts of the saga and the rationale for using British Museum (now British Library) Add II, 127 as the basis for her edition.

they might present a scene where a cutting observation in verse is recited in the presence of silent but impressed witnesses.

Þorgils saga ok Hafliða famously describes in some detail the entertainments at a wedding feast at Reykjahólar in 1118 – but none of the performed works, not even a snippet of them, is quoted in the saga. As well as mainly non-verbal entertainments like dancing and wrestling, the saga narrator describes the telling of a saga about Hrǫngviðr the viking, King Óláfr, the mound-breaking of Þráinn the berserkr and Hrómundr Gripsson (Þorgils saga ok Hafliði pp. 17–18).[11] In addition to significant details about the subject matter of the saga that was recited, the narrator divulges that it included many verses (vísur margar) and was performed by Hrólfr from Skálmarnes. Hrólfr had been introduced earlier in the saga as being a wealthy lawman and a good friend of Þorgils as well as his þingman, known as both an active lawman and a man-of-sagas (sagnamaðr), who, in addition, composed poetry well (orti skipuliga) (ÞsH, p. 3). In a series of convoluted asides in his description of the entertainments at the wedding feast (ÞsH, p. 19), the saga narrator also reflects on the truth value of Hrólfr's saga, noting that King Sverrir called such lying sagas the most entertaining, 'ok kallaði hann slíkar lygisǫgur skemtiligastar' – a qualitative assessment rather than a generic classification as such.[12] Another saga is also listed as part of the entertainment at the feast (saga Orms Barreyjarskálds), the saga of Ormr, poet of Barra, an island in the Hebrides. This saga is also characterised as including a lot of poetry: many verses (vísur margar) – presumably an indication that the saga was prosimetrum – as well as a good poem (flokkr) at the end. In this case we are told not just the identity of the performer – the priest Ingimundr Einarsson – but more specifically that he had composed the poem himself: 'ok flokk góðan við enda sǫgunnar, er Ingimundr hafði ortan'. Judging from these details, it may be that the performance of oral prosimetrum allowed for dilated poetic recitation, something that is rarely evident in textualised saga prosimetrum where few poems are quoted in their entirety as a single utterance. In view of the length of some literary sagas, it may furthermore be inferred that textualisation favoured the elaboration of prose as well as the truncation of poetic quotation.

The narrator of Þorgils saga ok Hafliða emphasises the fact that the performers – the priest and the lawman – were also accomplished poets. Ingimundr had also been introduced earlier in the saga, where he was de-

---

[11] All quotations of the saga (hereafter ÞsH) are taken from the edition by Ursula Brown; unless otherwise indicated, translations are my own. See also Males' quotation in extenso and discussion of this passage in Chapter 4 of this volume.

[12] The scholarship on this passage is extensive: see Peter Foote, 'Sagnaskemtan: Reykjahólar 1119', SBVS 14 (1953–57), 226–39; Stephen Mitchell, Heroic Sagas, pp. 92–98; and Margaret Clunies Ross, The Cambridge Introduction to the Old Norse-Icelandic Saga (Cambridge, 2010), pp. 18–20.

scribed as a good poet (*skáld gott*), a learned man (*frœðimaðr mikill*) who entertained with poetry as well as composing it: 'ok fór mjǫk með sǫgur ok skemti með kvæðum ok orti' (*ÞsH*, pp. 2–3). To cement his status as a poet of worth, it is reported that he had received payment for his poetry abroad, ('Kvæði góð gerði hann sjálfr ok þá laun fyrir útanlands', *ÞsH*, p. 3). Just as importantly for the feud narrative of the saga, he was a kinsman of Þorgils and had transferred his *goðorð* to him (*ÞsH*, p. 3). The social milieu the saga describes is that of the political elite, and it is in fact at Hafliði's farm, according to ch. 10 of *Íslendingabók*, that the first written laws in Iceland were produced around the same time as the saga is set.[13]

Back at Ingimundr's farm, a merry time was being had by all at the wedding feast, or almost all. For all the detail of the performers' identity and the emphasis that these were prosimetric works, the saga narrator was not moved to quote anything at all from the performance, nor to comment specifically on the audience reception except in the context of introducing the entertainment as an example of the boisterously festive nature of the feast ('Þar var nú glaumr ok gleði mikil', *ÞsH*, p. 17). The narrator's description of the entertainments, however, comes after a detailed account of what was going on during the eating of the meal: guests at the wedding taunted one of the other guests, Þórðr Þorvaldsson, who was Hafliði's son-in-law and very much on the other side of the feud, to the point where he walked out of the feast.

The account of the conversation over the meal is a highy realistic rendering of social interaction, told at a blow-by-blow tempo. The pace of telling, in other words, reproduces the pace at which the conversation develops, creating the mimetic effect of more or less unmediated access to the scene for the audience who hear each verse as it is performed. The necessary background to the jibes is provided as part of the introductory scene setting, during which the narrator describes in some detail Þórðr's digestive problems, as a result of which he belched foul air after eating meat. The narrator also builds tension by reporting Þórðr's apprehensive comment, when he first sat down at his bench and sensed he was among enemies, that he would rather be anywhere else. Þórðr's companions offered polite reassurances and the feast got underway, with everyone except Þórðr drinking heavily.

Ingimundr the priest leant across the table and asked rhetorically – in an improvised *alhent* couplet (v. 4) – where the horrible smell was coming from, providing in the second line of his couplet the response: it was Þórðr breathing. Everyone thought this was hilarious and when the laughter died down, Þórðr offered an impromptu couplet, also in *dróttkvætt*,

---

13 See *Íslendingabók*, ed. Jakob Benediktsson, ÍF 1 (Reykjavík, 1968), p. 23. On the intellectual and social milieu of the poets mentioned in *Þorgils saga ok Hafliða*, see Guðrún Nordal, *Tools of Literacy: The Role of Skaldic Verse in Icelandic Textual Culture of the Twelfth and Thirteenth Centuries* (Toronto, 2001), pp. 149–54.

in response (v. 5). He retorted that Ingimundr's own breath was not so pleasant. The banter got livelier, with an unnamed speaker aiming four derisive lines at Þórðr or, more particularly, the *goði*'s bald head on top of his wheezing windpipe (v. 6). Þórðr laughed heartily at this and, in response, he summed up the situation as a lot of hot air (v. 7) – or, in his words, increasing blasts of unpleasant-smelling air from all the belching, 'Raunillr gerisk þefr af ropum yðrum'. When the host, Þorgils, could not himself be drawn into responding – though the narrator reports that he smiled at the performances – Ingimundr invited other guests to respond. A voice which is later identified as that of Óláfr Hildisson offered a stanza (v. 9), claiming that the foul smell emanated not from the other beef-eating guests but from Þórðr's gut: 'Reptir Þórðr Þorvaldsson Kjartanssonar af kana sínum'. Óláfr had in fact played an important role in the earlier escalation of the feud between Þorgils and Þórðr's ally Hafliði and as a result had been conditionally outlawed, with the consequence that once Þórðr discovered the speaker's identity he demanded that he be ejected from the feast. Þorgils refused and Þórðr took his leave, sighing heavily as he passed along the benches, his breath the subject of a further two anonymous verses (vv. 9–10), the first in *dróttkvætt* and the second half-stanza in the artful metre of *stýfð rúnhenda*. They both reiterate how foul-smelling the *goði*'s breath was, the last onomatopoeic word (*fý*) the equivalent of English 'pyoo'!

While the description of the impromptu performances at the feast seems very much like an eye-witness account, certain details reveal that the information on which the account is based is incomplete. The angle of vision that permits Þorgils' smile to be reported, for instance, does not extend to the identification of the speakers of more than half of the verses that are heard above the boisterous revelry. In its own way, this limitation constructs verisimilitude, since even the central player, Þórðr, had to go to considerable lengths to identify the speaker of one of the rejoinders to his own versifying. The narrator explains that upon hearing the verse, Þórðr tried to locate the bench from which it had come and suspected it had been spoken by someone who is described as a powerful man with a good head of hair, sitting on one of the moveable benches in front of Þorgils. Þórðr then had to ask Yngvildr (the mother of the bride) the identity of the suspected speaker. The detail of the account draws attention to how confusing the scene of performance was and the critical disconnect between the aural reception of verses and the identification of reciting poets.

From our perspective as readers, saga narrators walk a fine line between authoritative objectivity and the kind of narratorial omniscience that is an expected convention of the modern genre of literary fiction. Just before Ingimundr initiated the trading of crude insults that so delighted the wedding guests, the narrator observes:

> Gerask nú málgir, ok má kalla, at hverr styngi annan nǫkkurum hnœfilyrðum, ok er þó fátt hermt af þeira keskiyrðum í þessarri frásǫgn. (*ÞsH*, p. 15)
>
> [People became garrulous and it might be said that everyone was aiming some kind of taunt at someone else, but few of these witticisms are repeated in this account.]

Self-reflexively aware that others may put it differently – 'ok má kalla' – the narrator highlights the selectivity of his own rendering of events. He actually begins his description of Ingimundr leaning across the bench as report: 'Nú er þess getit ... ', reinforcing the sense that, for all the mimetic effects he masters, he is crafting a revised account based on others' say-so.[14]

By choosing particular verses to quote, the narrator stages a performance which gives the audience the impression of being 'present' – or at least of being able to experience the words recited in real time – and cultivates the stance of a reliable reporter. Of course reference to what is not reported can stray into wry understatement, as the remarks that bracket the last verse that is uttered as Þórðr leaves the feast demonstrate:

> Eigi er þess getit, at Þórðr andœpti þessarri vísu ...
>
> ... Er svá sagt, at Þórðr væri með þessum kveðlingi út leystr. En ekki er getit, at neitt yrði at gjǫfum við hann. (*ÞsH*, p. 17)
>
> [It is not reported that Þórðr responded to this verse ...
>
> ... It is said that Þórðr was accompanied out by this little verse. But it is not reported that any gifts were given to him.]

That which is *getit* or *sagt* constitutes the transmitted story material about the feud between Hafliði and Þorgils which the narrator manipulated into his saga, even to the point where he can amusingly turn the conceit around to comment ironically on what is not included in the transmitted story. At a later point in the saga, the narrator lists the names of men who offered surety in a legal case, conceding at the end of the list 'at því sem mik minnir' (as far as I remember, *ÞsH*, p. 43), a concession that enhances rather than undermines the trustworthiness of the narrating voice. The illusion is created through the saga text that the narrator is in some sense 'present' as the story unfolds, even if he is only present in his performed recollection of the traditional material. This illusion in turn enables the saga audience to gain a cumulative sense that the account is believable.

---

14  For a discussion of the oral traditions and localised knowledge the saga author seems to have had access to, see Peter Foote, 'Sagnaskemtan', p. 68; see also Ursula Brown, 'Introduction', p. xliv–xlv.

The artifice of narration – especially in relation to the manipulation of the audience's sense of time passing – is brought to the surface of the text of *Þorgils saga ok Hafliða* on a number of other occasions. At a later stage of the feud, Hafliði gathered a force together during the autumn – an event that occasioned the quotation of another anonymous stanza, as we shall see – but nothing of importance to the narrative happened until the following spring. The narrator's observation in the meantime registers both his exactitude and his impatience: 'Ok nú liðu af misserin, ok er flest seinna en segir' (*ÞsH*, p. 30) (And now the seasons went by and most things are slower than the telling of them).

During the ensuing manoeuvres, when Hafliði and his men lie in ambush, the narrator seems to bridle against the delay caused when members of the party discuss their options: 'ok var alt um seinna en segir ... Ok margt varð til dvala' (*ÞsH*, pp. 31–32) (and everything happened more slowly than the telling of it ... And there was a long delay).

When the narrator styled the material he had about the wedding feast at Reykjahólar, he made a deliberate choice to focus on a breath-by-breath account of the poetic insulting of Þórðr and to speed up the account of the other entertainments: the banter that might have lasted no more than half an hour fills three pages of the edited text while the other entertainments that must have lasted several hours are accounted for in half a page. The amount of poetry quoted is striking: the seven quotations are well in excess of what is necessary to set the scene or develop the plot. The narrator clearly wanted to stage the performance, with space for different voices to exhibit their poetic skill, and the malodorous breath stanzas are judged to be more significant than the highly entertaining but presumably less barbed compositions that Ingimundr and other party-goers recite. The narrator patently enjoys exploiting the performative effect of restaged poetic recitation, using a simulacrum of orality within his markedly literary work, in order to develop the complex interpersonal animosity that drives the feud.

The very first run of stanzas quoted in the saga, in Chapter 8, is conspicuous in the degree to which the verses reiterate the same content, each verse displaying different metrical and lexical features (vv. 1–3). Such poetic variations on a theme probably indicate a competitive performance context, though that is not explored by the saga narrator, who simply quotes the verses after the result of a legal case has been reported, introducing them in this way: 'Þar um váru kveðnar vísur þessar' (*ÞsH*, p. 11) (These verses were composed about that).[15] The three verses, quoted in uninterrupted succession, comment on Þorgils' successful prosecution of a case against Hafliði over the death of his relative, Hneitir, with one poet apparently besting an-

---

15 For a discussion of verse capping in another episode described in *Sturlunga saga*, see Jonathan Grove, 'Skaldic Verse-Making in Thirteenth-Century Iceland: The Case of the Sauðafellsferðarvísur', *VMS* 4 (2008), 85–131.

other by saying a similar thing more cleverly. The first verse, which identifies Hafliði, Þorgils Oddson and Stranda-Hneitir by name, has a somewhat erratic pattern of internal rhyme; the second repeats the names but features kennings and a high proportion of *aðalhendingar* (internal rhymes); while the third, also repeating the names, uses end-rhyme rather than internal rhyme. The verses are all anonymously introduced, they seem to represent the work of three different poets demonstrating their art and their slightly different perspectives on the event, as well as playing around with rhythmic and phonic patterns to express basically similar content.[16]

All three verses express admiration for Þorgils in winning the case. While the stance of the speaker of the first stanza is that of one reporting news – 'Sátt var sǫgð á sumri' (*ÞsH*, p. 11) (the agreement was declared in the summer) – in the second the stakes are raised, both in the temper of the verse and with the broadening of the scope to include the appraisal of Þorgils by the people of the district: 'hringbaldr djarfr sásk Odda arfa' (*ÞsH*, p. 11) (the bold god of rings [> MAN] feared the heir of Oddi) and 'Játti slíkum sáttum sveit ... afreks kunni at unna alvísum Þórgisli' (*ÞsH*, p. 11) (The people approved this settlement ... they were able to acknowledge the great achievement of all-wise Þorgils). The third stanza reiterates how much Þorgils' reputation has been enhanced by the case, moving the focus beyond the immediate audience to future memorialisation of his fame, and along with that shift in focus, the poet draws attention to his ongoing importance to the process: 'reyndisk seggr inn svinni – slíkt hefir ǫld í minni; óð geri ek opt – með sanni at ágætismanni' (*ÞsH*, p. 12) (The clever man proved himself in truth a man of distinction. People keep such things in memory. I often perform praise).

In opting not to describe the original performance context of these compositions – nor to record the names of the poets who composed with the memorialisation of their patrons and themselves in mind – the saga narrator keeps the focus steadily on the feud and its central agents.[17] The expression of the impact of the feud on the community within which it is played out is nonetheless too important not to record, and the proliferation of verses is testament to the excitement it aroused among contemporary poets as well as the interest their compositions held for the saga writer. As is the case with the bad-breath verses, a single example of the kind of performances that took place is clearly not enough in the eyes of the saga narrator, and superfluity seems to be a characteristic of this style of documenting

---

16 As Ursula Brown observed in the introduction to her edition of the saga, 'It is surprising that all three verses should be preserved, but they are probably genuine; were they attempts by the saga-writer himself, he would surely have omitted his poorest version', 'Introduction', p. xlvii.
17 It is of course impossible to know whether the saga author knew the identity of the poets who composed these stanzas; it may be that they were transmitted as anonymous works, although the clustering of compositions about a common event suggests a situation in which different poets played off one another.

stories of the past. Unlike the wedding-feast verses, however, there is no attempt to stage the poetic compositions as interactive recitations between named speakers. The stanzas instead close the chapter as a kind of extended poetic coda to the episode, locking Þorgils' besting of Hafliði into the audience's memory.

A similar coda occurs at the end of an account of a later legal case in which compensation is awarded to Hafliði for an axe injury inflicted on him by Þorgils (*ÞsH*, ch. 31). Once again poetry serves to round off the report – 'Ok þá er lokit var málum þessum, þá var sú vísa kveðin' (*ÞsH*, p. 43) (And when this case was ended, the following stanzas were composed) – and the anonymous poets are not themselves present on the scene except as disembodied voices. And once again, the wording of one stanza is played on in the other, with clear verbal echoes between the two (vv. 16–17):

| | |
|---|---|
| *Máttit seigum sáttum* | *Máttit mága sáttum,* |
| *Sandkorn fyrir standa,* | *mál dragask ljót til bóta,* |
| *þó latti mjǫk mága,* | *geigr varð við svað, seigum* |
| *mál at greiða tœki.* | *Sandkorn fyrir standa.* |
| | |
| [Grain-of-Sand could not stand in the way of agreement, though it was difficult to achieve. Yet he strongly urged his kinsman to let the case be settled.] | [Grain-of-Sand could not prevent his kinsman from coming to an agreement, though it was achieved with difficulty; settlement is being reached in the ugly lawsuit; disaster was imminent.][18] |

The gist of the second half of each stanza varies, however, with the first reporting that *Sandkorn* urged men to battle, and the second that he urged them to leave as quickly as possible. *Sandkorn* (literally, 'grain of sand') is a disparaging play on the name of Hafliði's's relative, the chieftain Hallr Teitsson (*hallr* means 'stone' or 'boulder'), whose intransigence forms a strong current in the narration of the feud. It is possible that the two anonymous stanzas were variations on a theme by the same poet, although it seems more likely that one or other of them was composed in response to the other in the same kind of competitive performance environment that produced vv. 1–3. Interestingly, the prose *inquit* to the quotation of v. 16 introduces only one stanza (*sú vísa*), suggesting that the second stanza may have been an impromptu addition at some point in the text's transmission.[19]

---

18   The translations of these two verses are from the 'Notes' to Ursula Brown's edition of the saga, pp. 93–94.
19   It is also possible that the wording of the *inquit* is in error; see Ursula Brown, 'Notes', p. 95.

The same taste for riddling identification of major players in the feud is also evident in an earlier quotation of an anonymous stanza (v. 13), again positioned as a coda at the end of a narrative episode (ch. 20) and introduced without any information about the context of composition, 'ok var þetta þar um kveðit' (ÞsH, p. 30) (then this was recited about that). As the feud between Þorgils and Hafliði escalated, forces were mustered by the coalition of chieftains uniting against Þorgils. After a blunt account in prose, in which it is reported that Hafliði, Hallr Teitsson and Þórðr Þorvaldsson met together, a coded verse is quoted in which each of the chieftains is identified through animal imagery and the direction from which they have approached: Gull-head from the north, Seal-head from the south and Hart-head from the west.[20] The anonymous stanza stresses secrecy and stealth and the growing resentment building up in Hafliði, whose heart, it is said, has become wolfish: 'þó var úlfúð œrin í Ambhǫfða brjósti' (the wolfish spirit was fierce enough in Hawkhead's breast).[21] This stanza must once have been performed in a context where intrigue and oblique identification were potent discursive devices and it may well have been electrifying, given the violence the amassed forces would have presaged. As the stanza is staged in the prosimetrum of the saga, however, all that is defused because the prose assumes a retrospective position and divulges the players' identities in advance. There were nonetheless compensatory aspects that a written narrative afforded, since the saga narrator was able to stud the account with verifying quotations from eyewitnesses – albeit anonymous ones – to intensify the political intrigue and quicken the pace of the unfolding plot. It is in fact immediately after this quotation that the narrator commented that most things happen more slowly than the telling of them (ÞsH, p. 30).

In contrast to the quotation of anonymous verses to bracket off episodes in the narrative are quotations that are staged as mimetic renderings of encounters in the unfolding plot.[22] Angered by Hafliði's aggression in destroying Þorgils' booth at the *þing* (general assembly), for instance, the latter's supporters beat on their shields, urging him to announce a response (ch. 27). Þorgils is reported to have recited a verse ('Þá kvað Þorgils vísu'), after which he is reported to have said – in prose – that the company should ride on, however things might turn out, 'Ok munum vér ríða verða . . . eigi at síðr, ok verða fǫr sem má', (ÞsH, p. 40). The verse he recited (v. 15) celebrates his reputation as a warrior (someone who can

---

20 See *ibid.*, pp. 85–86.
21 See Ursula Brown, 'Introduction', p. xlix and 'Notes', pp. 85–86.
22 For discussions of the different uses of verse in prosimetrum, see Bjarni Einarsson, 'On the Role of Verse in Saga-Literature', *Mediaeval Scandinavia* 7 (1974), 118–25; and Diana Whaley, 'Skalds and Situational Verses in *Heimskringla*', in *Snorri Sturluson. Kolloquium anläßlich der 750. Wiederkehr seines Todestages*, ed. Alois Wolf (Tübingen, 1993), pp. 245–66.

provide so much carrion for the eagle that it bursts) and his avowal not to shy away from an arranged meeting:

> Munat óssvita ásum
> arnsprengjandi lengi,
> – þat segi ek, gulls ins gjalla
> Gerðr – þinglogi verða.

> [The one who causes the eagle to burst [> WARRIOR] will not be an assignation-defaulter for long with the gods of the fire of the river-mouth [> GOLD > MEN] – that is what I declare, goddess of the resounding gold [> WOMAN].]

While addressing such a proud assertion of valour to a woman is a well-attested convention of skaldic martial poetry, the apostrophe strikes an odd note in the prosimetric staging of the recitation: Þorgils' spies are depicted reporting back to him at a spot in the countryside, specified as being below Ármannsfell but above Sleðaás (*ÞsH*, p. 39), not somewhere a goddess-of-the-resounding-gold was likely to be on hand to hear and transmit his poetry.[23] This is a clear example of how the effects of poetic quotation that can be aligned with the generic concept of keying that was mentioned earlier: shifting a text from one generic context to another 'suspends the primary generic force of the text, but not its generic structure', as Frow has put it.[24] When the performance is resituated, the apostrophe remains, echoing through the landscape.

The verse Þorgils recites is, in terms of sophisticated diction, one of the most accomplished in the saga and the restaging of such poetic agility was no doubt intended to reflect well on its composer. As Ursula Brown noted, the poetry that is quoted throughout *Þorgils saga ok Hafliða* promotes the reputation of Þorgils and his supporters and is conspicuously biased against Hafliði – despite the many provocative and dishonourable moves made by Þorgils reported in the prose narrative.[25] As such, the poetry creates a kind of undertow in the narrative which otherwise seems to aspire to impartiality in its account of the feud between Þorgils and Hafliði. A further example of the partisan nature of the quoted poetry occurs earlier in this phase of manoeuvres (ch. 24), when Þorgils' kinsman and ally, the priest Ingimundr Einarsson is depicted reciting a *dróttkvætt* stanza of praise for Þorgils in his presence and that of his band of supporters (v. 14). Þorgils is described as 'mætr Odda sonr' (the respected son of Oddi) as he rode at the head of his troop, with Ingimundr recording,

---

23 For a discussion of the convention of addressing boasts of martial prowess to a woman, see Roberta Frank, 'Why Skalds Address Women', in *Poetry of the Scandinavian Middle Ages. Atti del 120 congresso internazionale di studi sull'alto medioevo* (Spoleto, 1990), pp. 67–83.
24 John Frow, *Genre*, p. 50.
25 See Ursula Brown, 'Introduction', p. xlix.

for posterity, his assessment of Þorgils' prowess: 'málmrýri tel ek skýran orðinn' (*ÞsH*, p. 35) (I declare the destroyer of metal [> WARRIOR] to have grown clever).

The injury inflicted on Hafliði by Þorgils mentioned above is also the subject of an apparently *ex tempore* composition by Ingimundr (v. 12), staged as a reply to men who asked for news of the encounter (ch. 18). Ingimundr reported that Hafliði had lost three fingers in the incident – a serious enough injury, he notes, though the privileged man should, in his opinion, have been deprived of even more: 'þó skyldi mun fleiri sundr á sælings hendi (*ÞsH*, p. 27) (though more should have been taken from the wealthy man). Both of Ingimundr's verses (v. 12 and v. 14) could have been deployed by the saga narrator in the style of a concluding poetic coda but instead are staged as live interactions in the presence of witnesses, a prosimetric technique which is more vivid and foregrounds the authority of Ingimundr's pronouncements.

After the incident, Hafliði himself regretted having ignored his wife Rannveig's advice not to take his axe with him when he left his booth (*ÞsH*, ch. 18), pointing up an interesting preoccupation with axes in the poetry by some of the main figures in the saga, including a verse preserved outside the saga. A praise-poem about Hafliði Másson, *Hafliðarmál*, is named in the *Third Grammatical Treatise* where two lines of it are quoted anonymously.[26] The metre of the lines is *ljóðaháttr*, which probably indicates that the poem was cast as dramatised advice:

> Rístu nú, Fála, farðú í búð hinig;
> þó es málsgengi mikit.
>
> [Get up now Fála, go over there to the booth; there is nonetheless great support for the case.]

'Fála' is a *heiti* for a giantess and hence can denote an axe.[27] It may well be that the incident referred to in this verse is the same as the one in which Hafliði ended up losing some of his fingers, in which case the saga narrator's decision not to include it in the saga and to quote only Ingimundr's rather cynical response to Hafliði's loss may be significant.[28] The same word, *fála*, occurs in another stanza quoted in *Þorgils saga ok Hafliða* by

---

26 Tarrin Wills, ed., '*Hafliðamál*', *Poetry from Treatises on Poetics*, ed. Kari Ellen Gade, *SkP* 3 (Turnhout, 2017), pp. 533–34; see also Ursula Brown, 'Introduction', p. xlvi.

27 For a discussion of the conceit of denoting an axe with the name of a giantess, see Judy Quinn, 'The "Wind of the Giantess": Snorri Sturluson, Rudolf Meissner and the Interpretation of Mythological Kennings along Taxonomic Lines', *VMS* 8 (2012), 221–29.

28 On the other hand, the possibility cannot be ruled out that the saga narrator had only partial access to the full body of poetic compositions for which the feud was a stimulus.

the poet Þórðr Rúfeyjarskáld (v. 11). As is so often the case, the prose casts Þorgils in a rather poor light, reporting that Þórðr had composed a poem about him without being rewarded for it: 'Þórðr hafði ort kvæði um Þorgils ok var eigi launat' (ÞsH, p. 20). When Þorgils later visited the poet, Þórðr openly coveted a fine axe Þorgils had with him and intimated that it would make a suitable reward for his poem. Throwing good poetry after bad as far as the stingy Þorgils was concerned, Þórðr elaborated his thoughts in a stanza ('Þorðr kvað vísu'):

> Ok fagrslegin fála
> fastleggs virði hála
> semdi sjá fyr kvæði ...

[And the beautifully-wrought giantess [AXE] would indeed be a fitting gift for the man who values the fire of the limb [GOLD] for his poem ...]

This incident is spliced into the narrative of ch. 12 between the death of the outlaw Óláfr – he accidentally dropped his axe which was then seized by his assailant, who used it to kill him – and the moment when his protector, Þorgils, found out about the killing which had been orchestrated by Hafliði. Like the rest of the poetry quoted in the saga, the stanza may have had its origins in Þorgils' political circle although the effect here of quoting the stanza is not straightforwardly partisan.[29] Þorgils' disinclination to follow social norms of reciprocity in fact extends beyond the rewarding of poetry into the legal arena of feud resolution, as so much of the prose narrative elaborates. This cluster of verses mentioning axes, and indeed using the same *heiti* to denote one, make it tempting to imagine that variations on the axe-theme were in circulation among the community touched by the feud and may have involved some form of sparring performances by poets, a seemingly popular genre through which political reputations could be damaged or enhanced. Given how partial and fragmentary the records of these kinds of compositions are, it is difficult to establish a full classification of types within the poetic genre of the (apparently) *ex tempore* political verse.[30] Reading them in the context of the narratives in which they are preserved, however, provides an enabling framework for thinking about the generic complexity of saga prosimetrum.

The saga narrator clearly chose not to tell the story of the feud between Þorgils and Hafliði exclusively through the channel of prose and in a number of places preferred to quote a superfluity of stanzas rather

---

29 Compare Ursula Brown, 'Introduction', p. xlix.
30 A number of different terms for occasional poetic compositions are recorded in the saga (for example, *hnæfilyrði* and *keskiyrði*, ÞsH, p. 15), though whether they should be regarded as emic terms for poetic sub-genres is debatable.

than just a single token to authenticate his account. In this regard, I was struck by the fact that in the foundational methodological chapter of his book, *The Partisan Muse*, Theodore Andersson discusses *Þorgils saga ok Hafliða* at considerable length without once mentioning the seventeen verses that are quoted in it.[31] In this essay, I have attempted to tune into the aesthetic of the saga narrator's prosimetrum in order to track how the quoted poetic voices of the past complicate the narrative and render a more complex political representation of feuding between powerful chieftains. Using poetry – their own and that of their supporters – chieftains no doubt sought to influence perceptions of their agonistic behaviour and through that to influence public opinion (and posterity) against their competitors. Judging from the written record, Þorgils won at this game and was successful in getting poetry which valourised his actions remembered and recited. Yet the saga narrator was not entirely won over by the points of view the transmitted poetry expressed: as he charted the feud right up to its final resolution in the last paragraphs of the saga, he quoted verses composed about it by various poets without apparently reformulating the drift of his narrative under their influence.

The restaged oral performances in the saga can therefore be said to maintain their integrity, both formally and ideologically, at the same time as they complicate the reader's understanding of the feud narrative. When the saga was first read to audiences still in touch with the broader oral traditions about the feud, the performativity of the quoted verses would have been potent: re-stagings that may have triggered further recitations by members of the audience or by the saga reciter of other verses about the incident or further verses of poems from which stanzas had been excerpted. To some extent we might therefore regard the poetic parts of the saga text as potentially more porous than the prose.

Overall, the prosimetric form, as we have seen, allows for considerable flexibility in restaging oral compositions within saga narrative and represents a creative hybridisation of poetic and prose modes, one that proved to be extremely productive across medieval Icelandic literary genres. Saga prosimetrum can itself be viewed as a manifestation of the oral and the literary interacting, as moments of past oral performances were incorporated into stylised literary prose, with a consequent array of prosimetric genres arising as varied oral traditions were brought into play by literary authors. Keying from prose to poetry was a manifest characteristic of the saga genre, to which contemporary audiences were acclimatised even if the shifting perspectives make for more challenging reading nowadays.

---

31 The omission is particularly stark given that the subject of the chapter is the 'Oral Prelude to Saga Writing'; Theodore M. Andersson, *The Partisan Muse in the Early Icelandic Sagas (1200–1250)*, Islandica 55 (Ithaca, 2012), pp. 1–34.

# Manuscripts and Codicology
*Jóhanna Katrín Friðriksdóttir*

Should you order a manuscript to the reading room of one of the several libraries in the world where medieval Icelandic manuscripts are kept, the book will probably look very different from what it once was. Even in the best of cases you will see stiff or fragile parchment, holes, tears, damage from damp, soot and mould, repairs, loose and fragmentary leaves, faded ink, scribbles, and it may have been rebound in a modern binding. Nevertheless, when up close to a manuscript, the reader feels a tangible connection to a time hundreds of years gone by, a time when to own a book – even one with the lowest production value – was the preserve of the few. Whatever its state now, it is immediately apparent from any medieval manuscript that making a codex demanded a substantial quantity of raw material (animal hides, ink and pigments, twine, leather and wood), special tools and labour. The hides needed to be processed into parchment of the correct size, the layout painstakingly prepared, the text laboriously copied, the leaves and quires sewn together and attached to the external binding, which was also custom-made. The page format (sometimes called *mise-en-page*) varied: the text was arranged in one or two columns, with wide or narrow margins, the hand was spaciously or densely spaced, and the design incorporated paratext such as rubrics, majuscules and decorated initials, even large illuminations. The way a manuscript was designed is no coincidence. Rather, the material features, which are often not rendered in a printed edition, convey meaning no less than the text itself: they indicate where the text fits into the literary polysystem, steer the reader through the book and articulate which aspects are more important than others.[1] When working with a medieval text in a modern edition, it can be easy to forget how differently medieval readers experienced it, but as I will discuss in this chapter, taking material aspects into account in the analysis of any given text can enhance our understanding of its genre, and the literary and historical context from which it emerged.

---

1   See for example Emily Lethbridge, 'Authors and Anonymity, Texts and Their Contexts: The Case of Eggertsbók', in *Modes of Authorship in the Middle Ages*, ed. Slavica Rankovic et al., Papers in Medieval Studies 22 (Toronto, 2012), pp. 343–64; Stefka Georgieva Eriksen, *Writing and Reading in Medieval Manuscript Culture: The Translation and Transmission of the Story of Elye in Old French and Old Norse Literary Contexts*, Medieval Texts and Cultures of Northern Europe 25 (Turnhout, 2014), pp. 178–99.

For many Icelandic medieval manuscripts, very little explicit knowledge exists about where they were originally produced, by whom, for whom, and what the patrons thought about the texts in them. However, information about a book's origins and provenance can be gauged with some certainty from internal evidence, such as palaeographical features. The manuscript as an artefact provides clues about the views held by the people who paid for it, individually and as members of a wider culture. That is, it tells us indirectly about the way its patron(s) thought about the world and their place in it. Was a manuscript visually impressive, suggesting that it was intended to be displayed – and thereby make a pronounced statement about the patron's social standing and wealth? Was it a utilitarian volume, to be read from aloud to the farm's inhabitants during the long winter evenings? Was it used in teaching children to read and write and perhaps simultaneously to instil privileged moral values into them? Did the book even exist in its present form in the medieval period, or is it a later construct? The more we know about these issues, the better we can understand the abstract qualities and cultural functions of a text.

## Medieval Icelandic Literary Manuscripts: A Brief Overview

Medieval Icelandic book production began in the late eleventh or twelfth century with the copying of charters, computational texts and laws, but the earliest extant saga manuscripts date to the mid-thirteenth century. 868 Icelandic manuscripts written in the vernacular have been preserved from the earliest days until *c*. 1600, ranging between thick codices of up to 248 leaves to small fragments.[2] Calculations show that around a third of these – fewer than 300 – are 'sizable books', meaning that they are relatively well preserved and fall on the upper scale in the number of leaves they contain.[3] At the other end, *c*. 40–50% of the corpus consists only of one to three leaves, or fragments of leaves, of otherwise lost codices, often severely damaged from cutting and folding when they were repurposed for binding. The remaining share, *c*. 15–25%, represents defective manuscripts, from which are missing a large number of leaves or quires. These items preserve most, though not all, of medieval Iceland's most important texts, but a few, e.g. the so-called *Íslendingabók* (*The Book of Icelanders*), are only extant in later paper manuscripts.

The earliest evidence for celebrated sagas from the thirteenth century such as *Egils saga Skalla-Grímssonar* or *Laxdæla saga* is often a fragmentary

---

2 Guðvarður Már Gunnlaugsson, 'Brot íslenskra miðaldahandrita,' in *Handritasyrpa: Rit til heiðurs Sigurgeiri Steingrímssyni sjötugum, 2. október 2013*, ed. Rósa Þorsteinsdóttir, Rit 88 (Reykjavík, 2014), pp. 121–40, at p. 127.
3 *Ibid*, pp. 129–30; Már Jónsson, 'Manuscript Design in Medieval Iceland', in *From Nature to Script: Reykholt, Environment, Centre and Manuscript Making*, ed. Helgi Þorláksson and Þóra Björg Sigurðardóttir, Rit 7 (Reykholt, 2012), 232–43, at p. 233.

leaf or two (here, AM 162 A θ fol., *c.* 1240–60, and AM 162 D 2 fol., *c.* 1250–1300, respectively; see fig. 1), while the works' complete text dates to decades or even centuries later.

Despite a manuscript's dire condition, each one can, from its codicological, palaeographical and paratextual features, give us some information, however limited, about medieval Icelandic culture and book production. Many of the earliest manuscripts of *Íslendingasögur* (sagas of Icelanders) were single-columned and plain, probably intended for reading to a household rather than for display, but an early fragmentary copy of *Njáls saga*, Þormóðsbók (AM 162 B δ fol., *c.* 1290–1310, 24 leaves; see fig. 2), is laid out in two columns, with chapter headings in red rubrics and modestly decorated initials, suggesting that it was originally a fine book, if not in the top tier of highly valuable works.[4] Fragments from the second half of the thirteenth century show that there was no standard format for *Íslendingasögur*, and one could conjecture from Þormóðsbók's relative costliness (compared with the simpler appearance of the two *Egils saga* and *Laxdæla* fragments) that *Njáls saga* reached a privileged status on the literary scene very soon after its composition in the late thirteenth century.[5]

The fourteenth century is considered the golden age of manuscript production, when luxurious, illuminated books containing laws, kings' sagas and biblical material were made both for the Icelandic market and export to Norway. Broadly speaking, the output from the fifteenth and sixteenth centuries is characterised by smaller, simpler books produced for domestic consumption only; many of these contain entertaining secular texts in both prose and poetic form: a variety of sagas or *rímur*, the popular late medieval ballads which are mostly based on earlier sagas. However, this period could and should be regarded as a second golden age: it saw the production of several splendid volumes, and many of the less impressive books preserve the first extant complete (or near-complete) version of sagas whose composition is dated to circa two hundred years earlier. Although Icelanders kept enthusiastically copying manuscripts for hundreds of years, the Reformation and the arrival of the printing press and paper as writing material in the second half of the sixteenth century had a profound impact. The organisation and layout of books changed – they now began to have title pages and other innovative paratextual features – and although paper was not cheap, it was still more readily available

---

4   Svanhildur Óskarsdóttir and Ludger Zeevaert, 'Við upptök *Njálu*: Þormóðsbók, AM 162 B δ fol.', in *Góssið hans Árna: Minningar heimsins í íslenskum handritum*, ed. Jóhanna Katrín Friðriksdóttir (Reykjavík, 2014), pp. 165–74, at p.168.

5   See images on handrit.is; Svanhildur Óskarsdóttir and Emily Lethbridge, 'Whose *Njála*? *Njáls saga* Editions and Textual Variance in the Oldest Manuscripts', in *New Studies in the Manuscript Tradition of Njáls saga: The Historia Mutila of Njála*, ed. Emily Lethbridge and Svanhildur Óskarsdóttir, The Northern Medieval World: On the Margins of Europe (Kalamazoo, 2018), pp. 1–28, at p. 11.

than parchment. Admittedly these developments had less of an impact on saga manuscripts than 'non-fiction', particularly theological-religious and computational texts, but they provide a useful cut-off point for the purposes of this chapter.[6]

In many ways, famous manuscripts such as Möðruvallabók (AM 132 fol., mid-fourteenth century) are not representative of the heterogeneity of the medieval corpus.[7] In fact, Möðruvallabók's contents are arguably unusual: sagas that have been considered the pinnacle of Icelandic literature – a small subsection of the 30-odd *Íslendingasögur* (depending how you count them) – are otherwise seldom preserved in isolation from texts that fall on the margins of or outside this genre. In many manuscripts, quintessential Norse heroes such as Gísli Súrsson and Egill Skalla-Grímsson keep company with Örvar-Oddr, Mágus the wizard and other mythical, legendary and romance figures, rather than their countrymen such as Hallfreðr or Víga-Glúmr. Many other codices with seemingly 'mismatched' texts affirm that medieval readers probably categorised literature differently from later scholars, emphasised different aspects of them and read them in dialogue with texts that many later critics have sidelined in their analysis. From another point of view, codicological similarities between manuscripts containing texts from different genres can draw links between or reframe works usually discussed separately.

The disparity between the critical and popular view of genre (which is strongly conditioned by nineteenth-century editorial decisions), and what actually appears in the historical record, prompts questions about the definition and use of genre as an analytical category. While not rejecting the concept's usefulness, in the following, I will survey some of the different types of Icelandic manuscripts and discuss the challenges that their preservation presents. I will contemplate which of their features are particularly significant for discussions about genre, and address different methods of interpreting the genre of texts in medieval manuscripts. This chapter will thus pivot between the fields of codicology and the literary study of texts, with particular regard to showing generic hybridity, it will aim to illuminate how the materiality of manuscripts can be incorporated with the analysis of their contents and enrich the conclusions that can be drawn from both approaches.

6   Silvia Veronika Hufnagel, 'Projektbericht "Alt und Neu": Isländische Handschriften, Bücher und die Gesellschaft des 16. und 17. Jahrhunderts', in *Quelle & Deutung III: Beiträge der Tagung Quelle und Deutung III am 5. November 2015*, ed. Sára Balázs, Antiquitas, Byzantium, Renascentia 24 (Budapest, 2016), pp. 147–68, at p. 155.
7   AM 132 fol., nicknamed 'Möðruvallabók' because of a marginal note that locates it at Möðruvellir at one point in time, contains *Brennu-Njáls saga, Egils saga Skalla-Grímssonar, Finnboga saga ramma, Bandamanna saga, Kormáks saga, Víga-Glúms saga, Droplaugarsonar saga, Ölkofra þáttr, Hallfreðar saga, Laxdæla saga* and *Fóstbræðra saga*.

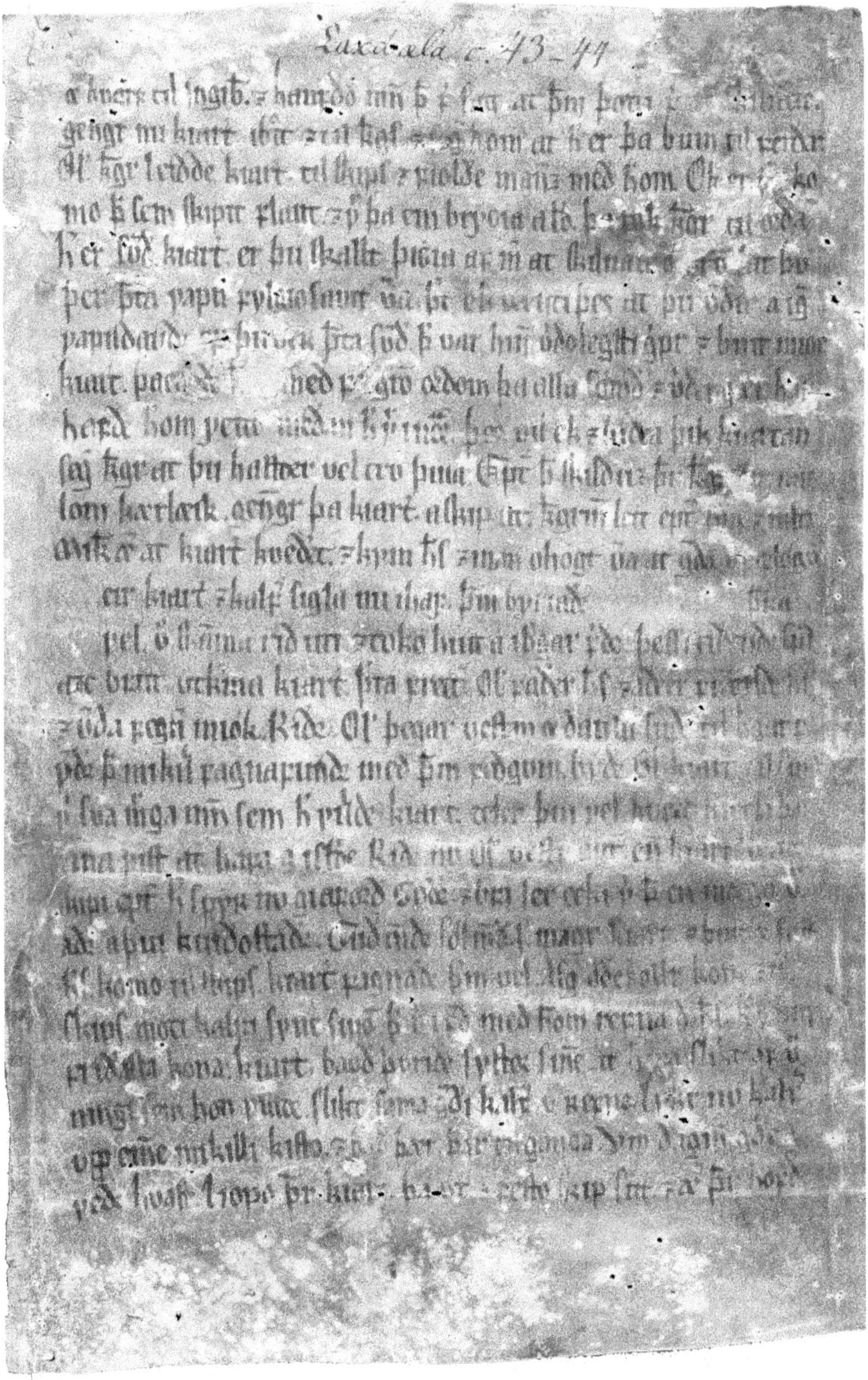

FIGURE 1: A fragment of *Laxdæla saga*. AM 162 D 2 fol., *c.* 1250–1300. 1r.

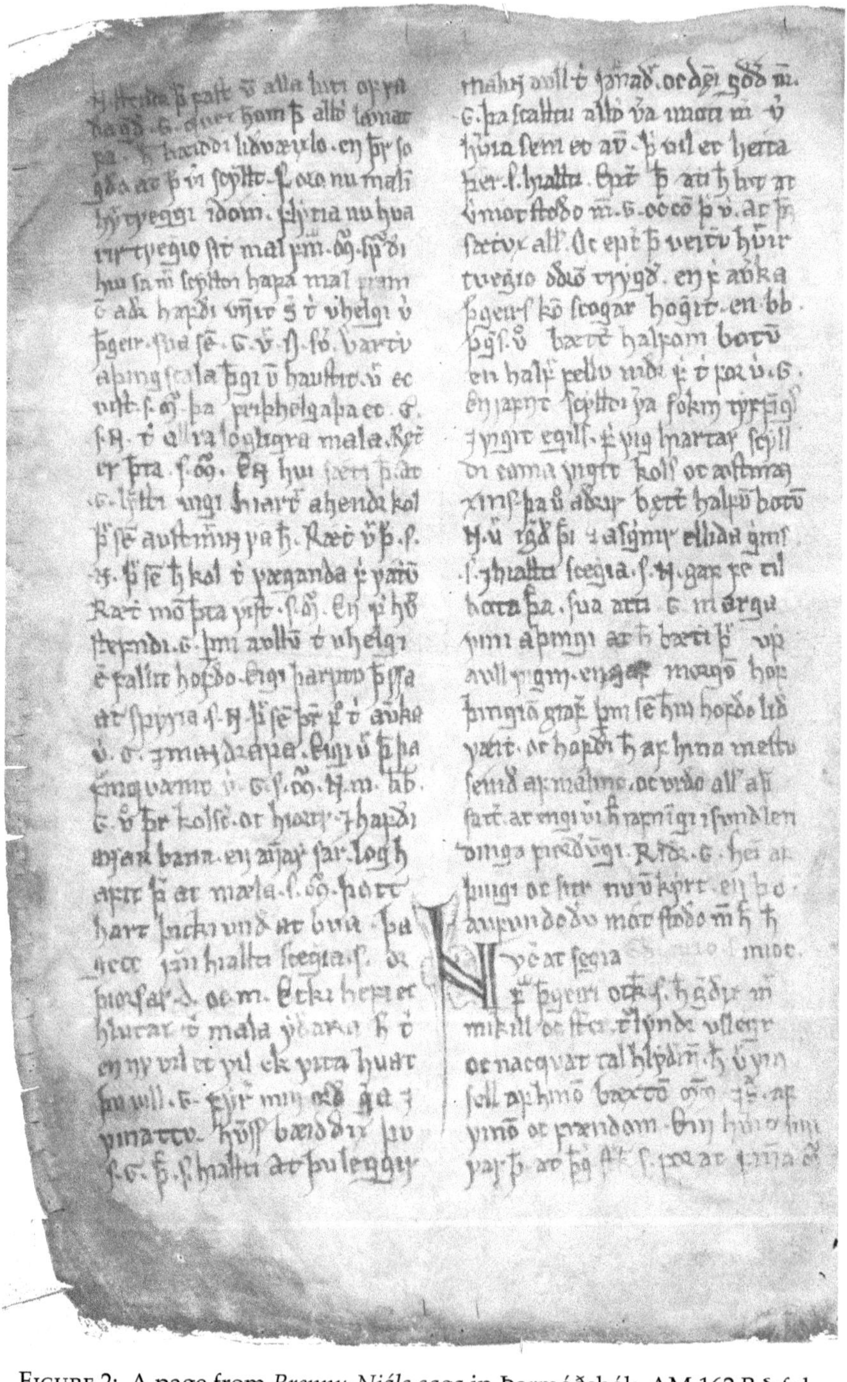

FIGURE 2: A page from *Brennu-Njáls saga* in Þormóðsbók. AM 162 B δ fol., c. 1290–1310. 13v.

## Codicological (Dis)unity and its Implications for Genre

First, however, we must ask, for what sort of analysis is a given manuscript a useful source? Manuscripts which fall into the category of sizeable books may not always have been created in the form in which they have reached us. Individual texts may have been copied out in medieval scriptoria and stored in loose quires for longer periods, with the intention to bind them with other texts to produce a larger book, perhaps when the patron was satisfied with their collection or a buyer came forward. Producing manuscripts 'on speculation' was probably not common due to the large financial risks involved, but as studies in the last few decades have shown, this may be the case for Möðruvallabók (see fig. 3).[8] The book probably came to Denmark in the seventeenth century as a stack of loose quires; it was protected by and later bound in wooden covers that were smaller than the pages (i.e., not originally made to fit this particular volume), and held together with a leather strap. *Njáls saga* and *Egils saga Skalla-Grímssonar* were almost certainly not originally supposed to be among the volume's nine other sagas, and there is no evidence that it was bound together in its present form until hundreds of years after it was copied.

This trajectory problematises the codex's evidentiary value in support of the view that medieval Icelanders would have considered its sagas as belonging to a single, culturally privileged, genre. On the other hand, nor does it offer any proof that this category would have included the remaining c. 25–30 sagas the *Íslendingasögur* traditionally encompass, nor the sundry *þættir* sometimes thrown into the bargain by modern editors.[9] In fact, the medieval preservation elsewhere of those sagas about Icelandic retainers of St Óláfr preserved in Möðruvallabók – *Hallfreðar saga* and *Fóstbrœðra saga* – throws their straightforward categorisation as *Íslendingasögur* into doubt. In Flateyjarbók (GKS 1005 fol.) and other manuscripts, parts of these sagas were inserted into the saga about the king; the lack of any paratextual features in Flateyjarbók or AM 61 fol. to indicate that they formed a separate entity suggests that they are regarded as parts of *Óláfs saga Tryggvasonar*, rather than independent units that can be separated from it in any meaningful way.[10] The composite text in such manuscripts could be seen as a new 'text work' that has its own internal logic and

---

8   Michael Chesnutt, 'On the Structure, Format, and Preservation of Möðruvallabók', *Gripla* 21 (2010), 147–67, provides a summary of growing scholarly consensus on this point.
9   See for example the Íslenzk fornrit series, and the two-volume Svart á hvítu and three-volume Mál og menning editions published in the 1980s and '90s, which include 49 *þættir*, and translations into English such as the popular Leifur Eiríksson edition (Reykjavík, 1997) and the Scandinavian-language translations based on these editions.
10  Emily Lethbridge, '"Hvorki glansar gull á mér / né glæstir stafir í línum": Some Observations on *Íslendingasögur* Manuscripts and the Case of *Njáls Saga*', *ANF* 129 (2014), 53–89, at pp. 71–72, 84–88.

coherence.¹¹ It follows that these two sagas might have been regarded, at least by some, as kings' sagas, or that there was no clear distinction between the genres, at least for some audiences.

Despite these problems, the fairly uniform layout of Möðruvallabók's different parts (two columns, red and green initials, similar line density, one main hand) could, on the other hand, indicate that, whether or not the book was planned as a coherent unit from the outset, its texts do have something in common.¹² In other words, if these sagas were originally produced in smaller units, i.e. as one or more loose quires, to be 'mixed and matched' according to the wishes of a buyer, the redactor considered it appropriate to have them laid out in a similar fashion so that they would match visually when it came to putting together a book. Although many manuscripts containing *Íslendingasögur* are less luxurious, the similarities in layout between Möðruvallabók (see fig. 3), Þormóðsbók (see fig. 2), and what remains of the so-called Pseudo-Vatnshyrna (see below, fig. 4) suggest that their patrons considered it likely that a potential buyer would wish to assemble these particular texts into a composite manuscript.

While these books achieve a degree of visual unity both internally and with each other, AM 309 4$^{to}$ (c. 1500) – another manuscript containing four *Íslendingasögur*, a section of *Ólafs saga Tryggvasonar* copied straight from Flateyjarbók, and selected *þættir* from the same source – conversely does not achieve this by any stretch of the imagination. Rather, it is characterised by a mishmash of styles that clash with each other. The entire book seems to have been written by the scribe Jón Oddsson, but it was in pieces when Árni Magnússon acquired it in parts; the current binding is from 1969 but it is unclear how it was bound before that.¹³ In fact, recent codicological and palaeographical analyses by Emily Lethbridge and Ah Leum Kwon have demonstrated that it is highly unlikely that the manuscript was ever intended as a cohesive volume; it is, rather, a so-called composite manuscript.¹⁴ As is abundantly clear from the photos of the manuscript on the online catalogue Handrit.is, line density varies hugely between the three parts: the Flateyjarbók section, a portion containing *Eyrbyggja saga* and *Laxdæla saga*, and a third and remaining part with a fragment of *Njáls saga*. Moreover, while most of the manuscript is in

---

11 I use this concept following Karl G. Johansson, 'Compilations, Collections and Composite Manuscripts: Some Notes on the Manuscript Hauksbók', in *RE:writing: Medial Perspectives on Textual Culture in the Icelandic Middle Ages*, ed. Kate Heslop and Jürg Glauser (Zürich, 2018), pp. 121–41, at pp. 125–26.
12 The verses in *Egils saga* are written by another scribe, and the rubrics were copied by a rubricator, see Handrit.is and Andrea de Leeuw van Weenen, *A Grammar of Möðruvallabók* (Leiden, 2000), pp. 22–23.
13 See entry for AM 309 4$^{to}$ on handrit.is; Ah Leum Kwon, 'The Structure of AM 309 4$^{to}$: A Codicological and Paleographical Analysis', unpublished MA diss. (University of Iceland, 2017), p. 33.
14 *Ibid.*, pp. 31–51; Lethbridge, 'Hvorki glansar', 60.

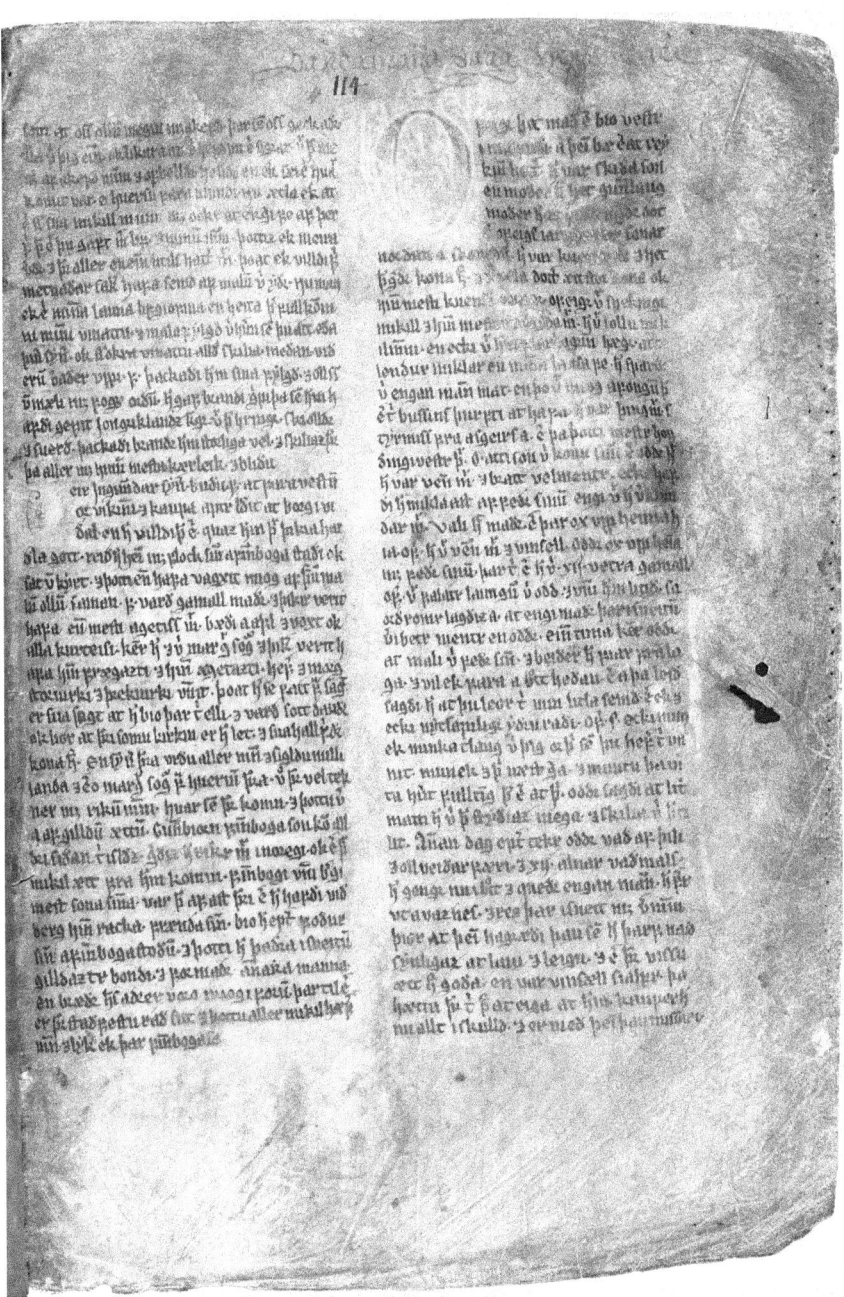

FIGURE 3: The beginning of *Bandamannasaga* in Möðruvallabók. AM 132 fol., mid-fourteenth century. 114r.

FIGURE 4: A page from *Þórðar saga hreðu* in the so-called Pseudo-Vatnshyrna, a fragmentary manuscript. AM 564 a 4to, ca. 1400. 3r

two columns, the last part is in a single column. Initials in the first section are much more elaborate than in the second two, and there are palaeographical differences between the parts too. The quality of the parchment also varies between them, and the first leaf of *Laxdæla saga* and last leaf of *Eyrbyggja saga* are darker than those on the inside of the section, suggesting that they were stored loose and exposed to light and wear and tear for an extended period before being bound with anything else. Judging from the striking discrepancies between the three parts (technically referred to as codicological units), AM 309 4to's sagas were not intended to be bound together at the outset. Although each section can be analysed as an individual codicological unit, any discussion about possible generic affinities between the contents of this codex as a whole should thus be undertaken with caution. It is easy to see why *Eyrbyggja saga* and *Laxdæla saga*, which share a geographical setting, characters and themes, would be copied together in the second unit, but it is a mystery how and when they came to be bound with the other two portions.

As this discussion has shown, manuscripts could be added to, split up and possibly combined with others at any point until Árni Magnússon or other collectors acquired them, or afterwards. Flateyjarbók, whose major section was copied in the late fourteenth century, was augmented by 23 leaves in the latter part of the fifteenth century, when it was in the hands of Þorleifur Björnsson of the Skarðverjar family.[15] Conversely, the manuscripts AM 471 4to, containing *Þórðar saga hreðu*, *Kjalnesinga saga*, *Króka-Refs saga*, the *Hrafnistumannasögur* and an indigenous romance, and the first part of AM 489 I–II 4to, with *Bárðar saga Snæfellsáss* and another romance, are believed to have once been a single volume. At some point it seems that one of the book's owners split it in two, perhaps because it was so thick as to be difficult to read.[16] The second part was then rebound with four romances, including two translated Arthurian texts, forming a separate manuscript which has the shelfmark AM 489 I–II 4to. There was thus clearly never any intention on part of the original redactor of keeping the *Íslendingasögur* in isolation from *fornaldarsögur* and romances; indeed, generic hybrids such as *Bárðar saga* and *Kjalnesinga saga* have much in common, thematically and structurally, with the *Hrafnistumannasögur*, in particular an interest in giant nature and heritage.[17] The movement of texts from one volume to another shows that whoever was responsible for this change considered placing the texts in this new configuration perfectly acceptable,

---

15  Jonna Louis Jensen, 'Den yngre del af Flateyjarbók', in *Afmælisrit Jóns Helgasonar: 30. júní 1969*, ed. Jakob Benediktsson *et al.* (Reykjavík, 1969), pp. 235–50.
16  Guðvarður Már Gunnlaugsson, 'Kjalnesingar, Króka-Refur og Hrafnistumenn', The Árni Magnússon Institute for Icelandic Studies, http://www.arnastofnun.is/page/kjalnesinga_saga, accessed March 1, 2019.
17  For a discussion of generic hybridity see Sif Rikhardsdottir's chapter in this volume.

and such manuscripts, comprising the majority of saga manuscripts, might indicate, as Margaret Clunies Ross has suggested, that ultimately, 'saga' is the only 'secure generic term' available to modern critics.[18]

More examples of shifting codicological units could be added to this brief discussion, but hopefully it is clear that researching Icelandic manuscripts presents scholars with a number of complications, including missing or partial information and unstable codicological boundaries. In sum, we must beware of basing conclusions on manuscripts' current state, for they should rather be based on the compilation's full history, insofar as it can be traced.

## Codicology and Genre

Since the 1990s, manuscripts have become increasingly studied as objects in their own right, rather than primarily as vessels which convey words from the scribe's pen to the eyes of a modern editor, who uses them to evolve a printed text. Some scholars investigate multiple codices as a group to uncover trends in size, script, layout, including the number of columns, width of margins, ruling, line density, initials, the thickness and quality of the vellum, and other material features. Analysing these variables quantitatively and identifying patterns in the data can yield a wealth of information, for instance about the development of book production as an industry, its international context and influences from abroad, localised manuscript culture and how books were organised and used. Another approach inspired by material philology is to study individual codices, incorporating textual analysis with evidence drawn from the manuscript itself. One component of such work can entail comparing one particular book with other manuscripts which contain the same text(s) and discussing how the individual volume fits into the larger picture. These methods can yield more knowledge about literary history, such as the attitudes different patrons and redactors held towards the texts they had copied.

The study of codicology has an important bearing on the study of genre, since disparate genres had different statuses in the literary polysystem at any given time.[19] This system was not a straightforward hierarchy running from elite and niche to popular, formulaic, low-status genres, but, rather, a three-dimensional universe where each category could rise and fall in status, depending on the perspectives and agendas of different social groups and individuals. It is not always clear to what extent the contents of a manuscript were the result of a concerted curatorial effort. Usually, a scribe says nothing about the circumstances in which the book was commissioned and the only evidence available on that topic is circumstantial:

---

18 'Interrogating Genre in the *fornaldarsögur*: Round-Table Discussion', ed. Judy Quinn, *VMS* 2 (2006), 275–96, at p. 277.
19 See further Bampi, this volume.

the book's material features. In some cases, a manuscript's contents might simply reflect which exemplars the redactor was able to get hold of.[20] Cheaper books might have more haphazard contents than expensive ones, and general trends in the production of less opulent volumes might tell us more about genre than a single book can. However, it seems reasonable that wealthy patrons, who were able to commission high-end manuscripts, would not simply have selected whatever random texts they had at hand for the books they put so much effort and cost into producing. Their books were bound to be seen and talked about, and so their contents would hardly have been left up to chance. Although we are usually not given an explicit rationale for the creation of a particular manuscript, it is easier to believe that wealthy patrons curated the contents carefully, whether for their own interest, to provide their household with the kind of amusement they found appropriate, or some other reason, such as when the manuscript was intended as a gift.

By actively choosing traditional or unconventional codicological features of the manuscript, patrons and redactors perpetuated or subverted the literary system, whether consciously or not. For example, many manuscripts of *fornaldarsögur* and romances—whether early (*c.* 1300) or late (16th-century)—are small, relatively cheap books probably intended for everyday reading. However, the widow Margrét Vigfúsdóttir (*c.* 1406–86) at Möðruvellir in Eyjafjörður probably commissioned a large, double-columned codex of translated and indigenous romances, Stockholm Perg. 7 fol., and another one, AM 243 a fol., with the thirteenth-century learned treatise *Konungs skuggsjá*, composed in Norway. Although these books are by no means as beautiful as some of the fourteenth-century show-stoppers, their luxuriousness relative to the homely books in which such texts were often found in the period suggests that she wanted to elevate them within the contemporary literary polysystem. Margrét was descended from the Norwegian king Hákon Hákonarson on her mother's side, and by promoting the types of texts that were fashionable in Hákon's time, she seems to have used the scriptorium at Möðruvellir to craft an image of herself as the king's legitimate successor and, by extension, the crown's rightful representative in Iceland.[21]

Similarly, none of the earliest extant copies of *Grettis saga Ásmundarsonar*, which date to the late fifteenth and early sixteenth centuries, are par-

---

20 The scribe carries out the work (though perhaps not all parts of it, such as rubrics or verses), while the redactor organises the production, i.e. he or she sources exemplars, chooses the redaction (if applicable), provides materials and so on. The patron is the person who commissions and pays for the work. These three roles might be fulfilled by one and the same person and there might also be some overlap or collaboration between them.
21 Jóhanna Katrín Friðriksdóttir, 'Konungs Skuggsjá [The King's Mirror] and Women Patrons and Readers in Late Medieval and Early Modern Iceland', *Viator* 49 (2019), 277–306.

ticularly fine, apart from the huge double-columned codex AM 152 fol., which was likely to have been sponsored by Björn Þorleifsson (the younger), a member of the rich Skarðverjar dynasty, and copied by his half-brother Þorsteinn. This manuscript is one of the two most illustrious books of the early sixteenth century, and the volume's privileging of *Grettis saga* – another generic hybrid – as well as *fornaldarsögur* and romances which all feature relationships between loyal brothers, suggests that Björn used the manuscript to cultivate a public image of his family as united and strong against aggressors, some of whom are rendered as monstrous.[22] For Björn and Þorsteinn, genre appears to have been less important than the sagas' themes and ideological messages. Although the layout of *Grettis saga* and the book's other texts links them to the other *Íslendingasögur* manuscripts discussed here, the decision to make the volume so costly was unlikely to have been based on generic attributes, unless, as previously noted, the only meaningful generic category for sagas is 'saga'. In sum, when texts appear in a much finer book than usual, and/or alongside texts that are typically assigned more prestige, this challenges our understanding of how genres were perceived in medieval Iceland, and suggests that shifts within the polysystem were underway.

## Compilations, Anthologies, Composite Manuscripts

In other cases, expensive books seem to reflect deliberate attempts to gather material into one volume that the manuscript's commissioner considered as belonging together, based on themes, narrative patterns, setting, chronotope and other textual features. Sometimes these compilations do suggest that medieval patrons of manuscripts had ideas about genre which broadly resemble modern ones. Kings' sagas tend to be copied separately (albeit sometimes interpolated with *þættir* and episodes from other genres), and religious-didactic material, laws, saints' lives, eddic texts and *rímur* are often collected in large compendia. The same is true for romances, e.g., the lost *Ormsbók (whose contents are known), Holm perg. 6 4$^{to}$ and Holm perg. 7 fol., all three of which contain translated or adapted and indigenous romances.[23] On the basis of these compendia we might be able

---

22  Jóhanna Katrín Friðriksdóttir, 'Ideology and Identity in Late Medieval Northwest Iceland: A Study of AM 152 fol.', *Gripla* 25 (2014), 87–128.
23  Records suggest that *Ormsbók (c. 1360–1400) contained *Parcevals saga, Ívens saga, Ereks saga, Bevers saga, Partalópa saga, Mágus saga, Flóvents saga, Trójumanna saga, Breta sögur, Mírmanns saga, Bærings saga, Rémundar saga, Enoks saga*; Stockholm Perg. 6 4$^{to}$ (c. 1400–25) contains *Parcevals saga, Ívents saga, Valvens þáttr, Möttuls saga, Elis saga ok Rósamundu, Amicus saga, Bevers saga, Mírmanns saga, Flóvents saga, Konráðs saga keisarasonar, Þjalar-Jóns saga, Clári saga*, 'erotic' poetry (filler at bottom of a page); Holm perg. 7 fol. (c. 1450–75) contains *Elis saga ok Rósamundu, Bevers saga, Partalópa saga, Sigurðar saga turnara, Rémundar saga keisarasonar, Konráðs saga keisarasonar, Hektors saga, Gibbons saga, Viktors saga ok Blávus, Sigurðar saga fóts, Adonias saga*.

to hypothesise that they show an inclination to organise books based on literary genre, notwithstanding that they also contain generic hybrids and outliers.[24]

Forming a distinct category, the *rímur* manuscripts are notable: ballads were likely popular beyond the élite, but although they tend to be very thick, their manuscripts are much smaller in terms of page size than the other books mentioned. In fact, the sixteenth-century Staðarhólsbók (AM 604 a–h 4[to]; see fig. 5) and the late thirteenth-century Codex Regius of eddic poetry (see fig. 6) have many similar features, including small size (around 20x14 cm), a line density of *c.* 32–34 lines per page, narrow margins and relatively simple page design (one column, majuscules indicating the beginning of stanzas, some decorated initials).

Although these manuscripts are separated by hundreds of years, the striking visual parallels between them (and other *rímur* manuscripts) could indicate that sixteenth-century redactors considered these kinds of poetry as generically related. The *rímur* also have many literary features in common with eddic poetry: they both narrate stories set in the legendary-mythical past, they are composed in relatively simple metres and employ kennings based on Norse mythology. Recent research is beginning to show that rather than being wholly inferior to eddic poetry, these poem's artistry has often gone unacknowledged, and future work will no doubt yield more of the *rímur*'s affinities with eddic verse.

What about *Íslendingasögur* manuscripts? The contents of Möðruvallabók in its present form might give the impression that the genre existed as a concept in the fourteenth century, but as outlined above, there are strong arguments against using it as a source to discuss genre from a codicological perspective.[25] It should be noted that while some of its sagas – *Laxdæla saga, Brennu-Njáls saga* and *Egils saga Skalla-Grímssonar* – are counted among the classical *Íslendingasögur*, others, e.g. *Finnboga saga ramma* and *Bandamanna saga*, might be considered generic outliers or imperfect specimens when measured against the 'gold standard' of classical sagas.

Two other manuscripts from around 1400 could seem, at first glance, to bring us back to the idea that *Íslendingasögur* constituted a separate genre. These are the lost *Vatnshyrna, which burned in a fire in the Copenhagen fire of 1728 but whose contents are recorded, and the so-called Pseudo-Vatnshyrna (AM 445 b 4[to], AM 445 c l 4[to] and AM 564 a 4[to], *c.* 1400). This is not one manuscript, but rather three fragments which, scholars have argued – based on their shared palaeographical and design characteristics – were once parts of a single volume.[26] Again, as might be

---

24 Eriksen, *Writing and Reading*, p. 176.
25 For a discussion about the medieval absence of generic terms corresponding to these categories see Rösli, this volume.
26 Stefán Karlsson, 'Um Vatnshyrnu', *Opuscula* 4 (1970), 279–303; John McKinnell,

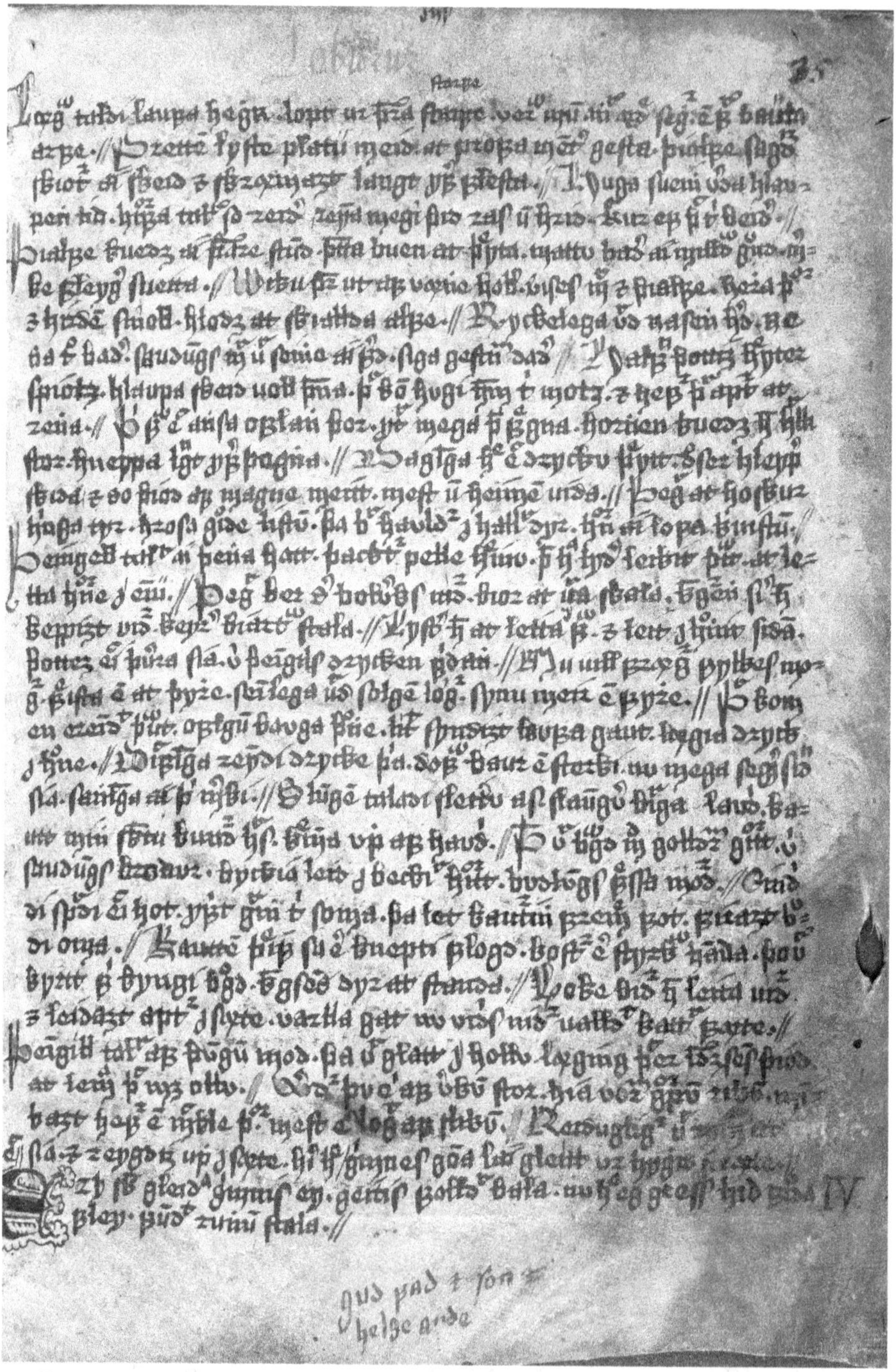

FIGURE 5: A page from *Lokrur*, late medieval *rímur*, in Staðarhólsbók. AM 604 g 4ᵗᵒ, mid-sixteenth century. 18r.

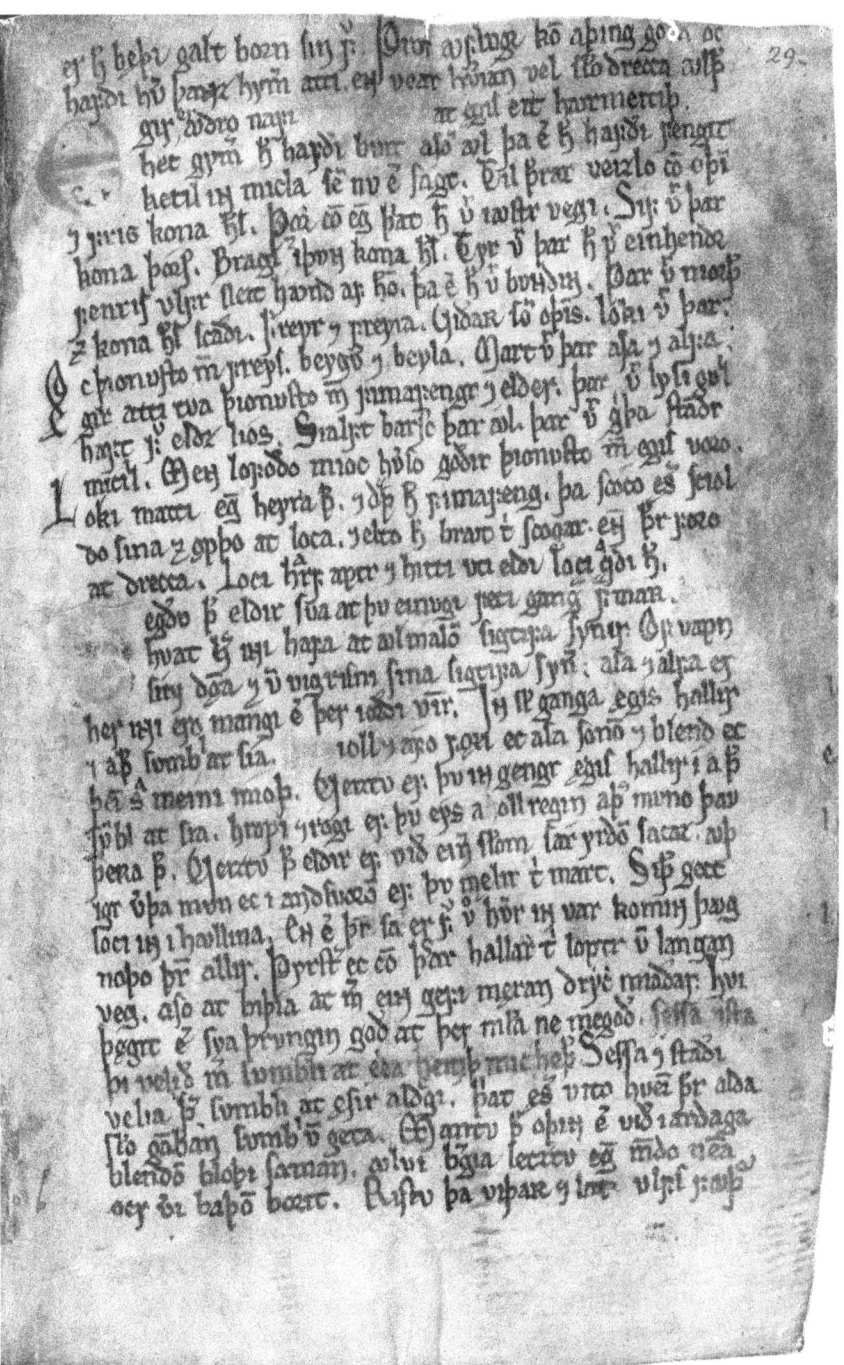

FIGURE 6: A page from *Lokasenna*, an eddic poem, in the Codex Regius of eddic poetry. GKS 2365 4$^{to}$, *c.* 1270. 15r

suspected, there are problems: *Vatnshyrna no longer exists and so it is impossible to ascertain whether it was a coherent codicological unit or pieced together in the manner of the books discussed previously. Similarly, as the parts of Pseudo-Vatnshyrna were found separately, it cannot be established beyond doubt that it was originally one book, rather than two or three similar volumes copied by the same scribe.[27] On the other hand, such features as its generous page size and double-columned layout does forge codicological connections to Möðruvallabók, the fragmentary Þormóðsbók and the second part of AM 309 4$^{to}$, but since many other genres also make use of this layout, it does not provide strong evidence for arguments about genre.

Using a non-existent and a fragmentary manuscript, respectively, as the basis for a discussion about medieval conceptions of genre, is then to argue from a flawed premise. Furthermore, how generically 'pure' are these compilations from a literary point of view? The presence of, first, *þættir* and sagas characterised by mythical-legendary or folkloric elements and structural affinities to *fornaldarsögur*, and, second, genealogies and *Landnámabók* (The Book of Settlements), a text about the settlement of Iceland, prompts questions about genre from yet another angle.[28] Do the contents of AM 445 b 4$^{to}$ (a part of the purported Pseudo-Vatnshyrna) suggest that we should expand the *Íslendingasögur* genre to include *Landnámabók*?[29] There are some arguments in favour of this idea, primarily the setting of all the texts in settlement-era Iceland, or the presence of folkloric and supernatural episodes, many of which are shared between the sagas and *Landnámabók*, sometimes even verbatim.[30] Second, how do the classical *Gísla saga Súrssonar* and *Eyrbyggja saga* – found in several late medieval compilations – fit with the 'young' and/or hybrid texts, i.e., sagas and *þættir* set partly or wholly in Iceland but which ex-

---

"The Reconstruction of Pseudo-Vatnshyrna', *Opuscula* 4 (1970), 304–37.
27 A somewhat related case is AM 162 C fol., a collection of 11 leaves that have been brought together into one book based on palaeographical aspects. The book – if it ever existed as a single unit – contained *Ljósvetninga saga, Vopnfirðinga saga, Droplaugarsona saga, Finnboga saga ramma, Þorsteins þáttr stangarhöggs* and *Sálus saga ok Nikanórs*, a romance.
28 *Vatnshyrna probably contained *Laxdæla saga, Flóamanna saga, Hænsna-Þóris saga, Vatnsdæla saga, Eyrbyggja saga, Kjalnesinga saga, Króka-Refs saga, Stjörnu-Odda draumr, Bergbúa þáttr, Draumr Þorsteins Síðu-Hallssonar;* Pseudo-Vatnshyrna (the fragments AM 445 b 4$^{to}$, AM 445 c 4$^{to}$ and AM 564 a 4$^{to}$) contains *Landnámabók, Vatnsdæla saga, Flóamanna saga, Eyrbyggja saga, Bárðar saga Snæfellsáss, Þórðar saga hreðu, Gísla saga Súrssonar, Víga-Glúms saga, Harðar saga ok Hólmverja, Bergbúa þáttr, Kumlbúa þáttr* and *Draumr Þorsteins Síðu-Hallssonar*.
29 AM 445 b 4$^{to}$ contains *Landnámabók* (the so-called Melabók text), *Vatnsdæla saga, Flóamanna saga* and *Eyrbyggja saga*.
30 See for example the episode about Ljót and Hrolleifr's antagonistic behaviour towards the Vatnsdælir, Geirríðr in Álftafjörðr's offerings of food to travellers, references to the younger Geirríðr being accused of witchcraft, and more.

hibit the characteristics of *fornaldarsögur* and/or other genres? Both sagas follow local feuds, but they also share motifs and thematic concerns in common with some *fornaldarsögur*, including proud but taciturn heroes (Gísli; Örvar-Oddr); hostile undead fathers (Þórólfr bægifótr; *Hervarar saga ok Heiðreks'* Angantýr), family tensions (Snorri goði and his stepfather; Gísli, his brother and brother-in-law; the bloodbath in *Völsunga saga*; *kolbítr* characters and their disgruntled fathers) and women prophesying doom (*Eyrbyggja saga'*s foster-mother; the prophetess in *Örvar-Odds saga*; Brynhildr), just to name a few motifs. Does this overlap mean that the boundaries between *Íslendingasögur* and *fornaldarsögur* were – and are – too vague as to be meaningful? Perhaps not, but considering all the questions that the manuscript evidence leads us to pose, it seems that none of the three codices discussed here that might be considered as *Íslendingasögur*-compendia provide strong literary evidence for the medieval genre '*Íslendingasögur*' as forming a distinct category. The label is thus probably anachronistic.

Does the perspective on genre change if we shift to the *fornaldarsögur*? Notably, no extant manuscripts contain only *fornaldarsögur*, defined according to the concept as used in modern criticism: based on Carl Christian Rafn's three-volume edition of legendary texts set in Viking-Age Scandinavia, published in 1829–30. The significantly damaged GKS 2845 4$^{to}$ (c. 1450) arguably gets the closest, with *Bandamanna saga* and the hybrid *Orms þáttr Stórólfssonar* as the only 'invaders' in what otherwise does seem to be a collection of *fornaldarsögur*.[31] However, the manuscript was bound at some point after many of its leaves were lost, so it is quite possible that it was arranged in a different configuration before this; thus it provides no solid foundation on which to build.[32] Otherwise, most of the larger manuscripts preserving texts commonly referred to as *fornaldarsögur* are notably diverse, containing mixtures of romances, *exempla*, which emerge from a clerical context but overlap significantly with romances, and *Íslendingasögur*, both classical and 'young' sagas.[33] Despite their common chronotope, the widespread and diverse manuscript distribution of sagas categorised as *fornaldarsögur* confirms their heterogeneity, or perhaps non-existence as a distinct genre. Importantly, the manuscript preservation highlights these sagas' complex affinities with all kinds of other texts, whether in terms of structure, stock motifs or ideology, and it suggests

---

31 The manuscript contains *Bandamanna saga*, *Norna-Gests þáttr*, *Orms þáttr Stórólfssonar* (a *fornaldarsaga-Íslendingasaga* hybrid), *Rauðúlfs þáttr*, *Hálfs saga ok Hálfsrekka*, *Göngu-Hrólfs saga*, *Yngvars saga víðförla*, *Eiríks saga víðförla*, *Hervarar saga ok Heiðreks*.

32 See handrit.is.

33 These are, most importantly, AM 343 a 4$^{to}$, AM 489 I 4$^{to}$ and AM 471 4$^{to}$ (see previous discussion about their moving parts), Holm perg. 7 4$^{to}$ and AM 580 4$^{to}$ (probably once one manuscript), AM 557 4$^{to}$, AM 589 a–f 4$^{to}$, AM 556 a–b 4$^{to}$, AM 152 fol., AM 586 4$^{to}$, AM 579 4$^{to}$ and AM 510 4$^{to}$.

that this label, too, is a modern one.

On the other hand, while romances – especially non-Arthurian ones – frequently appear in these eclectic saga collections, romance anthologies that contain no *fornaldarsögur* or other genres indicates that these manuscript redactors and patrons understood that these works were derived from a separate tradition. Whether they constitute a separate genre is less clear, and the overlap between some romances and *exempla* – e.g. the hybrid *Clári saga*, which blends some of the maiden-king sagas' attributes with the moralising *exempla* – underscores the flexibility of the genre.[34] AM 335 4$^{to}$ (*c*. 1400), AM 589 a–f 4$^{to}$ (1450–1500), AM 657 a–b 4$^{to}$ (1350–1400) and AM 343 a 4$^{to}$ (1450–75) all contain a mixture of *exempla* and sagas, both secular and devotional; while they are often introduced as *ævintýri*, in the last manuscript, an *exempla* is rubricated as *Perus saga meistara*. If the basic form of Icelandic literature is a saga – a long prose narrative set in the past – the appearance of *exempla* in saga manuscripts prompts the question whether our conceptualisation of a saga needs to be expanded even further to accommodate these narratives.

## Quantitative Approaches

As we have seen, the amount of data that Icelandic manuscripts present can quickly become dizzying in its volume and complexity. Although books with similar texts tend to have similar material properties, this is by no means consistent, and every manuscript which contains more than one text preserves them in a different order and combination from that in any other codex. This is not to mention textual variance, whether on the episodic or lexical level. The large number of medieval Icelandic manuscripts – many of which contain a number of texts – makes it difficult for the human mind to analyse and organise them in a systematic way. Even excluding law books, which make up a large portion of the corpus, there remain hundreds of manuscripts and fragments with sagas, treatises and poetry, each with their individual codicological features.[35] It follows that in order to group them into clusters and find structural patterns across the corpus – for example, to ascertain whether modern generic categories correspond to medieval ones – computer-based research methods are a valuable addition to our range of critical tools.

The rapidly developing methods offered by digital analysis are beginning to make an impact in the field of medieval Icelandic stud-

---

34 This was originally pointed out by Peter A. Jorgensen, 'The Icelandic Translations from Middle English', in *Studies for Einar Haugen Presented by Friends and Colleagues*, ed. Evelyn Scherabon Firchow *et al*. (The Hague, 1972), pp. 305–20, at pp. 315–19, and confirmed in several subsequent studies.
35 Mathias Blobel, '<Web>Scraping Parchment: Investigating Genre through Network Analysis of the Electronic Manuscript Catalogue *Handrit.is*', unpublished MA diss., (University of Iceland, 2015), p. 25.

ies, and projects using quantitative methods have the potential to nuance or disprove previously held convictions. For example, a recent network analysis study by Mathias Blobel of manuscripts copied before 1540 registered in the database Handrit.is (which contains data for manuscripts held in Reykjavík and Copenhagen) showed that texts assigned to the broader categories of modern genres are typically also found together in manuscripts.[36] The clusters identified in the study are: lives of saints and Apostles, Norwegian kings' sagas, learned literature (mostly Latin-derived), Icelandic history (*Sturlunga saga* and bishops' sagas) and 'secular narratives', by which is meant all sagas that are more literary than historical in character. Owing to limited data, it is not clear whether the indigenous learned material such as the Grammatical Treatises, Snorri Sturluson's *Edda* and, possibly, eddic poetry, should belong in their own cluster, or with European learned literature.[37] Despite a few more ambiguous cases, the manuscript evidence analysed broadly suggests that medieval Icelanders were in some way aware of the larger generic categories now in modern use. However, when it comes to the distinctions between *Íslendingasögur*, *fornaldarsögur* and romances, the evidence gives less clear results. This is mostly for reasons I outlined in the previous section: the few manuscripts that might indicate that these three genres existed are often too fragmented or their original form is too uncertain to provide useful evidence. Ultimately, there are very few facts from which to argue for a clear distinction between the first two of the three categories. There is some reason to believe that romances were seen as a separate genre, but conversely, there seems to have been nothing about them that was seen as to prevent redactors from juxtaposing them with northern material, whether Scandinavian or Icelandic.

One of the most intriguing parts of the study was that it identified manuscripts that were in some way 'anomalous': containing texts that are only found together in one manuscript, and notably including those texts which are normally at a great distance apart in the network. It may come as no surprise that the two books with the most eclectic content are Hauksbók (which is in three parts) and Flateyjarbók. These books have been intensively analysed as, respectively, a personal library, and a compilation containing a highly curated assortment of texts, both of which were *meant* to be disparate (though Karl G. Johansson has recently shown Hauksbók's original form to be quite as doubtful as Pseudo-Vatnshyrna and Möðruvallabók).[38] A third manuscript containing texts that with the

---

36 Ibid. The cut-off year 1540 was chosen because the *Ordbog over det norrøne prosasprog*'s data set ends there.
37 Ibid, p. 32.
38 See the overview of previous scholarship about Hauksbók in Johansson, 'Compilations'; Elizabeth Ashman Rowe, *The Development of Flateyjarbók: Iceland*

furthest 'distance' between them in terms of genre is AM 243 f 4$^{to}$, a late medieval book containing *Konungs skuggsjá* as its primary text. The scribe ended their copying with three pages to spare in the last quire, and they decided to fill the remaining space with Christian poetry: poems about the Virgin Mary and the deplorable state of the world, *Heimsósómi*. Stanzas of *Hugsvinnsmál* were copied in some of its margins, perhaps by a slightly later hand. It is not clear from the manuscript what these apparently disparate texts are doing together, and in such a situation, it seems that combining literary analysis with computer-based methods is a necessary next step.

Coincidentally, I discussed this neglected manuscript, AM 243 f 4$^{to}$, in my study of late medieval *Konungs skuggsjá* manuscripts, where I argued that although the appearance of these poems was unusual and unexpected, a literary analysis of the content of all these texts brings the didactic and moralising content of *Konungs skuggsjá* to the fore. Previous scholars have been interested in exploring the work's genesis in thirteenth-century Bergen, or its learned encyclopedic contents, but the treatise's strong ideological affinities with the poetry with which it was copied suggests that it came to be seen as appropriate reading for young people.[39] Another argument in favour of this interpretation was the codicological affinities between the *Konungs skuggsjá* manuscript GKS 1913 4$^{to}$ (1571), owned by Halldóra Sigurðardóttir, and AM 622 4$^{to}$ (*c.* 1549), a book with devotional, moralising poems copied for Helga Gísladóttir. Both books were made in the mid-sixteenth century for young upper-class girls; they were of similar size (16x12 cm), and laid out with striking similarity in one column, with a large, decorated initial in the upper-left corner at the beginning of the text(s). The visual aspects of these manuscripts reaffirm their related contents and objectives in the eyes of their patrons.

The methods employed in quantitative studies can both make general patterns clearer, and identify anomalies which could prompt us to reassess texts and their place in the literary system. Creating a more fine-grained database of manuscripts and fragments, e.g. by adding more information about codicological features such as layout, could develop our understanding of the corpus and even link fragments that were not previously connected. Network analysis could also be substantially enriched by the addition of chronology as a variable. The study mentioned previously presents as static a period of several centuries, from the dawn of writing until 1540, but the literary polysystem developed substantially over time and generic boundaries must have shifted in the course of several hundred years. Adding more variables to network analyses, especially a chronological dimension, would allow us to refine our understanding

---

*and the Norwegian Dynastic Crisis of 1389*, Viking Collection 15 (Odense, 2005).
39 Jóhanna Katrín Friðriksdóttir, '*Konungs skuggsjá*'. See also Schorn's chapter, this volume.

of Icelandic manuscript culture through the ages. Enabling a breakdown of regions and scriptoria would also give more insight into local variation in manuscript production. In this context, one could mention the late medieval volume AM 551 a 4$^{to}$ (*c.* 1500), which contains *Bárðar saga, Grettis saga* and *Víglundar saga*, which all have the same chronotope and setting in West and North-west Iceland, but all are generic hybrids, exhibiting affinities with *fornaldarsögur*, folklore, romances, *exempla* and hagiography. Are these sagas simply those that people around 1500 regarded as *Íslendingasögur*, are they understood as North-western sagas or sagas about unusual people whose nature is more giant than human, or are they simply sagas? In this chapter, I have tried to show how this fundamental question could be approached by looking at each manuscript as a material object: one which is a unique artifact but that is nevertheless located within a complex literary system. I have outlined some of the pitfalls to beware of when using manuscripts for this purpose, but I hope that this chapter has opened up the huge and mostly untapped potential in studying manuscripts from a multitude of angles.

# II
# THEMES

# The Body Politic
*Hans Jacob Orning*

In this study I intend to discuss how genre can contribute to our understanding of medieval Norwegian and Icelandic political processes, or their 'body politic'.[1] How did the socio-political structures of the medieval North influence the development of literary genres? On the one hand, the development of genres can be viewed as a reflection of politics, constituting its 'superstructure'. On the other hand, genres also contribute to the shaping and changing of politics through their function as vehicles for formulating ideologies that frame the ways in which politics is conceived and conducted. In Old Norse society, the growth of literacy in the Roman alphabet and state formation were parallel and interconnected processes. From the first Norwegian king Haraldr hárfagri (r. c. 872–930) onwards, various genres – both spoken and written – were utilised to formulate and legitimise their power and position in society. The same is true of other participants in the body politic, such as the secular and clerical elites. In this chapter, I will briefly trace the main trends in how kings and elites utilised various genres to establish and reinforce their authority and power from the Viking Age (c. 800–1050) throughout the high Middle Ages (c. 1050–1300) in Norway and Iceland, with a shorter section on the late Middle Ages (c. 1300–1500). Since this is a vast topic, emphasis will be placed on the saga genres and on the main ideological developments in Old Norse society. My hypothesis is that there was a shift towards more explicit definitions of genres and ideologies, and that these processes were interrelated, but that both genres and ideologies remained elusive concepts that were implicitly defined using overlapping and indistinct boundaries.

## Norway

Skaldic poems were probably the most important vehicles for transmitting and celebrating royal successes until the late twelfth century. In this predominantly oral society, skalds functioned both as preservers of mem-

---

1 The term 'body politic' was used by medieval authors such as John of Salisbury, and in Norway the anonymous author of *The Speech Against the Bishops* to envision society as an organic whole, see Erik Gunnes, *Kongens ære: Kongemakt og kirke i En tale mot biskopene* (Oslo, 1971), pp. 73–82. In modern historiography, the term is primarily associated with Ernst H. Kantorowicz, *The King's Two Bodies: A Study in Mediaeval Political Theology* (Princeton, 1957).

orable deeds and as embellishers of their patrons' – mostly kings' – feats in particular. The stability of the poems over time and their reliability as historical sources have been fervently debated, but there is a broad consensus on their pivotal role in formulating a type of heroic royal ideology.[2] King Haraldr hárfagri had several skalds in his entourage, and Haraldr harðráða (r. 1046–66) is described in *Morkinskinna* (written c. 1220) as surrounded by Icelandic skalds praising (and sometimes challenging) his honour. The image of the king transmitted by the skalds focused on his magnanimity, generosity and bravery. The king was the most powerful and impressive patron who surpassed everyone in appearance, wits and wisdom – a *primus inter pares* building his position on a combination of charismatic and traditional authority.[3] Kings also used some eddic poetry to strengthen their authority. For instance, Gro Steinsland has demonstrated how the *hieros gamos* myth in *Skírnismál*, which features a mythological marriage between god and giant, played a central role in royal ideology as a 'symbol of the king's intimate relationship with his land.'[4]

In the second half of the twelfth century there is an apparent multiplication of genres in Norway. This development was closely connected with the establishment of an archdiocese in Niðaróss in 1152/53; most of this literature was written in Latin and concerned Church matters, such as the foundation letter of the archdiocese and its rules (*Canones Nidrosiensis*).[5] The monarchy participated in this milieu from the very beginning. In 1163/64, Magnús Erlingsson (r. 1161–84) was crowned king of Norway by Archbishop Eysteinn in what constituted the first royal coronation in Scandinavia, as well as the first formalised alliance between monarchy and the Church. Here a Christian *rex iustus*-ideology was formulated in new modes of writing, such as in the coronation oath, where King Magnús pledged to

> exercise justice (*justiciam*) in correspondence with the laws of my fathers towards churches, ecclesiastical persons, my subjects, both high and low, and especially widows and orphans, both poor and rich [...].[6]

2   Shami Ghosh, *Kings' Sagas and Norwegian History: Problems and Perspectives*, The Northern World 54 (Leiden, 2011).
3   Sverre Bagge, *Society and Politics in Snorri Sturluson's Heimskringla* (Berkeley, 1991); Ármann Jakobsson, *A Sense of Belonging: Morkinskinna and Icelandic Identity, c.1220*, The Viking Collection 22 (Odense, 2014).
4   Gro Steinsland, *Det hellige bryllup og norrøn kongeideologi: En analyse av hierogamimyten i Skírnismál, Ynglingatal, Háleygjatal og Hyndluljóð* (Oslo, 1991), p. 349. On myths as vehicles of elite ideology in Iceland, see Margaret Clunies Ross, *Prolonged Echoes: Old Norse Myths in Medieval Northern Society: Vol. 2: The Reception of Norse Myths in Medieval Iceland*, The Viking Collection 10 (Odense, 1998).
5   Steinar Imsen, *Ecclesia Nidrosiensis 1153–1537: Søkelys på Nidaroskirkens og Nidarosprovinsens historie*, Skrifter Norges Teknisk-Naturvitenskapelige Universitet. Skrifter15 (Trondheim, 2003), in particular the article by Sverre Bagge.
6   'justitiam faciam ecclesiis, ecclasiasticis personis, populo mihi subdito maioribus

Whereas previous struggles for royal power had been contested between those sharing the heroic view of royalty transmitted in skaldic poetry, the coronation of King Magnús introduced a new set of rules and norms justifying royal rule, turning the traditional legitimation upside down, and stating that power came from God, not from popular support.[7] The amalgamation of royal and ecclesiastic ideology is evident in the writing of kings' sagas and *vitae* in Latin in the Niðaróss milieu, such as *Passio Olavi*, *Historia Norvegiae* and *Historia de Antiquitate regum Norwagiensium*.[8]

The first contemporary vernacular kings' saga, *Sverris saga*, was probably written as a response to the royal-ecclesiastic ideology of Magnús Erlingsson and Archbishop Eysteinn, and in particular against the rise of an independent Church.[9] *Sverris saga*, however, did not depart from the major aspects of the new ideology, such as the view of the king as chosen by God and the society as 'ecclesia'.[10] What characterises Sverrir's reign is foremost an 'ideologisation' of the saga genre by its application in a contemporary setting in which struggles were no longer fought as rivalries within a community of shared norms, but rather as clashes between different and contradictory ideologies.[11]

This 'ideologisation' of literary genres in the latter twelfth century was not, however, commonplace; in several kings' sagas written in the 1220s (*Fagrskinna*, *Morkinskinna* and *Heimskringla*) heroic kingship persisted apparently unaffected by the ideological struggles of the previous decades. It is true that these sagas were most likely written by Icelanders, but considering the strong ties between Iceland and Norway in this period, it would be wrong to suppose that the saga authors were not in touch with the norms of royalty in Norway. A common characteristic is that these saga authors built extensively on skaldic poems and took basi-

---

et minoribus et precipue viduis et orphanis et pupillis tam pauperibus quam divitibus.' *Latinske dokument til norsk historie fram til år 1204*, trans. and ed. Eirik Vandvik (Oslo, 1959), pp. 64–65.

7 Torfinn Tobiassen, 'Tronfølgelov og privilegiebrev', *(Norwegian) Historisk tidsskrift*, 43 (1964), 181–273; Sverre Bagge, *From Viking Stronghold to Christian Kingdom: State Formation in Norway, c. 900–1350* (København, 2010).

8 Inger Ekrem, Lars Boje Mortensen, and Karen Skovgaard-Petersen, *Olavslegenden og den latinske historieskrivning i 1100-tallets Norge: En artikelsamling* (København, 2000).

9 The first part of the saga was written by Karl Jónsson during King Sverrir's reign (1185–88). This was not the first time that a royal narrative was composed (cf. Eiríkr Oddsson, Sæmundr *fróði*), but now for the first time a fully fledged narrative was written about a king, this moreover, a contemporary king. See Sverre Bagge, *From Gang Leader to the Lord's Anointed: Kingship in Sverris Saga and Hákonar Saga Hákonarsonar*, The Viking Collection 8 (Odense, 1996).

10 Fredrik Charpentier Ljungqvist, 'Kristen kungaideologi i *Sverris saga*', *Scripta Islandica* 57 (2006), 79–96.

11 On 'ideologisation', see Bagge, *From Gang Leader to the Lord's Anointed*, p. 159; Hans Jacob Orning, *Unpredictability and Presence: Norwegian Kingship in the High Middle Ages*, The Northern World 38 (Leiden, 2008), pp. 329–43.

cally the same heroic view on kingship. As formulated by Sverre Bagge in his study of *Heimskringla*,

> [t]o get support, the king must do two things. He must rule in such a way as to promote the interests of the people [....] And he must form links to the leading magnates – make them his clients – so that their clients in turn will support him.[12]

Moreover, this conception of society 'is not subject to conflicts but taken for granted.'[13]

In the same decade – the 1220s – a new genre and ideology was introduced in Norway when King Hákon Hákonarson (r. 1217–63) in 1226 instigated the translation of the story of Tristan and Iseult into Old Norse. This translation was followed by further translations of chivalric romances as Old Norse texts, subsequently known as *riddarasögur* during the reigns of Hákon and his successors.[14] This chivalrous ideology was further 'politicised' in *Konungs skuggsjá*, a work belonging to the *mirror of princes* genre, written in the latter half of King Hákon's reign (1240–63) within the king's circle. This work launched an outright attack on traditional values by describing a society with joint rulership as associated with natural disaster, and made courtesy (*hæverska*) a central virtue for separating the legitimate elites surrounding the king and the illegitimate local elites considered to be ignorant and hostile to monarchy.[15]

---

12  Bagge, *Society and Politics in Snorri Sturluson's Heimskringla*, p. 135. On the relationship between skaldic poems and sagas, see Ghosh, *Kings' Sagas and Norwegian History*. There has been debate about the extent to which these sagas promoted a peaceful versus warrior-like royal ideal, and about the divergence in ideological outlook between the various sagas. See Theodore M. Andersson, 'The Politics of Snorri Sturluson', *JEGP* 93:1 (1994), 55–78; Ármann Jakobsson, *A Sense of Belonging*.

13  Bagge, *Society and Politics in Snorri Sturluson's Heimskringla*, p. 123. Birgit Sawyer criticised Bagge for underestimating the importance of ideology in *Heimskringla*, which she viewed as a mouthpiece for a limited royal power, formulated in line with his friend and ally Skúli Bárðarson's interests, see Birgit Sawyer, 'Samhällsbeskrivningen i *Heimskringla*', *(Norwegian) Historisk tidsskrift* 72 (1993), 223–37. In his reply, Bagge underlined that Snorri 'tells history from a fundamental, shared ideology'. See Sverre Bagge, 'Samfunnsbeskrivelsen i *Heimskringla*: Svar til Birgit Sawyer', *(Norwegian) Historisk tidsskrift* 73 (1994), 205–15, at p. 205.

14  Jürg Glauser, 'Romance (Translated *Riddarasögur*)', in *A Companion to Old Norse-Icelandic Literature and Culture*, ed. Rory McTurk, Blackwell Companions to Literature and Culture 31 (Oxford and Malden, 2005), pp. 372–87.

15  Sverre Bagge, *The Political Thought of the King's Mirror*, MS Supplements 3 (Odense, 1987); Hans Jacob Orning, 'The *King's Mirror* and the Emergence of a New Elite in 13th-Century Norway', in *Speculum Septentrionale: Konungs skuggsjá and the European Encyclopedia of the Middle Ages*, ed. Karl G. Johansson and Elise Kleivane, Bibliotheca Nordica 10 (Oslo, 2018), pp. 245–64. See also Schorn's chapter in this volume for further discussion of *Konungs skuggsjá*.

*Hákonar saga Hákonarsonar*, composed by Sturla Þórðarson in 1264–65, is the last extant kings' saga.[16] Sturla was able to draw on a variety of genres and ideologies in his account, for as an Icelandic chieftain he had been raised in the Icelandic secular-heroic saga tradition, and as a royal chronicler he was well-versed in the royal-ecclesiastic ideology of the king as God's elect. Moreover, the courtly world-view had become strongly established through the translated *riddarasögur* and *Konungs skuggsjá*. It must have been a difficult task to accommodate these differing concerns. *Hákonar saga* has been labelled a 'dull' saga with the politics left out.[17] It could be argued that one reason why the kings' sagas genre did not continue after the late thirteenth century was that its focus on dramatic encounters was incompatible with a royal ideology where the king was viewed as God's elect and court(ly) leader, raised above the rest of the population.

After 1319 Norway shared a king with Sweden. This implied that Iceland – the centre of saga writing – became more peripheral, since the political centre now moved eastwards. When Swedish kings began to have their deeds documented in the early fourteenth century, the writers whose patrons they were did not choose the saga form. Rather, the authors opted instead for the chivalric genres. *Erikskrönikan* (written *c.* 1320), the first major literary work from Sweden, was much more profoundly influenced by chivalric romances than by sagas both in form (*knittelvers*) and content (chivalric culture). Eufemia, queen of King Hákon Magnússon (r. 1299–1319), was also patron of the translation or writing of three chivalric romances – the so-called *Eufemia-visor* – into Old Swedish, a further indication of a shift in genre.[18]

## Freestate Iceland

Whereas the Norwegian political context in the later twelfth century produced a clash between opposing ideologies and genres, Iceland experienced fewer battles of principle between differing and contradictory ways of legitimising political power. This may have been a result of Iceland having no kings (before 1262/64), and of the clashes following the later Church reform movement (in the later thirteenth century). However, this does not mean that there was general agreement on how to legitimise political action and power, only that such struggles took the form

---

16 Excerpts from *Magnúss saga lagabætis* (written shortly after 1280) have survived, but the saga evidently did not become popular.
17 Knut Helle, 'Innleiing', *Soga om Håkon Håkonsson* (Oslo, 1963), p. 12. Bagge, *From Gang Leader to the Lord's Anointed*, pp. 94–107.
18 Olle Ferm *et al.*, *The Eufemiavisor and Courtly Culture: Time, Texts and Cultural Transfer*, Konferenser / Kungl. Vitterhets Historie Och Antikvitets Akademien 88 (Stockholm, 2015). For one of the works (*Hertug Fredrik*) we have no identifiable European model.

of implicit tensions, rather than of ideological battles. The divergences in how to legitimise politics are reflected in the two main genres that flourished in the thirteenth century: the sagas of Icelanders and contemporary sagas (so-called *samtíðarsögur*). Whereas these saga genres have usually been distinguished from one another on the basis of their chronological settings, what is interesting here is the different ways in which these genres sought to validate elite power.[19]

The sagas of Icelanders were mostly written in the thirteenth century with the Saga Age (*c.* 930–1030) as their temporal frame of reference. It is of course a simplification to treat these sagas as a single corpus, but from a general point of view they share several assumptions about the legitimisation of political power. Above all, they portray chieftains whose power is precarious and concerned more with people than with territories. Chieftains had to fulfil the needs of local farmers (*bændr*), who were able to seek out an alternative leader if they were displeased with their current one. This state of affairs implies that a successful chieftain had to offer protection and gifts in order to gain supporters. Hence, the sagas' emphasis is on how power is built from below on a local level. Even if the option for the *bændr* to choose freely among chieftains was restricted by the latter's superior power and their own need for protection, the rivalry among chieftains for power and support put the *bændr* in an unusually strong position.[20]

The contemporary sagas were compiled in the collection known as *Sturlunga saga* around 1300, and they described 'contemporary' events, occurring between 1117 and 1264. In contrast, these sagas deal relatively little with the theme of power from below. Chieftains in *Sturlunga saga* are more firmly established as local leaders over larger territories, and they are mainly depicted in interaction with other chieftains. In the sagas of Icelanders, such struggles were multiparty conflicts, in which there were several different contenders, and where alliances and conflicts varied over time and cut across different social groupings.[21] In *Sturlunga saga*, such conflicts increasingly occurred between two parties; this implied that the dividing line between different factions became more clear-

---

19 Other genres were of course active in medieval Iceland, such as eddic poems, grammatical treatises, saints' sagas, legendary sagas and laws (dating is uncertain in most cases). The point here is however not to offer an extensive list of genres, but rather to investigate the relationship between major genres and political ideologies. See McTurk, ed., *A Companion to Old Norse-Icelandic Literature and Culture*, for a survey of various genres in Iceland.
20 This argument builds on William Ian Miller, *Bloodtaking and Peacemaking: Feud, Law, and Society in Saga Iceland* (Chicago, 1990); Jesse L. Byock, *Viking Age Iceland* (London, 2001); Jón Viðar Sigurðsson, *Chieftains and Power in the Icelandic Commonwealth*, The Viking Collection 12 (Odense, 1999).
21 On multiparty conflicts and their dynamic, see Fotini Christia, *Alliance Formation in Civil Wars* (Cambridge, 2012).

cut and that options for staying outside conflicts were more limited. For instance, in *Þórðar saga kakala*, instead of trying to persuade people in border zones to support them, the two main protagonists used brute force to compel them, and if they resisted they were plundered. In the sagas of Icelanders, mediators played a key role in such conflicts and it was possible to remain impartial. In *Sturlunga saga*, the principle was 'either you are with us or you are against us,' and the scope and position of mediators were severely restricted.[22]

Do we find a correspondence between genre and political ideology in medieval Iceland? According to Preben Meulengracht Sørensen, the sagas of Icelanders promoted a view of honour that was incompatible with living under a monarchy. In his view, Icelanders had a horizontal concept of honour operating between equals, contrasting with Norway's hierarchical idea of honour which emanated from the king.[23] However, it is difficult to sustain a view that the sagas of Icelanders and the contemporary sagas expressed a consistently negative view of Norwegian kings. First, Icelanders throughout the Freestate period served as royal skalds, authors of kings' sagas and as royal retainers, without any objections on principle. Norwegian kings do indeed appear in the sagas of Icelanders, and were more often presented as attractive patrons than as threats to Icelandic chieftains. Second, the reading of *Sturlunga saga's* account of Iceland's submission to the Norwegian king in 1262/64 as a tragedy is a modern interpretation that finds no support in the sources. Even if the Norwegian king and archbishop placed increasing pressure on Icelandic chieftains, the same chieftains were eager to seek out the Norwegian king and Church as sources of power and prestige.[24]

The best examples of Icelandic ambiguity towards Norway are Snorri Sturluson (1179–1241) and his nephew Sturla Þórðarson (1214–84), who were politicians and prolific writers in both Iceland and Norway. Snorri is thought to be the author of *Heimskringla* and The *Prose Edda* and has been proposed as the author of *Egils saga Skalla-Grímssonar*.[25] He was the most powerful man in Iceland in the 1220s, when he served as *lendr maðr*

22 This builds on Jón Viðar Sigurðsson, *Chieftains and Power*; Viðar Pálsson, *Language of Power: Feasting and Gift-Giving in Medieval Iceland and Its Sagas*, Islandica 60 (Ithaca, 2017); Sverrir Jakobsson, 'The Process of State-Formation in Medieval Iceland', *Viator* 40:2 (2009), 151–70.
23 Preben Meulengracht Sørensen, *Fortælling og ære: Studier i islændingesagaerne* (Aarhus, 1993), p. 144: 'enhver afgivelse av selvbestemmelsesrett under tvang sætter ham ind i et andet socialt system, hvor den ære, der bygger på personlig frihed og integritet ikke længere gjælder.' (my translation: 'any waiving of sovereignty under compulsion puts him into another social system, where the honour, based on personal freedom and integrity, is no longer valid').
24 Jón Viðar Sigurðsson, 'The Icelandic Aristocracy after the Fall of the Free State', *Scandinavian Journal of History* 20:3 (1995), 153–66.
25 Torfi H. Tulinius, *Skáldið í skriftinni: Snorri Sturluson og Egils saga*, Íslensk Menning (Reykjavík, 2004).

(liegeman) for the Norwegian king, Hákon Hákonarson, and as lawman for three periods; he married off three daughters into the most prominent competing chieftain families in Iceland. However, his marriage alliances broke down, and as a result of his support for Duke Skúli Bárðarson against King Hákon Hákonarson he was slain by the men of his former son-in-law Gizurr Þorvaldsson in 1241. Sturla Þórðarson was a more prudent man, and attempted to stay out of the conflict as long as possible. However, in the final years before Iceland came under the Norwegian king, he opposed Gizurr, and as a result he was sent to King Hákon to be tried and convicted for his opposition. Here he obtained the commission of writing the deceased king's saga from King Magnús *lagabætir*. Sturla returned to Iceland as a lawman and aided in the acceptance of *Járnsiða* as the new law book for Iceland in 1271. During this period he composed *Íslendinga saga*, the major saga in the *Sturlunga saga* compilation, covering the period 1183–1262, and edited *Landnámabók*.

Both Snorri and Sturla were confronted at some point in their lives by the king's demands in a very dramatic manner – Snorri even lost his life through the conflict, whereas Sturla received the king's mercy – as would Snorri, had Gizurr not seized the opportunity to eliminate a troublesome rival.[26] However, these clashes did not reverberate in their literary works; in these we can hardly identify any trace of a struggle or a contradiction between heroic and royal ideologies. In Snorri's case, there have been numerous discussions and opinions about whether *Heimskringla* should be reckoned as a royalist or anti-royalist work; this in itself testifies to a lack of explicit ideology.[27] As for Sturla, it is easier to see how he took on different roles during his career. *Hákonar saga Hákonarsonar* is a work written as a royal commission, one that does not necessarily reflect his own attitudes; whereas he wrote *Íslendinga saga* later, a narrative that describes many of the same events from the perspective of Icelandic chieftains. Sturla's writing appears to accommodate opposing views.[28] Both Snorri and Sturla wrote within a number of genres while taking part in contemporary politics. As such, they were both writers and politicians, authors and historians, Icelanders and Norwegians, royalists and anti-royalists.

## Iceland in the Late Middle Ages

The fall of the Icelandic Freestate in 1262/64 constituted no sudden shock or rupture in the development of genres, and the sagas of Icelanders and contemporary sagas continued to be written well into the fourteenth century. *Fornaldarsögur*, describing an even more distant past than the

---

26 *Hákonar saga Hákonarsonar II*, ed. Þorleifur Hauksson, Sverrir Jakobsson and Tor Ulset, ÍF 31 (Reykjavík, 2013), p. 119.
27 For references, see fns 12 and 13 above.
28 *Sturla Þórðarson: Skald, Chieftain, and Lawman*, ed. Jón Viðar Sigurðsson and Sverrir Jakobsson, The Northern World 78 (Leiden, 2017).

sagas of Icelanders, were probably written from the early thirteenth century onwards, and became increasingly popular in the late Middle Ages.[29] Moreover, the translation of chivalric romances as Old Norse *riddarasögur*, which had originated at the royal Norwegian court, soon became a productive genre in Iceland.[30] In the early fourteenth century a new genre of indigenous *riddarasögur* (or *fornsögur Suðrlanda*) appeared. These can be viewed as a kind of hybridisation of *riddarasögur* and *fornaldarsögur* in that they feature European princes undertaking courtly adventures in the settings related to the latter saga genre.[31] Two ideological trends are evident in the development of new genres in the late Middle Ages. First, the new genres attest to a widening of the geographical horizon. Whereas the action in the sagas of Icelanders and contemporary sagas mainly played out in Iceland, now the saga chronotope included the Nordic area (*fornaldarsögur*), Europe (*riddarasögur*), and eventually the whole world (indigenous *riddarasögur*).[32] Second, these genres depicted a society dominated by kings and nobles. The elite character of the political struggles in these genres were in accordance with the concept of the body politic as described in *Sturlunga saga*, contrasting with the bottom-up perspective of the sagas of Icelanders.[33]

Various saga genres delineated different ways of legitimising political power and defining the political body. Power could emanate from below, where the obligations of giving protection and showing generosity to local *bændr* (farmers) was a prime concern of chieftains. Power could also originate from above, in relations of subordination towards kings and the Church, or it could operate 'horizontally' in struggles between chieftains or kings of roughly equal status. However, despite all their variations, the sagas present their political views as neither explicit nor comprehensive ideologies. This is reflected in the fact that most manu-

---

29  Stephen A. Mitchell, *Heroic Sagas and Ballads*, Myth and Poetics (Ithaca, 1991); Torfi H. Tulinius, 'Sagas of Icelandic Prehistory (Fornaldarsögur)', in *A Companion to Old Norse-Icelandic Literature and Culture*, ed. McTurk, pp. 447–61.
30  Jürg Glauser, 'Romance', pp. 372–87.
31  Matthew Driscoll, 'Late Prose Fiction (*lygisögur*)', in *A Companion to Old Norse-Icelandic Literature and Culture*, ed. McTurk, pp. 190–204. The question of whether indigenous *riddarasögur* are closer to *riddarasögur* or *fornaldarsögur* is heavily debated. See Marianne E. Kalinke, '*Riddarasögur, Fornaldarsögur* and the Problem Of Genre', in *Les Sagas de Chevaliers (Riddarasögur): Actes de la V*$^e$ *Conférence Internationale sur les Sagas*, ed. Régis Boyer, Civilisations (Paris, 1985), pp. 77–91.
32  For a discussion of the chronotope see Torfi Tulinius's chapter in this volume.
33  Torfi H. Tulinius, *The Matter of the North: The Rise of Literary Fiction in Thirteenth-Century Iceland*, The Viking Collection 13 (Odense, 2002); Sigríður Beck, *I kungens frånvaro: Formeringen av en isländsk aristokrati 1271–1387*, (Göteborg, 2011); Jón Viðar Sigurðsson, 'Historical Writing and the Political Situation in Iceland 1100–1400', in *Negotiating Pasts in the Nordic Countries: Interdisciplinary Studies in History and Memory*, ed. Anne Eriksen and Jón Viðar Sigurðsson (Lund, 2009), pp. 59–78.

scripts dating from the fourteenth and fifteenth centuries can be classified as 'composite manuscripts', comprising a variety of ideologically incompatible saga genres.[34]

An example of this comes from the extensive manuscript production at Möðruvellir, a large farm in Eyjafjörður in northern Iceland, in the mid-fifteenth century when the farm was headed by Margrét Vigfúsdóttir, widow and member of Iceland's uppermost elite.[35] This environment produced a number of different genres that communicated very different views on politics and society. Some genres elevated the Norwegian monarchy and its ideology. Manuscripts AM 81a fol. and AM 243a fol. were probably produced here and were preserved together. They contained the Norwegian contemporary kings' sagas: *Sverris saga*, *Böglunga sögur* and *Hákonar saga Hákonarsonar*, as well as *Konungs skuggsjá*. It is not surprising that Margrét and the audience at her farm appreciated the history of the Norwegian monarchy and its ideology, as Iceland was now part of Norway and Margrét's own family had previously enjoyed close connections to the Norwegian monarchy.[36] This, however, did not contradict Margrét's own interest in her Icelandic past. Fragments of *Egils saga Skalla-Grímssonar* (AM 162 Aη fol.) and *Svarfdæla saga* (AM 445c II 4ᵗᵒ) traced the lineage of her family and inhabitants of her farm back to the Saga Age, and signalled more 'patriotic' Icelandic sentiments. Yet the genres that Margrét Vigfúsdóttir must have preferred were legendary sagas about Nordic and European kings and warriors, as she had three large manuscripts (one in fragments) compiled in her lifetime containing thirty-one sagas in total – ten *fornaldarsögur*, sixteen indigenous *riddarasögur*, four *riddarasögur* and one *ævintýri* (moral fable). In these manuscripts legend blended with history and European with Nordic realms, without any strict demarcation. What they show is that when defining their 'ideology', or their conception of how society and politics were supposed to work, Icelanders (at least Margrét and her copyist) drew on a variety of resources.

---

34 On composite manuscripts, see Jonas Carlquist, *Handskriften som historiskt vittne* (Stockholm, 2002); Barbara Shailor, 'A Cataloguer's View', in *The Whole Book: Cultural Perspectives on the Medieval Miscellany*, ed. Stephen G. Nichols and Siegfried Wenzel, Recentiores: Later Latin Texts and Contexts (Ann Arbor, 1996), pp. 153–67.

35 See Hans Jacob Orning, *The Reality of the Fantastic: The Magical, Geopolitical and Social Universe of Late Medieval Saga Manuscripts*, The Viking Collection 23 (Odense, 2017) for a more thorough analysis of this environment. For further discussion of Margrét Vigfúsdóttir see Jóhanna Katrín Friðriksdóttir's chapter in this volume.

36 Both her father, grandfather and father-in-law had served as *hirdstjóri*, the highest royal official in Iceland, and Margrét had relatives in western Norway who might have been related to the Norwegian royal family. It is also no surprise that a manuscript of *Jónsbók*, the Icelandic law code under Norwegian rule from 1281, was produced at Möðruvellir in Eyjafjörður (AM 132 4ᵗᵒ). See Orning, *The Reality of the Fantastic*, pp. 224–26.

Genre and politics are in some sense two sides of the same coin, at least if the definition of politics is expanded to include conceptions of how society operates. For one thing, it is impossible to evade the question of genre in the analysis of medieval politics, since what we know about Old Norse society is formulated through texts in various genres. For another, people formulated their views and aspirations in writing, and in this way various genres can be studied as sources for the ideologies and opinions of the people who produced and listened to them. It also becomes evident that just as 'politics' concerns more than 'kings and wars', 'genres' are more than ideological vehicles expressing political views or agendas. The assemblage of the sagas of Icelanders, *fornaldarsögur* and indigenous *riddarasögur* in the same manuscript, for instance, shows that there were no contradictions between enjoying local stories and legends about Old Norse giants as well as stock tales of European knights and kings. Icelanders cherished their own uniqueness and their participation in a common European culture. This indicates that both 'genres' and 'ideologies' are terms which can easily become too rigid for the description and analysis of the complicated and varying ways in which elites used writing to legitimise their positions.

# Geography
*Dale Kedwards*

The link between place and narrative has been fundamental to our construction of genre in Icelandic saga literature. The sagas' prevailing geographical attachments have been used as a basis to categorise the *Íslendingasögur* (sagas of Icelanders), *fornaldarsögur* (legendary sagas) and *riddarasögur* (romances or knight's sagas); as Massimiliano Bampi puts it, 'the temporal and geographical setting of the action plays the foremost role in distinguishing one saga genre from another'.[1] The *Íslendingasögur* are characterised by their precise locatedness in the Icelandic landscape, their main action ranging across Iceland, Greenland, Scandinavia and the British Isles in the period c. 870–1050. The *fornaldarsögur* and *riddarasögur*, stories of quest and adventure that sometimes resemble romance, locate their action in landscapes mostly outside the mundane experience of saga audiences. These saga subgenres may sometimes elude classification on structural or thematic grounds, but are placed according to random 'accidents of geographic setting'.[2] Generally, the *riddarasögur*, which include translations of French *chansons de geste* and Latin histories as well as original Icelandic compositions, traverse a wide world centred on the southern European courts, while the *fornaldarsögur* situate their main action in a legendary Scandinavia before the Norse discovery of Iceland. These sagas' broad attachments to southern and northern geographies are among their main generic characteristics, the genre terms conventionally coupled with the geographically contrastive *norðrlanda* (of northern lands) and *suðr-*

1 Massimiliano Bampi, 'Genre', in *The Routledge Research Companion to the Medieval Icelandic Sagas*, ed. Ármann Jakobsson and Sverrir Jakobsson (London, New York, 2017), pp. 4–14, at p. 8.
2 Marianne Kalinke, 'Norse Romance (*Riddarasögur*)', in *Old Norse-Icelandic Literature: A Critical Guide*, ed. Carol J. Clover and John Lindow (Ithaca and London, 1985), pp. 316–64, at p. 326. On the relationship between the *fornaldarsögur* and *riddarasögur* see Beeke Stegmann, 'Árni Magnússon's Rearrangement of *fornaldarsaga* Manuscripts', in *The Legendary Legacy*, ed. Matthew Driscoll *et al.* (København, 2018), pp. 161–86, at p. 174; and Helen F. Leslie-Jakobsen, 'Genre and the Prosimetra of the Old Icelandic *fornaldarsögur*', in *Genre - Text - Interpretation: Multidisciplinary Perspectives on Folklore and Beyond*, ed. Kaarina Koski, Frog, Ulla Savolainen (Helsinki, 2016), pp. 251–75.

*landa* (of southern lands).³ These knots of place and time that localise action are sometimes called *chronotopes*.⁴

The Icelandic sagas provide insight into a capacious geographical imaginary that draws from the Norse explorations that precipitated Iceland's relatively late discovery, and, as importantly, the Icelanders' wider engagement with foreign and translated literatures.⁵ In earlier scholarship, interest in the geographical awareness that underlies the sagas was sometimes motivated by a modern preoccupation with their value as historical source material. Their geographical coverages were scrutinised in the easy assumption that historical regions described in the northern *fornaldarsögur* correspond seamlessly with, and can tell us something about the early histories of, their equivalents in modern political geography.⁶ The distinction between the historical medieval world and our modern one is further collapsed in the *Íslendingasögur*. The accuracy with which they describe 'real' places in the Icelandic landscape has become, as Emily Lethbridge notes, a mainstay of the introductions to the authoritative Íslenzk fornrit series.⁷ Conversely, the *riddarasögur*

3   Kalinke, 'Norse Romance', p. 323; Matthew James Driscoll, '*Fornaldarsögur Norðurlanda*: the stories that wouldn't die', in *Fornaldarsagornas Struktur och Ideologi*, ed. Ármann Jakobsson, Annette Lassen and Agneta Ney (Uppsala, 2003), pp. 257–69, at p. 257.
4   On the 'chronotope' in Old Norse literature see Bampi, 'Genre', p. 8; Fulvio Ferrari, 'Possible Worlds of Sagas: The Intermingling of Different Fictional Universes in the Development of the *Fornaldarsögur* as a Genre', in *The Legendary Sagas: Origins and Development*, ed. Annette Lassen, Agneta Ney, and Ármann Jakobsson (Reykjavík, 2012), pp. 271–90, p. 273; and Torfi Tulinius's chapter in this volume. On its use in Middle English literature see Kenneth Hodges, 'Introduction: Places of Romance', in *Mapping Malory: Regional Identities and National Geographies in Le Morte Darthur*, ed. Dorsey Armstrong and Kenneth Hodges (New York, 2014), pp. 1–18, at p. 2.
5   Stimulated by the Viking voyages of exploration and settlement, geography has long been considered a keynote of Old Norse literature. For an overview, see Judith Jesch, 'Geography and Travel', in *A Companion to Old Norse Icelandic Literature and Culture*, ed. Rory McTurk, Blackwell Companions to Literature and Culture 31 (Oxford and Malden, 2005), pp. 119–35. On the 'mental maps' of the Vínland voyages see Gísli Sigurðsson, *The Medieval Icelandic Saga and Oral Tradition: A Discourse on Method* (Cambridge MA, 2004), pp. 253–301. On the world-view of the Icelanders and the culmination of their inherited and observed geographical knowledge see Sverrir Jakobsson, *Við og veröldin: Heimsmynd Íslendinga 1100–1400* (Reykjavík, 2005).
6   On the nationalistic appropriations of the northern *fornaldarsögur*, see the introduction to *Illuga saga Gríðarfóstra: The Saga of Illugi, Gríður's Foster-Son*, ed. and trans. Philip Lavender (London, 2015), p. viii. On the entanglements between romance and incipient nationalisms see Sheryl McDonald Werronen, *Popular Romance in Iceland: The Women, Worldviews, and Manuscript Witnesses of* Nítíða Saga (Amsterdam, 2016), p. 93; and Hodges, 'Places of Romance', pp. 11, 14.
7   Emily Lethbridge, 'The Icelandic Sagas and Saga Landscapes: Writing, Reading and Retelling *Íslendingasögur* Narratives', *Gripla* 27 (2016), 51–92, at p. 67.

have been characterised, like the romance narratives they resemble, as 'having a geographical vagueness: locations in romance have sometimes been seen as ill-defined, or as having names that do not correspond to cities and countries in the real historical medieval world, or that, when they do, represent them in an entirely unrealistic fashion'.[8] Our modern saga genres remain predicated on *geographies* that are never surely medieval or modern.

The sagas, however, were not written primarily to be geographically informative or to provide their audiences with a complete and unobstructed view of their own sense of the physical world. Literary representations of geographical space are necessarily fictionalised in that they describe the world selectively and adapt it to the requirements of narrative. Geography is not simply the world exterior to literature, a fundamentally neutral and unchanging reality to which it merely refers, but is a category of literary composition in itself, that has sometimes been described as a literary genre.[9] *Geography* is a major generic classifier, but, like *genre*, it is also a modern analytical category with no precise equivalent in Old Norse or medieval Latin.[10]

The sagas' prevailing geographical attachments are usually focalised in their opening chapters.[11] The *Íslendingasögur* declare their spatial interests early on, relating the early Icelanders' migrations from Norway, and scrupulously delineating their settlements and wider territorial interests in the Icelandic landscape. The opening chapters of the northern *fornaldarsögur* and roving *riddarasögur* sometimes require a more expansive statement of geographical range. The compilation of *konungasögur* (kings' sagas) known as *Heimskringla* takes its name from *Ynglinga saga*'s open-

---

8   Robert Rouse, 'What Lies Between? Thinking Through Medieval Narrative Spatiality', in *Literary Cartographies: Spatiality, Representation, and Narrative*, ed. Robert T. Tally Jr. (London, 2014), pp. 13–29, at p. 19; Robert Rouse, 'Walking (between) the Lines: Romance as Itinerary/Map', in *Medieval Romance, Medieval Contexts*, ed. Michael Cichon and Rhiannon Purdie (Cambridge, 2011), pp. 135–47, at p. 136. For similar on Icelandic romance, see Ármann Jakobsson, *Illa fenginn mjöður: Lesið í Miðaldatexta* (Reykjavík, 2009), p. 179.
9   James S. Romm, *The Edges of the Earth in Ancient Thought: Geography, Exploration, and Fiction* (Princeton, 1992), p. 3.
10  In the classical world, geography could be distilled into three scaled categories: *topography* (from *topos*, 'place'), *chorography* (from *choros*, 'region'), and *geography* (from *geos*, the 'entire earth'). For Robert Rouse, medieval strategies of representing the world are more usually topographical or chorographical, focalising place or region, than they are classically geographical. See Rouse, 'What Lies Between', pp. 16–17. See also Andy Merrills, 'Geography and Memory in Isidore's *Etymologies*', in *Mapping Medieval Geographies: Geographical Encounters in the Latin West and Beyond, 300–1600*, ed. Keith D. Lilley (Cambridge, 2013), pp. 45–65.
11  The geographical introduction is not unique to medieval Icelandic literature, but is an ancient literary device. See Andrew H. Merrills, *History and Geography in Late Antiquity* (Cambridge, 2005).

ing words, which describe the division of the known world, the 'kringla heimsins' (the circle of the world) into the three continents, Europe, Africa, and Asia, centred on the Mediterranean Sea.[12] The saga writer locates the saga's action in the world as it was conceptualised by ancient bookish authorities, whose works had been canonised for the high Middle Ages by anthologists of late antique learning like Isidore of Seville (c. 560–636). This bookish world is explicitly invoked in the opening words to the fourteenth-century popular romance *Dínus saga drambláta*, the narrator contextualising the saga's action, which takes place in exoticised Egyptian and African kingdoms, with a statement that 'ysidorus hefer sua skrifat i fiortanda bok ethimologiarum at heimrinn se skiptr i þria parta' (Isidore has so written in the fourteenth book of *Etymologies* that the earth is divided into three parts).[13]

Geography permeates narrative – all stories happen *somewhere* – but more than simply providing a backdrop to narrative events, 'the space of action', as Kenneth Hodges has shown, 'determines what actions are possible and what they mean'.[14] Geographical descriptions in literature do more than specify the space of the ensuing action. As Guðrún Nordal writes of the landscape descriptions in the *Íslendingasögur*,

> the inclusion of the stories of the migration to and settlement of Iceland in a saga clearly affects its beginning and determines through which door the reader or listener enters the house of the narrative.[15]

Geography is generically coded, the geographical descriptions we encounter in the main saga subgenres eliciting a horizon of expectations that conditions the ways in which an audience engages the narrative.

## Iceland

The forty or so *Íslendingasögur* vary considerably at a thematic and stylistic level, but have in common their deep-rootedness in the Icelandic landscape. There are twenty-four *Íslendingasögur* that begin with *landnám* (land-taking) accounts, and around seventeen that open with the family's life in and migration from Norway.[16] These *landnám* episodes scrupulous-

---

12 Snorri Sturluson, *Heimskringla*, ed. Bjarni Aðalbjarnarson, vol. 1, ÍF 26 (Reykjavík, 1941), p. 10.
13 Geraldine Barnes, *The Bookish Riddarasögur: Writing Romance in Late Mediaeval Iceland* (Odense, 2014), p. 31.
14 Hodges, 'Places of Romance', p. 16.
15 Guðrún Nordal, 'Skaldic Citations and Settlement Stories as Parameters for Saga Dating', in *Dating the Sagas: Reviews and Revisions*, ed. Else Mundal (København, 2013), pp. 195–212, at p. 204.
16 See Nordal, 'Skaldic Citations', for a detailed taxonomy of the *Íslendingasögur* based on the prominence of their settlement accounts. See also Ann-Marie Long, *Iceland's Relationship with Norway c. 870 – c.1100: Memory, History and Identity* (Leiden, 2017), pp. 86–87.

ly delineate the land claims of the early Icelandic colonists through localisable anecdotes about the settlers and their activities and customs. These histories are frequently told through names in the Icelandic landscape, for which the sagas provide explicit narratorial explanation.[17] In *Egils saga Skalla-Grímssonar*, Skalla-Grímr's settlement, and the lands he distributes among his twelve followers, occupies the saga for a full three chapters, which describe the Icelandic landscape through the visions and experiences of its early explorers.[18] The place they make their landing in Iceland they name Knarrarnes (Ship-Ness), and seeing some swans gathered on a peninsula, call it Álftanes (Swan-Ness). The settlers' wonder at the extraordinary colour of glacial melt water is an anecdote that becomes attached to the place-name Hvítá (White-River): 'Hvítá, því at þeir fǫrunautar hǫfðu eigi sét fyrr vǫtn þau, er ór jǫklum höfðu fallit; þótti þeim áin undarliga lit' (Hvítá, because the companions had not seen before those waters that have flowed out of glaciers; they thought the river was an extraordinary colour).[19] In *Bárðar saga Snæfellsáss*, Bárðr discovers a cave on Snæfellsness where echoes (Old Norse *dvergmála*, 'dwarf-talk') seem to answer all that is said. Bárðr called this cave Sǫnghelli (Song-Cave), and subsequently 'gerðu þar ǫll ráð sín' (held all his councils there).[20] The settlement of lands by a principal settler, and their grant of smaller parcels of land among their followers, establishes a hierarchy of people and places that Icelandic place-names helped people remember.[21]

The complex motivations for spatial construction in the *Íslendingasögur* arise in part from the newness of Iceland and its people. Iceland had been discovered by Norse seafarers in c. 870, and was a *terra nova* with no native culture or human prehistory. It is not clear whether the place-name etymologies we encounter in the *Íslendingasögur* are 'authentic' descriptions of how a place was named, or were fabricated by a saga writer to strengthen the association between the landscape and its settlers, who may have been the ancestors of that region's thirteenth- or fourteenth-century inhabitants. Through such onomastic asides, however, the Icelandic landscape *quickens* – its rivers and headlands become cultural spaces with their

---

17  Margaret Clunies Ross, 'Land-Taking and Text-Making in Medieval Iceland', in *Text and Territory: Geographical Imagination in the European Middle Ages*, ed. Sylvia Tomasch and Sealy Gilles (Philadelphia, 1998), pp. 159–84, at p. 159.
18  David Stevens, 'Trouble with the Neighbours: The Problem of Ánabrekka in Skalla-Grímr's Land Claim', *SBVS* 35 (2011), 25–38. See also Lethbridge, 'Saga Landscapes', p. 61.
19  *Egils saga Skalla-Grímssonar*, ed. Sigurður Nordal, ÍF 2 (Reykjavík, 1933), pp. 74–75; my translation. See Eleanor Rosamund Barraclough, 'Land-naming in the Migration Myth of Medieval Iceland: Constructing the Past in the Present and the Present in the Past', *SBVS* 36 (2012), 79–101.
20  *Bárðar saga*, p. 112; my translation.
21  See, for example, *Laxdæla saga* (chapters 5–6), *Kjalnesinga saga* (chapters 2–3), and *Bárðar saga Snæfellsáss* (chapters 3–4). Barraclough, 'Land-naming', p. 86.

own local histories, and a recently discovered rocky prominence in the North Atlantic becomes properly *Iceland*. Jürg Glauser has called the work of translating Iceland's physical geography into a new cultural space the 'semioticization of the landscape'.[22] As Margaret Clunies Ross has shown, Iceland's settlement required the socialisation of the new geographical area, as 'immigrant society was obliged to 'produce' its own social space in an entirely new environment'.[23] The settlement episodes created for Icelanders a new historical record, but may have also addressed geopolitical preoccupations at the time the sagas were recorded. Seventeen of the *Íslendingasögur* emphasise how Iceland's colonisation was linked to the Norwegian homeland, an assertion of the historical kinship shared by Icelandic and Norwegian aristocratic elites in the period of social insecurity and civil war that culminated in the end of the Icelandic republic in 1264.[24] Through these *landnám* episodes, the Icelandic landscape became an archive of anecdotes and stories about the pioneer settlers, their families, and their ties to Norway.

The *landnám* episodes in *Landnámabók* and the *Íslendingasögur* sought to give written record to, or 'canonise', to use Ann-Marie Long's term, the Icelandic *landnám*. But the Icelandic landscape they sought to canonise was not an unchanging reality that existed wholly outside the *Íslendingasögur*, and to which they merely refer.[25] The variant versions of *Landnámabók*, and the *Íslendingasögur* written in their presence, vary in their construction of the Icelandic landscape, which may have been as much created as it was remembered. Christopher Callow has shown that depictions of the same area of western Iceland vary between *Laxdæla saga* and the *samtíðarsögur* (contemporary sagas), as each conveys its own time's views of their regional geography.[26] *Landnámabók*, whose variance is sometimes recognised with the plural, *Landnámabækur*, is an unstable text that has come down to us in three medieval versions – Melabók, Sturlubók and Hauksbók – attributed to post-Commonwealth Icelandic lawmen with strong connections to Norway, as well as two versions based on lost

---

22 Jürg Glauser, 'Sagas of Icelanders (*Íslendinga sögur*) and *þættir* as the Literary Representation of a New Social Space', in *Old Icelandic Literature and Society*, ed. Margaret Clunies Ross, Cambridge Studies in Medieval Literature 42 (Cambridge, 2000), pp. 203–20, pp. 214, 209.
23 Clunies Ross, 'Land-Taking', p. 159. See also Christopher Callow, 'Putting Women in their Place? Gender, Landscape, and the Construction of *Landnámabók*', *VMS* 7 (2011), 7–28.
24 Nordal, 'Skaldic Citations', p. 204. These sagas are: *Bárðar saga Snæfellsáss, Egils saga, Eyrbyggja saga, Flóamanna saga, Gísla saga Súrssonar, Grettis saga, Harðar saga, Hrafnkels saga, Kjalnesinga saga, Kormáks saga, Laxdæla saga, Reykdæla saga, Svarfdæla saga, Vatnsdæla saga, Víga-Glúms saga, Þórðar saga hreðu, Þorskfirðinga saga*. See also Long, *Iceland's Relationship with Norway*, pp. 85–86.
25 Lethbridge, 'Saga Landscapes', p. 54.
26 Chris Callow, 'Reconstructing the Past in Medieval Iceland', *Early Medieval Europe* 14:3 (2006), 297–324.

seventeenth-century texts.²⁷ The varying accounts of Skalla-Grímr's land claim, as related in *Egils saga Skalla-Grímssonar* and in the extant versions of *Landnámabók*, demonstrate how descriptions of the Icelandic landscape are historically and culturally contingent. David Stevens has shown that the Sturlubók version of *Landnámabók* followed, or developed in parallel with, *Egils saga*, as both present a 'maximalist' account of Skalla-Grímr's settlement. Sturlubók's compiler, Sturla Þórðarson (1214–84) was a direct descendant of Egill, and his grandiose portrayal of his family's settlement in the Viking Age supported the territorial claims of the Sturlungar, a powerful family whose control extended from western Iceland and the Vestfirðir to north-eastern Iceland. The Melabók version of *Landnámabók*, however, which was compiled on the other side of Borgarfjörður, confines Skalla-Grímr's settlement to the areas north of the fjord, a more modest account that may have been an attempt to de-emphasise the Mýrar region, the Sturlungs' heartlands, in favour of the Melar region on the south.²⁸ The geography that these histories sought to canonise was as unstable as the texts that encoded it. This literature emphasises the social nature of geographical space, and thus dulls the distinction between landscape and the textualised world of narrative.

The Icelandic landscape and its place-names, and the various oral and written traditions attached to them, were elaborated upon in the remembering and telling of *Íslendingasaga* narratives.²⁹ Their narrators sometimes invoked continuities between the allegedly historical world of saga narrative and the present to authenticate the narrative, so that some landmarks can 'still be seen' at the time the saga was composed.³⁰ In *Laxdæla saga*, for example, the farm Unnr djúpúðga establishes 'er síðan heitir í Hvammi' (has since been called Hvamm), quietly asserting that the account of Unnr's settlement there is transparent and authentic.³¹ It is of course unclear whether such statements were thought to be true, or were unspoken fabrications that enabled the narrator to shore up, or even create, a history advantageous to the time the saga was recorded. This semblance of continuity, however, is one of the main authenticating mechanisms that endows the *Íslendingasögur*, as Lethbridge puts it, with 'their famous sense of realism and verisimilitude'.³² As Lethbridge sees it, the landscape becomes 'a crucial vehicle for the transmission of these narratives, alongside the parchment and paper manuscripts that were produced and circulat-

---

27 Jesch, 'Geography and Travel', p. 122.
28 Stevens, 'Problem of Ánabrekka', pp. 28–29.
29 Lethbridge, 'Saga Landscapes', p. 58.
30 Carol Hoggart, 'A Layered Landscape: How the Family Sagas Mapped Medieval Iceland', *Limina: A Journal of Historical and Cultural Studies* 16 (2010), 1–8, at p. 1.
31 *Laxdæla Saga*, p. 53.
32 Lethbridge, 'Saga Landscapes', pp. 66, 69.

ed from the thirteenth century'.[33] Such moments configure the Icelandic landscape as a witness to its own narratives, the *Íslendingasögur* appearing to derive from the Icelandic landscape even as they produce it.

That the compilers of the *Íslendingasögur* sought to canonise the Icelandic landscape can also be seen within single-volume compilations of sagas, which embody the correspondence between place and narrative in their selection and arrangement of narratives. The sumptuous saga manuscript in Reykjavík's Stofnun Árna Magnússonar with the shelf mark AM 152 fol., for example, seems to have been compiled with a particular interest in sagas associated with north-western Iceland.[34] The mid-fourteenth-century Möðruvallabók (Reykjavík, Stofnun Árna Magnussonar, AM 132 fol.) from Möðruvellir in Eyjafjörður, the largest known single collection of Icelandic sagas of the Middle Ages, contains eleven sagas arranged in topographical sequence. From south-western *Njáls saga*, whose action is localised around the farms at Bergþórshvoll and Hlíðarendi, the compilation enacts a clockwise survey of the island's saga narratives to the eastern *Droplaugarsona saga*, focused on Arneiðarstaðir.[35] Möðruvallabók's circular narration of the Icelandic landscape imitates the model for describing Icelandic geography established by *Landnámabók*, which counts Iceland's earliest settlers by quarter, in a clockwise motion starting in the west and ending in the south. These compilations embody the geographical awareness of their compositors and readers, and demonstrate that geography, as well as genre, was an important part of the archival framework medieval audiences used to think about sagas and their relationships to one another.

## Diaspora

The *Íslendingasögur*'s prevailing geographical attachments are focalised in their opening chapters, which tend to relate the migration of aristocratic families from Norway to Iceland, and name narratives that evidence their settlements. Saga genres other than the *Íslendingasögur* focalise other geographies, locating their action predominantly in landscapes outside the mundane experience of the saga's audience. The geographical introduction, however, is a literary device that recurs across saga subgenres. Like many of the *Íslendingasögur*, *Ynglinga saga* describes the migrations of a ruling elite into a new cultural area, whose

---

33 *Ibid.*, p. 52.
34 Jóhanna Katrín Friðriksdóttir, 'Ideology and Identity in Late Medieval Northwest Iceland: A Study of AM 152 fol.', *Gripla* 25 (2014), 87–128, and see her chapter in this volume.
35 These sagas are *Njáls saga*, *Egils saga*, *Finnboga saga ramma*, *Bandamanna saga*, *Kormáks saga*, *Víga-Glúms saga*, *Droplaugarsona saga*, *Ölkofra Þáttr*, *Hallfreðar saga*, *Laxdæla saga* and *Fóstbrœðra saga*. On Möðruvallabók, see Leslie-Jakobsen, 'Genre', p. 253.

movements through the landscape leave a mark in its place-names.

*Ynglinga saga* resembles other *fornaldarsögur* in that its main matter is legendary Scandinavian prehistory, but its opening chapters focalise a Central Eurasian geography that centres on the estuary of the River Tanais (Don) and its surrounding regions. The saga relates the primeval migrations of the legendary Swedish Yngling dynasty into Scandinavia, its author arguing that their descendants among the Norse gods, the Æsir and the Vanir, were not truly divinities but exceptionally cunning people from Central Eurasia. The Norse god Óðinn, who possessed knowledge about the future, knew that he would find posterity in the world's northern regions, and so travels through Garðaríki (Russia) and Saxland (Saxony) to establish himself on the island of Fyn in Denmark. His progeny, through his son Freyr, become the Ynglings, whose legendary descendants are the Scandinavian royal lines.

The saga's geographical description contextualises Óðinn and the Æsir's transcontinental migrations from Central Eurasia into Scandinavia. Its opening statement, 'kringla heimsins, sú er mannfólkit byggir' (the circle of the world, which humanity inhabits), emphasises that this space contains all human civilisation and history, and that the Scandinavians' history and distant origins necessarily place them a wider world. The world's rivers and seas divide the *kringla heimsins* into its three continental parts: 'Sá skilr heimsþriðjungana. Heitir fyrir austan Ásíá, en fyrir vestan kalla sumir Európá, en sumir Enea' (this divides the world's three regions: the east is called Asia, and the west is called by some Europe, and others *Enea*).³⁶ The saga's description of continental space emphasises east and west, describing the trajectory of the Æsir's migrations from Asia into Europe. The saga further inscribes a global north and south onto the *kringla heimsins*, 'Inn nørðri hlutr Svíþjóðar liggr óbygðr af frosti ok kulða, svá sem inn syðri hlutr Blálands er auðr af sólar bruna' (the northern part of Sweden lies unsettled because of the frost and cold, just as the southern part of Bláland [sub-Saharan Africa] is empty because of the sun's intensity). These latitudinal distinctions between the northern hemisphere's hot and cold regions had been laid out by the classical system of zonal division, which had theorised that regions around the globe's equator were too hot for human inhabitation, and the regions under the poles, in both the northern and southern hemispheres, were too cold.³⁷ Its narrator situates the *kringla heimsins*, the space known to medieval Europeans, within the mild midlatitudes of the northern hemisphere. The geographical description accommodates Óðinn's transcontinental migrations to northern Europe, which the author locates within learned Latin models for conceptualising global geography: the lie of the three continents, and the earth's climatic zones.

36  Snorri Sturluson, *Heimskringla*, ed. Bjarni Aðalbjarnarson, I, p. 9.
37  Snorri Sturluson, *Heimskringla*, ed. Bjarni Aðalbjarnarson, I, p. 10; my translation.

The legendary geography that accommodates the Æsir's migrations out of Central Eurasia is related through a series of onomastic asides, through which the author provides etymological proofs of their historical settlements. The name *Enea*, which the author poses as an alternative name for Europe, is unattested outside the introductions to *Ynglinga saga* and *Snorra Edda*, and appears to have been invented by an Icelandic author, possibly Snorri Sturluson himself, to associate Europe with an eponymous founder in the Trojan hero Aeneas.[38] European ruling elites frequently traced their origins to Trojan heroes. Brutus, a legendary descendant of the hero Aeneas, was celebrated as the eponymous founder of Britain in Geoffrey of Monmouth's *Historia Regum Britanniae* (*History of the Kings of Britain*) and its related vernacular literatures.[39] In *Skáldskaparmál*, Snorri identifies the Norse 'god' Víðarr with the Trojan Aeneas: 'Hann er Eneas, hann kom braut af Troju ok vann síðan stór verk' (he is Aeneas, he came out of Troy, and accomplished then great deeds), demonstrating the Icelanders' connectedness to other European ruling elites who claimed descent from Troy.[40]

The alternative names for the Tanais estuary and its surroundings are the subject of a lengthier onomastic aside.

> Fellr á um Svíþjóð, sú er at réttu heitir Tanais. Hon var forðum kǫlluð Tanakvísl eða Vanakvísl. Hon kømr til sjávar inn í Svartahaf. Í Vanakvíslum var þá kallat Vanaland eða Vanaheimr.

> [a river flows into Sweden (the Great, i.e. Russia), which is correctly called the Tanais. It was previously called the Tana-estuary or Vana-estuary. It comes to the sea in the Black Sea. Around the Vana-estuary was then called Vana-land or Vana-home.][41]

---

38 Rudolf Simek, 'Snorri als Kosmograph', in *Snorri Sturluson: Beiträge zu Werk und Rezeption*, ed. Hans Fix (Berlin, 1998), pp. 255–66, at pp. 262–64.
39 On the myth of Trojan origins in medieval European literatures, see Sylvia Federico, *New Troy: Fantasies of Empire in the Late Middle Ages* (Minneapolis, 2003); and Emily Wingfield, *The Trojan Legend in Medieval Scottish Literature* (Cambridge, 2014). On euhemerism and other mechanisms for a *translatio imperii* in Icelandic literature see Diana Whaley, 'A Useful Past: Historical Writing in Medieval Iceland', in *Old Icelandic Literature and Society*, ed. Margaret Clunies Ross, Cambridge Studies in Medieval Literature 42 (Cambridge, 2000), pp. 161–202, at p. 178; Sverrir Jakobsson, 'Hauksbók and the Construction of an Icelandic Worldview', *SBVS* 31 (2007), 22–38, at p. 27; and Jonas Wellendorf, 'Zoroaster, Saturn and Óðinn: The Loss of Language and the Rise of Idolatry', in *The Performance of Christian and Pagan Storyworlds*, ed. Lars Boje Mortensen and Thomas M. S. Lehtonen with Alexandra Bergholm (Turnhout, 2013), pp. 143–70.
40 Snorri Sturluson, *Edda: Skaldskáparmál*, ed. Anthony Faulkes (London, 2005), p. 6, lines 27–28. My translation. See Simek, 'Snorri als Kosmograph', pp. 262–64.
41 Snorri Sturluson, *Heimskringla*, ed. Bjarni Aðalbjarnarson, p. 10.

These apparently alternative or earlier names for the Tanais estuary and the areas around it also appear to have been fabricated by the Icelandic author, who turns Tanakvísl into Vanakvísl to create an authenticating link between Central Eurasia and the divinities called the *Vanir*, whom the saga claims had their ancestral home there.[42] In *Gylfaginning*, Snorri similarly links the Æsir to their ancestral home in Asia on confected etymological grounds, maintaining that the *Æsir* (singular *Ás*) were *Asiamenn* (Asians).[43]

Place-names and their etymologies were, as we have seen, a frequently used authenticating mechanism in Icelandic saga literature. The onomastic asides in the introductory chapters to *Ynglinga saga* resemble the narratorial explanations of place-names in the *Íslendingasögur*. As in the example of *Tanakvísl*, the place-names written into the *Íslendingasögur* may well have preceded the etymologies created to explain their origins; or like *Enea*, have been created by saga authors to associate regions with events and people they allege to be historical. Both are concerned with Scandinavian origins and attempt to demonstrate, through etymology, the migration of aristocratic elites – from Central Eurasia to Scandinavia; from Norway to Iceland – into a new social space. These two *diasporas*, the Trojan and the Viking, are historical propositions mapped onto geography. They bestow a founding identity on the elite patrons of Icelandic saga literature by invoking wider geographies, looking outward from Iceland to Scandinavian and European cultures.

## Provincialising Iceland

Genres other than the *Íslendingasögur* sometimes enabled their audiences to look on Iceland from less commonly seen perspectives. *Illuga saga Gríðarfóstra*, which is numbered among the *fornaldarsögur*, focalises a legendary Scandinavian prehistory centred on the Danish kingdom.[44] The saga traverses, as Philip Lavender notes, 'a rag-tag assemblage of locations' in Scandinavia and areas surrounding the White Sea, and is strewn with moments of 'geographical incongruity' that do not seem to have troubled its audience.[45] Illugi and Prince Sigurðr, for example, set sail 'til Orkneyja og Skotlands og gjörðu hvorutveggjum miklar árásir og vinna mikinn sigur á Skotum og fá nú ofurfjár' (to the Orkney Islands and Scotland and made daring attacks on both places and win

---

42 Snorri Sturluson, *Heimskringla*, ed. Bjarni Aðalbjarnarson, p. 10.
43 Snorri Sturluson, *Edda: Prologue and Gylfaginning*, ed. Anthony Faulkes (London, 2005), p. 6.
44 *Illuga saga Gríðarfóstra* survives in thirty-seven manuscripts written between the sixteenth and nineteenth centuries. On its genre see Philip Lavender, '*Illuga saga* as *fornaldarsaga, riddarasaga*, and *Íslendingasaga*: Generic Fluidity in the Late Development of Sagas and Rímur', in *The Legendary Legacy*, ed. Driscoll *et al.*, pp. 187–214.
45 Lavender, 'Introduction', *Illuga saga*, ed. Lavender, pp. v–xxxvvi, at pp. x–xi.

a great victory over the Scots and get a large amount of wealth).[46] However, at least two of the saga's surviving manuscripts have Illugi and Sigurður setting sail for the less likely locality of *Ungaria* (Hungary) and Scotland.[47] The saga's narrator takes a similarly relaxed approach to the description of Denmark, the saga's focal region, placing a *sel* (a shieling on a mountain pasture, where cows were kept in the summer months) in mountainless Denmark.[48] The narrator has, it seems, unthinkingly inserted details of the familiar Icelandic landscape into a description of narrative events taking place in more distant lands.

In contrast to the precise locatedness of the *Íslendingasögur*, these sagas traverse an indistinct romance landscape that sometimes 'blurs into forests of adventure and unnamed castles'.[49] The Icelandic romances, however, differ from their Continental and English relations, as Geraldine Barnes has shown, in their openness to material from bookish and scholarly sources. Icelandic authors borrowed from these sources to invest their translated and original romance sagas with a capacious geographical imaginary. As we saw in the opening lines of *Dínus saga drambláta*, saga authors consulted encylopedic sources, like Isidore's *Etymologies*, to create 'opportunities for the narrative players themselves to step directly into the world as constructed in learned texts'.[50] Through the integration of this material, Icelandic romances in turn enabled the wider transmission and popularisation of information and learned speculation about the world and its places.

*Nítíða saga*, a popular romance composed in Iceland in the fourteenth century, traverses a wide world.[51] The saga conveys its 'impressive geographical awareness', as Sheryl McDonald Werronen notes, through its thirty-one named places.[52] Its action centres on the Parisian court of the maiden-king Nítíða, which the narrator places 'í norður hálfu veraldarinnar' (in the northern region of the world).[53] The saga's episodic narrative ranges between indistinct and conventionalised courtly settings in Paris, Apulia, Constantinople and India, as Nítíða wars against and eventually brings about the reconciliation between these eastern kingdoms. The narrator locates this romance landscape within the world as it was conceptualised by learned authorities: in the course of the saga's action, the

46 *Illuga saga*, ed. Lavender, pp. 6–7.
47 Ibid., p. x.
48 Ibid., pp. 4–5.
49 Hodges, 'Places of Romance', p. 3.
50 Barnes, *Bookish Riddarasögur*, p. 28.
51 Sheryl McDonald, '*Nítíða saga*: A Normalised Icelandic Text and Translation', *Leeds Studies in English* 40 (2009), 119–45. See also Geraldine Barnes, 'Margin vs. Centre: Geopolitics in *Nitida saga* (A Cosmographical Comedy?)', in *The Fantastic in Old Norse/Icelandic Literature: Sagas and the British Isles, Preprint Papers of the Thirteenth International Saga Conference, Durham and York, 6–12 August 2006*, 2 vols. ed. John McKinnell, David Ashurst, and Donata Kick (Durham, 2006), I, pp. 104–12.
52 McDonald Werronen, *Popular Romance*, p. 95.
53 McDonald, '*Nítíða saga*', p. 124.

audience glimpses an island under the North Pole, and the lands at the earth's equator. In the Apulian court, Nítíða hears travellers' tales about a fabulous island named Visio (vision), under the rule of an earl named Virgilius and lying 'út undan Svíþjóð hinni köldu, út undir heimsskautið, þeirra landa er menn hafa spurt af' (out beyond cold Sweden, out by the North Pole, the edge of those lands of which people have had reports).[54] As is usual within the sagas, which tend to focalise dramatic events and mute the more ordinary realities of travel, Nítíða arrives at Visio as it were between the lines.[55] The narrator disclaims that 'hef ég ei heyrt sagt frá þeirra ferð né farlengd fyrr en þau taka eyna Visio' (I have not heard tell of their journey, nor of their journey's length, before they reached the island of Visio).[56] The island of Visio epitomises Icelandic romance's approach to geography, being at once beguilingly vague and indistinct, situated somewhere, almost beyond report, at the edge of lands and story, and at the same time locatable within bookish models for conceptualising global space, lying somewhere in the vicinity of the North Pole.

The broad geographical attachments that characterise medieval romance manifest in *Nítíða saga* through three geographical visions.[57] On the island of Visio, Nítíða obtains four extraordinary stones (*náttúrusteinar*) that enable her, among other things, to see 'allar hálfar veraldarinnar' (all the regions of the world).[58] Nítíða uses these stones' visionary qualities to her tactical advantage, and especially, in one of the saga's several perspectives on the northern world, 'að sjá um veröldina ef víkingar kæmi og vildi stríða á hennar ríki' (to see throughout the world if vikings were coming to attack her kingdom).[59] At the culmination of Nítíða's struggle against King Liforinus, Nítíða uses the stones to locate her adversary who, apparently unbeknown to her, stands at her side disguised as the princely Eskilvarðr. She raises them in turn to reveal three interlocking visions of world geography that reveal to her the totality of the known world.

---

54 *Ibid.*, pp. 124–25. Despite its northern position, Visio is described as a verdant garden with an abundance of trees, fruit and healing herbs, perhaps, as McDonald Werronen, *Popular Romance*, p. 119 notes, in the widespread *locus amoenus* tradition.
55 Barnes has noted the tendency in the *riddarasögur* for 'virtually instant transportation across continents', *Bookish Riddarasögur*, p. 190. On the laconic handling of travel in other saga genres, see Eleanor Rosamund Barraclough, 'Sailing the Saga Seas: Narrative, Cultural, and Geographical Perspectives in the North Atlantic Voyages of the *Íslendingasögur*', *Journal of the North Atlantic* 7 (2012), 1–12.
56 McDonald, '*Nítíða saga*', pp. 124–25. For a thoughtful commentary on the significance of the narrator's interjection here, see McDonald Werronen, *Popular Romance*, pp. 210–11.
57 For this episode see McDonald, '*Nítíða saga*', pp. 140–41. On the variant witnesses within this episode see McDonald Werronen, *Popular Romance*, pp. 48–50.
58 McDonald, '*Nítíða saga*', p. 124.
59 *Ibid.*, pp. 124–25.

The first vision focalises southern Europe, showing Nítíða and Eskilvarðr 'Frakkland, Provintiam, Ravenam, Spaniam, Hallitiam, Friisland, Flandren, Norðmandiam, Skottland, Grikkland, og allar þær þjóðir þar byggja' (France, Provence, Ravenna, Spain, Hallitia, Frisia, Flanders, Normandy, Scotland, Greece, and all the people living there).[60] Raising the second stone, 'sáu þau norður hálfuna alla, Noreg, Ísland, Færeyjar, Suðureyjar, Orkneyjar, Svíþjóð, Danmörk, England, Írland, og mörg lönd önnur, þau er hann vissi ei skil á' (they saw all the northern regions, Norway, Iceland, the Faroes, the Hebrides, Orkney, Sweden, Denmark, England, Ireland, and many other lands which he could not distinguish). The third vision completes their vision of world geography, 'sjáandi þá nú austur hálfuna heimsins, Indíaland, Palestinam, Asiam, Serkland, og öll önnur lönd heimsins, og jafnvel um brúnabeltið, það sem ei er byggt' (then they saw the eastern regions of the world: India, Palestine, Asia, Serkland, and all the other lands of the world, and even around the burning belt, which is uninhabited).[61] Collectively, these interlocking visions reveal all that is not in the viewers' most immediate presence, as Nítíða knowingly coaxes Liforinus to reveal himself: 'nú sjást öll úthöfin um lá og leynivoga, hvorgi er hann þar, og hvorgi er hann í öllum heiminum útan hann standi hér hjá mér' (now everything is visible, from the oceans to the shoals and hidden coves; neither is he there nor is he anywhere in the whole world, unless he is standing here beside me).[62]

These three visions, which Barnes describes as a virtual *mappamundi*, epitomise medieval geographical knowledge, dividing the world's regions into near continental thirds, and into climatic zones bounded by the polar region, where these stones originate, and the equator.[63] The visions focalise three world regions: the lands and cities belonging largely to southern Europe; the northern regions, Iceland and the islands of the North Atlantic; and a loose assemblage of regions that extends from India to Saharan Africa. The third vision completes the saga's conspectus of world geography up to the equator (*brúnabeltið*), which marks the limits of the world's habitability, emanating from the classical system of zonal division that gave us the description of the sun's intensity in Bláland (sub-Saharan Africa) in the above passage from *Ynglinga saga*. The term the saga's author uses for the equator, *brúnabeltið*, appears elsewhere in the vernacular in the Norwegian *Konungs skuggsjá* (c. 1265), which calls the equator 'boginn rinng brænnannda vægar' (the curved ring of the burning belt) and the climatically hot zone around it *brennubeltið* (the

---

60 Ibid., pp. 140–41. The appearance of Scotland in this list may reveal the saga author's awareness of the Franco-Scottish alliance (1295–1560), established to resist the territorial ambitions of the English Edward I.
61 Ibid., pp. 140–41.
62 Ibid.
63 Barnes, *Bookish Riddarasögur*, p. 37.

burning belt).⁶⁴ Between these equatorial lands and the stones' origin on the island of Visio, under the North Pole, 'út undir heimsskautið', the saga's action encompasses the latitudinal entirety of the Earth's inhabitable area. These three visions appear to divide the world's parts in contravention of the classical division of the known world into the three continents: Africa, Asia and Europe.⁶⁵ Southern Europe and the environs of Nítíða's Parisian court are now translocated to the world's centre, normally understood in medieval cosmology as Jerusalem or Rome; while Iceland and northern Europe, compassed in the second vision, are elevated to the distinction of being a global third of the world.⁶⁶ Asia and Africa, from India to Serkland, are collapsed into a single vision. Barnes describes the saga as a 'cosmographical comedy' – a dispute between eastern and western powers resolved through a lavish triple wedding – that 'redraws the hierarchy of global power' in order to recast the relationship between the world's northern regions and its centre.⁶⁷

*Nítíða saga* repeatedly emphasises the correspondence between place and narrative, as well as the obvious pleasure in sharing stories about distant countries. In the guise of Eskilvarðr, Liforinus delights Nítíða and her court with travellers' tales, having something to say about each of the world's lands; 'hann kunni af hvoru landi að segja nokkuð'.⁶⁸ The triple wedding and extravagant celebrations at the saga's end brings together courtiers from India, Byzantium, and France. The narrator reminds the audience of their distance from the Parisian court at this world's narrative centre:

> Er og ei auðsagt með ófróðri tungu í útlegðum veraldarinnar, svo mönnum verði skemmtilegt, hvor fögnuður vera mundi í miðjum heiminum af slíku hoffólki samankomnu.
>
> [Indeed, it was so entertaining for everyone that it is not easily said with an unlearned tongue in the outer regions of the world what joy there may be in the middle of the world when such courtiers come together].⁶⁹

---

64 Dale Kedwards, 'The World Image of the *Konungs skuggsjá*', in *Speculum Septentrionale: Konungs skuggsjá and the European Encyclopaedic Tradition*, ed. Karl Gunnar Johansson and Elise Kleivane (Oslo, 2018), pp. 71–92. The theory of the world's climatic zones at its intersection with ancient and medieval theories of race can be seen in *Gylfaginning*, where Snorri Sturluson situates Muspell and the fiery Surtr in the far south, in harmony with what he knew from ancient authoritative texts. See Richard Cole, 'Racial Thinking in Old Norse Literature: The Case of the *Blámaðr*', *SBVS* 39 (2015), 21–40, at pp. 29–30.
65 Barnes, 'Margin vs. Centre', p. 110.
66 *Ibid.*, pp. 109–10; and Barnes, *Bookish Riddarasögur*, pp. 38–39.
67 Barnes, 'Margin vs. Centre', p. 111.
68 McDonald, '*Nítíða saga*', p. 138.
69 *Ibid.*, pp. 142–43. See Barnes, 'Margin vs. Centre', p. 111.

The saga's narrator encourages the Icelandic audience to see themselves from a romance perspective; the narrator provincialises Iceland and its vernacular literary culture, the relationship between Iceland and the Parisian court configured as one of both debt and distance. The narrator characterises Icelandic as the backwater language of a global periphery, which can at best do a poor service to the vibrant profusion of romance narratives in European languages shared among courtiers (*hoffólk*) at the world's centre (*í miðjum heiminum*). This statement, however, is a hoax; the false characterisation dissolves when we recognise *Nítíða saga*'s status as an original Icelandic example of the romance genre that is not at all provincial in its themes. The narrator confronts the saga's audience with a vision of itself as a community created through its enjoyment of romance, closing the gap between the *útlegðum veraldarinnar*, the outer regions of the world, and its centre.

The three visions participate in the saga's analysis of the relationship between place and narrative. As sequences of place-names, the visions resemble the textualised world of narrative more so than aerial views of physical topography, and thus resemble the chronotopes that are the basis for the main saga subgenres, such as the *Íslendingasögur* and romance. The world revealed to Nítíða and Eskilvarðor by the first stone is the normative world of romance, the regions and cities of southern and Continental Europe. This is the only vision to include the names of cities, and is expressive of the courtly settings and cosmopolitan audiences of the romance genre. Conversely, the second vision, centred on Iceland, is coextensive with the world of the *Íslendingasögur*. The third vision, which completes the world to the limits of terrestrial habitability, represents the world as it was constructed by medieval bookish authorities, and into which Icelandic authors arranged their narrative material. When Nítíða asks Eskilvarðor whether the famous King Liforinus would sail into the northern lands: 'mun Liforinus kóngur hinn frægi ekki sigla í þessi lönd', Eskilvarðor knowingly responds that his alter ego is far from them: 'hann er fjarlægur þessum löndum'. Eskilvarðor's response invokes the relationship between geography and genre to deny the appearance of a romance king in the sphere of the northern world, a chronotope incompatible with the appearance of romance actors. In excluding King Liforinus from the world's northern regions, the narrator alludes to the obvious generic limitations on the movements of romance kings, which are geographically specific. Indeed, when Eskilvarðor looks upon these regions in Nítíða's second vision, he sees, in addition to all the stable parts of the northern world 'mörg lönd önnur' (many other lands) that 'hann vissi ei skil á' (he is unable to discern).[70] Despite the stones' apparently panoptic qualities, these geographically contrastive visions do not emanate from a perspective that is universal. Rather,

---

70 McDonald, '*Nítíða saga*', pp. 140–41.

we see the world of the *Íslendingasögur* from a romance perspective that dissembles and disorientates, and from which the northern regions are envisioned as the most shadowy. The world of the *Íslendingasögur* is reimagined as a distorted periphery that is strange for being partially but not fully discernible.

Icelandic geography also surfaces in the romance *Sigrgarðs saga frækna*, in which the valiant Sigrgarðr quests from his father's kingdom in Garðaríki (Kievan Rus') to Tartaría (Tartary, on the Eurasian Steppe) in pursuit of the maiden-king Ingigerðr.[71] In the course of his adventures, Sigrgarðr travels to a strange place called Lóar, which the saga's editors characterise as 'an otherworld associated with supernatural beings and magic, marked by mirroring and inversion'.[72] This inversion is articulated in geographical terms, as Sigrgarðr's experiences in this otherworld are described in an unusually heightened degree of topographic detail. Characterised by *sléttirvellir* (valleys) and 'hömrum nökkurum. Þeir váru brattir ok hávir ok svá sléttir at eigi mátti klífa' (mountain cliffs, steep and high, and so smooth that no-one would be able to climb them), these landscapes are unusual for romance but, as the saga's editors note, strongly evocative of the Icelandic upland interior.[73] In *Sigrgarðs saga frækna*, the Icelandic landscape is harnessed in the creation of otherworlds, which, as in *Nítíða saga*, appear strange precisely because they are generically displaced, belonging to the *Íslendingasögur*.

## Conclusion

Narrative setting has sometimes provided the basis for the distinction of literary kinds, as modern genre distinctions have come to emphasise the sagas' prevailing geographical attachments. The tendency to foreground geography in a saga's opening chapters is one that transcends subgenre; in the *Íslendingasögur* and the Icelandic romance sagas alike, these spatial interests are categorically stated in their introductory chapters. Their introductions contextualise the ensuing action and, perhaps more importantly, alert the audience to the kind of saga they are reading or hearing.

Icelandic saga authors were certainly aware of the relationship between place and narrative. The *landnám* episodes in the *Íslendingasögur* show how places come into being through their entry into narrative, while geographically-organised compilations of *Íslendingasögur* demonstrate that geography sometimes provided a logical structure for the ordering of saga narratives in manuscript books, and perhaps also the minds of their compilers and audiences. The landscape could have an

---

71 '*Sigrgarðs saga frækna*: A Normalised Text, Translation, and Introduction', ed. Alaric Hall, Steven D. P. Richardson, and Haukur Þorgeirsson, *Scandinavian-Canadian Studies / Études Scandinaves au Canada* 21 (2012–2013), 81–155, at p. 84.
72 Ibid., pp. 92–93.
73 Ibid., p. 133.

indexical relationship to the sagas written to describe its settlement, enabling audiences to order and relate saga narratives to one another. The *riddarasögur*, romances that are occasionally distinctive for their learned construction of the world and its places, likewise demonstrate an ability to sort through and relate their various sources – literary and encyclopedic – on a geographical basis. Their stories about the world's distant regions were enlarged upon through the adaptation and incorporation of material from the learned, scholarly sources to which educated Icelanders had access. The *Íslendingasögur* and bookish romances alike show how Icelanders used literature to think about geographies ranging from their own landscapes, to the wider European and global spaces in which they sought their place.

There is, however, no single geography that underlies all saga narratives, one that is revealed by stitching saga subgenres together to complete their geographical coverage. For these geographies are not neutral representations of geographical area, but constructs premised on generic expectations. These geographical and generic horizons sometimes converged within the space of individual saga narratives. The normative landscapes of the *Íslendingasögur* appear remote, provincial or strange from the perspective of romance; while the set pieces of romance, such as magically disguised Indian kings, do not generally appear in narratives centred on the world's northern regions. Geography in the sagas is not so much fictionalised as it is fiction, the world not so much described as created.

The main distinction between the geographies of the *Íslendingasögur* and those of romance-affiliated subgenres is not that between familiar and unfamiliar. Icelandic audiences engaged with romances, both original and adapted, as voraciously with as their *Íslendingasögur*, and were wholly fluent in understanding their characteristics. Geography operates as a generic indicator, and its capacity to mean within a narrative is dependent on its characteristics – be they features in the Icelandic landscape, or in the courtly centres of medieval romance – being recognisable. Romance landscapes, with their nameless castles, sumptuous courts, and adventurous forests, were no less familiar to Icelanders than their fjords and fells.

# Time and Space
*Torfi H. Tulinius*

It is useful to think of genre from a pragmatic point of view. When communicating something to somebody, we follow conventions that determine both form and content. An example is the greeting card. A person we know is getting married, graduating from school, or has lost somebody close to him. Sending the appropriate greeting card will provide us with a medium in which we can express our feelings of sympathy to that person. Though not a literary genre, the greeting card is analogous in the sense that it conveys a message via a specific form and content that are both fixed and adaptable to circumstances. From among the fixed forms of the greeting card, we will choose the option that is best adapted to the situation in which the recipient finds him- or herself. A product of convention, the card also fulfils a social requirement: that of people who want to stay in touch with each other through the expression of different types of feelings. Like genres, moreover, the greeting card is made possible by a society where people, though separated by space, can be in contact with each other by way of a postal system as well as through the services of a publishing industry providing people with a variety of different cards for various occasions.

Literary genres are not different from simpler forms in this respect. Indeed, the premise of this chapter is that the literary genres of medieval Iceland also grew out of social circumstances and evolved as society changed. They provided a medium for communication within society and were made possible by the advent of literacy among laymen and enough economic affluence for books to be produced and made available to major households in the country.[1]

Mikhail Bakhtin's many contributions to our understanding of culture, particularly literature, concern the social nature of language and linguistic production. Any linguistic communication involves at least two participants, i.e. the one communicating the message and the recipient, as well as the context in which the communication occurs. Language and linguistic communications are moreover by necessity community-specific as they derive from and are intended for members of a particular linguistic

---

1 Torfi H. Tulinius, 'The Social Conditions for Literary Practice in Snorri's Lifetime', in *Snorri Sturluson and Reykholt: The Author and Magnate, his Life, Works and Environment at Reykholt in Iceland*, ed. Guðrún Sveinbjarnardóttir and Helgi Þorláksson (København, 2018), pp. 389–405.

community. For Bakhtin the literary work of art is dialogic, in the sense that some types of literature represent hugely different and at times contradictory discourses in the same text, a phenomenon for which he coins the term 'heteroglossia'.[2] More importantly for the purposes of this chapter, literature is also a dialogic co-creation of authors, performers, audience and/or readership.[3] As a product of this co-creation, Bakhtin's concept of the chronotope is a useful tool to describe and understand how the community communicates through the literary work of art.[4]

In the literary work, says Bakhtin, 'spatial and temporal indicators are fused into one carefully thought-out, concrete whole. Time, as it were, thickens, takes on flesh, becomes artistically visible; likewise, space becomes charged and responsive to the movements of time, plot and history'.[5] Each literary genre is characterised by one or several specific chronotopes. To illustrate this, Bakhtin studies the novels of ancient Greece, identifying three types, each typified by its own chronotope. An example of a chronotope taken from more familiar literature is that of Agatha Christie's Hercule Poirot stories. Here the chronotope is England in the early twentieth century, with spaces characteristic of the social group involved, most probably those familiar to the intended readership of these novels. These spaces are different parts of London, country estates in England, trains, and so on. An example of a chronotope from medieval literature would be that of Chrétien de Troyes' chivalric romances. Here the chronotope is characterised by a distant legendary time, that of the reign of King Arthur. Its dominant spaces are the court, the forest and castles, with the occasional medieval town. The intended readership of these romances, i.e. members of princely courts in what today are now France and England, would have considered the reign of King Arthur as an ideal time for chivalry, projecting on it their values and worries.[6] The spaces characteristic of the romance's chronotope would have been familiar to this social group. Whether the modern detective story or the medieval romance, each of these different genres explores and expands their specific chronotopes. This means that the authors working within the genres will tend to exploit new aspects of the time and space that characterise it. In the case of chronotopes set in different times and places from those occupied by the authors and their intended audience, the material exploited is the product of collective representations and memory.

2  *Bakhtin and Medieval Voices*, ed. Thomas J. Farrell (Gainesville, 1996), p. 3.
3  Mikhail M. Bakhtin, *The Dialogic Imagination: Four Essays by M. M. Bakhtin*, ed. Michael Holquist, trans. Caryl Emerson and Michael Holquist (Austin, 1981), p. 253.
4  Ibid., pp. 84–258.
5  Ibid., p. 84.
6  Ibid., pp. 151–56; Erich Köhler, *Ideal und Wirklichkeit in der höfischen Epik: Studien zur Form der frühen Artus- und Graldichtung* (Tübingen, 1970).

In this chapter, an attempt will be made to use the chronotope concept to describe the Icelandic genre system and then to understand its development. The main idea is that the saga literature developed from the need of a community to tell stories about a past that was relevant to it. This past was not only that of the inhabitants of the island, but a past they shared with other members of what has recently been called the 'Viking diaspora'.[7] This is the geographical area inhabited, invaded and/or settled by Norse people during the period from the eighth to the eleventh century. As Old Norse-Icelandic literature developed, it explored and extended the different chronotopes inherent to the different spaces that were the areas of deployment of the Viking expansion, emphasising however those spaces which were closest to Iceland and subsequently most travelled and most familiar to Icelanders.

A telling example of the saga authors' awareness of the geographical extent of this expansion can be found in *Færeyinga saga*, a thirteenth-century saga found in the Flateyjarbók codex written in the late fourteenth century. The saga is incompletely preserved, as parts of it were inserted into a larger narrative about Norwegian rulers. Though it seems to have been composed in Iceland, it narrates conflicts between chieftains in the Faroe Islands shortly before and after the inhabitants of the archipelago converted to Christianity around the year AD 1000. Two noble boys are sold into slavery after their fathers have been killed by their enemies. The merchant, named Hrafn, who takes them from the islands out in the North Atlantic has a home base in Viken, today's Oslo Fjord in Norway, but he also spends part of the year trading in Hólmgarðr, i.e. the Norse settlements in today's Russia.[8] The chronotope of *Færeyinga saga* can therefore be described as that of the sphere of activity of the Viking diaspora around the year AD 1000 as it was construed by people living two to three centuries later.

## Bakhtin and the Sagas

Despite the vogue for Bakhtin's theories in literary studies in the 1980s and 1990s, the concept of the chronotope does not seem to have been applied to the Old Norse-Icelandic literary corpus until the very end of the last century. In a book chapter, later translated and published in English, I proposed the concept as a useful way to characterise the sagas about early Icelanders or *Íslendingasögur*.[9] Their settings and time periods are

---

7 Judith Jesch, *The Viking Diaspora* (London and New York, 2015).
8 *Færeyinga saga, Ólafs saga Tryggvasonar eptir Odd munk Snorrason*, ed. Ólafur Halldórsson (Reykjavík, 2005), p. 18.
9 Torfi H. Tulinius, 'Framliðnir feður: Um forneskju og frásagnarlist í *Eyrbyggju, Eglu* og *Grettlu*', in *Heiðin minni*, ed. Baldur Hafstað and Haraldur Bessason (Reykjavík, 1999), pp. 283–316; Torfi H. Tulinius, 'Returning Fathers. Sagas, Novels and the Uncanny.' *Scandinavian-Canadian Studies* 21 (2012–14), 3–23.

Iceland and countries to which Icelanders were likely to travel to, in the period from the settlement of Iceland around AD 900 to shortly after its conversion to Christianity in AD 1000. These times and places constitute their specific chronotope, which has a certain number of properties. The social and physical world is identical to that of their authors and intended audience. It is likely that this is due to the sagas presenting themselves as history, even though their historical truth is disputable.[10] They nevertheless share a feature which distinguishes them from the other saga genres, most notably from the sagas of the *Sturlunga saga* compilation; these also have Icelanders as their main characters but they are accounts of events happening in the twelfth and thirteenth centuries, i.e. contemporary with the time of writing. This feature is an inherent ambiguity attached to the characters and events of the sagas about early Icelanders; one which has been called 'ontological uncertainty' and is related to the role of the paranormal in the sagas, as well as to the social identity of the characters.[11]

In the first decade of this century, Carl Phelpstead developed the first full-blown application of Bakhtin's theories to the saga corpus in his study of saints' lives and their relationship to the kings' sagas.[12] The question he was attempting to answer is: to what extent the saints' lives shaped the way kings' sagas were written. Using Bakhtin's concept of dialogism, Phelpstead considered whether some types of hagiography – introduced into Old Norse-Icelandic culture via translation – provided examples of heteroglossia, presenting the saga writers with models for kings' sagas, and later other saga genres, which are arguably dialogic.[13] The kings' sagas are 'host texts' in the sense that they display features of several genres at a time.[14] Similarly, the sagas are shown to incorporate several chronotopes. The Bakhtinian idea that genre and chronotope are intrinsically related provides an explanation for the 'generic hybridity' of many sagas: that is, how their narrative changes with the geographical setting. This has already been remarked upon by several scholars and is developed further in a later article by Phelpstead in which he charts how the narrative of the legendary saga *Yngvars saga víðförla* changes as its heroes move further east into territory unknown to the general audience of the sagas.[15]

---

10 Jónas Kristjánsson, *Eddas and Sagas: Iceland's Medieval Literature*, trans. Peter G. Foote (Reykjavík, 1988), pp. 204–06.
11 Torfi H. Tulinius, 'The Matter of the North: Fiction and Uncertain Identities in Thirteenth-Century Iceland,' in *Old Icelandic Literature and Society*, ed. Margaret Clunies Ross, Cambridge Studies in Medieval Literature 42 (Cambridge 2000), pp. 242–65, at p. 253.
12 Carl Phelpstead, *Holy Vikings: Saints' Lives in the Old Icelandic Kings' Sagas* (Tempe, 2007).
13 Ibid., pp. 69–70, 220.
14 Ibid., p. 75.
15 Carl Phelpstead, 'Adventure-time in *Yngvars saga víðförla*', in *Fornaldarsagaerne: myter og virkelighed: Studier i de oldislandske fornaldarsögur Norðurlanda*, ed. Agneta

In a later study of a similar subject to that investigated by Phelpstead in his 2007 book, i.e. the saints' sagas and their influence on saga writing, Siân Grønlie shows a preference for Even-Zohar's polysystem theory over Bakhtin's, while nevertheless acknowledging the usefulness of the concept of the chronotope.[16] The added value of polysystem theory lies in how well it explains the changes brought into a cultural system by the influx of translations. Grønlie therefore posits that there had been a tradition of storytelling previous to saga writing in Iceland and that exposure to the genres of saints' lives and later to romance caused the incorporation of these new kinds of writing into the pre-existing genre systems. According to her, polysystem theory is more useful in explaining the relationship between local narrative and imported literature. It also has the advantage of foregrounding the power relations in the interaction between the two, as hagiography is a central genre in the European medieval literary system whereas sagas are peripheral. Polysystem theory allows a more dynamic understanding of genre and literary history.[17] Inspired also by Hans Robert Jauss's influential article 'Theory of Genres' as well as by Alistair Fowler's *Kinds of Literature*, Grønlie sees genres as 'historically mutable and flexible' and 'located at the interface between audience expectation and individual innovation'. It is a 'dynamic force in literary creativity'.[18]

The same year that Grønlie published her book, Lena Rohrbach applied Bakhtin's chronotope to the saga corpus in a different way from previous attempts.[19] The difference lay on the one hand in her choice of text to study and on the other in her distinction between several types of chronotopes (local, major and generic), building on several commentators on Bakhtin's original work.[20] Her study focuses on the contemporary saga *Íslendinga saga*, commonly attributed to the Icelandic chieftain and historian Sturla Þórðarson (1214–84), demonstrating how the concept helps us to understand the relationship between literary representation and the reality in which saga authors and audience lived. Her choice of a contemporary saga serves her purpose well as the types of spaces in which the

---

Ney, Ármann Jakobsson, Annette Lassen (København, 2009), pp. 331–46. See also Torfi H. Tulinius, 'Landafræði og flokkun fornsagna', *Skáldskaparmál* I (Reykjavík), 142–56; Elizabeth Ashman Rowe, 'Generic Hybrids: Norwegian "Family Sagas" and Icelandic "Mythic-Heroic sagas"', *SS* 65:4 (1993), 539–54; Marianne Kalinke, 'Textual Instability, Generic Hybridity, and the Development of Some *Fornaldarsögur*', in *The Legendary Sagas. Origins and Development*, ed. Annette Lassen, Agneta Ney and Ármann Jakobsson (Reykjavík, 2012), pp. 201–28. See also Chapter 2 in this volume.

16 Siân Grønlie, *The Saint and the Saga Hero: Hagiography and Early Icelandic Literature*, Studies in Old Norse Literature 2 (Cambridge, 2017), pp. 27–31.
17 Grønlie, *The Saint and the Saga Hero*, pp. 32–36.
18 *Ibid.*, p. 25.
19 Lena Rohrbach, 'The Chronotopes of *Íslendinga saga*: Narrativizations of History in Thirteenth-Century Iceland', *SS* 89:3 (2017), 351–74.
20 *Ibid.*, p. 355.

narratives take place are not only familiar to the authors and intended audience of the sagas, but are in fact those of their own lives. This underlines how strongly grounded saga literature is in the experience of thirteenth- and fourteenth-century Icelanders.

However, Rohrbach also shows that the contemporary sagas did not exist in a literary vacuum and their authors used literary resources provided by other genres, not only to construct their texts, but also to expand the limits of the saga genre by narrativising types of spaces not usually present in the sagas. Thus, there are 'narrative potentials that underlie the spatial framework of events'. That is why for her the concept of chronotope is, more than any other, the 'active determinant of narrative'.[21]

Rohrbach and Grønlie concur on the dynamism of the literary system. However, Rohrbach's argument that the chronotope concept shows how the representational potential of the literary genre can be expanded by incorporating new spaces, or 'local chronotopes', is an interesting addition to the discussion of genre in the sagas. In the following pages, an attempt will be made to build on this to further our understanding of the development of Icelandic literature in the thirteenth and fourteenth centuries.

## The Chronotope and the Genre System

The genre distinctions within the saga corpus that scholars are accustomed to are partly based on spatial and temporal categories. Carl Christian Rafn had already used such criteria when selecting the sagas that he published under the title 'fornaldarsögur Norðrlanda' or 'sagas of Northern antiquity'.[22] In an influential essay on 'saga literature', Sigurður Nordal established a temporal distinction between 'samtidssagaer', 'fortidssagaer' and 'oldtidssagaer', based on the distance between the period of composition and the time the events portrayed are supposed to take place.[23] The terms translate as follows: 'contemporary sagas', 'sagas from the past', and 'sagas from the distant past', the first taking place in or near the lifetimes of their authors, the second in the period when Iceland was settled and the Nordic countries were transitioning to Christianity and the third in a more or less legendary past before the Viking expansion into the North Atlantic.

Sigurður Nordal's distinction between a distant and a closer past is an interesting one, implying that the worlds portrayed in the two genres are to some extent different from each other; this was due on the one hand to the scarcity of information available about a distant and somewhat

21 Ibid., p. 352.
22 *Fornaldarsögur Norðrlanda, eptir gömlum handritum* I–III, ed. Carl Christian Rafn (København, 1829–30).
23 Sigurður Nordal, 'Sagalitteraturen', in *Litteraturhistorie B. Norge og Island*, Nordisk Kultur 8B (Stockholm, 1953), p. 181.

vague past, as well as by the fact that this information was transmitted through material such as heroic poetry and legends. On the other hand, there was a wealth of information to be had about the historical past, in the form of skaldic poetry and oral tales transmitted across a relatively limited number of generations.

This temporal distinction is useful as it helps to explain not only the differences between sagas set in different times, but also the links between sagas set in the same period but belonging to different genres. This is particularly true of the relationship between kings' sagas and the sagas about early Icelanders as the same characters can appear in both genres and similar events tend to take place in them. For the purpose of this chapter, the most interesting aspect of Sigurður Nordal's distinction is that it attends to the point of view of the authors and intended audience. There is therefore a qualitative difference in the events and the world in which they take place, the further back in time they occur.

Spatial distinctions function in a similar way. If the events portrayed in legendary sagas cannot but be situated outside Iceland, as they take place before its discovery and settlement, the same applies to kings' sagas, but for a different reason: there were never any kings in Iceland. However, sagas can be about legendary, historical and contemporary kings, transcending the temporal distinctions mentioned above, and the kings' sagas vary hugely in content and style depending on the period in which they are set.

The table on the following page shows how the saga genres, as they are traditionally defined by scholars, can be mapped: distance in time forms the vertical axis and distance in space the horizontal one. The closer the events are in space and time to their authors and first audience, the further down and to the left the saga genres are placed. Several observations can be made drawing on this table. The first is that it contains significant empty spaces. Some are obvious, such as the fact, already mentioned, that there is no legendary past for Iceland. It is however remarkable that no sagas are devoted to the history of those parts of Europe that are relatively close to Iceland but do not belong to the geographical area dominated by the Viking diaspora. The chivalric sagas derived from the French *chansons de geste* could be considered as taking place in a historical period from the point of view of medieval Icelanders, as Charlemagne and his men were alive shortly prior to the settlement of Iceland. However, their stories are understood as legendary in the way they are told in the originals, as well as when recast in saga form. The same can be said of contemporary times, since no Old Icelandic chronicles of events in countries outside the Northern world have been preserved and there is no indication that they ever existed.

|  | ICELAND | NORDIC COUNTRIES | FURTHER AWAY |
|---|---|---|---|
| Distant past |  | Kings' sagas about kings of antiquity<br>Legendary sagas<br>Snorri's *Edda* | Saints' sagas<br>Sagas of chivalry, translated and autochtonous<br>Sagas of antiquity.<br>Biblical sagas (*Gyðinga saga*). |
| Settlement and Conversion period | Sagas about early Icelanders, *Íslendingabók*, *Landnámabók* | Kings' sagas about historical kings (Óláfr Tryggvason, St Óláfr, Haraldr harðráði, etc.)<br>Sagas from other parts of the Viking diaspora (*Jómsvíkinga saga*, *Orkneyinga saga*, *Færeyinga saga*, *Eiríks saga rauða*, *Grænlendinga saga*) |  |
| Present of twelfth-fourteenth century Icelanders | *Sturlunga saga* and other contemporary sagas<br>Bishops' sagas | Kings' sagas about contemporary kings (Sverrir, Hákon, etc.) |  |

## Reality, Identity and Ideology

This observation leads to a second one: the genre system seems to have grown out of the experience of a community, that of Icelanders in the twelfth and thirteenth centuries, who were themselves part of a larger community, the very one referred to as the Viking diaspora in the opening section of this chapter. This was however not the only community to which they belonged; they were also very much part of Western Christendom, having converted in the year 1000 AD, more than a century before writing began in the vernacular and almost two centuries before the advent of saga-writing.

Bakhtin's theory of the chronotope, as presented above, provides significant help in understanding the links between genre and the experience of the community. The physical and social world in which the Icelanders participated, both at home and in other parts of the Nordic world, is heavily represented in the genre system. Indeed, the sagas set in contemporary and historical times are exclusively devoted to this area. It is tempting to propose that these different types of narrative represent various forms of discourse about the Icelanders' social and physical world that underlie the narratives. The sagas set in contemporary times are attempting to make sense of *reality*, the ones portraying historical times are exploring *identity*, while the sagas set in the distant past are conveying *ideology*.

All three of these concepts are complex and must be used carefully. They also mesh with each other, since ideology influences the way meaning is given to reality, while plain facts are known to challenge ideology. Identity can also be described as the subject's self-image when ideology encounters reality. Furthermore, all three concepts are in one way or another pertinent in dealing with all genres. However, I believe these are useful ways of thinking about space and time in the saga corpus and that this approach clarifies some aspects of genre in the sagas without oversimplifying a complex issue. The contemporary sagas that form *Sturlunga saga*, as well as the sagas of twelfth- and thirteenth-century kings such as *Sverris saga* and *Hákonar saga Hákonarsonar*, are descriptions of real events, presumably for the most part based on accounts by those who participated in them. Nevertheless, no narrative is a pure transcription of events. Out of the infinite number of things that happen, the author of the narrative necessarily chooses what she or he deems relevant. The choice implies an attempt to ascribe meaning to the events narrated. Recent scholarship on these sagas has shown that, though they are constrained in what they say by their audience's knowledge about the events described, they are also influenced by literary conventions and provide an interpretation of the recent history they are narrating.[24] Ideology nevertheless has a powerful impact upon narratives of contemporary people and events. A good example of this are the sagas of Icelandic contemporary bishops such as the different versions of *Þorláks saga* or even the separate version of *Hrafns saga Sveinbjarnarsonar*.[25]

The important place given to narratives about kings, especially Norwegian kings, in the saga corpus should come as no surprise, since medieval Icelanders perceived themselves as coming mainly from Norway, and they maintained a continuous relationship with that country, participating in its history as well as their own. Furthermore, when saga-writing was in its infancy, Icelanders were in the process of becoming subjects of the Norwegian king. The historical kings, especially the missionary kings, Óláfr Tryggvason and Óláfr Haraldsson, were constructed as playing a decisive role in shaping the identity of Icelanders and other denizens of the North Atlantic as Christians. In addition, the origins of the political world in which thirteenth-century Icelanders lived were to be found in this period, not only with the discovery and settlement of Iceland and Greenland, and the establishment of societies there, but also with the development of the Norwegian monarchy from Harald hárfagri onwards. In his book on kings' sagas, Carl Phelpstead makes cogent remarks about the 'polyphony' of sagas such as Snorri Sturluson's *Saga of Saint Óláfr*, which develops a lucid staging of power politics with which the king is involved, while at the same time it adheres to the ideological message underlying sainthood, resulting in a 'realistically paradoxical portrait of Óláfr as a holy viking'.[26] Inspired by polysystem theory, Grønlie presents this as a dynamic dialectic between genres.[27] In the terms used in the present chapter, the chronotope of these sagas is one where ideology meets reality in an attempt to establish identity.

Narratives exploiting the chronotope of Iceland and the Nordic countries during the period from the settlement and into the early years of the Christian era had the potential to establish the identity of those in the present. This was particularly true of the sagas about early Icelanders with their narrative convention of telling stories of settlers and of their immediate descendants. One of the earliest representatives of the genre, *Egils saga Skalla-Grímssonar*, describes in detail how Skalla-Grímr comes to an uninhabited part of Iceland and claims it as his own, distributing the land among his followers. He and his descendants ensure that

---

24 Úlfar Bragason, *Ætt og saga: Um frásagnarfræði Sturlungu eða Íslendinga sögu hinnar miklu* (Reykjavík, 2010); Ármann Jakobsson, 'King Sverrir of Norway and the Foundations of His Power: Kingship Ideology and Narrative in *Sverris saga*', *Medium Ævum* 84 (2015), 109–35.
25 Ásdís Egilsdóttir, 'Hrafn Sveinbjarnarson, Pilgrim and Martyr', in *Sagas, Saints and Settlements*, ed. Gareth Williams and Paul Bibire (Leiden, Boston, 2004), pp. 29–39.
26 Phelpstead, *Holy Vikings*, pp. 118 and 156–58.
27 Grønlie, *The Saint and the Saga Hero*, p. 36.

they maintain their power in the area.[28] Their identity, and by implication that of their descendants, has therefore been established, but this saga, as well as many others, also explore the ambiguities of identity. Indeed, the chronotope of the sagas of Icelanders lends itself particularly well to such an exploration: the characters leave one country to settle in another, with potential changes of social status, also exacerbated by the ongoing competition between dominant members of the society. The country in which the saga characters settle is unknown to them and is potentially inhabited by paranormal beings. They also live in a period which either immediately precedes the Conversion of Iceland to Christianity or is contemporary with it. They are pagans or recently converted and many aspects of a pagan culture survive, adding to the ambiguity of the people living in these times. This ambiguity is enhanced by the stylistic conventions of saga writing, given their reluctance to describe inner states and preference for external focalisation.[29] We could say that in the chronotope of the northern countries during the settlement and conversion period, the saga authors explore their own identity and that of the political world they inhabit, as well as their inherent ambiguities.

Among the stories taking place far away in a distant past, it is obvious that ideology is transmitted by saints' lives. The Christian saint is the embodiment of the ideology promoted by the medieval Church in medieval times. The same applies to the sagas of chivalry, translations and adaptations of French *chansons de geste*, all promoting an ideology which had developed among the armed aristocracy of medieval Europe and which Scandinavian rulers seem to have been eager to promote among their retinues.[30] The so-called autochthonous *riddarasögur* (romances), composed in Iceland, but set in a chronotope very similar to that of the translated sagas, also participate in this ideology.[31] A similar ideology is promoted in the sagas about legendary kings and heroes, whether these are ascribed to the kings' saga or legendary saga genre. The beginning of *Ynglinga saga*, for example, is based on the ideological motif of *translatio*, i.e. the common idea in twelfth-century Europe that models of knowledge and rulership originating in the Middle East were brought to the West and North by immigrants.[32]

For all these sagas it is nevertheless somewhat reductive to suggest that they are exclusively promoting a particular ideology. They also explore its limits and

---

28 *Egils saga Skalla-Grímssonar*, ed. Sigurður Nordal, ÍF 2 (Reykjavík 1933), pp. 72–77, 283 and 286.
29 Torfi H. Tulinius, 'The Matter of the North', in *Old Icelandic Literature and Society*, ed. Margaret Clunies Ross, Cambridge Studies in Medieval Literature 42 (Cambridge, 2000), pp. 242–65; Ármann Jakobsson, 'Some Types of Ambiguity in the Sagas of the Icelanders,' *ANF* 119 (2004), 37–53.
30 Geraldine Barnes, 'Romance in Iceland', in *Old Icelandic Literature and Society*, ed. Clunies Ross, p. 276.
31 Henric Bagerius, *Mandom och mödom: sexualitet, homosocialitet och aristokratisk identitet på det senmedeltida Island* (Göteborg, 2009).
32 For a recent and useful discussion of the importance of the motif of 'translatio' in medieval Icelandic literature, see Gunnar Harðarson, 'Old Norse Intellectual Culture: Appropriation and Innovation', in *Intellectual Culture in Medieval Scandinavia, c. 1100–1350*, ed. Stefka Georgieva Eriksen (Turnhout, 2016), pp. 35–73.

sometimes its contradictions. The greatest representatives of the genres in question do this in a memorable way. The *Rúnzivals þáttr* in *Karlamagnús saga*, based on the French *Chanson de Roland*, opposes Roland's overblown heroism to Olivier's more measured one. The Icelandic *Völsunga saga*, based on eddic poetry, exposes the tragic absurdity of an ethics of revenge. The preoccupation with ideology does not exclude the texts' concerning themselves with social matters, but this is analysed in a more abstract way, or, in other words, in terms of ideology.[33]

In my *Matter of the North*, I stated as a conclusion of my investigation into the 'rise of literary fiction' that the contemporary sagas, the sagas about early Icelanders and the legendary sagas represent different ways of mediating a contemporary reality, but that the reality remains the same.[34] This could be challenged by pointing to the influx of translated romances and the impact they seem to have had on literary development, as even *Egils saga Skalla-Grímssonar*, by all accounts an early example of a saga about early Icelanders, can be shown to acknowledge their impact.[35] It is perhaps better, following Grønlie, to use polysystem theory to explain this. If, however, we consider the genres that I have placed in the uppermost right-hand corner of the table above to be principally ideological, then they all participate in a set of ideological constructs that, I would argue, are the same. They should therefore not be understood in terms of the still persistent scholarly construct of an opposition between a formerly pagan North and the rest of Christian Europe, as Grønlie does – albeit in a finely nuanced way – as she opposes the ideology of the saints' lives to that of the sagas.[36] I do not believe this clarifies or explains the development of Old Norse-Icelandic literature. There is an advantage to thinking of saints' lives and chivalric literature from an ideological point of view, as it makes it easier to understand their place within the genre system without resorting to the opposition between foreign and autochthonous literature. The saints' lives were an essential influence in creating Old Norse-Icelandic literature as both Phelpstead and Grønlie have convincingly shown. At the same time, they promoted Christian values among their authors and audience, as they did elsewhere in Europe. The same can be said of the romances. They had an impact on how sagas were composed, but they also served to make the audiences of these sagas more sensitive to chivalric values, just as they had done for their original audiences in Europe. When saga-writing

---

33 Torfi H. Tulinius, *The Matter of the North: The Rise of Literary Fiction in Thirteenth-Century Iceland* (Odense, 2002), p. 41.
34 *Ibid.*, pp. 293–95.
35 Torfi H. Tulinius, 'Writing Strategies: Romance and the Creation of a New Genre in Medieval Iceland', in *Textual Production and Status Contests in Rising and Unstable Societies*, ed. Massimiliano Bampi and Marina Buzzoni (Venice, 2013), pp. 33–42.
36 Grønlie, *The Saint and the Saga Hero*, p. 37.

began, at the end of the twelfth century, the authors and audience of the sagas were thoroughly permeated by Christianity and had already been exposed to courtly culture.[37] In this respect, they were participating in the same general evolution as the rest of the dominant secular ranks in Western society. In this case, translation is not to be understood as the sign of a submission by a peripheral culture to a dominant one, rather it was the result of Icelanders and Norwegians participating in the culture of the high Middle Ages.

## Dynamics of the Chronotope

The study of the chronotope is therefore a way to show how grounded the different saga genres are in a dynamic social reality quite like that of other parts of contemporary Western Europe. As a conclusion to this chapter, an understanding of development within genres will be proposed, based on the concept of the local chronotope as presented by Rohrbach. If a genre is defined by a major chronotope, such as Iceland and the North Atlantic in the settlement period for the sagas about early Icelanders, this chronotope can contain a number of local chronotopes, for example the farmstead, the assembly, or the royal court in Norway, to name just a few examples.[38]

In the last decade there has been renewed interest in the role played by the landscape in the sagas about early Icelanders.[39] The natural and human environments are particularly interesting in these sagas, as they are almost identical to those of the saga authors and audience, thereby creating a link between past and present. By sketching a timeline for the sagas about early Icelanders, it might be possible to show how the genre expands its artistic potential by exploring new aspects of the chronotope that defines it. As will be shown, specific local chronotopes that belong to Iceland and other parts of the Nordic world in the historical period become progressively included in the genre's general chronotope. The examples that will be given are from *Egils saga*, composed before 1250, *Eyrbyggja saga*, composed between 1250 and 1270, and *Grettis saga*, composed at the earliest around 1300. This is a tentative line of inquiry which needs to be followed up more thoroughly. Its results are however encouraging.

*Egils saga* has relatively few local chronotopes, especially in Iceland. Outside Iceland, they are mainly halls belonging to chieftains or kings, forest routes, sailing routes and battle-fields. In Iceland, we find essentially the farm at Borg and its surroundings, such as places of assembly

---

37 Torfi H. Tulinius, *The Matter of the North*, pp. 46–49.
38 Rohrbach, 'The Chronotopes of *Íslendinga saga*', p. 355.
39 Eleanor Rosamund Barraclough, 'Inside Outlawry in *Grettis saga Ásmundarsonar* and *Gísla saga Súrssonar*: Landscape in the Outlaw Sagas', *SS* 82:4 (2010), 365–88; Emily Lethbridge, 'The Icelandic Sagas and Saga Landscapes. Writing, Reading and Retelling *Íslendingasögur* Narratives,' *Gripla* 27 (2016), 51–92.

or outdoor social gatherings, the coast where ships are moored, pasture and routes between farms, as well as the site where Skalla-Grímr's grave-mound is erected. Within the farms, there are relatively few places that play a role in the narrative: the hall and the sleeping chamber where Egill retires to grieve for his lost son. In addition, the area surrounding the farm of Mosfell, where Egill spends his old age, is rather diversified, with different types of landscape described as potential hiding-places for Egill's chests of silver. Finally, the church built after Egill's death serves as an interesting example of a place that remains the same for a period exceeding a normal lifespan as when it is taken down Egill's bones are discovered, more than a century later.

*Eyrbyggja saga* has fewer episodes taking place abroad than *Egils saga*. The settings are similar. On the other hand, the types of places found in Iceland are much more diverse, both within farms and outside them, in the natural landscape. The main type of internal space is still the hall, but there is also a temple, corridors, storage rooms, a steam bath and even a communal toilet. The natural landscape includes routes between farms, assembly places, as in *Egils saga*, but also headlands, marshes, highland routes, caves in the mountains, hayfields and a variety of coastal landscapes, such as islands, landing-places or sea-cliffs. *Eyrbyggja saga* is strikingly different from the older saga in that it portrays an environment, both human and non-human, in which the paranormal plays a strong role in the narrative, especially with the different avatars of Þórólfr's revenants and the hauntings at Fróðá.

Composed at least three decades later than *Eyrbyggja saga*, *Grettis saga* uses a significantly expanded chronotope of the sagas about early Icelanders. Whether it is in Iceland, Norway or even at sea, the narrative potential is increased by an innovative use of local chronotopes, both those found in other sagas but also by new ones. Examples of the former are the fight using 'skyr', a local variety of yoghurt, in the communal room of a farm, or the transformation of the hall of another farm into a ruin by the fight between Grettir and the revenant Glámr. Examples of new local chronotopes in Iceland are all the episodes that take place in the highlands, in obscure glacier valleys or in caves under waterfalls. On a ship to Norway, the saga dwells on Grettir's on-board behaviour, his taunting of his shipmates and his prowess when bailing water. In Norway, the author innovates by setting a scene in a public drinking establishment, within a grave-mound or in a fishing hut, giving texture to the chronotope and bringing his hero into another world of the living dead. In the final series of episodes, devoted to Þorsteinn's quest for revenge for his brother, the chronotope moves to Constantinople where local chronotopes from kings' sagas and romances seem to be incorporated into the general chronotope of the sagas about early Icelanders.

## Conclusion

In conclusion, I will return to my comparison with the greeting card from the beginning of this chapter. Literature is a form of communication and different genres provide different ways to communicate. The literature of medieval Icelandic society is remarkable for its wealth, diversity and sophistication. The different genres that it spawned, adapted and incorporated were also different ways of communicating about themes, values and issues important to Icelanders from the twelfth century onwards. When we send a greeting card, we are not only communicating, but also projecting an image of ourselves. In the same way, the literary production of medieval Icelanders, in all its diversity, was a way to explore and construct their identity.

The literary record shows a real fascination among thirteenth- and fourteenth-century Icelanders for the period in which the country was settled and later converted to Christianity. The writing of *Íslendingabók* in the early twelfth century was probably decisive in giving a chronological framework to the chronotope of the sagas of early Icelanders. The 'narrativization' of *Landnámabók* is probably contemporary with the development of the sagas about early Icelanders as a genre, with its systematic description of how the country was settled from one region to another.[40] The earlier lost versions of the work would therefore also have contributed to the formation of this chronotope. However, the literature produced by medieval Icelanders also shows an awareness that they belonged to a larger Nordic world, that of the Viking diaspora, and also to Western Christianity in general. The chronotopes characterising the different genres are a testimony to this and to the role of literature in communication about reality, identity and ideology.

---

40 Sveinbjörn Rafnsson, *Sögugerð Landnámabókar. Um íslenska sagnaritun á 12. og 13. öld* (Reykjavík, 2001), pp. 32–36.

# Memory
*Pernille Hermann*

In this essay genre will be treated in the context of memory. It will be of particular interest to discuss how genres generate, and function as repositories of, cultural memory.[1] Many Old Norse genres, both prose and poetry, are preoccupied with events of the past, making it relevant to treat them as media of cultural memory. The focus will be on a few examples only, but my reflections have broader implications and it will be possible to apply them to other cases. 'Cultural memory' is a much-debated concept; here it is understood to cover situations from the past that are believed to be important for collective identities and self-images, or more broadly speaking, it is a concept that covers 'the interplay of present and past in socio-cultural contexts'.[2]

## Composition in Early Literary Culture

The discussion of genre in Old Norse scholarship has long roots. Old Norse-Icelandic genre divisions are often the results of nineteenth- and twentieth-century scholarship, and the terms that are used nowadays to cover the medieval texts and the various branches of the Icelandic sagas are rarely to be found in the texts themselves.[3] Consequently, some uncertainty attaches itself to the generic categories that may or may not have existed in the minds of medieval authors and their audiences. Even if it is a contested matter, it seems to me as if literary production in twelfth- to fourteenth-century Iceland was to a relatively high degree guided by knowledge of generic conventions and features, and medieval and post-medieval manuscripts indicate that the authors chose specific generic markers related to time, space, content, mode, etc., when composing narratives about the past.[4] Saying this

---

1 *Genres as Repositories of Cultural Memory*, ed. Hendrik van Gorp and Ulla Musarra-Schroeder (Amsterdam and Atlanta, 2000).
2 Jan Assmann, 'Collective Memory and Cultural Identity', *New German Critique* 65 (1988), 125–33; Astrid Erll, 'Cultural Memory Studies: An Introduction', in *Cultural Memory Studies: An International Handbook*, ed. Astrid Erll and Ansgar Nünning (Berlin and New York, 2008), pp. 1–18, at p. 2.
3 Lars Lönnroth, *European Sources of Icelandic Saga-Writing: An Essay Based on Previous Studies* (Stockholm, 1965), pp. 3–38.
4 Other opinions have claimed that saga-writers 'did not have any very definitive concepts about different genres of sagas' (Lars Lönnroth, *European Sources of Icelandic Saga-Writing*, p. 7). While this may be true in the sense that that they did

does not imply, for instance with regard to the saga genre, that there was no development and gradual refinement over time, nor that the saga genre was a static phenomenon; It is highly likely that we have to reckon with 'a century of experimentation with the long narrative form'.[5] A relevant definition of genre in this context goes back to Hans Robert Jauss' definition of medieval genres, which takes into account, among other features, existing norms and expectations, and which sees genres: 'as intrinsically dynamic, as categories of literary expression that change over time and, as such, display a varying amount of variability in content and form'.[6]

At the same time, however, a blending of repertoires of generic features is more often the norm than the expectation, and more and more often scholars emphasise that many individual texts are modally mixed and can be characterised as generic hybrids.[7] In other words, it seems as if both constraint (convention) and flexibility (invention) guided literary production. Massimiliano Bampi has noted that generic features and heterogeneity go together, or put this way:

> Heterogeneity is indeed not necessarily to be understood as proof of the non-existence of distinctive generic features […] the constraints which appear to regulate the construction of various fictional worlds are unaltered by the tendency towards a variable degree of hybridity.[8]

This point of view indicates that the authors were conscious of literary form at the same time as they experimented with generic features. Also, it should be kept in mind that compositional, or copyist, activities, were based on knowledge of other texts. Even if most of the authors are anonymous to us they would not have been so in their own times, as Carol Clover has written:

> saga authors must […] have been writing for each other. To concede the literary artistry of the saga is to concede a self-conscious artist, one who presumably studied the work of others with an eye to imitation or improvement.[9]

---

    not directly label their texts, there is still reason to believe that they approached their material with a consciousness about generic typologies.

5   Theodore M. Andersson, *The Growth of the Medieval Icelandic Saga (1180–1280)* (Ithaca and London, 2006), p. 208.

6   Massimiliano Bampi, 'Genre', in *The Routledge Research Companion to the Medieval Icelandic sagas*, ed. Ármann Jakobsson and Sverrir Jakobsson (London and New York, 2017), pp. 4–14, at p. 7.

7   Cf. Margaret Clunies Ross, *Prolonged Echoes: Old Norse Myths in Medieval Northern Society*, vol. 2: *The Reception of Norse Myths in Medieval Iceland* (Odense, 1998), pp. 50–51; Elizabeth Ashman Rowe, 'Generic Hybrids: Norwegian 'Family' Sagas and Icelandic "Mythic-Heroic" Sagas', SS 65:4 (1993), 539–54.

8   Bampi, 'Genre', p. 9.

9   Carol J. Clover, *The Medieval Saga* (Ithaca and London, 1982), p. 200.

That saga authors read and studied the works of others – and sometimes took a stance and reacted to those works either playfully or politically – does not mean that all aspects of a given text can be explained as the result of deliberate authorial choices. Here the point of view that intertextuality is a qualification of all texts is relevant to the genre discussion, it is to be expected that dialogues are generated between texts, even behind the author's back so to speak. Each individual text will remember other texts and will display intertextual connections.

Before entering into the discussion of genre and cultural memory more specifically, one characteristic of early literary culture can be adduced in support of the idea that the deliberate organisation of various fictional worlds was an integral part of literary composition. Authorial comments reveal that during the twelfth to fourteenth centuries much literary activity aimed at a transferring into written form of the knowledge that had otherwise been stored in the authors' own or in other peoples' memories. In a text like *Íslendingabók* (1122–33) and in some of the sagas, e.g., in the subgenres called the *byskupasögur* and the *konungasögur*, the authors sometimes refer to named informants who had remarkably good memories; in other cases the authors explicitly mention that they were transferring knowledge kept in their own memory to the written texts.[10] In other situations again, as in the *Íslendingasögur*, the memories transmitted were anchored in an unpersonalised communal tradition. The comments indicate that authorial activity was carried out by people who possessed both writing skills and mnemonic competences, that is, by authors who made use both of the Roman alphabet (and were acquainted with literacy and book cultures) and mnemonic devices (and were acquainted with mnemonic principles). In other words, aware of the fact that much Old Norse-Icelandic literature developed in a transformative culture between orality and writing, it is likely that mnemonic competences thrived in environments where literacy was in use, supporting the conviction that mnemonic principles would have been woven into written compositions. Mary Carruthers has emphasised that sorting methods and organizing structures were essential to and among the dominant principles of mnemonic culture:

> Without the sorting structure, there is no invention, no inventory, no experience and therefore no knowledge – there is only a useless heap, what is sometimes called silva, the pathless 'forest' of chaotic material.[11]

10 Pernille Hermann, 'Saga Literature, Cultural Memory, and Storage', *SS* 85:3 (2013), 332–54, at pp. 346–50.
11 In medieval culture sorting methods were expressed as containers of memories and with reference to storage metaphors and to different types of compartments (bins, cells, pigeon-holes, etc.), or sometimes to spatial structures often, but not exclusively, in the form of architectonic structures. See Frances A. Yates, *The Art*

The inclination to organise and sort knowledge, and to use compartments for storage of knowledge, does not indicate that mnemonic composition was a rigid and tedious technicality, rather – as suggested in the quote above – invention thrived exactly because of the existing sorting structures. We may here see an analogue to literary composition. This consists partly in the idea that the past worlds of different genres were organised, that is, represented with the use of relatively many similar constitutive generic features and characteristics. Partly the comparison lies in the conviction that invention and change are possible only when at one and the same time there is an awareness of conventions: or invention and convention go together as two sides of the same coin.[12] More to the point, if sorting devices were an integral part of mnemonic compositional activity, it is highly likely that they remained so also in writing culture: without those organizing devices, the information gathered and transmitted by the authors would have been nothing else than a 'pathless forest of chaotic material'. We may add to this, that when knowledge (about the real or the imagined past) that had otherwise been kept in memory was sorted and organised in written texts, each genre would have functioned as a sort of mnemonic compartment. As I will come back to, the development of medieval genres went hand in hand with a construction of the past and the development of an historical awareness. Even if this general implication would have been beyond the individual authors' immediate horizons, the relatively many authorial comments that reflect on the transferring of memories to the written records adds to the conviction that the memories that went into the creation of the past worlds of different kinds would have been deliberately selected and carefully organisised.

## Historiography as 'fictions of memory'

While the above reflections concern mnemonic culture and indicate, first, that knowledge that had been stored in people's memories was an important source for literary texts, and, second, that mnemonic principles entwined with authorial composition, cultural memory is a slightly different matter: one specifically concerned with how the past, and the relationship between past and present, is constructed. It has been suggested that the

---

*of Memory* (Chicago and London, 1974, orig. 1966); Mary Carruthers, *The Book of Memory* (Cambridge, 1990), p. 33.

12 When discussed in connection with genres the 'pigeon-hole metaphor' has been criticised, mostly in contexts where the metaphor has been expected to refer to static divisions and closed boxes, that is, where the notions of invention and creativity have not been included. For a discussion that underlines the inadequacy of considering genres as 'pigeon holes', see Vésteinn Ólason, 'The Icelandic Sagas as a Kind of Literature with Special Reference to Its Representation of Reality', in *Learning and Understanding in the Old Norse World. Essays in Honour of Margaret Clunies Ross*, ed. Judy Quinn, Kate Heslop, and Tarrin Wills (Turnhout, 2007), pp. 27–47.

term 'fictions of memory' can be used to define texts or genres that in one way or other are preoccupied with memory:

> The term 'fictions of memory' deliberately alludes to the double meaning of fiction. First, the phrase refers to literary, non-referential narratives that depict the workings of memory. Second, in a broader sense, the term 'fictions of memory' refers to the stories that individuals or cultures tell about their past to answer the question 'who am I, or collectively, who are we?' These stories can also be called 'fictions of memory' because more often than not, they turn out to be an imaginative (re-)construction of the past in response to current needs. Such conceptional and ideological fictions of memory consists of predispositions, biases and values, which provide agreed upon codes for understanding the past and present.[13]

Particularly, the second meaning of the term 'fictions of memory' is relevant in our context, since it allows for inclusion of multiple genres, representing historical, mythical and fictional events and worlds, when discussing which text types participated in the production of cultural memory in medieval Iceland.[14]

Scholarly literature about cultural memory often makes a distinction between memory and history, assuming that they represent two contrasting discourses.[15] However, it is equally productive to view history, not in opposition to cultural memory, but as one of its important media,[16] thus to consider works of history as 'fictions of memory' and to integrate them among the genres that feed into cultural memory.[17] The already mentioned text *Íslendingabók*, an early work of Icelandic history composed by Ari Þorgilsson, took part in the construction of cultural memory in the Middle Ages. It has often been talked about as a work of (local and secular) history. The text did indeed deal with local Icelandic history, but – as its title indicates – it did so with reference to a broader perspective of medieval book learning. The world that it presented was constructed from knowledge of Latin

---

13 Birgit Neumann, 'The Literary Representation of Memory', in *Cultural Memory Studies*, ed. Erll and Nünning, pp. 333–43, at p. 334.
14 The relevance of including multiple genres when discussion cultural memory corresponds to the idea that cultural memory is generated through a wide range of different media, not only counting verbal media (and with that multiple genres), but also material and visual ones.
15 Pierre Nora, 'Between Memory and History: *Les Lieux de Mémoire*', *Representations* 26 (1989), 7–24.
16 Erll, 'Cultural Memory Studies: An Introduction', p. 7; Marek Tamm, 'Beyond History and Memory: New Perspectives in Memory Studies', *History Compass* 11:6 (2013), 458–73, at p. 463.
17 'History writing is simply a very specific medium of cultural memory with its own rules and traditions – one of the most important for as comprehensive an understanding of the past as possible, but certainly not the only or necessarily the most influential one' (Tamm, 'Beyond History and Memory', p. 463).

works, and the information that it contains was contextualised by, and merging with, Christian universal history. *Íslendingabók*'s way of formally presenting its information, for example, the bringing of legal culture to the new society echoes biblical source texts, and the bringer of the law, Úlfljótr, looks like a type of Moses.[18] Since the knowledge (*fræði*) preserved in this book (*bók*) was selected, structured and organised with references to biblical text, we may say that this early work of history organised the Icelandic past typologically.[19] Sverrir Jakobsson notes:

> Although it is not surprising to see a mediaeval cleric holding this view, its appearance in the works that can be attributed to Ari demonstrates that Icelandic historiography was from the outset part of the universal, Roman-Catholic world view in which this structure of the world history was embedded.[20]

This relatively new take on *Íslendingabók* makes it relevant to consider the work in the context of other texts that imposed a similar broad time/space configuration onto the past, presented local history in a universal perspective, and prioritised a similar pool of source texts, or to use Gérard Genette's terminology, similar hypertexts. One such text is the so-called World History, most often referred to by a later name, *Veraldar saga* (1152–90). Drawing its knowledge from a number of Latin texts, this work represented the past in Christian universal categories and gave literary form to a world that was distant in both time and space. The world chronicle evoked a universal time/space configuration based on Augustinian ideas, and traced the origin of the world to the founding figure Moses and to events related in the Bible. It has been suggested that *Íslendingabók*'s author worked on a world history, *Heimsaldrar*, of this type,[21] which would, if it could be proved, underscore the relevance of universal historical perspectives for the earliest Icelandic literary production. Another text that focused on universal principles was the prologue to the *Prose Edda*, a text which – like *Íslendingbók* – was discussed in the manuscripts as a *bók* (book). It combined a biblical beginning of the world (e.g. with reference to Adam and Eve and Noah's Ark) and Scandinavian prehistory, presenting the latter as a development from one common, biblical, source. *Íslendingabók* (as well as the other texts just mentioned) created a vision of a past that drew on a universal time/space configuration, re-used a number of (Latin) source texts, and – in as much as they

---

18 *Íslendingabók*, in *Íslendingabók. Landnámabók*, ed. Jakob Benediktsson, ÍF 1 (Reykjavík, 1986), pp. 3–28, at pp. 6–7.
19 Pernille Hermann, '*Íslendingabók* and History', in *Reflections of Old Norse Myths*, ed. Pernille Hermann, Jens Peter Schjødt and Rasmus Tranum Kristensen (Turnhout, 2007), pp. 17–32.
20 Sverrir Jakobsson, 'Iceland, Norway, and the World', ANF 132 (2017), 75–99, at p. 85.
21 Stefán Karlsson, 'Fróðleiksgreinar frá tólftu öld', *Afmælisrit Jón Helgasonar 30. júní 1969* (Reykjavík, 1969), pp. 328–49.

revealed their predispositions to envisage the past in universal-Christian schemata – preferred a typological mode when remembering the past.

*Íslendingabók* can be considered as a 'fiction of memory', in as much as it creates an imaginative version of the past, that is ideologically biased and in line with how a group of medieval clerics and historians perceived of the past: First, it was articulating a certain discourse about the past, while at the same time it constructed a particular relationship between the past and the present, linking events of the (heathen) past with the Christian present. Secondly, the author of *Íslendingabók* frequently repeats that he gained his knowledge from the memory of a number of informants, and the text is not only interpreting the relationship between past and present, but is also engaged with the mnemonic culture of its time. What it actually facilitated was a channelling of, or a transportation of, those memories through generic (world historiographic) conventions and modes, consequently offering genre-dependent memories. Another quality attaches itself to the term 'fiction of memory', namely the ability to offer new perspectives on the past through 'the negotiation of cultural memory'.[22] The texts in this category are not necessarily mimetic, in the sense that they imitate existing versions of memory, rather they 'produce in the act of discourse, that very past that they purport to describe'.[23] While filtering memories through genre-specific criteria, a text like *Íslendingabók* does not simply reflect pre-existing ways of thinking about the past, but generates cultural memory by creating a version of the past that fits the present situation. The term 'fictions of memory' is a reminder that historiographies, and other genres that function of as media of cultural memory, do not give access to unfiltered memories, but first of all to 'genre memories' and to the priorities of the memory cultures from where the texts emanate.

## Genre and Cultural Memory: Synchronic Perspectives

Two interrelated perspectives, one synchronic the other diachronic, are relevant when discussing genres as repositories of cultural memory.[24] While the synchronic perspective focusses on the interrelation between literary genres and text-external contexts, the diachronic perspective is concerned with internal literary processes, such as intertextuality and the reuse of modes in new literary contexts, and with reception of genres. Both types promote discussions of how new genres come into existence, and how they grow, change and ramify either in response to particular historical situations or in response to their literary contexts. The synchronic perspective takes into account the particular historical context of a generic category. What follows is that, for example, the development

---

22 Neumann, 'The Literary Representation of Memory', p. 335.
23 *Ibid.*, p. 334.
24 Van Gorp and Musarra-Schroeder, *Genres as Repositories of Cultural Memory*, p. ii.

of the medieval Icelandic sagas at the beginning of the thirteenth century cannot be understood simply as the result of a literary process, but also as a response to historical and social conditions.[25] Around the year 1200 there was an awareness in reading communities of the new genre, and there are indications that the sagas were seen as different from works of history. An illustration of this is to be found in the church history of the bishopric in Skálholt, *Hungrvaka* (1200), where the author makes a distinction between *mannfræði* (historical knowledge) and *sögur* (sagas).[26] The term *saga* (deriving from the verb *segja* 'to say') reveals that the new genre that was coming into existence had an affinity with orally told stories, and it draws the attention to other source texts than those which ascribed meaning to the past, as presented in *Íslendingabók*. While the gradual implementation of Christian ideologies among learned elite groups supported the development of historiographical genres like *Íslendingabók*, social and political experiences (the relationship with Norway, the civil war of the so-called Age of the Sturlungs, the loss of political independence, etc.) become yet another background against which we can understand the development of the sagas. The coming into being of the new genre is likely to have been indebted to secular elites and their interest in the medium of literature. As Torfi Tulinius has written:

> Crucial to this development is the gradual process whereby literature extricated itself from clerical control to serve the needs of a lay aristocracy that was coalescing in the last decades of the twelfth century ... little by little their actions as lay rulers receive greater stress than religious mission.[27]

The sagas reveal an interest in local, Icelandic, history (in the *Íslendingasögur*), in Norwegian history (documented particularly in the so-called *konungasögur* and *þættir*), and in broader Scandinavian history (like in the *fornaldarsögur*). The *Íslendingasögur*, to take one example, narrowed down the focus and were much concerned with regions in Iceland and the worlds of individuals and families who traced their origin back to

---

25 Clunies Ross, *Prolonged Echoes*; Vesteinn Ólason, 'The Icelandic Sagas as a Kind of Literature'; Bampi, 'Genre'; Torfi H. Tulinius, *The Matter of the North: The Rise of Literary Fiction in Thirteenth-Century Iceland* (Odense, 2002), pp. 58–59.

26 *Hungrvaka*, in *Biskupa sögur* II, ed. Ásdís Egilsdóttir, ÍF 16 (Reykjavík, 2002), pp. 3–43, at p. 3. We do not know which texts (*fræði* or *sögur*) the author was referring to. It is possible that a text like *Veraldar saga* was among them as this historiography may be traced back to the bishopric of Skálholt, see Stefanie Würth, 'Historiography and Pseudo-History', in *A Companion to Old Norse-Icelandic Literature and Culture*, ed. Rory McTurk, Blackwell Companion to Literature and Culture 31 (Oxford and Malden, 2005), pp. 155–72, at p. 169). For the wider meaning and uses of the Old Norse terms *fræði* and *saga* see, e.g., Preben Meulengracht Sørensen, *Saga and Society* (Odense, 1993) and Lars Lönnroth, *European Sources of Icelandic Saga-Writing*, p. 10.

27 Torfi H. Tulinius, *The Matter of the North*, p. 59.

the Icelandic *landnám* and to heroic founding figures.[28] However, this narrow focus is to be understood as part of a broader perspective that is created within the scope of the saga genre as a whole. The memories that were transmitted in the various subgenres of the saga were passed through a dense and tightly woven network (a filtering process that is illustrated by the different priorities of the subgenres), and – along with fictions and facts – they became organised according to certain principles, yet with a constant eye to invention. Altogether the subgenres organise Icelandic history spatially and temporally and by so doing they create a coherent vision of the relatively recent as well as the more distant past.[29] This strongly indicates that the coming into being of the saga genre went hand in hand with the development of a historical consciousness. Joseph Harris has interpreted the introduction of Christianity as the 'historical moment' that changed historical conception in, or more directly, introduced historical conception to, Iceland. He writes:

> it is likely that it was in fact the historical moment of the conversion that created the necessary conditions for the body of historical fiction the saga authors were cultivating.[30]

Others have focused on the political situation, and the coming into being of the *Íslendingasögur*, explained as result of a crisis experience or as a response to the Norwegian rulership of the thirteenth century.[31] Moreover, the saga genre interprets the relationship between past and present, and it involves a retrospective look at the past, its social institutions, ethics and forms of behaviour. To take a very few out of many examples among the *Íslendingasögur*, a saga like *Hrafnkels saga Freysgoða* problematised belief in heathen gods and pagan religion, while sagas such as *Valla-Ljóts saga* and *Gísla saga Súrssonar* represented traditional systems of honour in ways that laid bare how the ethical system of the past was actually a threat to orderly society, producing, as it did, disastrous conflicts between regional groups and even within families.[32]

---

28 Guðrún Nordal, 'The Sagas of Icelanders', in *The Viking World*, ed. Stefan Brink with Neil Price (London and New York, 2012), pp. 315–18.
29 Cf. Clunies Ross, *Prolonged Echoes*, p. 50–53.
30 Joseph Harris, 'Sagas as Historical Novel', in *Structure and Meaning in Old Norse Literature: New Approaches to Textual Analysis and Literary Criticism*, ed. John Lindow, Lars Lönnroth and Gerd Wolfgang Weber (Odense, 1986), pp. 187–219, at p. 194.
31 Thomas Fechner-Smarsly, *Krisenliteratur: Zur Rhetorizität und Ambivalenz in der isländischen Sagaliteratur* (Frankfurt am Main, 1996); Jürg Glauser, 'Saga of Icelanders (*Íslendinga sögur*) and *þættir* as the Literary Representation of a New Social Space', in *Old Icelandic Literature and Society*, ed. Margaret Clunies Ross, Cambridge Studies in Medieval Literature 42 (Cambridge, 2000), pp. 203–20.
32 E.g. Hermann Pálsson, *Art and Ethics in Hrafnkel's Saga* (København, 1971); Marlene Ciklamini, 'The Concept of Honor in Valla-Ljóts saga', *JEGP* 65:2 (1966), 303–17.

The relatively intense preoccupation with saga-writing in Iceland during the thirteenth and fourteenth centuries indicates that remembrance of the past became closely linked to the literary form of the saga. It illustrates how a literary genre may offer a space for interpretation of historical change (this change being religious, social or political) – and for defining collective identities:

> Cultural memory is generated and transmitted by 'memory genres'. Understanding historical processes, conceiving of shared values and norms, establishing and maintaining concepts of collective identity – all these activities of cultural remembering are linked to genres.[33]

Those genres that are prioritised within a culture are significant instruments for ascribing meaning to that same culture, and in the case of the sagas such meaning-making activity came about through a so-called memory genre that was broad enough to encompass multiple time-layers and multiple spatial platforms.

For the saga genre, similar principles are relevant, it seems, as were germane with regard to the historical novel, which developed in various places in Europe in the nineteenth century.[34] Both the saga genre and the historical novel interpreted historical processes against the backdrop of wavering and unstable historical moments and both helped to shape ideas of collective identities.[35] Like the historical novel, the subgenres of the saga, say the *Íslendingasögur* and the *fornaldarsögur*, to different degrees fused imagination and reality and negotiated between memory and forgetting and by doing so they offered imagined versions of the past that had an impact on cultural memory, that is, on how groups of people defined their image of self. The sagas too are 'fictions of memory', in the sense that they represent imaginative views of the past, and in the sense that the past worlds presented in them are not predominantly mimetic of, but more often than not, are producers and generators of cultural memory.

The ability of a genre to define cultural self-images is not solely to be understood from experiences contemporary with the time of writing, but also to the genre's reception history. While the coming into being of a genre, its development and ramifications, among other factors can be explained by a need to interpret critical historical situations, the lasting impact of a genre, that is, its 'canonization',[36] goes hand in hand with, and depends upon, a con-

---

33 Astrid Erll and Ansgar Nünning, 'Concepts and Methods for the Study of Literature and/as Cultural Memory', in *Literature and Memory: Theoretical Paradigms, Genres, Functions*, ed. Ansgar Nünning, Marion Gymnich, and Roy Sommer (Tübingen, 2006), pp. 11–28, at p. 18.
34 Harris, 'Sagas as Historical Novel'; Torfi H. Tulinius, *The Matter of the North*, p. 294.
35 Erll and Nünning, 'Concepts and Methods for the Study of Literature and/as Cultural Memory', p. 18.
36 Aleida Assmann, 'Canon and Archive', in *Cultural Memory Studies*, ed. Erll and

tinued interest in the narrated worlds that are preserved in these particular genres. Demonstrating the function of the sagas as important media for cultural memory beyond their initial time of composition, manuscript transmission history indicates that their function as repositories of cultural memory remained intact beyond the thirteenth and fourteenth centuries, and well into post-medieval times.[37] The canonisation of a particular genre has a stabilizing function, in the sense that a canon is 'independent of historical change' and 'outlives generations'. The manuscript transmission of the sagas indicates that copyist activity took over from creativity: the preoccupation with the sagas over time did not involve the writing of completely new sagas. We may also note that the canonisation of one genre potentially causes the suppression, or rejection, of other memories; it is a process that implies hierarchical evaluation and that may overrule alternative points of view about historical processes or about the past – until, eventually, new genres may develop and challenge an existing cultural memory.

## Genre and Cultural Memory: Diachronic Perspectives

The diachronic perspective deals with internal literary mechanisms such as the reuse of textual elements in new literary contexts. Renate Lachmann has written that 'The memory of the text is formed by the intertextuality of its references'.[38] Genres can be seen as the 'result of fundamental processes of memory',[39] they develop out of repetitions of style, setting, subject, etc. While a steady reuse of identical features will confirm the existence of conventional genres, the severing of text-relations and the establishing of new relations may destabilise genres. This perspective draws attention to the dialogues and relations between texts that are established through respectively remembering and forgetting of elements from other texts, a theme that is indeed relevant both with regard to historiographies, as represented by *Íslendingabók*, *Veraldar saga* and the prologue of the *Prose Edda*, and to the sagas. It raises the question to what extent texts placed within the same genre 'remember' the same texts, and to what extent a sharing of source texts should be considered as a genre-criterion. Moreover, each individual saga creates its own mnemonic space, which is inspired by a variety of textual influences from oral and written sources. So, for instance, *Njáls saga* reuses and merges elements from multiple other sagas, as well as European literature, assembling all these source texts in a new design. In this particular sense, *Njáls saga* possesses a large inner-literary mnemonic capacity.

---

Nünning, pp. 97–107, at p. 100.
37  Glauser, 'Saga of Icelanders (*Íslendinga sögur*) and *þættir*'.
38  Renate Lachmann, 'Mnemonic and Intertextual Aspects of Literature', in *Cultural Memory Studies*, ed. Erll and Nünning, pp. 301–10, at p. 304.
39  Erll and Nünning, 'Concepts and Methods for the Study of Literature and/as Cultural Memory', p. 17.

When we look at the dialogues between individual texts that are classified as sagas it becomes clear that the genre as such is by no means a static textual space; it is dynamic in the sense that individual texts often re-negotiate generic features and constitute new configurations, e.g. become hybrids. As mentioned above, the transformation of generic features, and the merging of elements that are considered to belong to different subgroups, do not imply that generic features are not recognised by authors. Elizabeth Ashman Rowe has written that, 'the saga authors ... chose to compose their narratives within generic hybrids not because they did not know what genres were, but because they knew all too well'.[40] Of relevance in this context is Alastair Fowler's argument against the conviction that genres are static forms of classification; he has suggested talking about 'types' instead of genres:

> The literary genre [...] is a type of a special sort. When we assign a work to a generic type, we do not suppose that all its characteristic traits need be shared by every other embodiment of the type. In particular, new works in the genre may contribute additional characteristics. In this way a literary genre changes with time, so that its boundaries cannot be defined by any single set of characteristics such as would determine a class. [...] the notion of type is introduced to emphasise that genres have to do with identifying and communicating rather than with defining and classifying.[41]

Like the notion of hybridity, also the notion of literary types draws the attention to the dynamic dimension of genres and, as the latter part of the quote touches upon, to their communicative potential, as I will come back to below.

The saga genre is dynamic in the sense that individual texts cross between available genre repertoires, but it is also noticeable that the sagas refer to, and engage in a dialogue with many other genres: laws, learned texts, annals, genealogies, poetry, etc. When the author of *Hungrvaka* referred to the texts that had been written in the Old Norse language, apart from *sǫgur* and *mannfræði* he also mentioned the laws: *Lǫg eða sǫgur eða mannfræði* (laws or sagas or human knowledge).[42] While the quote admittedly seems to indicate that the *Hungrvaka*-author kept the categories apart, the textual corpus itself seems to illustrate absorption rather than exclusion, the laws being one generic form that was transported massively into the sagas. The legal knowledge that is quoted in the sagas is integrated into the storylines; in the *Íslendingasögur* this citation of laws is dominant enough to make one of the generic particularities of that

---

40 Rowe, 'Generic Hybrids', p. 553.
41 Alastair Fowler, *Kinds of Literature: An Introduction to the Theory of Genres and Modes* (Oxford, 1982), p. 38.
42 *Hungrvaka*, ed. Ásdís Egilsdóttir, p. 3.

sub-group. Also the author of a text that is slightly older, namely the *First Grammatical Treatise* talked about genres written in Old Norse, once again mentioning *lǫg* (laws) this time together with *áttvísi* (genealogies), *þýðingar helgar* (interpretations of sacred writings) and the *frœði* (historical knowledge) written by Ari Þorgilsson.[43] Like the laws these genres were included into the sagas, the genealogies being yet another generic marker, together with the interpretations of sacred writings (presumably referring to hagiographical texts), which in some cases inspired structure and characterisation (like, to take just one out of many examples, in the description of Njál's death in *Njáls saga*).

At times other learned information is cited, imported into, and transformed within sagas, as is the case in *Fóstbrœðra saga* when anatomical knowledge is used for characterisation. This consistent dialogue with other genres, or this blurring of boundaries between genres, reveals that the saga genre has an immensely large storage potential; its capacity to 'remember' other texts is wide-ranging, and the genre constitutes a tremendously comprehensive, even endless, mnemonic space. One of the attractive traits of the saga genre in the Middle Ages may very well relate to its mnemonic capacity, and its status as a repository that absorbed multiple important genres known within this culture. If new genres come into existence in the space in-between existing genres, the saga indeed seems to fill out such spaces by establishing connections between multiple different texts. The incorporation of poetry into the sagas is yet another indication of the fact that the saga genre remembers other genres. Many of the *fornaldarsögur*, the so-called legendary sagas, developed out of an older narrative tradition, especially the poems of the Poetic Edda.[44] While in some cases the poetic form is dissolved and transformed into the prose narrative, in other cases the older layer continued to be visible, and the palimpsest-character of the narratives transpires through the poems quoted in the prose narratives.

In the context of (cultural) memory we may consider genres as communicative strategies. While the focus so far has been on the authors behind the text, it is crucial to consider recipients of the texts. This involves the conviction that in medieval Iceland, historiographies and sagas, among other genres, functioned as communicative acts that, at various times and in different contexts, mediated cultural memory. Texts are always situated in certain contexts, they are institutionalised and audiences approach them with certain predefined expectations. Like authors, audiences are aware of generic conventions, which essentially form an integral part of a society's cultural memory.[45] Recipients are guided by

---

43 *The First Grammatical Treatise*, ed. Hreinn Benediktsson (Reykjavík, 1972), pp. 208–09.
44 Torfi H. Tulinius, *The Matter of the North*, p. 19.
45 Cf. Erll and Nünning, 'Concepts and Methods for the Study of Literature and/

knowledge of generic characteristics when reading texts, or when listening to oral performances of texts. The implied message of a genre, expressed in individual texts that either repeated (remembered) or changed (forgot) generic repertoires, would have been understood only by an audience familiar with the genre. Reception is guided by horizons of expectations, and any changes, say from a heroic to a comic mode, would have been noted. This would presumably have been the case when, in *Fóstbrœðra saga*, a reference to learned anatomical knowledge was inserted into a description of one of the character's emotional reactions. Such a combination of elements from different generic categories (i.e., different mnemonic compartments) would have caused a reaction from the audience, in this case the presumably playful mixing of generic features would have caused a humorous response.[46] Equally importantly, these changes could potentially influence and re-negotiate the cultural memory constructed by the genre and the rhetoric used when referring to the past. To the extent that genres and cultural memory are interrelated and mutually influence each other, we can say that the dynamic aspect of genres, that is hybridity and other kinds of generic change, will be indicative of a memory culture's new interests.

## Conclusion

The function of genres in cultures depends on their double-sided quality, both their regulative character and their stretchability, as well as their communicative potential and the familiarity with which they are met by authors and recipients:

> On the one hand, the usefulness of genres in culture has to do with their strongly regulative character. On the other hand, it derives from their flexibility, which allows everyone to modify genres in order to serve his or her own communicative needs. [...] familiarity with the genre of an utterance is a necessary prerequisite for understanding it. But it is not sufficient in itself – and only in the simplest of cases, and perhaps not even in those, is it possible to identify a text as belonging to one genre and one genre only.[47]

The mnemonic potential of medieval genres stretches in many directions, pointing to their function as storage-sites for memories as well as their role in the construction of cultural memory. Each genre, displaying certain characteristics, can be considered as a template or a container of a

---

as Cultural Memory'.
46 Preben Meulengracht Sørensen, 'On Humour, Heroes, Morality, and Anatomy in *Fóstbræðra Saga*', in *Twenty–Eight Papers Presented to Hans Bekker-Nielsen on the Occasion of his Sixtieth Birthday 28. April 1993* (Odense, 1993), pp. 395–418.
47 Sune P. Auken, Schantz Lauridsen and A. Juhl Rasmussen, 'Introduction,' *Genre and...*, ed. Sune Auken et al. (Valby, 2015), pp. vii–viii.

selection of memories, each genre, e.g., historiographies and sagas, at the same time digests memories, that is, by absorbing, filtering and recreating the knowledge of the culture, and produces genre-dependent cultural memories. At a particular historical moment the saga genre gave literary form to a chronologically organised past that was conceptualised as different yet complementary units, or, we could say, a number of 'mnemonic compartments'; these facilitated a cultural self-understanding based on storage and especially on interpretation of the past. In conclusion a few words can be said about poetry, a genre that was equally important as a medium of memory. Like the prose genres treated already eddic and skaldic poetry have the same twofold relation to the memory cultures of their times, partly being indebted to a mnemonic culture, partly being relevant for taking part in the shaping of the past that supported medieval self-images. Skaldic and eddic poetry bear evidence of mnemonic devices, both in the form of verbal qualities (such as metre, diction, rhyme, listing, etc.) and (for some poems more than others) performative cues (direct speech, characters' movements, props, etc.) all constitutive elements that illustrate their links with a mnemonic culture.[48] Moreover, the genre of poetry played an important role in the thirteenth century in representing past worlds that were relevant for definitions of identity. The treatment of the poetic materials in the *Prose Edda* and the wish to secure skaldic art are indications of that, as is the Codex Regius manuscript (c. 1270). This manuscript, which talks about the poems it contains as *fornfræði* (knowledge of old), shows that an effort went into the recording of traditions of the past that could represent the roots of the culture, just as its collection of eddic poems is indicative of the idea that a genre-sensibility existed among the writers and recipients of its time.

---

48 E.g. Thomas Dubois, 'Oral Poetics: The Linguistics and Stylistics of Orality', in *Medieval Oral Literature*, ed. K. Reichl (Berlin 2016), pp. 201–24; and Terry Gunnell, *The Origins of Drama in Scandinavia* (Cambridge, 1995).

# The Human Condition
*Stefanie Gropper*

Old Norse-Icelandic sagas tell about individual characters, their families and relations between these families. Literary representations of social and cultural conditions, which we may call 'the human condition', therefore play an important role in these texts. The idea of the human condition encompasses a very broad range of features that are all essential to human existence, for example: birth, growth, emotionality, conflict and/or death. In literary texts these features are also important for the narrative because they can determine the plot or change the course of action. Saga characters, as characters in medieval literature in general, are quite puzzling to modern readers because they do not develop in the sense of modern psychology. The identities of these characters are mainly determined by social relationships and by their behaviour, depending on the literary genre or subgenre and on the story to which they belong.[1]

Since the human condition is a spectrum far too wide to be dealt with in one short chapter, I want to limit myself to the cornerstones of family life: the aspects of marriage and death, and the emotions connected with these events, for instance love or sorrow. These will be explored in a selected number of *Íslendingasögur* (sagas of Icelanders); these are chosen with the aim of covering 'classical' texts as well as the so-called 'post-classical' sagas. Although each saga deals with the human condition in its very own specific way we may suppose that they nevertheless may display some common – or generic – characteristics.[2] In this chapter I want to complement previous scholarship and investigate the ways in which representations of the human condition and emotions are important for the saga narrative and why the narrators may have chosen a particular way of literary representation in the genre of the *Íslendingasögur*.

## Previous Scholarship

For a long time, the topic of the 'human condition' was treated in saga scholarship mainly from a historical, a sociological or an anthropological point of view.[3] These early works dealt with the history of the hu-

---

1 Armin Schulz, *Erzähltheorie in mediävistischer Perspektive* (Berlin, München and Boston, 2015), p. 2.
2 Sif Rikhardsdottir, *Emotion in Old Norse Literature: Translations, Voices, Contexts*, Studies in Old Norse Literature 1 (Cambridge, 2017), p. 20.
3 See for example on love and sexual relationships Thomas Bredsdorff, *Chaos and*

man condition and the history of emotions rather than with their literary functions. It has been only relatively recently that the specifics of literary representations of emotions have come into focus. This rather new research encompasses questions of the relationship of body and emotion, language and emotion or about the social dynamic of emotions.[4] While earlier research claimed that medieval texts are quite often void of emotions, scholars have now shown that many texts do not explicitly talk about emotions, but rather they perform emotion, for example in rituals, special gestures or in conventional interactions.[5] Ritual behaviour and bodily expressivity are especially important in representations of grief, which, besides anger and love, is one of the most frequent emotions in medieval literature.[6]

With regard to the Icelandic sagas a long-enduring stereotype is that the *Íslendingasögur* show less emotionality than continental medieval literature. Emotions, especially the emotion of love, were thought to be found only in the translated *riddarasögur* (romances) with their contents derived from continental courtly literature and in sagas either derived from the *riddarasögur* or in the later family sagas influenced by the *riddarasögur*. Emotionality seemed to be rather a sign of a younger text than of the classical Icelandic texts. Up to the late twentieth century thorough studies of emotionality in medieval Icelandic literature were scarce. In 1992 William Ian Miller presented the first approach to the study of emotions in the Icelandic sagas with an article about the concept of shame. Shortly afterwards in a number of essays he proved the

---

*Love: The Philosophy of the Icelandic Family Sagas*, trans. John Tucker (København, 2001, orig. 1971); Aðalheiður Guðmundsdóttir, '"How Do You Know If It Is Love or Lust?": On Gender, Status, and Violence in Old Norse Literature', *Interfaces* 2 (2016), 189–209; on marriage, Jenny Jochens, 'Germanic Marriage: The Case of Medieval Iceland', in *The Medieval Marriage Scene: Prudence, Passion, Policy*, ed. Sherry Roush and Cristelle Louise Baskins (Tempe, 2005), pp. 55–65; Roberta Frank, 'Marriage in Twelfth-and Thirteenth-Century Iceland', *Viator* 4 (1973), 473–84; on family relationships, Kári Gíslason, 'Within and Without: Family in the Icelandic Sagas', *Parergon* 26:1 (2009), 13–33; on children, Robin Waugh, 'Language, Landscape, and Maternal Space: Child Exposure in Some Sagas of Icelanders', *Exemplaria* 29:3 (2017), 234–53.

4   For a survey of different types of research on emotions in medieval literature see Jutta Eming, 'Emotionen als Gegenstand mediävistischer Literaturwissenschaft', *Journal of Literary Theory* 1:2 (2007), 251–73.

5   For more details see Ingrid Kasten *et al.*, 'Zur Performativität von Emotionalität in erzählenden Texten des Mittelalters', *Encomia: Encomia-Deutsch, Sonderheft der deutschen Sektion der International Courtly Literature Society* (2000), pp. 42–60.

6   For examples from medieval High German literature see Elke Koch, *Trauer und Identität: Inszenierungen von Emotionen in der deutschen Literatur des Mittelalters* (Berlin and New York, 2006); for examples from medieval literature in general see the contributions in *Codierungen von Emotionen im Mittelalter / Emotions and Sensibilities in the Middle Ages*, ed. Stephen C. Jaeger and Ingrid Kasten, (Berlin and New York, 2003).

importance of social conduct within honour-based saga society.[7] Then in 1997 Daniel Sävborg published a study of the eddic elegies, claiming that they recall old Germanic conventions of lament in their literary representations of grief. Ten years later, Sävborg presented his comprehensive book about love and emotion in Old Norse literature. Analysing examples of different Old Norse genres, he concludes that the texts do not represent a common Germanic literary tradition of love scenes, but rather the literary representation of love has different specific characteristics in each genre. According to his analyses of the *Íslendingasögur*, love and the erotic are not very important in these sagas, except when 'they guide the intrigue and dominate the whole in a smaller number of works'.[8]

In contrast to other scholars, Sävborg postulates an indigenous saga tradition for the literary representation of love.[9] The generic representation of love in the *Íslendingasögur* consists of a number of repeating clichés, i.e. specific formulas and motifs, such as 'the conversation cliché, the visit cliché, the formula: *sitja hjá* and the motif of the dress gift'.[10] In the elaboration of these motifs, different literary techniques could be used, and in this respect Sävborg points out the importance of verse stanzas for the expression of love. The literary technique rather than the motifs is where Sävborg sees an influence from the continental courtly literature, albeit in his opinion only a very limited one.[11]

A somewhat different approach is pursued by Sif Rikhardsdottir, based on the concept of the 'emotive script', which enables her to 'analyse the emotionality of a text, i.e. the way in which emotions are manifested through words, expressions or dialogue'.[12] Since emotive scripts are both socially and culturally encoded, new scripts – as for instance those derived from the courtly romances – should be expected to be modified and adapted to their new literary surrounding. But nevertheless, as the co-existence of different genres in Old Norse-Icelandic literature suggests, the audience was quite capable of understanding a variety of literary emotive codes. It is therefore not surprising that the literary representation of emotions in Old Norse-Icelandic literary genres is quite flexible and diverse, although some emotive scripts do seem to have generic significance. According to Sif

---

7   William Ian Miller, *Humiliation: And Other Essays on Honor, Social Discomfort, and Violence* (Ithaca, 1993).
8   Daniel Sävborg, *Sagan om kärleken: Erotik, känslor och berättarkonst i norrön litteratur*, Acta universitatis upsaliensis, Historia litterarum 27 (Uppsala, 2007), p. 624, my translation.
9   Sävborg had already come to the same conclusion in his 'Kärleken i *Laxdœla saga* – höviskt och sagatypiskt', *Alvíssmál* 11 (2004), 75–104.
10  Sävborg, *Sagan om kärleken*, p. 623.
11  *Ibid.*, p. 627.
12  Sif Rikhardsdottir, *Emotion in Old Norse Literature*, p. 12.

Rikhardsdottir there are tendencies which indicate a generic emotive script for the *Íslendingasögur*. Perhaps most striking is their laconic mode, related to a relatively low frequency of words describing or expressing emotions. Compared to other genres of European literature the characters in Icelandic sagas quite often express their feelings by being silent, laughing or through some other physical reaction. The audience must have been able to fill these semantic gaps from their own experience as well as from their literary knowledge. The better the audience's knowledge of different literary genres and their respective representations of emotions the easier it was to detect the details of an emotive script.[13]

Both Sif Rikhardsdottir and Daniel Sävborg point out that the literary representation of emotions is important for the construction of meaning in saga narrative. Emotive scripts serve as catalysts of the plot, for example when grief turns into the action of revenge or when love outside marriage leads to a conflict between two families. But despite their literary function the emotive scripts as elements of the saga world can only be understood against the background of their audience's ideas about the extratextual world.[14]

When we look at the *Íslendingasögur* as a genre we find increasing influence from courtly romances, proving the permeability of genre borders and their flexibility; this keeps them at the centre of the literary system.[15] In what follows I would like to show that, although the literary techniques in emotive scripts change over time due to increasing influence from other genres, they nevertheless maintain their function as 'social manipulators'.[16] The generic characteristics of the literary representations of emotions can be seen rather in the sagas' reflections of social concepts than in their wording or literary style.

## Private and the Public Sides of the Human Condition

Saga characters often hide or mask their feelings or they express them through some physical reaction.[17] Youthful male characters are expected to convert their feelings into action; mostly it is grief that is turned into an action of vengeance. Older male characters, however, resort to frustration or melancholy. Women who are not allowed to act themselves either mask their grief with a smile or laughter or they may turn their

---

13 Cf. Sif Rikhardsdottir, *Emotion in Old Norse Literature*, p. 100.
14 Schulz, *Erzähltheorie*, p. 292.
15 Cf. Massimiliano Bampi, 'Genre', in *The Routledge Research Companion to the Medieval Icelandic Sagas*, ed. Ármann Jakobsson and Sverrir Jakobsson (London and New York, 2017), pp. 4–14, at p. 9.
16 Sif Rikhardsdottir, *Emotion in Old Norse Literature*, p. 177.
17 See the many examples in Sif Rikhardsdottir, *Emotion in Old Norse Literature*, pp. 117–44.

grief into action by whetting their male relatives to take revenge.[18] These behaviours also correspond to the spatial relations of the interior and the exterior, as much of the body as of the house, and thus they also correspond to the private and the public sphere. Quite often saga characters react differently to emotional situations, depending not only on their personalities but also on the function of these situations for the narrative.

## Private and Public Mourning

In the sagas, mourning is usually connected to the death of a character. One of the most famous passages concerning emotive scripts is when Guðrún is goading her sons to revenge their father's death.[19] She summons her sons 'í laukagarð sinn' (into her leek-garden), which seems to be a secluded place near the house.[20] Guðrún's behaviour is a perfect orchestration of grief for her dead husband and the father of her children. She shows her sons the bloody clothes of their father, which she has kept for many years and her manner of speaking seems both formalised and conventionalised.[21] From the formality of her words and her behaviour, it becomes clear that Guðrún performs a widow's official grief. She presents her outer or public side, but does not show her inner side or her real sorrow regarding or stemming from the loss of her husband. The semi-private location of the *laukagarðr*, however – reminiscent of a monastery garden, a closed place for contemplation – suggests that Guðrún herself has contemplated her situation very deeply, but she locks away her personal feelings in favour of maintaining her family's honour, i.e. that of her husband and sons.[22] Guðrún's objective in this scene is, however, to evoke emotions in her sons and induce them to turn their emotions into action. Both her words and symbols have indeed an effect on her young sons. During the following night they cannot sleep and tell Þorgils that they cannot any longer bear their grief nor their mother's confrontational action. In their bedroom, the safe and private space of the house, the brothers may speak about their personal unhappiness, but they are also aware of their public duty to avenge their father. They have to show the public – *menn* – that they are capable of turning their private emotions into revenge.

18 Ibid., 69.
19 *Laxdœla saga, Halldórs þáttr Snorrasonar, Stúfs þáttr*, ed. Einar Ólafur Sveinsson, ÍF 5 (Reykjavík, 1934), pp. 179–80.
20 *Laxdœla saga*, ed. Einar Ólafur Sveinsson, p. 179; all translations from Old Norse are my own.
21 On the significance of Bolli's bloody clothes, see Sif Rikhardsdottir, *Emotion in Old Norse Literature*, p. 128.
22 The fact that at the end of her life Guðrún becomes a recluse in a monastery is indeed suggestive. She is no longer active in Icelandic society, but rather devotes herself to her inner spiritual life.

In the sagas, personal feelings are restricted to spaces outside public life like the *laukagarðr* mentioned above. Kjartan's wife Hrefna secludes herself from the centre of the saga and stays in the private space of her brothers' farm. She is filled with sorrow, but hides her grief from other people. According to the narrator 'hon lifði litla hríð, síðan er hon kom norðr, ok er þat sǫgn manna, at hún hafi sprungit af stríði' (she only lived for a short time, after she came to the north, and people tell the story that she had burst from grief).[23] In a similar way, Egill withdraws after the death of his son Bǫðvarr to mourn in the secluded space of his bed-closet in *Egils saga Skalla-Grímssonar*.[24]

Personal feelings, that is, exactly those traits of a character that seem the most interesting to a modern reader, are firmly restricted in the *Íslendingasögur* to the inner space of a character or to the interior spaces of a house. This holds true for female characters as well as for male characters. After having killed Kjartan, Bolli is swept away by his mourning for Kjartan. Until the trial is over, he restricts himself to the private sphere. He uses direct speech only with Guðrún and he secludes himself together with Guðrún's brothers in a secret earthhouse. The saga does not tell whether he stays there all the time until the trial, but we do learn that he does not show up at a peace-meeting.[25]

The saga narrators observe and present the characters from outside; they report what happens on the public stage of the narration. We can only get a glimpse of a character's interior or behind their emotional masks in direct speech and in poetry, as is the case with Egill Skalla-Grímsson's famous poem *Sonatorrek*. Despite different interpretations of this poem, all scholars agree that it is a very personal expression of Egill's feelings.[26] Most of the secular skaldic poems and stanzas are about persons, intended either as praise-poems for kings and rulers or as poems expressing the personal experiences of the *skáld* (poet). The art of skaldic poetry thus is an intensely self-conscious one and is quite often used in sagas as a means to express a character's internal emotion.[27] According to skaldic kennings the human chest is the 'house' or the 'hall' where emotions as well as the heart and the mind are to be found.[28] From this private room within his body

---

23 *Laxdœla saga*, ed. Einar Ólafur Sveinsson, p. 159.
24 Cf. the detailed analysis of this episode in Sif Rikhardsdottir, *Emotion in Old Norse Literature*, pp. 71–78.
25 *Laxdœla saga*, ed. Einar Ólafur Sveinsson, pp. 153–59.
26 Within her own interpretation of the poem Sif Rikhardsdottir also gives an overview of previous scholarship. Cf. Sif Rikhardsdottir, *Emotion in Old Norse Literature*, pp. 85–97.
27 Diana Whaley, 'Skaldic Poetry', in *A Companion to Old Norse-Icelandic Literature and Culture*, ed. Rory McTurk, Blackwell Companion to Literature and Culture 31 (Oxford and Malden, 2005), pp. 479–502, at p. 483, and see Sif Rikhardsdottir, *Emotion in Old Norse Literature*, p. 85
28 Rudolf Meißner, *Die Kenningar der Skalden: Ein Beitrag zur skaldischen Poetik*

Egill releases his inner feelings into a poem about his dead sons.[29] Skaldic poetry with its complicated kennings thus provides another safe space for a character's feelings by turning them into art.

In contrast to the examples above, saga narrators in many cases deal rather summarily with a character's death. In *Laxdæla saga*, Unnr in djúpúðga, the female ancestor of a huge number of the saga's characters, dies during the wedding of one of her grandchildren. After having heard the news the family celebrates the funeral feast and the wedding together.[30] The narrator does not mention her family's grief; Unnr was a famous and thus public person, her death is also a public event. Later in the saga, the death of her grandson Óláfr pái, one of the most impressive characters in *Laxdæla saga*, is noted in one single, rather dry sentence.[31] Even Egill Skalla-Grímsson, the eponymous hero of one of the most famous Icelandic sagas, dies rather unspectacularly.[32]

Dying from old age is not considered to be something noteworthy in the sagas. The rather sober way of relating these characters' death does not mean that it did not cause any grief. The funeral feast as a public event demonstrates the worthiness of a character. In old age death has to be expected and does not disrupt the life of the survivors as much as the sudden death of a young character. With respect to the end of the human life, the sagas are mainly interested in its public side, when grief turns into action, as revenge or legal action. The characters' emotions are generally kept private and concealed, either within secluded spaces in the house or inside the body.

## Love in Public and in Private

Love scenes and episodes in the *Íslendingasögur* are often suspected of being influenced by other genres. This is because the courtly romances brought a new genre to Iceland, in which emotions play an important role. The number of surviving manuscripts of the translated *riddarasögur* as well as the number of the indigenous *riddarasögur* show that the new genre soon became very popular.[33] Different elements from courtly literature had an impact on other Icelandic genres.[34] *Laxdæla saga* in particular has been thought to show quite some influence from courtly romances.[35]

---

(Bonn and Leipzig, 1921), p. 134.
29 *Egils saga Skalla-Grímssonar*, ed. Sigurður Nordal, ÍF 2 (Reykjavík, 1933), pp. 244–56.
30 *Laxdæla saga*, ed. Einar Ólafur Sveinsson, p. 13.
31 *Laxdæla saga*, ed. Einar Ólafur Sveinsson, p. 159.
32 *Egils saga Skalla-Grímssonar*, ed. Sigurður Nordal, p. 298.
33 Stefka G. Eriksen, 'Courtly Literature', in *The Routledge Research Companion to the Medieval Icelandic Sagas*, ed. Ármann Jakobsson and Sverrir Jakobsson (London and New York, 2017), pp. 59–73, at p. 62.
34 Bampi, 'Genre', p. 9.
35 Cf. for instance Rolf Heller, *Literarisches Schaffen in der Laxdæla saga: Die Entstehung*

In courtly romances, love plays a central role as an emotional bond between a woman and a man, independent of marriage. Courtly love poses its own rules against the rules of society, and courtly love is an art, represented as a code of gestures, actions and words, operating within the frame of the lover's service towards the beloved woman. This service has to be displayed in public, although the identity of the beloved woman has to remain unknown to the public.[36] In the *Íslendingasögur*, however, love as a motif that dominates the characters' lives is fairly rare.[37]

As is the case with grief, there is a public and a private side of love. *Laxdœla saga* has an unusually high frequency of words for 'love', but as is the case in other *Íslendingasögur* these words are only used for the relationship between family members or close friends.[38] Although the love between Kjartan and Guðrún in *Laxdœla saga* is considered to be one of the most famous stories of saga literature, it is never stated explicitly that they loved each other, whereas the text states expressly that: 'Þeir Kjartan ok Bolli unnusk mest' (Kjartan and Bolli loved each other dearly).[39] Only the occurrence of some of the clichés that Sävborg mentions, such as the conversation cliché or the visit cliché, indicates that Kjartan and Guðrún might be in love with each other. Kjartan and Guðrún do not hide their relationship, which at this point is not disruptive; it follows the rules of society as a test for a possible future marriage. The narrator, who seems mainly interested in this public realm, reports only what can be seen in public and he never allows a private space for Kjartan and Guðrún.[40] All knowledge about Kjartan's and Guðrún's feelings is mere conjecture that is, moreover, dependent on their public behaviour. Even later, when Guðrún declines Bolli's marriage proposal, she does not say explicitly that she loves Kjartan, but only states that she would never marry anybody else as long as Kjartan is alive.[41] It is the frequency of these hints in Guðrún's behaviour that signals an emotional relationship between her and Kjartan. The winter after Kjartan returned home to Iceland, Guðrún goes very quiet – as does in fact Kjartan too – and the narrator tells us how the public interpreted her silence: 'en þat var auðfynt, at henni líkaði illa,

---

*der Berichte über Olaf Pfaus Herkunft und Jugend*, SAGA: Untersuchungen zur nordischen Literatur- und Sprachgeschichte, ed. Walter Baetke, vol. 3 (Halle an der Saale, 1960); Heinrich Beck, '*Laxdœla saga* – A Structural Approach,' SBVS 19 (1974–77), 383–402; Susanne Kramarz-Bein, '"Modernität" der *Laxdœla saga*', *Studien zum Altgermanischen: Festschrift für Heinrich Beck*, ed. Heiko Uecker (Berlin and New York, 1994), pp. 421–42. More skeptical, however, is Sävborg, 'Kärleken i Laxdœla saga'.

36 Schulz, *Erzähltheorie*, pp. 53–54.
37 Sävborg, *Sagan om kärleken*, p. 627.
38 Sävborg, Kärleken i *Laxdœla saga*, p. 84.
39 *Laxdœla saga*, ed. Einar Ólafur Sveinsson, p. 112.
40 Ibid., pp. 112, 114–15.
41 Ibid., p. 128.

þvíat þat ætluðu flestir men, at henni væri enn mikil eftirsjá at um Kjartan, þó at hon hyldi yfir' (but it was easy to see that she was unhappy, because most people thought that she was still longing for Kjartan, even though she hid it).[42] Since the narrator obviously feels obliged to explain how and why to understand her silence, even if she wanted to hide her feelings, this must be something rather unknown in contemporary literature. In the sagas the silence of the other characters signals the momentous emotive significance of an event or a situation.[43] The audience has to fill the semantic void of silence with emotive content drawn from their own personal experiences as well as from previous literary encounters and the generically stipulated signifying horizon of the saga world.[44] In the Íslendingasögur silence because of grief is usually caused by the death of a character – Guðrún's grief for the loss of love must have been something new within in the genre, maybe inspired by the riddarasögur, as for instance Tristrams saga ok Ísöndar, a story about the destructive force of love. But Laxdœla saga nevertheless sticks to the convention of grief turning into action when Guðrún start to provoke Hrefna because of her precious headdress. While Guðrún's feelings for Kjartan are hidden inside her, she shows her animosity towards Hrefna in public.

Neither does the skáld Kormákr in Kormáks saga mention his love explicitly. When he meets Steingerðr for the first time at a gathering, their closest friends suspect that they are flirting with each other. As Kormákr afterwards comes to see Steingerðr frequently and talks to her it is obvious to the public that their relationship is becoming closer, but when Kormákr also wants to see Steingerðr in private, her father demands that Kormákr marry her.[45] As a skáld Kormákr can resort to the private space of his poetry for expressing his emotions, but his stanzas are less about his love for Steingerðr than about his love for poetry.

As these examples show, in Kormáks saga and Laxdœla saga, two 'classical' Íslendingasögur, there is no private space for love outside marriage. Even if it can be inferred that the characters meet in private, the narrators never relate any details of these meetings. In contrast to the courtly romances, the feelings between two people do not have to be hidden, but emotions are not talked about and they are expected to lead to marriage. In the Íslendingasögur emotional relationships are only narrated when they are the starting point of a conflict, as when the bride is reluctant or an expected marriage does not take place or when it might cause another suitor's jealousy.

This generic convention also holds true for Víglundar saga, a late or 'post-classical' Íslendingasaga. The influence of courtly romance on

---

42 Ibid., p. 134.
43 Sif Rikhardsdottir, Emotion in Old Norse Literature, p. 73.
44 Ibid., p. 65.
45 Kormáks saga, ed. Einar Ól. Sveinsson, ÍF 8 (Reykjavík, 1939), p. 216.

*Víglundar saga*'s structure, themes and vocabulary is so strong that the question whether the saga should still be considered an *Íslendingasaga* has been raised.[46] The saga recounts two love stories in two subsequent generations; in each part of the saga the lovers have to overcome great difficulties until they manage to get married. As in courtly romances, love is engendered by sight and reaches the heart through the eye, without other people noticing.[47] Þorgrímr and Ólöf want to legitimise their love as fast as possible, but since Ólöf's father wants to prevent their marriage they are forced to meet secretly and to live against the rules of society. Only after they have fled to Iceland and are living outside the Norwegian social context can they get married. The narrator emphasises that their first son is born the year after their wedding – an implicit hint about their chaste relationship during the time before.[48] The second part of the saga deals with the love between Víglundr, son of Ólöf and Þorgrímr, and his foster sister Ketilríðr.[49] The description of their love contains many formulations and metaphors reminiscent of courtly romances, such as the heat and fire of love or the heart as the location of love.[50] Like Þorgrímr and Ólöf, Víglundr and Ketilríðr want to legitimise their love by marriage. They meet in private, talk about their love (in prose as well as in verse), they kiss each other and they cry: they freely show and verbalise their affections. Their problem is less to find a private space for their love than to achieve their aim of marriage. When at last Víglundr and Ketilríðr are able to get married, Ketilríðr is still a virgin. Despite all their previous private meetings their love (as a physical act) is only consummated in the private space of a legitimate marriage.

Although love in *Víglundar saga* is more explicitly narrated than in *Laxdœla saga* and *Kormáks saga*, it is not disruptive of societal rules. In none of these examples is love subversive. The characters' final objective is always marriage – marriage is the private space for love. The emotive script of love turns into the emotive script of marriage, which means that it does not only involve the lovers but also their families.

## The Individual and Society

In the *Íslendingasögur* the characters' lives are mostly seen from the public vantage-point, in relation to other people. Although we perceive saga characters as personalities with very distinct traits, in the texts we do not

---

46 Marianne Kalinke, '*Víglundar saga*: An Icelandic Bridal-Quest Romance', *Skáldskaparmál* 3 (1994), 119–43.
47 *Víglundar saga*, ed. Jón Halldórsson, ÍF 14 (Reykjavík, 1959), p. 70.
48 Ibid., p. 75.
49 This structure of the saga recalls the 'double cursus' in Arthurian romances, but in contrast to the Arthurian texts, in *Víglundar saga* each 'cursus' has its own main characters.
50 *Víglundar saga*, ed. Jón Halldórsson, p. 82.

see them evolve from childhood through youth and adulthood as in a modern *Bildungsroman*. Medieval identities are determined by their social relationships and by their history.[51] In the sagas this is indicated by the importance of genealogies. The *Íslendingasögur* are less about individual characters and their individual problems in life than about conflicts arising within one family or between two families. Marriage and death are important events for a family, and they affect the ties between two or even more families.

*Death causes Action*

As stated above, personal grief is mostly hidden and restricted to the private space. In public space grief is turned into action: revenge or legal action. Death from old age is followed by a memorial feast and possibly discussions about inheritance. Although sorrow might not be explicitly mentioned, the importance of the loss can be deduced from the number and intensity of the actions following. Revenge or a legal move are the usual actions when death is caused by violence. The death of a young character, therefore, attracts most attention in the *Íslendingasögur*, since the consequent actions determine the plot of a saga.

The emotive scripts in the episodes following Kjartan's death contain an interesting mixture of different elements. Immediately after Bolli has struck Kjartan the deadly blow, he sits down and takes Kjartan's body in his lap – recalling a *pietà* and signalling Bolli's private grief for his dead friend.[52] Later we are told how individual characters, such as Óláfr or Hrefna, are dealing with the loss.[53] At the same time the saga reports how everyday life carries on, according to the conventions connected to a person's death: burial, legal process, feud. These procedures help to re-establish order within the family and the balance between the families involved in the killing. While the passages concerned with private mourning only cover a short span of time and take only a little space in the narration, the plot advances over a longer period of time with the families' actions and reactions after Kjartan's death. These actions are determined by each family member's relation to Kjartan. It is his father Óláfr who organises the measures taken. Relationship and genealogical connections do not only determine but can also complicate actions, as can be seen from *Gísla saga*: Gísli is forced to take revenge for his brother-in-law, who was killed by Gísli's other brother-in-law.[54]

In the *Íslendingasögur* the death of a young man is a threat to the stability and to the future of a family. Death causes grief for the individual loss as well as anxiety about the family's future. When Egill Skalla-Gríms-

---

51 Schulz, *Erzähltheorie*, p. 2.
52 *Laxdœla saga*, ed. Einar Ólafur Sveinsson, p. 153.
53 *Laxdœla saga*, ed. Einar Ólafur Sveinsson, pp. 154–55.
54 *Gísla saga*, ed. Björn K. Þórólfsson and Guðni Jónsson, ÍF 6 (Reykjavík, 1943), pp. 43–44.

son loses two of his three sons he expresses his personal sorrow and his worries in his poem *Sonatorrek*. He has trouble speaking: 'Mjǫk erum tregt / tungu at hrœra' (Very slow is / my tongue to be moved) because he realises that his kin-group might have to face its end: 'Þvít ætt mín / á enda stendr' (Because my family / is close to its end).[55] The unexpected death of a character is less important as an individual loss of a loved one than as a disruption of the family and a threat to its future. While one can prepare for the death of old people, the violent death of a young person damages the fragile construction of a family and demands public action to re-establish the family's balance.

## Love as a Family Matter

Love is a focus in the *Íslendingasögur* when it is the start of a conflict within one family, as the complicated relations in *Gísla saga* demonstrate, or between two or even more families, as in *Laxdœla saga* or *Víglundar saga*. Love causes conflict when the characters are torn between their feelings for the loved person and their loyalty towards their families.

Large parts of *Laxdœla saga* are narrated in paratactic sentences, which imply causality; they manipulate the audience to interpret cause and effect that is not explicit in the text. The love-story of Kjartan and Guðrún owes a large part of its drama to this implied causality. Kjartan never asks Guðrún to marry him, but she infers his intentions from his behaviour. To support this interpretation the narrator refers to public opinion and thus demonstrates how the characters are subject to social control.[56] As soon as the public notices that Kjartan and Guðrún are seeing each other, discussions start about a possible match. When Kjartan's father Óláfr is not very pleased about the idea of having Guðrún as a daughter-in-law, Kjartan replies that he does not want to act against his father's will, but that he is confident that everything will turn out better than Óláfr expects.[57] Kjartan's answer is as ambiguous as his actions. When Guðrún wants to come with him on his journey abroad, he asks her to wait for him for three years, but he does not ask her to marry him.[58] After his return from Norway Kjartan appears not to care that Guðrún is engaged to his best friend Bolli, but many people had worried that this might be the case.[59] The public is anxious about a possible conflict between

---

55 *Egils saga Skalla-Grímssonar*, ed. Sigurður Nordal, pp. 246–47.
56 On the narrative technique of using public opinion as a steering means for interpretation cf. Rebecca Merkelbach, 'Volkes Stimme: Interaktion als Dialog in der Konstruktion sozialer Monstrosität in den Isländersagas', in *Stimme und Performanz in der mittelalterlichen Literatur*, ed. Monika Unzeitig *et al.* (Berlin and Boston, 2017), pp. 251–75.
57 *Laxdœla saga*, ed. Einar Ólafur Sveinsson, p. 112.
58 *Ibid.*, p. 115.
59 *Ibid.*, p. 132.

the families and the associated societal disruption. Hrefna is well aware of public opinion and of her responsibility towards her family. At their first meeting Hrefna reprimands Kjartan for his flirtatious behaviour and tells him how he is judged by the public opinion.[60] When Kjartan asks for her hand in marriage her father asks Hrefna whether she wants to marry Kjartan, but she wants her father to decide. While Guðrún acts as an individual, driven by her own sense of well-being and her individual longing, Hrefna proves to be a well-behaved woman and a responsible member of society who subordinates her individual desires to her father's interests to keep the family's balance and peace. Kjartan's proposal is successful and after the wedding the narrator states: 'Tókusk góðar ástir með þeim Kjartani ok Hrefnu' (they became very fond of each other).[61]

In the *Íslendingasögur* women are usually asked by their fathers whether they are willing to marry a man, but the women's agreement does not mean they are madly in love with their future husband.[62] The woman's consent as well as the narrator's remark that after the marriage the couple come to love each other signifies to the audience that no problems are to be expected in the near future. The example of Guðrún's first marriage shows how problematically events may turn out when a woman is married against her will.[63] She does not like her husband and provokes him until he slaps her and thus gives her a reason for divorce. A marriage without consent might thus pose a threat to the future of this family.

In *Laxdœla saga* as well as in other sagas, love is thus a matter of public interest. Long-term bonding is more important than the short-term emotions before or outside marriage. Friendship between men is therefore at least as important as love between a man and a woman and it is referred to by the same word (*unnask*). Friendship, especially between sworn- or foster-brothers, is about loyalty and trust: more important in a long life than lust and passion.[64] Deception in a friendship can thus lead to similar conflicts as a failed love affair. In *Laxdœla saga* the friendship between Kjartan and Bolli is as important as the love between Kjartan and Guðrún. While Kjartan and Guðrún become opponents after their failed love affair, Bolli is torn between his loyalty towards his friend and his wife.

This emphasis on long-term and family relationships also structures the two love stories in *Víglundar saga*. In the first few chapters the saga

60 Ibid., p. 133.
61 Ibid., p. 139.
62 This might also have been influenced by the church, which sought to enforce consent in marriage, based on the friendly affection of both partners; *maritalis affectus* (Schulz, *Erzähltheorie*, p. 55).
63 *Laxdœla saga*, ed. Einar Ólafur Sveinsson, pp. 93–94.
64 See Carolyne Larrington, *Brothers and Sisters in Medieval European Literature* (York, 2015), pp. 210–16.

presents different models of families and social status. In each of these families, children play an important role as their fathers have certain plans for them, as embodying their families' promise for the future. In the first part of the saga, Þorgrímr and Ólöf prove disruptive to this family model, since they do not agree with their parents' plans and want to marry without their consent. They are forced to leave their home country and to move to Iceland, and Þorgrímr is outlawed by the Norwegian king. They have to start from scratch like many other families in the time of settlement, but without a supporting family network their life is not easy.[65] Some people, who are envious of Þorgrímr's success and his popularity in the new neighbourhood, plan to rape his wife Ólöf. But Ólöf is aware of a possible attack and manages to evade the aggression.[66] This episode demonstrates the fragility of a small family trying to survive without any larger genealogical network.

In the second part of the saga Víglundr and Ketilríðr, in contrast, abstain from getting married rather than marrying without consent. Ketilríðr finds herself caught in a dilemma between her loyalty to her parents and her love for Víglundr. Ketilríðr's father also finds himself in a dilemma, torn between his love for his daughter and his loyalty towards his wife and sons. Peace and solidarity within the family is more important than the love between two individuals. Víglundr accepts Ketilríðr's decision, albeit reluctantly. When Ketilríðr is married to another man against her will, Víglundr wants to kill this man. But his brother Trausti convinces Víglundr in a verse that the love of one woman should not destroy the good spirit of an honourable man.[67] Víglundr has learned the lesson of his father, who decided differently and was therefore outlawed.

The importance of kin solidarity is also reflected in Hólmkell's and Þorgrímr's friendship. Although Þorgrímr's wife and their sons try to prevent the marriage between Víglundr and Ketilríðr, even resorting to illegal measures, both men maintain their solidarity and try to resolve all the problems through compromise, without using force and without risking a continuous feud. In *Víglundar saga* peace within family and between families is more important than individual characters and their feelings this corresponds to the needs of a society that is based on kinship bonds.

Love as starting point for a character's dilemma, caught between individual desires and loyalty towards his family is also the focus of the *skálds*' sagas *Gunnlaugs saga Ormstungu* and *Kormáks saga*. Both *skálds* (poets) cause conflict because they do not fulfil their promises to marry the

---

[65] This is hinted at in the narrative by their genealogies: while the Norwegian families are introduced as courtly characters without any hint about their ancestors, the Icelandic neighbours of Þorgrímr and Ólöf are introduced with their genealogies (*Víglundar saga*, ed. Jón Halldórsson, p. 74).
[66] Ibid., p. 78.
[67] Ibid., p. 109–10.

women they proposed to. On his travel abroad Gunnlaugr enjoys his success as a *skáld* at foreign courts and is very self-confident about his personal worth. He therefore does not consider it necessary to return within the promised time-limit and thus has to face the fact that Helga is married to another man. Although Kormákr's failure to appear for his own wedding is caused by a sorcerer's spell, this is considered a dishonour by Steingerðr's family and a cause for revenge.[68] Both *skálds* are torn between their loyalty to the beloved women and their own careers. Although they are successful poets, their pursuit of their individual goals does not make them happy. When they die, they still have not found any purpose in their lives. In his last stanza, Kormákr complains that he has to die of old age rather than in battle.[69] Gunnlaugr dies in a fight in Norway and is buried far from home. Both sagas end with the death of their main characters. Since they have no family their deaths will not be revenged nor have any other consequences: their sagas have no continuation.

## Conclusion

Literary representation of the human condition in the *Íslendingasögur* is connected to interpersonal relations and thus is situated far more in public space than in the private life of the characters. Since individual characters are subordinate to their family relations, the emotive scripts of grief and love are adapted to the needs of the saga plots about conflicts within and between families and Icelandic society. In the sagas a character's private emotions centred on death or marriage are less important than the effects of these events on their families. Emotions function more often as 'social manipulators', entailing a certain social behaviour, and less as an expression of an interior feeling, although in some sagas, poetry is used as a means to express a character's inner emotions. In the sagas a character's death is important when it starts a new chain of actions, as in feud or in legal procedures. In this respect love is usually less significant in the sagas than the death of a character; nevertheless, love and marriage are the basis of the complicated family networks determining the chain of action after a violent death. Despite variations in the narrative techniques employed to express the human condition, the prioritisation of family relations over individual destiny remains stable as a generic characteristic from the 'classical' sagas to the 'post-classical' sagas.

---

[68] *Kormáks saga*, ed. Einar Ól. Sveinsson, pp. 224–25.
[69] *Ibid.*, p. 302.

# God(s)
*Carolyne Larrington*

Once the technology of writing had been established in the cultures of the Ancient Near East, Egypt and Greece, the first kinds of texts that seem to have been committed to clay tablet or papyrus were the laws and wisdom collections, and next, hymns of praise to the deities who guarded and guided humankind. Fragments of epics detailing the adventures of the gods also fall among the earliest kinds of writing. Sumerian hymns to such figures as Enlil and Inanna, and fragments of the Flood-myth are preserved among the oldest tablets from the mid-fourth millennium BC onwards.[1] Funeral inscriptions and hymns are preserved in the earliest form of the Egyptian language.[2] The Greek poet Hesiod probably composed his *Theogony* between 750 and 650 BC, at the same time as the Homeric epics that related interactions between gods and heroes were also composed. The *Theogony* is a hymn invoking Zeus and the Muses; it describes how the gods came into existence and how they gained control over the cosmos.[3] Using writing on different media to record information about, invocations of, and hymns of praise to, the gods seems an obvious application of the new technology; the act of inscription itself may have been viewed as meritorious, and reading and reciting the hymns pleased the gods and brought their favour.

In western European cultures, tracing the historical associations between perceptions of the divine and the development of different genres in which to transmit such material is complicated by the close relationship between literacy and Christianity. Nevertheless in Scandinavia, some early runic inscriptions have religious functions; the Rǫk stone, dating from the mid-eighth century, makes cryptic allusion to Þórr and to Gunnr, thought to be a valkyrie. We might assume that hymns in praise of the Norse gods were composed and sung by their devotees, but such poems would have been highly unlikely to be written down by the Christian antiquarians who preserved pre-Conversion material in various contexts.[4]

---

1  See *The Literature of Ancient Sumer*, ed. Jeremy Black *et al.* (Oxford, 2004).
2  *Ancient Egyptian Literature: A Collection of Poems, Narratives and Manuals of Instructions from the Third and Second Millennia BC*, ed. Adolf Erman, trans. Aylward M. Blackman (New York, 2005).
3  *Hesiod: Theogony*, ed. Martin L. West (Oxford, 1966).
4  An exception is a skaldic fragment of Bragi Boddason, in which he directly invokes Þórr and alludes to his slaying of the giant Þrivaldi. Bragi inn gamli

Yet the eddic prosimetrum known as *Sigrdrífumál* gives a sense of how such praise-songs might have sounded when, delighted to have been woken from her enchanted sleep by the hero Sigurðr, the valkyrie Sigrdrífa invokes the gods, goddesses and cosmic powers:

> Heill dagr!         heilir dags synir,
>       heill nótt ok nipt!
> Óreiðum augum      lítið okkr þinig,
>       ok gefið sitjǫndum sígr!
>
> Heilir æsir,       heilar ásynjur
>       heil sjá fjǫlnýta fold!
> mál ok mannvit     gefið okkr mærum tveim
>       ok læknishendr meðan lífum! (*Sigrdrífumál*, sts 3–4)[5]

[Hail to the day! Hail to the sons of day! Hail to night and her kin! With gracious eyes may you look upon us two, and give victory to those sitting here!

Hail to the Æsir! Hail to the goddesses! Hail to the mighty, fecund earth! May you give eloquence and native wit to this glorious pair and healing hands while we live!].

## Eddic Mythological Poetry and its Genres

Mythological eddic poetry is principally recorded in the Codex Regius manuscript (GKS 2365[to]), hereafter R, dating from around 1270, and the related AM 748 4[to] manuscript (A) from the early fourteenth century; this contains six complete mythological poems and a fragment of the prose prefacing *Vǫlundarkviða*.[6] The eleven poems in R, along with *Hynd-*

---

Boddason, *Fragments*, st. 3, ed. Margaret Clunies Ross, in *Poetry from Treatises on Poetics*, ed. Kari Ellen Gade and Edith Marold, 2 vols, *SkP* 3 (Turnhout, 2017), I: 57–58.

[5] Cited from *Eddukvæði*, ed. Jónas Kristjánsson and Vésteinn Ólason, 2 vols, ÍF (Reykjavík, 2014), vol. 2, p. 314. My translation. Cf. *Lokasenna* st. 11/1–3 where Bragi toasts all the gods present at the feast with a similar formula: 'Heilir æsir, heilar ásynjur / ok ǫll ginnheilog goð!' (Hail to the Æsir, hail to the goddesses / and all the most sacred gods). The titles of Eddic poems are abbreviated as is conventional, according to the abbreviations used in Neckel and Kuhn, 4th edn.

[6] A contains the following mythological poems in this order: *Hárbarðsljóð*, the only text of *Baldrs Draumar*, *Skírnismál*, *Vafþrúðnismál*, *Grímnismál* and *Hymiskviða*. An exemplary discussion of genre and mode in eddic poetry is Brittany Schorn, 'Eddic Modes and Genres', in *A Handbook to Eddic Poetry: Myths and Legends of Early Scandinavia*, ed. Carolyne Larrington, Judy Quinn and Brittany Schorn (Cambridge, 2016), pp. 231–51.

*luljóð*, *Rígsþula* and *Baldrs Draumar*, preserved in a range of other manuscript contexts, relate information about the gods within a variety of poetic genres.[7] Here of course several caveats must be entered. The medievally attested categorisations available for cataloguing poetic genres are not 'ethnic' in the sense that Joseph Harris has adduced; the oral poets who composed the surviving mythological poems may not have thought of the kinds of poetry they were producing in the terms – generally referring to different kinds of speech-act – that the thirteenth-century copyists used to designate the texts they had to hand.[8] Nor, as Brittany Schorn astutely notes, do we know whether audiences, reciters and poets who encountered these poems in the same thirteenth-century contexts as the manuscript compilers might not have understood them differently and ascribed different titles and genre affiliations to them.[9]

*Vǫluspá* (The Seeress's Prophecy), the first poem in R (and preserved in different recensions in Hauksbók and the various manuscripts of the *Prose Edda*) imparts a particular version of the creation myth and the anthropogony, and, by selective juxtaposition of particular myths, demonstrates how the gods' bad faith towards other beings – in some ways epitomised by Loki – precipitates the death of Baldr and the inevitability of *ragna rǫk*. This key account of the parameters of the Old Norse mythic universe is presented as a prophecy (*spá*), a generic designation shared by two other surviving poems, neither of which deal with mythological material. The probably late poem *Grípisspá*, copied later in R, is a proleptic summary of the adventures of Sigurðr Fáfnisbani, delivered by his maternal uncle Grípir, while *Merlínusspá* is a translation of the Latin *Prophetiae Merlini* made by Gunnlaugr munkr in the thirteenth century and uniquely preserved in Hauksbók (AM 544 4[to]). The generic designation entails no particular formal qualities (though the poems are all composed in the typical eddic metre of *fornyrðislag*); rather it shows that content – vatic pronouncements about the future – constitute the main genre identifier.

The other mythological poems of R also attract manuscript titles, many of which simply record who is speaking: these end in *–mál*, *–kviða*

---

7   Ten of the eleven mythological poems in R have medieval titles: the exception is *Vǫlundarkviða* whose status as a mythological poem is debateable. Of the three mythological poems preserved in other manuscripts, *Baldrs Draumar* and *Rígsþula* lack medieval titles; *Hyndluljóð* names itself. See Judy Quinn, 'The Naming of Eddic Mythological Poems in Medieval Manuscripts', *Parergon* n.s. 8 (1990), 97–115, at pp. 112–15.
8   Joseph Harris, 'Genre in Saga Literature: A Squib', *SS* 47:4 (1975), 427–36. cf. also Else Mundal, 'Theories, Explanatory Models and Terminology: Problems and Possibilities in Research on Old Norse Mythology', in *Old Norse Religion in Long-Term Perspectives*, ed. Anders Andrén, Kristina Jennbert and Catharina Raudvere, Vägar til Midgårds 8 (Lund, 2006), pp. 285–88; Bernt Øyvind Thorvaldsen, 'The Generic Aspect of Eddic Style', in *Old Norse Religion in Long-Term Perspectives*, pp. 276–79.
9   Schorn, 'Eddic Modes and Genres', p. 236. Compare *Skírnismál* versus *Fǫr Skírnis* as titles for the same poem in its two medieval witnesses.

or -*ljóð*.¹⁰ Of interest is here is *Lokasenna*, a poem that dramatises an episode in mythological history, in which Loki demands admission to a feast held at the sea-deity Ægir's hall and proceeds to insult in turn each of the gods and goddesses present. The *senna* is a type of 'flyting' as the international genre is known; normally two opponents exchange insults, each trying to claim credit for his own deeds, to denigrate the other, and to defend or refute the accusations made by the opponent.[11] Both *Lokasenna* and *Hárbarðsljóð* broadly conform to this pattern, but both poems introduce significant structural variations. *Lokasenna* presents one antagonist (Loki) and an array of other deities; this situation allows the poet to refer glancingly to a range of mythological 'facts', only some of which are preserved in other sources. Allusions are thus made to the circumstances surrounding the deaths of Þjazi and Baldr, along with various allegations against the goddesses suggesting that they have had sexual liaisons with Loki. In the Codex Regius prosimetrum within which the poem is presented, Loki's intrusion and insults result in his being seized and bound: a necessary precursor to *ragna rǫk*. That Loki's intention within the poem was precisely to provoke the gods into making this crucial move has been argued by John McKinnell. However, this kind of systematic chronological connection between various events in mythic history seems more likely to be the product of antiquarian compilers in the thirteenth-century context.[12] *Hárbarðsljóð* too departs from presumed generic models; the disguised Óðinn lays claim to exploits that would normally seem disgraceful rather than honour-enhancing – seducing women, preciptating enmity between peoples – while his son and interlocutor, Þórr, brags of slaying giants and harrying supernatural figures to keep Miðgarðr and the realm of the gods safe. Yet, somehow, even in the face of Óðinn's barefaced lies, Þórr still fails either to win the contest or to gain passage across the fjord to speed him home.[13]

Four other mythological eddic poems fall broadly into the 'wisdom poetry' generic category that is the focus of Schorn's article in this volume. *Vafþrúðnismál* takes the form of a wisdom contest in which Óðinn and the giant Vafþrúðnir wager their heads on the wisdom. Comparable dialogic contests are found elsewhere in early medieval European literature, and indeed a similar framing is used for the presentation of riddles by

10 See Schorn, 'Eddic Modes and Genres', pp. 234–41, and Margaret Clunies Ross, *A History of Old Norse Poetry and Poetics* (Cambridge, 2005), pp. 29–30.
11 Karen Swenson, *Performing Definitions: Two Genres of Insult in Old Norse Literature* (Columbia, 1991); Antje Frotscher, 'The War of the Words: A History of Flyting from Antiquity to the Later Middle Ages', unpublished DPhil thesis (Oxford, 2004).
12 John McKinnell, 'Motivation in *Lokasenna*', *SBVS* 22:3–4 (1987–88), 234–62.
13 Carol Clover, '*Hárbarðsljóð* as Generic Farce', *SS* 51 (1979), 124–45; Marcel Bax and Tineke Padmos, 'Two Types of Verbal Duelling in Old Icelandic: The Interactional Structure of the *senna* and the *mannjafnaðr*', *SS* 55 (1983), 149–74.

a disguised Odinic figure in *Hervarar saga ok Heiðreks*. *Grímnismál* presents arcane mythological facts, some pertaining to the creation of the world, others as diverse as the (enumerated) dwelling-places of the gods, the rivers of the Other World, or the culminating list of Óðinn-*heiti* with which the god ends his monologue and finally reveals his identity. *Hávamál* too, very likely a composite of separate poems engaging with human and divine wisdom, depends for its poetic unity on the figure of Óðinn as speaker, an identity only gradually revealed in the course of the poem as the topics progress from advice about how to behave in hall to a full apotheosis as the myth of the mead of poetry is allusively retold.[14]

The remaining mythological poems of R recount different adventures of the gods and their allies: in obtaining the consent of the giantess Gerðr to a liaison with Freyr, gaining a mighty cauldron for the brewing of ale, preventing a dwarf from marrying Þórr's daughter, or the recovery of Þórr's stolen hammer, Mjǫlnir, from the giant Þrymr. The three mythological poems from other manuscripts that are conventionally included in the Poetic Edda find their place there in part because of their generic similarities to the mythological poems of Codex Regius. *Hyndluljóð* is a kind of wisdom poem within which a good number of mythological or legendary facts are elicited from the giantess Hyndla; one section, known as *Vǫluspá in skamma*, focusses in particular on mythological origins. *Baldrs Draumar*, another question and answer dialogue poem, preserved in A, relates how Óðinn questions a dead giantess at the edge of Hel's kingdom to confirm the import of his son's bad dreams: that Baldr's death is imminent. *Rígsþula* accounts for human social ranking through the activities of the god Heimdallr, visiting three representative households and engendering an ancestor on each of the wives.

Judging by the limited number of poems that were preserved so fortuitously in the two manuscripts, and which can only represent a small proportion of the poems about the Old Norse pantheon that must once have existed, the gods, their adventures and their fate were addressed within a limited range of genres. Of these, wisdom poetry in various forms – dialogue, monologue, catalogue – is pre-eminent; the *spá* sketches the broad parameters in terms of time and space in which the pre-Christian gods operated; two examples of *senna*-type poetry allusively transmit knowledge about the gods and goddesses and characterise major divine figures in ways that – at least in the case of *Lokasenna* – have opened up questions about parodic intention on the part of a Christian poet.[15] The remaining poems narrate discrete divine adventures, usually structured as quests,

---

14 Carolyne Larrington, *A Store of Common Sense: Gnomic Theme and Style in Old Icelandic and Old English Wisdom Poetry* (Oxford, 1993); Brittany Schorn, *Speaker and Authority in Old Norse Wisdom Poetry* (Berlin, 2017).
15 Barbro Söderberg, 'Lokasenna: egenheter och ålder', *ANF* 102 (1987), 18–99.

undertaken in order to win or recover prized cultural items in the possessions of the *jǫtnar*.¹⁶

## Skaldic Treatment of Mythological Subjects

Skaldic poetry, the complex formal court-poetry ascribed generally to named poets, encodes mythological information at the heart of its imagery system; the distinctive kennings that are integral to the form are very often dependent on the possession of knowledge about the gods and their histories for the poets' encoding and the audience's understanding. I discuss below (pp. 204–05) this convention and its importance to Snorri Sturluson's *Edda*, in which Old Norse's major mythographic treatise is embedded.

The god Óðinn is regarded as the patron of human poets – and thus the iteration of the myth of the mead-winning becomes crucial to poetic self-presentation. The poet Egill Skalla-Grímsson pictures himself as bringing a cargo of poetic praise, 'Óðins mjǫð' (st. 2/3) across the sea to Eiríkr bloodaxe in the poem *Hǫfuðlausn*, a cargo that he must discharge successfully in order to save his life:

> Vestr fór ek of ver,
> en ek Viðris ber
> munstrandar mar;
> svá er mitt of far.
> Dró ek eik á flot
> við ísa brot;
> hlóð ek mærðar hlut
> míns knarrar skut. (*Hfl* st. 1)¹⁷

> [I came westwards over the ocean and I bear Viðrir's [Óðinn's] mind-strand's sea, my state is so; I set the oak-vessel afloat at ice-thaw; I carry a load of praise at my trading-ship's stern].

The *hǫfuðlausn* is a particular functional subgenre of praise-poetry, defined by its extratextual purpose: to save the poet's life in the face of a king's wrath.¹⁸ Later, in perhaps his greatest poem, the powerful lament

---

16 See Margaret Clunies Ross on the concept of 'negative reciprocity' in *Prolonged Echoes: Old Norse Myths in Medieval Northern Society*, 2 vols, The Viking Collection 7 (Odense, 1994), vol. I, pp. 103–43.
17 Cited from *Egils saga*, ed. Bjarni Einarsson (London, 2003), p. 106. My translation. Abbreviations for skaldic poems are those used in *SkP*.
18 Alison Finlay, 'Risking One's Head: *Vafþrúðnismál* and the Mythic Power of Poetry', in *Myths, Legends, and Heroes: Essays on Old Norse and Old English Literature in Honour of John McKinnell*, ed. Daniel Anlezark (Toronto and London, 2011), pp. 91–108. Óttarr svarti also composed such a poem for Óláfr Haraldsson, king of Norway, having fallen foul of the ruler by composing a *mansǫngsdrápa* (poem

*Sonatorrek*, Egill suggests that he has relinquished his faith in his patron, given the terrible loss he has suffered in the deaths of two of his sons. Yet, even as he castigates the god, he acknowledges that the gift of poetry has brought him consolation.

> Blœt ek því
> bróður Vílis,
> goðjaðar,
> at ek gjarn sék.
> Þó hefr Míms vinr
> mér of fengnar
> bǫlva bœtr,
> ef it betra telk. (*Son*, st. 23)[19]

[I do not sacrifice to Víli's brother [Óðinn], gods' bulwark, because I am willing. Yet Mímr's friend [Óðinn] has got for me a remedy for ills, if I reckon up the better].

Despite the important role played by the Old Norse deities in the lexis and imagery system of skaldic poetry, surprisingly little of the skaldic poetry preserved deals directly with the gods or their adventures; its complex, riddling style makes skaldic verse perhaps less suited than eddic metres for rendering straightforward narrative. One remarkable exception is *Þórsdrápa*, composed by Eilífr Goðrúnarson, mainly preserved in *Skáldskaparmál* in the *Prose Edda*.[20] The circumstances under which the poem came into existence are unknown, though it is possible that it was intended as a praise-poem for Hákon jarl (*c.* 937–95), among whose court-poets Eilífr is listed, in the list of well-known poets, *Skáldatal*.[21] This argument has been put forward by Edith Marold, and rests in part on what we know of Hákon – that he particularly venerated Þórr – and in part on the frequent use of ethnic base-words in the kennings denoting the giants against whom Þórr battles.[22] Marold argues that these words evoke peoples

---

about a woman) about Óláfr's wife. Þórarinn loftunga is credited with another, of which only one stanza survives, a penalty elicited by King Knútr of Denmark. See Matthew Townend, 'Introduction to Óttarr svarti, *Hǫfuðlausn*', in *Poetry from the Kings' Sagas 1: From Mythical Times to c. 1035*, gen. ed. Diana Whaley, SkP 1 (Turnhout, 2012), pp. 739–40, and Matthew Townend, 'Introduction to Þórarinn loftunga, *Hǫfuðlausn*', in *Poetry from the Kings' Sagas 1*, gen. ed. Whaley, SkP 1, pp. 849–50.

19 *Egils saga*, ed. Bjarni Einarsson, p. 153.
20 See Edith Marold *et al.*, transl. John Foulks, 'Introduction to Eilífr Goðrúnarson, *Þórsdrápa*' in *Poetry from Treatises on Poetics*, gen. ed. Gade and Marold, SkP 3, I: pp. 68–75. Marold gives full details of the preservation contexts.
21 This list, probably dating from around 1260, was transmitted in the Kringla manuscript of *Heimskringla* (destroyed in the Copenhagen fire of 1728) and survives in the Codex Upsaliensis (DG 11 4^to) of the *Prose Edda*. See *The Uppsala Edda*, ed. Heimir Pálsson, trans. Anthony Faulkes (London, 2012), pp. 100–18.
22 Edith Marold, 'Skaldedichtung und Mythologie', in *Atti del 12. Congresso*

'who mostly had been enemies of Hákon jarl, such as the Danes (st. 13/6, 8) in the battle of Hjǫrungavágr and the Swedes (st. 13/2) in the viking expeditions in his youth and on his way through Götaland'.[23]

Þjóðólfr ór Hvínir's ekphrastic poem *Haustlǫng* from around 900 AD offers a detailed account of the abduction of Iðunn by the giant Þjazi, and the battle between Þórr and Hrungnir.[24] Ekphrastic poems comprise a small but notable subgenre of skaldic poetry.[25] A number of other mythological episodes, including Gefjon's winning of Sjælland from Gylfi, Baldr's funeral and Þórr's battle with the Miðgarðsormr, listed by Clunies Ross, are either recounted or alluded to in ekphrastic poems.[26] Such scenes were popular themes for the decoration of shields (Bragi Boddason's *Ragnarsdrápa*) or carved panels (Úlfr Uggason's *Húsdrápa*). A number of *lausavísur* variously attributed to Bragi, Úlfr and Þjóðólfr by Snorri also engage with mythological incidents.[27] The Miðgarðsormr fight is well evidenced in Viking-Age sculpture from sites as far apart as Gotland, Gosforth and the Isle of Man, as Clunies Ross notes; its distinctive details of course make it easy to identify in material contexts. Likewise, it and other episodes scenes chosen for depiction on shields or carved panels, and recounted in the ekphrastic verses are lively and dramatic, agonistic in Clunies Ross's terms: 'the skalds in most of these instances have adopted a narrative style of extreme economy, representing a known story at its most dramatic point'.[28] The encounters between god and other beings often take place in liminal and contested space, a criterion suggesting that this genre has more complex ideological work to do than simply celebrating and recording the rich and significant artworks within patrons' halls: 'hlaut innan svá minnum' (Memorable things were thus allotted inside [the hall]), as the refrain of *Húsdrápa* has it (sts 6/8, 10/8).[29] The poets' apparently simple equation between patron –

---

*Internazionale di Studi sull'Alto Medioevo: Poetry in the Scandinavian Middle Ages. The Seventh International Saga Conference*, ed. Teresa Pàroli, (Spoleto, 1990), pp. 107–30, at pp. 119–27.

23 Marold, 'Introduction to Eilífr Goðrúnarson', pp. 73–74.
24 Margaret Clunies Ross, 'Þjóðólfr ór Hvini, *Haustlǫng*', in *Poetry from Treatises on Poetics*, gen. ed. Gade and Marold, SkP 3, I: pp. 431–63.
25 Margaret Clunies Ross et al. 'Stylistic and Generic Identifiers of the Old Norse Skaldic Ekphrasis', VMS 3 (2007), 159–92.
26 Ibid., p. 166; see also Signe Horn Fuglesang, 'Ekphrasis and Surviving Imagery in Viking Scandinavia', VMS 3 (2007), 193–224.
27 Ǫlvir hnufa, Gamli gnævarðarskáld and Eysteinn Valdason also treat the theme of Þórr and the Miðgardsormr in fragmentary form; see Clunies Ross, 'Stylistic and Generic Identifiers', p. 169.
28 Clunies Ross, 'Stylistic and Generic Identifiers', p. 172.
29 Russell Poole, 'Ekphrasis: its "Prolonged Echoes" in Scandinavia', VMS 3 (2007), 245–67; Edith Marold et al., transl. John Foulks, 'Úlfr Uggason, *Húsdrápa*' in *Poetry from Treatises on Poetics*, gen. ed. Gade and Marold, SkP 3, I: pp. 402–24, at p. 424.

king or jarl – and Þórr in his many triumphs over giant enemies can thus be read as symbolising different kinds of transitions and initiations in human lives: whether emerging into full maturity, assuming new social positions, or even – as in *Húsdrápa*, passing into the next life, as figured by the procession of gods riding to Baldr's funeral pyre (sts 7–11). The tales of the gods related in these poems are indeed a kind of praise-poetry, but one that – through metonymy – addresses and celebrates the patron, not the god. For Úlfr Uggason, this is Óláfr 'pái' Hǫskuldarson at Hjarðarholt in Western Iceland. Like Egill in *Hǫfuðlausn* Úlfr identifies the speech-act in which he is engaged, but in the final rather than first stanza: 'æri ... bark mærð af hendi ... sverðregns' (I gave praise to the sword-rain's messenger [warrior]) (st. 12), he claims. Gods and great men are thus closely aligned; celebration of the divine is subordinated to the pragmatics of the patronage relation.

## Christianity and the Polysystem

When Christianity finally became the recognised religion in Iceland and Norway at the turn of the eleventh century, new textual traditions came into contact with native oral and genres, instigating fundamental shifts in the generic polysystem. Icelanders in particular became part of a 'textual community', travelling abroad to ecclesiastical centres in Europe and they were trained to read the texts imported in the country by missionaries and other priests.[30] Episcopal sees and monastic foundations became important centres for manuscript production; interaction between Latin and vernacular genres reshaped the native polysystem through – importantly – the different kinds of formal and stylistic possibilities offered by prose. Vernacular hagiography and homiletic texts were the first fruits of the systemic re-organisation of genre; these were of course largely translations, evidenced by the very early *Norwegian Homily Book*, *Maríu saga*, *Niðrstígninga saga* (the apocryphal Gospel of Nicodemus, known in Latin as *Descensus Christi ad inferos*), the *Dialogues* of Gregory the Great and the *Elucidarius*.[31] These texts were key for Christian teaching, for pastoral care and for inspiration. The translated lives – more accurately, the passions of important early Christian martyrs – were later augmented by the lives of more recent figures; four different versions of *Thómas saga erkibyskups*, the saga of Thomas Becket (*c*. 1120–70), were composed in the thirteenth

---

30 See Pernille Hermann, 'Literacy' in *The Routledge Research Companion to the Medieval Icelandic Sagas*, ed. Ármann Jakobsson and Sverrir Jakobsson (London and New York, 2017), pp. 34–47; Brian Stock, *Literacy in Theory and Practice* (Cambridge, 1984), p. 90.
31 See Jonas Wellendorf, 'Ecclesiastical Literature and Hagiography', in *The Routledge Research Companion to the Medieval Icelandic Sagas*, ed. Jakobsson and Jakobsson, pp. 48–58.

and fourteenth centuries.[32] *Thómas saga 1* was probably written by a Norwegian in the latter half of the thirteenth century; the other versions (of which sagas 3 and 4 only exist now in fragments) were composed in Iceland. *Thómas saga 2* is a composite work, containing sections translated from a now-lost life of Thomas, composed by Robert of Cricklade, prior of St Frideswide in Oxford between 1173–80; this work was translated in Iceland as early as 1200.

Hagiography, argues Siân Grønlie, 'constitutes an unexpectedly wide-ranging and heterogeneous set of genres': epic, history-writing and the tripartite integral elements of the Latin saint's life.[33] Indeed, notes Lars Lönnroth, 'the generic concepts of hagiography dealt with *parts* of saints' lives, (the *vita* part, the *passio* part, the *miracula* part) rather than the saint's life as a whole.'[34] Hagiographical writings, both translated and indigenous in origin, became extraordinarily popular very quickly in Iceland.[35] 'Of the 420 manuscripts containing sagas, 156 contain saints' lives, as opposed to only 52 containing sagas of Icelanders', Grønlie observes. An early and quirky example of the vernacular response to the impact of hagiography within the polysystem is Oddr Snorrason's biography of Óláfr Tryggvason, 'the failed saint' as Grønlie calls him. This was first written in Latin around 1190, and translated into Old Icelandic shortly afterwards; 'it draws on an eclectic mix of genres, which have been variously identified as saint's life, secular biography, romance, heroic epic and folktale.'[36] Oddr does his best to present his hero within the paradigms of the saint's life, 'as a man whose heroic violence on the mission field had exemplary value, even if it meant that he fell short of sainthood.'[37] Nevertheless, Oddr's pioneering work and his translator's readiness to innovate in the vernacular long prose form within the newly reconfigured generic system would have far-reaching effects.

For, thereafter, Scandinavian royal saints' careers began to be chronicled in historiographical works that recounted the history of the Norwegian or Danish monarchies, or the political events across several centuries in the earldom of Orkney. The life of St Óláfr Haraldsson, the Norwegian king who died at the Battle of Stiklastaðir in 1030 is recounted in Snorri Sturluson's *Heimskringla*, and also in a separately preserved version, known as the *Separate Saga of Saint Olaf*.[38] The life of St Magnus of Orkney is simi-

---

32 Haki Antonsson, '*Thomas saga erkibyskups* ('The Saga of Archbishop Thomas')', in *The Oxford Dictionary of the Middle Ages* (Oxford, 2010). Online.
33 Siân Grønlie, *The Saint and the Saga Hero: Hagiography and Early Icelandic Literature*, Studies in Old Norse Literature 2 (Cambridge, 2017), p. 6.
34 Lars Lönnroth, 'The Concept of Genre in Saga Literature', *SS* 47:4 (1975), 419–26, at p. 425.
35 Grønlie, *The Saint and the Saga Hero*, p. 34.
36 *Ibid.*, p. 39, citing Theodore Andersson, *The Growth of the Medieval Icelandic Sagas (1180–1280)* (Ithaca, 2006), p. 25.
37 Grønlie, *The Saint and the Saga Hero*, p. 76.
38 Carl Phelpstead, *Holy Vikings: Saints' Lives in the Old Icelandic Kings' Sagas* (Tempe,

larly woven into the secular historiographical and prosimetrical account of *Orkneyinga saga*, probably composed first around 1200.[39] Carl Phelpstead's important work on the sagas of Scandinavian royal saints draws upon Bakhtin's concepts of heteroglossia, dialogue and polyphony to address the hybrid nature of those *konungasögur* (kings' sagas) that relate the lives of these saintly men; using Heather Dubrow's concept of the 'host genre', Phelpstead shows how the genre conventions of hagiography are imported within the larger historiographical project in order to build the case for sanctity.[40] Thus, verse prosimetrum, saga prose, miracle stories, and confrontational dialogue between the saint and his opponent all become incorporated within these texts: 'narrative meets homily, prose meets verse', and, in the case of St Knútr in the Danish *Knýtlinga saga*, 'Saga Style meets Court Style'.[41]

These innovative genres were influential for the emergence of the secular Icelandic saga. Jonas Wellendorf traces in some detail Gabriel Turville-Petre's arguments, proposing that the early Christian prose texts gave rise to the kings' sagas, and these in turn shaped the *Íslendingasögur*. Turville-Petre's often-quoted dictum, 'the learned literature did not teach the Icelanders what to think or what to say, but it taught them how to say it', has offered a persuasive model of generic influence, but one which is, as Wellendorf notes, hard to prove.[42] Indeed, it seems just as likely that the direction of influence was not as linear and chronological as Turville-Petre, and also Jónas Kristjánsson, suggest.[43] It is entirely possible that the writers of the different saga subgenres rubbed shoulders in the same monastic, episcopal or secular chieftainly centres, turning their hand to different kinds of works in a roughly similar time frame. This alternative model, proposed by Sverrir Tómasson 'has the advantage of being more flexible and it allows for mutual and dynamic influences between the two groups of writings', notes Wellendorf, but firm evidence for the provenance of

---

    2007), pp. 17–23; 117–58. Other versions of Óláfr's life include the fragmentary *Oldest saga* and the so-called *Legendary saga*, composed in Norway around 1250, Phelpstead, *Holy Vikings*, pp. 19–22.

39 Phelpstead, *Holy Vikings*, pp. 77–115; see also Haki Antonsson, *St Magnus of Orkney: A Scandinavian Martyr-Cult in Context*, Northern World 29 (Leiden, 2007).

40 Heather Dubrow, *Genre*, Methuen Critical Idiom 42 (London, 1982), p. 116. Phelpstead, *Holy Vikings*, pp. 61–75, citing Lönnroth's remarks, noted above, that, in genre terms, the saint's life was understood in its constituent parts. 'The same is true of secular prose', Lönnroth contends ('Concept of Genre', p. 425).

41 Phelpstead, *Holy Vikings*, p. 215.

42 Gabriel Turville-Petre, *Origins of Icelandic Literature* (Oxford, 1953), p. 142; Wellendorf, 'Eccelesiastical Literature', pp. 49–51.

43 Jónas Kristjánsson, 'Learned Style or Saga Style?', in *Speculum Norrœnum: Norse Studies in Memory of Gabriel Turville-Petre*, ed. Ursula Dronke et al. (Odense, 1981), pp. 260–92.

early secular and religious compositions of this kind is lacking.[44] Grønlie argues for a continuing relationship between the saints' life genre and the *Íslendingasögur*; the Christian genre does not only play a vital role in the saga subgenre's genesis, rather *Íslendingasaga* and saint's life remain interwoven as long as the former continues to be written:

> it might be better to think of the relationship ... in terms of dialogue, interdependence, active and willing engagement on the part of the sagas with one of the central narrative genres of the Christian Middle Ages.[45]

This dialogic model explains how Christian themes, motifs and moralisation became so thoroughly absorbed into the apparently more secular saga subgenres.[46]

## Mythography

The Old Norse gods were not, of course, extirpated by the arrival of Christianity. The *Prose Edda*, designed as a treatise on traditional skaldic poetics, is composed of four distinct sections. The final part, *Háttatal*, catalogues different varieties of skaldic metre; it is a poem intended to praise Duke Skúli Bárðarson of Norway (d. 1240) and King Hákon Hákonarson (d. 1263). *Háttatal* is preceded by an account of kennings that, perforce, has to explain the references to the pre-Christian gods that these metaphorical coinages employ. This section, *Skáldskaparmál*, begins as a dialogue between Bragi, the god of poetry, and Ægir, characterised as a 'maðr ... mjǫk fjǫlkunnigr' (a man ... very well-versed in knowledge).[47] The dialogic structure soon breaks down once Bragi has related a couple of important myths: the gods' dealings with Þjazi and the story of the mead of poetry. Bragi then launches upon a systematic account of the kenning system. This part of the treatise is itself preceded by *Gylfaginning* (The Deception of Gylfi), a mythographical account of the pantheon, the creation of the universe, the anthropogony, key adventures of various deities and the fullest account we have of *ragna rǫk*, the end of the world and its aftermath.[48] Here Snorri harnesses a learned European understanding of the antithetical principles of ice and fire that gave rise to the universe to the differing mythic traditions preserved in the various eddic stanzas that

---

44 Wellendorf, 'Ecclesiastical Literature', p. 51; Sverrir Tómasson, 'The Hagiography of Snorri Sturluson, Especially in the *Great Saga of St Olaf*', in *Saints and Sagas: a Symposium*, ed. Hans Bekker-Nielsen and Birte Carlé (Odense, 1994), pp. 49–72.
45 Grønlie, *The Saint and the Saga Hero*, p. 264.
46 See further, Haki Antonsson, *Damnation and Salvation in Old Norse Literature*, Studies in Old Norse Literature 3 (Cambridge, 2018).
47 Snorri Sturluson, *Edda: Skáldskaparmál*, ed. Anthony Faulkes (London, 2005), p. 1.
48 Snorri Sturluson, *Gylfaginning*, ed. Anthony Faulkes, 2nd ed. (London, 2005).

he cites.[49] The entire mythographic and poetic treatise is prefaced by a *Prologue* in which Snorri offers a euhemeristic explanation of the Old Norse gods – as refugees from Troy, one which situates the entire work within the European tradition of *translatio studii*; he also makes use of contemporary theories of natural religion to explain how humanity had become so forgetful of the Christian god that humans might be accorded worship.[50] Snorri's unparalleled text presents all kinds of information about the gods, encoded in poetic stanzas or brief kennings, and also vividly narrated in fully realised prose adventures, all subordinated to a explanatory model that emphasises that these figures are neither real nor powerful in creating anything other than illusion (*sjónhverfingar*).[51] The *Prose Edda* draws upon the kinds of systematic modes of organisation typical of the grammatical treatises, creative prose narratives, the kind of prosimetrum that the Codex Regius would later employ, and which may already have been in use in *fornaldarsögur*, prefaced by a learned, speculative and perhaps playful discussion of the gods' origins that served to authorise the entire project.

## Christian Poetics

Critical to the development of vernacular genres in which religious content could be engaged with was an emerging understanding of the importance of communicative function. High style, elaborate, ornate and complex, was deemed appropriate for praise-poetry; skaldic poetry had indeed always been the mode of choice to eulogise kings and to recount divine exploits. It was, as discussed above, often composed in an immediate social context that called for artful praise of high-status patrons. One of the earliest skaldic Christian compositions is a hymn of praise for St Óláfr: *Geisli* (Light-beam), composed by Einarr Skúlason around 1153.[52] Just as poems like *Þórsdrápa* and the ekphrastic genre discussed above ei-

---

49   See on Snorri's poetics, Clunies Ross, *A History of Old Norse Poetry and Poetics* and her earlier *Skáldskaparmál: Snorri Sturluson's ars poetica and Medieval Theories of Language*, The Viking Collection 4 (Odense, 1987).
50   See Kevin Wanner, *Snorri Sturluson and the Edda: the Conversion of Cultural Capital in Medieval Scandinavia* (Toronto, 2008) for a full account of Snorri's possible aims in writing the *Edda*. Wanner takes note of Elias Wessén's suggestion that the text may have been composed in effect backwards, with *Háttatal* as the starting point. Interpretation of the poem would then successively have required an explanation of metre, of the kenning system and consequently of the mythographical traditions, if its dedicatees were to make sense of the culminating poem. Elias Wessén, 'Introduction' to *Codex Regius of the Younger Edda: MS No. 2367 4° in the Old Royal Library of Copenhagen*, Corpus Codicum Islandicorum Medii Ævi 14 (København, 1940), pp. 15–16, 29–32, and Wanner, *Snorri Sturluson*, pp. 99–103.
51   Snorri Sturluson, *Gylfaginning*, ed. Faulkes, p. 1; Snorri Sturluson, *Edda: Skáldskaparmál*, ed. Faulkes, p. 1.
52   For further discussion of the emergence of Christian poetic genres in the twelfth century, see Chapter 15 in this volume.

ther retold in full or recounted more allusively the exploits of gods and heroes, so Christian poets adapted the traditional kinds of poetry, such as the *drápa*, in order to relate the exploits of saints. An early example is the *vita* of St John the Evangelist in *Jónsdrápa*, a twelfth-century poem only partially preserved. The thirteenth century saw a brief flurry of composition in eddic metre – the translation of the *Distichs of Cato*, *Hugsvinnsmál* (The Wise One's Speech), and the extraordinary hybrid wisdom-vision poem, *Sólarljóð* (Song of the Sun) – as well as the remarkable anonymous *dróttkvætt* poem, *Líknarbraut* (The Way of Grace), a long *drápa* that draws on such eclectic influences as the Cross hymns of Venantius Fortunatus, the Good Friday liturgy and traditional exegesis, in order to celebrate the Cross and its role in Christ's passion.[53] The poem's first verse demonstrates how the Christian poet now prays for inspiration rather than boldy announcing his own poetic prowess; as in earlier praise-poems the subject is directly named:

> Einn, lúk upp, sem ek bæni,
> óðrann ok gef sanna
> mér, þú er* alls átt ærit,
> orðgnótt, himins dróttinn.
> Þinn vil ek kross, sem kunnum,
> (Kristr styrki mik) dýrka
> (örr, sá er ýta firrir
> allri nauð ok dauða). (*Lik* st. 1)[54]

> [Heaven's Lord [> GOD], you who alone possess a fullness of all, open up my poetry-house [> BREAST], as I pray, and give me true word-abundance. I desire to glorify your Cross as [well as] we [I] can; may Christ strengthen me, the bountiful one, who removes men from all distress and death.]

This verse shows vividly how far kennings have been simplified: *óðrann* (poetry-place) for 'breast', for example, or *himins dróttinn* for 'God'. While this stanza with its intercalated clauses retains typical skaldic syntax, overall the poem has fewer such embedded comments, or sentences split across the *helmingr*.

The fourteenth century would see more propitious circumstances for the preservation of Christian skaldic poetry, as the mode not only flourished but developed into a flexible and highly aesthetic system of related poetic genres. The *drápa* form continued to be employed to celebrate

---

53 George S. Tate, 'Introduction to Anonymous, *Líknarbraut*', in *Poetry on Christian Subjects*, ed. Margaret Clunies Ross, 2 vols, *SkP* 7 (Turnhout, 2007), I: pp. 228–29; George S. Tate, 'Good Friday Liturgy and the Structure of *Líknarbraut*', *SS* 50:1 (1978), 31–38.
54 Text and translation from *Líknarbraut*, ed. Tate, *Poetry on Christian Subjects*, ed. Clunies Ross, p. 230.

the saints. The Virgin Mary is a popular subject for fourteenth-century poems, as in the anonymous *Maríudrápa* (*Drápa* of Mary) and *Drápa af Maríugrát* (*Drápa* of Mary's lament). *Pétrsdrápa* (*Drápa* of Peter) and *Andreasdrápa* (*Drápa* of Andrew) celebrate the brother Apostles. Kálfr Hallsson is the only named poet for this period; his substantial *Katrínardrápa* (*Drápa* about St Catherine) is a versification of the Old Norse prose *vita* of Saint Catherine of Alexandria.[55] Two substantial poems list a range of male and female saints in the fragmentary *Heilagra manna drápa* (*Drápa* of Holy Men) and the better-preserved *Heilagra meyja drápa* (*Drápa* of Holy Maidens).[56] Composed in *hrynhent*, in 26 whole or part-stanzas, *Heilagra manna drápa* catalogues the most popular saints in Iceland, including two English saints venerated in the North: St Thomas Becket and St Edmund, along with Scandinavian saints: St Hallvarðr of Vík (Oslo), King Knútr of Denmark, and his brother Benedikt.[57]

> Börðuz menn, þar Benedict varði
> bróður sinn af drengskap góðum;
> Knútr var staddr í musteri mætu
> mildr og eigi stríða vildi. (*HMD* st. 20/1–4)[58]

> [Men fought, where Benedikt defended his brother with great manliness; gentle Knútr was situated in the magnificent church and did not want to fight.]

The most impressive among the fourteenth-century Christian poems is *Lilja* (The Lily), 'an impeccably wrought *drápa*, a *tour de force* of poetic technique' as its editor remarks.[59] The poem marks a major stylistic turning-point in the history of Icelandic poetics; it is composed in *hrynhent*, a metre with a longer eight-syllable line, as exemplified in the *Heilagra manna drápa* stanza cited above. Up to the point where *Lilja* was composed, as Chase notes, most Christian poetry was in *dróttkvætt*; thereafter, the more expansive *hrynhent* became the more popular metre. It seems likely that the longer line began to be preferred because it was more similar to the poets' Latin models. In *Lilja*, the new style is very successful. Its

> lines are more supple and often seem to accommodate extra syllables in a way that earlier *hrynhent* and *dróttkvætt* do not. The syntax is more natural, the vocabulary less exotic, and the use of kennings is kept to

---

55 Kirsten Wolf, 'Introduction to Kálfr Hallsson, *Kátrínardrápa*', in *Poetry on Christian Subjects*, ed. Clunies Ross, II: pp. 931–64; *Heilagra meyja sögur*, ed. Kirsten Wolf, Íslenzk trúarrit 1 (Reykjavík, 2003).
56 Kirsten Wolf, ed. and trans., 'Anonymous, *Heilagra manna drápa*', in *Poetry on Christian Subjects*, ed. Clunies Ross, II: pp. 872–90.
57 Wolf, 'Introduction', p. 872.
58 Text and translation from *Heilagra manna drápa*, ed. Wolf, p. 886.
59 Martin Chase, 'Introduction to Anonymous, *Lilja*', in *Poetry on Christian Subjects*, ed. Clunies Ross, pp. 544–677, at p. 558.

a minimum.[60]

That the poem has 100 stanzas is noteworthy, for 100 was a significant number in Christian numerology.[61] The poet justifies his simpler style in sts 97 and 98 as conducive to clarity in communicating Christian doctrine:

> Veri kátar nú, virða sveitir;
> vætti þess, í kvæðis hætti,
> várkunni, að verka þenna
> vanda eg minnr, en þætti standa.
> Varðar mest, að allra orða
> undirstaðan sie riettlig fundin,
> eigi glögg þó að eddu regla
> undan hljóti að víkja stundum.
>
> Sá, er óðinn skal vandan velja,
> velr svá mörg í kvæði að selja
> hulin fornyrðin; trautt má telja;
> tel eg þenna svá skilning dvelja.
> Vel því að hier má skýr orð skilja,
> skili þjóðir minn ljósan vilja;
> tal óbreytiligt veitt að vilja;
> vil eg, að kvæðið heiti Lilja. (*Lil* sts 97–8)[62]

[Hosts of men, be glad now; I expect this, that they will excuse, that I execute this poem less well in poetic form than it would seem to merit. It is of great importance that the right meaning of all words be found, even though the obscuring rule of the Edda must at times give way. / He who must execute the elaborate poem chooses to put into the verse so many obscure archaisms one can hardly count them; I say that he thus impedes understanding. Because one here can understand clear words well, let people understand my transparent intent, this ordinary speech given freely; I desire that the poem be called 'Lilja'.]

The *right* meanings of words must be employed to mediate the poet's meaning, even if the high style represented by *eddu reglur* – a reference to Snorri Sturluson's poetic treatise – must be abandoned or modified: *skilning* (understanding) and *ljósan vilja* (clear intention) are more important than the ostentatious deployment of *hulin fornyrðin* (obscure archaisms). The term *óðinn* in the first line of st. 98, although in context meaning 'elab-

---

60 *Ibid.*, p. 558.
61 *Lilja* thus evokes comparison with the 101-stanza anonymous Middle English poem *Pearl*, a highly wrought dream-vision in which the nature of the heavenly life is revealed to a bereaved father.
62 *Lilja*, ed. and trans. Chase, pp. 672–73.

orate', must surely also pun on the name of the god of poetry, the deity who has been thoroughly displaced by the 'Almáttugr guð ... yfirbjóðandi engla og þjóða' (st. 100/1–2) (Almighty God ... supreme ruler of angels and nations) who is invoked in the poem's final stanza.[63]

Here, perhaps, the patterns of generic development that have been traced across this chapter have come full circle. In poetry, simplicity and directness is once more prized, as in the eddic poetry that chronicled the deeds of the gods and in which Sigrdrífa invoked the higher powers. Edda and Óðinn are invoked here only to be repudiated; the elaborate kennings and coinages, the dense and brilliant word-play exhibited by Eilífr Goðrúnarson in his *Þórsdrápa* is now regarded as an impediment to effective communication. The bold experimentalism with which Einarr Skúlason creates his newly minted Christian kennings in honour of St Óláfr in *Geisli* gives way to a more direct, if no less vivid language, drawing, like other medieval lyric traditions, on conventional European Catholic epithets for Mary:

> Þú ert hreinlífis dygðar dúfa,
> dóttir guðs, og lækning sótta,
> giftu vegr, og geisli lofta,
> gimsteinn brúða og drotning himna. (*Lilja*, st. 89/1–4)[64]

> [You are the dove of the virtue of chastity, daughter of God and healing of sicknesses, path of good fortune and light-beam of the skies, jewel of women and queen of the heavens].

Praising divine figures, narrating their adventures, composing hymns to honour them, explaining the ways in which their stories should be understood were key activities for both Norwegian and Icelandic authors in the pre- and post-conversion north. Poetry, in both eddic and skaldic modes, was regarded as appropriate for addressing the functions and histories of the pagan gods; these modes were repurposed to Christian ends after the Conversion. Skaldic poetry adapted its kenning system, a prominent convention of the mode, in order to forge new epithets for the new religion. Eddic poetry had a more limited role in Christian versifying; as we shall see in Chapter 15, it was adapted to communicate particular kinds of wisdom.

Prose writing meanwhile seems to have begun in response to imported Latin models and rapidly diversified into an extraordinary number of genres. Not all of these are used for Christian or religious purposes – the chronotope of the *fornaldarsaga*, for example, largely excludes the possibility of Christian characters.[65] Nevertheless, the prose genre system in

---

63 Ibid., p. 676.
64 Ibid., p. 662.
65 See, however, Haki Antonsson, *Damnation and Salvation*, pp. 82–95, on two texts that may represent a kind of Christianisation of the genre, *Yngvars saga*

medieval Iceland encompassed not only native equivalents of prominent Christian Latin genres, such as the *visio* (*leiðzla*), the exemplum (*ævintýri*), the sermon and homily, and, above all, the saint's life, along with the mythographical treatise, but also encouraged the inventive and imaginative treatment of every kind of Christian theme, infused within the main saga subgenres: the *Íslendingasögur, konungasögur, samtíðarsögur* and the *þættir*.

---

*víðfǫrla* and *Eiríks saga víðfǫrla*; see also Haki Antonsson, 'Salvation and Early Saga Writing in Iceland: Aspects of the Works of the Þingeyrar Monks and their Associates', *VMS* 8 (2012), 71–140.

# Wisdom
*Brittany Schorn*

Wisdom in Old Norse denotes two things. On the one hand, wisdom describes maxims, proverbs, riddles and the like: abstracted pronouncements about humanity and the world it inhabits that might occur in a range of texts. On the other, wisdom describes a genre of texts that are concerned in whole or large part with the conveyance and context of such wisdom material. The two need to be understood together, like words and the typeface in which they are written, and as a pair the two sides of wisdom encapsulate a particular cultural urge to relate generalised knowledge to particular or collective experience. Wisdom literature in one sense derives from wisdom content, since the former perforce contained reams of the latter, but the relationship between the two was symbiotic. Wisdom as a genre stemmed from what was considered to be valued knowledge – and in turn helped valorise that knowledge, and situate its acquisition, exchange and deployment within a relatable framework. By this means knowledge was arranged and categorised, as well as contextualised with voice and setting.

The way in which wisdom texts encoded information inevitably depended on specific cultural, historical and literary circumstances. Both wisdom and the literature that conveyed it tended to be highly diverse, reflecting shifting tastes in what knowledge mattered and why. These variations can be perceived in a great many medieval and world cultures. In part that is because wisdom – and the desire to record it – is a response to universal social situations, and the inherent human desire to provide a structure for defining reality, knowledge and truth, in a sense doing what the concept of genre does in relation to literary compositions.[1] Another reason for the heterogeneity of wisdom and literature is that it is an analytic category, not an ethnic one, which is to say that it is based on analogy with the textual product of a particular culture and then exported into others. In this instance the base category is ultimately the Biblical books of wisdom.[2] If one takes Biblical wisdom as the pro-

---

1 Amy J. Devitt, 'Generalizing about Genre: New Conceptions of an Old Concept', *College Composition and Communication* 44 (1993), 573–86 and Amy J. Devitt, *Writing Genres* (Carbondale, 2004), pp. 1–32.
2 Brittany Schorn, *Speaker and Authority in Old Norse Wisdom Poetry* (Berlin, 2017), pp. 1–16. On the distinction between 'analytic' and 'ethnic' categories or genres, see Daniel Ben-Amos, 'Analytic Categories and Ethnic Genres', *Folklore Genres*,

totype from which all others diverge, the expression of wisdom in other cultures will inevitably seem highly diverse.

Such is the case in Old Norse. Christian denizens of medieval Scandinavia would have been familiar with Biblical wisdom texts, but they also inherited quite different concepts and materials that modern scholarship collectively brackets together as 'wisdom'. It must be underlined that while taking all of the texts which package this content as a single genre is an artificial exercise, doing so highlights recurring elements of what wisdom meant and how it should be presented. Paradoxically, the coherence of the genre is reflected in the relative ease with which wisdom passages can be identified embedded in more complex genres, from *Íslendingasögur* and *fornaldarsögur* to the prosimetric sequence on Sigurðr's youth in the Codex Regius of the Poetic Edda. This brief survey will consider four major aspects of this body of literature, constructed around the dynamic between wisdom genre and wisdom content. The first looks at the most primal associations of wisdom, exemplified by its deployment in abstracted form in texts that belong to other genres. It establishes what it was that made wisdom, for want of a better word, wise. The main part of the chapter then moves on to look at texts which build on these associations to present quantities of wisdom in a more structured way. This begins with what might be described as the 'traditional' end of the wisdom continuum, the largest group of wisdom-focused texts, which consists of eddic poems relating to gods and heroes of the mythic past. Aspects of these texts are thought to be deeply rooted in the oral literature of the Viking Age, even though its surviving representatives include many which respond more or less overtly to the influence of Christian culture. The next part of the chapter reverses this approach: it considers examples of what might be loosely considered as 'learned' wisdom, in which the primary point of reference is western European literature of the Christian Middle Ages, inspired more directly by Biblical wisdom and its offshoots. What is striking is that one can see cross-contamination between the expectations and associations of these seemingly quite distant forms of wisdom. Traditional eddic verse and learned compositions display similar conventions of content and presentation. It is for this reason that these otherwise quite distinct strands can be put side by side. At its core, wisdom material was remarkably versatile. The reverberating echoes of its characteristic voice and associations connect a varied yet permeable set of literary genres, turning them into a loose whole. This point is developed in the final part of the chapter, in which select case-studies in the terminology and content

---

ed. Daniel Ben-Amos (Austin, 1975), pp. 264–91. For the background of biblical wisdom literature, see James L. Crenshaw, *Old Testament Wisdom: an Introduction*, 3rd edn (Louisville, 2010) and James L. Crenshaw, 'The Wisdom Literature', in *The Hebrew Bible and its Modern Interpreters*, ed. Douglas A. Knight and Gene M. Tucker (Philadelphia, 1985), pp. 369–407.

of wisdom are pursued to illustrate how the meaning of wisdom was continually reformulated in response to cultural change and the innovation of new generic forms.

## Wisdom as Utterance: 'Applied Wisdom'

Wisdom at its most basic in Old Norse was something spoken, and was hence closely tied to simple genres and speech-acts such as the riddle and the proverb. In order for wisdom to be wise, it had to *sound* right according to traditional criteria. In this sense, as a kind of didactic mode instead of a developed genre, it is to be found everywhere, including the most productive prose genres. Digested and contextualised nuggets of wisdom are a key feature of saga style, and can be found in a large number of diverse texts, typically put into the mouths of specific characters.[3]

Applied wisdom is not so detached from more elaborate representatives of the genre as might be supposed. It exemplifies the oral and situational character of Norse wisdom. In a saga context, wisdom tended to work on two levels. Ostensibly it lent weight to acts and opinions, since proverbs or other expressions of wisdom drew their force from an implied sense that they reflected a general, traditional truth: not one person's words, but the consensus of human experience fitted to a specific moment in time. Yet at the same time, the decision to call upon wisdom and put it in the mouth of a particular character at a particular point represented an act of judgement. In genres that eschewed direct comment on the events and personalities of the narrative, wisdom therefore served a valuable function as a way of indirectly expressing opinion. Wisdom passages might have served this role since the oral or written origins of any given saga, though it is also clear from differences between recensions that wisdom content was particularly amenable to addition or adjustment by copyists and editors as they introduced their

---

3   I use John Frow's distinction between a mode detached from particular structural embodiments, and genre (or subgenre) with more specific thematic, rhetorical and formal dimensions: John Frow, *Genre*, 2nd edn (London and New York, 2015), p. 71. An excellent illustration of this can be gleaned from Richard Harris's database of proverbs in the sagas (www.usask.ca/english/icelanders/, consulted 7 January 2019), with Richard Harris, '"Mér þykkir þar heimskum manni at duga, sem þú ert": Paremiological Sub-Categories and the *Íslendingasögur*: Some Applications of the Concordance to the Proverbs and Proverbial Materials in the Old Icelandic Sagas', *Scandinavian-Canadian Studies* 16 (2005–06), 28–54. For further specific examples of how proverbs are deployed in texts, see *idem*, 'The Literary Uses of Proverbs in *Njáls saga*', *Proverbium* 18 (2001), 149–66 and *idem*, 'The Proverbs of *Vatnsdæla saga*, the Sword of Jokull and the Fate of Grettir: Examining an Instance of Conscious Intertextuality in *Grettis saga*', in *The Hero Recovered: Essays in Honor of George Clark*, ed. James Weldon and Robin Waugh (Kalamazoo, 2010), pp. 150–70.

own take on a text. *Gísla saga Súrssonar*, for example, contains a famous proverb, 'ok eru opt kǫld kvenna ráð'.⁴ In all three main versions of the saga this relates to Þórdís Súrsdóttir's shocking revelations to her husband about her brother Gísli's deeds. But it is uttered (with small variations in formulation) by a different character in each version, with subtle yet significant consequences for how one understands the narrative and motivations of the characters.⁵ By raising debate about the world-view of the characters and the applicability of the wisdom they invoke, saga authors also led their audiences to examine the framework of their own expectations about the world and human behaviour.

## 'Traditional' Wisdom

The applied wisdom seen in saga texts – general information spoken for particular purposes – is writ large in texts that are assigned to the loose category of wisdom genre. The particular constellation of thematic, rhetorical and formal features that characterise this genre can be summarised as follows: wisdom is the central theme of a number of texts (or extended parts of larger texts) that set out to provide some kind of *systematic* framework for understanding individual existence and experience. There were many blueprints for how that framework might be constructed, each adhering to its own intellectual architecture; as many as there were ways of understanding the nature of humanity and the limits of its knowledge. For this reason wisdom exists as a genre only as a cluster of different approaches to contextualising and valorising a particular kind of information. These clusters include several kinds of verse as well as prose, and range in tone and setting from the mythic past to Christian contemplation, learned exposition and courtly romance. They can be cut in several ways, and many can themselves be further subdivided on various criteria.

The largest of these clusters in terms of number of representatives consists of eddic poems that situate wisdom debate or exposition in the legendary world of gods and heroes. To call these texts' contents diverse would be an understatement. They run from spells for raising the dead to reflections on the difficulties of chasing reindeer down thawing hillsides. Topics include: observations about and advice for navigating social interactions; properties of all worlds, including what we (but not necessarily medieval audiences) would classify as the natural, the human and the mythological; moral instruction; numinous knowledge (including runes and spells); names for things, places and beings and their characteristics;

4   *Vestfirðinga sǫgur*, ed. Björn K. Þórolfsson and Guðni Jónsson, ÍF 6 (Reykjavík, 1943), *Gísla saga Súrssonar*, ch. 14, p. 61.
5   Emily Lethbridge, '*Gísla saga Súrssonar*: Textual Variation, Editorial Constructions and Critical Interpretations', in *Creating the Medieval Saga: Versions, Variability and Editorial Interpretations of Old Norse Saga Literature*, ed. Judy Quinn and Emily Lethbridge (Odense, 2010), pp. 123–52, at pp. 146–49.

and knowledge of events, past, present and future. The particular combination of these types of wisdom varies by poem, with the probably composite *Hávamál* containing the greatest variety. With a title that signifies simply 'Sayings of the High One' (i.e. Óðinn) and running to 164 stanzas, it has a complicated structure. More than half the poem consists of generalised, decontextualised gnomic observations; these are followed by two short narratives about Óðinn's sexual adventures, and then by another series of wisdom admonitions, this time framed as advice for an otherwise unknown individual named Loddfáfnir. The poem ends with two shorter sections themed around magic, the first an apparent account of Óðinn's quest for runic knowledge, the second a numbered list of spells. All these types of wisdom represent information that is of broad interest and can be briefly encapsulated in universal terms, be it as admonition, observation, personal experience or a list. What bound these miscellaneous contents together was association with Óðinn.[6]

Within this category of 'wisdom' one can also identify further genres or subgenres that often seem more coherent, such as the Odinic wisdom contests and expositions of eddic poetry. These might be represented by free-standing texts as well as discrete episodes within a larger text, such as the various gnomic exchanges of the young Sigurðr poems (the lengthy prosimetric sequence divided and titled in modern editions as *Reginsmál, Fáfnismál* and *Sigrdrífumál*). Such sequences take for granted a certain amount of background knowledge about, for instance, the role of Óðinn and the significance of particular formulaic phrases and rhetorical stances. Thus characterisation of Sigurðr occurs primarily through dialogue and our understanding of his initial successes depends on an expected range of possibilities.[7] The impression of diversity is enhanced by the difficulty of pinning most relevant compositions down in terms of origin and transmission beyond their first manuscript appearance. Whatever historical spectrum there may have been is largely inaccessible. Suspended in a chronological soup, Old Norse eddic wisdom poetry presents a false sense of homogeneity: what we see very probably consists of many generations and layers of literary activity, flattened by a reluctance to divulge details about time and place of composition. This is a widespread feature of Old Norse literature, but is particularly acute in the case of poetic expressions of wisdom, which drew their authority from an inherently conservative aura of antiquity.

Bearing these difficulties in mind, about ten eddic texts can be wholly or in large part categorised as wisdom on the basis of centring around extensive wisdom material. These cut across a number of other formal

---

6 Schorn, *Speaker and Authority*, pp. 61–84.
7 See Carolyne Larrington, *A Store of Common Sense: Gnomic Theme and Style in Old English and Old Icelandic Wisdom Poetry* (Oxford, 1993), pp. 73–96; and Schorn, *Speaker and Authority*, pp. 103–07 with references.

or generic divisions.⁸ Most are cast in *ljóðaháttr*: a metre which lent itself to simple, repetitive syntax as well as other mnemonic strategies, and which furthermore provided an appropriately archaic rhetorical posture for the speakers and the imagined world of the ancient past to which they belonged.⁹ The majority of the relevant poems deal with the exploits of mythical gods and heroes (among them *Hávamál* and *Sigrdrífumál*), though one can add a smaller number of poems that use eddic forms and metres to present wisdom but do so in a Christianised setting, such as *Sólarljóð*.¹⁰ Perhaps more distinctive than the thematic content of Old Norse wisdom was its rhetorical structure. This was the vessel within which the fluid concept of Old Norse wisdom swirled, and which hence served to signal wisdom discourse to audiences across a variety of texts. Such passages could be put into the mouths of giants and gods in eddic verse, or those of men, women or narrators in a range of saga texts; they could also be deployed in didactic literature, and in other contexts. Despite the often pithy quality of Old Norse wisdom, its literary framing repeatedly stressed that it could not stand alone. The display or exchange of wisdom is always situational, with a specified speaker (and it is almost always couched in oral terms) and addressee. Even if only one voice is heard as in *Grímnismál*, the identity of the addressed party is key for establishing the tone and indicating the significance of wisdom, as well as its correct interpretation. The importance of the relationship between speaker and addressee is often underlined in the highly developed narrative frames which are particularly characteristic of the more extended presentations of wisdom. Thus in *Grímnismál* knowledge about the mythological world and its inhabitants has immediate and profound consequences for the Gothic dynasty: the death of a king and the divinely mandated succession of his son. Moreover, the relationship between participants is almost always combative: a worthy source of wisdom is a dangerous, and usually hostile, one. Riddles are hence a good fit rhetorically as well as thematically, as they pit one participant against another, both trying simultaneously to conceal and uncover truth. Contests such as that of *Vafþrúðnismál* provided a natural model for the riddles of Gestumblindi in *Hervarar saga ok Heiðreks*.¹¹

---

8   Alternative categorisations are discussed in Brittany Schorn, 'Eddic Modes and Genres', in *A Handbook to Eddic Poetry*, ed. Carolyne Larrington, Judy Quinn and Brittany Schorn (Cambridge, 2016), pp. 231–51.
9   See further Schorn, 'Eddic Style' in *A Handbook to Eddic Poetry*, pp. 278–82.
10  Schorn, *Speaker and Authority*, pp. 124–33; see further discussion in Chapter 15 in this volume.
11  Hannah Burrows, 'Introduction to sts 48–85, *Heiðreks gátur*' in *Poetry in Fornaldarsögur*, gen. ed. Margaret Clunies Ross, 2 vols, SkP 8 (Turnhout, 2017), II: pp. 406–10, and further Hannah Burrows, 'Wit and Wisdom: The Worldview of the Old Norse-Icelandic Riddles and their Relationship to Eddic Poetry' in *Eddic, Skaldic and Beyond: Poetic Variety in Medieval Iceland and Norway*, ed. Martin

Inherent in these contests is a certain tension. The competitive quality of knowledge was only partially a matter of how much information each party possessed; on a deeper level, combatants had to have the wit and discernment needed to use it effectively. These qualities were closely intertwined. Thus a list of *heiti* for *vit* (wisdom) in Snorri Sturluson's *Skáldskaparmál* includes, among other nouns, *minni*, *ráð* and *skilning*:[12] these terms express the concepts of memory, counsel and discernment. They exemplify a recurring concern with how information was retained, processed and expressed in order to be classed as wisdom. For Snorri, therefore, wisdom collapsed together information and knowledge, but also the judgement needed to utilise that information effectively, and the ability to express it. This complex process was best accomplished through brevity. The expression of wisdom tended towards short, simple declarative sentences with repetitive syntax that presented content as self-evident and universal, anticipating potential value in contexts beyond that of its coinage and rendering the words memorable and amenable to listing. Wisdom was, more often than not, expressed impersonally, presenting its truth value as self-evident and irrefutable. The verb too indicated observation of the world as it is (or should be), usually with either a simple present tense or *skal*, and conditional phrases take the place of imperatives.[13] These features come together in *Hávamál* st. 35, which presses its argument by juxtaposing two maxims making the same essential point:

> Ganga skal, skala gestr vera
> ey í einum stað;
> ljúfr verðr leiðr, ef lengi sitr
> annars fletjum á.[14]

> [A man must go, he must not remain a guest always in one place; the loved man is loathed if he sits too long in someone's hall.]

This is certainly memorable advice, as the poetic form is exploited to highlight the operative words with alliteration, and parallel syntax expresses the contrasting possibilities. It also exemplifies the most elusive of Snorri's criteria, *skilning*: the *gestr* is reliant on his own judgement to know when he has outstayed his welcome.

---

Chase (New York, 2014), pp. 114–35.
12 Snorri Sturluson, *Skáldskaparmál*, ch. 109 (*Snorri Sturluson, Edda: Skáldskaparmál*, ed. Anthony Faulkes, 2 vols. (London, 2005), p. 109).
13 See further Larrington, *A Store of Common Sense*, pp. 7–9.
14 *Eddukvæði*, ed. Jónas Kristjánsson and Vésteinn Ólason, 2 vols (Reykjavík, 2014), I: p. 328; *The Poetic Edda*, trans. Carolyne Larrington, 2nd edn (Oxford, 2014), p. 17). All further references to the *Poetic Edda* will be to this edition and translation. *Skal* in the first line is supplied by all editors, as Jónas Kristjánsson and Vésteinn Ólason note, without controversy.

It was when confronting the gulf between wisdom as knowledge and wisdom as discernment that contests became most lethally unequal and competitive. Eddic wisdom frequently played on this crux, sometimes turning it into a narrative or rhetorical device. Would wisdom actually do its speakers or listeners any good? Or, to put it differently, would the use of wisdom really show anyone to be wise? In *Vafþrúðnismál*, for example, the giant Vafþrúðnir fails to realise that he has got himself into a wisdom contest with Óðinn until it is too late: his judgement lets him down.[15] The need for discernment in the exploitation of wisdom is also one of the central messages of *Hávamál*. It throws vast amounts of decontextualised wisdom at the audience, but reminds them with the refrain used repeatedly in the so-called *Loddfáfnismál* portion of the poem that:

> Ráðumk þér, Loddfáfnir, at þú ráð nemir,
>   njóta mundu ef þú nemr,
> þér munu góð ef þú getr. (*Háv* sts 112 etc.)
>
> [I advise you, Loddfafnir, to take this advice, it will be useful if you learn it, do you good, if you have it.]

In principle, individuals who identified relevant guidance from their inner bank of wisdom could learn from it, like the enigmatic Loddfáfnir, and encode that information in a manner that would allow others – including audiences – to do the same. But one had to be able to sift such cases from the background noise, and for this very reason wisdom had the potential to distance and mislead as well as enlighten. It was the art of relating particular situations to general precepts in a way that would be of practical, intellectual or moral benefit. As both a thing and a quality, eddic wisdom could be conceived of as a commodity to be hoarded, sought after and fought over. Deception hence abounds in such texts, reflecting the power of language to mislead as easily as edify. This frequent play on the relationship between universal wisdom and the dangers of its specific deployment meant that Óðinn – the cunning, inscrutable and often disguised god – was a particularly appropriate interlocutor in wisdom contexts and by far the most frequently recurring one. The exceptions even seem to require this background knowledge about the conventions of the genre to achieve their full force in subverting expectations. Thus a presumptuous dwarf calls himself All-wise in *Alvíssmál*, a valkyrie takes over patronage of the hero in *Sigrdrífumál* and the wise words of the *heiðinn maðr* (heathen man) of *Hugsvinnsmál* are to the moral benefit of all who hear them.[16] Ultimately the authority of wisdom is produced by the kind of voices that are imagined as speaking it. And what all speakers of wisdom have in common is a cer-

---

15 Schorn, *Speaker and Authority*, pp. 87–92.
16 *Hugsvinnsmál* st 1, ed. and trans. Tarrin Wills and Stephanie Gropper, in *Poetry on Christian Subjects*, ed. Clunies Ross, 2 vols, *SkP* 7 (Turnhout, 2007), I: p. 361.

tain distance from their audience: where speakers are specified, they are figures from a distant past, and when not given a name they represent a generalised voice of common knowledge so generic that its sources are unknowable and its truth value indisputable. Proverbial utterance is by definition repeated, even if one has to create that repetition oneself.

## 'Learned' Wisdom

Extended presentations of wisdom were not exclusively confined to eddic verse. A range of native and foreign generic models was available for the communication of wisdom in Old Norse, and their selection and combination indicated the authority of their content to audiences. One might compare the idiosyncratic skaldic poem *Málsháttakvæði*, in which proverbs are used to construct a sort of satire of courtly love.[17] Other kinds of parallel can be drawn with prose encyclopedic texts. These sought to package a different kind of knowledge drawn form western European learned tradition. Thus the *Elucidarius*, an elementary textbook of Christian theology written in the eleventh century and translated into Norse before about 1200, used an oral, dialogic form of exposition that harked back to 'traditional' wisdom.[18] Another text translated into Norse around the same time was the *Physiologus*, which offered pithy moral judgements based on allegorical interpretation of creatures and other natural phenomena.[19] Many of the wisdom elements in the Norse were supplements introduced during a comparatively loose translation process; thus, for example, *Physiologus A* concludes its description of the onocentaur with the statement that 'Réttor skal góðr maðr of all hluti ávalt, hvárt sem er auðigri eða snauðr' (good men, both rich and poor, must always be sincere) – a maxim which is not found in the Latin, but expands on the scriptural quotations given in support of the onocentaur's proclivity to falsehood (2 Tim 3:5 and Ps. 48:21), which are themselves only paraphrased in the Norse.[20]

---

17 Roberta Frank, *Sex, Lies and Málsháttakvæði: An Old Norse Poem from Medieval Orkney* (Nottingham, 2004) and Roberta Frank, 'Introduction to *Málsháttakvæði*', in *Poetry from Treatises on Poetics*, gen. ed. Kari Ellen Gade and Edith Marold, SkP 3 (Turnhout, 2017), II: pp. 1213–15.
18 *The Old Norse Elucidarius: Original Text and English Translation*, ed. Evelyn Scherabon Firchow (Woodbridge, 1992).
19 The text – including its fascinating illustrations in both surviving fragments – is best consulted in the collection of facsimiles and discussions assembled in *Romanske stenarbejder* 2 (1984). See also Dora Faraci, 'The *Gleða* Chapter in the Old Icelandic *Physiologus*', *Opuscula* 9 (1991), 108–26.
20 *The Icelandic Physiologus*, ed. Halldór Hermansson (Ithaca, 1938), p. 17, with discussion and translation in Vittoria Dolcetti Corazza, 'Crossing Paths in the Middle Ages: The *Physiologus* in Iceland', in *The Garden of Crossing Paths: the Manipulation and Rewriting of Medieval Texts*, ed. Marina Buzzoni and Massimiliano Bampi (Venice, 2007), pp. 225–48, at pp. 231–36.

The Old Norse *Physiologus* translations gave a mainstream European view of the natural world a new twist, and in the process expanded on the proverbial dimension of its didactic message. An even more elaborate reconstruction of learned European wisdom is presented in the prose text *Konungs skuggsjá* (King's Mirror). Unique in many ways, this educational dialogue on moral and political themes, written for the benefit of the king of Norway's son, offers a quite different take on wisdom; one which draws more on developments in western European literature than on Scandinavian literary tradition, and relies on royal associations for authority. Yet it still cleaved to some of the associations of wisdom seen elsewhere in Old Norse literature.

With content sanctioned by the highest secular and divine authorities, *Konungs skuggsjá* revolves around the theme of wisdom, but draws on literary conventions associated with 'mirrors of princes'.[21] When compared analytically with biblical wisdom literature, this text comes theoretically from the same stable as the traditional poetry that has been focused on so far, albeit by a very different route, and *Konungs skuggsjá* comprehends something rather different in its notion of wisdom. Beyond similar concerns with mapping the world and its qualities – though the subject in this case is real-world places that traders might visit – *Konungs skuggsjá* concerns itself largely with correct behaviour in moral and courtly terms. It is far more systematic in its conception and organisation than any of the wisdom poetry and formally, of course, it is fundamentally different as a prose text. The style too bears little resemblance to the pithy maxims of *ljóðaháttr*: figurative language abounds in *Konungs skuggsjá*, and complex learned allegory is sustained at length, for example, in the speech of personified wisdom (*speki*). In general *Konungs skuggsjá* lies much closer to instructive texts from the rest of medieval Europe, especially *specula principis* aimed at the edification of kings or prospective kings (though these too were a varied crop).[22]

Like the eddic wisdom poems discussed above, *Konungs skuggsjá* presents a scene of oral instruction, recollected from the memory of the narrator and stresses the importance of learning from the information collected and mediated.[23] Rhetorically there is a marked difference from eddic wisdom in the set-up of *Konungs skuggsjá*'s dialogue between a son and his *vitr ok góðviljaðr* (wise and kind) father who gives *ástsemðar ráð* (loving advice), and their interplay is better explained by learned peda-

21 Karl G. Johansson and Elise Kleivane, '*Konungs skuggsjá* and the Interplay between Universal and Particular', in *Speculum septentrionale: Konungs skuggsjá and the European Encyclopedia of the Middle Ages*, ed. Karl G. Johansson and Elise Kleivane (Oslo, 2018), pp. 9–34.
22 Both the heterogeneity of the genre as a whole and the absence of a direct model for *Konungs skuggsjá* should be stressed, e.g. Johansson and Kleivane, '*Konungs skuggsjá*', pp. 16–19.
23 Ibid., pp. 14–15.

gogical methods.²⁴ Scenes of instruction in traditional Old Norse wisdom literature are hardly ever straightforwardly benevolent; power struggles between imperfect human or mythological participants and some element of deception are the more usual model.²⁵ The best Norse parallel to the scene of instruction in *Konungs skuggsjá* is *Hugsvinnsmál*, which goes much further in adapting other aspects of its Latin source material to native conventions.²⁶ This poem is based on the well-known *Disticha Catonis*, and Jens Eike Schnall has argued that *Konungs skuggsjá* owes much to that text.²⁷ Yet, as with *Hugsvinnsmál* and the *Disticha*, Johansson and Kleivane have noted that in *Konungs skuggsjá* 'the speculum genre is not simply translated into Norse, it is appropriated and presented as an indigenous genre'.²⁸

## Wisdom and its Variation in Practice

A series of different perspectives on wisdom have been identified, broadly categorised as abstracted, traditional and learned. All three presented broadly similar material, and did so in a manner that laid claim to ingrained, long-established authority, often in fact using the same rhetorical and verbal tools. The varied perspectives of these subgenres of wisdom can be understood most effectively by pursuing how select terms were redeployed by each – specifically, words for wisdom itself. What one sees is that even though wisdom kept the same names, it took on new baggage as it travelled. References to wisdom provide one barometer for how valued knowledge was imbued with new significance. In other words, while wisdom literature consisted of often highly conservative wisdom content, rendered timeless through use of style and syntax, that content's meaning was subtly reimagined in new generic contexts. Wisdom, whatever one did with it, was not as monumental as its conservative expression implied.

---

24  *Konungs skuggsjá*, ed. Ludvig Holm-Olsen (Oslo,1945), ch. I–II; *The King's Mirror (Speculum Regale- Konungs skuggsjá)*, trans. Laurence M. Larson (New York, 1917), pp. 73 and 78. All further references to *Konungs skuggsjá* will be to this edition and translation. See recently e.g. Stefka Eriksen 'Pedagogy and Attitudes towards Knowledge in the *King's Mirror*', *Viator*, 45:3 (2014), 143–68 and Alessia Bauer, 'Encyclopedic Tendencies and the Medieval Educational Programme: The Merchant's Chapter of *Konungs skuggsjá*', in *Speculum septentrionale*, ed. Johansson and Kleivane, pp. 222–36.

25  This is not to say that inequalities of power were not at issue in the text: Alessia Bauer argues that 'this text seems to suggest that the possibility of participating respectively in *mannvit* "understanding, wit" or *speki* "wisdom" was intimately related to the social order and the position a subject assumed in it', 'Encyclopedic Tendencies', pp. 217–19.

26  Schorn, *Speaker and Authority*, pp. 133–42.

27  Jens Eike Schnall, '*Nunc te, fili carissime, docebo* — Anfang und Aufbau der *Konungs skuggsjá*', in *Speculum regale: der Altnorwegische Königsspiegel (Konungs skuggsjá) in der Europäischen Tradition*, ed. Jens Eike Schnall and Rudolf Simek (Vienna, 2000), pp. 63–89.

28  Johansson and Kleivane, '*Konungs skuggsjá*', pp. 10 and 19.

The Old Norse language had a remarkably rich vocabulary for talking about wisdom; here, discussion will focus on two closely related compound nouns that belong to the semantic field of wisdom formed on the common noun *vit*: *mannvit* or *manvit* (original first elements *maðr* 'man' and *munr* 'mind' appear to have effectively fallen together). A further variant *mannsvit* is constructed on the genitive. Dictionaries and glossaries take varying approaches to whether these words represent distinct lexemes and which instances are to be identified with which. *Vit* is a neuter noun formed on a common Germanic root, cognate with, for instance, Old High German *giwiz* 'knowledge'.[29] It derives from the preterite-present verb 'to know'. This sense comes from a perfective use 'to have seen' (from the root *\*ueid*) of an Indo-European verb 'to see'.[30] It is indeed possible to detect a deep-seated sense that seeing in a way was knowing, and therefore that this type of wisdom was the experiential product of an individual's faculties. *Vit* is attested in a variety of senses relating to innate intelligence, and can be translated as 'consciousness', 'sense', 'wit', 'understanding', 'reason' or similar. In the case of *mannsvit*, the first element modifies this meaning in a straightforward and transparent way similar to other *mann-* compounds: the *vit* that defines humanity. The word was often understood more or less straightforwardly along such lines in texts from diverse genres. Thus in *Brennu-Njáls saga*, Gunnarr is promised that the dog Sámr will be just as valuable as any human companion and has the quality of human intelligence, 'þat fylgir ok at hann hefir mannsvit'.[31] Óláfr cites as evidence of this the dog's unerring ability to separate friend from foe by reading facial expressions. Similarly in *Strengleikar*, the Old Norse adaptation of the *Lais* of Marie de France, the king recognises Bisclaret's essential humanity despite his wolfish form: 'Þetta kvikvendi hefir mannz vit' (that animal has a man's intelligence; French *sen d'ume*).[32] *Vit* comes across as a uniquely human capacity, a facet of sentience.

*Mannvit* is the form attested more frequently, and is especially common in eddic poetry where it occurs with the generalised sense 'understanding, intelligence, reason'. Again, the reference is to the innate intelligence of sentient beings, but the implicit contrast between humanity and other forms of life is missing in such texts. It is a quality of human and

---

29 Vladimir Orel, *A Handbook of Germanic Etymology* (Leiden, 2003), s.v. *\*witan*; see further Elmar Seebold, *Vergleichendes und etymologisches Wörterbuch der germanischen starken Verben*, Janua Linguarum, series practica, 85 (The Hague and Paris, 1970), s.v. *wait*.
30 Guus Kroonen, *Etymological Dictionary of Proto-Germanic* (Leiden, 2013), s.v. *\*witan*.
31 *Brennu-Njáls saga*, ed. Einar Ól. Sveinsson ÍF 12 (Reykjavík, 1954), ch. 70, p. 173.
32 *Strengleikar* IV: *Bisclarets lioð*, ch. 6, in *Strengleikar: An Old Norse Translation of Twenty-One Old French Lais*, ed. Robert Cook and Mattias Tveitane (Oslo, 1979), p. 90; cf. Marie de France, *Lais: Bisclavret*, l. 154 (*Die Lais der Marie de France*, ed. Karl Warnke and Reinhold Köhler, 3rd edn (Halle, 1925), p. 80).

mythological beings alike, and when it is remarked on, it is in the context of individuals who possess it to a particularly high degree. Thus *Hávamál*'s refrain 'Byrði betri berrat maðr brautu at, enn sé man mikit' (No better burden a man bears on the road than a store of common sense) refers to the quality necessary to apply one's wit and discernment to potentially hazardous social situations, and to Guðrún's admirable, but futile, ability to anticipate the destructive consequences of the men's actions in *Atlamál*:

> Horsk var húsfreyja, hugði at manviti,
> lag heyrði hon orða, hvat þeir á laun mæltu. (*Am* st. 3)
>
> [The lady of the house was clever; she used her common sense, she heard what they were saying, though they spoke in secret.]

Like life itself, wisdom is ultimately a gift from the gods and in particular Óðinn.

> Gefr hann sigr sumum, enn sumum aura
> mælsku mǫrgum ok manvit firum. (*Hyndl* st. 3)
>
> [He gives victory to some, to some riches, eloquence to many, and common sense to the living.]

Though a universal quality of personhood, the distribution of wisdom is uneven; and while it can be given, valued and applied, there is no mention of it being cultivated as such. La Farge and Tucker's gloss 'mother wit, native intelligence, common sense, good sense, worldly wisdom' is representative of how most commentators have taken *mannvit* in an eddic context.[33] The Cleasby-Vigfusson dictionary goes further, defining *mannvit* specifically 'as opposed to *bók-vit*'.[34] This is not a distinction that is ever made explicitly in texts though (even if one allows for synonyms like *bók-nám*). On the contrary, *Konungs skuggsjá* argues that 'því at þar er raunar at allra annarra er vit minna en þeirra er af bokum taka manvit' (For it is clear that those who gain knowledge from books have keener wits than others).[35] In a Christian context *manvit* might even become a limitation: human wit, to be contrasted with divine omniscience. The poem *Lilja* uses *manvit* in this way in the course of its reflections on Christian salvation, so as to make a point about human limitations in the face of divine mysteries:

> Finn eg, alt að manvit manna
> mæðiz, þegar er um skal ræða

---

33 Beatrice La Farge and John Tucker, *Glossary to the Poetic Edda, Based on Hans Kuhn's Kurzes Wörterbuch* (Heidelberg, 1992), s.v. *mannvit*.
34 Richard Cleasby and Guðbrandur Vigfússon, *An Icelandic-English Dictionary*, 2nd ed. (Oxford, 1957), s.v. *mannvit*.
35 *Konungs skuggsjá*, ed. Holm-Olsen, ch. III, pp. 4–5; trans. Larson, p. 81. My normalisation.

máttrinn þinn, inn mikli drottinn;
meiri er hann en gjörvalt annað. (*Lil* st. 38)

[I find that all the understanding of men becomes exhausted as soon as your might shall be spoken about, great Lord.][36]

As well as facilitating the rhyme and alliteration, the modification of *manvit* with *manna* – 'the *human* wit of *humans*' – highlights the first element of the compound and emphasises the gulf between the human and the divine. This is the exact opposite of Sámr the wonder-dog: human ability is simply not able to comprehend heavenly mysteries. Yet *manvit* still carried weight. A counter example is Arnórr jarlaskáld's depiction of St Michael as *mannvitsfróðr*, (translated as 'wise with discernment') as he sits in judgement on men's deeds, just as God himself does.[37] Elsewhere in skaldic poetry, *manvit* is a secular virtue.[38]

Its meaning was further renegotiated by the author of *Konungs skuggsjá*. Jens Eike Schnall, who has offered the most thorough analysis of the text's didactic philosophy and strategies, notes that the concept of *manvit* in the text corresponds roughly to the cardinal virtue *prudentia*, and is the required foundation for the acquisition of *siðgœði* (good manners) and *hœverska* (courtly bearing).[39] Comparing *Katrínar saga* and the bilingual king's prayer in *Konungs skuggsjá*, he concludes that *manvit* is defined in particular by *skilning* (discernment), which is associated with Latin *intellectus, intelligentia* and *discretio*.[40] This maintains the sense of worldly wisdom, as opposed to *sapientia*, but, significantly, the possibility of instruction in *manvit* is introduced. Such instruction requires more complex strategies of exemplification than the simple listing of rules one encounters in the likes of *Hávamál*: only a broad training in encyclopedic knowledge, memory and eloquence can provide a basis for it.

The capacity to learn is repeatedly said to be a God-given (and limited) ability which individuals are responsible for cultivating and acting on. The portions of wisdom given out to men are varied and

er sá auðr svá sem hann er elskaðr til. Sá er mjök vill elska þenna auð ok örliga veita þá hlýtr hann mykit af. Því at þessi auðæfi hafa þá nát-

---

36 *Lilja*, ed. and trans. Martin Chase, in *Poetry on Christian Subjects*, gen. ed. Margaret Clunies-Ross, 2 vols. *SkP* 7 (Turnhout, 2007), II, pp. 607–08.
37 Arnórr jarlaskáld Þórðarson, 'Fragment 1', ed. and trans. Diana Whaley, in *Poetry from Treatises on Poetics*, gen. ed. Gade and Marold, *SkP* 3, I: p. 3.
38 E.g. Markús Skeggjason's praise of the various traditional martial and intellectual accomplishments of King Eiríkr Sveinsson of Denmark in *Eiríksdrápa* st. 7 alongside his particular virtues as a Christian ruler, *Eiríksdrápa*, ed. and trans. Jayne Carroll, in *Poetry from the Kings' Sagas*, gen. ed. Kari E. Gade, *SkP* 2 (Turnhout, 2009), p. 439.
39 Jens Eike Schnall, *Didaktische Absichten und Vermittlungsstrategien im altnorwegischen »Konigsspiegel«* (Konungs skuggsjá) (Göttingen, 2000).
40 *Ibid*, pp. 65–77.

> túru at þau dragask þeim mest til handa, er mest elskar þau ok þeirra neytir með mestum örleik ... ok sá er eignask vill þessi auðæfi þá skal hann þat upphaf at hafa at hræðask almáttkun guð ok elska hann um fram hvetvetna.
>
> [these riches have their value according to how they are loved. He who is sure to appreciate this wealth and share it freely receives a large amount; for the nature of this possession is such that it is most attracted to him who loves it most and uses it most liberally ... But he who wishes to secure this wealth must begin in this way: he must fear Almighty God and love Him above all things.][41]

Each person who wishes to be wise must actively acquire wisdom through a combination of seeking out appropriate sources and applying logic to new information. Thus the Father helps his son make the transition from knowledge to understanding:

> Þat má ek vel gera eptir því sem ek hefi heyrt or fróðra manna munni, ok mér þykki likast vera eptir því viti sem guð hefir mér gefit.
>
> [I can indeed give such an explanation, just as I have heard it from the lips of well-informed men, and as seems most reasonable according to the insight that God has given me.][42]

Andrew Hamer has argued the text in fact is most successful at speaking to the broad audience for which the *Prologue* indicates it was intended when viewed as an exemplum for the correct process of wisdom acquisition in the face of the potential hazards posed by intellectual ambition (in contrast to the actual content of much of what follows).[43]

*Konungs skuggsjá* brought something new to the experiential understanding of wisdom: the idea that one must apply oneself specifically to virtue in order to become wise. Ultimately what we find in *Konungs skuggsjá* is not an alternative conception of wisdom but rather an expanded one. By electing to write in the vernacular, the author necessarily had to mediate between the Norse vocabulary and trappings of wisdom on one side, and an alternative literary form on the other. This means that the same concepts of wisdom can be found in *Konungs skuggsjá* as *Hávamál* and other 'classic' wisdom poems, despite differences in how each understood the origin and significance of those concepts.

The shifting connotations of *manvit* illustrate very well that the idea of wisdom in Old Norse had a recognisable semantic core. This sat along-

---

41 *Konungs skuggsjá*, ed. Holm-Olsen, ch. XL, p. 65; trans. Larson, p. 230.
42 *Ibid.*, ch. V, p. 7; trans. Larson, p. 87.
43 Andrew Hamer, 'Searching for Wisdom: The King's Mirror', in *Speculum regale*, ed. Schnall and Simek, pp. 47–62.

side common syntactic elements such as a taste for depersonalisation, and deeply entrenched formal associations, among them the idea that wisdom was something that should be spoken, with an utterer and a listener. This selection of simple central features made wisdom highly elastic in application. It could be embedded in texts of many kinds, and in a number of generic categories of more systemic wisdom literature. Even though the grouping of all these texts together under a single heading is an artificial, analytical exercise, and there is no clear sense that they were ever thought of as a whole, they nonetheless shared common ground. Wisdom as content bled into wisdom as theme. By putting these texts side by side from the perspective of genre, we see how, in a way, wisdom gains interest from its awkwardness. Medieval Scandinavian authors wrestled with some of the same problems as modern scholars, in that they were heirs to multiple different traditions – native, biblical and others – which all had a claim to broadly similar content, and which all provided different ways to valorise that information. Their innovative and varied approaches to the generic affiliations of wisdom continually interrogated and reinvented traditional material and hence kept it vital and relevant across the centuries.

# III
# GENRE IN FOCUS

# Skaldic Poetry – A Case Study:
The Poetry of Torf-Einarr Rǫgnvaldsson of Orkney

*Erin Michelle Goeres*

A variety of genres are expressed in the skaldic mode, including praise-poetry, love-poetry, hagiography, mockery and slander, travelogue, and political commentary. One of the most popular genres, however, is verse that describes armed conflict, which we might term 'battle-poetry'. As Norman Ingham observes, genre reflects the interactions between literature and the society in which it is produced, and the sheer quantity of skaldic poetry about armed conflict must be due in large part to the courtly context in which so much of it originated: particularly during the early medieval period, skaldic verse was primarily composed by and for a warrior elite.[1] Poetry about armed conflict offered a means through which to praise rulers, castigate enemies, and emphasise the shared values and experiences of the warrior community.[2] Indeed, the very ubiquity of battle-stanzas in the skaldic corpus can make the genre seem somewhat amorphous. Descriptions of armed conflict appear in many of the generic contexts listed above: love-poetry, for example, may describe a warrior's prowess as a means of impressing a woman; poetic slander may describe a man's defeat in battle or his failure to engage in conflict at all. Battle-poetry is particularly closely connected to praise-poetry, as many Viking-Age rulers are eulogised for their fighting abilities, and the line between these two genres is often blurred. This does not mean, however, that the concept of 'battle-poetry' as a genre should be discarded; it is, rather, an illustration of Kevin Whetter's argument that 'what distinguishes a genre is not the presence of certain elements but the emphasis and significance given to each of them'.[3] Battle-poetry is, in essence, poetry in which the description of armed conflict is of primary importance; battle-poetry in

---

1   Norman W. Ingham, 'Genre-Theory and Old Russian Literature', *The Slavic and East European Journal* 31.2 (1987), 234–45, at p. 244.
2   A good overview of skaldic verse is given by Margaret Clunies Ross et al. in the 'General Introduction' to *Poetry from the Kings' Sagas 1: From Mythical Times to c. 1035*, gen ed. Diana Whaley, 2 vols, SkP 1 (Turnhout, 2012), pp. xiii–xciii. On the social function of skaldic verse, see Erin Michelle Goeres, *The Poetics of Commemoration: Skaldic Verse and Social Memory, c. 890–1070* (Oxford, 2016), pp. 1–17.
3   Kevin Whetter, *Understanding Genre and Medieval Romance* (Aldershot and Burlington, 2008), p. 20.

the skaldic mode also tends to incorporate a series of related features that further signal its generic identity.[4] This chapter will discuss the genre of battle-poetry as manifested in five stanzas attributed to the early skaldic poet Torf-Einarr Rǫgnvaldsson, earl of Orkney. These stanzas are in many ways typical of the genre of skaldic battle-poetry, but they also exemplify the difficulties of delineating that genre, particularly when the stanzas are considered in the context of the later prose sagas in which they are now preserved.

The story of Torf-Einarr is told in both *Orkneyinga saga* and in Snorri Sturluson's compendium of the Norwegian kings, *Heimskringla*; a shorter version also appears in the anonymous kings' saga *Fagrskinna*.[5] Differences between the three sagas will be discussed in more detail below, but all three agree that the verses centre on the vengeance taken by Torf-Einarr on Hálfdan háleggr, son of King Haraldr hárfagri of Norway, for the killing of Einarr's father, Rǫgnvaldr, earl of Mœrr. Set during the early tenth century, the story takes place against the tumultuous backdrop of King Haraldr's efforts to extend royal control over the entire kingdom, as well as early attempts at Scandinavian expansion into the North Atlantic islands. As *Orkneyinga saga* relates, however, the Scottish islands are claimed by marauding vikings as a base from which to attack Norway, and Haraldr soon leads an expedition west to subdue them. On this expedition Rǫgnvaldr's eldest son, Ívarr, is killed, and the king grants Rǫgnvaldr rule over Orkney and Shetland in compensation. Rǫgnvaldr in turn appoints first his brother, then his brother's son, and finally his own son Hallaðr to govern the islands, but none lasts for long. Hallaðr finally tires of his inability to defend his territory against the vikings and choses instead to give up the title of earl and return to Norway. As the saga author wryly notes, 'þótti hans ferð in hæðiligsta' (his journey was thought to be most ridiculous).[6]

Enraged by his son's failure, Rǫgnvaldr summons his remaining offspring to decide who should take over the earldom. Einarr, the youngest of Rǫgnvaldr's illegitimate sons, volunteers; although dismissed by his father as 'þrælborinn' (descended from slaves), Einarr becomes earl of Orkney, eventually driving the vikings from the islands.[7] His nickname is

---

4 Cf. Whetter's discussion of generic features and the many examples given there (*Understanding Genre*, pp. 20–21).
5 In the prose context, the stanzas are edited as part of the Íslenzk fornrit series: Finnbogi Guðmundsson, ed. *Orkneyinga saga*, ÍF 34 (Reykjavik, 1965), pp. 12–16; Bjarni Aðalbjarnarson, ed., *Heimskringla*, vol. 1, ÍF 26 (Reykjavik, 1941), pp. 131–34; and Bjarni Einarsson, ed., *Ágrip af Nóregskonunga sǫgum. Fagrskinna – Nóregs konunga tal*, ÍF 29 (Reykjavik, 1985), pp. 291–93.
6 *Orkneyinga saga*, ed. Finnbogi Guðmundsson, p. 10.
7 *Ibid.*, p. 11. In contrast to Einarr's rather folkloric status as the youngest of three in *Orkneyinga saga*, Snorri identifies Einarr as the second-born of three illegitimate brothers, all of whom are older than Rǫgnvaldr's three legitimate sons (*Heimskringla*, I, ed. Bjarni Aðalbjarnarson, p. 123).

explained in both *Orkneyinga saga* and *Heimskringla* as deriving from his idea to burn peat (*torf*) rather than firewood in the scarcely forested islands. The two sagas are also alike in describing him in distinctly Odinic tones, foreshadowing his poetic ability: 'Einarr var mikill maðr ok ljótr, einsýnn ok þó manna skyggnstr' (Einarr was a tall man and ugly, one-eyed and yet the most sharp-sighted of men).[8] Unsurprisingly, Einarr becomes the most successful of Rǫgnvaldr's offspring and, despite the frosty relationship between father and son, it is he who avenges Rǫgnvaldr's death when the earl of Mœrr is killed by two of the sons of King Haraldr, Hálfdan háleggr and his brother Guðrøðr. Hálfdan flees to Orkney; after briefly retreating to the Scottish mainland, Einarr defeats Hálfdan in battle and executes him through the gruesome – and no doubt highly sensationalised – practice of blood-eagling: the prince's ribs are cut along the spine and the lungs pulled outside his body.[9] Five skaldic stanzas are attributed to Torf-Einarr, and all are associated with this victory over, and killing of, Hálfdan háleggr.

The third of theses stanzas (following their order in *Orkneyinga saga*) exemplifies many of the characteristics associated both with the skaldic mode in general and the genre of battle-poetry in particular:

> Ey munk glaðr, síz geirar
> – gótts vinna þrek manni –
> bǫðfíkinna bragna
> bitu þengils son ungan.
> Þeygi dylk, nema þykki
> – þar fló grár at sǫrum
> hræva nagr of holma –
> hól undvala gœli.[10]

---

8 *Orkneyinga saga*, ed. Finnbogi Guðmundsson, p. 11; see also *Heimskringla*, I, ed. Bjarni Aðalbjarnarson, p. 129. Óðinn, the god of both poetry and battle, was famously one-eyed, having given one of his eyes in exchange for a drink of Mimir's well, a source of wisdom. See Snorri Sturluson's account in *Edda: Prologue and Gylfaginning*, ed. Anthony Faulkes (London, 2005), p. 17. Einarr's appearance is typical of many skalds in the Old Norse-Icelandic corpus; see further Margaret Clunies Ross, 'The Art of Poetry and the Figure of the Poet in *Egils saga*', in *Sagas of the Icelanders: A Book of Essays*, ed. John Tucker (New York, 1989), pp. 126–45.

9 This discussion looks mainly at the first stanza of Sigvatr Þórðarson's Knútsdrápa; see Roberta Frank, 'Viking Atrocity and Skaldic Verse: The Rite of the Blood-Eagle', *English Historical Review* 99:391 (1984), 332–43. See also the discussion prompted by this article between Bjarni Einarsson and Frank; Bjarni Einarsson, 'De Normannorum atrocitate, or on the Execution of Royalty by the Aquiline Method', *SBVS* (1986), 79–82; Roberta Frank, 'The Blood-Eagle Again', SBVS (1988), 287–9; Bjarni Einarsson, 'The Blood-Eagle Once more: Two Notes. A. Blóðörn: An Observation on the Ornithological Aspect', SBVS 23 (1990), 80–1; and Roberta Frank, 'The Blood-Eagle Once more: Two Notes. B. Ornithology and the Interpretation of Skaldic Verse', SBVS 23 (1990), 81–3.

10 The stanzas are edited by Russell Poole in *Poetry from the Kings' Sagas*, ed. Whaley, 1: pp. 129–38, largely drawing on his work in *Viking Poems on War and Peace: A*

[I will always be glad, since the spears of the battle-eager men – it is good for a man to accomplish a courageous deed – pierced the young son of the prince. I do not deny that it seems – the grey bird of corpses [> CARRION BIRD > EAGLE or RAVEN] flew there, away from the wounded, over the islands – like bragging to the comforter of the wound-falcons [> WARRIOR, i.e. King Haraldr]].

This stanza is a gleeful boast about Torf-Einarr's bloody revenge in which the focus is firmly on the speaker and the accomplishment of his heroic deed. His victim, Hálfdan, is nameless, identified only by his rank as the son of the king (*sonr þengils*) and dismissively described as *ungr* (young); he is no match for Einarr or for the battle-eager men (*boðfíknir bragnar*) who comprise Einarr's troops. The poet makes deft use of the two-part structure of the skaldic stanza: the two four-line sections, known as *helmingar* (halves), play off each other to emphasise Einarr's triumph and his enemy's defeat in the conflict. That is, both begin with a deceptively understated pronouncement in the first person: *Ey munk glaðr* (I will always be glad) and *Þeygi dylk* (I do not deny [that it seems like bragging]). Litotes is characteristic of much skaldic verse, but in this stanza Einarr's seeming modesty is mere pretence, serving to emphasise his military victory over the prince. The young earl himself is the subject of both main verbs, a structure that reminds his audience of the central role he has played in Hálfdan's death: Einarr asserts his agency both as the man who led the killing and as the poet who memorialises that killing in verse. As is also common in the skaldic corpus, both *helmingar* are structured in an envelope pattern in which an intercalary clause – a phrase inserted into the main sentence – interrupts the flow of the verse. In battle-poetry, this structure allows the poet to play with his audience, temporarily withholding crucial information about the conflict described. In this stanza, the identity of the person who has borne the brunt of Einarr's actions is delayed until the end of each half-stanza. That is, in the first *helmingr*, the reason for the poet's glee is revealed only in line four to be the death of the king's son. Similarly, in the second, the fact that Einarr cannot deny is revealed only in the final line: it is the harm he has caused King Haraldr by killing the king's son. Such interruptions momentarily leave the audience in suspense as they wait for the conclusion of each half-stanza; the delay in naming the victim further emphasises the heroism and agency of the speaker, while at the same time reinforcing the apparent passivity of his enemies.

The intercalary clause is a key feature of the skaldic mode, as poets exploit the flexibility of Old Norse syntax to weave further information into their sequences. Such additions can include extra details about the events described, descriptions of the poets' own reaction to events, or simply a reit-

---

*Study of Skaldic Narrative* (Toronto, 1991), pp. 161–72. All translations are my own. Block quotations are cited as in the edition, while citations integrated in the main text of the chapter are cited in prose word-order for ease of reading.

eration of the main sentence, but couched in highly poetic language. In this battle-stanza, Einarr's intercalary clauses are a mixture of all three. In the first *helmingr*, the quasi-gnomic utterance that 'gótts vinna þrek manni' (it is good for a man to accomplish a courageous deed) further enhances the poet's reputation, framing the killing of the king's son as something that ought to be universally approved. In the second *helmingr*, the intercalary clause expands to fill up two full lines, or half of the *helmingr* itself. The expansive nature of this clause matches the elevated poetic register as Einarr uses the kenning *grár nagr hræva* (grey bird of corpses) to describe a bird flying over the battlefield. The 'bird of corpses' is a carrion bird, such as an eagle or raven; such birds were said to fly over the battlefield hoping to feast on the bodies of dead men. This 'beast of battle' motif is a common generic marker of skaldic battle-poetry and the kenning itself relatively conventional. Nevertheless, although the expression would have been easily understood by Einarr's audience, kennings often have a riddling or metaphoric quality that demands a process of active decoding on the part of the poet's audience; the inclusion of this kenning in a clause that has already broken into the structure of the main sentence adds a further sense of fragmentation to the verse, perhaps mirroring the disarray of battle and the imminent disintegration of the prince's dead body. In this way, Einarr employs several of the hallmarks of the skaldic mode – the double *helmingar*, the envelope pattern, the intercalary clause, and the kenning – in the context of poetry about armed conflict to emphasize his own prowess and his enemy's defeat.

The kenning *grár nagr hræva* (grey bird of corpses) is closely related to that which concludes the stanza, in which Einarr describes King Haraldr as a *gælir undvala* (comforter of wound-falcons). This second example is typical of the warrior-kennings used in battle-poetry, in which men are frequently portrayed as 'comforting' or 'feeding' carrion birds through the slaughter of their enemies. Here, however, the kenning is deeply ironic as the 'comfort' offered to the birds actually consists of the body of Haraldr's son; it has certainly not been the king's choice to 'comfort' the scavengers in this way. In this context, it is possible that the use of the verb *bíta* in the first *helmingr* should be understood in its most literal meaning, that is, 'to bite', with the pointed spear-ends that pierce the prince's body perhaps evoking an uncanny resemblance to the pointed beak of the eagle or raven. It is notable too that the spears themselves are the subject of the verb *bíta*: they are not imagined as merely the instruments used by Einarr's forces but seem rather to take on a life of their own as they pierce or 'bite' the prince's body. Weapons seeming to act of their own accord is another generic feature of skaldic battle-poetry, and Einarr uses this trope to great effect, extending the image of carrion birds feasting on Hálfdan's corpse throughout the stanza. On the whole, the two kennings in the second *helmingr* stand in marked contrast to the simpler poetic diction of the first. Although the first *helmingr* does employ specialist poetic vocabulary – the noun *boð* (battle) in the compound adjective *bǫðfíkinn* (battle-eager) and the word *þengill* (king or prince) are almost never encountered in prose – such language pales in comparison to the intricate circumlocutions of the second *helmingr*. The second intercalary clause also stands out from the stanza in which it appears through the poet's use of internal rhyme in the phrase *grár at sǫrum* (grey [birds flew] from the wounded). Although such patterns are a regular feature of the most common skaldic metre, known as *dróttkvætt* (court-metre), Einarr's stanzas are cast in a slightly different form, known as *munnvǫrp* (mouth-throwings). *Munnvǫrp* typically employs less internal rhyme than *dróttkvætt*, and the use of full rhyme in this phrase is therefore notable.[11] It is possible too that Einarr's decision not to use *dróttkvætt* is a subtle rejection of the courtly context with which that metre is so closely associated: as will be discussed in more detail below, Einarr is as yet a marginal figure operating on the fringes of courtly society. A metre associated with the formal encomia addressed to rulers at the height of their powers is perhaps not yet appropriate for this upstart hero; the use of a less common metre may signal instead Einarr's violent disruption of the Norwegian courtly community. In other ways, however, the stanza is a masterful example of skaldic battle-poetry. While the second *helmingr* is essentially a reiteration of the first – in both, Einarr gloats about killing the king's son – the impact of that act intensifies as the stanza progresses: syntax, diction, and rhyme work together to elevate the poetic register of the second *helmingr*, centred around the image of carrion birds feasting on the body of Hálfdan. By the end of the verse we are caught in a moment of high drama that marks Einarr's absolute dominance over his defeated enemies.

The third stanza marks the climax of Einarr's confrontation with the sons of Haraldr, but the four accompanying verses add important context to the act of killing the king's son. While it is not possible to consider all of these stanzas in as much detail as st. 3, above, a brief overview of their principal themes further illustrates the ways in which Einarr engages further with the generic conventions of skaldic battle-verse. The verse that follows st. 3 in *Orkneyinga saga* describes how Einarr's men bury Hálfdan's body in a grave-mound:

Rekit hefk Rǫgnvalds dauða
– rétt skiptu því nornir –

---

11 In Snorri's description of *munnvǫrp* in *Háttatal*, even lines contain *skothendingar* (half rhymes) while odd lines generally lack rhyme altogether; see *Edda – Háttatal*, ed. Anthony Faulkes (London, 1999), p. 28–29. Einarr's verses are more varied: some odd lines also contain *skothendingar*, while even lines generally employ *skothendingar* and a few *aðalhendingar* (full rhymes, as in this example). Some have no rhyme at all, however. In contrast, *dróttkvætt* tends to follow a regular pattern, with *skothendingar* in odd lines and *aðalhendingar* in even ones. For a brief overview of skaldic metre, see the 'General Introduction' to *Poetry from the Kings' sagas*, ed. Whaley, 1: pp. li–lxvii.

- nús folkstuðill fallinn –
at fjorðungi mínum.
Verpið, snarpir sveinar,
þvít sigri vér róðum,
(skatt velk hónum harðan)
at Háfœtu grjóti

[I have avenged Rǫgnvaldr's death – the fates have arranged this rightly – now the people's pillar [> RULER, i.e. Hálfdan] has fallen – for my quarter share. Throw stones, brave boys, as we have won victory – I choose a bitter tax for him – at Long-Legs [Hálfdan]].

The erection of a burial mound was a common way of memorialising a dead ruler and is referred to in a number of skaldic sequences.[12] Here, however, the practice is described in mocking tones, with Einarr urging his troops – jocularly addressed as *snarpir sveinar* (brave boys) – to chuck rubble (*verpa grjóti*) at Hálfdan's lifeless body. The prince is named through an insultingly feminised version of his nickname, *Háfœta* (Long-Legs), and the stones that build his mound ironically become the only tax (*skatt*) this ineffective ruler is able to secure from his erstwhile Orcadian subjects. Unlike other commemorative verses that celebrate the ruler and the building of his mound, the stanza becomes a memorial for the act of revenge. The name of Einarr's father, Rǫgnvaldr, appears in the first line of the stanza, mirroring but far outweighing in importance the name *Háfœta* in the final line. Einarr's revenge has, moreover, been orchestrated by the *nornir* (figures who determine fate) themselves, the influence of these powerful, mythological creatures standing in sharp contrast to the haphazard throwing of stones that comprises Hálfdan's burial. In this stanza, then, Einarr turns the usual function of commemorative verse on its head: the building of Hálfdan's mound and its memorialisation in verse serve not to glorify the man buried inside, but to proclaim the warrior-poet's successful revenge on his defeated enemy.

Einarr's curious description of revenge as *fjórðungr minn* (my quarter share) in this verse is presumed to be a mocking reference to his three older brothers, all of whom failed to avenge their father. As noted above, the prose of *Orkneyinga saga* sets up an almost folkloric structure that pits Einarr, the despised younger son, against his more privileged siblings, and rivalry between the brothers is a theme that appears in the first two stanzas of the sequence as well. Indeed, in the first verse of the sequence the focus of Einarr's anger is not Prince Hálfdan but his own brothers:

Sékat Hrolfs ór hendi
né Hrollaugi fljúga
dǫrr á dolga mengi;

---

12 See further examples in Goeres, *The Poetics of Commemoration*, pp. 20–54.

dugir oss fǫður hefna.
En í kveld, meðan knýjum,
of kerstraumi, rómu,
þegjandi sitr þetta
Þórir jarl á Mœri.

[I do not see spears flying from Hrólfr's hand into the multitude of enemies, nor from Hrollaugr's; it is right for us to avenge our father. But tonight, while we press forward into battle, Earl Þórir silently sits it [i.e., the battle] out, over his cup-stream [> DRINK] in Mœrr.]

The contrast between those who seek out battle and those who stay at home, either feasting or in the company of women, is a common trope in skaldic battle-poetry; it is also employed in other antagonistic speech-acts such as the *senna* (verbal duel) and the *mannjafnaðr* (comparison of men).[13] In this stanza, however, Einarr employs that trope to criticise not his enemies but his own family; in so doing, he rejects the suggestion that he is worth less than his brothers and shames them for not fulfilling their filial obligations. Einarr himself scorns the leisurely life enjoyed by Þórir and, in contrast, relishes the danger his pursuit of revenge occasions. As he boasts in the second stanza,

Hætt segja mér hǫlðar
við hugfullan stilli;
Haralds hefk skarð í skildi
– skala ugga þat – hǫggvit.

[Men say there is danger for me from the courageous ruler; I have hewed – I shall not fear that – a notch in Haraldr's shield [i.e., by killing Hálfdan].]

As this verse makes clear, Einarr does not expect the cycle of revenge to conclude with his killing of Hálfdan; unlike Einarr's brothers, King Haraldr appears more than willing to hunt down those who kill his family members. Although enemies, it seems that the king and the earl have more in common than Einarr has with his own brothers. Placing himself on a level with King Haraldr in this way allows Einarr to transcend the problem of illegitimacy and to claim nobility through deeds rather than birth. Mirror-

---

13 See further Roberta Frank, 'Why Skalds Address Women', in *Atti del 12. Congresso Internazionale di Studi sull' Alto Medioevo: Poetry in the Scandinavian Middle Ages. The Seventh International Saga Conference*, ed. Teresa Pàroli (Spoleto, 1990), pp. 55–66; on *senna* and *mannjafnaðr* see Marcel Bax and Tineke Padmos, 'Two Types of Dueling in Old Icelandic: the Interactional Structure of the *senna* and the *mannjafnaðr* in *Hárbarðsljóð*', SS 55:2 (1983), 149–74. Cf. also the broader generic category of the flyting, the ritualised exchange of insults, found both in Old Norse and Old English poetry, as well as more broadly throughout medieval literature.

ing the repetitive structure of individual stanzas – such as st. 3, in which the second *helmingr* repeats but intensifies the rhetoric of the first – the final stanza of the sequence returns to this theme on a grander scale, as the victorious Einarr awaits the vengeance not only of King Haraldr but of the wider aristocratic community:

> Eru til míns fjǫrs margir
> menn of sannar deilðir
> ór ýmissum ǫttum
> ósmábornir gjarnir.

> [There are many who are eager for [i.e. to take] my life because of justified conflicts, men of various families, not lowly born.][14]

In this way, Torf-Einarr's sequence articulates the necessity of vengeance and the glory to be won from it, but also acknowledges the inevitable repercussions caused by further killing as the cycle of violence continues. It is somewhat ironic that the killing of his father is the making of Einarr, at least according to the skaldic sequence. Einarr demonstrates a subtle understanding of the conventions of the skaldic mode and of battle-poetry in particular; he employs the formal structures of the skaldic stanza – the two-part stanzaic structure, the intercalary clause, the kenning – to craft battle-verse that subverts such generic markers as the 'beasts of battle' motif, the formal commemoration of rulers, and the ritualised insult of one's enemies. Even the use of the first person plays with the conventions of battle-poetry, which is more frequently expressed in the third person as the poet praises not his own actions but those of his leader or comrades. A young and unproven leader, Einarr has yet to attract the service of poets who might honour him in verse. Nevertheless, his verses also demonstrate the self-sufficiency that enables his unexpected rise to power: he has no need of a poet to chronicle his battles for him. Through his verse, Einarr rejects his marginalised social position and claims instead a series of heroic roles: the dutiful son, the victorious battle-commander, the *agent provocateur* of an ongoing cycle of vengeance and violence. Verse allows him a degree of agency and the opportunity to craft his own story: in this, he is indeed the ideal progenitor for the new earldom of Orkney.

The story of Einarr's conflict with the sons of Haraldr is thus a story of killing and counter-killing, of the struggle between young, ambitious noblemen as they attempt to forge new states in the semi-lawless environ-

---

14 Two of the extant *Orkneyinga saga* manuscripts substitute *fréttir* (reports) for *deilðir* (conflicts) in this stanza. The meaning in this case seems to be that 'true reports' of Hálfdan's killing have reached Norway, in line with comments in both *Orkneyinga saga* and *Heimskringla* that Hálfdan's brothers have heard of his death and are planning to seek revenge (*Orkneyinga saga*, ed. Finnbogi Guðmundsson, pp. 15–16 and *Heimskringla*, I, ed. Bjarni Aðalbjarnarson, pp. 133–34). See further Poole, *Viking Poems*, pp. 171–72.

ment of the tenth-century northern world. The inclusion of Einarr's stanzas in the prose narrative of the sagas lends the texts a dramatic sense of immediacy, as the young earl of Orkney appears to speak directly to the saga audience: whether exulting in the gory details of Hálfdan's death or gleefully excoriating his brothers for their lack of action, Einarr's first-person commentary breaks into the laconic saga prose, demanding the reader's attention and engagement. Despite this, details in the poetry do not always match those given in the prose, nor do the three sagas in which the stanzas are now preserved present them in the same way. As noted above, much skaldic verse, and nearly all battle-poetry, is now preserved in a prosimetric context: questions about the relationship between prose and verse, the order of the stanzas themselves, and the degree to which the extant sequence might differ from its presumed 'original', tenth-century form all complicate the study of Torf-Einarr's work; in this too, however, the verses are typical of the skaldic corpus and of the challenges modern scholars face when approaching the genre of battle-poetry in particular.

A division is often made between skaldic stanzas that appear to be spoken in the heat of the moment, usually by one of the characters featured in the saga (sometimes called 'situational verses'), and those quoted by the saga author to demonstrate the veracity or reliability of his account ('authenticating verses').[15] Verses about armed conflict appear frequently in both contexts, and yet their presentation by the saga author can have a significant impact on how readers interpret both the meaning of the stanzas and the verses' generic identity. Stanzas recited by a character in the heat of battle can add immediacy and excitement to the prose narrative; like Torf-Einarr's, they are generally expressed in the first person and were ostensibly composed during the battle described. Verses cited by a saga author to corroborate his description of an armed conflict are, by contrast, more commonly presented as having been composed after its conclusion; the focus of such verses is generally not the speaker's personal experience of battle but rather the deeds performed by his noble patron. Unlike the apparently impromptu, single-stanza compositions known as *lausavísur*, or 'loose verses', such stanzas are often drawn from longer poetic sequences such as the *drápur* (long, formal poems with one or more refrains) composed about the lives of individual rulers or in *flokkar* (series of verses) about specific battles, campaigns, or expeditions. These longer sequences seem to have been held in significantly higher esteem than the *lausavísur*, and an account of battle could therefore be endowed with significantly more cultural cachet if it formed part of lengthy, structured sequence than if it appeared in a single verse. In the prose context, however,

---

15 See Diana Whaley in 'Skalds and Situational Verses in *Heimskringla*', in *Snorri Sturluson: Kolloquium anläßlich der 750 Wiederkehr seines Todestages*, ed. Alois Wolf, ScriptOralia 51 (Tübingen, 1993), pp. 245–66; and Margaret Clunies Ross, *A History of Old Norse Poetry and Poetics* (Cambridge, 2005), pp. 78–80.

the differences between a sequence of *lausavísur* and the fragments of a *drápa* are not always clear, while the same stanza may be employed in a 'situational' context in one saga and an 'authenticating' one in another. Torf-Einarr's verses are a case in point.

As quoted in *Heimskringla* and *Orkneyinga saga*, Einarr's verses are broadly employed in a 'situational' context. In both texts, the verses are introduced as impromptu compositions through such phrases as 'Þá kvað Einarr vísu' (then Einarr spoke a verse) and 'Þá kvað Einarr þetta' (then Einarr said this).[16] They are cited in relatively quick succession and in generally the same context; this has led some scholars to suggest that the verses are not *lausavísur*, as one might expect from such a context, but that they once formed part of a single skaldic poem. Pointing to a number of inconsistencies between the verse and the prose, Klaus von See has observed that all of the major characters – Einarr, his three brothers, as well as Haraldr and Hálfdan – are named, but that each proper name appears only once in the poetic sequence; variations such as *þengill* (prince, i.e. Haraldr) and *allvalds sonr* (all-powerful ruler's son, i.e. Hálfdan), are elsewhere used to avoid repeating those names. This, he argues, suggests that the verses were intended to be performed together, and that the prose narratives that now enclose them were composed later.[17] In response, however, Dietrich Hofmann argues that the verses must always have been enclosed within a prose frame because they present the conflict between Einarr and Hálfdan from two different chronological perspectives: the first stanza appears to describe the battle as it takes place but the others clearly describe events that happen afterwards.[18] Hofmann suggests that some sort of narrative explanation would have been necessary to bridge this gap; that explanation might even have become embellished over time, leading to the type of extended narrative we see in *Orkneyinga saga*. More recently, Russell Poole has offered an intriguing combination of these two positions. He observes that the verses are preceded in both *Orkneyinga saga* and *Heimskringla* by a couplet in *munnvǫrp*, the same relatively unusual metre as the five stanzas attributed to Einarr.[19] Nevertheless, this couplet refers to the earl in the third person

---

16  *Orkneyinga saga*, ed. Finnbogi Guðmundsson, pp. 12–15 and *Heimskringla*, I, ed. Bjarni Aðalbjarnarson, pp. 132–33. The only exception to this is the citation of the first stanza ('Sékat Hrólfs ór hendi') in *Heimskingla*, which is, rather unusually, presented as something Einarr composed a few hours earlier than the moment of its actual citation in the saga: 'Einarr jarl kvað vísu þessa um aptaninn, áðr hann lagði til orrustu' (Earl Einarr spoke this verse in the evening, before he fought the battle) (*Heimskringla*, I, ed. Bjarni Aðalbjarnarson, p. 131).
17  Klaus von See, 'Der Skalde Torf–Einar Jarl', *Beiträge zur Geschichte der deutschen Sprache und Literatur* 82 (1960), 31–43, esp. pp. 42–43.
18  Dietrich Hofmann, 'Sagaprosa als Partner von Skaldenstrophen', *Medieval Scandinavia* 11 (1978–79), 68–81, esp. pp. 77–78. See further Poole's discussion of both von See's and Hofmann's work in *Viking Poems*, pp. 165–69.
19  'Hann gaf Tréskegg trollum; / Torf-Einarr drap Skurfu' (He gave Tréskegg [the viking Þórir 'Wood-beard'] to the trolls; Torf-Einarr killed Skurfa [Þórir's

and is therefore unlikely to be his own work. For this reason, Poole suggests that the couplet and the five complete stanzas all derive from a longer sequence, now lost, that contained a mix of third-person narrative and direct speech. This, he argues, might have led to a confusion between the author of the sequence and its protagonist, Einarr, thus accounting for the attribution of the five main stanzas to the Orkney earl himself by the later saga authors. The status of Einarr's verses as *lausavísur* is therefore far from certain.

If, however, the verses did once comprise a discrete skaldic sequence – that is, a formal battle-poem rather than off-the-cuff improvisations – in what order did they appear? The most recent edition of the sequence follows the order given in *Orkneyinga saga*, and that is the order referred to in this chapter. Nevertheless, *Heimskringla* and *Fagrskinna* each present the stanzas in a different order, suggesting that the sagas are highly unreliable guides to the verses' original configuration.[20] The different order of the stanzas also demonstrates how saga authors may have misunderstood, or even manipulated, the presentation of individual verses. This can most clearly be seen in the 'blood-eagle' episode, described both in *Orkneyinga saga* and in *Heimskringla*. As *Orkneyinga saga* relates, 'lét Einarr rísta ǫrn á baki honum með sverði ok skera rifin ǫll frá hrygginum ok draga þar út lungum ok gaf hann Óðni til sigrs sér' (Einarr had an eagle carved on his [Hálfdan's] back with a sword and all the ribs cut from the spine and the lungs pulled out from there, and dedicated him to Óðinn [in thanks for] his victory).[21] *Heimskringla* contains a near-verbatim account, albeit without the explicit reference to Óðinn.[22] Although both sagas then cite stanzas by Torf-Einarr, there is no reference in any of those verses to the more grotesque manner of killing described in the prose. That is, the author of *Orkneyinga saga* quotes sts 2 and 3 in short succession, but in st. 2 Einarr merely brags in general terms about Hálfdan's death and focuses instead on the damage he has caused to King Haraldr by killing his son (*hefk hǫggvit skarð í skildi Haralds*); in st. 3 Einarr states explicitly that the prince's death was caused by spears (*geirar bitu ungan son þengils*). Snorri takes a different approach in *Heimskringla* by quoting st. 4, in which Einarr boasts that he has avenged his father's death and urges his followers to build Hálfdan's burial mound (*verpið grjóti at Háfœtu*,

---

companion, Kálfr 'the scabby']). Edited by Kari Ellen Gade in *Poetry from the Kings' sagas*, ed. Whaley, 1: p. 1070.

20 Using the stanza numbers assigned by Poole (who follows their order in *Orkneyinga saga*), *Heimskringla* cites the stanzas in the following order: st. 1 ('Sékat Hrólfs ór hendi'), st. 4 ('Rekit hefk Rǫgnvalds dauða'), st. 5 ('Eru til míns fjǫrs margir'), and st. 2 ('Margr verðr sekr at sauðum'. *Fagrskinna* cites st. 1 ('Sékat Hrólfs ór hendi'), 4 ('Rekit hefk Rǫgnvalds dauða') and then st. 3 ('Ey munk glaðr, síz geirar').

21 *Orkneyinga saga*, ed. Finnbogi Guðmundsson, p. 13.
22 *Heimskringla*, I, ed. Bjarni Aðalbjarnarson, p. 132.

*snarpir sveinar*). In none of these stanzas is Hálfdan portrayed as having been killed in an unconventional or ritualistic manner; the quotation of verse at this point does little to substantiate – and at times actively contradicts – the accounts given in the prose.

Is it possible that the reference to the blood-eagle does, nevertheless, derive from one or more of Einarr's verses? As noted above, st. 3 contains the kenning *grár nagr hræva*, which denotes a carrion bird such as an eagle or raven and is an example of the 'beast of battle' motif so common to the genre of skaldic battle-poetry. This bird is depicted as flying over the islands (*þar fló of holma*) and is clearly a reference to an actual carrion bird that is imagined to be feasting on the bodies of the dead. Do the prose accounts perhaps suggest that the saga authors misunderstood this kenning, or the related image in st. 5, in which Einarr threatens that other noblemen may likewise 'stand under the eagle's claws' (*standa undir ilþorna arnar*) if they attempt to attack him? In her analysis of the earliest apparent reference to the blood-eagle in skaldic verse, Roberta Frank argues that authors of the sagas, writing at a considerable remove from the poets they cite and blinded by an antiquarian desire to detect more savagery in tales of their Viking-Age ancestors than the texts themselves warrant, may have interpreted such poetic language in an overly literal manner.[23] Russell Poole similarly argues that the addition of the blood-eagle to the prose narrative of Hálfdan's death represents a 'late romanticizing addition' to the saga text; indeed, he suggests that Snorri deliberately left st. 3, with its explicit mention of death-by-spear, out of *Heimskringla* because it contradicted the more lurid account of the prose.[24]

While it is difficult to determine exactly what process led to the inclusion of the blood-eagle in the sagas, it is clear that the citation of different verses at the moment of Hálfdan's death has profound consequences for the way in which the two sagas present that death and, consequently, the use to which these battle-stanzas are put by the saga authors. While the stanzas cited in *Orkneyinga saga* emphasise the theme of revenge and, in particular, Einarr's successful attack on King Haraldr's son, the stanza in *Heimskringla* widens the scope of that conflict: the group action of throwing stones over Hálfdan's body emphasises the collective nature of the Orcadian defence, while Hálfdan's brothers are said to be planning an attack of their own. In *Orkneyinga saga*, therefore, the citation of battle-verse presents Hálfdan's death as vengeance accomplished, emphasising the young earl's autonomy from Norwegian rule and his now-firm control over the Orkney Islands. As such, the episode offers a suitable climax to the first part of the saga narrative, which focuses on the founding of a relatively independent Orkney earldom. In *Heimskringla*, however, Hálfdan's death

---

23 Frank's discussion looks mainly at the first stanza of Sigvatr Þórðarson's *Knútsdrápa* ('Viking Atrocity and Skaldic Verse', 332–43, esp. 339–43).
24 Poole, *Viking Poems*, p. 166.

becomes one more event in the ongoing struggle between Einarr's family and the sons of King Haraldr; the broader scope of this perspective befits Snorri's lengthy compendium in which the kings of Norway come into conflict not only with the Orkney earls, but with a number of powerful Norwegian families, as well as the royal dynasties of Denmark, Sweden and England. Thus while the stanzas cited do not differ significantly in the information they communicate, the way they present that information clearly speaks to the broader themes of the sagas in which they are preserved. Although presented by the saga authors as improvised *lausavísur*, the stanzas' broadly historicising function in these works is more typical of the way verses from long, formal, battle-poems are employed in the prosimetric context. As the scholarly debate detailed above indicates, Torf-Einarr's stanzas seem to slip uneasily between these two categories.

To complicate matters still further, the use to which these verses are put in *Fagrskinna* differs markedly from that in *Heimskringla* and *Orkneyinga saga*. This text is much shorter than *Heimskringla*, although it covers much of the same material and is thought to have been one of Snorri's sources for at least part of the longer work. Unlike *Heimskringla* and *Orkneyinga saga*, however, *Fagrskinna* employs Einarr's verses in a purely 'authenticating' fashion almost entirely separate from the story of the young earl himself: that is, they provide corroboration for the saga author's description of William, Duke of Normandy and Conqueror of England. As with many a saga hero, William is introduced by way of a lengthy genealogy that details not only his Norman predecessors but also his more distant Scandinavian ancestors:

> Hans faðir var Rotbertr longespée, en hans faðir var Ríkarðr, sonr annars Ríkarðar, en hans faðir var Vilhjálmr, sonr Gǫngu-Hrólfs. Hann vann þat ríki í Vallandi, er síðan var kallat Norðmandí, ok var þar yfir jarl síðan ok allir þeir langfeðr. Gǫngu-Hrólfr jarl var sonr Rǫgnvalds Mœrajarls, bróðir Þóris jarls þegjanda ok Torf-Einars í Orkneyjum, ok Hrollaugr hét einn, svá sem Einarr segir, þá er hann hafði drepit Hálfdan hálegg, son Haralds ens hárfagra, er áðr hafði drepit fǫður hans.[25]

> [His father was Robert Longsword, and his father was Richard, son of a second Richard, and his father was William, son of Gǫngu-Hrólfr (Hrólfr the Walker). He won that kingdom in France that was afterwards called Normandy, and he was then earl over it, along with all of his descendants. Earl Gǫngu-Hrólfr was the son of Earl Rǫgnvaldr of Mœrr, the brother of Earl Þórir þegjandi (the Silent) and of Torf-

---

25 *Fagrskinna*, ed. Bjarni Einarsson, p. 291. A similar account of William's genealogy is given in *Heimskringla*, where it is placed much earlier in the chronology of the saga as part of the story of Gǫngu-Hrólfr and the founding of Normandy (*Heimskringla*, I, ed. Bjarni Aðalbjarnarson, 124–25).

Einarr of Orkney, and Hrollaugr was the name of the man who had earlier killed [Torf-Einarr's] father, as Einarr said when he had killed Hálfdan hálegg (Longleg), son of Haraldr hárfagri (Fair-hair).]

*Fagrskinna* then cites three of the verses discussed above: st. 1, in which Einarr castigates his brothers for not avenging their father's death; st. 4, with its description of Hálfdan's burial mound; and the climactic st. 3, in which Einarr brags about killing Hálfdan and the harm this act of revenge will cause to Hálfdan's father, King Haraldr. In the first of these verses, Einarr explicitly names and shames his brother Hrólfr, from whom the dukes of Normandy were descended; this is the Gǫngu-Hrólfr (Hrólfr the Walker) mentioned in the prose text of *Fagrskinna*. In this way, the saga introduces Duke William of Normandy as the descendant of a famous ancestor, Hrólfr, who failed to defend his family's honour, despite his clear obligation to do so. Although *Fagrskinna* does not directly mention Einarr's illegitimacy, the text twice mentions William's nickname, *bastarði* (bastard), perhaps reminding an audience familiar with *Orkneyinga saga* that the Norman duke came, like Torf-Einarr, from less than conventional beginnings. When the saga author goes on to detail the other side of William's family and his kinship with the kings of England, the implications are clear: the invasion of 1066 is William's opportunity to redress his ancestor's inaction, to provide the descendants of Hrólfr with an inheritance equal to that of the illegitimate – but successful – Earl Einarr.[26] That this opportunity comes at the expense of another King Haraldr, the Anglo-Saxon leader Harold Godwineson, further emphasises William's affinity with his Scandinavian ancestors and, in particular, with the first successful earl of Orkney, Torf-Einarr Rǫgnvaldsson.

In this way, the author of *Fagrskinna* creates an illustrious genealogy for William, one that locates the dukedom of Normandy firmly within the history of the great Viking-Age migrations and the Norwegian colonisation of the North Atlantic territories. In *Fagrskinna*, Einarr's battle-verses demonstrate that genealogy alone does not ensure success: one must be ready to defend one's honour with force, and to kill those who get in the way. The ancient conflict between Einarr and the sons of King Haraldr also encourages the audience of *Fagrskinna* to consider the broader historical context of such processes as colonisation, conquest, and revenge. In

---

26 'Vilhjálmr bastarðr ok Játvarðr enn helgi Englakonungr váru systkina synir. Rotbertr jarl ok Emma dróttning, þau váru Ríkarðs bǫrn bæði. Emmu átti áðr Aðalráðr Englakonungr. Þeira synir váru Játmundr ok Játvarðr enn helgi. Síðan átti Emmu Knútr gamli. Þeira sonr var Haraldr ok Hǫrða-Knútr' (William the Bastard and Edward the Confessor, king of the English, were first cousins. Earl Robert and Queen Emma were both children of Richard [Duke of Normandy]. Emma had earlier married Æthelred, king of the English. Their sons were Edmund and Edward the Confessor. Later Emma married Cnut the Old. Their sons were Harold and Harthacnut) (*Fagrskinna*, ed. Bjarni Einarsson, p. 293).

so doing, the saga author creates a link between Einarr and Duke William that the poet himself could not have foreseen, but which the saga's readers cannot ignore. While maintaining their generic affiliation as battle-poetry, the stanzas reveal new and different meanings in their various prosimetric contexts.

In this way, the stanzas of Torf-Einarr Rǫgnvaldsson offer a useful illustration of the complex processes of adaptation, appropriation, and reinterpretation that accompanied the integration of skaldic poetry into the later prose sagas. In this, they are typical not only of the genre of battle-poetry but of the skaldic corpus in general. As a poetic mode, skaldic verse emerges as highly malleable, its meanings changeable and the significance of individual stanzas constantly evolving throughout the Viking and medieval periods. Such movements reflect the various 'communities of users', to use Whetter's term, to engage with the genre of battle-poetry over that time.[27] It is difficult to know for certain how the poet's tenth-century audience (if such existed) interpreted the stanzas in terms of a category like genre, but Einarr's use of multiple features found in other works about battle suggests that this was a meaningful category for that early audience. Indeed, the stanzas suggest a sophisticated and even playful approach to the concept of skaldic battle-poetry: Einarr's mastery of the formal structures of the skaldic mode, such as the two-part stanza and the intercalary clause, contrasts with his slyly unconventional use of generic markers such as the 'beasts of battle' motif, warrior-kennings, the ritualised insult of one's enemies, and themes of violence, revenge, and memorialisation. Unlike so many battle-stanzas composed by and for members of the courtly community, Einarr's verses invoke the genre of battle-poetry only to subvert its key features, signalling his marginal social status and antagonistic relationship with the Norwegian royal court. The disruptive nature of his verse continues into the later medieval period, when his stanzas are integrated into the prosimetric context of three different sagas; there, they seem to play with the reader's expectations of how battle-poetry contributes to the construction of a historical narrative. Slipping between 'situational' and 'authenticating' functions, the stanzas appear at times to be occasional verses composed during the heat of battle, and at others the remnants of a formal poetic sequence looking back at the conflict. Their use in the sagas suggests an evolution in the function of battle-poetry in the later medieval period. As part of the prosimetric text, the stanzas give voice to more than Einarr's personal experience; they help to articulate broader concerns about the effects of migration, colonisation and conquest, and the ways in which those processes are encoded in the later written record. Einarr's stanzas thus demonstrate the surprising flexibility of battle-poetry as a genre, as well as the ongoing interest in that genre on the part of multiple communities of users.

---

27 Whetter, *Understanding Genre*, pp. 21–22.

# Eddic Poetry – A Case Study: *Sólarljóð*

Carolyne Larrington

## Christian Genres

The long processes of the Scandinavian and Icelandic conversion to Christianity over the tenth and eleventh centuries had an unparalleled effect on the Old Norse-Icelandic literary polysystem, in Even-Zohar's terminology.[1] The new religion's institutions not only imported manuscript literacy to the North, they also brought Latin texts, most notably the Bible. New genres: saints' lives, hymns and moral tales were introduced alongside other less distinctively Christian kinds of writing, such as annals and written versions of the law. In association with the new genres came, of course, new topics and subjects. These could be mediated through the newly introduced literary forms, but they were also adopted into existing Old Norse literary genres. After a hiatus in skaldic composition, as poets reformulated kennings in order to incorporate Christian concepts, praise-poetry, now adapted for characteristic Christian purposes, had a triumphant relaunch in the mid-twelfth century.[2] Four important and closely related *drápur* (a long stanzaic poem with a refrain) are preserved from this period. These include *Geisli*, composed by Einarr Skúlason most likely in 1153 and Gamli kanóki (canon)'s *Harmsól*.[3] This is both 'a praise-poem addressed to Christ, whose purity, magnificence, creative power and holiness are stressed throughout the work in a series of magnificently crafted kennings', and a sermon on Christian values, harnessing the poet's sense of his own sinfulness to instruct and inform his audience.[4] The other two poems are anonymous: *Leiðarvísan* is a version of the so-called

---

1. See for a representative outline of polysystem theory Itamar Even-Zohar, 'Polysystem Theory', *Poetics Today* 11:1 (1990), 9–94.
2. See Diana Edwards (Whaley), 'Christian and Pagan References in Eleventh-Century Norse Poetry: The Case of Arnórr Jarlaskáld', *SBVS* 21 (1982–85), 33–53.
3. Martin Chase, 'Introduction to Einarr Skúlason, *Geisli*', in *Poetry on Christian Subjects*, ed. Margaret Clunies Ross, 2 vols, *SkP* 7 (Turnhout, 2007), I: pp. 5–6. See also Chase's independent edition, *Einarr Skúlason's Geisli: A Critical Edition*, Toronto Old Norse and Icelandic Studies 1 (Toronto, Buffalo and London, 2005)
4. Katrina Attwood, 'Introduction to Gamli kanóki, *Harmsól*', in *Poetry on Christian Subjects*, ed. Clunies Ross, I: pp. 70–72, at p. 70. Gamli also composed *Jónsdrápa*, a praise-poem in honour of St John the Evangelist, of which four stanzas survive. Beatrice La Farge, 'Introduction to Níkulás Bergsson, *Jónsdrápa postula*', in *Poetry on Christian Subjects*, ed. Clunies Ross, I: pp. 66–67.

'Sunday letter', in which Christ adjures his followers to keep the Church's festivals and to mediate on his own suffering and sacrifice; *Plácitusdrápa* is a fragmentary account of the life of St Plácitus (Placitus, later St Eustace), a Roman general who converts to Christianity after encountering Christ in the form of a stag.[5] Unlike the other three *drápur* in this group, *Plácitusdrápa* is a vivid narrative – indeed, a saint's life; the surviving stanzas relate how Eustace converts his family, how his wife and children were abducted, and tell of the family's reunion, breaking off just before they are martyred for their faith. While the move from praising kings to praising God, Christ and the Apostles does not demand a huge conceptual leap, it is notable that the dramatic narrative of Plácitus should also be so mediated. *Plácitusdrápa* is however an outlier among these early Christian poems. Many contemporary saints' lives, translated and adapted usually from Latin prose sources, were mediated in saga prose form.[6] The fourteenth century would see the composition of ambitious narrative *dróttkvætt* poems such as *Petrsdrápa* and the fragmentary *Andreasdrápa*, relating and celebrating the lives and achievements of two important saints.[7]

*Dróttkvætt* then, as the highest-status poetic metre, seems to have been regarded as the worthiest form for Old Norse-Icelandic's first surviving Christian compositions, capable of fittingly honouring the principal figures of the new faith. Writers who wished to address Christian themes and topics faced a tradeoff between employing an ornamented high style with involuted metaphors and syntactic complexity or maximising comprehensibility and memorableness through the use of the simpler, paratactic prose medium.[8] Mastery of the prestigious poetic form no doubt produced social and cultural capital, yet plain style was more readily grasped by ordinary lay-folk. Between the obscurities of skaldic poetry and the emerging medium of saga prose lay the possibility of composition on Christian wisdom and teaching about the fundamentals of belief in so-called eddic metres. Although it is difficult to establish the age of the mythological and heroic poetry preserved in *fornyrðislag*, *ljóðaháttr*

---

5   Katrina Attwood, 'Introduction to Anonymous, *Leiðarvísan*', in *Poetry on Christian Subjects*, ed. Clunies Ross, I: pp. 137–40; Jonna Louis-Jensen and Tarrin Wills, 'Introduction to Anonymous, *Plácitus drápa*', in *Poetry on Christian Subjects*, ed. Clunies Ross, I: pp. 179–81.
6   See Jonas Wellendorf, 'Ecclesiastical Literature and Hagiography', in *The Routledge Research Companion to the Medieval Icelandic Sagas*, ed. Ármann Jakobsson and Sverrir Jakobsson (London, 2017), pp. 48–58.
7   These poems, edited by Ian MacDougall, are also to be found in *Poetry on Christian Subjects*, ed. Clunies Ross, II: pp. 796–851.
8   See Margaret Cormack, 'Poetry, Paganism and the Sagas of Icelandic Bishops', in *Til heiðurs og hugbótar: Greinar um trúarkveðskap fyrri alda*, ed. Svanhildur Óskarsdóttir and Anna Guðmundsdóttir, Snorrastofa Rit 1 (Reykholt, 2003), pp. 33–51. Cormack argues here that the Church was reluctant to sponsor skaldic hagiographical compositions; see *contra* Margaret Clunies Ross, 'Introduction' to *Poetry on Christian Subjects*, ed. Clunies Ross, I: pp. xliv–xlix.

and *málaháttr* in such thirteenth-century manuscripts as GKS 2365 4$^{to}$ or AM 748 4$^{to}$, it is clear that these metres remained available to contemporary authors, whether for long-form independent poems or for the composition of *lausavísur* as individual verses or in short sequences to insert into such prosimetrical compositions as the *fornaldarsögur*.[9]

*Fornyrðislag*, like the four-stress alliterative verse metres of other Germanic languages (Old Saxon, Old High German or Old English), tends to be used for sustained narratives, while *ljóðaháttr* with its marked *helmingr* (two-half) structure and its expansive long lines has a strong association with the dissemination of wisdom.[10] This then might allow us to hypothesise a thirteenth-century 'generic *community* of users', as Kevin Whetter terms it: one that was able to recognise the distinctive features and emphases that constitute wisdom poetry as genre; this capability ensured that the genre remained productive.[11]

Only two explicitly Christian poems in eddic metres have survived from the thirteenth century: *Hugsvinnsmál* (The Wise-minded One's Speech), a loose translation into *ljóðaháttr* of the second or third-century AD Latin prose text known as the *Distichs of Cato*, and the oddly hybrid *Sólarljóð* (The Song of the Sun), also composed in *ljóðaháttr*.[12] It should be noted that the oldest and incomplete extant manuscript of *Hugsvinnsmál*, AM 624 4$^{to}$, dates from the fifteenth century, while *Sólarljóð*'s oldest surviving witness, AM 166b 8$^{vo}$, is a paper manuscript from the mid-seventeenth century.[13] *Sólarljóð*, the subject of this case study, is an imaginative repurposing of the eddic wisdom poetry genre, brought into productive collision with the continental Other World vision genre – the sinner's journey through the Other World (Type I as labelled by Peter Dinzelbacher), and the creative literary vision.[14] For, as Whetter comments,

9   See the chapters by Margaret Clunies Ross, 'The Transmission and Preservation of Eddic Verse'; Carolyne Larrington, 'Eddic Poetry and Heroic Legend' and, particularly, Brittany Schorn, 'Eddic Modes and Genres', in *A Handbook to Eddic Poetry: Myths and Legends of Ancient Scandinavia*, ed. Carolyne Larrington, Judy Quinn and Brittany Schorn (Cambridge: Cambridge University Press, 2016), pp. 12–32; 147–72; 231–51.
10  For discussion of eddic metrical forms see R. D. Fulk, 'Eddic Metres', in *A Handbook to Eddic Poetry*, ed. Larrington, Quinn and Schorn, pp. 252–70.
11  Kevin Whetter, *Understanding Genre and Medieval Romance* (Aldershot and Burlington, 2008), p. 21 (his italics).
12  Eddic metre is also used for the thirteenth-century *Merlínusspá*, a version of the Latin *Prophetiæ Merlini*, in *fornyrðislag*. For a wide-ranging discussion of these poems as Christian wisdom compositions, see Brittany Schorn, *Speaker and Authority in Old Norse Wisdom Poetry*, Trends in Medieval Philology 34 (Berlin and Boston, 2017), pp. 117–48, especially pp. 124–42.
13  A full account of the poem and its manuscript contexts is given in Carolyne Larrington and Peter Robinson, 'Introduction to Anonymous, *Sólarljóð*', in *Poetry on Christian Subjects*, ed. Clunies Ross, I: pp. 287–95. All citations and translations of the poem are from this edition.
14  Peter Dinzelbacher, *Vision und Visionsliteratur im Mittelalter*, Monographien zur

elements associated predominantly with one genre may be found in many other genres, so that what distinguishes a genre is not only the presence of certain elements but the emphasis and significance given to each of them. ... Equally, such features and emphases, when sufficiently manipulated, can sometimes reveal or create generic hybrids.[15]

*Sólarljóð* offers a striking example of just such a generic hybrid; a poem that, arguably, is neither a kind of wisdom poem nor a kind of Other World vision. For its understanding requires, as Moritz Baßler notes, that the audience invoke distinctive 'Vergleiches-Korpora mit ihren jeweiligen Prototypen' (comparative corpora, each with their own prototypes), such that 'zwei Sätze von generischen Diskursusregeln aufgerufen werden' (two (or more) sets of generic discourse rules are summoned up).[16] The audience must engage in creative interpretation across genre and subgenre, each listener or reader deciding which (sub)genre is currently in play and what the consequences for meaning might be.

## *Sólarljóð* and its Subgenres

The poem's closing sequence, in particular sts 78 (cited later), 81 and 82, appears to offer the key to *Sólarljóð*'s generic identity:

> Kvæði þetta, er þér kent hefi,
> skaltu fyr kvikum kveða:
> Sólarljóð, er sýnask munu
> minnst at mörgu login. (*Sól* st. 81)

[This poem which I have taught you, you shall recite before living men: 'Songs of the sun' which will appear to be the least lying in many ways.]

> Hér vit skiljumk ok hittask munum
> á feginsdegi fira;
> dróttinn minn gefi þeim dauðum ró,
> ok hinum líkn er lifa. (*Sól* st. 82)

[Here we part and we shall meet on men's day of joy. May my Lord give the dead peace, and grace to those who live.]

In these final verses, the poem is revealed as a father-son dialogue

---

Geschichte des Mittelalters 23 (Stuttgart, 1981). Dinzelbacher's Type II is later in development; a spirit returns from Purgatory to warn, and to ask for the help (often intercession) of the living. Compare also Christian Carlsen, *Visions of the Afterlife in Old Norse Literature* (Oslo, 2015), pp. 115–23.

15 Whetter, *Understanding Genre*, p. 14.
16 Moritz Baßler, 'Gattungsmischung, Gattungsübergänge, Unbestimmbarkeit', in *Handbuch Gattungstheorie*, ed. Rüdiger Zymner (Stuttgart and Weimar, 2010), pp. 52–54, at p. 53. My translation.

(though, in fact, the son does not speak).[17] The structure occurs also in didactic works as – in Old Norse –*Hugsvinnsmál* and *Konungs skuggsjá*, and the Old English wisdom poem *Solomon and Saturn* II. The Old English poem entitled *Precepts,* a wisdom monologue in which a father addresses his son, offers a closer formal analogue. These parallel texts suggest that the poem that the audience has just heard should be retrospectively understood as a wisdom dialogue, or more precisely, like *Precepts,* as a one-sided wisdom monologue, in which a father imparts vital wisdom of various kinds to a silently listening son. To some extent *Sólarljóð*'s overarching generic type is precisely that of the Christian wisdom poem. Yet, in its central section, *Sólarljóð* is an extraordinary journey through the experience of the Four Last Things: death, judgement, heaven and hell, and thus it clearly partakes in the European Christian tradition of the Other World vision.[18] The Norwegian ballad *Draumkvæde*, with which *Sólarljóð* is often compared, is explicitly framed as a dream vision; *Sólarljóð*'s concluding st. 83, thought to be a later addition, also claims it as a dream-utterance, but there is no trace of this conceptualisation anywhere earlier in the poem.[19]

> Dásamligt fræði var þér draumi kvatt
>   en þú sást it sanna;
> fyrða engi var svá fróðr skapaðr
>   er áðr hefði heyrt Solarljóðs sögu. (*Sól* st. 83)

[Admirable advice was imparted to you in a dream, and you saw the truth. No man was created so wise that he has heard *Song of the Sun*'s tale before.]

In a book chapter published in 2001, I argued that *Sólarljóð*'s affinities lie predominantly with the *literary* vision, also often framed as a dream, such as Dante's *Divina Commedia* or the Chaucerian dream visions, a form that allows the author remarkable imaginative freedom.[20] Nevertheless, the poem also draws upon the well-known Type I vision within which itineraries through Other World geographies and targeted punishments and rewards were well established topoi. *Sólarljóð* is thus a remarkable generic hybrid whose textual affiliations place it within two very different traditions. It also subsumes a number of subgenres (or *undergenerer* as Bjarne Fidjestøl called them): as well as the wisdom poem, vision poem and visionary journey, Fidjestøl identifies: the exemplum, advice, lyric, allegory, the apocalypse or revelation, and even the riddle.[21] *Sólarljóð*'s long

---

17 See Carlsen, *Visions of the Afterlife*, pp. 82–88.
18 See Bjarne Fidjestøl, *Sólarljóð: Tyding ok tolkningsgrunnlag* (Bergen, 1979), p. 10.
19 Schorn, *Speaker and Authority*, p. 120.
20 Carolyne Larrington, 'Freyja and the Organ-Stool: Neo-Paganism in *Sólarljóð*', in *Germanisches Altertum und christliches Mittelalter*, ed. Bela Broyanyi (Hamburg, 2001), pp. 177–96.
21 Fidjestøl, *Sólarljóð*, pp. 30–31.

manuscript history links the work with other, more unexpected generic types: magical knowledge imparted by the dead and the bridal-quest romance. I begin, however, by situating the poem squarely within the Old Norse native wisdom genre. The poet's opening sequence offers powerful intertextual encouragement to hear and read it as a particular type of gnomic wisdom poem, structured around telling exempla.

## *Sólarljóð* as Wisdom Poem

*Sólarljóð*'s principal wisdom-poem model is the eddic poem *Hávamál*, perhaps known by the poem's author in a form much like the already hybrid sequence of stanzas preserved in the Codex Regius. *Hávamál* reminds us that generic hybridity need not only be produced by the adaptation of native genre systems to imported models, but was very likely already endemic in Old Norse poetics.[22] Since wisdom poetry by definition lacks the structuring cohesion imparted by narrative, variety and eclecticism has always been integral to it, underpinned by a powerful cultural belief that more wisdom must be a good thing: 'the idea of open-endedness, of infinite extension'.[23] Wisdom subgenres, as exemplified in *Hávamál* and eddic wisdom poetry more generally, are thus to be understood as constituted by interactions between form and content. Mnemonically effective framing and structuring devices, such as the dialogue or contest, the catalogue or enumerated list, are employed to encode and present varying types of wisdom: human or nature gnomes, mythological arcana, religious teaching, or the names of the runes.

*Sólarljóð* adopts the preferred metre of *Hávamál*, and other eddic wisdom sequences, *ljóðaháttr*, making regular, though in places flexible, use of it. The poem begins strikingly in *medias res*, like its model, with an extended anecdote about a repentant robber, and follows this with a series of representative micro-narratives or case-studies which explore more or less complex human situations. Brittany Schorn has noted how this beginning

> is deliberately ambiguous, and invites the audience to understand it as the start of a narrative poem, or at least a narrative frame, and speculate about the genre of the poem.[24]

Only at st. 8 is the anecdote revealed as an exemplum. This vivid illustrative technique may have been taken over from *Hávamál* st. 78, where the narrator demonstrates the fleeting nature of earthly wealth by contrasting the before-and-after condition of Fitjungr's sons.

---

22 Cf. Klaus von See, *Die Gestalt der Hávamál: Eine Studie zur eddischer Spruchdichtung* (Frankfurt am Main, 1972).
23 Carolyne Larrington, *A Store of Common Sense: Gnomic Themes and Style in Old Icelandic and Old English Wisdom Poetry* (Oxford, 1993), p. 129.
24 Schorn, *Speaker and Authority*, p. 127.

> Fullar grindr sá ek fyr Fitjungs sonum,
>   nú bera þeir vánar vǫl;
> svá er auðr sem augabragð,
>   hann er valtastr vina. (*Háv* st. 78)
>
> [Fully stocked folds I saw for Fitjungr's sons, now they carry a beggars' staff; wealth is like the twinkling of an eye, it is the most unreliable of friends.]

The brothers were once prosperous, their sheep-folds crammed with animals a visible sign of affluence, but, for unexplained reasons, they are now reduced to beggary. The *Sólarljóð*-poet adopts this technique of brief exempla that sketch before-and-after situations from *Hávamál*, along with quasi-allegorically inflected names: here in st. 78 *Fitjungr*, probably deriving from a root meaning 'fat'. Thus Ráðný and Véboði (st. 16), whose names suggest 'new counsel' and 'sanctuary offerer', thought that they were secure in their arrogance, trusting in themselves and obsessed with gold, but now they cower in hellfire. The exemplary vignettes, often gesturing towards motifs typical of *Íslendingasögur*, along with the 'speaking' names, effectively make concrete everyday situations in which foolish judgement or the vicissitudes of fate change human circumstances in predictable, but nevertheless, distressing ways. This use of exempla signals a particular kind of situational ethics prevalent in the poetics of Old Norse wisdom, and particularly apparent in the tale of Sörli and Vígólfr in sts 19–24.[25] The first stanza in the sequence warns against trusting the promises of enemies:

> Óvinum þínum trú þú aldri,
>   þó fagrt mæli fyr þér;
> góðu þú heit, gótt er annars
>   víti hafa at varnaði. (*Sól* st. 19)
>
> [Never trust your enemies, though they speak fair words to you; promise good things, it is good to have another's punishment as warning.]

Vígólfr killed Sörli's brother and, despite legal settlement and convivial drinking together, he murders Sörli too. The native common sense of st. 19 seems to be vindicated; yet in st. 24, Sörli's act of Christian forgiveness and his peacemaking intentions send his soul straight to heaven while his betrayers are hell-bound. Traditional wisdom and new Christian ethi-

---

25 For a fuller account of this approach, see Carolyne Larrington, 'New Thoughts on Old Wisdom: Norse Gnomic Poetry, the Narrative Turn and Situational Ethics', in *Proverbia Septentrionalia: Essays on Proverbs in Medieval Scandinavian and English Literature*, ed. Michael Cichon and Yin Liu, Medieval and Renaissance Texts and Studies 542 (Tempe, 2019), pp. 55–68.

cal injunctions pull interestingly against one another; ideological changes slant and inflect the anecdote.

After these exempla, dealing with transience, sexual desire, arrogance and gullibility, respectively, comes a list of seven precepts, tallied up in st. 32, with a typical wisdom adjuration to remember them and to put them into practice.

> Vinsamlig ráð ok viti bundin
>   kenni ek þér sjau saman;
> görla þau mun ok glata aldri;
>   öll eru þau nýt at nema. (*Sól* st. 32)

> [I teach you friendly advice, bound together with wit, seven (counsels) in all. They must be learned and never let slip; they are all useful to learn.]

Wisdom-poem generic markers (apart from the anaphoric catalogue of sts 39–45) now vanish, to reappear in the poem's closing sequence as noted above. The poem takes on a new direction in st. 33, with an explicit change of subject, 'Frá því er at segja' (It is to be told), as the speaker begins to narrate an account of his own spiritual condition before he embarked on his final illness and death. The themes of the earlier wisdom material thus find reflection in the speaker's own autobiographical situation before a plaintive tone emerges. Now the speaker describes his death, culminating in st. 39 with the first of the celebrated 'Sól ek sá' stanzas; their anaphoric openings unify them in a list of successive apprehensions of the speaker's inexorable journey into death.

> Sól ek sá sanna dagstjörnu
>   drúpa dynheimum í;
> en helgrind heyrða ek annan veg
>   þjóta þungliga. (*Sól* st. 39)

> [I saw the sun, the true day-star, bow down in the noisy world; and in the other direction I heard the gate of Hell roaring mightily.]

The symbolic valence of these verses has been much debated, but Fidjestøl is, I think, right to point to a crucial lyric element as the narrator's consciousness registers his last moments in the world.[26] Nevertheless, this sequence (sts 33–53) is difficult to place generically. Aphorisms emerge from time to time, encapsulating the general wisdom that explains and underpins the suffering and regret that the narrator experiences:

---

26 Fidjestøl, *Sólarljóð*, 'andre hoveddelen, str. 33–52, er meir sentrallyrisk ... Men i den samanhengen det er integrert her, fungere dette også dette som eit slags exemplum' (the second main section, sts 33–52, is more centrally lyrical ... but in the context into which it is integrated here, it too functions as a kind of exemplum) (my translation) (p. 31).

Hörundar hungr tælir hölða opt,
  hann hefr margr til mikinn;
lauga vatn er mér leiðast var
  eitt allra hluta. (*Sól* st. 50)

[The hunger of the flesh often entraps men, many a man has too much of it. A bath of warm water which alone of all things was most loathsome to me.]

The quasi-allegorical mode also returns with references to the *vánarstjarna* (star of hope) (st. 46), the *norna stóll* (norns' seat) (st. 51) and the *sjau sigrheimar* (seven victory-worlds) (st. 52). These terms produce vivid, immediate images; these connote mystical and unknowable aspects of postmortem existence, gesturing towards the arcane and inexpressible which can only be hinted at through metaphor and analogue.

## The Other-World Vision

From st. 55 onwards, a new generic model emerges: the narrator journeys through hell and heaven, observing the punishments of the damned and the pleasures of the saved. Accounts of Other-world visions had already been translated into Old Norse: *Duggals leizla*, a translation of the Irish *Visio Tnugdali* (composed in Latin in 1149 and translated into Icelandic at some point in the thirteenth century), is the best known, but Icelandic versions of the visions of Paul, Gundelinus, Furseus and Dryhthelm were also made.[27] The genre became productive within the native literary system, evidenced by 'Rannveigar leizla', an episode preserved in *Guðmundar saga Arasonar* as a brief prose account, conforming closely to the archetypal features of the religious vision-journey. The protagonist falls unconscious, is taken on a tour of the Other World, receives individualised warnings about her own sinful behaviour and prophetic information about the heavenly rewards awaiting the bishop after death. 'Rannveigar leizla' shares the political and ideological interests of its continental models, underlined by its inclusion in the hagiographical saga of Guðmundr.[28] Christian Carlsen notes how thoroughly the features of the vision genre – the journey through heaven and hell and scenes of reward and punishment among them – had been assimilated to Icelandic tradition: there is no clear source text for this section of the saga.[29]

*Sólarljóð*, in contrast, does something quite different with the genre, and indeed the poem is frequently not even considered alongside the

---

27  See Jonas Wellendorf, *Kristelig visionlitterature i norrøn tradition*, Bibliotheca Nordica 2 (Oslo, 2009).
28  Carolyne Larrington, '*Leizla Rannveigar*: Gender and Politics in the Other World Vision', *Medium Ævum* 64 (1995), 230–49.
29  Carlsen, *Visions of the Afterlife*, p. 40.

translated *leizlur*.³⁰ Traditional features such as the other-world guide are omitted, so too are the alternations between fire and frost (in fact incorporated in the earlier exempla at st. 18) or the Other-World bridge. The protagonist's swoon or quasi-death is rendered as a permanent state, impelling him to speak from beyond the grave with an enhanced authority. Nevertheless, the speaker's journey through the Other World incorporates a range of specific motifs found elsewhere in European visions: the grinding of food with earth to make it inedible (st. 57) occurs in the English 'Vision of the Monk of Wenlock'; limbs pierced with red-hot nails (st. 65) and the damned clad in burning clothes (st. 66), are both motifs from *Visio Thurkilli*, already known in Iceland at the putative date of composition.

The pleasures of heaven in vision accounts tend to be less unique and vivid than the torments of hell. They generally include features of the *locus amoenus* – meadows, fountains, sweet-smelling flowers, brilliant light – and splendid buildings. *Sólarljóð*'s conception of heaven is unusual, employing the distinctive accoutrements of Christian ecclesiastical practice. Angels bow low before the elect, books and inscriptions in *himna skript* (heavenly writing), candles are specifically mentioned, contrasting with earlier references to runes, ogress's blood and poisonous dragons, the pagan symbols which characterise hell.³¹

The penultimate section of the poem (sts 76–80) is the most obscure in the poem. In an inchoate, nightmarish sequence the poet invokes demonic supernatural figures with strangely pagan names and attributes, such as the rune-carving daughters of Njörðr (st. 79) *Óðins kván* (Óðinn's wife) (st. 77) and valkyrie-like figures (st. 76). These combine with homiletic images – *jarðar skipi* (the ship of the world) (st. 77) and even an organ-stool (st. 76). Suggestively symbolic references, exemplified in st. 78, introduce the return of the wisdom-format:

> Arfi, faðir einn ek ráðit hefi,
>   ok þeir Sólkötlu synir
> hjartarhorn, þat er ór haugi bar
>   inn vitri Vígdvalinn. (*Sól* st. 78)

> [Heir, I alone, the father, and the sons of Sólkatla, have interpreted the hart's horn which the wise Dvalinn carried out of the burial mound.]

Here at last is the generic convention of father imparting *ráð* to his son, but it is also clear that the supervening vision of hell and heaven has reconfigured the language in which the received wisdom is formulated. The riddling diction, harking back to the key image of the *sólar hjörtr* in

---

30  See, for example, Eldar Heide, 'The Term *leizla* in Old Norse Vision Literature – Contrasting Imported and Indigenous Genres', *Scripta Islandica* 67 (2016), 37–63.
31  Larrington, 'Freyja and the Organ-Stool', p. 189.

st. 55, poses a hermeneutic challenge to son and audience alike. Fidjestøl included the riddle as one of the *undergenrer* that he identified in the poem, and it is indeed productive to read the poem's series of obscure references, some incorporating speaking names, some not, in terms of kennings. It is not self-evident however, judging from the poem's critical history that there is a single key conceptualisation that could unlock the referential system, revealing a sustained allegory as shaping the poem's second half. For, as Whetter notes, while genre is 'a communicative resource leading to understanding', it is also one whose 'fluidity has often led to errors in communication and interpretation'.[32] Instead, such figurations as 'the sons of the dark of the moon' (*niðja synir*, st. 56), the well of Baugreyrir, (*brunnr Baugreyris*, also st. 56) or the sons of Sólkatla (Sun-kettle probably denoting heaven) in st. 78, cited above, seem to depend on local and immediate metaphorical associations rather than systematic correspondences. The author apparently invents eddic-sounding names, possibly without much reference to their other contextual senses; thus, a number of commentators have linked their interpretations of st. 78 to the Harrowing of Hell, and read the name *Vígdvalinn* (literally 'Slaughter-Delayer'), as conceivably a kenning for Christ, the death of Death. Perhaps inevitably, the name retains an unsettling association with the archetypal dwarf, mentioned several times in eddic poetry.[33] These sinister quasi-mythological nonce-formations connect this sequence with *Svipdagsmál*, likely composed around the same time, but where *Svipdagsmál* is a playful literary experiment in adapting Celtic story material in an Icelandic context, *Sólarljóð* warns those audience members with antiquarian interests of the perils of dabbling in the pagan past, invoking dangerously demonic forces in an already uncertain world.[34] While the wisdom monologue represents a traditional pre-Christian genre that still demonstrably possess usefulness, the cryptic mythological arcana of, for example, *Grímnismál*, is stigmatised, made terrifying and confusing, in the new eschatological and apocalyptic framework.

## *Sólarljóð* in Its Manuscript Context

Other kinds of genre information can be gleaned from the codicology of the manuscripts in which *Sólarljóð* is preserved. The poem is sometimes, and not unexpectedly, found alongside *Hugsvinnsmál* (as in Lbs 1199 4to from the late seventeenth century or ÍB 13 IV 8vo from the eighteenth century). Interestingly however, thirty-two manuscripts contain

32 Whetter, *Understanding Genre*, p. 14.
33 Dvalinn the dwarf appears in *Vsp*(K) st. 14, *Vsp*(H), sts 11, 14; *Vsp*(SnE). st. 5; *Háv* st. 143, *Alv* st. 16; *Fm* st. 13; *Dvalinn* is found as a deer-name in *Grm* st. 33.
34 Peter Robinson, 'An Edition of *Svipdagsmál*', unpublished DPhil thesis, (Oxford, 1991), is the most substantial study of *Svipdagsmál* to date. See also Larrington, 'Freyja and the Organ-Stool', pp. 190–92.

both *Sólarljóð* and the two neo-eddic poems *Gróugaldr* and *Fjölsvinnsmál*. These poems, collectively known as *Svipdagsmál*, represent a kind of pastiche, or at least a reappropriation of eddic lexis and motifs.[35] *Gróugaldr* also takes wisdom-poem form; structured around the enumerating list it has strong links to the 'Ljóðatal' section of *Hávamál* and *Sigrdrífumál*. *Gróugaldr* features a dead protagonist: Gróa, the mother awakened in her tomb to chant protective spells over her son who must journey on a dangerous bridal-quest at the behest of his stepmother. The magically knowledgeable, dead female being is an eddic staple, found in *Baldrs Draumar*, *Vǫluspá* and possibly *Hyndluljóð*. Gróa does not impart gnomic or mythological wisdom as do the male protagonists of eddic wisdom poetry, but her nine spells sketch out the perils awaiting Svipdagr on a journey that will take him to the Other World where his bride awaits. Dangerous rivers (st. 8) will course back towards Hel(l), mountain-frost and carrion-cold (st. 12) will not avail against him and the odd menace of a 'kristin dauð kona' (st. 13) will be averted. The terrors that Svipdagr must contend with are not demonstrably infernal, yet they share some of the traditional features of hell: frost and cold, and rushing rivers.

While *Gróugaldr* clearly belongs among the multiform genres of eddic wisdom poetry, *Fjölsvinnsmál* takes off from Gróa's anticipation that her son may be obliged to 'bandy words with the spear-magnificent giant', *við inn naddgöfga / orðum skipta jötun* (st. 14). Svipdagr's long exchange with Fjölsvinnr contains riddling elements, mysteriously symbolic-sounding names, and even three sons of the suggestively named Sólblindi, as well as arcane information about names and origins. *Fjölsvinnsmál* compares stylistically rather than generically with *Sólarljóð*, but the common preservation context suggests that later readers and manuscript compilers recognised the similarities between them, for both *Svipdagsmál* and *Sólarljoð* harness and hybridise the genres of wisdom poetry and the Other World journey: while the first poem sequence is inflected by a pastiche pagan sensibility, the second transmits a deeply serious Christianity.

## Conclusion

Why, given eddic metres' flexibility, strong association with the didactic, and their directly communicative stylistic features, more Christian poetry was not composed in them remains an interesting question. In part, perhaps, eddic poetry fell between two stools, as neither richly ornamented enough for high-status poetical composition in honour of the greatest king and lord of all, nor as simple and comprehensible enough to compete in clarity and directness with saga prose. Moreover, although narrative in *fornyrðislag* is possible, most poetry preserved in that metre is in fact dia-

---

35 Recently edited in *Eddukvæði*, ed. Jónas Kristjánsson and Vésteinn Ólason, 2 vols, ÍF (Reykjavík, 2014), II: pp. 437–50.

logue; so too the *ljóðaháttr* form tends to mediate directly voiced wisdom, whether as monologue or dialogue. Comparable Old English wisdom poems, such as *Precepts*, the arcane *Solomon and Saturn* II, and the Exeter and Cotton *Maxims* are composed in four-stressed alliterative verse; the first two in monologue / dialogue format, also present vestigially in the Exeter *Maxims*.[36] Old English however has no equivalent to *dróttkvætt*; either poetry or prose could equally be employed to mediate biblical paraphrase, as too saints' lives and homiletic material. Wisdom, soul and body dialogues and prayers tend to be preserved exclusively in verse.

Reading *Sólarljóð* against some different works from its usual comparanda of *Hávamál* and *Hugsvinnsmál* raises new and interesting questions about the way genre categories may have operated in the mid-thirteenth century, if that is when the poem was composed. Eddic wisdom poetry made use of shared frameworks and structures to deliver wisdom that might include mythological and supernatural arcana, common-sense human gnomes, protective spells, and runic lore, as well as exemplary anecdotes. These content categories might be pre-Christian or Christian; the landscapes and halls of *Grímnismál* finding their counterpart in the multiple geographies of *Sólarljóð*, the everyday human wisdom of *Hávamál* matched in *Sólarljóð*'s warnings against trusting in worldly goods or adjurations about the value of prayer. Runic lore is transformed into the different scripts of heaven and hell, while the exemplary micronarrative of Fitjungr's sons intersects effectively with the Christian exemplum tradition, and the plot-motifs shared with the *Íslendingasögur* to generate the vivid stories of Unnarr and Sævaldi or Ráðný and Véboði.

*Sólarljóð* represents a productive encounter between native wisdom modes and Christian visionary literature; the impact of learned tradition has reconfigured, at least in this instance, the Icelandic wisdom-poetry genre. '(G)eneric intermingling is sufficient and serious enough to create a generic hybrid', as Whetter defines the phenomenon.[37] But, as *Hávamál* and, in its way, *Svipdagsmál* teach us, the indigenous genre was already eclectic, expansive and innovative in its readiness to incorporate new subjects and new generic features into one of its oldest and most enduring literary forms. Creative and innovative as *Sólarljóð* is, it represents an evolutionary dead end within the Old Norse-Icelandic genre categorisation system. The *Svipdagsmál* model would inspire mythological-heroic pastiches well into the eighteenth century in poems that take up eddic mythological persons and styles.[38] Yet *Sólarljóð*'s hybridisation of wisdom and vision, innovative and creative though it was, generated no imitators,

---

36 See Larrington, *A Store of Common Sense*.
37 Whetter, *Understanding Genre*, p. 23.
38 Shaun F. D. Hughes, '"Where are all the eddic champions gone?" The Disappearance and Recovery of the Eddic Heroes in Late Medieval Iceland Literature, 1400–1800', *VMS* 9 (2013), 37–67.

as Wellendorf notes: 'ikke har (det) sin lige andre steder i den norrøne litteratur' ((there is) nothing like it anywhere else in Norse literature).[39] Thus the generic transformation of the kind of poem *Sólarljóð* is – from hybrid-form to *Mischgattung* – is arrested.[40] Preserved in seventy-seven extant manuscripts, the poem remains both unique and popular: a quirky outcrop in the Icelandic generic polysystem landscape.

---

39  Wellendorf, *Kristelig visionlitteratur*, p. 325.
40  See Baßler, 'Gattungsmischung', p. 53.

# Þættir – A Case Study: *Stjörnu-Odda draumr*

## Elizabeth Ashman Rowe

When considering the contribution of *þættir* studies to the question of genre in Old Norse literature, we can begin by remembering that it was a debate about these short prose narratives that sparked the articulation of some long-standing concerns about genre more broadly, namely whether it was valid to impose modern analytical categories on medieval literature whose authors did not seem to think in those terms.[1] The *þættir* are also an example of a 'necessary' genre. Ármann Jakobsson challenged *fornaldarsaga* scholars to start afresh and only use genres that are arguably needed, and he had already shown how this could be done in other areas of Old Norse literature by demonstrating that he needed the genre of *þættir* to talk about *Morkinskinna*.[2]

Like the sagas, the *þættir* (sing. *þáttr*) present us with the problem of disentangling corpus from genre, for the modern consciousness of 'short prose narrative' as a category of Old Norse literature has been shaped by nineteenth-century editorial choices and is not the product of rigorous analysis.[3] Unlike long literary prose narratives, however, which all fall into the single broad category of 'saga', short literary prose narratives can fall into one of two categories: *þættir* and 'ordinary' episodes, and it may be more accurate to postulate a spectrum going from *þættir* through *þáttr*-like episodes to ordinary episodes.[4] *Þættir* thus present a particular problem in regard to

---

1  This debate appeared in *SS* 47:4 (1975): Lars Lönnroth, 'The Concept of Genre in Saga Literature', 419–26; Joseph Harris, 'Genre in the Saga Literature: A Squib', 427–36; Theodore M. Andersson, 'Splitting the Saga', 437–41. For a survey of scholarship on the *þættir* from 1989 to 2006, see Elizabeth Ashman Rowe and Joseph Harris, 'Short Prose Narrative (þáttr)', in *A Companion to Old Norse-Icelandic Literature and Culture*, ed. Rory McTurk, Blackwell Companion to Literature and Culture 31 (Oxford and Malden, 2005), pp. 462–87. The *þættir* have most recently been discussed by Elizabeth Ashman Rowe, 'The Long and the Short of It', in *The Routledge Research Companion to the Medieval Icelandic Sagas*, ed. Ármann Jakobsson and Sverrir Jakobsson (London, 2017), pp. 151–63.
2  Ármann Jakobsson, 'Interrogating Genre in the *Fornaldarsögur*: Round-Table Discussion', ed. Judy Quinn, *VMS* 2 (2006), 282–83. For his discussion of *þættir*, see Ármann Jakobsson, 'King and Subject in *Morkinskinna*', *Skandinavistik* 28 (1998), 101–17, at p. 105.
3  Ármann Jakobsson, 'The Life and Death of the Medieval Icelandic Short Story', *JEGP* 112 (2013), 257–91.
4  For a discussion of 'saga', see Margaret Clunies Ross, *The Cambridge Introduction to the Old Norse-Icelandic Saga* (Cambridge, 2010), pp. 27–36.

genre, in that the base category as well as any subcategories need to be defined and identified. This is usually done on the basis of theme and structure or on the basis of rubric, but both methods are problematic. Theme and structure do not always clearly distinguish a *þáttr* from an episode, and few of the putative examples are referred to as *þættir* by the scribes who copied them, which undermines the validity of the term as a label for this category. Texts that are part of the corpus of *þættir* can be rubricated in terms of their content alone, as with *Auðunar þáttr vestfirzka*, which is headed 'Fra þvi er Avþvn enn vestfirðzki førþi Sveini konvngi biarndyri' (Concerning this, when Auðun the Westfjorder brought King Svein a bear), or *Albani þáttr ok Sunnifu*, which is headed 'Af lífláti Albani ok Sunnifu' (Of the death of Albanus and Sunnifa).[5]

The word *þáttr* means 'strand' (as in 'a strand of rope') and was generalised to mean 'a part (of a larger whole)', but it was only in the thirteenth century that 'þáttr' began to be used to refer to parts of sagas or to other textual units.[6] By the end of that century, the term 'þáttr' designated something different from a saga, with the two kinds of narratives being combined in a variety of ways. *Þættir* appear as prologues, epilogues, episodes within a saga, and independent works.[7] And as will be discussed below, *þættir* were an adaptable form: dependent *þættir* could be revised to stand alone, and independent *þættir* could be revised for interpolation. Flateyjarbók shows that the use of the term *þáttr* to identify a literary category remained imprecise during the fourteenth century, for the rubricator uses 'þáttr' to designate chapters of sagas, short narratives interpolated into sagas, sagas interpolated into other sagas, and independent short narratives.[8]

Even though 'þáttr' is not a very precise term, and even though not every text that we might call a *þáttr* is so labelled by the scribes, scribes upheld a consistent distinction between texts denominated as sagas and texts denominated as *þættir*: the average length of a saga is twenty-one to thirty-five pages, whereas out of forty-nine *þættir*, 88% are ten pages or less, and only one is as long as fifteen pages.[9] In some ways this is not surprising, but

5  *Morkinskinna*, ed. Finnur Jónsson, Samfund til Udgivelse af Gammel Nordisk Litteratur 53 (København, 1932), p. 180; *Flateyjarbók: En Samling af norske Konge-Sagaer med inskudte mindre Fortællinger om Begivenheder i og udenfor Norge samt Annaler*, ed. Guðbrandur Vigfússon and C. R. Unger, I (Christiania [Oslo], 1860), p. 242.
6  John Lindow, 'Old Icelandic *Þáttr*: Early Usage and Semantic History', *Scripta Islandica* 29 (1978), 3–44.
7  For examples, see Rowe, 'The Long and the Short of It', p. 155.
8  For example, 'Þaattr Otto keisara ok Gorms konungs' rubricates chapter 81 of *Óláfs saga Tryggvasonar*; 'Þaattr Þorleifs' rubricates a short narrative interpolated into *Óláfs saga Tryggvasonar*; 'Her hefr vpp Jomsvikinga þaatt' rubricates the beginning of *Jomsvikinga saga* (interpolated into *Óláfs saga Tryggvasonar*), and 'Þáttr frá Sigurði konungi slefu' rubricates an independent short narrative (*Flateyjarbók*, ed. Guðbrandur Vigfússon and Unger, pp. 107, 207, 96, 19).
9  Rowe, 'The Long and the Short of It', pp. 156–58.

it is doubly significant because it correlates with the contention that size is a generic marker, and it indicates medieval Icelandic consciousness of two kinds of prose narrative.[10] Whatever *þættir* might be as a literary category, they are not short sagas.

Nonetheless, *þættir* have multiple relationships to sagas that must be considered in theorisations of *þáttr* genre. First, the fact that most of the corpus is found embedded in kings' sagas is significant for the broader understanding of genre in Old Norse literature, insofar as this literature is notable for deploying genres in tandem: *þættir* in kings' sagas, eddic-style poetry in *fornaldarsögur*, and prosimetrum overall. Second, when Harris identified groups of *þættir* on the basis of shared characteristics, he associated four of his seven groups with saga genres: mytho-heroic *þættir* have elements in common with the *fornaldarsögur*, and feud *þættir*, skald *þættir*, and dream *þættir* have elements in common with the sagas of Icelanders.[11] Third, the (sub)genre of a *þáttr* may be determined by its function within its host saga. For example, *Þorsteins þáttr uxafóts* if taken in isolation is very much like a *fornaldarsaga*, but it is never found in isolation – it is only found in Flateyjarbók, in the saga of Óláfr Tryggvason, and there it is deployed as a conversion *þáttr*.[12] Its generic identity is not internal (or fully internal) to itself; instead its generic identity emerges from its relationship to *Óláfs saga*. Yet medieval audiences did not always read long works from start to finish, and dependent *þættir* may well have been read out of context.[13] Especially in Flateyjarbók, where the compiler of the Olaf sagas explains his reasons for including additional material, it is possible that the genre of a *þáttr* might differ according to individual perspective: the compiler intended *Þorsteins þáttr uxafóts* to be a conversion *þáttr*, but a reader who declines to wade through 600 pages of *Óláfs saga Tryggvasonar en mesta* might take it for a *fornaldarsaga*.[14]

---

10  Alastair Fowler, *Kinds of Literature: An Introduction to the Theory of Genres and Modes* (Cambridge MA, 1982), pp. 62–64; for discussions of medieval Icelandic consciousness of genre, see n. 1 above and also Massimiliano Bampi, 'Genre', in *The Routledge Research Companion to the Medieval Icelandic Sagas*, ed. Ármann Jakobsson and Sverrir Jakobsson (London, 2017), pp. 4–14.

11  Harris's other categories were king-and-Icelander *þættir*, conversion *þættir*, and journey-to-the-Otherworld *þættir*; see Joseph Harris, 'Þættir', *Dictionary of the Middle Ages*, ed. Joseph R. Strayer (New York, 1989), vol. 12, pp. 1–6. Since then, some *þættir* have been put into different categories, and the categories of feud *þættir*, journey-to-the-Otherworld *þættir*, and mytho-heroic *þættir* have been argued to be unnecessary (Rowe, 'The Long and the Short of It', pp. 153–54).

12  Elizabeth Ashman Rowe, '*Þorsteins þáttr uxafóts*, *Helga þáttr Þórissonar*, and the Conversion Þættir', *SS* 76:4 (2004), 459–74.

13  John Dagenais, *The Ethics of Reading in Manuscript Culture: Glossing the Libro de Buen Amor* (Princeton, 1994); Elizabeth Ashman Rowe, *The Development of Flateyjarbók: Iceland and the Norwegian Dynastic Crisis of 1389* (Odense, 2005), pp. 90–92.

14  Compare Glauser's chapter in this volume.

*Þættir* also demonstrate the necessity for the literary understanding of Old Norse genre to be well grounded in history and material culture. For example, aspects of the *þættir* that are deemed generically significant, such as a shared structure, theme, and ethos, could result from non-literary circumstances such as the geography of Iceland and Norway and the political structure of the Norwegian court.[15] And because nearly all *þættir* are found in just seven manuscripts, we risk concretising the interests of a single individual as literary genres or subgenres.[16] It may be valid to do so, but it should be done with full knowledge of the transmission of the texts.

Even though king-and-Icelander *þættir* might be dismissed as a category of historical reality rather than literature, the various kinds of conversion *þættir* do comprise true literary subgenres.[17] They clearly have their origins in textual culture, and they fit my preferred definition of a genre well. This is the definition proposed by Alistair Fowler, who argues that genres are identified by markers that include scale, subject, setting, values, mood, attitude, plot structure, and style.[18] Fowler also sees genres as inevitably evolving over time, as each new example can change subsequent authors' understanding of the category.[19] Another cause of change is the ability of authors to compose between genres as well as within them. The conversion *þættir* exemplify these processes. Composition within the genre is seen in the case of *Tóka þáttr*, where the existence of a story about King Óláfr Tryggvason encountering a man who could tell him first-hand about the pagan age (*Norna-Gests þáttr*) seems to have inspired the composition of a similar story about King Óláfr Haraldsson (*Tóka þáttr*).[20] Evolution of the genre is seen in the case of *Helga þáttr ok Úlfs*, which arguably was written in response to the conversion *þættir* associated with Óláfr Tryggvason and Óláfr Haraldsson.[21] This new kind of conversion *þáttr* is still about the conversion of a Norseman, but it is an independent narrative rather than an embedded one, the structure is bipartite rather than tripartite, and the theme is the power of St Peter rather than the power of Norwegian kings. Composition between genres

---

15 Rowe, 'The Long and the Short of It', pp. 154–55.
16 The chief manuscripts containing *þættir* are Morkinskinna, Flateyjarbók, Hulda, Hrokkinskinna, Jöfraskinna, Vatnshyrna, and Möðruvallabók; see Ármann Jakobsson, 'The Life and Death'.
17 Joseph Harris, 'Folktale and Thattr: The Case of Rognvald and Raud', *Folklore Forum* 13 (1980), 158–98; Rowe, '*Þorsteins þáttr uxafóts*'; Rowe, *The Development of Flateyjarbók*, p. 60; Rowe and Harris, 'Short Prose Narrative', p. 471; Rowe, 'The Long and the Short of It', pp. 152–54.
18 Fowler, *Kinds of Literature*, pp. 60–74. On these aspects of genre distinctions see also Chapter 9 and Chapter 17 in this volume.
19 Fowler, *Kinds of Literature*, p. 164; see also Chapter 2 in this volume.
20 Joseph Harris and Thomas D. Hill, 'Gestr's "Prime Sign": Source and Signification in *Norna-Gests þáttr*', *ANF* 104 (1989), 103–22.
21 Rowe, *The Development of Flateyjarbók*, pp. 275–79.

or hybridisation is seen in the case of the narrative about Þorsteinn *bæjarmagn*, which transforms elements of the conversion *þættir* into a short *fornaldarsaga*.[22] And yet another way in which the genre evolved was the change in context of transmission: the earliest conversion *þættir* are embedded into larger narratives in the manner of sermon exempla, but by the fourteenth century they are found as independent works.

The *þættir* can also be understood in terms of other genre theories. Postmodern theories that locate genre entirely within the world of literature help explain the *þættir* deployed in conjunction with sagas of Icelanders and the contemporary sagas, in that they share their cast of characters with those genres, even if they differ in size and structure. If the king-and-Icelander subgenre in fact began as history, it too engaged with the world of literature, as seen in *Orms þáttr Stórólfssonar*. This account of an unusual Icelander's interactions with powerful men in Norway makes a particular point about a king and an Icelander, and in this regard it resembles *Auðunar þáttr vestfirzka*.[23]

Social theories of genre such as polysystem theory, the oral origins of the material, and 'traditionality' and 'factuality' as generic markers are highly productive when analyzing the *þættir*.[24] Polysystem theory illuminates the *þættir* that are about competition for dominance over a centre, as with the *þættir* that depict Icelanders as the favoured spiritual sons of the missionary kings of Norway, the *þættir* that illustrate how to get ahead at court, and the *þættir* that promote the benefits of Christian literary culture.[25] The question of oral origins pertains as well, as mentioned for the *þættir* of *Morkinskinna* and as will be discussed for the skald *þættir* and dream *þættir*. 'Traditionality' and 'factuality' as generic markers can certainly be applied to the *þættir* and are particularly useful for thinking about subgroups, given that king-and-Icelander *þættir* rate high in factuality, whereas the conversion *þættir* rate low, but both groups rate low in traditionality.

The *þættir* can also be used to critique particular theories of genre. Scholars uncomfortable with rigid definitions of genre have invoked Wittgenstein's concept of 'family resemblance':

---

22  Fowler, *Kinds of Literature*, p. 183; Elizabeth Ashman Rowe, 'Generic Hybrids: Norwegian "Family" Sagas and Icelandic "Mythic-Heroic" Sagas', *SS* 65:4 (1993), 539–54.
23  Rowe, *The Development of Flateyjarbók*, pp. 83–84.
24  For polysystems, see Massimiliano Bampi, 'The Development of the *Fornaldarsögur* as a Genre: A Polysystemic Approach', in *The Legendary Sagas: Origins and Development*, ed. Annette Lassen, Agneta Ney, and Ármann Jakobsson (Reykjavík, 2012), pp. 185–99; for oral origins, see Aðalheiður Guðmundsdóttir, 'Interrogating Genre in the *Fornaldarsögur*', ed. Judy Quinn, 287–89; for 'traditionality' and 'factuality', see Stephen Mitchell, 'Interrogating Genre in the *Fornaldarsögur*', ed. Judy Quinn, 286–87.
25  E.g. *Þorsteins þáttr skelks*, *Brands þáttr örva*, and 'Óðinn kom til Óláfs konungs með dul ok prettum', respectively.

Like the members of a family, the texts in a given genre resemble other texts in that 'family' in various ways, but it may well be that no one text shares all the defining features with any other one text.[26]

The case of the *þættir* suggests that genre theories drawing on Wittgenstein's concept fail to take into account the dynamism of genre: if all instances of a genre are compared regardless of their date of composition, of course some will not share all the defining features.

Theories that make use of Wittgenstein's conceptualisation similarly fail to take into account the dynamism between genres, another reason why some examples of a genre may not share all the defining features. Hybrid, multigeneric, or multimodal *þættir* are certainly to be found. *Orms þáttr Stórólfssonar* and *Þorsteins þáttr uxafóts* change from *Íslendingasaga* to *fornaldarsaga* before coming to rest as a king-and-Icelander *þáttr* in the case of *Orms þáttr* and a conversion *þáttr* in the case of *Þorsteins þáttr*.[27] Another variety of multimodalism is heteroglossia, which is also found in the *þættir*.[28] For example, *Norna-Gests þáttr* presents three competing voices. One is the heroic tragedy of the eddic poem *Helreið Brynhildar*, which Gestr evidently recites with deep sincerity, as he had been the devoted servant of Sigurðr, whose death Brynhildr caused. Set against this is the response of King Óláfr Tryggvason's retainers, who take a gleeful delight in the verbal conflict between Brynhildr and the giantess: 'Gaman er þetta ok segþu enn flæira' (That's fun – recite still more).[29] Contrasting with both is the voice of King Óláfr himself, who cuts off his retainers and turns the entertainment to a topic of Christian morality: 'Ægi er naudzsyn at segia flæira fra þuilikum hlutum... vartu nǫkkut með Lodbrokar sonum' (It is not needful to say more about such things ... Were you with the sons of Loðbrók at all?).[30]

The difficulty of *establishing* a generic framework for the *þættir* is exemplified by the skald *þættir* and dream *þættir*, which have been associated with the *Íslendingasögur*. In keeping with Ármann Jakobsson's point about the *þættir* overall, the association of skald *þættir* with the *Íslendingasögur* should be revisited, for although the *þættir* involve Icelandic skalds, the narratives are entirely found in the contexts of kings' sagas.[31]

---

26 Carl Phelpstead, 'Interrogating Genre in the *Fornaldarsögur*', ed. Judy Quinn, 279; see also Marianne Kalinke, 'Interrogating Genre in the *Fornaldarsögur*', ed. Judy Quinn, 275–76, and Stephen Mitchell, 'Interrogating Genre in the *Fornaldarsögur*', ed. Judy Quinn, 286–87.
27 See Elizabeth Ashman Rowe, '*Fornaldarsögur* and Flateyjarbók', *Gripla* 14 (2003), 93–105, at p. 99, note 10 (*Orms þáttr*), and 100 (*Þorsteins þáttr*); Rowe and Harris, 'Short Prose Narrative', pp. 472–73 and 475.
28 On heteroglossia see also Chapter 5 in this volume.
29 *Flateyjarbók*, ed. Guðbrandur Vigfússon and C. R. Unger, p. 357.
30 *Ibid*. Norna-Gestr goes on to relate the miracle by which the sons of Loðbrók were dissuaded from attacking Rome.
31 Ármann Jakobsson, 'The Life and Death', pp. 258–59. *Morkinskinna* is the earliest

## Þættir – Stjörnu-Odda draumr

An association with the *Íslendingasögur* is more plausible for the dream *þættir*, which are set in Iceland, and the protagonist of *Þorsteins draumr Síðu-Hallssonar* even has his own saga. It might be objected that these two groups should not be considered together, given that the skald *þættir* are dependent works about living human poets composing in a historical setting during waking hours, whereas the dream *þættir* are independent works about poetry heard in dreams or during the night, in all but one case composed by a supernatural creature.[32] Nonetheless, the two groups arguably sprang from a common origin.

The earliest extant versions of nearly all the skald *þættir* are found as elements of more or less unified sagas composed between 1185 and 1225 (*Sverris saga*, the saga about St Óláfr attributed to Styrmir Kárason, and *Morkinskinna*), but presumably the skaldic verses had previously been preserved in oral tradition, along with the names of the poets and something about the circumstances of composition. In the late fourteenth century, the interpolation of *Þorleifs þáttr jarlsskálds* into the Flateyjarbók *Óláfs saga Tryggvasonar* suggests that skald *þættir* could be composed or elaborated for deployment in a saga, and this in turn suggests that skald *þættir* had developed into a genre, a productive category of literature. In the fifteenth century, the development of the genre continued when some skald *þættir* were extracted from their saga matrices, revised to be read separately, and transmitted as independent works.

If skaldic poetry accompanied by relevant information gave rise to skald *þættir*, dream *þættir* appear to form a parallel or secondary development of prosimetric narratives containing non-narrative poetry. That is, new *þættir* could be created on the model of the skald *þættir*. Composing a poem from a giant's point of view and devising a frame tale for it accounts for *Bergbúa þáttr*, and *Þorsteins draumr Síðu-Hallssonar* could be an attempt

---

extant context of *Arnórs þáttr jarlaskálds* (ch. 21), *Einars þáttr Skúlasonar* (ch. 97), *Sneglu-Halla þáttr* (ch. 43), *Stúfs þáttr hinn skemmri* (ch. 47) and *Þórarinns þáttr stuttfeldar* (ch. 72). *Sverris saga* is the earliest extant context of *Mána þáttr skálds* (ch. 85). Flateyjarbók is the earliest extant context of *Óttars þáttr svarta* (*Viðbætir við Óláfs saga helga*, ch. 6), *Þorleifs þáttr jarlsskálds* (*Óláfs saga Tryggvasonar*, chs. 168–74), and *Þormóðar þáttr* (*Óláfs saga helga*, chs. 148–50). The *Viðbætir* are excerpts from the *Óláfs saga helga* attributed to Styrmir *fróði* Kárason, composed c. 1210–25 but preserved only in Flateyjarbók.

32  In *Bergbúa þáttr*, two Icelanders taking shelter in a cave are required to memorise a poem recited by what seems to be a giant; in *Kumlbúa þáttr*, an Icelander who has taken a sword from a grave mound is threatened in poetry by the dead warrior; in *Þorsteins draumr Síðu-Hallssonar*, dream-women utter verses indicating that Þorsteinn will shortly meet a violent end; and in *Stjörnu-Odda draumr*, Stjörnu-Oddi dreams he is a saga character named Dagfinnr who composes praise poetry for King Geirviðr of Gautland. For a discussion of these works, see Ralph O'Connor, 'Astronomy and Dream Visions in Late Medieval Iceland: *Stjörnu-Odda draumr* and the Emergence of Norse Legendary Fiction', *JEGP* 111 (2012), 474–512.

to improve an existing narrative by composing poetry for it.[33] The verses in *Kumlbúa þáttr* could date from the late twelfth century, when Þorsteinn Þorvarðsson was supposed to have heard them, or they could be later medieval compositions.[34]

The fourth dream *þáttr*, *Stjörnu-Odda draumr*, must be discussed separately, as it is very much a 'generic outlier', to use O'Connor's phrase.[35] It begins with a frame tale about the twelfth-century farm-worker/astronomer Stjörnu-Oddi (Star-Oddi), who is described as truthful and not a poet. He is sent to Flatey to supervise some fishing, and at night he dreams that someone is telling a saga. The saga in the dream – about young King Geirviðr of Gautland and his court-poet Dagfinnr – is in the style of the late medieval, romance-inflected *fornaldarsögur*. It also boasts other generically significant features. As a nested story of the fantastic, it resembles *Hálfdanar saga Brönufóstra*; because Oddi dreams that he is Dagfinnr, the *þáttr* resembles the dream visions of thirteenth- and fourteenth-century Europe in which the dreamer is an active character in his dream; and because Oddi remembers some of the skaldic verses that he as Dagfinnr composed in the king's honour, the *þáttr* can be grouped with the dream *þættir*, although it is much more elaborate.

The peculiarities of *Stjörnu-Odda draumr* have elicited a range of critical interpretations. Its modern editor sees the dream-saga as an allegory of the twelfth-century dispute over the Reykjadalur chieftancy; Andrén sees it as inspired by the 1404 Battle of Slite; Allard argues for it being a parody of a *lygisaga* composed by the historical Oddi in the twelfth century; and the highly artistic nature of the work and its extensive connections to the *fornaldarsögur* are demonstrated by O'Connor and by Hui.[36] Two source-critical issues have further complicated our understanding of the work. One is that the verses seem to be much older than the prose,

---

33 For a discussion of some examples of awkward composition in *Þorsteins saga*, see *Norse–Gaelic Contacts in a Viking World: Studies in the Literature and History of Norway, Iceland, Ireland, and the Isle of Man*, ed. Colmán Etchingham et al. (Turnhout, 2019), pp. 223–24. If *Þorsteins draumr* is a kind of addition to the extant saga, it is no longer necessary to suppose that it is an excerpt from a saga that is otherwise lost.

34 Þorsteinn Þorvarðsson is mentioned in *Sturlu saga* (ch. 28), in the midst of events taking place in the 1170s (*Sturlunga saga*, ed. Jón Jóhannesson, Magnús Finnbogason, and Kristján Eldjárn, 2 vols (Reykjavík, 1946), I, p. 102).

35 O'Connor, 'Astronomy and Dream Visions', p. 490.

36 *Harðar saga*, ed. Þórhallur Vilmundarson and Bjarni Vilhjálmsson, pp. ccxv–ccxxi; Anders Andrén, 'Is it possible to date a *fornaldarsaga*? The Case of Star-Oddi's Dream', in *Nordic Mythologies: Interpretations, Intersections, and Institutions*, ed. Timothy R. Tangherlini (Berkeley, 2014), pp. 173–83; Joe Allard, 'Oral to Literary: Kvöldvaka, Textual Instability, and All That Jazz' (2004), http://tobias-lib.uni-tuebingen.de/volltexte/2004/1073; O'Connor, 'Astronomy and Dream Visions'; Jonathan Y. H. Hui, 'The *Fornaldarsaga* in a Dream: Weaving Fantastical Textures in *Stjörnu-Odda draumr*', *Quaestio Insularis* 17 (2016), 48–73.

and the second is that the work is only preserved in copies of the now-lost manuscript Vatnshyrna. The manuscript has been dated to between 1391 and 1395, and most scholars assume that this constitutes the *terminus ante quem* for the composition of the *þáttr*.[37] In support of his argument for a fifteenth-century date of composition, Andrén suggests that material was added to Vatnshyrna after its original phase of production.[38]

Pace Allard, a late medieval context of composition seems far more likely than a twelfth-century one. *Lygisögur* were certainly being composed as early as 1119, as described in the well-known account of the wedding at Reykjahólar, but the dream-saga in *Stjörnu-Odda draumr* has so many parallels with late *fornaldarsögur* and indigenous *riddarasögur*, and the interaction of dreamer and dream is so typical of late medieval European and English literature, that a late medieval context of composition is eminently plausible, whereas there are no parallels at all extant from the twelfth century. Moreover, as Allard points out, the conceit of the poetry being *stirðr* (stiff, wooden) because it was composed by a non-poet while he was asleep is perfectly paralleled by the character of Chaucer the pilgrim in the *Canterbury Tales*, who only knows one poem and that one so dreadful that the Host cuts short the recitation.[39] I would argue that the verses in *Stjörnu-Odda draumr* are a late medieval imitation of early praise-poetry, and it is part of the joke that any shortcomings are excused by its author's being not just untalented, but asleep to boot. Allard argues that this witty author is none other than the historical Oddi, who in reality must have been the opposite from how he is described in the *þáttr*: not a poor worker and no poet at all, but on the contrary hard-working and a gifted versifier.[40] Given the late medieval characteristics of the work, I would instead extend Allard's Chaucerian interpretation and see the figure of Oddi as the *þáttr*-author's equivalent of Lollius, the fictitious *auctour* (author, authority) from whose work Chaucer claims to have obtained the story of Troilus and Criseyde. In this case the *auctour* is in fact historical, rather than simply believed to be historical, but as O'Connor shows, an astronomer is just the kind of person who is likely to have a dream vision, and I would add that this scenario makes it more likely that the real Oddi was in fact not known to have composed poetry.[41]

Given the literary case for late medieval authorship, can Andrén's argument for composition after 1404 find any further support? The argument is not without flaws: Hui points out that the Battle of Slite took place on the island of Gotland, whereas the dream-saga describes a battle in

---

37 For the date of the manuscript, see Stefán Karlsson, 'Um Vatnshyrnu', *Opuscula* 4 (1970), 279–303.
38 Andrén, 'Is it possible', pp. 173–74.
39 Allard, 'Oral to Literary', p. 9.
40 *Ibid*.
41 O'Connor, 'Astronomy and Dream Visions', p. 498.

Gautland (Götaland in modern Sweden), and Andrén himself notes that the *þáttr* is not historically accurate in depicting Geirviðr as the defender of Gautland against the forces of the warrior maiden Hléguðr (whom Andrén argues was inspired by Margareta I), as the real Geirviðr (the Gotlandic magistrate Geirvid Lauk) had died more than twenty years before the battle over Gotland between Margareta's forces and the Teutonic Order.[42] The confusion of Gotland and Götaland noted by Hui is not in itself reason to dismiss Andrén's historicist reading, for the author might have deliberately transposed the battle from Gotland to Gautland, as Gautland was a frequent setting for fantastic adventures, whereas Gotland was not. A much more substantial objection is that the Icelandic annals, which report on contemporary events from around 1200 to 1430, mention Gotland only once, so it is highly unlikely that Icelanders had heard of Geirvid Lauk or the Battle of Slite.[43] Indeed, the Icelanders had never heard of anyone named Geirviðr, for the name is not found in any medieval Iceland work. However, names ending in -viðr are to be found in the *fornaldarsögur*, and the name Geirviðr is perhaps modelled on that of Russian King Hreggviðr (*Göngu-Hrólfs saga*) or the Swedish Jarl Þorviðr (*Sörla saga sterka*).[44] And if any of Margareta's battles were the inspiration for the dream-saga account of Hléguðr's attempt to obtain through battle her inheritance in Gautland, it would have been the Battle of Falköping, in Västergötland on 24 February 1389. This great victory, which resulted in the capture of King Albrecht and which made Margareta undisputed ruler of all Sweden except the German stronghold of Stockholm, was known to the Icelanders, took place in Gautland/Götaland, and fits unproblematically into the dating of Vatnshyrna.[45]

The literary interpretation of *Stjörnu-Odda draumr* is also relevant to questions of *þættir* and genre. Although acknowledging Allard's reading of the dream-saga as bordering on parody, O'Connor considers the work as a whole 'a literary *tour de force*' and a bold experiment in *fabu-*

---

42 Hui, 'The *Fornaldarsaga* in a Dream', p. 51, n. 8; Andrén, 'Is it possible', p. 182.
43 A miracle of St Óláfr in Visby is reported in Skálholts-annaler, *s. a.* 1314 (*Islandske Annaler indtil 1578*, ed. Gustav Storm (Christiania [Oslo], 1888), p. 203).
44 *Fornaldar Sögur Norðurlanda*, ed. Guðni Jónsson, 4 vols (Reykjavík, 1950), III, pp. 164, 387. Less likely as a model are the names in the family of the early rulers of Sunnmøre in Norway, according to *Hversu Noregr byggðisk* (*Flateyjarbók*, ed. Guðbrandur Vigfússon and Unger, I, p. 23): Þorviðr, Arnviðr, Slæviðr, and Bráviðr. For a discussion of the genre of this work, see Rowe, *The Development of Flateyjarbók*, pp. 316–31.
45 Lögmanns-annáll, *s. a.* 1387; Flatø-annaler, *s. a.* 1388 (*Islandske Annaler*, ed. Storm, pp. 283, 415); *Flateyjarbók*, ed. Guðbrandur Vigfússon and Unger, I, p. 29). The year designations in Icelandic annals are sometimes incorrect due to errors in numbering, the use of confusing abbreviations instead of long *anno domini* dates in Roman numerals, and the retrospective compilation of notices. See Rowe (forthcoming).

la.[46] Intrinsic to the genre of dream vision, O'Connor argues, is the difficulty in ascertaining the point of the narrative; whereas most dreams in Old Norse literature are later interpreted, O'Connor sees no obvious polemical or ideological purpose in the dream-saga.[47] Instead, it is escapist entertainment of a strongly fictional (rather than historiographical) nature. O'Connor's subtle, perceptive, and wide-ranging reading of the *þáttr* misses the mark in one important respect: it does not fully account for the author's choices regarding the subject matter of the dream-saga and the style in which it is treated, for the fictionality of any kind of saga could have been explored equally well. As the Continental and English dream literature shows, the form can be used for serious narratives about Christian morality (*Piers Plowman*) and courtly love (*Le Roman de la Rose*) as well as for satire (*The House of Fame*; 'Sir Thopas').[48]

In my view, the choice of a fanciful *fornaldasaga* is at the heart of the author's project. As O'Connor discusses, *Stjörnu-Odda draumr* is escapist entertainment, but the points made by Allard and Hui are vital as well: with its extensive borrowing from earlier sagas and heroic legends, its untalented skalds, and its absurdly young heroes and brides, Oddi's Otherworld is satirical rather than serious. The composition, although certainly innovative, is not experimental for the sake of experiment. Rather, like Chaucer in his 'Sir Thopas', the author deploys considerable artistry in the construction of a literary entertainment that is often entertaining precisely because it is not very good. The author presumably thought that his audience would find Stjörnu-Oddi as an unexpected but understandable choice of protagonist and would work out why his Gautland alter ego is named Dagfinnr. The author probably also thought that his audience would be diverted by the multiple layers of the narrative, would appreciate the geography of workaday Breiðafjörður reappearing in legendary Gautland, would be amused at the piling of *fornaldarsaga* cliché upon cliché, would relish the lameness of the verse (which, like 'Sir Thopas', I believe is deliberately incomplete), would cheer at the defeat of the monstrous Hléguðr, and would laugh aloud at the punchline: 'Má ok eigi undrast, þótt kveðskaprinn sé stirðr, því at í svefni var kveðit' (And although the poetry is wooden, one must not wonder at this, because it was composed while asleep).[49]

To conclude, the *þættir* contribute in significant ways to our understanding of literary genre in Old Norse. The case-study offered here – the postulated development of the skald *þættir* and the dream *þættir* – shows

---

46  O'Connor, 'Astronomy and Dream Visions', pp. 474 and 512.
47  *Ibid.*, p. 485.
48  Compare Larrington's chapter on '*Sólarljóð*', this volume.
49  *Harðar saga*, ed. Þórhallur Vilmundarson and Bjarni Vilhjálmsson, pp. ccxiv (the geography) and 481 (the quotation). For a discussion of Margareta's unpopularity in Iceland, see Rowe, *The Development of Flateyjarbók*, pp. 290–92, 333–36.

the necessity of including change over time in any theory of Old Norse literary genre. It also exemplifies how a corpus-based analysis can produce important insights into specific genres. Above all, it explores the extremely dynamic nature of Old Norse literature. The oral transmission of the compositions of historical poets not only developed into independent skald *þættir* but also became a model for a new variety of prosimetric narrative, the dream *þættir*. This in turn was drawn on by the author of *Stjörnu-Odda draumr* for a highly inventive parody of a late *fornaldarsaga*. *Þættir* provide clear evidence of medieval Icelandic awareness of different kinds of prose literature, and the different ways in which *þættir* relate to sagas highlight the flexible linking of genres as a fundamental characteristic of Old Norse literature. Although dream *þættir* developed from kings' sagas, they could be composed in connection with the genres of *Íslendingasaga* (*Þorsteins draumr*), *samtíðarsaga* (*Kumlbúa þáttr*), and *fornaldarsaga* (*Stjörnu-Odda draumr*).

# Íslendingasǫgur – A Case Study: *Vatnsdœla saga*

## Russell Poole

*Vatnsdœla saga*, a text long stigmatised as transgressing certain norms, at least in the eyes of modern scholarship and literary criticism, forms the subject of this case study. Its composition is thought to have occurred before 1280, because Sturla Þórðarson (d. 1284) used it in his redaction of *Landnámabók*, and after 1260, because the saga shows awareness of *Hallfreðar saga* and other works that are believed to have been written before 1260.[1] It is known in full only from transcriptions of Vatnshyrna, a now-lost early fourteenth-century manuscript.[2] Sturla appears to have used a different, superior manuscript for his redaction of *Landnámabók* and the Melabók redactor used a different manuscript again (*Vatnsdœla saga*, p. lvii). The present case study will contend that if we eschew normative genre approaches *Vatnsdœla saga* has the potential to add to our understanding of the saga genre.[3]

I start with some remarks by Norman W. Ingham. How, he asks, does the community recognise that a work belongs to a certain genre? In most cases, he contends, 'by a set of features the text displays – features of structure, mode, subject matter, style, commonplaces, implied functions, and more.' He concludes that classification by shared features is unavoidable, even though the common set of features may not be inclusive or always decisive.[4] In this spirit, I shall itemise some features that *Vatnsdœla saga* has in common with other sagas that have Icelanders as their principal personages, looking first at narrative material.

MULTI-GENERATIONAL NARRATIVE: *Vatnsdœla saga* chronicles the direct line of descendants of Ketill raumr over five generations.[5] The lead-

---

1 Vésteinn Ólason, '*Vatnsdœla saga*', in *Medieval Scandinavia: An Encyclopedia*, ed. Phillip Pulsiano (New York, 1993), p. 689; *Vatnsdœla saga*, ed. Einar Ól. Sveinsson, ÍF 8 (Reykjavík, 1939), p. xli (henceforward page references to this edition will be given inline in the form *Vatnsdœla saga*, p. xli); cf. Bjarni Einarsson, *Skáldasögur. Um uppruna og eðli ástaskáldsagnanna fornu* (Reykjavík, 1961), pp. 176, 214–22.
2 Jan de Vries, *Altnordische Literaturgeschichte* II, Grundriß der Germanischen Philologie 16, 2nd edn (Berlin, 1964), p. 399.
3 Cf. Massimiliano Bampi, 'Genre', in *The Routledge Research Companion to the Medieval Icelandic Sagas*, ed. Ármann Jakobsson and Sverrir Jakobsson (Abingdon and New York, 2017), pp. 4–14, at p. 7.
4 Norman W. Ingham, 'Genre-Theory and Old Russian Literature', *The Slavic and East European Journal* 31:2 (1987), 234–45, at p. 237.
5 Theodore M. Andersson, *The Growth of the Medieval Icelandic Sagas (1180–1280)*

ing figures in each generation are respectively Þorsteinn Ketilsson, Ingimundr inn gamli Þorsteinsson, Þorsteinn Ingimundarson ins gamla, Ingólfr Þorsteinsson and Þorkell krafla Þorgrímsson. In Iceland the family were known as the Hofverjar.

EMIGRATION FROM NORWAY TO ICELAND: *Vatnsdœla saga* recounts the family's move from northern Norway, led by Ingimundr inn gamli, to settle Vatnsdalr (modern Vatnsdalur) in the north of Iceland.

INCLUSION OF THE CONVERSION TO CHRISTIANITY: The account of this decisive moment, which occurs in the generation of Þorkell krafla, takes in both regional missionary activity and the decision at the Althing.

REGIONAL FOCUS: The district of Vatnsdalr, its chieftains and the *goðorð* based at Hof first assumed by Ingimundr inn gamli lie at the heart of this saga, which aside from its Norwegian prelude contains very little by way of excursions into other districts or references to other bases of power or influence (*Vatnsdœla saga*, pp. xxvii–xxviii).[6]

DETAILED DESCRIPTIONS OF LOCALITIES AND SPATIAL RELATIONSHIPS: An instance is the following: 'Ingimundr [inn gamli] nam Vatnsdal allan fyrir ofan Helgavatn ok Urðarvatn. Þórdísarlœkr fellr vestan í Smiðjuvatn' (*Vatnsdœla saga*, pp. 41–42, ch. 15), (Ingimundr [the old] took the entirety of Vatnsdalr above Helgavatn and Urðarvatn. Þórdísarlœkr runs from the west into Smiðjuvatn).

PLACE-NAME AETIOLOGIES: Names such as Hrútafjǫrðr, Borðeyri, Vatnsdalr, Víðidalr, Sauðadalr and Þórdísarholt are explained with respect to either natural features or events that take place at the locality. Thus when Ingimundr inn gamli sees a bear with her two cubs (*húna*) walking on an icy lake, he declares that it will be henceforth known as Húnavatn (ch. 15).

TAUNTS AND INCITATIONS: In a lengthy harangue, Ketill raumr admonishes his son Þorsteinn for lassitude in taking up the duties of a warrior (ch. 2). Uni, a farmer in Unadalr, more briefly incites his son Oddr to resist Hrolleifr Arnaldsson (ch. 19).

GRIEVANCES AND VENGEANCE: The most protracted case in this saga, running from ch. 22 to ch. 27, is the vengeance taken by the sons of Ingimundr inn gamli after his killing by Hrolleifr.

INVOCATIONS OF FATE AND DESTINY: It is noted that 'Þorsteini [Ketilssyni] var annarra forlaga auðit en vera þar drepinn' (*Vatnsdœla saga*, p. 8, ch. 3), (for Þorsteinn [son of Ketill] were different destinies decreed than to be slain there). Associated with these invocations in some way are repeated references to the family *hamingja* or *fylgja*, terms signifying something between 'attendant spirit' and 'inherent magical strength or giftedness'.[7]

---

(Ithaca, 2006), pp. 154–55.
6   Cf. de Vries, *Altnordische Literaturgeschichte* II, p. 399.
7   Gabriel Turville-Petre, 'Liggja fylgjur þínar til Íslands', in Gabriel Turville-Petre, *Nine Norse Studies* (London, 1972), pp. 52–58, esp. p. 57. For further discussion

## Íslendingasǫgur – Vatnsdœla saga

MAGICAL AND SUPERNATURAL OCCURRENCES: The saga contains numerous examples, amounting to a virtual narrative thread.[8] Related to these as a saga standby are dreams and their rival interpretations (ch. 42).

COMMERCE WITH THE GODS: Freyr is the god of this saga, just as Þórr is the god of *Eyrbyggja saga*. A silver object in Ingimundr inn gamli's purse, stamped with the image of Freyr, disappears and he subsequently finds it in Iceland as he places the high-seat pillars in his new temple (chs 10, 15). His sons Þorsteinn, Jǫkull and Þórir hafrsþió (goat's thigh) are given the use of a strong fearless horse called Freyfaxi which despite wintry weather, said to have been caused by magical powers, gets them safely to their destination (ch. 34).[9]

COURTING AND LOVE-MAKING: Ingólfr Þorsteinsson is a classic example of a saga personage with special attractiveness for women.

I turn now to extradiegetic features – i.e. stylistic and self-referential features that do not directly constitute narrative – that are equally constitutive of the saga genre.

MANIFESTATIONS OF A SENSE OF HISTORY: Explicit comment is made on such ancient and obsolete customs and practices as regional kingship in Norway (ch. 1); ship burials (ch. 23); the use of the *jarðarmen* or arch of turf in certain rituals (ch. 33); and succession to the *goðorð* (ch. 41).

EMBEDDED VERSES: The single example in this saga is used, as in many other sagas, partly to corroborate a statement and partly, it seems, for its entertainment value.[10] 'Ingólfr þótti konunum vænstr svá sem kveðit var: Allar vildu meyjar / með Ingólfi ganga / þær er vaxnar váru; / vesǫl kvazk hon æ til lítil' (*Vatnsdœla saga*, p. 100, ch. 38), (Ingólfr was regarded by women as most attractive, as was said: 'All the maidens who were grown up wanted to go with Ingólfr. The girl who was too little was forever saying she was desolate').

REFERENCES TO THE STATEMENTS OF INFORMANTS: Although opinions vary as to the significance of these references there is no doubting their pervasiveness in the saga genre. As pointed out by Bill Manhire, 'they often accompany unusual claims or extravagant details which might seem excessive to … a pragmatic audience'.[11] Typical is this example in *Vatnsdœla saga*: 'Úlfheðinn

---

of the two terms, and a possible distinction between them, see Clive Tolley, *Shamanism in Norse Myth and Magic*, 2 vols, Folklore Fellows Communications 296 (Helsinki, 2009), I, p. 228.

8   Bernadine McCreesh, 'The Structure of *Vatnsdœla saga*', SBVS 34 (2010), 76–83. For a specific instance, see Terry Gunnell, '"Magical Mooning" and the "Goatskin Twirl": "Other" Kinds of Female Magical Practices', in *Nordic Mythologies: Interpretations, Intersections, and Institutions*, ed. Timothy R. Tangherlini (Berkeley and Los Angeles, 2014), pp. 133–56, at p. 147.

9   On these and other allusions to Freyr see Lars van Wezel, 'Mythology as a Mnemonic and Literary Device in *Vatnsdœla saga*', in *Old Norse Religion in Long-Term Perspectives: Origins, Changes, and Interactions*, ed. Anders Andrén, Kristina Jennbert and Catharina Raudvere, Vägar till Midgård 8 (Lund, 2006), pp. 289–92 and references there given.

10  The classic study is Bjarni Einarsson, *Skáldasögur*.

11  W[illiam] Manhire, 'The Narrative Functions of Source-References in the Sagas

var mikill vinr Hólmgǫngu-Starra, ok þat segja menn, þá er Þórarinn illi skoraði á hann til hólmgǫngu, at Úlfheðinn fór með honum til hólmstefnunnar ok í þeiri ferð gerði at þeim veðr illt, ok ætluðu þeir vera gørningaveðr' (*Vatnsdœla saga*, p. 127, ch. 47), (Úlfheðinn was a great friend of Dueller-Starri, and men say that when Þórarinn the Evil challenged Starri to a duel Úlfheðinn accompanied him to the duelling place, and on that journey the weather turned foul, and they believed it was a witch's storm).[12]

REFERENCES TO (OTHER) SAGAS: 'Þeirar konu fekk Gríss Sæmingsson, en þó lék it sama orð á með þeim Hallfreði, sem segir í sǫgu hans' (*Vatnsdœla saga*, p. 122, ch. 45), (Gríss Sæmingsson married this woman but there were rumours about her and Hallfreðr, as is told in his saga).[13]

OVERLAPS IN CONTENT WITH OTHER SAGAS: The writer of *Vatnsdœla saga* used material also found, albeit with significant differences, in *Finnboga saga ramma* in describing Finnbogi's enmity with the sons of Ingimundr inn gamli.[14]

QUASI-FORMULAIC ELEMENTS: In this phenomenon, an action or event is stereotypical and can be described in semi-formulaic language. Examples are 'síðan vanði Hrolleifr þangat gǫngur sínar ok settisk á rœður við Hróðnýju' (*Vatnsdœla saga*, p. 52, ch. 18), (after that Hrolleifr got into a habit of going there and chatting with Hróðný);[15] 'ok er hann fann Harald konung, þá var honum vel fagnat' (*Vatnsdœla saga*, p. 44, ch. 16), (and when he reached King Haraldr he was given a good reception). Sexual dalliance and royal reception are two stereotypical components in sagas.

EXPLICIT TRANSITIONS: Examples of this prevalent stylism are 'Nú er þat at segja frá Ingimundarsonum, at þeir fóru heim um kveldit' (*Vatnsdœla saga*, p. 62, ch. 23), (Now is this to be said about the sons of Ingimundr that they went home in the evening) and 'Nú skal segja frá þeim manni, er fyrr var nefndr, er hét Þórólfr sleggja' (*Vatnsdœla saga*, p. 72, ch. 28), (Now must be told about the man mentioned previously called Þórólfr sleggja).

VARIATIONS IN STYLE: The style of *Vatnsdœla saga* is intermittently copious, sometimes even verbose, in both direct narration and dialogue. Some sentences are complex and multiply embedded. Paired alliterating nouns

---

of Icelanders', SBVS 19 (1974–77), 170–90, at p. 178.
12 Translation adapted from Andrew Wawn, 'The Saga of the People of Vatnsdal', in *The Sagas of Icelanders* (London, 2001), pp. 185–270, at p. 267.
13 Adapted from Wawn, 'The Saga of the People of Vatnsdal', p. 264.
14 Anton Gerard van Hamel, '*Vatnsdœlasaga* and *Finnbogasaga*', JEGP 33 (1934), 1–22. Also Gísli Sigurðsson, 'Another Audience — Another Saga: How Can We Best Explain Different Accounts in *Vatnsdœla* saga and *Finnboga* saga *ramma* of the Same Events?', in *Text und Zeittiefe*, ed. Hildegard L. C. Tristram, ScriptOralia 58 (Tübingen, 1994), pp. 359–75, at p. 364.
15 Cf. Daniel Sävborg, *Sagan om kärleken: Erotik, känslor och berättarkonst i norrön litteratur*, Acta Universitatis Upsaliensis. Historia Litterarum 27 (Uppsala, 2007), pp. 45–57.

and adjectives occur, as in the *riddarasǫgur* and religious writings (*Vatnsdœla saga*, pp. xxi–xxiii). Such stylistic features are sometimes said not to belong in saga style[16] but that claim is hard to sustain unless one prescriptively invokes notions of a 'classic' saga style.[17]

LOOSE STRUCTURE: Jónas Kristjánsson faults the construction of *Vatnsdœla saga* as 'rather loose', with the work falling into 'a series of tenuously linked sections',[18] but once again this looseness is an intermittent genre characteristic, also evident in such works as *Eiríks saga rauða* and *Eyrbyggja saga*. It can also be argued, as I shall presently, that the looseness is more apparent than real.

The sum of these features is sufficient, on the logic of Massimiliano Bampi and others, for us to classify *Vatnsdœla saga* confidently as belonging to the saga genre.[19] Here and elsewhere I pointedly avoid a narrower categorisation as 'sagas of Icelanders' (*Íslendingasögur*), since, as Margaret Clunies Ross notes, that term represents a 'fuzzy' rather than a firm demarcation.[20] If we accept Kevin S. Whetter's view that 'generic mixture is indeed ubiquitous' and consequently 'much of it does not require specific sub-classifications', then the pursuit of minute demarcation seems unlikely to be productive.[21]

Naturally many scholars have attempted, using a variety of methods, to impose definitions and tidy up our conceptualisation of the genre. Notable in this regard is Theodore Andersson's highly influential *The Icelandic Family Saga. An Analytic Reading* of 1967. Andersson sought to generalise a particular case of saga structure and content, the through-composed and highly plot-driven narrative of a long-running feud or vendetta, into an almost universal generic characteristic of sagas.[22] While this pattern is indeed fairly prevalent, and Andersson's achievements in analysing saga structure are undoubted, he himself noted that *Vatnsdœla saga*, 'like *Eyrbyggja saga*, fails to conform'.[23]

---

16  De Vries, *Altnordische Literaturgeschichte* II, p. 402.
17  The classic study is Jónas Kristjánsson, *Um Fóstbræðrasögu*, Rit Stofnun Árna Magnússonar á Íslandi 1 (Reykjavík, 1972), pp. 251–91. Cf. also Margaret Clunies Ross, *The Old Norse-Icelandic Saga* (Cambridge, 2010), p. 70.
18  Jónas Kristjánsson, *Eddas and Sagas: Iceland's Medieval Literature*, transl. Peter Foote (Reykjavík, 1988), p. 234.
19  Bampi, 'Genre', p. 8.
20  Judy Quinn *et al.*, 'Interrogating Genre in the *Fornaldarsögur*: Round-Table Discussion', *VMS* 2 (2006), 275–96, p. 278; cf. Bampi, 'Genre', p. 7, and John Tucker, 'Introduction: Sagas of the Icelanders', in *Sagas of the Icelanders: A Book of Essays*, ed. John Tucker (New York, 1989), pp. 1–26, at p. 3 n. 10.
21  Kevin.S. Whetter, *Understanding Genre and Medieval Romance* (Aldershot, 2008), p. 18.
22  Theodore M. Andersson, *The Icelandic Family Saga. An Analytic Reading*, Harvard Studies in Comparative Literature 28 (Cambridge, 1967), p. 5.
23  Andersson, *The Icelandic Family Saga*, p. 221, though contrast Margaret Clunies Ross, *The Old Norse-Icelandic Saga*, p. 129.

In his time Jan de Vries also found failings in *Vatnsdœla saga*. To account for them he developed a complex hypothesis, building on earlier work such as that of Anton Gerard van Hamel.[24] In what could be termed a 'stratigraphic' approach to the saga he invoked two authors (or redactors) of very different character: one from the early thirteenth century, who wrote in laconic style, and one from nearer the end of the century, who wrote in a more prosy sententious style and had lost touch with traditional understandings of *hamingja* and fate.[25] But in reality this dichotomy has only a weak evidential basis, resting chiefly on comparisons of the extant *Vatnsdœla saga* with the Sturlubók redaction of *Landnámabók*. The relationships postulated between the two texts are purely inferential and could easily be differently constructed (cf. *Vatnsdœla saga*, p. xxxviii). Additionally, as de Vries himself admitted, his two posited versions contain substantial overlaps in content, e.g. that relating to magic, which detracts from their supposed distinctness. Equally subjective were de Vries's distinctions, like those of van Hamel before him, between purportedly genuine oral tradition and fictional confabulation.

The methodologies adopted by de Vries and Andersson, although sharply differing, both rely upon essentially negative perceptions of this saga, positing failures that then require explanation. Instead, I propose adopting an affirmative approach, whereby *Vatnsdœla saga* challenges us to reach a more inclusive understanding of the saga genre. Specifically, it calls on us to recognise that individual works within the saga genre can develop distinctive and individual emphases.[26] Andersson's overarching vendetta plot is in fact an instance of these differential emphases: although such a plot is well attested in the genre it represents a special development that does not apply to all sagas. Another well-known instance of a special emphasis is the rich prosimetrism developed in some members of the genre, such as *Grettis saga*, *Egils saga* and *Kormáks saga*, when other sagas, including *Vatnsdœla saga*, have few verses or none. In *Kormáks saga* this particular elaboration is so marked that the saga has struck many readers as deficient in other respects.

The special emphasis to be identified in *Vatnsdœla saga* is the thematising of leadership. If we consider the successive heads of the dynasty central to the saga – Þorsteinn Ketilsson, Ingimundr inn gamli, Þorsteinn Ingimundarson, Ingólfr Þorsteinsson and Þorkell krafla – we observe that they exhibit consistent qualities of an exceptional nature. Their key

---

24 De Vries, *Altnordische Literaturgeschichte II*, pp. 403–04; van Hamel, 'Vatnsdœlasaga and Finnbogasaga'. It is to be noted that van Hamel avowedly disregards the opening Norwegian episodes of the saga (p. 2).
25 A similar approach is used by van Wezel, 'Mythology as a mnemonic and literary device in *Vatnsdœla saga*', pp. 291–92.
26 Whetter makes a related observation, 'What distinguishes a genre is not only the presence of certain elements but the emphasis and significance given to each of them' (*Understanding Genre and Medieval Romance*, p. 20).

function is, as Vésteinn Ólason remarks, to cleanse 'the land of alien and disruptive elements' that seek to misappropriate that which is not theirs.[27] Þorsteinn Ketilsson slays the mountain-man Jǫkull, who has been robbing travellers on an essential trade route (ch. 3). Þorsteinn Ingimundarson sends Þórólfr sleggja, a thief protected by his magical powers, to his death (ch. 28). Þorsteinn also moves to check the misappropriation of land (ch. 29). The sons of Ingimundr humiliate and finally kill Þórólfr heljarskinn, who has been stealing livestock (ch. 30). Þorsteinn imposes outlawry on Bergr, who has grazed his horses in Þorsteinn's hayfield (chs 31–5). Ingólfr attacks robbers and outlaws against great odds and defeats them, though he later dies of his wounds (ch. 41). Þorkell krafla kills Þorkell silfri when the latter repeatedly uses magic in an attempt to misappropriate the position of *goði* (ch. 42). Thus each holder of the *goðorð*, except possibly Þórir hafrsþió, whose tenure of it is somewhat equivocal, can be credited with the assertion of the law in the face of misappropriation and aggression.

This rectitude does not operate, be it noted, to the exclusion of the dynasty itself occasionally engaging in misappropriations. Þorsteinn Ketilsson and Ingjaldr and, in the next generation, Ingimundr inn gamli engage in Viking raids, the latter in partnership with Grímr Ingjaldsson and later also Sæmundr inn suðreyski (the Hebridean), before they all settle down to become respected landowners (ch. 7). The same holds true of Þorkell krafla, the last member of the dynasty to be chronicled (ch. 43). On a more individual scale Ingimundr inn gamli tricks a Norwegian guest, Hrafn, into forfeiting his sword, which becomes the ancestral heirloom Ættartangi (ch. 17); in this case the implication is that the Norwegian's excessive behaviour makes his property fair game.

Equally, in countering magical powers members of the dynasty sometimes avail themselves of magic. Thus Þórdís the seeress instructs Þorkell krafla to strike the cheek of Guðmundr Eyjólfsson, his opponent in a legal suit, three times, with the result that Guðmundr magically forgets to pursue the case (ch. 44). On the other hand, they do not go in whole-heartedly for magic. When Ingjaldr has a Lappish woman (Finna) attend a feast to foretell men's destinies and most guests take up the opportunity, Ingimundr and Grímr abstain: 'Þeir lǫgðu ok engan hug á spár hennar' (*Vatnsdœla saga*, p. 29, ch. 10), (they also paid no heed to her prophecies), as befits their noble heathen status. Reinforcing them in this restraint is perhaps the family's special luck or giftedness that protects them as they counter their adversaries. When Jǫkull's mother spares Þorsteinn's life she speaks of him seeking *gipta* (good fortune) from her son (ch. 5), and this could be seen as the originary *gipta* for the dynasty. It is renewed from another Norwegian source when King Haraldr gives Ingimundr, the founder of the Hofverjar, the lucky ship Stígandi (ch. 16).

---

27  Vésteinn Ólason, '*Vatnsdœla saga*', p. 689.

Another key attribute of the leading personages is an avoidance of excess in conflict and acquisition, complemented by a penchant for seeking and creating settlements. When struck his deathblow by Þorsteinn Ketilsson the robber Jǫkull says he was about ready to give up his wicked ways in any case – 'nú var ek á brott búinn at hverfa frá þessu óráði' (*Vatnsdœla saga*, p. 9, ch. 3) – and proposes that Þorsteinn marry his sister Þórdís. De Vries understandably wonders at the singular figure of the noble Viking, who at the hour of his death finds the spiritual power to forgive his adversary (die eigentümliche Figur des edlen Wikings Jǫkull, der im Augenblick des Todes die seelische Kraft findet, seinem Feinde zu vergeben).[28] This 'noble Viking' is part of the saga's thematisation; although not a member of the dynasty, he foreshadows their forbearance and temperance – perhaps indeed it could be seen as part of his 'gift' to them. Þorsteinn returns home from killing Jǫkull with angry accusations against Ketill, his father, but after some dispute the two are reconciled (ch. 4). Þorsteinn then summons people to an assembly where he makes restitution of their goods, reserving for himself only what others have not claimed and certainly not invoking any principle of 'to the victor go the spoils' (ch. 4). In his last illness he states, 'uni ek því bezt við ævi mina, at ek hefi verit engi ágangsmaðr við menn' (*Vatnsdœla saga*, p. 32, ch. 11), (The thing which I hold best in my life is that I have not been aggressive towards others).[29]

This ethos persists into the ensuing generations. On a visit from Ingimundr inn gamli to his father Þorsteinn some initial tension is soon smoothed over. Ingimundr and Grímr, on their expedition, engage in battle with a Norwegian called Sæmundr but soon agree to reconcile and join forces (ch. 7). As a *goði* Ingimundr maintains the peace without need for combat or litigation (ch. 17). Þorsteinn Ingimundarson restrains his characteristically hot-headed brother Jǫkull from taking drastic action against Þorgrímr skinnhúfa (Skin-hood), a magician who has encouraged Már Jǫrundarson to misappropriate valuable grazing land from the sons of Ingimundr (ch. 29).[30] Þorsteinn also promises his brother Þórir hafrsþió to call on 'the one who created the sun' to eradicate Þórir's berserk fits (ch. 37).[31] In his Viking days Þorkell krafla offers his entire booty to his munificent kinsman Sigurðr jarl rather than simply appropriating it himself or sharing it with his men (ch. 43). During his tenure of the *goðorð* he improvises a stratagem whereby Hermundr Ávaldason can escape after killing Galti and then prevails on the opposing parties to reach a peaceful settlement (ch. 45). Once again, there

---

28 De Vries, *Altnordische Literaturgeschichte* II, p. 399.
29 Wawn, 'The Saga of the People of Vatnsdal', p. 206.
30 On the possible connection of this land with the fertility god Freyr see van Wezel, 'Mythology as a mnemonic and literary device in *Vatnsdœla saga*', pp. 289–90.
31 Cf. van Hamel, who speaks of Þorsteinn's 'sentimental humility' and notes that 'it is represented by the author as a christian virtue' ('*Vatnsdœlasaga* and *Finnbogasaga*', p. 2).

Íslendingasǫgur – Vatnsdœla saga

are occasional lapses from this measured behaviour; thus Ingólfr joins with Jǫkull in breaking up the assembly violently to prevent Óttarr Þorvaldsson bringing his justifiable case against Ingólfr (ch. 37). In stopping short of outright idealisation the narrative exhibits quite a marked sense of history, perhaps because it was founded upon family or regional memories and confabulations which the writer could tone down but not simply bypass; as we have seen, the incorrigible womaniser and intermittently violent but highly popular *goði* Ingólfr is also remembered in *Hallfreðar saga*.

It is in keeping with this general tendency that *Vatnsdœla saga* is, as already noted, not one for narratives of protracted feuds. The one such episode that does occur (chs 18-27) goes to exemplify moderation in two generations of leaders. Hrolleifr Arnaldsson, a nephew of Sæmundr, settles in the district and, along with his mother, a sorceress, immediately causes trouble. When he starts courting Hróðný Unadóttir, her father incites his son Oddr to check the intruder but Oddr is killed. Uni is given Hrolleifr's land in compensation. Remarkably, Ingimundr takes in Hrolleifr and his mother when nobody else would but then, finding them as incompatible as others have done, moves them to a farm on the other side of the river. Here Hrolleifr causes trouble with the sons of Ingimundr by abusing the fishing rights and when Ingimundr rides up to intervene Hrolleifr fatally spears him. Again remarkably, and in the spirit of the Jǫkull of old, Ingimundr forgives his killer and tries to save his life.[32] Þorsteinn the younger reflects on this action:

> En við þat megu vér huggask, at mikill manna munr er orðinn með þeim Hrolleifi, ok njóta mun faðir minn þess frá þeim, er sólina hefir skapt ok allan heiminn, hverr sem sá er. En þat má vita, at þat mun nǫkkur gǫrt hafa (*Vatnsdœla saga*, p. 62, ch. 23).

> [We can take comfort in the huge difference that there is between my father and Hrolleifr, and for this my father will be rewarded by him who created the sun and all the world, whoever he is – we can be sure that someone must have been its creator.][33]

Eventually, impatient with Þorsteinn's measured pace in pursuing vengeance, Jǫkull beheads Hrolleifr. Þorsteinn nonetheless claims honour equivalent to the *goðorð* and the homestead at Hof as his reward for his leadership in this vengeance. Once more remarkably, the brothers not merely consent but also share the other main items of property amicably, including the sword Ættartangi, in such a way as to benefit Þorsteinn as well as themselves. Þorsteinn's brother Þórir is awarded titular rather than full tenure of the *goðorð* and holds it for some years before volun-

---

32 Böðvar Guðmundsson *et al.*, *Íslensk bókmenntasaga* II (Reykjavík, 1993), p. 114; the author of this section is Vésteinn Ólason.
33 Wawn, 'The Saga of the People of Vatnsdal', p. 225.

tarily yielding it to Þorsteinn. This story of the succession to Ingimundr inn gamli epitomises the triumph of moderation.

Moderation is likewise shown in Ingimundr's avoidance of conflict with the reigning power, namely Haraldr lúfa (more commonly known as Haraldr hárfagri). This characterisation runs against the grain of the majority of sagas, whose foundation legend normally shows settlers as resisting or evading the king, an ideologeme that is here enacted by Sæmundr. Ingimundr, as a close friend and ally of Haraldr, expresses reluctance to emigrate to Iceland (ch. 10). The mysterious flight of the silver object from his purse effectively takes the decision out of his hands (or, to put it differently, annuls his agency) but even so he undertakes that he would never emigrate without the king's permission (ch. 12).

No doubt registering these special features of the saga, Einar Ól. Sveinsson proposes that it is a 'mirror for princes' intended for the behoof of chieftains at the author's time (*Vatnsdæla saga*, p. xxxii).[34] It does seem that the author devised the main thread of the saga as a series of examples, if not exempla in the strict sense – some illustrating moderation and some excess.[35] A well-known thematic parallel is seen in *Hrafnkels saga*, where it is said, 'Á þetta lǫgðu menn mikla umrœðu, hversu hans ofsi hafði niðr fallit, ok minnisk nú margr á fornan orðskvið, at skǫmm er óhófs ævi' (People talked a great deal about this, how his arrogance had fallen away, and many now recalled the old proverb that the life of intemperance is short).[36] The leaders in *Vatnsdæla saga* look like noble heathens imperfectly incarnating virtues inculcated by St Paul in his Epistle to the Romans ch. 12: not rendering evil for evil (v. 17); having peace with all men so far as it lies within one to do so (v. 18); eschewing vengeance (v. 19 ); being generous to one's enemy in the knowledge by so doing you are heaping coals of fire upon his head (v. 20); and not being overcome by evil but overcoming evil by good (v. 21).[37]

---

34 A possible indication of this purpose is Þorsteinn's statement, addressing Ingimundr, an earl and the father of the robber Jǫkull, that 'er þat ok hǫfðingja siðr, at veita þeim líf, er sjálfkrafa ganga upp á þeira náð' (ch. 5), (it is also the custom of princes to spare the lives of those who approach them of their own free will).

35 On the increasing currency of literary exempla in the thirteenth century, see Conrad van Dijk, *John Gower and the Limits of the Law* (Woodbridge, 2013), p. 19. On the Icelandic reflexes of that development see Shaun F. D. Hughes, 'The Old Norse Exempla as Arbiters of Gender Roles in Medieval Iceland', in *New Norse Studies: Essays on the Literature and Culture of Medieval Scandinavia*, ed. Jeffrey Turco (Ithaca, 2015), pp. 255–300.

36 'Hrafnkels saga Freysgoða', in *Austfirðingar sǫgur*, ed. Jón Jóhannesson, ÍF 11 (Reykjavík, 1950), pp. 93–133, at p. 122.

37 For knowledge and use of the Epistles in twelfth- and thirteenth-century Iceland, cf. Ian Kirby, 'Bible and Biblical Interpretation in Medieval Iceland', in *Old Icelandic Literature and Society*, ed. Margaret Clunies Ross, Cambridge Studies

In considering possible contexts for this special thematisation, we can note that *Vatnsdœla saga* is widely regarded as reflecting the influence of the Benedictine monastery at Þingeyrar, situated at the mouth of Húnaflói north of Vatnsdalr (*Vatnsdœla saga*, p. lv). Founded in 1133, Þingeyrar was the first monastery in Iceland; its monks and their associates may well represent the first generation of saga writers.[38] Historically, the *goðorð* of the Hofverjar family had pertained to the public assembly at Þingeyrar and so what had been their domain fell within the ambit of the monastery once it was established.[39]

A clear textual link between *Vatnsdœla saga* and Þingeyrar is material the saga shares with *Þorvalds þáttr víðfǫrla*. In the *þáttr* Friðrekr, the missionary bishop, is challenged by two berserks to ordeal by fire, which he wins when they are burnt to death and he survives unharmed. This is one of two episodes in *Þorvalds þáttr víðfǫrla* explicitly attributed to Gunnlaugr Leifsson, reputedly the most learned of the monks at Þingeyrar.[40]

It is tempting to speculate further on possible connections with Gunnlaugr. An outstanding work of his is *Merlínusspá*, a rendering of Geoffrey of Monmouth's *Prophetiae Merlini* (Prophecies of Merlin). In this lengthy poetic translation Gunnlaugr catalogues the dynasties that rule Britain. He follows Geoffrey in focusing on the contrasting temperaments of the rulers and the effect of their character upon the people they rule.[41] While there is no suggestion that Gunnlaugr participated directly in the composition of *Vatnsdœla saga* it is possible that more generally the attitudes held by Gunnlaugr and his colleagues to secular leadership influenced the shaping of this saga set in his region of Iceland.

In summary, *Vatnsdœla saga* is not easily accounted for if we adhere to normative genre approaches. If we eschew them this saga has the potential to add to our understanding of the saga genre by letting us see its potential for thematic elaboration.

---

in Medieval Literature 42 (Cambridge, 2000), pp. 287–301, at pp. 294, 296.

38 Haki Antonsson, 'Salvation and Early Saga Writing in Iceland: Aspects of the Works of the Þingeyrar Monks and their Associates', VMS 8 (2012), 71–140, at p. 77.

39 Thor Hjaltalín, 'The Historic Landscape of the Saga of the People of Vatnsdalur: Exploring the Saga Writer's Use of the Landscape and Archaeological Remains to Serve Political Interests', *Medieval Archaeology* 53 (2009), 243–70, at p. 248.

40 *Biskupa sögur*, ed. Sigurgeir Steingrímsson, Ólafur Halldórsson and Peter Foote, ÍF 15 (Reykjavik, 2003), pp. 72, 84; Haki Antonsson, 'Salvation and Early Saga Writing in Iceland', pp. 121–22.

41 *Merlínusspá*, ed. Russell Poole, in *Poetry in Fornaldarsögur*, ed. Margaret Clunies Ross, SkP 8 (Turnhout, 2017), pp. 38–189.

# Byskupasögur and heilagra manna sögur – A Case Study

Kevin J. Wanner

Byskupasögur and heilagra manna sögur have long been labels used for, respectively, accounts of 'hinn fyrstu biskups í Skálholti og á Hólum' (the first bishops in Skálholt and in Hólar), and of Old Norse 'stories and legends of holy men and women'.[1] As the only traditional saga genres defined by a focus on religious actors, bishops' sagas and saints' sagas seem ripe for direct comparison. If, however, we shift attention from what these texts *are about* to what they *are*, we may find ourselves trying to compare two quite unlike concepts. I suggest that these sets of texts do not just differ in the way that all non-identical members of a class must, but that they perhaps will not fit in the same categorical box(es).

Yet before considering whether terms like *saga* and *genre* apply, in the same way or with the same meaning, to both sets of texts, it must first be acknowledged that, even if this is assumed, we are not here dealing with two distinct 'saga genres'. Rather, we have one genre that is fairly unified and homogenous, and another that is split between two other genres, one of which happens to be the first we are addressing. Since the category's inception, some *byskupasögur* have been classed among *samtíðarsögur* or 'contemporary sagas', a temporally defined genre dominated by the *Sturlunga saga* compilation, and covering events in the twelfth and thirteenth centuries. Others are placed among *heilagra manna sögur*, for the simple reason that their subjects are saints as well as bishops. As most who make this division observe, however, no *byskupasaga* is ever purely one or the other. Rather, each is an unbalanced hybrid or chimera, with bits and pieces of a secondary genre jutting out, in often obvious and sometimes incongruous ways, from the dominant one. The upshot of this is that our terms for comparison have shifted: what really needs to be compared are the qualities of contemporary sagas with those of saints' sagas.

---

1   Jón Sigurðsson and Guðbrandur Vigfússon, 'Formáli' to *Biskupa sögur*, I, ed. Jón Sigurðsson and Guðbrandur Vigfússon (København, 1858), p. v; *Heilagra manna søgur: Fortællinger og legender om hellige mænd og kvinder*, ed. C. R. Unger, 2 vols (København, 1877).

Another complication faced in comparing these saga groups is that each fits very differently among or within other genres. Joshua Rothman, writing about modern literature, remarks that one reason:

> [i]t's hard to talk in a clear-headed way about genre ... [is that g]enres themselves fall into genres: there are period genres (Victorian literature), subject genres (detective fiction), form genres (the short story), style genres (minimalism), market genres ('chick-lit'), mode genres (satire), and so on. How are different kinds of genres supposed to be compared?[2]

To keep things simple, one could say that *byskupasögur* and *heilagra manna sögur* are both subject-based subgenres of a culturally-defined subgenre ('saga') of the form genre of written prose (or, though rarely in these cases, prosimetric) narrative. Yet *heilagra manna sögur* also need to be described as a culturally-defined form subgenre of a subject genre (stories about saints or hagiography) that extends across many cultures, and manifests in many forms of media.[3] *Byskupasögur*, in contrast, are not part of a transcultural and multimedia subject genre: they are nothing more (or less) than a slice of the *saga* pie.

But what of the category of *saga*? While it seems like mere tautology to claim that bishops' sagas and saints' sagas are, indeed, both types of sagas, some doubt whether this is so. This stems from thinking of *saga* not just as a literary form, but as a specifically Icelandic genre defined by a gamut of stylistic, formal and substantive criteria. By this measure, some decide that saints' sagas do not fit into this category. For example, Kurt Schier declares that *Heiligensagas* may count only when '*saga* ... bedeutet ... "Geschichte" im weitesten Sinn. Das Wort sagt also zunächst nichts aus über den Inhalt oder die Gestalt eines Prosatextes' ('saga' ... means ... 'story' in the broadest sense. The word therefore says next to nothing about the content or the form of a prose text).[4] However, Schier also notes that:

> Im engeren Sinn ... [*saga* refers to] die in Island etwas von der Mitte des 12. Jhs bis in die erste Hälfte des 14. Jhs entstanden erzählenden Prosawerke, sofern sie nicht Übersetzungen sind. Sie bilden die klassischen Gruppen von Sagas, nämlich die *Islendingasögur*, *Konungasögur* ..., *Fornaldarsögur*, *Bykupasögur* [sic] und die *Sturlunga saga* ...

---

2   Joshua Rothman, 'A Better Way to Think about the Genre Debate', *The New Yorker* (Nov. 6, 2014): https://www.newyorker.com/books/joshua-rothman/better-way-think-genre-debate.
3   '[E]very source that says something about a saint, also an image or a material object, is a hagiographic source': Anneke B. Mulder-Bakker, 'The Invention of Saintliness: Texts and Contexts', in *The Invention of Saintliness*, ed. Anneke B. Mulder-Bakker (London, 2002), p. 13.
4   Kurt Schier, *Sagaliteratur* (Stuttgart, 1970), p. 1.

[E]s sind Werke über Ereignisse der eigenen, näheren oder weiter zurückliegenden Vergangenheit ..., denen man einen gewissen, wenn auch nicht immer gleich großen Wahrheitsgehalt beigemessen hat.

[In the narrower sense ... [*saga* refers to] narrative prose works originating in Iceland from around the middle of the twelfth century until the first half of the fourteenth century, provided they are not translations. They constitute the classical groups of sagas, namely *Íslendingasögur*, *Konungasögur* ..., *Fornaldarsögur*, *Byskupasögur* and *Sturlunga saga* ... These are works about events in their [Icelanders'] own nearer or more distant past ..., to which a definite, if not always equal, truth-value is assigned.][5]

Schier denies that sagas in the narrow sense include translated *riddarasögur* (sagas of knights or romances) or *Märchensagas* (fairytale sagas also known as *lygisögur*, about which more below), and 'Am seltensten rechnet man ... die Heiligengeschicheten zur Sagaliteratur' (least often have ... saints' stories been counted as saga literature).[6]

Thus, bishops' sagas and saints' sagas, despite their similar and overlapping subject matter, appear very different once one starts to think about how each fits into genre classification systems, as well as about whether their subject genres extend through other forms of media or into other cultures. Next, I will suggest another way in which *byskupasögur* – here, those that are essentially a subset of *samtíðarsögur* – significantly, perhaps fundamentally, differ from *heilagra manna sögur*, by drawing on insights from modern media studies. Specifically, I will consider a frequently made distinction between *textual genres*, an all-inclusive term whose noun serves simply as a synonym for *class* or *type*, and *genre texts*, a differentiating term whose adjective separates texts into two mutually exclusive camps. In so doing, I will not limit myself to analyses of written literature, but will also draw liberally from discussions focusing on film and television. Doing so seems justifiable since my primary intention is simply to differentiate generic from non-generic styles or modes of storytelling, and the nature of this distinction seems to hold fairly steady across different media forms. Thus, in this instance at least, analyses of genre in relation to audiovisual media have as much, and perhaps sometimes more, potential as those focusing on print or purely literary media to inform our understanding of pre-modern narratives such as those found in Old Icelandic literature.

5  *Ibid.*, pp. 3, 5.
6  *Ibid.*, 4. Schier is, of course, aware that saints' lives were among the earliest written prose narratives produced in Iceland, so that, even if one tries to exclude them from the genre, they were likely among the principal prototypes of the 'classical' saga form (pp. 121–22).

## Generic versus Non-Generic Storytelling

Above, I quoted a literary critic worrying about how different genres of genres are to be compared. Problems of comparison grow even more acute if zones in fields of cultural production are cultivated where genre itself is weeded out. Rothman suggests that the result is a true case of comparing apples and oranges: '"Literary fiction" and "genre fiction", one senses, aren't really comparable categories'.[7] *Genre fiction* refers to works that employ stock characters, settings, elements, tropes, and story patterns; standard examples include science fiction, fantasy, spy thriller, and horror. *Literary fiction* (or *mainstream* or *general fiction*, though these labels carry less of a whiff of prestige or promise of quality) refers to works that avoid conventions in pursuit of being *sui generis*. Literary fiction also, because it eschews period, futuristic, exotic, or otherworldly settings as well as fantastical elements, and emphasises characterisation over plot, typically 'focus[es] … on the commonplace dramas of our everyday lives'.[8] This same division applies to another fiction-dominated medium, that of film. As Thomas Sobchack writes:

> [a] genre film … differs fundamentally from other films by virtue of its reliance on preordained forms, known plots, recognizable characters, and obvious iconographies … Other fiction films are not genre films precisely because … they go out of their way to be original, unique, and novel. They appear more realistic, more true to life. Their characters are more highly individualized, their actions … more believable, and the events of the plot, employing random events and inconsequential details, well within the realm of possibility.[9]

Also worth considering here is television criticism. According to Su Holmes, 'the conceptual status of genre remains more contested in television studies' than in studies of other media because a borrowing of genre categories from film has 'made for a primary emphasis on television's narrative and fictional genres, leaving the applicability of the concept to non-fiction television … ambiguous'.[10] When watching television, we encounter not just sitcoms or dramas, but news programmes, commercials, sports broadcasts, game shows, cooking tutorials, or shows

---

7  Rothman, 'A Better Way to Think about the Genre Debate'.
8  Harvey Chapman, 'What is Genre Fiction?', *Novel Writing Help*: https://www.novel-writing-help.com/genre-fiction.html.
9  Thomas Sobchack, 'Genre Films: A Classical Experience', *Film Genre Reader IV*, ed. Barry Keith Grant (Austin, 2012), p. 124.
10 Su Holmes, '"A Term Rather Too General to be Helpful": Struggling with Genre in Reality TV', in *The Shifting Definitions of Genre: Essays on Labeling Films, Television Shows and Media*, ed. Lincoln Geraghty and Mark Jancovich (Jefferson, 2008), p. 161.

about non-actors house-buying, ghost-hunting or hoarding. While all of these can be considered genres, many reserve the term *genre television* for works of fiction (or also for reality shows in which 'reality' has been so carefully staged and selectively edited that any pretence of capturing things as they happened has been abandoned). As Jason Mittell puts it, 'studying *television genres* is distinct from studying *genre television*'.[11]

Clearly, in modern media criticism, great weight is attached to making 'genre' the adjective rather than noun when it is paired with the name of a form or medium. The formulation 'genre —' is usually restricted to works of fiction because only these can be expected to 'tell familiar stories with familiar characters in familiar situations'.[12] Conversely, non-fiction is non-genre for the simple reason that actual events and people will not conform to standardised patterns. As for invented stories that seek to imitate real life, these are classified as non-genre fiction owing to what Barry Keith Grant calls a long 'accepted separation of historical verisimilitude ... from the analysis of genre'.[13]

Can this distinction apply, however, in analysis of sagas? Does it make sense to think that there are not just 'saga genres', but also 'genre sagas'? Since works that aim to represent or resemble reality are not regarded as genre works, the first question to ask when considering whether there are 'genre sagas' is whether there are any fictional ones – or, rather, whether any were *regarded as* fiction, since the issue is not whether a story is true, but whether native opinion viewed it as such or as invention. Matthew Driscoll argues that,

> while not recognizing our modern generic distinctions, Icelanders did ... distinguish between narratives on the basis of their historicity and degree of verisimilitude, between what we might call 'history' and 'fiction'. Their term for the latter ... was *lygisaga*, or 'lying saga'.[14]

Driscoll goes on to suggest that *lygisögur* are, indeed, much like modern genre fiction, in terms not just of form and features, but of their enduring popularity, and the disdain they often receive from critics:

> They are, as has been said, all of a given type, the narrative possibilities of which are somewhat limited, but this same criticism can be

---

11 Jason Mittell, *Genre and Television: From Cop Shows to Cartoons in American Culture* (London, 2004), p. 201.
12 Barry Keith Grant, 'Introduction', in *Film Genre Reader IV*, pp. xvii–xxii at p. xvii.
13 *Ibid.*, p. xviii.
14 Matthew Driscoll, 'Late Prose Fiction (*lygisögur*)', in *A Critical Companion to Old Norse-Icelandic Literature and Culture*, ed. Rory McTurk, Blackwell Companion to Literature and Culture 31 (Oxford and Malden, 2005), pp. 190–204, at p. 193.

– and often is – levelled against, say, murder mysteries, country and western songs, 'Bollywood' – or for that matter Hollywood – films.[15]

Not only, then, are *lygisögur* fictional, but it seems valid to view them as a type of genre saga.

But how might this relate to bishops' or saints' sagas? Since both purport to report on reality, it seems they must be 'saga genres' rather than 'genre sagas'. Yet if we consider how some scholars have described them and the classes into which they fall, a different conclusion suggests itself. Theodore M. Andersson observes that, in comparison to 'sagas set in the Saga Age', *samtíðarsögur* 'are narratively flatter' and 'more chroniclelike', and Peter Hallberg describes them as presenting 'the raw material of life in all its overwhelming fullness …; the many authentic details threaten to blur the main outlines'.[16] Hallberg further notes that not only contemporary but also 'classical' sagas 'are encumbered with things that look more like remnants of a historical tradition than the contribution of a creative author'.[17] Such characterisations are reminiscent of how media critics describe both non-fiction narratives and non-genre fiction, even if these sagas claim only ever to be the former.

As for hagiography, while everyone recognises 'the diversity within the uniformity', no one doubts that here patterns trump representing or imitating life.[18] '[S]aints were the heroes of the Church, whose lives were illustrations of Christian perfection', and so 'the saint's life avoids the individualized portrait … rather present[ing] … an idealized type'.[19] Since 'saints inevitably share the same personal features and deeds, their written lives strongly resemble each other'.[20]

---

15 *Ibid.*, p. 198.
16 Theodore M. Andersson, *The Growth of the Medieval Icelandic Sagas (1180–1280)* (Ithaca, 2006), p. 13; Peter Hallberg, 'Sturlunga saga', in *Medieval Scandinavia: An Encyclopedia*, ed. Phillip Pulsiano and Kirsten Wolf (New York, 1993), pp. 616–18, at p. 618.
17 Peter Hallberg, *The Icelandic Saga*, trans. Paul Schach (Lincoln NE, 1962), p. 57. See also Schier, *Sagaliteratur*, p. 61. These scholars all build upon the analysis in Knut Liestøl, *The Origin of the Icelandic Family Sagas*, trans. A. G. Jayne (Oslo, 1930).
18 Ásdis Egilsdóttir, 'The Beginnings of Local Hagiography in Iceland: The Lives of Bishops Þorlákr and Jón', in *The Making of Christian Myths in the Periphery of Latin Christendom (c. 1000–1300)*, ed. Lars Boje Mortensen (København, 2006), pp. 121–33, at p. 131.
19 Margaret Cormack, 'Sagas of Saints', in *Old Icelandic Literature and Society*, ed. Margaret Clunies Ross, Cambridge Studies in Medieval Literature 42 (Cambridge, 2000), pp. 302–25 at p. 302; Margaret Cushing Hunt, 'A Study of Authorial Perspective in *Guðmundar saga A* and *Guðmundar saga D*: Hagiography and the Icelandic Bishop's Saga', unpublished DPhil thesis (Indiana University, 1985), p. 121.
20 Ásdis Egilsdóttir, 'Beginnings of Local Hagiography', p. 131.

These translated sagas tend to conform to their originals' content and tone, and '[t]he first Icelandic saints' lives show that the hagiographers ... were familiar with and could copy both the structure and the ideology of hagiography'.[21] In such descriptions, hagiography is assigned the same qualities as genre fiction. Indeed, the similarity is so pronounced that Sobchack could just as well be describing saints' sagas/lives when he writes that

> genre films attempt to embody once again the essence of a well-known story ... [While] other films may have the whole of life experience to choose from, the genre film must be made from certain well-known and immediately recognizable plots — plots usually ... in which obvious villains and heroes portray the basic conflict of good versus evil ... Genre films ... are made in imitation not of life but of other films.[22]

If saints' sagas join *lygisögur* as a type of genre saga, we must still come to grips with media studies' consensus that there are no non-fiction genre texts. While one way of removing this difficulty is to assert, not unreasonably, that saints' stories are mostly fiction, this does not really clarify the issue, which, again, is not the stories' objective truth-status, but the claims made by or for them to verity.

A better way to proceed is to suppose that saints' lives were regarded as both truth and fiction, albeit not in the latter term's usual sense. Rather, we must look to the obsolete meaning of 'fiction' as '[t]he action of fashioning or imitating'.[23] Saints' stories record events, but only ones realised according to a model. Thinking of them in this way requires 'the understanding of a world-view embracing direct supernatural intervention in human affairs'.[24] More precisely, it depends upon a belief that there are not just human authors, but also a divine one, who writes his stories not just in words, but in reality. And nowhere are God's plotting, characterisation, and presentation of themes supposed to be more evident or tightly controlled than in the lives of saints, who, because 'sanctity is derived from the sacred, which is radically singular, ... are fundamentally alike'.[25] And so saints' lives are not just 'true fictions', but fictions of the most generic sort.

---

21 *Ibid.*, p. 130.
22 Sobchack, 'Genre Films', p. 122.
23 'fiction, *n.*', *OED Online* (Dec., 2018): http://www.oed.com/view/Entry/69828. This entry also notes that 'fiction' derives ultimately from the Latin verb '*fingĕre*, to fashion or form'.
24 Diana Whaley, 'Miracles in the Sagas of Bishops: Icelandic Variations on an International Theme', *Collegium Medievale* 7 (1994), 155–84, at p. 156.
25 Thomas J. Heffernan, *Sacred Biography: Saints and their Biographers in the Middle Ages* (Oxford, 1988), pp. 7, 12.

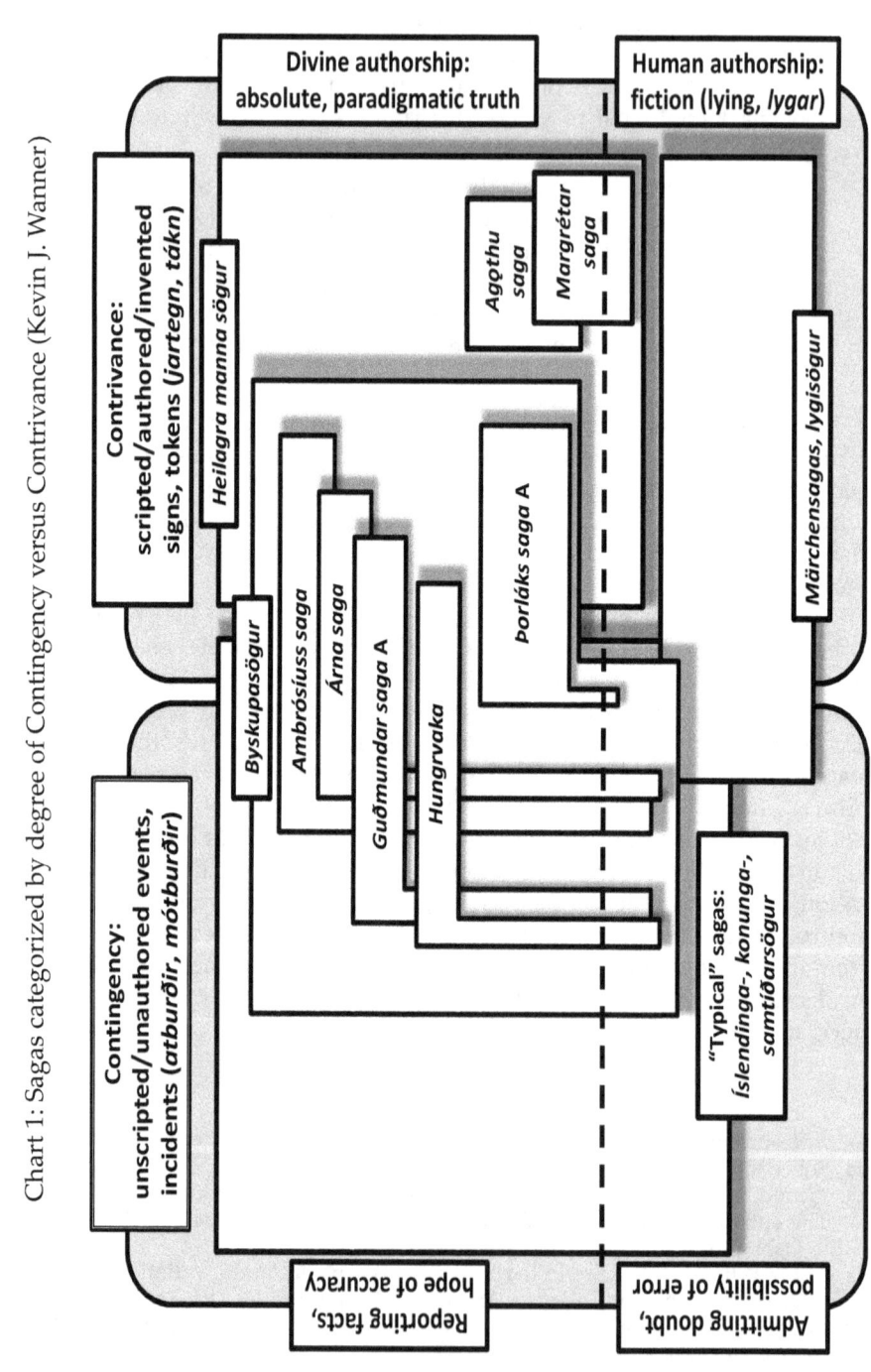

Chart 1: Sagas categorized by degree of Contingency versus Contrivance (Kevin J. Wanner)

## Charting Some Types of Saga Genres and Genre Sagas

At this point, a chart will prove useful. As I have suggested, in distinguishing narrative genres from genre narratives, the perception of an author, not just of a story's form but of the elements comprising it, is decisive. My chart (see Chart 1) thus starts with two underlying boxes: one labelled 'contingency' contains reports of unauthored incidents (*atburðir*, 'happenings', and *mótburðir*, 'coincidences', in native parlance); another labelled 'contrivance' holds scripted arrangements of carefully selected elements and invented incidents, which thus constitute meaningful signs or tokens (*jartegn* or *tákn*). A dotted line marks off both compartments' lower portions. The upper-left quadrant is a zone of certainty or at least reasonable confidence in reported facts; beneath the line lies a quadrant of doubt or potential error. On the right, this line separates our two sorts of authors: God perches above it, defining a quadrant of absolute and paradigmatic truth, while humans sit beneath it, working in a quadrant of fiction, or lying. Naturally, *lygisögur* or *Märchensagas* lie in the lower right, though I have indicated some seepage of these into the quadrant of uncertainty, to reflect sources' suggestions that some of what they relate *could* be true.[26]

The major genres of Schier's narrow corpus – *Íslendingasögur*, *konungasögur*, and *samtíðarsögur* – all fall largely in the quadrant of fact-reporting, with some spillover into the zones of error or, in the case especially of sagas of saintly kings, divine contrivance. As Massimiliano Bampi suggests, 'what is common to most saga genres is an interest in the representation of the past', and surely this includes these three: their readers expected a good-faith effort at an accurate and mostly non-editorialised recounting of events.[27] That the stories are artful, or ornamented with dialogue that must be regarded 'essentially as fiction' does not negate their intention to represent actuality.[28] Authors of such sagas were not in this respect very different, I suspect, from me when I repeat an amusing anecdote that I am well aware I have refined and embellished, or from a reporter who has no qualms about approximating or fabricating quotations so as to 'captur[e] the spirit of what was said'.[29] All of us simply navigate within our differing 'norms of what is permissible within the bounds of truth'.[30]

---

26 See examples cited in Driscoll, 'Late Prose Poetry', p. 194.
27 Massimiliano Bampi, 'Genre', in *The Routledge Research Companion to the Medieval Icelandic Sagas*, ed. Ármann Jakobsson and Sverrir Jakobsson (New York, 2017), pp. 4–14, at p. 8.
28 Hallberg, *Icelandic Saga*, p. 59.
29 Mark Liberman, 'Journalists: Stop Passing Off a Paraphrase as a Direct Quotation', *Slate* (Oct. 17, 2013): http://www.slate.com/blogs/lexicon_valley/2013/10/17/gay_talese_there_s_no_excuse_for_journalists_to_paraphrase_sources_in_direct.html.
30 M. I. Steblin-Kamenskij, *The Saga Mind*, trans. Kenneth H. Ober (Odense,

Placing *heilagra manna sögur* squarely within the quadrant of divine authorship is, of course, an oversimplification. Most saints' sagas contain random details or items of historical interest, and many admit to gaps in knowledge and the possibility of mistakes. Yet what I wish to highlight is, again, the genre's intention, which Jørgen Højgaard Jørgensen describes well:

> when writing ... [a] saint's life it is only reasonable to concentrate on those aspects that are of significance to God and then only by the way ..., to touch upon his dealings with the world, as they are irrelevant to the main theme.[31]

Two sagas of maiden martyrs will serve as illustrations. *Agǫthu saga* concerns Agatha of Sicily (*c.* 231–51), and *Margrétar saga*, Margaret of Antioch (*c.* 289–304). Both exist as more or less 'faithful' and often 'slightly abridged translation[s]' of *vitae*.[32] A single synopsis serves for both: a highborn, young, Christian virgin resists a nobleman's efforts to make her his wife or concubine and sacrifice to his gods. She is imprisoned and tortured, experiences visions and visitations in her cell, asks God for and is granted death and entry into heaven, performs posthumous miracles, and becomes the focus of a cult.

As rather lean genre texts, neither saga really contains anything incidental, and each is clear that God is the sole author of the saint's character and life. Agatha's saga expresses this theme very directly. When her tormenters try 'hug hennar snua mega fra heilagri fyrirætlan' (to turn her mind from holy design), she informs them: 'Hugr minn er fastr ok uppsmidadr af Kristi ... En ... grundvoll hus mins, þa mun þat eigi falla, þviat þat er smidat yfir stein' (My mind is firm and has been built like a house by Christ ... And ... my house's foundation ... will not fall, because it is built on stone).[33] And in her last prayer, she implores 'drottinn, er mik skapadir ok vardveittir mik fra æsko allt hingat til' (the Lord, who has shaped me and preserved me from my youth all the way until now), now 'latir mik skiliazt vit verolld' (let me depart from this world).[34] Because they are so similar, these sagas overlap on the chart. I also show, however, a portion of *Margrétar saga* dipping beneath the line separating divine from human invention. This is because its scene of Margaret being swallowed by a

---

1973), p. 33. Obviously, I disagree with Steblin-Kamenskij's overall thesis that the 'saga mind' operated with a notion of truth fundamentally different from that of modern people.

31 Jørgen Højgaard Jørgensen, 'Hagiography and the Icelandic Bishop Sagas', *Peritia* 1 (1982), 1–16, at p. 11.
32 Kirsten Wolf, *The Legends of the Saints in Old Norse-Icelandic Prose* (Toronto, 2013), p. 16.
33 *Agǫthu saga meyiar* I, ch. 1, in *Heilagra manna søgur*, I, ed. Unger, p. 1.
34 *Ibid.*, ch. 5, p. 5.

devil in dragon's form has been flagged as 'apocryphal', presumably because it stretched credulity.[35]

As for *byskupasögur*, true to the genre's divided nature these are placed in the chart's centre, with a rotated 'L' shape indicating their unequal extension into three of the four quadrants. This is because bishops' sagas tend to combine, on the one hand, the notion of the world being 'authored' and thus depictions of lives and events as stereotyped or patterned with, on the other, honest reporting of situations and occurrences that inevitably reveal the world to be full of accidents and elements to which it is hard to assign any inherent meaning or purpose.

One near exception to this is *Þorláks saga* A. As characterised by Jørgensen, this saga gives readers

> the impression that the hero [Þorlákr Þórhallsson of Skálholt (d. 1198)] managed to lead a life in complete harmony with all the prescriptions of scripture ... [He] is guided by his love of God, and only features of his life that serve to illustrate this, or God's love of him, are recorded.[36]

While many of the saga's elements are doubtless drawn from reality, it manages to ascribe virtually everything it reports to God's will. Even when this is not made explicit, events are often given a theodical twist. For example, when covering the uncomfortable fact of Þorlákr's parents' divorce, the saga suggests that this formative experience led the bishop to work to ensure that lack of funds would not cause marriages to end, mainly by using fines for adultery to help couples in crisis make ends meet. Thus, the bishop's misfortune is shown ultimately to result in good for others.

As for the most secular and historically minded *byskupasögur*, they still seem best depicted as stretching across regions of the chart. For example, Þorleifur Hauksson describes *Árna saga* (about Árni Þorláksson of Skálholt, d. 1298) as 'a political document and a traditional biography' that, using many 'letters and documents', provides 'a meticulous account' of part of Iceland's history'.[37] Yet Haki Antonsson argues that its dominant theme is 'how God's providence guided the bishopric through a period of uncertainty'.[38] This theme is developed less by conforming Árni's story to hagiographical tropes, than through extensive use of biblical parallel-

---

35 *Margrétar saga*, ch. 5, in *Heilagra manna søgur*, I, ed. Unger, pp. 477–79. I am cheating a bit here, since the editorialising in question is not in the saga, but in Jacobus de Voragine's *Legendus aurea*. Still, I think the point stands.
36 Jørgensen, 'Hagiography', p. 9. For similar comments, see Hunt, 'Study of Authorial Perspective', pp. 50–51.
37 Þorleifur Hauksson, 'Árna saga biskups', in *Medieval Scandinavia: An Encyclopedia*, p. 20.
38 Haki Antonsson, '*Árna saga biskups* as Literature and History', *JEGP* 116 (2017), 261–85, at p. 285.

ism.³⁹ *Árna saga* thus maintains the looseness of structure that signals a 'journalistic' commitment to reporting things as they happened, while insisting that all is yet 'written' and thus revealing of an authorial will.

A text that is in these respects similar to and thus sits near to *Árna saga* is *Ambrósíuss saga*, a life of Bishop Ambrose of Milan (d. 397) ultimately deriving from Paulinus's *vita* (c. 422). While not a *byskupasaga*, it is included here to show that a mixture of generic and non-generic properties may also be found in stories of non-Icelandic saintly ecclesiastics who, because the matters in question are too well-known and significant to ignore or reshape, are shown engaging in real-life or verisimilitudinous situations.⁴⁰ Like *Árna saga*, Ambrose's saga maintains a chronological rather than thematic structure, while also imbuing most of its episodes with divine purpose. For instance, in a chapter narrating the Empress Justina's and her Arian backers' efforts to harass Ambrose and his congregation, they fail time and again 'þviat guds vili stod i moti' (because God's will stood against it) and 'til auka gudligs takns' (to allow for an increase of divine signs).⁴¹ The saga also omits details that make Ambrose seem less remote in his concerns and dealings from Iceland's activist bishops: this includes near elimination of theological formulations, debates with heretics, castigations of Jews and references to his books. Finally, there are episodes so much like ones in bishops' sagas that they were likely perceived as 'stock scenes' that God has 'recycled' in his saints' lives. To give a few examples: the Holy Spirit's flame is seen in the mouths of both Ambrose and Guðmundr Arason of Hólar (d. 1237);⁴² Ambrose and Þorlákr are both threatened with a church they wish to control being used as a stable (*hrossahús*);⁴³ and an Icelandic chieftain's inability to hear church bells ringing the day before he dies in an assault against Bishop Guðmundr is matched by an imperial functionary who prevented Ambrose from advocating at a man's trial failing to see the open doors of a church wherein he hopes to find sanctuary.⁴⁴

The last texts I will discuss are centremost in the chart because of their pronounced hybridity. *Guðmundar saga* A is a patchwork of earlier accounts, and so its noticeable shifts in focus and tone are unsurprising. In her dissertation comparing *Guðmundar sögur* A and D, Margaret Cushing Hunt writes that A has 'a puzzling mixture of features' and an

---

39 Ibid., pp. 277–79, 283.
40 This similarity was not lost on writers of bishops' sagas, several of whom explicitly compare their subjects with Ambrose.
41 *Ambrósíuss saga*, ch. 5, in *Heilagra manna søgur*, I, ed. Unger, p. 32.
42 *Guðmundar saga* A, ch. 30, in *Guðmundar sögur biskups* I: *Ævi Guðmundar biskups*, *Guðmundar saga A*, Editiones Arnamagnæanæ B6, ed. Stefán Karlsson (København, 1983), p. 69; *Ambrósíuss saga*, ch. 23, p. 48.
43 *Þorláks saga* B, ch. 23, in *Biskupa sögur* II, ÍF 16, ed. Ásdís Egilsdóttir (Reykjavík, 2002), p. 170; *Ambrósíuss saga*, ch. 15, p. 42.
44 *Guðmundar saga* A, ch. 131, p. 156; *Ambrósíuss saga*, ch. 9, p. 36.

overall 'generic ambiguity'.⁴⁵ She emphasises A's reporting aspects: it is organised 'in strict chronological order', often offers 'a remarkably unbiased and truthful account of events', displays a fascination with 'minutiae [that] bespeak an interest in facts *per se*', and provides its main characters with 'individualized' and evolving rather than idealised, fixed, and God-given personalities.⁴⁶ Yet the saga also features, especially before Guðmundr becomes bishop, many miracles and prophecies. And affirmations of divine guidance of events are sprinkled throughout, such as when God is said to watch out for Guðmundr in a human fight that breaks out at a horse-fight, or when Bishop Brandr Sæmundarson interprets a fire at Hólar as God warning him against stinginess.⁴⁷

When undeniable tragedy strikes, however, the text's providential assumptions seem less confident, or consoling. In a harrowing account of Guðmundr's party getting caught in a snowstorm, many die, including children. The only (implied) miracle is that a girl wrapped in his cloak suffered frostbite only on an uncovered toe, and two boys' deaths are mitigated by a vision of them happy in heaven.⁴⁸ Elsewhere, theodicy is not even attempted, and mishaps are simply reported or treated naturalistically. Too much cannot be made of borrowings from annals, though the question of why God took no interest in preventing many deaths from illness in one year is at least raised when this fact is closely preceded by a story of him gently rebuking an old woman who dozed off during mass.⁴⁹ Some cases are well integrated into the whole, however, such as when Snorri Sturluson's daughter Hallbera takes ill, and Guðmundr, rather than having recourse to his holy water, enlists a priest who 'kallaðiz vera lecnir goðr' (declared himself to be a good physician); despite the priest's efforts, Hallbera dies, and the text simply reports that Kolbeinn Arnórsson could now get a new wife.⁵⁰

A similar, and sometimes more jarring, combining of contrivances and contingencies characterises *Hungrvaka*, a short account of Skálholt's first five bishops (1056–1176). As in Guðmundr's saga, the text is rife with incidentals (like Ísleifr Gizurarson giving a polar bear to an emperor in Saxony), annalistic passages, and attention to its subjects' activities not just in the socio-political arena, but in regard to administrative and fiscal duties. Also like Guðmundr's saga, *Hungrvaka* has strongly generic elements and passages, including stock scenes, such as when an episcopal candidate's reluctance gives way to acceptance that his election is God's will (of course, this scenario likely often played out for real,

---

45 Hunt, 'Study of Authorial Perspective', pp. 247–48.
46 *Ibid.*, pp. 91, 106–07, 133 (see also pp. 122, 164).
47 *Guðmundar saga* A, chs 20, 47, pp. 54–56, 83–84.
48 *Ibid.*, chs. 41–5, pp. 77–82.
49 *Ibid.*, chs 36, 38, pp. 73–74.
50 *Ibid.*, ch. 245, p. 247.

as an instance of life imitating art), as well as hagiographic tropes such as miracles and allusions to God's will and assistance.

The most striking similarity between these texts, however, is when real-life tragedies do not receive the response expected from a religious perspective. *Hungrvaka* recounts Bishop Magnús Einarsson's death in a huge housefire in Hítardalr.[51] While the text deploys a hagiographical commonplace by claiming that his body was hardly burned, its attempt to explain this calamity (*óhamingja*) – that God had Magnús die in a fire to grant his prayer that he not have to suffer a lingering death – seems rather uncomforting, more in line with the be-careful-what-you-wish-for moral of the cautionary fable 'The Monkey's Paw' than the comforting theodicy of the self-help classic *When Bad Things Happen to Good People* (It's also not said whether the eighty-two other casualties had made similar petitions…).

Even odder is the tale of another bishop's death earlier in the same chapter. *Hungrvaka* relates that when Ketill Þorsteinsson of Hólar was invited to Skálholt to a lavish feast,

> fóru byskupar báðir til laugar … eptir náttverð. En þar urðu þá mikil tíðendi. Þar andaðisk Ketill byskup, ok þótti mǫnnum þat mikil tíðendi … En með fortǫlum Magnúss byskups ok drykk þeim inum ágæta er menn áttu þar at drekka, þá urðu menn nǫkkut afhuga skjótara en elligar myndi.
>
> [both bishops went to the hot spring … after the evening meal. And then great tidings happened there. Bishop Ketill died there, and that seemed to men to be great tidings … But by the persuasions of Bishop Magnús and that excellent drink which men had there to drink, the men put it from their minds somewhat more quickly than they otherwise would have done.][52]

Camilla Bassett calls this passage 'blackly comic', but this hardly does it justice: 'sardonic', or perhaps 'absurdist', seems nearer the mark.[53] It is hard to say which bishop appears less dignified: the one who dropped dead while bathing, or the one who refused to let this ruin his party. More to the point, *Hungrvaka* makes no attempt to assign any deeper or higher meaning to what it twice in rapid succession calls *mikil tíðendi*, an astonishing turn of events.

A feature of the *byskupasögur* in the chart's centre, then, is their allowing random and tragic events to break the spell of a benevolent authorial will. They thus make room for – alluding to Sighvatr Sturluson and

---

51 *Hungrvaka*, ch. 8, *Biskupa sögur* II, pp. 31–23.
52 *Ibid.*, p. 31. Translation adapted from Camilla Bassett, trans., *Hungrvaka*, unpublished MA thesis, (University of Iceland, 2013), p. 64.
53 *Ibid.*, p. 19, n2.

Arnórr Tumason's famous exchange in Guðmundr's sagas – *atburðir* and *mótburðir* alongside *jartegn* or *tákn*.[54] Whether or not this juxtaposition is taken as a distinctive quality of this genre, it is certainly a paradoxical one. In worlds in which everything is given its place and purpose by an omnipotent and omniscient narrator, there can be no coincidences or accidents, or assignments of value or meaning that contradict those that have been assigned by the storyteller. This is what Rothman, Sobchack and Mittell understand about genre specimens of literature, film or television, and the chasm separating these from their non-genre counterparts. One cannot really compare (let alone combine) a realistic novel like *The Grapes of Wrath* with a fantasy epic like *The Lord of the Rings*, a biographical film like *Won't You Be My Neighbor?* with a superhero extravaganza like *Avengers: Infinity War*, or a scientific docudrama like *Cosmos* with a paranormal detective series like *The X-Files*, at least not when it comes to the worlds these stories profess or pretend to be true. And in the case of 'genre texts' that refuse to recognise themselves as fiction – which is one way of describing religion – meaning-filled plots escape the confines of human invention and are placed at the centre of reality.[55] What makes the most hybridised of the *byskupasögur* hard to understand in genre terms, then, is that they seek to combine the incommensurate, a generic and non-generic sensibility, in the same narrative. Or, in religious terms, they simultaneously believe and do not believe, or switch between these states at a sometimes giddying rate.

---

54 *Guðmundar saga* A, ch. 172, p. 187; cf. *Guðmundar saga* D, in *Biskupa sögur*, II, ed. Jón Sigurðsson and Guðbrandur Vigfússon (København, 1878), p. 113.
55 Brian Boyd calls religion 'invented stories that people take as true' in *On the Origin of Stories: Evolution, Cognition, and Fiction* (Cambridge MA, 2009), p. 199.

# Romance – A Case Study

*Jürg Glauser*

## The Origins of a Medieval Genre

The generic term 'romance', used to designate a specific group of medieval narratives, goes back to the Old French expression *mettre en romanz* 'to translate into the vernacular French', lit. 'to put into Romance language'.[1] The first French romances from the middle of the twelfth century were actually the result of translations of Latin chronicles and epics. It is worth noting that at the very origin of the French *romans* as a literary category, the activity of translating a narrative from one language (Latin) to another (French) was highlighted to such a degree that it gives the new genre its name.[2] The importance of the process of interlinguistic translation (and by extension transformation, adaptation, rewriting) which from the beginning was an integral part of the genre was underscored in countless romances in many different languages by comments which contribute to the innovative awareness that narratives written in the vernacular could and did exist in more than one language, change their forms and styles, adapt accordingly different meanings and functions, and were narrated by the self-conscious figure of a narrator.

Such meta-fictional features became generically constitutive and are found throughout the corpus.[3] They were part of romance's specific nar-

---

1  For an excellent introductory overview see Roberta L. Krueger, 'Introduction', in *The Cambridge Companion to Medieval Romance*, ed. Roberta L. Krueger (Cambridge, 2000), pp. 1–9; cf. also Simon Gaunt, 'Romance and Other Genres', ibid., pp. 45–59, and also the *Handbook of Arthurian Romance: King Arthur's Court in Medieval European Literature*, ed. Leah Tether and Johnny McFadyen, with Keith Busby and Ad Putter (Boston, 2017) with chapters by Stefka G. Eriksen, Sif Rikhardsdottir, Carolyne Larrington, Sofia Lodén and others.
2  Krueger, 'Introduction', p. 2.
3  The topical statement that a story was translated into the Nordic language (*norræna*) is also displayed at the beginnings or endings of numerous Norwegian, Icelandic, Swedish and Danish romances, especially early ones; see for example the prologue to the Norwegian translation of *lais*, *Strengleikar*: 'hinn virðulege hacon kononogr let norrœna or volsko male' (the esteemed King Hákon had [this book] translated into Norse from the French language) (*Strengleikar: An Old Norse Translation of Twenty-one Old French Lais. Edited from the Manuscript Uppsala De la Gardie 4–7 – AM 666 b, 4°*, ed. Robert Cook and Mattias Tveitane, Norrøne tekster 3 (Oslo, 1979), pp. 4–5; or the epilogue to the Old Swedish version of *Yvain*, *Hærra Ivan*: 'Eufemia drotning ... / læt þæssa bokena vænda svo/ af valske tungo

rative mode which is characterised by a great degree of explicit (meta-) fictionality; this was introduced and further developed by such writers as Chrétien de Troyes, Marie de France, Hartmann von Aue, Gottfried von Strassburg, or Wolfram von Eschenbach. Hence, medieval romance is often considered to be one of the prerequisites for the emergence and evolution of the genre of the modern novel.

Other essential criteria that are applied to define the corpus of romance on the thematic level are a set of common themes and contents such as: the focus on a royal universe, in which chivalric behaviour by individual knights is staged; the importance of adventures and physical fights which the knight has to endure; the love between the knight and a lady; and, more generally, the essential role of gender issues, emotions, and imaginations. On the formal level, the early European romances were written in verse, while prose romances are usually a later phenomenon.

One of the pre-eminent traits of the textual group, as well as the terminology used to delineate it, is the fact that neither were stable or consistent; this makes defining romance as a homogeneous genre with clear and neat boundaries even more difficult, if not impossible. The varying narrative modes and styles play on the historical, hagiographical, heroic, courtly, popular and so on. This structural and thematic fluidity opened the romance to permanent dialogues with other more or less closely related genres, allowed it to participate in a discursive framework and 'was a major factor in the evolution of romance and in the formation of its own generic specificity'.[4] In addition to this, the tangible material manuscript tradition contributed to further blurring the genre boundaries; romances

---

ok a vart mal' (Queen Eufemia ... / had this book translated/ from French into our language) (*Hærra Ivan*, ed. Henrik Williams and Karin Palmgren, in *Norse Romance*, ed. Marianne E. Kalinke, vol. 3, Arthurian Archives IV (Woodbridge, 1999), pp. 298–99). But later Icelandic romances also use the topos, e.g. *Viktors saga ok Blávus*: 'Marga merkiliga hluti heyrdum vær sagda af herra Hakoni Norges konungi Magnussyne einkannliga at hann hiellt mikid gaman af fogrvm frasögnvm. ok at hann liet venda morgum riddara sögvm j norænu vr girdzku eda franzeisv' (We heard told many remarkable things of Hákon, the king of Norway, son of Magnus, in particular that he took great pleasure in pleasant story-telling, and that he had many chivalric stories translated into Norwegian from Greek or French), (*Saga af Viktor ok Blavus, a Fifteenth Century Icelandic Lygisaga: An English Edition and Translation*, ed. Allen H. Chappel, Janua Linguarum. Series Practica 88 (The Hague, Paris, 1972), pp. 36–37). See also Jürg Glauser, 'Staging the Text: On the Development of a Consciousness of Writing in the Norwegian and Icelandic Literature of the Middle Ages', in *Along the Oral-Written Continuum: Types of Texts, Relations and their Implications*, ed. Slavica Ranković, Leidulf Melve and Else Mundal, Utrecht Studies in Medieval Literacy 20 (Turnhout, 2010), pp. 311–34; and Glauser, 'The Colour of a Sail and Blood in a Glove: Medial Constellations in the *riddarasǫgur*', in *Riddarasǫgur: The Translation of European Court Culture in Medieval Scandinavia*, ed. Karl G. Johansson and Else Mundal, Bibliotheca Nordica 7 (Oslo, 2014), pp. 199–224.

4 Cf. Gaunt, 'Romance and Other Genres', particularly p. 45.

were as a rule transmitted in manuscripts which also contained other text groups and genres, particularly *chansons de geste* and hagiographical texts; these supported an intertextual reading of the narratives.

There thus existed within the context of early French literature a traditional – so to speak 'ethnic' and not 'analytic' – term for this specific genre which however competed with other generic terms such as *contes* (tales) or *estoires* (stories/histories);[5] related French genres were *chansons de geste* (heroic songs/legends), *lais* (short narratives supposedly of Breton origin), *fabliaux* (short comic texts, often bawdy) and hagiography.[6] While the French term *romans* has its analogy in the ubiquitous English term *romance*, there is no adequate equivalent for it in German or any of the Scandinavian languages. In saga scholarship, the diverse French generic terms are therefore usually all subsumed under the indigenous Norse umbrella term *riddarasögur* (sagas of knights), on which more below.[7]

## An Innovative Genre in Medieval and Early Modern Scandinavia

Within a few decades after the first romances were written down in France in the second half of the twelfth century, the genre began to spread across most West and South European countries and by the beginning of the thirteenth century found its way into the north of Europe. If the chronological dating and channels of dissemination usually accepted in saga scholarship are correct, translations of Old French and Anglo-Norman and, to a lesser degree, Latin *chansons de geste* and romances were being made relatively shortly after 1200, first in Norway, then in Iceland, around 1300 in Sweden and towards the end of the fifteenth century also in Denmark.

Most if not all of the generic features of medieval romance mentioned above were represented within this increasingly vast and heterogeneous body of romance in medieval and early modern Scandinavia. The Nordic romances, i.e. the translations, adaptations and reworkings of quite a few French texts in the West and East Nordic languages (Old Norwegian, Old and Middle Icelandic on the one hand, and Old Swedish, Old and Middle Danish on the other) were able to invade, mainly because of their generic capability for connecting with many kinds of narrative modes, other genres

---

5  Krueger, 'Introduction', p. 1.
6  Cf. Gaunt, 'Romance and Other Genres', *passim*, particularly pp. 49–51.
7  The closest German correspondence to romance would be *höfische Dichtung*, or *höfische Romane*, (courtly poetry), (courtly novels). The Modern Icelandic *rómansa*, pl. *rómönsur*, is a recent neologism, see Torfi H. Tulinius, 'Kynjasögur úr fortíð og framandi löndum', in *Íslensk bókmenntasaga*, ed. Böðvar Guðmundsson, Sverrir Tómasson, Torfi H. Tulinius and Vésteinn Ólason, vol. II (Reykjavík, 1993), pp. 165–246, particularly 'Íslenska rómansan – fornaldarsögur og frumsamdar riddarasögur', pp. 218–44. Examples of the *chansons de geste* in the corpus of Norse romance are *Karlamagnús saga* or *Elis saga*, of the *lais*, the so-called *Strengleikar*-collection, of the *fabliaux: Mǫttuls saga*.

and in a literary historical perspective, they became more and more ubiquitous.⁸ By the middle of the thirteenth century romance in general and romance themes in particular were an inherent part of the Old Norse-Icelandic (prose and verse) generic system.⁹ The difference in form (verse in the French and Anglo-Norman texts, prose in the Norwegian and Icelandic saga translations and adaptations) is usually explained by the fact that a written vernacular prose-tradition had emerged in Norway and Iceland in the twelfth century. In the following centuries, Icelandic romance expanded into verse-forms such as *rímur* (narrative ballads) and *kvæði* (dance ballads), while the three primary examples of romances in the East Norse tradition, the so-called *Eufemiavisor* (romances commissioned by Queen Eufemia of Norway), were translated into *knittel verse*, marking, in their metrical proximity to the French texts, a distinct formal difference from the sagas' prose renderings.¹⁰ The simple metrums of the ballads were often close to that of

8   The metaphor of the 'invasion of romance' was launched by Gaunt, 'Romance and Other Genres', p. 57. For a telling example of how Geoffrey of Monmouth's *Historia regum Britanniae* in its Old Icelandic translation, *Breta sögur* (Sagas of the Britons), was adapted in two redactions in different styles and genres – one as historiography, the other one as romance – which were circulating simultaneously in manuscripts from the thirteenth century and later, see Stefanie Gropper, '*Breta sögur* and *Merlínusspá*', in *The Arthur of the North: The Arthurian Legend in the Norse and Rus' Realms*, ed. Marianne E. Kalinke, Arthurian Literature in the Middle Ages V (Cardiff, 2011), pp. 48–60.
9   Cf. Massimiliano Bampi, 'Genre', in *The Routledge Research Companion to the Medieval Icelandic Sagas*, ed. Ármann Jakobsson and Sverrir Jakobsson (London, 2017), pp. 4–14, provides a concise research review of earlier and recent attempts at defining medieval Icelandic prose genres and suggests methodologically fresh approaches to solve the main issues of genre definition in the corpus of the Icelandic sagas on the basis, among others, of reception theory, intertextuality, polysystem theory, material philology and memory studies. There can be no doubt that this is the way to go forward in future analysis of literary genres in medieval Iceland.
10  Matthew J. Driscoll, 'Arthurian Ballads, *rímur*, Chapbooks and Folktales', in *The Arthur of the North*, ed. Kalinke, pp. 168–95, and William Layher, 'The Old Swedish *Hærra Ivan Leons riddare*', in *ibid.*, pp. 123–44, treat aspects of the Arthurian romance in these genres. Recent research results with regard to Norse romance are also to be found in Sif Rikhardsdottir, *Medieval Translations and Cultural Discourse: The Movement of Texts in England, France and Scandinavia* (Cambridge, 2012); *Rittersagas: Übersetzung, Überlieferung, Transmission*, ed. Jürg Glauser and Susanne Kramarz-Bein, Beiträge zur Nordischen Philologie 45 (Tübingen, 2014); *Riddarasǫgur: The Translation of European Court Culture in Medieval Scandinavia*, ed. Karl G. Johansson and Else Mundal, Bibliotheca Nordica 7 (Oslo, 2014); 'Arthur of the North: Histories, Emotions, and Imaginations', special issue of *SS* 87.1 (2015), ed. Bjørn Bandlien, Stefka G. Eriksen and Sif Rikhardsdottir; Marianne E. Kalinke, *Stories Set Forth with Fair Words: The Evolution of Medieval Romance in Iceland* (Cardiff, 2017). The impressive number of studies dealing with *riddarasögur* in the broadest sense mirrors the increasing popularity of romance studies in recent Old Norse-Icelandic scholarship quite well. The field of East Norse romance has also attracted renewed scholarly interest in the past years,

the *Eufemiavisor*, while *rímur* – called by Ralph O'Connor 'the true representatives of romances in Iceland' – came to display a rich variety of complex metres and verse-forms.[11]

In the second half of the thirteenth century, the system of Icelandic prose genres consisted of a number of different types in terms of date, scope, narrative modes, structure and so on, of which *heilagra manna sögur* (saints' lives), sagas of antiquity, *konungasögur* (kings' sagas), *Íslendingasögur* (sagas of Icelanders), *byskupasögur* (bishops' sagas), Icelandic saints' lives, *samtíðarsögur* (contemporary sagas), *fornaldarsögur* (mythical-heroic or legendary sagas), *riddarasögur* (knights' sagas) are the most prominent. The terminology is documented only for *heilagra manna sögur*, *konungasögur*, and *riddarasögur* in pre-modern manuscripts; the other terms are coined by modern scholarship.

Kurt Schier's widely used subdivision and (German) terminology of the sagas from 1970 are mainly based on the thematic categories and are at times somewhat rigid.[12] Compared with this, Stephen A. Mitchell's diagram which shows '"ideal types" of each saga genre' on the axes 'Fabulous'–'Factual' / 'More traditional'–'Less traditional' has the advantage of being dynamic and allowing for zones of transgression between various subgenres.[13]

The genre of Norse romance consists then of several, thematically, medially, and chronologically defined subgroups:

1) The 'core group' would encompass those eleven Old Norwegian and Icelandic *riddarasögur* and *Eufemiavisor* for which there is a Latin, Old French or Anglo-Norman model. These are *Tristrams saga ok Ísöndar*, *Erex saga*, *Ivens saga/ Hærra Ivan* (Old Swedish), *Parcevals saga*, *Strengleikar* (a collection of twelve *lais* in Old Norwegian translation), *Flóres saga ok Blankiflúr / Flores och Blanzaflor* (Old Swedish and Middle Danish), *Möttuls saga*, *Partalópa saga*, *Karlamagnús saga* (a compilation of several *chansons de geste*), *Elis saga ok Rósamundu*, *Bevers saga*, and *Flóvents saga*.[14]

---

see e.g. Sofia Lodén, *Le chevalier courtois à la rencontre de la Suède médiévale: Du Chevalier au lion à Herr Ivan*, Forskningsrapporter/Cahiers de la Recherche 47 (Stockholm, 2012); Virgile Reiter, '*Flores och Blanzeflor*. L'amour courtois dans la Suède du XIV$^{ème}$ siècle', PhD dissertation (Paris, 2015); Olle Ferm *et al.*, eds., *The Eufemiavisor and Courtly Culture: Time, Texts and Cultural Transfer. Papers from a symposium in Stockholm 11–13 October 2012*, Konferenser 88 (Stockholm, 2015); Anna Katharina Richter and Jürg Glauser, eds., 'Transmission und Transformation. Die Historie von Floire et Blanchefleur in der skandinavischen und niederländischen Überlieferung.' *TijdSchrift voor Skandinavistiek* 36:1 (2018). online.

11 Ralph O'Connor, 'Introduction', in *Icelandic Histories & Romances*, trans. Ralph O'Connor (Stroud, 2002), p. 19.
12 Kurt Schier, *Sagaliteratur*, Sammlung Metzler 78 (Stuttgart, 1970).
13 See Stephen A. Mitchell, *Heroic Sagas and Ballads* (Ithaca and London, 1991), p. 17.
14 The late medieval Swedish and Danish prose renderings of the Charlemagne-

2) A limited group of early Icelandic romances from the beginning of the fourteenth century shares stylistic similarities with the translated *riddarasögur*, but no known foreign-language source text exists for them. These sagas are usually called 'original', 'indigenous', 'native', 'Icelandic', or 'younger' *riddarasögur*.[15] To this subgenre belong *Klári saga*, *Mágus saga jarls*, *Bærings saga*, *Mírmanns saga*, *Konráðs saga keisarasonar*, *Rémundar saga*, as well as the Old Swedish and Middle Danish *Eufemiavisa*, *Hertig Fredrik av Normandie*.[16] These texts form a kind of transitionary space which includes a very large group of even younger *riddarasögur* assumed to be written later than the translated *riddarasögur* and equally characterised by their being composed in the Icelandic language.[17] The boundary between the older and the younger original, indigenous, Icelandic *riddarasögur* is extremely unstable, and it can be debated whether a distinction between these two groups actually can and should be drawn at all.

3) The group of younger indigenous *riddarasögur* from the Icelandic late Middle Ages and extant in medieval manuscripts numbers about thirty narratives, among them, to name but a few, *Dínus saga*, *Gibbons saga*, *Kirjalax saga*, *Nitida saga*, *Sálus saga ok Nikanors*, *Sigrgarðs saga frœkna*, *Sigurðar saga þögla*, *Vilhjálms saga* and *Vilmundar saga viðutan*. While many of these sagas share common narrative structures and subject matters, their style and intergeneric relationships differ substantially. Most of the non-translated Icelandic *riddarasögur* seem to have enjoyed a considerable popularity, since many of them were transmitted in large numbers of manuscripts (an average of forty and above) and in addition

---

cycle are the subject of a recent study by Elena Brandenburg, *Karl der Große im Norden: Rezeption französischer Heldenepik in den altostnordischen Handschriften*, Beiträge zur Nordischen Philologie 65 (Tübingen, 2019).

15 Cf. also Hendrik Lambertus, *Von monströsen Helden und heldenhaften Monstern: Zur Darstellung und Funktion des Fremden in den originalen Riddarasögur*, Beiträge zur Nordischen Philologie 52 (Tübingen and Basel, 2013). Lambertus, who uses the term *originale Riddarasögur*, speaks of a 'bunte Vielgestaltigkeit ihres Erzählens' (the colourful multiplicity of their narratives) which makes the sagas 'nur schwer einzugrenzen' (only to be delimited with difficulty) (p. 43).

16 The Danish manuscript Holm K47 (c. 1500) contains, besides the Danish translations of the three Swedish *Eufemiavisor* (*Ivan Løveridder*, *Hertug Frederik af Normandi*, and *Flores og Blanseflor*), two translations from the German, *Dværgekongen Laurin* and *Persenober og Konstantianobis*, as well as *Den kyske dronning*, another romance-like narrative without a known foreign-language original. The codex comprises the majority of the romances extant from the Danish Middle Ages.

17 These sagas are sometimes called *Märchensagas*, see Schier, *Sagaliteratur*; Jürg Glauser, *Isländische Märchensagas: Studien zur Prosaliteratur im spätmittelalterlichen Island*, Beiträge zur nordischen Philologie 12 (Basel and Frankfurt am Main, 1983), but the term is mostly used in German scholarship only, if at all. On *lygisögur* see below.

were versified in *rímur*-cycles.[18] In contrast to other genres of Old Norse-Icelandic literature, e.g. skaldic or eddic poetry, Norse romance can not be defined by means of form alone; romances took changing shapes in verse or prose narratives.[19]

The total number of medieval Old Norse-Icelandic prose romances amounts to roughly fifty sagas. It is usually conjectured that another *c.* 200 sagas in the romance-style were composed in Iceland between the sixteenth century and the beginning of the twentieth century.[20] In late medieval and early modern times romance was the most productive numerically and the longest-lasting of the Icelandic prose genres. This is even more the case, if one considers that the category of 'romance' can not at all be confined only to complete narratives. Rather, individual parts of romances would be loaned to and would influence stories from related genres. The sagas that had the closest affinities with the *riddarasögur* were certainly the *fornaldarsögur*, but if one broadens the spectrum even more, not a few hagiographic texts, *konungasögur* and *Íslendingasögur* (*Laxdæla saga*, *Grettis saga*, *Víglundar saga*, *Bárðar saga Snæfellsáss* and many others), and even some of the eddic heroic poems and skaldic poetry feature romance elements.[21]

Margaret Schlauch, in her by now classic and still invaluable monograph *Romance in Iceland* (1934), based her descriptive method on an implicit preconception of romance and made no attempt at defining the genre theoretically or even systematically.[22] Neither did any of the fol-

---

18 See Marianne E. Kalinke and P. M. Mitchell, *Bibliography of Old Norse-Icelandic Romances*, Islandica 44 (Ithaca and London, 1985).
19 In the prologue to *Klári saga*, the fact that Latin and French romances were composed in verse is commented on explicitly.
20 To compare these numbers with the totality of medieval romances in other countries, see Krueger, 'Introduction', p. 4. Krueger estimates over 200 French romances, *c.* 100 Italian romances, over 100 English romances, and well over 50 German romances. On the late, post-medieval Icelandic romances see Matthew James Driscoll, *The Unwashed Children of Eve: The Production, Dissemination and Reception of Popular Literature in Post-Reformation Iceland* (Enfield Lock, 1997), and 'Late Prose Fiction (*lygisögur*)', in *A Companion to Old Norse-Icelandic Literature and Culture*, ed. McTurk, pp. 190–204.
21 Matthew J. Driscoll, 'Introduction: The Transmission and Reception of the Fornaldarsögur Norðurlanda', in *The Legendary Legacy. Transmission and Reception of the Fornaldarsögur Norðurlanda*, ed. Matthew J. Driscoll et al., The Viking Collection 24 (Odense, 2018), pp. 9–10. There are about thirty-five legendary sagas, transmitted in *c.* 1700 individual *fornaldarsögur*-texts in *c.* 1000 manuscripts from the beginning of the fourteenth to the beginning of the twentieth centuries. See also in the same volume Philip Lavender, '*Illuga saga* as *fornaldarsaga*, *riddarasaga* and *Íslendingasaga*: Generic Fluidity in the Late Development of Sagas and *rímur*', pp. 187–213.
22 Margaret Schlauch, *Romance in Iceland* (New York, 1934, reissued, 1973). Among the studies which focus on dividing the bulk of romances into sub-groups or pooling various, traditionally separated saga-groups is Marianne E. Kalinke's

lowing works on romance in medieval Scandinavia succeed in giving a satisfying and convincing full genre definition. So far, no systematic genre theory defining romance has been put forward. This absence and failure has partly to do with the difficulties inherent in the corpus. The elusiveness which makes it difficult to tell exactly what a romance is is also the result of the sheer mass of individual narratives and the number of manuscripts, as well as a consequence of the many refashionings, changes and shifts of media, interweavings, overlaps and constant crossovers that have been going on. As in other languages, in the Norse genre system romance is an extraordinarily hybrid, unstable and heterogeneous phenomenon. Accordingly, most recent studies fall back on romance definitions that stress its character of family resemblance in intertextual relationships, networks between narratives, and rhizomatic constellations more than rigid traditional genre concepts. These features make romance, also in its Norse forms, the prototypical representatives of open texts.[23]

While strict analytic genre definitions in the case of (Norse) romance might be difficult if not impossible to achieve, a look at the codicological evidence may perhaps offer a way to approach at least some elements indicating a potential medieval genre awareness. The same might hold true for the evidence provided by terminologies found in medieval manuscripts.[24] In terms of discourse theory, medieval and early modern collective manuscripts open up the space for discussion of aesthetic, psychological, cultural, political, ideological and other issues and offer excellent evidence of how texts were received and arranged according to certain patterns. The important lost Icelandic manuscript *Ormsbók (c. 1360–1400) whose content is to a large extent preserved in paper copies, for example, follows a compilation pattern that was observed by Sylvia Huot

---

    book on the bridal-quest theme in *riddarasögur* and *fornaldarsögur*; Kalinke proposes to subsume those sagas whose structure and themes are characterised by the hero's quest for a bride into a common new sub-genre, see Marianne E. Kalinke, *Bridal-Quest Romance in Medieval Iceland*, Islandica 46 (Ithaca and London, 1990). O'Connor, 'Introduction', identifies specific features of *riddarasögur* as narratives between romances and histories.

23 On this see also Bampi, 'Genre'; on fluidity, Sif Rikhardsdottir's chapter in this volume. For the concept of the 'text' as opposed to the 'work', see Roland Barthes, 'From Work to Text', in *Textual Strategies: Perspectives in Post-Structuralist Criticism*, ed. Josué V. Harrari (Ithaca, 1976), pp. 73–81; for Jacques Derrida's critique of the classical genre doctrine and his concept of transgression of generic boundaries, see his 'The Law of Genre', *Critical Inquiry* 7:1 (1980), 55–81.

24 Cf. Sylvia Huot, 'The Manuscript Context of Medieval Romance', in *The Cambridge Companion to Medieval Romance*, ed. Krueger, pp. 60–77, and Gaunt, 'Romance and Other Genres', particularly pp. 48–50. For the Norse romances see Kalinke, *Stories Set Forth with Fair Words*, passim, and especially Katharina Seidel, *Textvarianz und Textstabilität: Studien zur Transmission der* Ívens saga, Erex saga *und* Parcevals saga, Beiträge zur Nordischen Philologie 56 (Tübingen, 2014), who offers the hitherto most exhaustive study of genre consciousness and manuscript transmission.

in the French material.²⁵ Like in many continental miscellanies containg romances in this manuscript there is a chronological progression of texts which begin with narratives about antiquity, here *Trójumanna saga* (and probably also *Breta sögur*), followed by ten *riddarasögur*, including three Arthurian sagas (about Erec, Iven, and Parceval), and one example from Petrus Alphonsi's *Discplina clericalis* collection of moral fables. *Mágus saga jarls, Flóvents saga, Bærings saga, Rémundar saga, Erex saga, Ívens saga, Bevers saga, Mírmanns saga, Partalópa saga, Enoks saga,* and *Parcevals saga* follow. Also two translated *chansons de geste* (of Flovent and Bever) belong to the collection. The late medieval Icelandic codex thus presented the history of ancient Greece and Britain and then went over to include translated and original *riddarasögur*. Read in such a context, the sagas gained additional meaning. In German scholarship, such miscellanies are often quite aptly called *Überlieferungsverbünde* (transmission clusters).

Another important medieval romance-manuscript is DG 4-7 fol./ AM 666b 4ᵗᵒ (*c*. 1270, made in south-western Norway or Bergen). It contains *Pamphilus* (translation of a Latin dialogue), *Elis saga ok Rósamundu* (translation of a *chanson de geste*), *Strengleikar* (translation of *lais*), and a fragment of a dialogue between 'Courage' and 'Fear' which is in accordance with many continental romance manuscripts that mix romances with hagiographical and didactic materials.

There are rather few Icelandic codices which only contain romances, but the Icelandic codex Holm perg 7 fol., a manuscript that again blends translated and original *riddarasögur*, is one of them. In her dissertation on this late fifteenth-century manuscript, Karoline Kjesrud undertakes an analysis of the geographies and wisdom culture of the eleven sagas in the manuscript, *Rémundar saga, Elis saga ok Rósamundu, Sigurðar saga turnara, Bevers saga, Konráðs saga keisarasonar, Ectors saga, Gibbons saga, Viktors saga ok Blávus, Sigurðar saga fóts, Partalópa saga, Adonias saga*.²⁶ In her study on textual variance and stability in three Icelandic Arthurian romances, Katharina Seidel argues convincingly that generic patterns are observable on different levels of the transmission such as, obviously, the texts themselves, but also on the levels of patrons, scribes, and audiences, and not least on the material level of the manuscripts.²⁷ It is fascinating to see how the medieval and post-medieval manuscripts containing romances developed certain generic patterns in accordance with as well as demarcation from other related genres. The codicological evidence both indicates certain generic coherences and links romances to related external stories.

25 See Huot, 'The Manuscript Context of Medieval Romance', pp. 63–68. On Ormsbók see Gropper, '*Breta sögur* and *Merlínusspá*', p. 53.
26 Karoline Kjesrud, *Lærdom og fornøyelse: Sagaer om helter på eventyr* (Oslo, 2011).
27 Seidel, *Textvarianz und Textstabilität*, particularly pp. 103–19.

Another possible way to approach an 'ethnic' definition would be to scrutinise the medieval terminology and meta-narratological expressions found in medieval and early modern codices. As mentioned before, there is no implicit theory of Old Norse genres in the extant manuscript material, and generic terms for individual text groups from medieval times are sparse and isolated. A few do exist, however.

The main Old and Middle Icelandic word to describe romances is the general term *riddarasögur*. Its meaning and scope is expressed in *Skikkjurímur* (Mantle Rhymes), III, 78: 'riddara sögurnar rísa af því / að rekkar komu þrautir í' (tales of chivalry arise therefrom, / that men engage in great labors).[28] *Skikkjurímur*, a *rímur*-version of *Möttuls saga*, are extant in three manuscripts; one from 1470–80 (Codex Guelferbytanus 42.7 Augusteus 4$^{to}$), one probably from 1695 (AM Acc. 22), and one from the seventeenth century (Holm papp 4$^{to}$ nr 15). According to this passage, romances, or *riddarasögur*, have their origins in what other texts belonging to the genre called *aventiure*, *æwintyr* etc., a central generic feature of romance. From about the same time as the oldest *Skikkjurímur*-manuscript date the earliest manuscripts of *Viktors saga ok Blávus* (1450–75) where the prologue refers to the putative translation activities during the reign of King Hákon Magnússon quoted above: 'hann liet venda morgum riddara sögvm' (he had many chivalric stories translated). Here, no additional information about the character or contents of *riddarasögur* is given. In the epilogue to *Mágus saga jarls* (AM 152 fol., c. 1500–75), an equally often-quoted passage mentions *Þiðreks saga, Flóvents saga eða aðrar riddarasögur* (Þiðrek's saga, Flovent's saga or other chivalric tales) and characterises these as stories about famous men who dealt out blows and fought single combats: 'þeir vinna þau þrekvirki, sem slíkir eða aðrir þvílíkir frægðarmenn gerðu með stórum höggum og sterkum atreiðum' (they performed those heroic deeds as such and other famous men do, with great blows and powerful attacks).[29] A fourth and final instance of *riddarasögur* is found in an inventory of the bishop's see of Hólar in Hjaltadalur in North Iceland, dated 12$^{th}$ May, 1396. Here, after a list of 45 bound and 40 unbound religious text-books and school-books, a table of 'saga-books' (*soghubókr*) in the possession of the bishop's see is given:

---

28 *Skikkjurímur*, ed. and transl. Matthew J. Driscoll, in *Norse Romance*, II. The Knights of the Round Table, ed. Marianne E. Kalinke, Arthurian Archives IV (Cambridge, 1999), pp. 312–13 and pp. 267–325. See also Kalinke, *The Arthur of the North*, pp. 79–80.

29 'Mágus saga jarls hin meiri', in *Riddarasögur* II, ed. Bjarni Vilhjálmsson (Reykjavík, 1954), p. 429. The prologue to *Flóres saga konungs ok sona hans* mentions three types of sagas, *heilgra manna sögur* 'sagas about holy men', *sǫgur ... af ríkum konungum* 'sagas about mighty kings', and *(sögur) frá konungum þeim, sem koma í miklar mannraunir ok hafa misjafnt úr rétt* 'sagas about those kings who encountered big dangers and got out differently'. In scholarship, the second and third groups are usually considered to belong to or come close to (translated or original) romances.

Mariu sagha guds modur. olafuanna sǫghur. karla maghnus saga.
thomass sǫghur. ij. jacobi sagha. anndress sagha. gudmundar sogur.
ij. thorlaks sagha. liber regum. barláms sagha. Riddara sogur a
tueim bokum. postola sǫgur. jons sagha hola biskups

[Saga of Mary, mother of God, Olavssagas, Saga of Charlemagne,
Two sagas of Thomas, Saga of Jacobus, Saga of Andres, Two sagas of
Gudmund, Saga of Thorlak. Liber Regum. Barlaams saga. Knights'
sagas in two volumes. Sagas of the Apostles, Saga of Jon, the bishop
of Hólar].[30]

This inventory supports the findings that romances and *chansons de geste* were not only regularly transmitted in compilations of various contents, but were considered to belong to and subsequently placed on the same library shelves together with hagiographies and texts on the history of the Icelandic Church. In these passages a vague and rudimentary genre conception becomes identifiable.

Other lexemes such as *lygisögur* (lying sagas), *ýkjusögur* (exaggerating sagas), or *hégómasögur* (vanity sagas) which have sometimes been used as generic terms cannot be applied to the genre of romance; they express pejorative statements about certain types of narratives. The same is true of the many terms that designate and refer to the narrative, the plot, the book etc. which are found in both Old Norse-Icelandic sagas (particularly *riddarasögur*) and Swedish and Danish *Eufemiavisor*.[31] Examples are (in normalised spelling) *saga* (saga), *æwintyr* (equivalent to *aventiure*), *bok* (book), *dikt* (poem), *spil* (game, play) from the East Norse tradition; *bók* (book), *saga* (saga), *frásögn* and *frásaga* (narrative), *þáttr* (short story), *ljóðsöngr* (poem), *rœða* (speech), *ævintyr* (adventure), *fabula*, *frœði* (learning, knowledge), *atburðr* (happening) etc. from the West Norse saga-tradition. These are telling and highly interesting examples of how certain medieval stories developed a specific narratological terminology, but they can not be utilised as generic terms in the proper sense.

## The Story of Floire and Blanchefleur in the North

One of the few romances in the North that exist in both West Norse saga forms and *rímur* as well as in an East Norse *Eufemiavisa* is the story of Floire and Blanchefleur. A short sketch of this exemplary narrative's transmission can summarise some of the present reflections.

The French verse romance *Floire et Blanchefleur* dates from the middle of the twelfth century. It is not clear whether it was this version or a

---

30 *Islandske originaldiplomer indtil 1450. Tekst*, ed. Stefán Karlsson, Editiones Arnamagnæanæ A, 7 (København, 1963), No. 101, p. 125.
31 For a discussion of further examples see Glauser, 'Staging the Text', and 'The Colour of a Sail'.

lost Anglo-Norman version that was translated into Old Norse prose as *Flóres saga ok Blankiflúr*, presumably around 1280 in Norway. The exact date of the first Norwegian translation is unknown; a Norwegian text from the fourteenth century (NRA 65) has probably a version that is close to the first translation. The Norwegian prose saga was adapted in Iceland in the course of the fourteenth century. An equally fragmentary Icelandic manuscript from the end of the fourteenth century (AM 575 4$^{to}$, eight of originally twenty leaves are extant) and another Icelandic manuscript from *c*. 1450 (AM 489 4$^{to}$, complete, ten leaves, heavily shortened text) mark the starting point of the saga's transmission and success in Iceland (*c*. twenty-five manuscripts written between 1385–1900). Around 1300 (perhaps 1312 as the last of the three *Eufemiavisor*), the story was rendered in Old Swedish verse: *Flores och Blanzaflor*; whether the author/ translator of the Swedish *Eufemiavisa* only used the Old Norwegian or a French text as well is not certain.[32] Around 1500, the Swedish *visa* was translated into Danish (*Flores og Blanseflor*); this verse romance was printed in Copenhagen in 1504 and 1509 by Gotfred af Ghemen. In post-medieval Iceland, several *Rímur af Flóres og Blanzeflor* were composed, one of them, by Níels Jónsson (1782–1857), was printed in Akureyri in 1858.

Together with the English version, the Nordic story is part of the insular tradition of the romance. Its continental tradition consists of a wealth of versions in French, Flemish, Low German, Low Rhenish, High German, Yiddish, Italian, Spanish, Czech, and Greek. In fact, *Floire et Blanchefleur* was one of the most popular romances in medieval and early modern Europe. On the other hand, there are no ballads about the subject matter from the Faroe Islands or any of the other Scandinavian countries, even though the over 400 'Chivalric ballads' (*ridderballader*) constitute the most numerous type-group of the Scandinavian medieval ballads.

The Swedish *Eufemiavisor* to which *Flores och Blanzeflor* belong are traditionally considered to be the project of an aristocratic culture displaying many 'classical' features of romance in medieval Europe. It has been suggested that their Danish equivalents show some hagiographical influences. The West Norse tradition of the story about Flores and Blankiflúr was adapted to the formal and thematic features of the Old Norse and early modern genre system. The saga was well integrated in this system, as is not only manifest by the late *rímur*-cycles, but even more distinctly by the intertextual links it shared with other romances. In the extremely popular

---

32  See Helle Degnbol, '"Fair words": The French poem *Floire et Blancheflor*, the Old Norse prose narrative *Flóres saga ok Blankiflúr*, and the Swedish poem *Flores och Blanzaflor*', in *Rittersagas*, ed. Glauser and Kramarz-Bein, pp. 71–96, who considers it 'not unlikely that the saga was translated during the reign of Hákon Magnússon ([b.]1270–[r.]1299–[d.]1319) ... no less natural to see Queen Eufemia (around 1280–1312) as the promotor of the entire enterprise', that is, suggesting simultaneous translations of a lost Anglo-Norman text into Old Norwegian prose and a translation/ adaptation into Old Swedish *knittelvers*.

original *riddarasaga Sigurðar saga þögla*, for example, there is an explicit reference to *Flóres saga ok Blankiflúr*, and the two narratives are connected with each other by way of dynastic links; Sedentiana, the maiden-king in *Sigurðar saga þögla* and later the wife of the eponymous hero Sigurðr, is said to be the daugther of Flóres and Blankiflúr. Thus, not only do subgenres such as translated and original *riddarasögur* have open boundaries, some of the texts themselves offer comment upon intertextual relations and make new stories out of them.

To sum up, Nordic romance displays all the relevant features such as: subject matter and literary style, pluri-linguistic background and intercultural translation, narrative modes and self-reflexivity, time-depth of manuscript transmission, generic adaptability, hybridity, and permeability of boundaries, so specific to this genre with its roots in Breton oral storytelling and continental medieval aristocracy's literary culture, and its adaptations and creative reception in the post-Reformation and early modern era. As such, the Nordic *riddarasögur*, *Eufemiavisor* as well as the chivalric *rímur*, *kvæði*, and ballads are prototypical representatives of romance and thus contribute substantially to what according to Roberta L. Krueger is 'arguably the most influential and enduring secular literary genre of the European Middle Ages'.[33]

---

33 Roberta L. Krueger, 'Introduction', p. 1.

# ANNOTATED TAXONOMY OF GENRES

The list below contains an overview of the major generic categories currently in use in Old Norse literary studies. It is not intended to be exhaustive nor prescriptive, but instead to give a synopsis of the genres or generic taxonomies that are discussed more broadly (and frequently challenged) in this volume. It is divided into three sections; sagas, poetry and other prose. Not all Old Norse texts can be fitted into the categories listed below and many belong to more than one generic group or adhere only loosely or even problematically to the generic parameters of the relevant group(s). The difficulty associated with generic hybridity and generic and modal shifts, for instance in the translation of the Old French *chansons de geste* and the *lais* into romance form (cf. *Karlamagnús saga* and *Strengleikar*), the ambiguous classification of some of the translated historiographies and learned materials (such as *Breta sögur* and *Gyðinga saga*) and the problematic classifications of works such as *Yngvars saga víðfǫrla* or *Kirialax saga* calls attention to the malleability and plasticity of literary genres, while it simultaneously highlights an underlying sense of generic stipulations and how these both dictate how a work is framed and how it will be received. The list below should therefore be understood to reflect not rigid or defined categories, but standardised taxonomies that are customarily used to define a work's place within a literary history or a literary system.

## SAGAS

CONTEMPORARY SAGAS (*samtíðarsögur*): Prose narratives recounting events that purportedly took place in twelfth- and thirteenth-century Iceland and were written down shortly thereafter. Most have been preserved in the single compilation *Sturlunga saga*, which recounts the story of the Sturlungs, one of the major family clans during the violent strife for power in mid-thirteenth century Iceland, leading up to the end of the Commonwealth. (See Chapter 7)

FAIRY TALES (*ævintýri*): Shorter prose narratives that usually circulated orally before being written down. They often recount tales of magical or supernatural events and creatures. They are not the same as the exempla (*dæmisögur*), often referred to as *ævintýri* as well (see under OTHER PROSE).

KINGS' SAGAS (*konungasögur*): Prose narratives that recount the lives of both historical and semi-legendary (or mythical) Nordic kings. They were composed from the twelfth through the fourteenth centuries, mostly in Ice-

*Taxonomy*

land and Norway. Examples include the lost *Skjöldunga saga* (c. 1180), *Morkinskinna* (c. 1220), and *Hákonar saga Hákonarsonar* by Sturla Þórðarson (c. 1265). (See Chapter 7)

LAIS (*Strengleikar*): A compilation of twenty-one short prose stories translated from Old French in the mid-thirteenth century, either from anonymous Breton *lais* or from the collection of *lais* conventionally attributed to Marie de France. (See Chapter 19)

LEGENDARY SAGAS (*fornaldarsögur*): Prose narratives compiled largely in the thirteenth through the fourteenth centuries that take place primarily in Iceland, generally in an undetermined ancient (pre-colonisation) time period. They contain both historical (or pseudo-historical) personages and mythical figures and thus may preserve narrative motifs from the Germanic legendary heritage. Some feature verses, almost exclusively in the eddic mode. Examples include *Völsunga saga*, *Hrólfs saga kraka*, *Örvar-Odds saga*. (See Chapters 2, 8, 9)

MAIDEN KING ROMANCES (*meykónga sögur*): An apparently Icelandic subgenre of romance (both translated and local) written down in the fourteenth century and featuring stories of misogamous female rulers and their vanquishing by their would-be suitors. Examples include *Clári saga* and *Sigurðar saga þögla*. (See Chapter 2)

ROMANCES, INDIGENOUS/ NATIVE (*frumsamdar riddarasögur*): Prose narratives that deal normally with events occurring beyond Scandinavian geographic borders, featuring tales of knights or noble heroes and their adventures. They were composed in Iceland from the late thirteenth century onward (following the introduction of the romance as genre through translations) and flourished in the fourteenth century and beyond. Examples include *Mágus saga jarls* and *Gibbons saga*. (See Chapters 2, 8, 19)

ROMANCES, TRANSLATED (*þýddar riddarasögur*): Prose translations predominantly from Old French romance and *chansons de geste* and some Latin romances and histories and possibly Middle High German sources. They stem principally from Norway and Iceland in the thirteenth and possibly fourteenth centuries, with translations into Old Swedish occurring in the fourteenth century and later yet into Middle Danish. Examples include *Ívens saga* (translation of Chrétien de Troyes *Yvain*), *Alexanders saga* (translation of *Alexandreis*), and the *Eufemiavisor* for East Norse romance. (See Chapter 19)

SAGAS OF BISHOPS (*byskupasögur*): Prose accounts of the bishops of Skálholt and Hólar in Iceland stemming mainly from the thirteenth and early fourteenth centuries. Examples include *Hungrvaka* and *Þorláks saga helga*. (See Chapter 18)

*Taxonomy*

SAGAS OF ICELANDERS (*Íslendingasögur*): Prose narratives first written down in the thirteenth century that conventionally feature historical events associated with the settlement of Iceland and the lives of the settlers and their descendants in the ninth through the eleventh centuries. They frequently trace genealogical histories, legal disputes, conflicts and feuds, but also depict personal relationships and individual aspirations in pre- and post-conversation Iceland. They are closely related (and often intersect with) the kings' sagas and the legendary sagas and many contain verses, usually in skaldic metre. Noted examples are, for instance, *Egils saga Skalla-Grímssonar*, *Laxdæla saga* and *Brennu-Njáls saga*. (See Chapters 8, 9, 11, 17)

SAINTS' LIVES (*heilagra manna/meyja sögur*): Prose hagiographical accounts of male and female saints, largely based on Latin sources, but including a few local saints. Examples include *Thómas saga erkibiskups*, *Guðmundar saga* and *Margrétar saga*. (See Chapter 18)

SHORT NARRATIVES (*þættir*): Short prose narratives written typically in Iceland in the thirteenth and fourteenth century. They are frequently woven into or added to longer sagas, such as the *konungasögur* (e.g. *Morkinskinna*) or form part of longer prose generic groupings, such as the *Íslendinga þættir* (e.g. *Bolla þáttr Bollasonar*) and legendary *þættir* (e.g. *Norna-Gests þáttr*) or are independent (*Orkneyinga þáttr*). (See Chapter 16)

## OTHER PROSE

ANNALS: Written historical records of events in a community, arranged chronologically by year. The earliest known Icelandic annals date to around 1280.

ENCYCLOPEDIC AND LEARNED LITERATURE: Embraces a broad spectrum of learned, mostly non-fictional works (for the most part translated from Latin and other vernaculars) that cover a wide range of knowledge. It includes compendia (*Elucidarius*) and works about various aspects of the natural world (e.g. world description, time-reckoning, predictions) as well as bestiaries and lapidaries. Examples include the *Physiologus*, *Heimslýsing* (a description of the world) and *Algorismus* (a short treatise on mathematics). The manuscript known as Hauksbók contains a selection of works of this kind. (See Chapters 6 and 8)

EXEMPLA (*dæmisögur/ ævintýri*): Short prose narratives, mostly translated from Latin and based on the Latin convention of the exemplum, or a moral anecdote, used to illustrate a point as part of the sermon in Christian religious services. Translated exempla from both Latin and Middle English became the basis for local production of anecdotes often referred to as *ævintýri* (cf. Fr. *aventure*, not to be confused with fairy tales, see SAGAS).

*Taxonomy*

GRAMMATICAL TREATISES: Four prose works written in the twelfth and thirteenth centuries in which various aspects of the Icelandic linguistic system are treated, from phonology to stylistic and rhetorical devices employed for the composition of literary texts. The third treatise, attributed to Óláfr Þórðarson, and the fourth follow the classical model of grammatical treatises as established by the Latin authors Donatus and Priscianus. (See Chapter 4)

HAGIOGRAPHY: Includes a variety of genres of religious nature, e.g. legends, edifying anecdotes, miracle accounts and saints' lives. (See Chapter 18)

HISTORIOGRAPHY: Embraces a variety of works whose primary aim is to chronicle the most important events of Nordic and world history, from mythic and legendary times to the time of writing. Examples include *Íslendingabók* (The Book of Icelanders) and *Landnámabók* (The Book of Settlement). A number of works about world history such as *Gyðinga saga* (The Saga of the Jews), *Veraldar saga* (The Saga of the World), *Trójumanna saga* (The Saga of the Trojans), *Rómverja saga* (The Saga of the Romans) and *Breta sögur* (The Sagas of the Britons) are generally refererred to as pseudo-histories. (See Chapter 10)

HOMILY: A commentary taking a particular Biblical text as its starting point. A homily is usually delivered during a religious service. The two most important collections of homilies are the Norwegian and the Icelandic Homily Books. (See Chapter 12)

LAWS: Written collection of all rules used to regulate the actions of the members of a community (e.g. a country, a region or a town). In medieval Iceland, laws were traditionally passed down and recited orally during the *Alþingi* (General Assembly). One major written collection of laws is known: the so-called *Grágás* (lit. Grey Goose), from the second half of the thirteenth century. In 1271 a new law, based on the Norwegian laws of Frostaþing and Gulaþing and called *Járnsíða* (lit. Iron Side), was introduced.

MIRACLES: An account of miracles attributed to male and female saints when they intervene in human affairs. Consequently such accounts are widely present in hagiographic texts, most notably in saints' lives. A collection of the miracles attributed to the royal saint Óláfr Haraldsson is preserved in the Old Norwegian Homily Book. (See Chapter 18)

MORAL LITERATURE: Includes a broad scope of genres (e.g. *speculum principis*, *Minnereden*, love allegories, religious-didactic verse) that were meant to provide moral precepts by way of illustrating virtues and vices through exemplary stories. As such, moral literature was primarily concerned with promoting good conduct, both in the religious sphere and with regard to the social and political domain. The category intersects with wisdom literature. An Old Norse example of the *speculum principis* genre is *Konungs skuggsjá* (The King's Mirror). (See Chapter 13)

POETIC TREATISES: Prose works that illustrate and explain the categories of poetic diction (style, structure, metrics), primarily for the purpose of teaching poets how to write. In Old Norse literature, the *Prose Edda* is a fitting example. Attributed to Snorri Sturluson, the *Prose Edda* is generally described as a handbook for the Old Norse poets, called skalds. It is divided into four sections: a Prologue, *Gylfaginning* (The Deception of Gylfi, where the ancient myths are systematised and explained in dialogic form), *Skáldskaparmál* (about poetic diction), and *Háttatal*, which contains a list of verse forms.

SERMONS: Religious writing specifically designed to address thematic aspects of the Holy Scriptures and explain their meaning to an audience largely made up of lay people. It is thus intended to instruct people in matters of faith and morals.

VISIONS: Accounts of a supernatural experience during which the protagonist acquires revelatory knowledge by being in contact with an otherworld reality. Such experiences often take place during sleep (*dream visions*) or whilst in some other anomalous physical state. Visionary texts include works that relate full sensory experiences or physical journeys to a realm placed outside the earthly world. They can also describe a journey through hell and heaven or an event in which someone receives a supernatural visitation. Dream visions are attested across the whole corpus of Old Norse literature and abound especially in the sagas. Examples of visions include *Páls leizla* (Vision of Saint Paul) and *Duggals leizla* (an Old Norse translation of *Visio Tnugdali*). (See Chapter 15)

# POETRY

This section is divided into eddic and skaldic modes, though the distinction between these modes is by no means clear-cut. Conventionally, eddic verse is composed in alliterative metres similar to the common Germanic four-stress metre (although it is strophic), it is often anonymous and frequently dialogic in form. Those Old Norse-Icelandic poets whose names are known to us tend to compose in the skaldic mode, using the kinds of complex metrical forms described by Snorri Sturluson in *Háttatal*. Nevertheless, there is a marked area of overlap; poets such as Eyvindr skáldaspillir (destroyer of poets) compose *Hákonarmál* in an eddic metre; conversely *kviðuháttr* is a much simpler metre than other skaldic types. The division below then acknowledges the ways in which Old Norse poetry has normally been classified, but should by no means be regarded as prescriptive.

## *Eddic* MODE

AUTOBIOGRAPHICAL POEMS (*ævidrápur*): Longer poems recited by characters (very often in *fornaldarsögur*) giving a retrospective overview of their lives, including both triumphs and vicissitudes. A good example is the long poem uttered by Örvar-Oddr in his saga as he is about to die. *Víkarsbálkr*, in *Gautreks saga*, which summarises the events in the hero Starkaðr's life hitherto is another such.

CURSES (*formælingar* or *níð*): A kind of (often performative) speech-act that may form part of a longer narrative, as in *Skírnismál* or, as the case of *Buslabæn*, stand alone in a prosimetrical context.

DEATH-SONGS: Poems recited by characters (very often in *fornaldarsögur*) at the point of death. Closely related to AUTOBIOGRAPHICAL POEMS (*ævidrápur*). For example, the so-called 'Hjálmars Death-Song', preserved in *Örvar-Odds saga* and *Hervarar saga ok Heiðreks*.

FLYTING (*senna*): Aggressive exchanges between two or more antagonists, often but not always performed prior to battle. The best-known examples are *Lokasenna* and *Hárbarðsljóð*, but the form is also frequently found in prosimetrical *fornaldarsögur*, where the hero encounters a troll or troll-woman. (See Chapters 12 and 14)

FREE-STANDING VERSES (*lausavísur*): Often spoken by characters in *fornaldarsögur* to express a particular stance or feeling evoked by events within the plot. (See Chapters 12, 14 and 15)

LAMENT (sometimes designated as *grátr*): A poem which addresses the loss of one or more loved ones, usually identified by name. Examples include *Oddrúnargrátr*. (See Chapters 2 and 12)

MEMORIALISING POEMS: A poem that commemorates a high-status man who has died. The primary eddic examples are *Eiríksmál* and *Hákonarmál*, both of which feature the entry of the dead man into Valhöll.

NARRATIVE (may be designated by *–kviða* or *–mál*): Poems that relate events happening to particular characters. These often contain large quantities of dialogue and prose passages explaining changes of scene, as well as other subgenres, such as curses. *Atlakviða* and *För Skírnis* are examples of such poems.

PROPHECY (*spá*): Poems that relate future events, usually through a first-person speaker. For example, *Völuspá* in its various versions and *Grípisspá*. This genre also includes an example in the skaldic mode: the translated poem *Merlínusspá*. (See Chapters 12 and 15)

RIDDLES: Usually composed in the *ljóðaháttr* metre, these verses challenge the listener to guess the identity of an object or to work out a particular configuration of circumstances. The best-known collection of riddles is the sequence preserved in *Hervarar saga ok Heiðreks*; other verses in poems ascribed to different kinds of genre have also been identified tentatively as riddle-like (for example, *Baldrs Draumar* st. 12). (See Chapter 13)

WISDOM POEMS: Poems defined largely by their content, communicating human or divine wisdom or a combination of the two, often in dialogic or monologic form. Wisdom poems often use enumeration or other forms of framework to organise the wisdom material they communicate. Examples include *Vafþrúðnismál*, some of the constituent sections of *Hávamál*, such as the so-called 'Ljóðatal' or 'Loddfáfnismál', and the translation of the *Disticha Catonis*, *Hugsvinnsmál*. (See Chapters 13 and 15)

WHETTING (*hvǫt*): Poems in which a character urges other characters to vengeance. For example, *Guðrúnarhvöt*. (See Chapter 2)

## *Skaldic* MODE

BATTLE-POEMS: Poems narrating prowess in battle, sometimes proleptic, sometimes looking back on victory or defeat. These may be first-person or third-person narrations or they may be framed as dialogues about a battle. This genre intersects with PRAISE-POETRY. Examples include *Haraldskvæði*, also known as *Hrafnsmál* or *Liðsmannaflokkr*. (See Chapter 14)

FREE-STANDING VERSES (*lausavísur*): These are single verses or sequences of verse that cannot be ascribed to a named poem, and which occur in a prosimetrical context. They frequently express the feelings of the speaker in response to events in the text, or they may narrate and / or confirm happenings related in the surrounding prose. (See Chapter 5)

HEAD-RANSOM (*höfuðlausn*): A poem composed to assuage the wrath of a ruler and to effect some kind of reconciliation. Egill Skalla-Grímsson's poem is the best-known example, but Óttarr svarti also composed one for King Óláfr Haraldsson. (See Chapter 12)

HYMN (*sálmur* or *lofsöngur*): Christian poetry praising a figure worthy of veneration such as Jesus, the Virgin Mary or one of the saints. Examples include: Einarr Skúlason's *Geisli,* and *Lílja.* (See Chapters 12 and 15)

LOVE-SONGS (*mansöngsvísur*): Poetry about women was considered socially shameful to the woman's family and actionable under Icelandic law, thus the verses recorded as related to such cases may not be a direct reflection of what was actually composed. The verses of Kormákr Ǫgmundarson about Steingerðr Þorkelsdóttir, preserved in *Kormáks saga,* are a possible example.

MEMORIAL-POEMS (*erfidrápa*): Poems mourning and / or commemorating the loss of a significant figure who has died. Example: Þórmóðr Bersason Kólbrúnarskáld's *Þorgeirsdrápa* for his friend Þorgeirr Hávarsson.

NARRATIVE: Poems which relate a series of events, which may be autobiographical, biographical or fictional. Examples include: Eilífr Goðrúnarson's *Þórsdrápa* and Sigvatr Þórðarson's *Austfararvísur*. SAINTS' LIVES form a significant subgenre.

PRAISE-POEMS (*lofkvæði*): This genre intersects with BATTLE-POETRY and MEMORIAL-POETRY. Typically it praises the battle-prowess, generosity and strategic behaviour of its subject. Examples include Egill Skalla-Grímsson's *Arinbjarnarkviða*.

SAINTS' LIVES (*heilagra manna / meyja sögur*): The lives of Christian saints may be narrated in prose or in skaldic verse; poetic examples include Kálfr Hallsson's fourteenth-century *Katrínardrápa* or the anonymous *Heilagra manna drápur* from the same period. (See also under SAGAS)

SLANDER (*níð*): Verse composed to impugn an enemy and legally actionable. Consequently they may not be preserved as composed. For example, Sigmundr Lambason composes three or four slanderous verses at Hallgerðr's bidding in *Brennu-Njáls saga*, calling Njáll's sons *taðskegglingar* (little dung-beards), but these are not recorded in the saga.

## Other Poetic MODES

BALLADS (*rímur*): Later medieval narrative poems with a distinctive four-line end-rhyming stanzaic form, use of *heiti* or simple kennings, and traditionally beginning with an address to the speaker's lady. The ballads often versify material that also exists in prose. Examples include *Skikkjurímur* (The Mantel-Rhymes) which relate an Arthurian adventure also preserved in *Möttuls saga* and *Úlfhams rímur*, the adventures of a werewolf's son and his antagonistic mother. (See Chapters 6 and 19)

## Chronological Outline

| | |
|---|---|
| c. 800–1050 | Conventionally defined as the Viking Age. |
| 870–930 | Conventionally defined as the Age of Settlement in Iceland (Icel. *landnámsöld*). |
| c. 872–930 | Reign of Haraldr hárfagri, king of Norway. |
| 874 | Conventional date for the beginning of the settlement of Iceland by people from Scandinavia (particularly Norway) and the British Isles. |
| 930 | Establishment of the *Althing*, i.e. the General Assembly. |
| 995–1000 | Reign of Óláfr Tryggvason, king of Norway. |
| 1000 | Iceland becomes officially Christian. |
| 1015–28 | Reign of Óláfr Haraldsson, king of Norway. |
| 1046–66 | Reign of Haraldr harðráði, king of Norway. |
| 1056 | Ísleifr Gizurarson becomes the first bishop of Skálholt in Iceland. |
| 1106 | Jón Ögmundsson becomes the first bishop of Hólar. |
| 1112 | Foundation of Þingeyrar, the first monastery of Iceland. |
| 1118 | Wedding at Reykjahólar is supposed to have taken place according to *Þorgils saga ok Hafliða*. |
| 1153 | Probable composition of *Geisli* by Einarr Skúlason, the earliest preserved long Christian poem. |
| 1179 | Scholar and statesman Snorri Sturluson born. |
| 1184–1202 | Reign of Sverrir Sigurðarson, king of Norway. |
| 1200–50 | Conventionally defined as the Age of the Sturlungs (Icel. *Sturlungaöld*), a period of civil unrest and internal political turmoil in Iceland named after one the most powerful families (the Sturlungar) that took part in the fight for power. |
| 1217–63 | Reign of Hákon IV Hákonarson, king of Norway, probable patron of a number of translations into Old Norwegian. |
| c. 1220s | Writing of *Morkinskinna*, *Fagrskinna* and *Heimskringla*, important works of early Old Norse historiography. |
| 1241 | Death of Snorri Sturluson. |

## Chronological Outline

| | |
|---|---|
| 1260–80 | Compilation of the Codex Regius of the *Poetic Edda* (Gks 2365 4$^{to}$). |
| 1262–64 | End of the so-called Commonwealth period and the establishment of the Old Covenant (Icel. *Gamli sáttmáli*) as Iceland comes under the Norwegian crown. |
| 1263–80 | Reign of Magnús VI Hákonarson (known as Magnús lagabætir, 'Magnus the Law-mender'), king of Norway. |
| 1271–74 | The new law-code *Járnsíða* (lit. 'iron side') is introduced in Iceland by King Magnús Hákonarson to replace the old law-code (*Grágás*, lit. 'grey goose'). |
| 1299–1312 | Reign of Eufemia, Queen Consort of Norway, patroness of a number of translations into Old Swedish. |
| 1300–25 | Compilation of AM 748 1a 4to, an important manuscript containing eddic poems. |
| 1300–1325 | Compilation of the Codex Upsaliensis DG 11 of the *Prose Edda* |
| 1300–50 | Compilation of the Codex Regius of the *Prose Edda* (GKS 2367 4$^{to}$). |
| 1301–12 | The Old Swedish *Eufemiavisor* (*Herr Ivan lejonriddaren*, *Hertig Fredrik av Normandie*, *Flores och Blanzeflor*) are translated at the instigation of the Norwegian Queen Eufemia. |
| 1305–15 | Compilation of Hauksbók (AM 544 4$^{to}$), named after its owner, Haukr Erlendsson. Contains, amongst other things, a version of the eddic poem *Völuspá*. |
| 1330–70 | Compilation of Möðruvallabók (AM 132 fol.), an important collection of Sagas of Icelanders. |
| 1387–94 | Compilation of Flateyjarbók (GKS 1005 fol.), which contains, amongst other things, the oldest known example of the *rímur*-genre (*Óláfs ríma Haraldssonar*). |
| 1387–1412 | Reign of Margareta I, queen of Denmark, Norway and Sweden. During her reign, the three Scandinavian kingdoms were united under the Danish Crown initiating the so-called Kalmar Union. |
| 1397–1523 | Kalmar Union. |
| 1486 | Margrét Vigfúsdóttir, widow at Möðruvellir, dies. Margrét may have commissioned the production of manuscripts containing translated and indigenous romances and other material usually related to King Hákon IV's reign. |

# Works Cited

Manuscripts

*The Arnamagnæan Institute, Copenhagen*
AM 61 fol.
AM 66 fol. (Hulda)
AM 81 a fol.
AM 226 fol.
AM 243 f $4^{to}$
AM 243 a fol.
AM 309 $4^{to}$
AM 325 VIII 3 d $4^{to}$ (Jöfraskinna)
AM 544 $4^{to}$ (Hauksbók)
AM 575 a $4^{to}$
AM 580 $4^{to}$
AM 657 a–b $4^{to}$
AM 666 b $4^{to}$
AM 748 I a $4^{to}$
*Ormsbók
*Vatnshyrna

*The Árni Magnússon Institute for Icelandic Studies (Stofnun Árna Magnússonar), Reykjavík*
AM 122 a fol. (Króksfjarðarbók)
AM 122 b fol. (Reykjarfjarðarbók)
AM 132 $4^{to}$
AM 132 fol. (Möðruvallabók)
AM 152 fol.
AM 162 A η fol.
AM 162 A θ fol.
AM 162 B δ fol. (Þormóðsbók)
AM 162 C fol.
AM 162 D 2 fol.
AM 166 b $8^{vo}$
AM 335 $4^{to}$
AM 343 a $4^{to}$
AM 445 b $4^{to}$ (Melabók; Pseudo-Vatnshyrna)
AM 445 c I $4^{to}$ (Pseudo-Vatnshyrna)
AM 445 c II $4^{to}$
AM 471 $4^{to}$
AM 489 $4^{to}$
AM 489 I–II $4^{to}$
AM 510 $4^{to}$

AM 551 a 4<sup>to</sup>
AM 556 a–b 4<sup>to</sup>
AM 557 4<sup>to</sup>
AM 564 a 4<sup>to</sup> (Pseudo-Vatnshyrna)
AM 579 4<sup>to</sup>
AM 586 4<sup>to</sup>
AM 589 a–f 4<sup>to</sup>
AM 604 a–h 4<sup>to</sup> (Staðarhólsbók)
AM 604 g 4<sup>to</sup> (Staðarhólsbók rímna)
AM 622 4<sup>to</sup>
AM 624 4<sup>to</sup>
AM 748 I b 4<sup>to</sup>
AM 748 II 4<sup>to</sup>
AM Acc. 22
GKS 1005 fol. (Flateyjarbók)
GKS 2365 4<sup>to</sup> (Codex Regius of the *Poetic Edda*)
GKS 2367 4<sup>to</sup> (Codex Regius of the *Prose Edda*)
GKS 2845 4<sup>to</sup>

*The British Library, London*
MS Add. II, 127

*Herzog August Library, Wolfenbüttel*
Codex Guelferbytanus 42.7 Augusteus 4<sup>to</sup>

*National and University Library of Iceland (Landsbókasafn-Háskólabókasafn), Reykjavík*
ÍB 13 IV 8<sup>vo</sup>
JS 8 fol.
JS 27 fol.
Lbs 1199 4<sup>to</sup>

*The National Archives of Iceland (Þjóðskjalasafn Íslands) & The Árni Magnússon Institute for Icelandic Studies (Stofnun Árna Magnússonar), Reykjavík*
AM dipl. Isl. Fasc. V 18

*The National Archives of Norway (Riksarkivet), Oslo*
NRA 65

*The National Library of Sweden (Kungliga biblioteket), Stockholm*
Holm K47
Holm papp 4<sup>to</sup> nr 15
Holm perg 7 4<sup>to</sup>
Holm perg 6 4<sup>to</sup>
Holm perg 7 fol.

*The Royal Library (det Kgl. Bibliotek), Copenhagen*
GKS 1009 fol. (Morkinskinna)
GKS 1010 fol. (Hrokkinskinna)
GKS 1913 4^to

*Uppsala University Library (Uppsala universitetsbibliotek), Uppsala*
Codex Upsaliensis DG 11
De la Gardie 4-7 fol.

## Primary Texts

*Ágrip af Nóregskonunga sǫgum. Fagrskinna – Nóregs konunga tal*, ed. Bjarni Einarsson, Íslenzk fornrit 29 (Reykjavik, 1985)
*Ágrip af Nóregskonungasögum*, ed. Matthew J. Driscoll, 2nd edn (London, 2008)
Alighieri, Dante, *La Divina Commedia*, ed. Tommaso Di Salvo (Bologna, 1985)
*Andreasdrápa*, ed. Ian McDougall, in *Poetry on Christian Subjects*, SkP 7, pp. 845–51
'Arnórr jarlaskáld Þórðarson, *Fragments*', ed. Diana Whaley, in *Poetry from Treatises on Poetics*, SkP 3, p. 3
*Bárðar saga snæfellsáss*, in *Harðar saga*, ed. Þórhallur Vilmundarson and Bjarni Vilhjálmsson, Íslenzk fornrit 13 (Reykjavík, 1991)
*Biskupa sögur*, ed. Sigurgeir Steingrímsson, Ólafur Halldórsson and Peter Foote, Íslenzk fornrit 15 (Reykjavik, 2003)
*Biskupa sögur II*, ed. Ásdis Egilsdóttir, Íslenzk fornit 16 (Reykjavík, 2002)
'Bragi inn gamli Boddason, *Fragments*', ed. Margaret Clunies Ross, in *Poetry from Treatises on Poetics*, SkP 3, pp. 57–58
*Brennu-Njáls saga*, ed. Einar Ólafur Sveinsson, Íslenzk fornrit 12 (Reykjavík, 1954)
Chaucer, Geoffrey, *The Canterbury Tales*, in *The Riverside Chaucer*, ed. Larry D. Benson, 3rd edn (Boston, 1987), pp. 3–328
Cleasby, Richard and Guðbrandur Vigfússon, *An Icelandic-English Dictionary*, 2nd edn (Oxford, 1957)
Clunies Ross, Margaret, gen. ed., *Poetry on Christian Subjects*, 2 vols, SkP 7 (Turnhout, 2007)
———, gen. ed., *Poetry in the Fornaldarsögur*, SkP 8 (Turnhout, 2017)
*Donat et la tradition de l'enseignement grammatical. Étude sur l'"Ars Donati' et sa diffusion (iv^e–ix^e siècle) et édition critique*, ed. Louis Holtz (Paris, 1981)
*Edda. Die Lieder des Codex Regius nebst verwandten Denkmälern*, ed. Gustav Neckel, rev. Hans Kuhn, vol. 1. Text, 5. rev. edn (Heidelberg, 1983 [1914])
*Eddukvæði*, ed. Jónas Kristjánsson and Vésteinn Ólason, 2 vols (Reykjavík, 2014)

*Egils saga Skalla-Grímssonar*, ed. Sigurður Nordal, Íslenzk fornrit 2 (Reykjavík, 1933)
*Egils saga Skallagrímssonar*, ed. Bjarni Einarsson, Jón Helgason and Michael Chesnutt, vol. 1: A-Redaktionen, Editiones Arnamagnæanæ, Series A, vol. 19 (København, 2001; London, 2003)
*Egils saga Skallagrímssonar*, ed. Michael Chesnutt and Jón Helgason, vol. 3: C-Redaktionen, Editiones Arnamagnæanæ, Series A, vol. 21 (København, 2006)
*Einarr Skúlason's Geisli: A Critical Edition*, ed. Martin Chase, Toronto Old Norse and Icelandic Studies 1 (Toronto, Buffalo and London, 2005)
*Eiríksdrápa*, ed. Jayne Carroll, in *Poetry from the Kings' Sagas*, SkP 2, pp. 432–60
*'Elucidarius' in Old Norse Translation*, ed. Everlyn Scherabon Firchow and Karen Grimstad (Reykjavík, 1989)
Erman, Adolf, ed., *Ancient Egyptian Literature: A Collection of Poems, Narratives and Manuals of Instructions from the Third and Second Millennia BC*, trans. Aylward M. Blackman (New York, 2005)
*Eyrbyggja saga*, ed. Einar Ólafur Sveinsson, Íslenzk fornrit 4 (Reykjavík, 1935)
*Færeyinga saga, Ólafs saga Tryggvasonar eptir Odd munk Snorrason*, ed. Ólafur Halldórsson, Íslenzk fornrit 25 (Reykjavík, 2005)
*Finnboga saga ramma*, ed. Jóhannes Halldórsson, Íslenzk fornrit 14 (Reykjavík, 1959)
*The First Grammatical Treatise*, ed. Hreinn Benediktsson (Reykjavík, 1972)
*Flateyjarbók: En Samling af norske Konge-Sagaer med inskudte mindre Fortællinger om Begivenheder i og udenfor Norge samt Annaler*, ed. Guðbrandur Vigfússon and C. R. Unger, vol. I (Christiania [Oslo], 1860)
*Fornaldar sögur Norðurlanda*, ed. Guðni Jónsson, 4 vols (Reykjavík, 1950)
*Fornaldarsögur Norðrlanda, eptir gömlum handritum*, ed. Carl Christian Rafn, vol. I–III (København, 1829–30)
*The Fourth Grammatical Treatise*, ed. Margaret Clunies Ross and Jonas Wellendorf (London, 2014)
Gade, Kari Ellen and Edith Marold, gen. eds, *Poetry from Treatises on Poetics*, 2 vols, SkP 3 (Turnhout, 2017)
Gade, Kari Ellen, gen. ed., *Poetry from the Kings' Sagas 2: c. 1035 to c. 1300*, SkP 2 (Turnhout, 2009)
*Gísla saga Súrssonar, in Vestfirðinga sǫgur*, ed. Björn K. Þórólfsson and Guðni Jónsson, Íslenzk fornrit 6 (Reykjavík, 1943)
*Grettis saga Ásmundarsonar*, ed. Guðni Jónsson, Íslenzk fornrit 7 (Reykjavík, 1936)
*Guðmundar saga A, Guðmundar sögur biskups I: Ævi Guðmundar biskups, Guðmundar saga A*, ed. Stefán Karlsson, Editiones Arnmagnæanæ B, 6 (København, 1983), pp. 15–255

*Guðmundar saga* D, *Biskupa sögur*, ed. Jón Sigurðsson and Guðbrandur Vigfússon, vol. II (København, 1878), pp. 1–220

*Gunnlaugs saga ormstungu* in *Borgfirðinga sǫgur*, ed. Sigurður Nordal and Guðni Jónsson, Íslenzk fornrit 3 (Reykjavík, 1938)

*Hafliðamál*, ed. Tarrin Wills, in *Poetry from Treatises on Poetics*, SkP 3, pp. 533–34

*Hærra Ivan*, ed. Henrik Williams and Karin Palgrem, in *Norse Romance*, vol. III: *Hærra Ivan*, ed. Marianne E. Kalinke, Arthurian Archives IV (Woodbridge, 1999)

*Hákonar saga Hákonarsonar II*, ed. Þorleifur Hauksson, Sverrir Jakobsson and Tor Ulset, Íslenzk fornrit 31, Version Jubileumsutg. (Reykjavík, 2013)

*Harðar saga*, ed. Þórhallur Vilmundarson and Bjarni Vilhjálmsson, Íslenzk fornrit 13 (Reykjavík, 1991)

*Heilagra manna drápa*, ed. and trans. Kirsten Wolf, in *Poetry on Christian Subjects*, SkP 7, pp. 872–90

*Heilagra manna søgur: Fortællinger og legender om hellige mænd og kvinder*, ed. C. R. Unger, 2 vols (København, 1877)

*Heilagra meyja sögur*, ed. Kirsten Wolf, Íslenzk trúarrit 1 (Reykjavík, 2003)

*Heimskringla*, ed. Bjarni Aðalbjarnarson, 3 vols, Íslenzk fornrit 26–28 (Reykjavík, 1941–51)

*Hesiod: Theogony*, ed. Martin L. West (Oxford, 1966)

*Hrafnkels saga Freysgoða*, in *Austfirðingar sǫgur*, ed. Jón Jóhannesson, Íslenzk fornrit 11 (Reykjavík, 1950), 93–133

*Hugsvinnsmál*, ed. Tarrin Wills and Stephanie Gropper, in *Poetry on Christian Subjects*, SkP 7, pp. 358–449

*Hungrvaka* in *Biskupa sögur II*, ed. Ásdís Egilsdóttir, Íslenzk fornrit 16 (Reykjavík, 2002)

*Hungrvaka*, trans. Camilla Bassett, unpublished MA thesis, (University of Iceland, 2013)

*The Icelandic Physiologus*, ed. Halldór Hermansson (Ithaca, 1938)

*Illuga saga Gríðarfóstra. The Saga of Illugi Gríður's Foster Son*, ed. and trans. Philip Lavender (London, 2015)

Isidore of Seville, *The Etymologies of Isidore of Seville*, trans. Stephen A. Barney (Cambridge, 2006)

*Isidori Hispalensis episcopi Etymologiarum sive Originum libri XX*, ed. Wallace Martin Lindsay, 2 vols (Oxford, 1911)

*Islandske Annaler indtil 1578*, ed. Gustav Storm (Christiania [Oslo], 1888)

*Islandske originaldiplomer indtil 1450. Tekst*, ed. Stefán Karlsson, Editiones Arnamagnæanæ A, 7 (København, 1963), No. 101, pp. 124–27

*Íslendingabók. Landnámabók*, ed. Jakob Benediktsson, Íslenzk fornrit 1 (Reykjavík, 1986)

*The King's Mirror (Speculum Regale- Konungs skuggsjá)*, trans. Laurence M. Larson (New York, 1917)

*Konungs skuggsjá*, ed. Ludwig Holm-Olsen, 2nd edn (Oslo, 1983 [1945])

*Kormáks saga*, in *Vatnsdœla saga, Hallfreðar saga, Kormáks saga, Hrómundar þáttr halta, Hrafns þáttr Guðrúnarson*, ed. Einar Ólafur Sveinsson, Íslenzk fornrit 8 (Reykjavík, 1939)

Kroonen, Guus, *Etymological Dictionary of Proto-Germanic* (Leiden, 2013)

*Die Lais der Marie de France*, ed. Karl Warnke and Reinhard Köhler, 3rd edn (Halle, 1925)

*Latinske dokument til norsk historie fram til år 1204*, ed. and trans. Eirik Vandvik (Oslo, 1959)

*Laxdœla saga, Halldórs þáttr Snorrasonar, Stúfs þáttr*, ed. Einar Ólafur Sveinsson, Íslenzk fornrit 5 (Reykjavík, 1934)

*Líknarbraut*, ed. George Tate, in *Poetry on Christian Subjects, SkP 7*, pp. 228–86.

*Lilja*, ed. Martin Chase, in *Poetry on Christian Subjects, SkP 7*, pp. 544–677

*The Literature of Ancient Sumer*, ed. Jeremy Black *et al.* (Oxford, 2004)

*Mágus saga jarls hin meiri*, in *Riddarasögur*, ed. Bjarni Vilhjálmsson, vol. II (Reykjavík, 1954), pp. 135–429

*Merlínusspá*, ed. Russell Poole, in *Poetry in Fornaldarsögur*, ed. Margaret Clunies Ross, *SkP*, 8 (Turnhout, 2017), pp. 38–189.

*Mírmanns saga*, ed. Desmond Slay, Editiones Arnamagnæanæ A, 17 (København, 1997)

*Morkinskinna*, ed. Finnur Jónsson, Samfund til Udgivelse af Gammel Nordisk Litteratur 53 (København, 1932)

*The Old Norse Elucidarius: Original Text and English Translation*, ed. Everlyn Scherabon Firchow (Woodbridge, 1992)

*Orkneyinga saga*, ed. Finnbogi Guðmundsson, Íslenzk fornrit 34 (Reykjavik, 1965)

*Petrsdrápa*, ed. Ian McDougall, in *Poetry on Christian Subjects, SkP 7*, pp. 796–844

*The Poetic Edda*, trans. Carolyne Larrington, 2nd edn (Oxford, 2014)

Robinson, Peter M. W., 'An Edition of *Svipdagsmál*', unpublished DPhil thesis, (Oxford, 1991)

Robortello, Francesco, *In librum Aristotelis de arte poetica explications* (Firenze, 1548)

*Saga af Viktor ok Blavus, a Fifteenth-Century Icelandic Lygisaga. An English Edition and Translation*, ed. Allen H. Chappel, Series Practica 88 (The Hague, Paris, 1972)

'The Saga of the People of Vatnsdal', trans. Andrew Wawn, in *The Sagas of Icelanders* (London: Penguin, 2001), pp. 185–270

'Saga Óláfs konungs hins helga'. *Den store saga om Olav den hellige efter pergamenthåndskrift i Kungliga Biblioteket i Stockholm nr. 2 4to med varianter fra andre håndskrifter*, ed. Oscar Albert Johansen and Jón Helgason, 2 vols (Oslo, 1941)

'*Sigrgarðs saga frækna*: A Normalised Text, Translation, and Introduction', ed. and trans. Alaric Hall, Steven D. P. Richardson and Haukur Þorgeirsson, in *Scandinavian-Canadian Studies / Études Scandinaves au Canada* 21 (2012–13), 81–155

*Sigurðar saga þǫgla* in *Late Medieval Icelandic Romances*, ed. Agnete Loth, vol. 2, Editiones Arnamagnæanæ, Series B, vol. 21 (København, 1963)

*Sigurðar saga þögla: The Shorter Redaction*, ed. Matthew J. Driscoll (Reykjavík, 1992)

*Skikkjurímur*, ed. and trans. Matthew J. Driscoll, in *Norse Romance*, II. *The Knights of the Round Table*, ed. Marianne E. Kalinke, Arthurian Archives IV (Cambridge, 1999), pp. 267–325

Snorri Sturluson, *Edda: Skáldskaparmál, 1. Introduction, Text, and Notes*, ed. Anthony Faulkes (London, 1998)

——, *Edda – Háttatal*, ed. Anthony Faulkes (London, 1999)

——, *Edda*, trans. Anthony Faulkes (London, 2004)

——, *Prologue and Gylfaginning*, ed. Anthony Faulkes, 2nd edn (London, 2005)

——, *The Uppsala 'Edda'*, ed. Heimir Pálsson and trans. Anthony Faulkes (London, 2012)

*Soga om Håkon Håkonsson* trans. Knut Helle (Oslo, 1963)

*Sólarljóð*, ed. Carolyne Larrington and Peter M. W. Robinson, in *Poetry on Christian Subjects*, SkP 7, pp. 287–357.

*Sólarljóð: Tyding ok tolkningsgrunnlag*, ed. Bjarne Fidjestøl (Bergen, 1979)

*Strengleikar: An Old Norse Translation of Twenty-one Old French Lais*, ed. Robert Cook and Mattias Tveitane (Oslo, 1979)

*Sturlunga saga*, ed. Jón Jóhannesson, Magnús Finnbogason and Kristján Eldjárn, vol. I (Reykjavík, 1946)

'*Sturlunga saga' efter membranen Króksfjarðarbók udfyldt efter Reykjarfjarðarbók*, ed. Kristian Kålund, 2 vols (København, 1906–11)

*Den tredje og fjærde grammatiske avhandling i Snorres Edda tilligemed de grammatiske avhandlingers prolog og to andre tillæg*, ed. Björn M. Ólsen, Skrifter 12 (København, 1884)

Úlfr Uggason, *Húsdrápa*, ed. Edith Marold *et al.*, trans. John Foulks, in *Poetry from Treatises on Poetics*, SkP 3, pp. 402–24

*United States Supreme Court Reports from the Organization of the Court to 2000*, 524 vols. (New York, 1812), vol. 378, case no. 184 (Jacobellis v. Ohio, 1964)

*Vatnsdæla saga*, ed. Einar Ólafur Sveinsson, Íslenzk fornrit 8 (Reykjavík, 1939), pp. 1–131

*Vestfirðinga sǫgur*, ed. Björn K. Þórólfsson and Guðni Jónsson, Íslenzk fornrit 6 (Reykjavík, 1943)

*Víglundar saga*, in *Kjalnesinga saga, Jökuls þáttr Búasonar, Víglundar saga, Króka-*

*Refs saga, Þórðar saga hreðu, Finnboga saga, Gunnars saga keldugnúpsfífls*, ed. Jóhannes Halldórsson, Íslenzk fornrit 14 (Reykjavík, 1959)
*Viktors saga ok Blávus*, in *Riddarasögur*, ed. Jónas Kristjánsson, vol. II (Reykjavík, 1964)
Whaley, Diana, gen. ed., *Poetry from the Kings' Sagas 1: From Mythical Times to c. 1035*, 2 vols, SkP 1, (Turnhout, 2012)
*Yngvars saga víðförla* in *Fornaldarsögur Norðurlanda*, ed. Guðni Jónsson and Bjarni Vilhjálmsson, vol. III (Reykjavík, 1943–44), pp. 361–94
'Þjóðólfr ór Hvini, *Haustlǫng*', ed. Margaret Clunies Ross, in *Poetry from Treatises on Poetics*, SkP 3, pp. 431–63
*Þorgils saga ok Hafliða*, ed. Ursula Brown [Dronke] (Oxford, 1952)

## Secondary Texts

Aðalheiður Guðmundsdóttir, 'Interrogating Genre in the *Fornaldarsögur* Round-Table Discussion', *VMS* 2 (2006), 287–89
——, '"How Do You Know If It Is Love or Lust?": On Gender, Status, and Violence in Old Norse Literature', *Interfaces: A Journal of Medieval European Literatures* 2 (2016), 189–209
Ailes, Marianne, 'What's in a Name? Anglo-Norman Romances or *chansons de geste*', in *Medieval Romance*, ed. Purdie and Cichon, pp. 61–75
Allard, Joe, 'Oral to Literary: *Kvöldvaka*, Textual Instability, and All That Jazz' (2004), http://tobias-lib.uni-tuebingen.de/volltexte/2004/1073
Andersson, Theodore M., *The Icelandic Family Saga. An Analytic Reading*, Harvard Studies in Comparative Literature 28 (Cambridge MA, 1967)
——, 'Splitting the Sagas', *SS* 47:4 (1975), 437–41
——, 'The Politics of Snorri Sturluson', *JEGP* 93:1 (1994), 55–78
——, 'Kings' Sagas (*Konungasögur*)', in *Old Norse-Icelandic Literature. A Critical Guide*, ed. Clover and Harris, pp. 197–238
——, *The Growth of the Medieval Icelandic Sagas (1180–1280)* (Ithaca and London, 2006)
——, *The Partisan Muse in the Early Icelandic Sagas (1200–1250)*, Islandica 55 (Ithaca, 2012)
Andrén, Anders, 'Is it Possible to Date a *fornaldarsaga*? The Case of Star-Oddi's Dream', in *Nordic Mythologies*, ed. Tangherlini, pp. 173–83
Andrén, Anders, Kristina Jennbert and Catharina Raudvere, eds, *Old Norse Religion in Long-Term Perspectives*, Vägar til Midgårds 8 (Lund, 2006)
Ármann Jakobsson, 'King and Subject in *Morkinskinna*', *Skandinavistik* 28 (1998), 101–17
——, 'Some Types of Ambiguity in the Sagas of the Icelanders', *ANF* 119 (2004), 37–53
——, 'Interrogating Genre in the *Fornaldarsögur* Round-Table Discussion', *VMS* 2 (2006), 282–83
——, *Illa fenginn mjöður: Lesið í Miðaldatexta* (Reykjavík, 2009)
——, 'The Life and Death of the Medieval Icelandic Short Story', *JEGP* 112 (2013), 257–91

## Works Cited

———, *A Sense of Belonging: Morkinskinna and Icelandic Identity, c.1220*, The Viking Collection 22 (Odense, 2014)
———, 'King Sverrir of Norway and the Foundations of His Power: Kingship Ideology and Narrative in *Sverris saga*', *Medium Ævum* 84 (2015), 109–35
Ármann Jakobsson and Sverrir Jakobsson, eds, *The Routledge Research Companion to the Medieval Icelandic Sagas* (London, 2017)
Ásdís Egilsdóttir, 'Hrafn Sveinbjarnarson, Pilgrim and Martyr', in *Sagas, Saints and Settlements*, ed. Gareth Williams and Paul Bibire (Leiden, Boston 2004), pp. 29–39
———, 'The Beginnings of Local Hagiography in Iceland: The Lives of Bishops Þorlákr and Jón', in *The Making of Christian Myths in the Periphery of Latin Christendom (c. 1000–1300)*, ed. Lars Boje Mortensen (København, 2006), pp. 121–33
Assmann, Aleida, 'Canon and Archive', in *Cultural Memory Studies. An International Handbook*, ed. Erll and Nünning, pp. 97–107
Assmann, Jan, 'Collective Memory and Cultural Identity', *New German Critique* 65 (1988), 125–33
Attwood, Katrina, 'Introduction to Gamli kanóki, *Harmsól*', in *Poetry on Christian Subjects*, SkP 7, pp. 70–72
———, 'Introduction to Anonymous, *Leiðarvísan*', in *Poetry on Christian Subjects*, SkP 7, pp. 137–40
Auken, Sune, P. Schantz Lauridsen and A. Juhl Rasmussen, 'Introduction', *Genre and…*, ed. Sune Auken et al. (Valby, 2015)
Bagerius, Henric, *Mandom och mödom: sexualitet, homosocialitet och aristokratisk identitet på det senmedeltida Island* (Göteborg, 2009)
Bagge, Sverre, *The Political Thought of the King's Mirror*, Medieval Scandinavia Supplements, vol. 3 (Odense, 1987)
———, *Society and Politics in Snorri Sturluson's Heimskringla* (Berkeley, 1991)
———, 'Samfunnsbeskrivelsen i *Heimskringla*: Svar til Birgit Sawyer', (Norwegian) *Historisk tidsskrift* 73 (1994), 205–15
———, *From Gang Leader to the Lord's Anointed: Kingship in Sverris Saga and Hákonar Saga Hákonarsonar*, The Viking Collection 8 (Odense, 1996)
———, *From Viking Stronghold to Christian Kingdom: State Formation in Norway, C. 900–1350* (København, 2010)
Bakhtin, Mikhail M., *The Dialogic Imagination: Four Essays*, trans. Caryl Emerson and Michael Holquist (Austin, 1981)
Bampi, Massimiliano, 'The Development of the *Fornaldarsögur* as a Genre: A Polysystemic Approach', in *Legendary Sagas: Origins and Development*, ed. Lassen, Ney and Ármann Jakobsson, pp. 185–99
———, 'Literary Activity and Power Struggle. Some Observations on the Medieval Icelandic Polysystem after the Sturlungaöld', in *Textual Production and Status Contests*, ed. Bampi and Buzzoni, pp. 59–70
———, 'Genre', in *The Routledge Research Companion to the Medieval Icelandic Sagas*, ed. Ármann Jakobsson and Sverrir Jakobsson, pp. 4–14

Bampi, Massimiliano and Marina Buzzoni, eds, *Textual Production and Status Contests in Rising and Unstable Societies* (Venice, 2013)

Bandlien, Bjørn, Stefka G. Eriksen and Sif Rikhardsdottir, eds, 'Arthur of the North: Histories, Emotions, and Imaginations', *SS* 87:1 (2015), 1–7

Barnes, Geraldine, 'Romance in Iceland', in *Old Icelandic Literature and Society*, ed. Clunies Ross, pp. 266–286

——, 'Margin vs. Centre: Geopolitics in *Nitida saga* (A Cosmographical Comedy?)', in *The Fantastic in Old Norse/Icelandic Literature: Sagas and the British Isles, Preprint Papers of the Thirteenth International Saga Conference, Durham and York, 6–12 August 2006*, 2 vols, ed. John McKinnell, David Ashurst and Donata Kick, vol. 1 (Durham, 2006), pp. 104–12

——, *The Bookish Riddarasögur: Writing Romance in Late Mediaeval Iceland* (Odense, 2014)

Barraclough, Eleanor Rosamund, 'Inside Outlawry in *Grettis saga Ásmundarsonar* and *Gísla saga Súrssonar*: Landscape in the Outlaw Sagas', *SS* 82:4 (2010), 365–88

——, 'Land-naming in the Migration Myth of Medieval Iceland: Constructing the Past in the Present and the Present in the Past', *SBVS* 36 (2012), 79–101

——, 'Sailing the Saga Seas: Narrative, Cultural, and Geographical Perspectives in the North Atlantic Voyages of the *Íslendingasögur*', *Journal of the North Atlantic* 7 (2012), 1–12

Barthes, Roland, 'From Work to Text', in *Textual Strategies: Perspectives in Post-Structuralist Criticism*, ed. Josué V. Harrari (Ithaca, 1976), pp. 73–81

Baßler, Moritz, 'Gattungsmischung, Gattungsübergänge, Unbestimmbarkeit', in *Handbuch Gattungstheorie*, ed. Rüdiger Zymner (Stuttgart and Weimar, 2010), pp. 52–54

Bauer, Alessia, 'Encyclopedic Tendencies and the Medieval Educational Programme: The Merchant's Chapter of *Konungs skuggsjá*', in *Speculum Septentrionale*, ed. Johansson and Kleivane, pp. 217–44

Bax, Marcel and Tineke Padmos, 'Two Types of Verbal Duelling in Old Icelandic: The Interactional Structure of the *senna* and the *mannjafnaðr*', *SS* 55:2 (1983), 149–74

Beck, Heinrich, '*Laxdœla saga* – A Structural Approach,' *SBVS* 19 (1974–77), 383–402

Beck, Sigríður. *I kungens frånvaro: Formeringen av en isländsk aristokrati 1271–1387* (Göteborg, 2011)

Ben-Amos, Daniel, 'Analytical Categories and Ethnic Genres', *Genre* 2 (1969), 275–301. Reprinted in *Folklore Genres*, ed. Daniel Ben-Amos (Austin, 1975), pp. 264–91

Bjarni Einarsson, *Skáldasögur: Um uppruna og eðli ástaskáldsagnanna fornu* (Reykjavík, 1961)

——, 'On the Role of Verse in Saga-Literature', *Mediaeval Scandinavia* 7 (1974), 118–25

——, 'De Normannorum atrocitate, or on the Execution of Royalty by the Aquiline Method', *SBVS* 22 (1986), 79–82

———, 'The Blood-Eagle Once More: Two Notes. A. Blóðörn: An Observation on the Ornithological Aspect', *SBVS* 23 (1990), 80–1
Blobel, Mathias, '<Web>Scraping Parchment: Investigating Genre through Network Analysis of the Electronic Manuscript Catalogue *Handrit.is*.', unpublished MA diss., (University of Iceland, 2015)
Boyd, Brian, *On the Origin of Stories: Evolution, Cognition, and Fiction* (Cambridge MA, 2009)
Böðvar Guðmundsson, Sverrir Tómasson and Torfi Tulinius, eds, *Íslensk bókmenntasaga* (Reykjavík, 1993)
Brandenburg, Elena, *Karl der Große im Norden: Rezeption französischer Heldenepik in den altostnordischen Handschriften*, Beiträge zur Nordischen Philologie 65 (Tübingen, 2019)
Bredsdorff, Thomas, *Chaos and Love: The Philosophy of the Icelandic Family Sagas*, trans. John Tucker (København, 1971; 2001)
Brown, Ursula, 'The Saga of Hrómund Gripsson and *Þorgilssaga*', *SBVS* 13 (1947–48), 51–77
Burrows, Hannah, 'Wit and Wisdom: The Worldview of the Old Norse-Icelandic Riddles and their Relationship to Eddic Poetry', in *Eddic, Skaldic and Beyond: Poetic Variety in Medieval Iceland and Norway*, ed. Martin Chase (New York, 2014), pp. 114–35
———, 'Introduction to sts 48–85, *Heiðreks gátur*', in *Poetry from the Fornaldarsögur*, SkP 8, pp. 406–10
Busby, Keith, 'Narrative Genres', in *The Cambridge Companion to Medieval French Literature*, ed. Simon Gaunt and Sarah Kay (Cambridge, 2008), pp. 139–52
Butterfield, Ardis, 'Medieval Genres and Modern Genre Theory', *Paragraph* 13:2 (1990), 184–201
Byock, Jesse L., *Viking Age Iceland* (London, 2001)
Callow, Christopher, 'Reconstructing the Past in Medieval Iceland', *Early Medieval Europe* 14:3 (2006), 297–324
———, 'Putting Women in their Place? Gender, Landscape, and the Construction of *Landnámabók*', *VMS* 7 (2011), 7–28
Carlquist, Jonas, *Handskriften som historiskt vittne* (Stockholm, 2002)
Carlsen, Christian, *Visions of the Afterlife in Old Norse Literature* (Oslo, 2015)
Carruthers, Mary, *The Book of Memory* (Cambridge, 1990)
Chapman, Harvey, 'What is Genre Fiction?' *Novel Writing Help* (n.d.) https://www.novel-writing-help.com/genre-fiction.html.
Chase, Martin, 'Introduction to Anonymous, *Lilja*', in *Poetry on Christian Subjects*, SkP 7, pp. 544–677
———, 'Introduction to Einarr Skúlason, *Geisli*', in *Poetry on Christian Subjects*, SkP 7, pp. 5–6
Chesnutt, Michael, 'On the Structure, Format, and Preservation of Möðruvallabók', *Gripla* 21 (2010), 147–67
Christia, Fotini, *Alliance Formation in Civil Wars* (Cambridge, 2012)
Ciklamini, Marlene, 'The Concept of Honor in *Valla-Ljóts Saga*', *JEGP* 65.2 (1966), 303–17

# Works Cited

Clover, Carol J., '*Hárbarðsljóð* as Generic Farce', SS 51 (1979), 124–45
——, *The Medieval Saga* (Ithaca and London, 1982)
——, 'Hildigunnr's Lament', in *Cold Counsel: Women in Old Norse Literature and Mythology: A Collection of Essays*, ed. Sarah M. Anderson and Karen Swenson (New York and London, 2002), pp. 15–54
——, 'Icelandic Family Sagas (*Íslendingasögur*)', in *Old Norse-Icelandic Literature*, ed. Clover and Lindow, pp. 239–315
Clover, Carol J., and John Lindow, eds, *Old Norse-Icelandic Literature: A Critical Guide* (Toronto, Buffalo, and London, 2005),
Clunies Ross, Margaret, *Skáldskaparmál: Snorri Sturluson's ars poetica and medieval theories of language*, The Viking Collection 4 (Odense, 1987)
——, 'The Art of Poetry and the Figure of the Poet in Egils saga', in *Sagas of the Icelanders: A Book of Essays*, ed. John Tucker (New York, 1989), pp. 126–45
——, *Prolonged Echoes: Old Norse Myths in Medieval Northern Society*, 2 vols, Vol. I: *The Myths*, The Viking Collection 7 (Odense, 1994)
——, 'The Intellectual Complexion of the Icelandic Middle Ages: Toward a New Profile of Old Icelandic Saga Literature', SS 69 (1997), 443–53
——, *Prolonged Echoes. Old Norse Myths in Medieval Northern Society*, Vol. II: *The Reception of Norse Myths in Medieval Iceland*, The Viking Collection 10 (Odense, 1998)
——, 'Land-Taking and Text-Making in Medieval Iceland,' in *Text and Territory: Geographical Imagination in the European Middle Ages*, ed. Sylvia Tomasch and Sealy Gilles (Philadelphia, 1998), pp. 159–84
——, ed., *Old Icelandic Literature and Society* (Cambridge, 2000)
——, *A History of Old Norse Poetry and Poetics* (Cambridge, 2005)
——, 'Interrogating Genre in the *fornaldarsögur*: Round-Table Discussion', VMS 2 (2006), 276–78
——, 'Introduction' to *Poetry on Christian Subjects*, SkP 7, pp. xliv–xlix
——, *The Cambridge Introduction to the Old Norse-Icelandic Saga* (Cambridge, 2010)
——, 'The Transmission and Preservation of Eddic Poetry', in *A Handbook to Eddic Poetry*, ed. Larrington, Quinn and Schorn, pp. 12–32
Clunies Ross, Margaret, et al., 'Stylistic and Generic Identifiers of the Old Norse Skaldic Ekphrasis', VMS 3 (2007), 159–92
Clunies Ross, Margaret, Kari Ellen Gade, Guðrún Nordal, Edith Marold, Diana Whaley and Tarrin Wills, 'General Introduction', in *Poetry from the Kings' Sagas 1: From Mythical Times to c. 1035*, SkP 1, pp. xiii–xciii
Colbert, David, *The Birth of the Ballad: The Scandinavian Medieval Genre* (Stockholm, 1989)
Cole, Richard, 'Racial Thinking in Old Norse Literature: The Case of the *Blámaðr*', SBVS 39 (2015), 21–40
Cormack, Margaret, 'Poetry, Paganism and the Sagas of Icelandic Bishops', in *Til heiðurs og hugbótar: Greinar um trúarkveðskap fyrri alda*, ed. Svanhildur Óskarsdóttir and Anna Guðmundsdóttir, Snorrastofa Rit 1 (Reykholt, 2003), pp. 33–35

——, 'Sagas of Saints', in *Old Icelandic Literature and Society*, ed. Clunies Ross, pp. 302–25
Crenshaw, James L., 'The Wisdom Literature', in *The Hebrew Bible and its Modern Interpreters*, ed. Douglas A. Knight and Gene M. Tucker (Philadelphia, 1985), pp. 369–407
——, *Old Testament Wisdom: An Introduction*, 3rd edn (Louisville, 2010)
Crocker, Christopher, 'Emotions', in *The Routledge Research Companion to the Medieval Icelandic Sagas*, ed. Ármann Jakobsson and Sverrir Jakobsson, pp. 240–52
Dagenais, John, *The Ethics of Reading in Manuscript Culture: Glossing the Libro de Buen Amor* (Princeton, 1994)
Davenport, Tony, *Medieval Narrative. An Introduction* (Oxford, 2004)
Degnbol, Helle, '"Fair words": The French poem *Floire et Blancheflor*, the Old Norse prose narrative *Flóres saga ok Blankiflúr*, and the Swedish poem *Flores och Blanzaflor*', in *Rittersagas*, ed. Glauser and Kramarz-Bein, pp. 71–96
Derrida, Jacques, 'The Law of Genre', *Critical Inquiry* 7:1 (1980), 55–81
——, *Acts of Literature*, ed. Derek Attridge (London and New York, 1992)
de Vries, Jan, *Altnordische Literaturgeschichte II* (= *Grundriß der Germanischen Philologie*; 16), 2nd edn (Berlin, 1964)
Devitt, Amy J., 'Generalizing about Genre: New Conceptions of an Old Concept', *College Composition and Communication* 44 (1993), 573–86
——, *Writing Genres* (Carbondale, 2004)
van Dijk, Conrad, *John Gower and the Limits of the Law* (Woodbridge, 2013)
Dinzelbacher, Peter, *Vision und Visionsliteratur im Mittelalter*, Monographien zur Geschichte des Mittelalters 23 (Stuttgart, 1981)
Dolcetti Corazza, Vittoria, 'Crossing Paths in the Middle Ages: the *Physiologus* in Iceland', in *The Garden of Crossing Paths: the Manipulation and Rewriting of Medieval Texts*, ed. Marina Buzzoni and Massimiliano Bampi (Venice, 2007), pp. 225–48
Driscoll, Matthew James, *The Unwashed Children of Eve. The Production, Dissemination and Reception of Popular Literature in Post-Reformation Iceland* (Enfield Lock, 1997)
——, '*Fornaldarsögur Norðurlanda*: the stories that wouldn't die', in *Fornaldarsagornas struktur och ideologi*, ed. Ármann Jakobsson, Annette Lassen and Agneta Ney (Uppsala, 2003), pp. 257–69
——, 'Late Prose Fiction (*lygisögur*)', in *A Critical Companion to Old Norse-Icelandic Literature*, ed. McTurk, pp. 190–204
——, 'Arthurian Ballads, *rímur*, Chapbooks and Folktales', in *The Arthur of the North*, ed. Kalinke, pp. 168–95
——, 'Introduction: The Transmission and Reception of the *fornaldarsögur Norðurlanda*', in *The Legendary Legacy*, ed. Driscoll, Hufnagel, Lavender and Stegmann, pp. 9–17
Driscoll, Matthew J., Silvia Hufnagel, Philip Lavender and Beeke Stegmann, eds, *The Legendary Legacy. Transmission and Reception of the Fornaldarsögur Norðurlanda*, The Viking Collection 24 (Odense, 2018)

Dubois, Thomas, 'Oral Poetics: The Linguistics and Stylistics of Orality', in *Medieval Oral Literature*, ed. K. Reichl (Berlin, 2016), pp. 201–24

Dubrow, Heather, *Genre*, Methuen Critical Idiom 42 (London, 1982)

Duff, David, *Modern Genre Theory*, Longman Critical Readers (Harlow, 2001)

Ekrem, Inger, Lars Boje Mortensen, Karen Skovgaard-Petersen, *Olavslegenden og den latinske historieskrivning i 1100-tallets Norge: En artikelsamling* (København, 2000)

Eming, Jutta, 'Emotionen als Gegenstand mediävistischer Literaturwissenschaft', *Journal of Literary Theory* 1:2 (2007), 251–73

Eriksen, Stefka Georgieva, 'Pedagogy and Attitudes towards Knowledge in the *King's Mirror'*, *Viator* 45:3 (2014), 143–68

——, *Writing and Reading in Medieval Manuscript Culture: The Translation and Transmission of the Story of Elye in Old French and Old Norse Literary Contexts*, Medieval Texts and Cultures of Northern Europe 25 (Turnhout, 2014)

——, 'Courtly Literature', in *The Routledge Research Companion to the Medieval Icelandic Sagas*, ed. Ármann Jakobsson and Sverrir Jakobsson, pp. 59–73

Erll, Astrid, 'Cultural Memory Studies: An Introduction', in *Cultural Memory Studies. An International Handbook*, ed. Erll and Nünning, pp. 1–18

Erll, Astrid and Ansgar Nünning, 'Concepts and Methods for the Study of Literature and/as Cultural Memory', in *Literature and Memory. Theoretical Paradigms. Genres. Functions*, ed. Ansgar Nünning, Marion Gymnich, and Roy Sommer (Tübingen, 2006), pp. 11–28

——, eds, *Cultural Memory Studies. An International Handbook* (Berlin and New York, 2008)

Ernst, Ulrich, 'Gattungstheorie im Mittelalter', in *Handbuch Gattungstheorie*, ed. Rüdiger Zymner, pp. 201–02

Etchingham, Colmán, *et al.*, eds, *Norse–Gaelic Contacts in a Viking World: Studies in the Literature and History of Norway, Iceland, Ireland, and the Isle of Man* (Turnhout, 2019)

Even-Zohar, Itamar, 'Polysystem Theory', *Poetics Today* 11:1 (1990), 9–94

Faraci, Dora, 'The Gleða Chapter in the Old Icelandic *Physiologus'*, *Opuscula* 9 (1991), 108–26

Farrell, Joseph, 'Classical Genre in Theory and Praxis', *New Literary History* 34:3 (2003), 383–408

Farrell, Thomas J., ed., *Bakhtin and Medieval Voices* (Gainesville, 1996)

Fechner-Smarsly, Thomas, *Krisenliteratur: Zur Rhetorizität und Ambivalenz in der isländischen Sagaliteratur* (Frankfurt am Main, 1996)

Federico, Sylvia, *New Troy: Fantasies of Empire in the Late Middle Ages* (Minneapolis, 2003)

Ferm, Olle, Ingela Hedström, Sofia Lodén, Jonatan Pettersson and Mia Åkestam, eds, *The Eufemiavisor and Courtly Culture. Time, Texts and Cultural Transfer. Papers from a Symposium in Stockholm 11–13 October 2012*, Konferenser 88 (Stockholm, 2015)

Ferrari, Fulvio, 'Possible Worlds of Sagas: The Intermingling of Different Fictional

Universes in the Development of the *Fornaldarsögur* as a Genre', in *The Legendary Sagas: Origins and Development*, ed. Lassen, Ney and Ármann Jakobsson, pp. 271–90

Finlay, Alison, 'Jómsvíkinga Saga and Genre', *Scripta Islandica* 65 (2014), 63–79

——, 'Risking One's Head: *Vafþrúðnismál* and the Mythic Power of Poetry', in *Myths, Legends, and Heroes: Essays on Old Norse and Old English Literature in Honour of John McKinnell*, ed. Daniel Anlezark (Toronto and London, 2011), pp. 91–108

Foote, Peter, 'Notes on the Prepositions *of* and *um(b)* in Old Icelandic and Old Norwegian', *Studia Islandica* 14 (1955), 41–83

——, '*Sagnaskemtan*: Reykjahólar 1119', in *Aurvandilstá*, ed. Michael Barnes, Hans Bekker-Nielsen and Gerd Wolfgang Weber (Odense, 1984), pp. 65–83

Fowler, Alastair, *Kinds of Literature: An Introduction to the Theory of Genres and Modes* (Oxford, 1982)

Frank, Barbara, 'Innensicht und "Außensicht". Zur Analyse mittelalterlicher volkssprachlicher Gattungsbezeichnungen', in *Gattungen mittelalterlicher Schriftlichkeit*, ed. Barbara Frank, Thomas Haye and Doris Torphinke, ScriptOralia 99 (Tübingen, 1997), pp. 117–36

Frank, Roberta, 'Marriage in Twelfth- and Thirteenth-Century Iceland', *Viator* 4 (1973), 473–84

——, 'Viking Atrocity and Skaldic Verse: The Rite of the Blood-Eagle', *English Historical Review*, 99:391 (1984), 332–43

——, 'The Blood-Eagle Again', *SBVS* 22 (1988), 287–9

——, 'The Blood-Eagle Once More: Two Notes. B. Ornithology and the Interpretation of Skaldic Verse', *SBVS* 23 (1990), 81–3

——, 'Why Skalds Address Women', in *Poetry of the Scandinavian Middle Ages. Atti del 12° congresso internazionale di studi sull'alto medioevo* (Spoleto, 1990), pp. 67–83

——, *Sex, Lies and Málsháttakvæði: An Old Norse Poem from Medieval Orkney* (Nottingham, 2004)

——, 'Introduction to *Málsháttakvæði*', in *Poetry from Treatises on Poetics*, SkP 3, pp. 1213–16

Freund, Stefan, 'Gattungstheorie in der Antike', in *Handbuch Gattungstheorie*, ed. Rüdiger Zymner, pp. 199–200

Fricke, Harald, *Norm und Abweichung: Eine Philosophie der Literatur* (München, 1981)

Frotscher, Antje, 'The War of the Words: A History of Flyting from Antiquity to the Later Middle Ages', unpublished DPhil thesis (Oxford, 2004)

Frow, John, *Genre*, The New Critical Idiom (Abingdon, 2006; 2nd edn, London, 2015)

Fubini, Mario, *Entstehung und Geschichte literarischer Gattungen*, trans. Ursula Vogt (Tübingen, 1971)

Fuglesang, Signe Horn, 'Ekphrasis and Surviving Imagery in Viking Scandinavia', *VMS* 3 (2007), 193–224

Fulk, Robert D., 'Eddic Metres', in *A Handbook to Eddic Poetry*, ed. Larrington, Quinn and Schorn, pp. 252–70

Furrow, Melissa, *Expectations of Romance: The Reception of a Genre in Medieval England* (Cambridge, 2009)

Gade, Kari Ellen, 'Poetry and its Changing Importance in Medieval Icelandic Culture', in *Old Icelandic Literature and Society*, ed. Clunies Ross, pp. 61–95

Gaunt, Simon, 'Genres in Motion: Reading the *Grundriss* 40 Years On', *Medioevo Romanzo* 27 (2013), 24–43

——, 'Romance and Other Genres', *The Cambridge Companion to Medieval Romance*, ed. Krueger, pp. 45–59

Gayk, Shannon and Ingrid Nelson, eds, *Exemplaria* 27:1–2 (2015), special issue on *Theorizing Early English Genre*

Genette, Gérard, *The Architext: An Introduction*, trans. Jane E. Lewin (Berkeley, 1982)

——, *Paratexts: Thresholds of Interpretation*, trans. Jane E. Lewin (Cambridge, 1997)

Ghosh, Shami, *Kings' Sagas and Norwegian History: Problems and Perspectives*, The Northern World 54 (Leiden, 2011)

Gísli Sigurðsson, 'Another Audience — Another Saga: How Can We Best Explain Different Accounts in *Vatnsdœla* saga and *Finnboga saga ramma* of the Same Events?', in *Text und Zeittiefe*, ed. Hildegard L. C. Tristram, ScriptOralia 58 (Tübingen, 1994), pp. 359–75

——, *The Medieval Icelandic Saga and Oral Tradition: A Discourse on Method* (Cambridge MA, 2004)

Glauser, Jürg, *Isländische Märchensagas. Studien zur Prosaliteratur im spätmittelalterlichen Island*, Beiträge zur nordischen Philologie 12 (Basel and Frankfurt am Main, 1983)

——, 'Sagas of Icelanders (*Íslendinga sögur*) and *þættir* as the Literary Representation of a New Social Space', in *Old Icelandic Literature and Society*, ed. Clunies Ross, pp. 203–20

——, 'Romance (Translated *Riddarasögur*)', in *A Companion to Old Norse-Icelandic Literature*, ed. McTurk, pp. 372–87

——, 'The Speaking Bodies of Saga Texts', in *Learning and Understanding in the Old Norse World*, ed. Quinn, Heslop and Wills, pp. 13–26

——, 'Staging the Text: On the Development of a Consciousness of Writing in the Norwegian and Icelandic Literature of the Middle Ages', in *Along the Oral-Written Continuum: Types of Texts, Relations and their Implications*, ed. Slávica Rankovic (with Leidulf Melve and Else Mundal), Utrecht Studies in Medieval Literacy 20 (Turnhout, 2010), pp. 311–34

——, 'What is Dated, and Why? Saga Dating in the Histories of Old Norse-Icelandic Literature', in *Dating the Sagas*, ed. Mundal, pp. 9–30

——, 'The Colour of a Sail and Blood in a Glove. Medial Constellations in the *riddarasǫgur*', in *Riddarasǫgur*, ed. Johansson and Mundal, pp. 199–224

Glauser, Jürg and Susanne Kramarz-Bein, eds, *Rittersagas. Übersetzung, Überlieferung, Transmission*, Beiträge zur Nordischen Philologie 45 (Tübingen, 2014)

## Works Cited

Goeres, Erin Michelle, *The Poetics of Commemoration: Skaldic Verse and Social Memory, c. 890–1070* (Oxford, 2016)

Goffman, Erving, *Frame Analysis: An Essay on the Organisation of Experience* (New York, 1974)

van Gorp, Hendrik and Ulla Musarra-Schroeder, eds, *Genres as Repositories of Cultural Memory* (Amsterdam-Atlanta, 2000)

Gottskálk Jensson, 'Were the Earliest *fornaldarsögur* Written in Latin?', in *Fornaldarsagaerne: Myter og virkelighed*, ed. Ney, Ármann Jakobsson and Lassen, pp. 79–91

Grabmann, Martin, *Die Geschichte der scholastischen Methode*, 2 vols: *Die scholastische Methode im 12. und beginnenden 13. Jahrhundert* (Graz, 1957)

Grant, Barry Keith, 'Introduction', in *Film Genre Reader IV*, ed. Barry Keith Grant (Austin, 2012), pp. xvii–xxii

Greimas, Algirdas Julien and Joseph Courtés, *Sémiotique: Dictionnaire Raisonné de la Théorie de Langage* (Paris, 1979)

Gropper, Stefanie, '*Breta sögur* and *Merlínusspá*', in *The Arthur of the North*, ed. Kalinke, pp. 48–60

Grønlie, Siân E., *The Saint and the Saga Hero. Hagiography and Early Icelandic Literature*, Studies in Old Norse Literature 2 (Cambridge, 2017)

Grove, Jonathan, 'Skaldic Verse-making in Thirteenth-century Iceland: The Case of the Sauðafellsferðarvísur', *VMS* 4 (2008), 85–131

Grubmüller, Klaus, 'Gattungskonstitution im Mittelalter', in *Mittelalterliche Literatur und Kunst im Spannungsfeld von Hof und Kloster*, ed. Nigel F. Palmer and Hans-Jochen Schiewer (Tübingen, 1999), pp. 193–210

Gunnar Harðarson, 'Old Norse Intellectual Culture: Appropriation and Innovation', in *Intellectual Culture in Medieval Scandinavia, c. 1100–1350*, ed. Stefka Georgieva Eriksen (Turnhout, 2016), pp. 35–73

Gunnell, Terry, *The Origins of Drama in Scandinavia* (Cambridge, 1995)

———, 'Eddic Poetry', in *A Companion to Old Norse-Icelandic Literature*, ed. McTurk, pp. 82–100

———, '"Magical Mooning" and the "Goatskin Twirl": "Other" Kinds of Female Magical Practices', in *Nordic Mythologies*, ed. Tangherlini, pp. 133–56

Gunnes, Erik, *Kongens ære: Kongemakt og kirke i en tale mot biskopene* (Oslo, 1971)

Guðrún Nordal, *Tools of Literacy. The Role of Skaldic Verse in Icelandic Textual Culture of the Twelfth and Thirteenth Centuries* (Toronto, 2001)

———, 'The Sagas of Icelanders', in *The Viking World*, ed. Stefan Brink with Neil Price (London and New York, 2012), pp. 315–18

———, 'Skaldic Citations and Settlement Stories as Parameters for Saga Dating', in *Dating the Sagas*, ed. Mundal, pp. 195–212

Guðvarður Már Gunnlaugsson, 'Brot íslenskra miðaldahandrita', in *Handritasyrpa: Rit til heiðurs Sigurgeiri Steingrímssyni sjötugum, 2. október 2013*, ed. Rósa Þorsteinsdóttir, Rit 88 (Reykjavík, 2014), 121–40

———, 'Kjalnesingar, Króka-Refur og Hrafnistumenn', The Árni Magnússon Institute for Icelandic Studies, http://www.arnastofnun.is/page/kjalnesinga_saga

## Works Cited

Haki Antonsson, *St Magnus of Orkney: A Scandinavian Martyr-Cult in Context*, Northern World 29 (Leiden, 2007)

———, 'Thomas saga erkibyskups ('The Saga of Archbishop Thomas')', in *The Oxford Dictionary of the Middle Ages* (Oxford, 2010)

———, 'Salvation and Early Saga Writing in Iceland: Aspects of the Works of the Þingeyrar Monks and their Associates', *VMS* 8 (2012), 71–140

———, '*Árna saga biskups* as Literature and History', *JEGP* 116 (2017), 261–85

———, *Damnation and Salvation in Old Norse Literature*, Studies in Old Norse Literature 3 (Cambridge, 2018)

Hallberg, Peter, 'Sturlunga saga', in *Medieval Scandinavia: An Encyclopedia*, ed. Pulsiano and Wolf, pp. 616–18

———, *The Icelandic Saga*, trans. Paul Schach (Lincoln NE, 1962)

van Hamel, Anton Gerard, '*Vatnsdœlasaga* and *Finnbogasaga*', *JEGP* 33 (1934), 1–22

Hamer, Andrew, 'Searching for Wisdom: The King's Mirror', in *Speculum regale*, ed. Schnall and Simek, pp. 47–62

Harris, Joseph, 'Genre in Saga Literature: A Squib', *SS* 47:4 (1975), 427–36

———, 'Folktale and Thattr: The Case of Rognvald and Raud', *Folklore Forum* 13 (1980), 158–98

———, 'Sagas as Historical Novel', in *Structure and Meaning in Old Norse Literature. New Approaches to Textual Analysis and Literary Criticism*, ed. John Lindow, Lars Lönnroth, Gerd Wolfgang Weber (Odense, 1986), pp. 187–219

———, 'Þættir', in *Dictionary of the Middle Ages*, ed. Joseph R. Strayer, vol. 12 (New York, 1989), pp. 1–6

———, 'The Prosimetrum of Icelandic Saga and Some Relatives', in *Prosimetrum. Crosscultural Perspectives on Narrative in Prose and Verse*, ed. Joseph Harris and Karl Reichl (Cambridge, 1997), 131–63

Harris, Joseph and Thomas D. Hill, 'Gestr's "Prime Sign": Source and Signification in *Norna-Gests þáttr*', *ANF* 104 (1989), 103–22

Harris, Richard, 'A Concordance to the Proverbs and Proverbial Materials in the Old Icelandic Sagas', online database, www.usask.ca/english/icelanders/

———, 'The Literary Uses of Proverbs in *Njáls saga*', *Proverbium* 18 (2001), 149–66

———, '"Mér þykkir þar heimskum manni at duga, sem þú ert." Paremiological Sub-Categories and the *Íslendingasögur*: Some Applications of the Concordance to the Proverbs and Proverbial Materials in the Old Icelandic Sagas', *Scandinavian-Canadian Studies* 16 (2005–06), 28–54

———, 'The Proverbs of *Vatnsdœla saga*, the Sword of Jokull and the Fate of Grettir: Examining an Instance of Conscious Intertextuality in *Grettis saga*', in *The Hero Recovered: Essays in Honor of George Clark*, ed. James Weldon and Robin Waugh (Kalamazoo, 2010), pp. 150–70

Heffernan, Thomas J., *Sacred Biography: Saints and their Biographers in the Middle Ages* (Oxford, 1988)

Heide, Eldar, 'The term *leizla* in Old Norse Vision Literature – Contrasting Imported and Indigenous Genres', *Scripta Islandica* 67 (2016), 37–63

Helle, Knut, 'Innleiing', in *Soga om Håkon Håkonsson* (Oslo, 1963), pp. 7–15

## Works Cited

Heller, Rolf, *Literarisches Schaffen in der Laxdœla saga. Die Entstehung der Berichte über Olaf Pfaus Herkunft und Jugend* (Halle (Saale), 1960) [= *SAGA. Untersuchungen zur nordischen Literatur- und Sprachgeschichte*, ed. Prof. Dr. W. Baetke, Heft 3]

Hermann Pálsson, *Sagnaskemmtun Íslendinga* (Reykjavík, 1962)

——, *Art and Ethics in* Hrafnkel's Saga (København, 1971)

Hermann, Pernille, '*Íslendingabók* and History', in *Reflections of Old Norse Myths*, ed. Pernille Hermann, Jens Peter Schjødt, and Rasmus Tranum Kristensen (Turnhout, 2007), pp. 17–32

——, 'Saga Literature, Cultural Memory, and Storage', *SS* 85:3 (2013), 332–54

——, 'Literacy', in *The Routledge Research Companion to the Medieval Icelandic Sagas*, ed. Ármann Jakobsson and Sverrir Jakobsson, pp. 34–47

Heslop, Kate and Jürg Glauser, eds, *RE:writing. Medial Perspectives on Textual Culture in the Icelandic Middle Ages*, Medienwandel – Medienwechsel – Medienwissen 29 (Zürich, 2018)

Hiatt, Alfred, 'Genre without System', in *Middle English*, ed. Paul Strohm, Oxford Twenty-First Century Approaches to Literature (Oxford, 2007), pp. 277–94

Hjaltalin, Thor, 'The Historic Landscape of the Saga of the People of Vatnsdalur: Exploring the Saga Writer's Use of the Landscape and Archaeological Remains to Serve Political Interests', *Medieval Archaeology* 53 (2009), 243–70

Hodges, Kenneth, 'Introduction: Places of Romance', in *Mapping Malory: Regional Identities and National Geographies in Le Morte Darthur*, ed. Dorsey Armstrong and Kenneth Hodges (New York, 2014), pp. 1–18

Hofmann, Dietrich, 'Sagaprosa als Partner von Skaldenstrophen', *Medieval Scandinavia* 11 (1978–79), 68–81

Hogenbirk, Marjolein, 'The "I-Word" and Genre: Merging Epic and Romance in the *Roman van Walewein*', in *'Li premerains verse': Essays in Honor of Keith Busby*, ed. Catherine M. Jones and Logan E. Whalen (Amsterdam and New York, 2011), pp. 157–70

Hoggart, Carol, 'A Layered Landscape: How the Family Sagas Mapped Medieval Iceland', *Limina: A Journal of Historical and Cultural Studies* 16 (2010), 1–8

Holmes, Su, '"A Term Rather Too General to be Helpful": Struggling with Genre in Reality TV', in *The Shifting Definitions of Genre: Essays on Labeling Films, Television Shows and Media*, ed. Lincoln Geraghty and Mark Jancovich (Jefferson, 2008), pp. 159–78

Hufnagel, Silvia Veronika, 'Projektbericht "Alt Und Neu": Isländische Handschriften, Bücher und die Gesellschaft des 16. und 17. Jahrhunderts', in *Quelle & Deutung III: Beiträge der Tagung Quelle und Deutung III am 5. November 2015*, ed. Sára Balázs, Antiquitas, Byzantium, Renascentia 24 (Budapest, 2016), pp. 147–68

Hughes, Shaun F. D., '"Where are all the eddic champions gone?" The Disappearance and Recovery of the Eddic Heroes in Late Medieval Iceland Literature, 1400–1800', *VMS* 9 (2013), 37–67

——, The Old Norse Exempla as Arbiters of Gender Roles in Medieval Iceland', in

*New Norse Studies: Essays on the Literature and Culture of Medieval Scandinavia*, ed. Jeffrey Turco (Ithaca, 2015), pp. 255–300

Hui, Jonathan Y. H., 'The *Fornaldarsaga* in a Dream: Weaving Fantastical Textures in *Stjörnu-Odda draumr*', *Quaestio Insularis* 17 (2016), 48–73

Huot, Sylvia, 'The Manuscript Context of Medieval Romance', in *The Cambridge Companion to Medieval Romance*, ed. Krueger, pp. 60–77

Hunt, Margaret Cushing. 'A Study of Authorial Perspective in *Guðmundar saga A* and *Guðmundar saga D*: Hagiography and the Icelandic Bishop's Saga', unpublished DPhil thesis, (Indiana University, 1985)

Imsen, Steinar, *Ecclesia Nidrosiensis 1153–1537: Søkelys på Nidaroskirkens og Nidarosprovinsens historie*, Skrifter 15 (Trondheim, 2003)

Ingham, Norman W., 'Genre-Theory and Old Russian Literature', *The Slavic and East European Journal* 31:2 (1987), 234–45

Jaeger, Stephen C. and Ingrid Kasten, *Codierungen von Emotionen im Mittelalter / Emotions and Sensibilities in the Middle Ages* (Berlin and New York, 2003)

Jameson, Fredric, *The Political Unconscious: Narrative as a Socially Symbolic Act* (London, 1981)

Jauss, Hans Robert, *Literaturgeschichte als Provokation der Literaturwissenschaft* (Konstanz, 1967)

——, 'Literary History as a Challenge to Literary Theory', *New Literary History* 2 (1970), 7–37

——, 'Theorie der Gattungen und Literatur des Mittelalters', in *Alterität und Modernität der mittelalterlichen Literatur: Gesammelte Aufsätze 1956–1976*, ed. Hans Robert Jauss (München, 1977), pp. 327–58

——, *Toward an Aesthetic of Reception*, trans. Timothy Bahti (Minneapolis, 1982)

——, 'Theory of Genres and Medieval Literature', in *Modern Genre Theory*, ed. David Duff (Harlow, 2000), pp. 127–47

Jensen, Jonna Louis, 'Den yngre del af Flateyjarbók', in *Afmælisrit Jóns Helgasonar: 30. júní 1969*, ed. Jakob Benediktsson, *et al.* (Reykjavík, 1969), pp. 235–50

Jesch, Judith, 'Geography and Travel', in *A Companion to Old Norse Icelandic Literature*, ed. McTurk, pp. 119–35

——, *The Viking Diaspora* (London and New York, 2015)

Jochens, Jenny, 'Germanic Marriage: The Case of Medieval Iceland', in *The Medieval Marriage Scene: Prudence, Passion, Policy*, ed. Sherry Rouse and Cristelle Louise Baskins (Tempe, 2005), pp. 55–65

Jóhanna Katrín Friðriksdóttir, *Women in Old Norse Literature: Bodies, Words, and Power*, The New Middle Ages (New York, 2013)

——, 'Ideology and Identity in Late Medieval Northwest Iceland: A Study of AM 152 fol.', *Gripla* 25 (2014), 87–128

——, '*Konungs Skuggsjá* [The King's Mirror] and Women Patrons and Readers in Late Medieval and Early Modern Iceland', *Viator* 49 (2019), 277–306

Johansson, Karl G., 'Compilations, Collections and Composite Manuscripts: Some Notes on the Manuscript *Hauksbók*', in *RE:writing*, ed. Heslop and Glauser, pp. 121–41

## Works Cited

Johansson, Karl G. and Elise Kleivane, eds, *Speculum Septentrionale: Konungs Skuggsjá and the European Encyclopedia of the Middle Ages*, Bibliotheca Nordica 10 (Oslo, 2018)

——, 'Konungs skuggsjá and the Interplay between Universal and Particular', in *Speculum septentrionale*, ed. Johansson and Kleivane, pp. 9–34

Johansson, Karl G. and Else Mundal, eds, *Riddarasǫgur. The Translation of European Court Culture in Medieval Scandinavia*, Bibliotheca Nordica 7 (Oslo, 2014)

Jón Jóhannesson, *A History of the Old Icelandic Commonwealth: Íslendinga Saga*, trans. Haraldur Bessason, University of Manitoba Icelandic Studies 2 (Winnipeg, 1974)

Jón Sigurðsson and Guðbrandur Vigfússon, 'Formáli' to *Biskupa sögur*, I, ed. Jón Sigurðsson and Guðbrandur Vigfússon (København, 1858), pp. v–xc

Jón Viðar Sigurðsson, 'The Icelandic Aristocracy after the Fall of the Free State', *Scandinavian Journal of History* 20.3 (1995), 153–66

——, *Chieftains and Power in the Icelandic Commonwealth*, The Viking Collection 12 (Odense, 1999)

——, 'Historical Writing and the Political Situation in Iceland 1100–1400', in *Negotiating Pasts in the Nordic Countries: Interdisciplinary Studies in History and Memory*, ed. Anne Eriksen and Jón Viðar Sigurðsson (Lund, 2009), pp. 59–78

Jón Viðar Sigurðsson and Sverrir Jakobsson, *Sturla Þórðarson: Skald, Chieftain, and Lawman*, The Northern World 78 (Leiden, 2017)

Jónas Kristjánsson, *Um Fóstbræðrasögu*, Rit Stofnun Árna Magnússonar á Íslandi, 1 (Reykjavík, 1972)

——, 'Learned Style or Saga Style?', in *Speculum Norrœnum: Norse Studies in Memory of Gabriel Turville-Petre*, ed. Ursula Dronke et al. (Odense, 1981)

——, *Eddas and Sagas: Iceland's medieval literature*, trans. Peter Foote (Reykjavík, 1988; repr. 1997)

Jørgensen, Jørgen Højgaard, 'Hagiography and the Icelandic Bishop Sagas', *Peritia* 1 (1982), 1–16

Jorgensen, Peter A., 'The Icelandic Translations from Middle English', in *Studies for Einar Haugen Presented by Friends and Colleagues*, ed. Evelyn Scherabon Firchow, et al. (The Hague, 1972), pp. 305–20

Kalinke, Marianne E., 'Norse Romance (*Riddarasögur*)', in *Old Norse-Icelandic Literature*, ed. Clover and Lindow, pp. 316–364

——, '*Riddarasögur, Fornaldarsögur* and the Problem of Genre', in *Les Sagas de Chevaliers (Riddarasögur): Actes de la V$^e$ Conférence Internationale sur les Sagas*, ed. Régis Boyer (Paris, 1985), pp. 77–91

——, *Bridal-Quest Romance in Medieval Iceland*, Islandica 46 (Ithaca, 1990)

——, '*Víglundar saga*: An Icelandic Bridal-Quest Romance', *Skáldskaparmál* 3 (1994), 119–43

——, 'Interrogating Genre in the *Fornaldarsögur* Round-Table Discussion', *VMS* 2 (2006), 275–76

——, ed., *The Arthur of the North. The Arthurian Legend in the Norse and Rus' Realms*, Arthurian Literature in the Middle Ages V (Cardiff, 2011)

———, 'Textual Instability, Generic Hybridity, and the Development of Some *Fornaldarsögur*', in *The Legendary Sagas. Origins and Development*, ed. Lassen, Ney and Ármann Jakobsson, pp. 201–228

———, *Stories Set Forth with Fair Words. The Evolution of Medieval Romance in Iceland* (Cardiff, 2017)

Kalinke, Marianne and Philip M. Mitchell, *Bibliography of Old Norse-Icelandic Romances*, Islandica 44 (Ithaca and London, 1985)

Kantorowicz, Ernst Hartwig, *The King's Two Bodies: A Study in Mediaeval Political Theology* (Princeton, 1957)

Kári Gíslason, 'Within and Without: Family in the Icelandic Sagas', *Parergon* 26:1 (2009), 13–33.

Kasten, Ingrid *et al.*, 'Zur Performativität von Emotionalität in erzählenden Texten des Mittelalters', *Encomia. Encomia-Deutsch, Sonderheft der deutschen Sektion der International Courtly Literature Society* (2000), 42–60

Kedwards, Dale, 'The World Image of the *Konungs skuggsjá*', in *Speculum Septentrionale*, ed. Johansson and Kleivane, pp. 71–92

Kindermann, Udo, 'Gattungensysteme im Mittelalter', in *Kontinuität und Transformationen der Antike im Mittelalter*, ed. Willi Erzgräber (Sigmaringen, 1989), pp. 303–13

Kirby, Ian, 'Bible and Biblical Interpretation in Medieval Iceland', in *Old Icelandic Literature and Society*, ed. Clunies Ross, pp. 287–301

Kjesrud, Karoline, *Lærdom og fornøyelse: Sagaer om helter på eventyr* (Oslo, 2011)

Koch, Elke, *Trauer und Identität: Inszenierungen von Emotionen in der deutschen Literatur des Mittelalters* (Berlin and New York, 2006)

Köhler, Erich, *Ideal und Wirklichkeit in der höfischen Epik: Studien zur Form der frühen Artus- und Graldichtung* (Tübingen, 1970)

———, 'Gattungssystem und Gesellschaftssystem', in *Zum mittelalterlichen Literaturbegriff*, ed. Barbara Haupt (Darmstadt, 1985), pp. 111–29

Kramarz-Bein, Susanne, '"Modernität" der *Laxdœla saga*', in *Studien zum Altgermanischen. Festschrift für Heinrich Beck*, ed. Heiko Uecker (Berlin and New York, 1994), pp. 421–42

Kreutzer, Gert, *Die Dichtungslehre der Skalde:. Poetologische Terminologie und Autorenkommentare als Grundlage einer Gattungspoetik* (Kronberg, 1974)

Kristján Árnason, 'Um *Háttatal* Snorra Sturlusonar. Bragform og braglýsing', *Gripla* 17 (2006), 75–124

Krueger, Roberta L., ed., *The Cambridge Companion to Medieval Romance* (Cambridge, New York, Melbourne, Madrid, 2000)

———, 'Introduction', *The Cambridge Companion to Medieval Romance*, ed. Krueger, pp. 1–9

Kwon, Ah Leum, 'The Structure of AM 309 4to: A Codicological and Paleographical Analysis', MA diss (University of Iceland, 2017)

La Farge, Beatrice, 'Introduction to Níkulás Bergsson, *Jónsdrápa postula*', in *Poetry on Christian Subjects*, SkP 7, pp. 66–67

La Farge, Beatrice and John Tucker, *Glossary to the Poetic Edda, Based on Hans Kuhn's*

*Kurzes Wörterbuch* (Heidelberg, 1992)

Lachmann, Renate, 'Mnemonic and Intertextual Aspects of Literature', in *Cultural Memory Studies: An International Handbook*, ed. Erll and Nünning, pp. 301–10

Lambertus, Hendrik, *Von monströsen Helden und heldenhaften Monstern. Zur Darstellung und Funktion des Fremden in den originalen Riddarasögur*, Beiträge zur Nordischen Philologie 52 (Tübingen and Basel, 2013)

Larrington, Carolyne, *A Store of Common Sense: Gnomic Themes and Style in Old Icelandic and Old English Wisdom Poetry* (Oxford, 1993)

——, '*Leizla Rannveigar*: Gender and Politics in the Other World Vision', *Medium Ævum* 64 (1995), 230–49

——, 'Freyja and the Organ-Stool: Neo-Paganism in *Sólarljóð*', in *Germanisches Altertum und christliches Mittelalter*, ed. Bela Broyanyi (Hamburg, 2001), pp. 177–96

——, *Brothers and Sisters in Medieval European Literature* (York, 2015)

——, 'Eddic Poetry and Heroic Legend', in *A Handbook to Eddic Poetry: Myths and Legends of Ancient Scandinavia*, ed. Larrington, Quinn and Schorn, pp. 147–72

——, 'New Thoughts on Old Wisdom: Norse Gnomic Poetry, the Narrative Turn and Situational Ethics', in *Proverbia Septentrionalia: Essays on Proverbs in Medieval Scandinavian and English Literature*, Medieval and Renaissance Texts and Studies 542, ed. Michael Cichon and Yin Liu (Tempe, 2019), pp. 55–68

Larrington, Carolyne, Judy Quinn and Brittany Schorn, eds, *A Handbook to Eddic Poetry: Myths and Legends of Ancient Scandinavia* (Cambridge, 2016)

Larrington, Carolyne and Peter Robinson, 'Introduction to Anonymous, *Sólarljóð*', in *Poetry on Christian Subjects*, pp. 287–95

Lassen, Annette, Agneta Ney and Ármann Jakobsson, eds, *The Legendary Sagas: Origins and Development* (Reykjavík, 2012)

Lavender, Philip, '*Illuga saga* as *fornaldarsaga*, *riddarasaga* and *Íslendingasaga*: Generic Fluidity in the Late Development of Sagas and Rímur', in *The Legendary Legacy*, ed. Driscoll, Hufnagel, Lavender and Stegmann, pp. 187–214

Layher, William, 'The Old Swedish *Hærra Ivan Leons riddare*', in *The Arthur of the North*, ed. Kalinke, pp. 123–44

Leslie-Jacobsen, Helen F., 'Genre and the Prosimetra of the Old Icelandic *fornaldarsögur*', in *Genre –Text – Interpretation: Multidisciplinary Perspectives on Folklore and Beyond*, ed. Kaarina Koski and Frog with Ulla Savolainen, Studia Fennica, Folklorica 22 (Helsinki, 2016), pp. 251–75

Lethbridge, Emily, '*Gísla saga Súrssonar*: Textual Variation, Editorial Constructions and Critical Interpretations', in *Creating the Medieval Saga: Versions, Variability and Editorial Interpretations of Old Norse Saga Literature*, ed. Judy Quinn and Emily Lethbridge (Odense, 2010), pp. 123–52

——, 'Authors and Anonymity, Texts and Their Contexts: The Case of Eggertsbók', in *Modes of Authorship in the Middle Ages*, ed. Slavica Rankovic, *et al.*, Papers in Medieval Studies 22 (Toronto, 2012), pp. 343–64

——, '"Hvorki glansar gull á mér / né glæstir stafir í línum": Some Observations on *Íslendingasögur* Manuscripts and the Case of *Njáls Saga*', *ANF* 129 (2014), 55–89

——, 'The Icelandic Sagas and Saga Landscapes: Writing, Reading and Retelling *Íslendingasögur* Narratives', *Gripla* 27 (2016), 51–92

Libera, Alain de, *Denken im Mittelalter*, trans. Andreas Knop (München, 2003)

Liberman, Mark, 'Journalists: Stop Passing Off a Paraphrase as a Direct Quotation', *Slate* (Oct. 17, 2013) http://www.slate.com/blogs/lexicon_valley/2013/10/17/gay_talese_there_s_no_excuse_for_journalists_to_paraphrase_sources_in_direct.html.

Liestøl, Knut, *The Origin of the Icelandic Family Sagas*, trans. A. G. Jayne (Oslo, 1930)

Lindow, John, 'Old Icelandic *Þáttr*: Early Usage and Semantic History', *Scripta Islandica* 29 (1978), 3–44

Ljungqvist, Fredrik Charpentier, 'Kristen kungaideologi i Sverris saga', *Scripta Islandica* 57 (2006), 79–95

Lodén, Sofia, *Le chevalier courtois à la rencontre de la Suède médiévale. Du Chevalier au lion à Herr Ivan*, Forskningsrapporter/Cahiers de la Recherche 7 (Stockholm, 2012)

Long, Ann-Marie, *Iceland's Relationship with Norway c.870 – c.1100: Memory, History and Identity* (Leiden, 2017)

Lönnroth, Lars, *European Sources of Icelandic Saga-Writing. An Essay Based on Previous Studies* (Stockholm, 1965)

——, 'The Concept of Genre in Saga Literature', *SS* 47:4 (1975), 419–26

Louis-Jensen, Jonna and Tarrin Wills, 'Introduction to Anonymous, *Plácitus drápa*', in *Poetry on Christian Subjects*, *SkP* 7, pp. 179–81

Males, Mikael, *The Poetic Genesis of Old Icelandic Literature*, Ergänzungsbände zum Reallexikon der Germanischen Altertumskunde 113 (Berlin, 2020)

Már Jónsson, 'Manuscript Design in Medieval Iceland', in *From Nature to Script: Reykholt, Environment, Centre and Manuscript Making*, ed. Helgi Þorláksson and Þóra Björg Sigurðardóttir, Rit 7 (Reykholt, 2012), pp. 231–43

Marold, Edith, 'Skaldedichtung und Mythologie', in *Atti del 12. Congresso Internazionale di Studi sull'Alto Medioevo: Poetry in the Scandinavian Middle Ages. The Seventh International Saga Conference*, ed. Teresa Pàroli, (Spoleto, 1990), pp. 107–30

Marold, Edith, *et al.*, trans. John Foulks, 'Introduction to Eilífr Goðrúnarson, *Þórsdrápa*', *Poetry from Treatises on Poetics*, *SkP* 3, pp. 68–75

Manhire, William, 'The Narrative Functions of Source-References in the Sagas of Icelanders', *SBVS* 19 (1974–7), 170–90

McCreesh, Bernadine, 'The Structure of *Vatnsdœla saga*', *SBVS* 34 (2010), 75–86

McDonald, Sheryl, '*Nítíða saga*: A Normalised Icelandic Text and Translation', *Leeds Studies in English* 40 (2009), 119–45

McDonald Werronen, Sheryl, *Popular Romance in Iceland: The Women, Worldviews, and Manuscript Witnesses of Nitida Saga* (Amsterdam, 2016)

McKinnell, John, 'The Reconstruction of Pseudo-Vatnshyrna', *Opuscula* 4 (1970), 304–37

——, 'Motivation in *Lokasenna*', *SBVS* 22.3–4 (1987–88), 234–62

## Works Cited

McTurk, Rory, ed., *A Companion to Old Norse-Icelandic Literature and Culture* (Oxford and Malden, 2005)

Meißner, Rudolf, *Die Kenningar der Skalden. Ein Beitrag zur skaldischen Poetik* (Bonn and Leipzig, 1921)

Merkelbach, Rebecca, 'Volkes Stimme. Interaktion als Dialog in der Konstruktion sozialer Monstrosität in den Isländersagas', in *Stimme und Performanz in der mittelalterlichen Literatur*, ed. Monika Unzeitig *et al.* (Berlin and Boston, 2017), pp. 251–75

Merrills, Andrew H., *History and Geography in Late Antiquity* (Cambridge, 2005)

——, 'Geography and Memory in Isidore's *Etymologies*', in *Mapping Medieval Geographies: Geographical Encounters in the Latin West and Beyond, 300–1600*, ed. Keith D. Lilley (Cambridge, 2013), pp. 45–65

Meulengracht Sørensen, Preben, *Fortælling og ære: Studier i islændingesagaerne* (Aarhus, 1993)

——, 'On Humour, Heroes, Morality, and Anatomy in *Fóstbrœðra Saga*', in *Twenty-Eight Papers Presented to Hans Bekker-Nielsen on the Occasion of his Sixtieth Birthday 28. April 1993* (Odense, 1993), pp. 395–418

——, *Saga and Society* (Odense, 1993)

——, 'Social Institutions and Belief Systems of Medieval Iceland (c. 870–1400) and their Relations to Literary Production', trans. Margaret Clunies Ross, in *Old Icelandic Literature and Society*, ed. Clunies Ross, pp. 8–29

Miller, Carolyn, 'Genre Innovation: Evolution, Emergence, or Something Else?', *Journal of Media Innovations* 3:2 (2016), 4–19

Miller, William Ian, *Bloodtaking and Peacemaking: Feud, Law, and Society in Saga Iceland* (Chicago, 1990)

——, *Humiliation: And Other Essays on Honor, Social Discomfort, and Violence* (Ithaca, 1993)

Mitchell, Stephen, *Heroic Sagas and Ballads* (Ithaca and London, 1991; 1994)

——, 'Interrogating Genre in the *Fornaldarsögur* Round-Table Discussion', *VMS* 2 (2006), 286–87

Mittell, Jason, *Genre and Television: From Cop Shows to Cartoons in American Culture* (London, 2004)

Mulder-Bakker, Anneke B, 'The Invention of Saintliness: Texts and Contexts', in *The Invention of Saintliness*, ed. Anneke B. Mulder-Bakker (London, 2002), pp. 3–24

Müller, Claudia, *Erzähltes Wissen: Die Isländersagas in der Möðruvallabók (AM 132 fol.)*, Texte und Untersuchungen zur Germanistik und Skandinavistik 47 (Frankfurt am Main, 2001)

Mundal, Else, 'Theories, explanatory models and terminology: Problems and Possibilities in Research on Old Norse Mythology', in *Old Norse Religion in Long-Term Perspectives*, ed. Andrén, Jennbert and Raudvere, pp. 285–88

——, *Dating the Sagas: Reviews and Revisions* (København, 2013)

Neumann, Birgit, 'The Literary Representation of Memory', in *Cultural Memory Studies: An International Handbook*, ed. Erll and Nünning, pp. 333–43

Neumann, Birgit and Ansgar Nünning, 'Einleitung: Probleme, Aufagaben und Perspektiven der Gattungstheorie und Gattungsgeschichte', in *Gattungstheorie und Gattungsgeschichte*, ed. Birgit Neumann and Ansgar Nünning (Trier, 2007), pp. 1–28

Ney, Agnete, Ármann Jakobsson and Annette Lassen, eds, *Fornaldarsagaerne: Myter og virkelighed. Studier i de oldislandske fornaldarsögur Norðrlanda* (København, 2009)

Nora, Pierre, 'Between Memory and History: *Les Lieux de Mémoire*', *Representations* 26 (1989), 7–24

Nyboe, Jacob Ølgaard, 'The Game of the Name: Genre Labels as Genre and Signature', *SS* 88 (2017), 364–92

O'Connor, Ralph, 'Introduction', in Ralph O'Connor, *Icelandic Histories & Romances* (Stroud, 2002), pp.7–46

——, 'History or Fiction? Truth-Claims and Defensive Narrators in Icelandic Romance-Sagas', *Mediaeval Scandinavia* 15 (2005), 133–39

——, 'Interrogating Genre in the *Fornaldarsögur*: Round-Table Discussion', *VMS* 2 (2006), 291–93

——, 'Truth and Lies in the *fornaldarsögur*: The Prologue to *Göngu-Hrólfs saga*', in *Fornaldarsagaerne: Myter og virkelighed*, ed. Ney, Ármann Jakobsson and Lassen, pp. 361–78

——, 'Astronomy and Dream Visions in Late Medieval Iceland: *Stjörnu-Odda draumr* and the Emergence of Norse Legendary Fiction', *JEGP* 111 (2012), 474–512

O'Donoghue, Heather, *Old Norse-Icelandic Literature: A Short Introduction* (Malden and Oxford, 2004)

——, *Skaldic Verse and the Poetics of Saga Narrative* (Oxford, 2005)

*OED Online*, 'fiction, n.' (Dec., 2018) <http://www.oed.com/view/Entry/69828>

Orel, Vladimir, *A Handbook of Germanic Etymology* (Leiden, 2003)

Orning, Hans Jacob, *Unpredictability and Presence: Norwegian Kingship in the High Middle Ages*, The Northern World 38 (Leiden, 2008)

——, 'The *King's Mirror* and the Emergence of a New Elite in 13th-Century Norway', in *Speculum Septentrionale*, ed. Johansson and Kleivane, pp. 245–64

——, *The Reality of the Fantastic. The Magical, Geopolitical and Social Universe of Late Medieval Saga Manuscripts*, The Viking Collection 23 (Odense, 2017)

Paden, William D., *Medieval Lyric: Genres in Historical Context*, Illinois Medieval Studies 7, (Urbana and Chicago, 2000)

Phelpstead, Carl, 'Interrogating Genre in the *Fornaldarsögur* Round-Table Discussion', *VMS* 2 (2006), 278–79

——, *Holy Vikings. Saints' Lives in the Old Icelandic Kings' Sagas*, Center for Medieval and Renaissance Studies (Tempe, 2007)

——, 'Adventure-Time in *Yngvars saga víðförla*', in *Fornaldarsagaerne: Myter og virkelighed*, ed. Ney, Ármann Jakobsson and Lassen, pp. 361–78

——, 'Time', in *The Routledge Companion to the Medieval Icelandic Sagas*, ed. Ármann Jakobsson and Sverrir Jakobsson, pp. 187–97

Poole, Russell, *Viking Poems on War and Peace: A Study of Skaldic Narrative* (Toronto, 1991)

*Works Cited*

———, 'Ekphrasis: its "Prolonged Echoes" in Scandinavia', *VMS* 3 (2007), 245–67
Pugh, Tison. 'Queering Genres, Battering Males: The Wife of Bath's Narrative Violence', *Journal of Narrative Theory* 33:2 (2003), 115–42
Pulsiano, Phillip and Kirsten Wolf, eds, *Medieval Scandinavia: An Encyclopedia* (New York, 1993)
Purdie, Rhiannon and Michael Cichon, eds, *Medieval Romance, Medieval Contexts*, Studies in Medieval Romance (Cambridge, 2011)
Quinn, Judy, 'The Naming of Eddic Mythological Poems in Medieval Manuscripts', *Parergon* n.s. 8 (1990), 97–115
———, '"Ok er þetta upphaf": First Stanza Quotation in Old Norse Prosimetrum', *Alvíssmál* 7 (1997), 61–80
———, ed., 'Interrogating Genre in the *Fornaldarsögur*: Round-Table Discussion', *VMS* 2 (2006), 276–96
———, 'The "Wind of the Giantess": Snorri Sturluson, Rudolf Meissner and the Interpretation of Mythological Kennings along Taxonomic Lines', *VMS* 8 (2012), 207–59
Quinn, Judy, Kate Heslop and Tarrin Wills, eds, *Learning and Understanding in the Old Norse World: Essays in Honour of Margaret Clunies Ross*, Medieval Texts and Cultures of Northern Europe 18 (Turnhout, 2007)
Reiter, Virgile, '*Flores och Blanzeflor*. L'amour courtois dans la Suède du XIV$^{\text{ème}}$ siècle', PhD dissertation (Paris, 2015)
Richter, Anna Katharina and Jürg Glauser, 'Transmission und Transformation. Die Historie von Floire et Blanchefleur in der skandinavischen und niederländischen Überlieferung', *TijdSchrift voor Skandinavistiek* 36:1 (2018). Online.
Rohrbach, Lena, 'The Chronotopes of *Íslendinga saga*: Narrativizations of History in Thirteenth-Century Iceland', *SS* 89:3 (2017), 351–74
Romm, James S., *The Edges of the Earth in Ancient Thought: Geography, Exploration, and Fiction* (Princeton, 1992)
Rosenwein, Barbara H., *Emotional Communities in the Early Middle Ages* (Ithaca, 2006)
Rösli, Lukas, 'Manuscripts', in *Handbook of Pre-Modern Nordic Memory Studies. Interdisciplinary Approaches*, vol. 1, ed. Jürg Glauser, Pernille Hermann, and Stephen A. Mitchell (Berlin and Boston, 2018), pp. 406–13
———, 'Paratextual References to the Genre Term *Íslendingasögur* in Old Norse-Icelandic manuscripts', *Opuscula* 17 (2019), 151–67.
———, 'From *Schedæ Ara Prests Fróða* to *Íslendingabók*– When an Intradiegetic Text Becomes Reality', in *The Meaning of Media. Medieval Scandinavian Text Culture from Epigraphy to Typography*, ed. Anna Catharina Horn and Karl G. Johansson, Modes of Modification 1 (Berlin and Boston, forthcoming 2021)
Rothman, Joshua, 'A Better Way to Think about the Genre Debate', *The New Yorker* (Nov. 6, 2014) <https://www.newyorker.com/books/joshua-rothman/better-way-think-genre-debate.>
Rouse, Robert, 'Walking (between) the Lines: Romance as Itinerary/Map', in *Medieval Romance, Medieval Contexts*, ed. Cichon and Purdie, pp. 135–47

——, 'What Lies Between? Thinking Through Medieval Narrative Spatiality', *Literary Cartographies: Spatiality, Representation, and Narrative*, ed. Robert T. Tally Jr. (London, 2014), pp. 13–29

Rowe, Elizabeth Ashman, *The Development of Flateyjarbók: Iceland and the Norwegian Dynastic Crisis of 1389*, The Viking Collection 15 (Odense, 2005)

——, '*Fornaldarsögur* and Flateyjarbók', *Gripla* 14 (2003), 93–105

——, 'Generic Hybrids: Norwegian "Family" Sagas and Icelandic "Mythic-Heroic" Sagas', *SS* 65:4 (1993), 539–54

——, '*Þorsteins þáttr uxafóts*, *Helga þáttr Þórissonar*, and the Conversion *Þættir*', *SS* 76:3 (2004), 459–74

——, 'Interrogating Genre in the *Fornaldarsögur*: Round-Table Discussion', *VMS* 2, 284–86

——, 'The Long and the Short of It', in *The Routledge Research Companion to the Medieval Icelandic Sagas*, ed. Ármann Jakobsson and Sverrir Jakobsson, pp. 151–63

——, *The Medieval Annals of Iceland, Vol. 1: Introduction* (forthcoming)

Rowe, Elizabeth Ashman and Joseph Harris, 'Short Prose Narrative (þáttr)', in *A Companion to Old Norse-Icelandic Literature*, ed. McTurk, pp. 462–87

Sävborg, Daniel, *Sorg och elegi i Eddans hjältediktning*, (Stockholm, 1997) [= Acta universitatis Stockholmiensis, Stockholm Studies in History of Literature 36]

——, 'Kärleken i *Laxdœla saga* – höviskt och sagatypiskt', *Alvíssmál* 11 (2004), 75–104

——, *Sagan om kärleken. Erotik, känslor och berättarkonst i norrön litteratur* (Uppsala, 2007) [= Acta universitatis upsaliensis. Historia litterarum 27]

Sawyer, Birgit, 'Samhällsbeskrivningen i *Heimskringla*', (Norwegian) *Historisk tidsskrift* 72 (1993), 223–37

Schaeffer, Jean-Marie, *Qu'est-ce qu'un genre littéraire?* Poétique (Paris, 1989)

Schier, Kurt, *Sagaliteratur*, Sammlung Metzler 78 (Stuttgart, 1970)

Schlauch, Margaret, *Romance in Iceland* (New York, 1934 [1973])

Schnall, Jens Eike, *Didaktische Absichten und Vermittlungsstrategien im altnorwegischen "Konigsspiegel" (Konungs skuggsjá)* (Göttingen, 2000)

——, '*Nunc te, fili carissime, docebo* — Anfang und Aufbau der *Konungs skuggsjá*', in *Speculum regale*, pp. 63–89

Schnall, Jens Eike, and Rudolf Simek, eds, *Speculum regale: der Altnorwegische Königsspiegel (Konungs skuggsjá) in der Europäischen Tradition* (Vienna, 2000)

Schorn, Brittany, 'Eddic Modes and Genres', in *A Handbook to Eddic Poetry*, ed. Larrington, Quinn and Schorn, pp. 231–51

——, 'Eddic Style', in *A Handbook to Eddic Poetry*, ed. Larrington, Quinn and Schorn, pp. 271–87

——, *Speaker and Authority in Old Norse Wisdom Poetry*, Trends in Medieval Philology 34 (Berlin and Boston, 2017)

Schulz, Arnim, *Erzähltheorie in mediävistischer Perspektive* (Berlin, München and Boston, 2015)

von See, Klaus, 'Der Skalde Torf-Einar Jarl', *Beiträge zur Geschichte der deutschen*

*Sprache und Literatur* 82 (1960), 31–43

———, *Die Gestalt der Hávamál: Eine Studie zur eddischer Spruchdichtung* (Frankfurt am Main, 1972)

Seebold, Elmar, *Vergleichendes und etymologisches Wörterbuch der germanischen starken Verben*, Janua Linguarum, series practica 85 (The Hague and Paris, 1970)

Seidel, Katharina, *Textvarianz und Textstabilität: Studien zur Transmission der Ívens saga, Erex saga und Parcevals saga*, Beiträge zur Nordischen Philologie 56 (Tübingen, 2014)

Shailor, Barbara, 'A Cataloguer's View', in *The Whole Book: Cultural Perspectives on the Medieval Miscellany*, ed. Stephen G. Nichols and Siegfried Wenzel, Recentiores: Later Latin Texts and Contexts (Ann Arbor, 1996), pp. 153–67

Shuttleworth, Mark, 'Polysystem Theory', in *Routledge Encyclopedia of Translation Studies*, ed. Mona Baker and Kirsten Malmkjær (London, 1998), pp. 176–79

Sif Rikhardsdottir, 'Meykóngahefðin í riddarasögum: Hugmyndafræðileg átök um kynhlutverk og þjóðfélagsstöðu', *Skírnir* 184 (2010), 410–33

———, *Medieval Translations and Cultural Discourse: The Movement of Texts in England, France and Scandinavia* (Cambridge, 2012)

———, *Emotion in Old Norse Literature: Translations, Voices, Contexts*, Studies in Old Norse Literature 1 (Cambridge, 2017)

Sigurður Nordal, 'Sagalitteraturen', in *Litteraturhistoria B: Litteraturhistorie: Norge og Island*, ed. Sigurður Nordal (Stockholm, 1953), pp. 180–273

Simek, Rudolf, 'Snorri als Kosmograph', in *Snorri Sturluson: Beiträge zu Werk und Rezeption*, ed. Hans Fix (Berlin, 1998), pp. 255–66

Sobchack, Thomas, 'Genre Films: A Classical Experience', in *Film Genre Reader IV*, ed. Barry Keith Grant (Austin, 2012), pp. 121–32

Söderberg, Barbro, 'Lokasenna: egenheter och ålder', *ANF* 102 (1987), 18–99

———, 'Saga och bulla: fornsvenska genrebeteckningar och medeltida skriftmiljöer', *ANF* 109 (1994), 141–72

Steblin-Kamenskij, M. I., *The Saga Mind*, trans. Kenneth H. Ober (Odense, 1973)

Stefán Karlsson, 'Fróðleiksgreinar frá tólftu öld', *Afmælisrit Jón Helgasonar 30. júni 1969*, ed. Jakob Benediktsson *et al.* (Reykjavík, 1969), pp. 328–49

———, 'Um Vatnshyrnu', *Opuscula* 4 (1970), 279–303

Stegmann, Beeke, 'Árni Magnússon's Rearrangement of *Fornaldarsaga* Manuscripts', in *The Legendary Legacy*, ed. Driscoll, Hufnagel, Lavender and Stegmann, pp. 161–86

Steiner, Peter, 'Russian Formalism', in *The Cambridge History of Literary Criticism. From Formalism to Poststructuralism*, ed. Raman Selden (Cambridge, 1995), pp. 11–32

Steinsland, Gro, *Det hellige bryllup og norrøn kongeideologi: En analyse av hierogamimyten i Skírnismál, Ynglingatal, Háleygjatal og Hyndluljóð* (Oslo, 1991)

Stevens, David, 'Trouble with the Neighbours: The Problem of Ánabrekka in Skalla-Grímr's Land Claim', *SBVS* 35 (2011), 25–38

Stock, Brian, *Literacy in Theory and Practice* (Cambridge, 1984)

Svanhildur Óskarsdóttir and Emily Lethbridge, 'Whose *Njála*? *Njáls saga* Editions and Textual Variance in the Oldest Manuscripts', in *New Studies in the Manuscript Tradition of* Njáls saga: *The Historia Mutila of* Njála, ed. Svanhildur Óskarsdóttir and Emily Lethbridge, The Northern Medieval World: On the Margins of Europe (Kalamazoo, 2018), pp. 1–28

Svanhildur Óskarsdóttir and Ludger Zeevaert, 'Við upptök *Njálu*: Þormóðsbók, AM 162 B δ fol', in *Góssið hans Árna: Minningar heimsins í íslenskum handritum*, ed. Jóhanna Katrín Friðriksdóttir (Reykjavík, 2014), pp. 155–169

Sveinbjörn Rafnsson, *Sögugerð Landnámabókar. Um íslenska sagnaritun á 12. og 13. öld* (Reykjavík, 2001)

Sverrir Jakobsson, *Við og veröldin: Heimsmynd Íslendinga 1100–1400* (Reykjavík, 2005)

⸻, 'Hauksbók and the Construction of an Icelandic worldview', *SBVS* 31 (2007), 22–38

⸻, 'The Process of State-Formation in Medieval Iceland', *Viator* 40:2 (2009), 151–70

⸻, 'Iceland, Norway, and the World', *ANF* 132 (2017), 75–99

Sverrir Tómasson, 'The Hagiography of Snorri Sturluson, Especially in the *Great Saga of St Olaf*', in *Saints and Sagas: A Symposium*, ed. Hans Bekker-Nielsen and Birte Carlé (Odense, 1994), pp. 49–72

Swenson, Karen, *Performing Definitions: Two Genres of Insult in Old Norse Literature* (Columbia, 1991)

Tamm, Marek, 'Beyond History and Memory: New Perspectives in Memory Studies', *History Compass* 11.6 (2013), 458–73

Tangherlini, Timothy R., ed., *Nordic Mythologies: Interpretations, Intersections, and Institutions* (Berkeley and Los Angeles, 2014)

Tate, George S., 'Good Friday Liturgy and the Structure of *Líknarbraut*', *SS* 50:1 (1978), 31–38

⸻, 'Introduction to Anonymous, *Líknarbraut*', in *Poetry on Christian Subjects*, *SkP* 7, pp. 228–29

Tether, Leah, Johnny McFadyen, Keith Busby and Ad Putter, eds, *Handbook of Arthurian Romance: King Arthur's Court in Medieval European Literature* (Boston, 2017)

Thorvaldsen, Bernt Øyvind, 'The Generic Aspect of Eddic Style', in *Old Norse Religion in Long-Term Perspectives*, ed. Andrén, Jennbert and Raudvere, pp. 276–79

Tobiassen, Torfinn, 'Tronfølgelov og privilegiebrev', *Historisk tidsskrift* 43 (1964), 181–273

Todorov, Tzvetan, *The Poetics of Prose*, trans. Richard Howard (Ithaca, 1992 [1977])

Tolley, Clive, *Shamanism in Norse Myth and Magic*, 2 vols, Folklore Fellows Communications 296 (Helsinki, 2009)

Torfi H. Tulinius, 'Landafræði og flokkun fornsagna', *Skáldskaparmál* 1 (1990), 142–56

⸻, 'Kynjasögur úr fortíð og framandi löndum', in *Íslensk bókmenntasaga*, II, ed. Böðvar Guðmundsson *et al.* (Reykjavík, 1993), pp. 165–244

⸻, 'Framliðnir feður. Um forneskju og frásagnarlist í Eyrbyggju, Eglu og Grettlu', in *Heiðin minni*, ed. Baldur Hafstað and Haraldur Bessason (Reykjavík, 1999), pp. 283–316

——, 'The Matter of the North: Fiction and Uncertain Identities in Thirteenth-Century Iceland', in *Old Icelandic Literature and Society*, ed. Clunies Ross, pp. 242–65

——, *The Matter of the North: The Rise of Literary Fiction in Thirteenth-Century Iceland*, trans. Randi C. Eldevik (Odense, 2002)

——, 'Sagas of Icelandic Prehistory (Fornaldarsögur)', in *A Companion to Old Norse-Icelandic Literature*, ed. McTurk, pp. 447–61

——, *Skáldið í skriftinni: Snorri Sturluson og Egils saga*, Íslensk Menning (Reykjavík, 2004)

——, 'Returning Fathers. Sagas, Novels and the Uncanny', *Scandinavian-Canadian Studies* 21 (2012–14), 3–23

——, 'Writing Strategies. Romance and the Creation of a New Genre in Medieval Iceland', in *Textual Production and Status Contests*, ed. Bampi and Buzzoni, pp. 33–42

——, 'The Social Conditions for Literary Practice in Snorri's Lifetime', in *Snorri Sturluson and Reykholt. The Author and Magnate, his Life, Works and Environment at Reykholt in Iceland*, ed. Guðrún Sveinbjarnardóttir and Helgi Þorláksson (København, 2018), pp. 389–405

Townend, Matthew, 'Introduction to Óttarr svarti, *Hǫfuðlausn*', in *Poetry from the Kings' Sagas 1: From Mythical Times to c. 1035*, SkP 1, pp. 739–40

——, 'Introduction to Þórarinn loftunga, *Hǫfuðlausn*', in *Poetry from the Kings' Sagas 1*, SkP 1, pp. 849–50.

Treharne, Elaine, *Writing Gender and Genre in Medieval Literature: Approaches to Old and Middle English Texts* (Woodbridge, 2002)

Tucker, John, 'Introduction: Sagas of the Icelanders', in *Sagas of the Icelanders: A Book of Essays*, ed. John Tucker (New York, 1989), pp. 1–26

Turville-Petre, Gabriel, *Origins of Icelandic Literature* (Oxford, 1953)

——, 'Liggja fylgjur þínar til Íslands', in Gabriel Turville-Petre, *Nine Norse Studies* (London, 1972), pp. 52–58

Úlfar Bragason, *Ætt og saga. Um frásagnarfræði Sturlungu eða Íslendinga sögu hinnar miklu* (Reykjavík, 2010)

Vésteinn Ólason, *The Tradition of Ballads of Iceland* (Reykjavík, 1982)

——, 'Vatnsdœla saga', in *Medieval Scandinavia: An Encyclopedia*, ed. Pulsiano and Wolf, p. 689

——, 'Family Sagas', in *A Companion to Old Norse-Icelandic Literature*, ed. McTurk, pp. 101–18

——, 'The Icelandic Sagas as a Kind of Literature with Special Reference to Its Representation of Reality', in *Learning and Understanding in the Old Norse World*, ed. Quinn, Heslop and Wills, pp. 27–47

——, 'Old Icelandic Poetry', in *A History of Icelandic Literature*, ed. Daisy Neijman, Histories of Scandinavian Literature (Lincoln, 2006), pp. 1–63

Viðar Pálsson, *Language of Power: Feasting and Gift-Giving in Medieval Iceland and Its*

*Sagas*, Islandica 60 (Ithaca, 2017)
Voßkamp, Wilhelm, 'Gattungen', in *Literaturwissenschaft. Eine Einführung*, ed. Helmut Brackert and Jörn Stückrath (Reinbek, 1992), pp. 253–69
Wanner, Kevin, *Snorri Sturluson and the Edda: The Conversion of Cultural Capital in Medieval Scandinavia* (Toronto, 2008)
Waugh, Robin, 'Language, Landscape, and Maternal Space: Child Exposure in Some Sagas of Icelanders', *Exemplaria* 29:3 (2017), 234–53
van Weenen, Andrea de Leeuw, *A Grammar of Möðruvallabók* (Leiden, 2000)
Wellek, René and Austin Warren, *Theory of Literature* (New York, 1949)
Wellendorf, Jonas, *Kristelig visionlitterature i norrøn tradition*, Bibliotheca Nordica 2 (Oslo, 2009)
——, 'Ecclesiastical Literature and Hagiography', in *The Routledge Research Companion to the Medieval Icelandic Sagas*, pp. 48–58
——, 'Zoroaster, Saturn and Óðinn: The Loss of Language and the Rise of Idolatry', in *The Performance of Christian and Pagan Storyworlds*, ed. Lars Boje Mortensen and Thomas M. S. Lehtonen with Alexandra Bergholm (Turnhout, 2013), pp. 143–70
Wessén, Elias, 'Introduction' to *Codex Regius of the Younger Edda: MS No. 2367 4o in the Old Royal Library of Copenhagen*, Corpus Codicum Islandicorum Medii Ævi 14 (København, 1940)
van Wezel, Lars, 'Mythology as a Mnemonic and Literary Device in *Vatnsdœla saga*', in *Old Norse Religion in Long-term Perspectives*, ed. Andrén, Jennbert, and Raudvere, pp. 289–92
Whaley, Diana, 'Christian and Pagan References in Eleventh-Century Norse Poetry: The Case of Arnórr Jarlaskáld', *SBVS* 21 (1982–85), 33–53
——, 'Skalds and Situational Verses in *Heimskringla*', in *Snorri Sturluson. Kolloquium anläßlich der 750. Wiederkehr seines Todestages*, ed. Alois Wolf (Tübingen, 1993), pp. 245–66
——, 'Miracles in the Sagas of Bishops: Icelandic Variations on an International Theme', *Collegium Medievale* 7 (1994), 155–84
——, 'A Useful Past: Historical Writing in Medieval Iceland', in *Old Icelandic Literature and Society*, ed. Clunies Ross, pp. 161–202
——, 'Skaldic Poetry', in *A Companion to Old Norse-Icelandic Literature and Culture*, ed. McTurk, 479–502
Whetter, Kevin, *Understanding Genre and Medieval Romance* (Aldershot and Burlington, 2008)
Wingfield, Emily, *The Trojan Legend in Medieval Scottish Literature* (Cambridge, 2014)
Wolf, Kirsten, 'Introduction to Kálfr Hallsson, *Kátrínardrápa*', in *Poetry on Christian Subjects*, SkP 7, pp. 931–64
——, *The Legends of the Saints in Old Norse-Icelandic Prose* (Toronto, 2013)
Würth, Stefanie, *Elemente des Erzählens: Die þættir der Flateyjarbók*, Beiträge zur Nordischen Philologie 20 (Basel, 1991)
——, 'Historiography and Pseudo-History', in *A Companion to Old Norse-Icelandic, Literature and Culture*, ed. McTurk, pp. 155–72
Yates, Frances A., *The Art of Memory* (Chicago and London, 1974 [1966])

*Works Cited*

Zoëga, G. T. ed., *A Concise Dictionary of Old Icelandic* (Oxford, 1967 [1910])
Zymner, Rüdiger, *Gattungstheorie: Probleme und Positionen der Literaturwissenschaft* (Paderborn, 2003)
——, ed., *Handbuch Gattungstheorie* (Stuttgart and Weimar, 2010)
Þorleifur Hauksson, 'Árna saga biskups', in *Medieval Scandinavia: An Encyclopedia*, ed. Pulsiano and Wolf, p. 20

# INDEX

aðalhending   82; see also hending
Adonias saga   307
Ægir, deity   196, 204
Aeneas, Trojan hero   136
Æsir   66, 135, 136, 137, 194
ævintýri/æwintyr (fairy tale)   108, 124, 210, 308, 309, 313, 315
Agatha of Sicily   292
Agǫthu saga   290, 292
Ágrip   74, 230
Alexander the Great   5
Alexanders saga   314
Alexandreis   314
Albani þáttr ok Sunnifu   260
Algorismus   315
Allard, Joe   266, 267, 268, 269
allegory   220, 249, 255, 266
alliteration   68, 217, 224
Alvíssmál   75, 179, 218
Ambrose, Bishop of Milan   294
Ambrósíuss saga   290
Andersson, Theodore M.   35, 37, 38, 56, 88, 118, 202, 259, 271, 275, 276, 288
Andreasdrápa   207, 246
Andrén, Anders   195, 266, 267, 268, 273
anger   178, 235; see also emotion
Anglo-Norman   39, 30–3, 310; see also French
annals   172, 245, 268, 295, 315
aphorism   252
apocalypse   249
Ari Þorgilsson, fróði   165, 173
Arinbjarnarkviða   320
Aristotle   15, 18, 32, 49
   Poetics   49
Ármann Jakobsson   259, 264
Árna saga   290, 293, 294
Árni Magnússon   96, 99
Árni Þorláksson, Bishop   293
Arnórr Tumason   297
Arnórr Þórðarson, jarlaskáld   224
Arthur, King   39, 146

Atlakviða   318
Atlamál   223
Auðunar þáttr vestfirzka   260, 263
Austfararvísur   320

Bærings saga   304, 307
Bagge, Sverre   118
Bakhtin, Mikhail   8, 145–9, 153, 203,
Baldr, deity   195, 196, 197, 200, 201
Baldrs Draumar   195, 197, 256, 319
ballad   52, 91, 103, 249, 302, 310, 311, 320–1,
Bampi, Massimiliano   51, 127, 162, 275, 291
Bandamanna saga   103, 107
Bárðar saga Snæfellsáss   4, 99, 131, 305
Barnes, Geraldine   43, 138, 140, 141
Barra, Hebridean island   63, 77
Bassett, Camilla   296
Battle of Falköping   268
Battle of Slite   266, 267, 268
Battle of Stiklastaðir   202
Bergbúa þáttr   265
Bergen   110, 307
bestiaries   315
Bevers saga   303, 307
Bible   166, 245
Björn Þorleifsson, the younger   102
Blobel, Mathias   109
Bǫðvarr Egilsson   182
Bǫglunga sǫgur   124
Bolla þáttr Bollasonar   315
Bolli Þorleiksson   182, 184, 187, 188, 189
Bragi Boddason   200
Brandr Sæmundarson, Bishop   295
Breta sǫgur   307, 313, 316
Brennu-Njáls saga   34, 42, 94–96, 103, 134, 171, 173, 222, 315, 320
Britain   136, 281, 307
Brown, Ursula (Dronke)   85
Brutus   136
Brynhildr   107, 264
Buslabœn   318

*byskupasögur* (sagas of bishops); *see under* sagas

Callow, Christopher   132
canonisation   8, 56, 57, 170, 171
Carlsen, Christian   253
Carruthers, Mary   163
catalexis   70
Catherine of Alexandria, saint   207
Cervantes, Miguel de
   *Don Quixote*   45
*chansons de geste*   38, 127, 151, 155, 301, 303, 307, 309, 313, 314
Charlemagne, King and Emperor   39, 151, 309
Chase, Martin   207
Chaucer, Geoffrey   7, 34, 45, 267, 269
   *Canterbury Tales, The*   34, 45, 267
      'Tale of Sir Thopas'   269
      'Wife of Bath's Tale'   34
   *House of Fame, The*   269
Chrétien de Troyes   7, 38, 146, 300, 314
Christianity   2, 26, 27, 169, 193, 272
   and poetry   201, 204, 245, 246, 256
   impact of   147, 148, 150, 155, 157, 159
chronotope   8, 10, 35, 102, 107, 111, 123, 128, 142, 146–59, 209; *see also under Egils saga Skallagrímssonar*; romance, sagas of Icelanders
church, Catholic   73, 116, 117, 119, 121, 123, 155, 246, 288, 294, 309
*Clári saga*   108, 314
Clover, Carol   52, 53, 162
Clunies Ross, Margaret   23, 55, 100, 132, 200, 275
Codex Regius of the Poetic Edda; *see under* manuscripts
Codex Regius of the Prose Edda; *see under* manuscripts
codicology   10, 89, 92, 100, 255
Constantinople   138, 158
cultural memory; *see under* memory
curse   318

Dagfinnr, court poet   266, 269
Dante, Alighieri
   *Divina Commedia*   44, 249

*Descensus Christi ad inferos*   201
deity   196–209; *see also* God
Denmark   3, 34, 95, 135, 138, 140, 207, 242, 301, 324
dialogism   148
diaspora   134, 137
   Viking   147, 151, 152, 153, 159
Dinzelbacher, Peter   247
*Dínus saga drambláta*   130, 138
*Disciplina clericalis*   307
*Disticha Catonis (Distichs of Cato)*   206, 221, 247, 319
Donatus   68, 69, 316
   *Barbarismus*   68
*drápa* (long formal poem)   206, 207, 239
   *ævidrápa*   318
*Drápa af Maríugrát*   207
*Draumkvæde*   249
Driscoll, Matthew   287
*Droplaugarsona saga*   134
Dryhthelm   253
Dubrow, Heather   203
Duff, David   15
*Duggals Leizla*   253, 317

East Norse   3, 7, 302, 309, 314
*Ectors saga*   307
Edda, deity   209
Edmund, saint   207
Egill Skalla-Grímsson   92, 182, 183, 187, 198, 319, 320
*Egils saga Skallagrímssonar*   11, 121, 124, 131, 133, 276, 315
   and emotion   41, 182
   chronotope of   154, 156, 157, 158
   manuscript context   90, 91, 95, 103
Eilífr Goðrúnarson   199, 209, 320
Einar Ól. Sveinsson   280
Einarr Skúlason   205, 209, 245, 320, 323
Eiríkr bloodaxe, King   198
*Eiríksmál*   318
*Eiríks saga rauða*   152, 275
Ejchenbaum, Boris   24
ekphrasis   200–1
*Elis saga ok Rósamundu*   303, 307
*Elucidarius*   65, 201, 219, 315
emotion   10, 31, 41–43, 177–191, 300;

*see also* anger, emotionality; grief, love, sorrow; *under Egils saga Skallagrímssonar*; *Laxdœla saga*; romance; sagas of Icelanders
emotionality   177–191; *see also* emotion
England   140, 146, 242, 243
*Enoks saga*   307
epic   16, 49, 193, 202, 297, 299
*Erex saga*   303, 307
*Erikskrönikan*   119
*Erwartungshorizont* (horizon of expectations); *see* horizon of expectations
Eufemia, Queen   119, 302, 324
*Eufemiavisor*   7, 119, 302, 303, 304, 309, 310, 311, 314, 324
Even-Zohar, Itamar   24, 149, 245; *see also* polysystem theory
*exempla*   107, 108, 111, 250, 251, 252, 254, 257, 263, 280, 313, 315
*Eyrbyggja saga*   96, 99, 106, 107, 157, 158, 273, 275
Eysteinn, Archbishop   116, 117
Eyvindr skáldaspillir   317

*fabliau*   34, 301
*fabula*   309
*Færeyinga saga*   147, 152
*Fáfnismál*   215
*Fagrskinna*   117, 230, 240, 242–3, 323
fairy tales; *see* ævintýri
La Farge, Beatrice   223
Faroe Islands   147, 310
*Finnboga saga ramma*   4, 24, 103, 274
Finnbogi rammi   274
Fidjestøl, Bjarne   249, 252, 255
Fitjungr   250, 251, 257
*Fjölsvinnsmál*   256
Fjölsvinnr   256
Flatey   266
Flateyjarbók; *see under* manuscripts
*flokkr* (series of verses)   63–65, 77
*Floire et Blanchefleur*   309, 310
*Flores och Blanzaflor*   303, 310
*Flores og Blanseflor*   310
*Flóres saga ok Blankiflúr*   303, 310, 311
*Flóvents saga*   303, 307, 308
folklore   111

form   61–72; *see also under* generic
Formalism, Russian   16, 24–5, 29
*fornaldarsögur* (legendary sagas); *see under* sagas
*Fóstbræðra saga*   95
Fowler, Alastair   21, 36, 149, 172, 262
France   140, 141, 146, 242, 301
Frank, Roberta   241
French   7, 48, 127, 222, 299; *see also* Old French; Anglo–Norman
translations from   39, 40, 151, 155, 156, 301, 302, 307, 309, 310
Freyr, deity   135, 197, 273
Frideswide of Oxford, saint   202
Frow, John   32, 74, 85
functionality   5, 7, 11, 12, 33, 35, 38, 39, 41, 42, 45
*Fǫr Skírnis*   318

Gamli kanóki (Old canon)   245
Gaunt, Simon   20
Gautland; *see* Götaland
*Gautreks saga*   318
Gefjon   200
Geirvid lauk   268
Geirviðr of Gautland, King   266
*Geisli*   205, 209, 245, 320, 323
genealogy   65, 242, 243,
generic
  affiliations   10, 36, 38, 41, 43, 44, 226
  affinities   11, 99
  categories   5, 6, 7, 8, 9, 11, 31, 35, 41, 108, 109, 161, 174, 226, 313
  change   174
  characteristics   76, 127, 174, 180
  classifications   6, 8
  complexity   29, 87
  conformity   9, 11, 40
  context   8, 9, 10, 85, 221, 229
  fluidity   7
  form   4, 7, 34, 36, 37, 39, 40, 41, 43, 44, 45, 172, 213; *see also* form
  framework   9, 10, 31–45, 264
  hybridity   22, 31–45, 92, 148, 250, 313; *see also* hybridity
  identity   36, 38, 40, 42, 45, 230, 238, 248, 261
  marker   6, 8–9, 10, 11, 21, 28, 31–44, 61, 161, 173, 233, 237, 244, 252,

261, 263; *see also under* space
parameters   32, 36, 42, 44, 313
perceptions   10, 19
properties   10, 294
qualifications   8
repertoire   4, 8, 19, 21–26, 29, 32, 174
stability   10, 32
variety   5
versatility   5
Genette, Gérard   166
Geoffrey of Monmouth
  *Historia Regum Britanniae* (*History of the Kings of Britain*)   136
  *Prophetiae Merlini* (Prophecies of Merlin)   281
geography   10, 127–144, 262, 269
Gerðr, giantess   85, 197
Gestumblindi   216
*Gibbons saga*   304, 307, 314
*Gísla saga Súrssonar*   106, 169, 214
Gísli Súrsson   92
Gizurr Þorvaldsson   122
Glámr   158
Glauser, Jürg   11, 38, 132
God   117, 119, 193–210, 224, 225, 246, 289–296, 309; *see also* deity
Goeres, Erin   10
Goffman, Erving   74
Göngu-Hrólfr   242, 243
*Göngu-Hrólfs saga*   268
Götaland   200, 268
Gotland   200, 267, 268
Gottfried von Strassburg   300
Gottskálk Jensson   36
*Grammatica*   67, 68, 69, 70, 71
Grant, Barry Keith   287
*Grágás*   324
Greece   140, 146, 193, 307
Greek   49, 193, 310
Greenland   70, 127, 154
Gregory the Great   201
  *Dialogues*   201
*Grettis saga Ásmundarsonar*   101
grief   178–185, 187, 191; *see also* emotion
*Grímnismál*   197, 216, 255, 257
Grímr Ingjaldsson   277
Grípir   195
*Grípisspá*   195, 319

Grønlie, Siân   149, 150, 154, 156, 202, 204
Gropper, Stefanie   10
Gróa   256
*Gróugaldr*   256
*Guðmundar saga Arasonar*   253
Guðmundr Eyjólfsson   277
Guðmundr Arason, Bishop   294
Guðrøðr, son of King Haraldr hárfagri   231
*Guðrúnarhvǫt*   319
Guðrún Nordal   130
Guðrún Ósvífrsdóttir   181, 182, 184, 185, 188, 189
Gunnlaugr Leifsson, monk   281
Gunnlaugr Ormstunga   190, 191
*Gunnlaugs saga Ormstungu*   190
*Gyðinga saga*   152, 313, 316
*Gylfaginning*   137, 204, 317
Gylfi   200, 204, 317

*Hærra Ivan*   303
*Hafliðarmál*   86
Hafliði Másson   76, 86
hagiography   52, 61, 111, 148–9, 201–3, 229, 284, 288–9, 301, 316; *see also* saints' lives
Haki Antonsson   293
Hákon Hákonarson, King   101, 118, 122, 204, 323, 324
Hákon, Earl   199, 200
Hákon Magnússon, King   119, 308
*Hákonarmál*   317, 318
*Hákonar saga Hákonarsonar*   119, 122, 124, 153, 314
Hálfdan háleggr, son of King Haraldr hárfagri   230, 231
*Hálfdanar saga Brönufóstra*   266
Hallaðr Rǫgnvaldsson   230
Hallbera Snorradóttir   295
Hallberg, Peter   288
Halldór Laxness,
  *Gerpla*   45
Halldóra Sigurðardóttir   110
*Hallfreðar saga*   95, 271, 279
Hallr Teitsson   83, 84
Hallvarðr of Vík, saint   207
Hamel, Anton Gerard van   276
Hamer, Andrew   225

*Index*

Haraldr harðráði, King   152, 323
Haraldr hárfagri, King   115, 116, 230, 243, 280, 323
*Haraldskvæði*   319
Harold Godwineson, King   243
*Hárbarðsljóð*   196
*Harmsól*   245
Harris, Joseph   35, 169, 195, 261
Hartmann von Aue   300
*Háttalykill*   67, 70
*Háttatal*   66, 204, 317
*háttr* (mode); *see under* mode
Hauksbók; *see under* manuscripts
Haukr Erlendsson   324
*Haustlǫng*   200
*Hávamál*   197, 215, 216, 217, 218, 223–5, 250, 251, 256, 257, 319
*hégómasögur* (vanity sagas)   309
*Heilagra manna drápa*   207
*heilagra manna sögur* (saints' lives); *see* saints' lives
*Heilagra meyja drápa*   207
Heimdallr, deity   197
*Heimsaldrar*   166
*Heimskringla*   64, 117, 118, 121, 122, 129, 202, 230, 231, 239, 240, 241, 242, 323
*Heimslýsing*   315
*Heimsósómi*   110
*heiti*   86, 87, 197, 217, 320
Helga hin fagra   191
Helga Gísladóttir   110
*Helga þáttr ok Úlfs*   262
*Helreið Brynhildar*   264
*hending*   68, 69, 82
Hermann, Pernille   10
Hermundr Ávaldason   278
*Hertig Fredrik av Normandie*   304, 324
*Hervarar saga ok Heiðreks*   107, 197, 216, 318, 319
Hesiod   193
heterogeneity   3, 15, 18, 22, 23, 24, 29, 92, 107, 162, 211
heteroglossia   146, 148, 203, 264
High German   310, 314
Hildigunnr Starkaðardóttir   42
*Historia de Antiquitate regum Norwagiensium*   117
*Historia Norvegiae*   117

historiography   5, 52, 67, 70, 164, 166, 316, 323
  Latin   5
*Hjálmars Death Song*   318
Hléguðr, warrior maiden   268, 269
Hodges, Kenneth   130
Hofmann, Dietrich   239
*Hǫfuðlausn*   198, 201, 319
Hólar, bishop's see   283, 294, 295, 296, 308, 309, 314, 323
Holmes, Su   286
Hólmgarðr (Novgorod in Russia)   147
Hólmkell, farmer   190
homilies   61, 73, 316
*Homily Book*   201, 316
honour   42, 116, 121, 169, 181, 243, 266, 279
horizon of expectations   21, 22, 75, 174; *see also* Jauss, Hans Robert
*Hrafnistumannasögur*   99
*Hrafnkels saga Freysgoða*   169
*Hrafnsmál*   319
*Hrafns saga Sveinbjarnarsonar*   154
Hrefna Ásgeirsdóttir   182, 185, 187, 188, 189
Hróðný Unadóttir   274, 279
Hrólfr from Skálmarnes   62, 77
Hrolleifr Arnaldsson   272, 279
*Hrólfs saga kraka*   314
Hrómundr Gripsson   62, 63, 77
Hrǫngviðr, Viking   62, 77
Hrungnir, giant   200
*Hugsvinnsmál*   110, 206, 218, 221, 247, 249, 255, 257, 319
Hui, Jonathan Y. H.   266, 267, 268, 269
*Hungrvaka*   168, 172, 290, 295, 296, 314
Hunt, Margaret Cushing   294
Huot, Sylvia   306
*Húsdrápa*   200, 201
*hvǫt*   42, 319
hybridity   7–12, 22, 31–45, 56, 92, 148, 162, 172, 174, 250, 294, 311, 313; *see also under* generic; romance; sagas of Icelanders
hymn   193, 205, 206, 209, 245, 320
  Sumerian   193

*Index*

Hyndla, giantess   197
*Hyndluljóð*   195, 197, 256
ideology   4, 20, 35, 107, 115–125, 153, 154, 155, 157, 159, 289
Iðunn, deity   200
*Illuga saga Gríðarfóstra*   37, 137
Illugi Gríðarfóstri   137, 138
Ingham, Norman W.   20, 21, 229, 271
Ingimundr Einarsson   77, 85
Ingimundr inn gamli Þorsteinsson   272–4, 276, 277–80
Ingólfr Þorsteinsson   272
intertextuality   163, 167, 171
Isidore of Seville   49, 130
   *Etymologiæ*   49
Ísleifr Gizurarson   295, 323
*Íslendinga saga*   122, 149
*Íslendingabók*   78, 90, 152, 159, 163, 165, 166, 167, 168, 171, 316
*Íslendingasögur* (sagas of Icelanders); see under sagas
Íslenzk fornrit   56, 128
*Ivens saga*   303, 307, 314
Ívarr Rǫgnvaldsson   230

Jameson, Frederic   19, 32
*Járnsiða*   122, 316, 324
Jauss, Hans Robert   21–2, 24–5, 55, 149, 162
Jóhanna Katrín Friðriksdóttir   5, 10
Johansson, Karl G.   109, 221
John the Evangelist, saint   206
Jǫkull Ingimundarson ins gamla   273, 278–9
*Jómsvíkinga saga*   152
Jón Oddsson, scribe   96
Jón Ögmundsson   323
Jónas Kristjánsson   52, 203, 275,
Jónsbók   52
*Jónsdrápa*   206
Jørgensen, Jørgen Højgaard   292–3

Kálfr Hallsson   207
Kalinke, Marianne E.   41
*Karlamagnús saga*   156, 303, 313
*Katrínardrápa*   207
*Katrínar saga*   224
Kedwards, Dale   10
kenning   67, 82, 103, 182–3, 198, 199, 204–9, 233, 237, 241, 244–5, 255
Ketill raumr   271, 272, 278
Ketill Þorsteinsson of Hólar   296
Ketilríðr   186, 190
*Kirialax saga*   4, 313
*Kjalnesinga saga*   4, 99
Kjartan Ólafsson   182, 184–5,187–9
Kjesrud, Karoline   307
*Klári saga*   304
Kleivane, Elise   221
*knittelvers*   7, 110
knowledge   2, 10, 12, 23, 32, 59, 64, 155, 250, 292, 309, 315, 317; see also wisdom
   and memory   161, 162–8, 172–5
   geographical   135, 140
   in wisdom poetry   211–26
   mythological   197–8, 204,
Knútr, King and saint   203, 207
*Knýtlinga saga*   203
Kolbeinn Arnórsson   295
*Konráðs saga keisarasonar*   107, 304, 307
*konungasögur* (kings' sagas); see under sagas
*Konungs skuggsjá* (*Speculum regale*; King's Mirror)   101, 110, 118–19, 124, 140, 220–5, 249, 317; see also *speculum principis*
Kormákr Ögmundarson   185, 191, 320
*Kormáks saga*   185, 186, 190, 276, 320
Kristján Árnason   70
*Króka-Refs saga*   99
Krueger, Roberta L.   311
*Kumlbúa þáttr*   266, 270
*kvæði* (dance ballads)   302, 311
Kwon, Ah Leum   96

Lachmann, Renate   171
*lais*   38–9, 222, 301–03, 307, 313, 314; see also under Marie de France
lament   42, 179, 198, 207, 318: see also poetry, eddic
*landnám*   130–3, 143, 169, 323; see also settlement
*Landnámabók*   106, 122, 132–4, 152, 159, 271, 276, 316

lapidaries 315
Larrington, Carolyne 10, 11
Latin
  disciplines 69
  models 135, 166, 207, 209, 245, 303
  translations from, 65, 68, 127, 195, 201–2, 245–7, 299, 301, 303, 307, 314–6
  vitae 117
lausavísa (single verse) 200, 238–40, 242, 247, 318, 319
Lavender, Philip 37, 137
laws 52, 78, 90, 91, 102, 116, 172–3, 193, 316
Laxdœla saga 11, 37, 132, 133, 305, 315
  emotions in 183–6, 188–89
  manuscript context 90, 91, 93, 96, 99, 103
Leiðarvísan 245
Lethbridge, Emily 96. 128, 133
Liðsmannaflokkr 319
Líknarbraut 206
Lilja 207–9, 223, 320
literature
  biblical 91, 152, 166, 211–12, 220, 226, 257, 293, 316
  courtly 61, 178–80; see also romance
    ideology 119, 124, 157, 219–20, 229
    romance 39–40, 44, 183–6, 214
    settings 138, 142, 144, 234, 244
  encyclopaedic 110, 144, 219, 224, 315
  learned 52, 101, 109–10, 172, 174, 203, 212, 219–21, 257, 313, 315
  moral 108, 110, 124, 204, 214, 219–20, 245, 264, 269, 307, 315, 316–7
Litla Skálda 67, 70
liturgy 73, 206
Ljóðatal 256, 319
Loddfáfnir 215, 218
Loddfáfnismál 215, 218, 319
Long, Ann–Marie 132
Lönnroth, Lars 35, 202
Lokasenna 105, 196, 197, 318
Loki, deity 195–6
love 177–80, 183–6, 188–91, 219, 269, 273, 300; see also emotion
  courtly 219, 269, 300; see also romance; under literature
Low German 310
Low Rhenish 310
lygisögur 62, 77, 266–7, 285, 287–9, 290, 309
lyric 16, 49, 209, 249, 252

magic 143, 215, 250, 256, 272, 273, 276–8, 313
Magnús Einarsson, Bishop 296
Magnús Erlingson, King 116–7
Magnús Hákonarson (Magnús lagabætir), King 122, 308, 324
Magnus of Orkney, Saint 203
Mágus, wizard 92
Mágus saga jarls 304, 307, 308, 314
Males, Mikael 9
Málsháttakvæði 219
Manhire, Bill 273
mannjafnaðr 236
manuscript 3, 5–7, 17, 315, 324, 325–7
  and codicology 300, 306–8, 310, 311
  and generic terminology 50–1, 57–9
  and memory 171, 175
  compilation 89–111, 109, 121, 124–5, 134, 194–6, 303, 306, 314, 324
  production 124, 201
  AM 61 fol. 95, 325
  AM 81a fol. 124, 325
  AM 132 fol. (Möðruvallabók) 50, 92, 95–6, 97, 103, 106, 109, 134, 324, 325
  AM 152 fol. 50, 102, 134, 308, 325
  AM 162 A η fol. 124, 325
  AM 162 A θ fol. 91, 325
  AM 162 B δ fol. (Þormóðsbók) 91, 94, 325
  AM 162 D 2 fol. 91, 93, 325
  AM 166b 8$^{vo}$ 247, 325
  AM 226 fol. 5, 325
  AM 243 f 4$^{to}$ 110, 124, 325
  AM 243a fol. 101, 325
  AM 309 4$^{to}$ 96, 99, 106, 325
  AM 335 4$^{to}$ 108, 325

AM 343 a 4to   108, 325
AM 445 b 4to (Pseudo-
   Vatnshyrna)   96, 103, 106, 109, 325
AM 445 c 4to (Pseudo-
   Vatnshyrna)   96, 106, 109, 325
AM 445 c II 4to   325
AM 471 4to   5, 99, 325
AM 489 4to   99, 310, 325
AM 489 I–II 4to   99, 310, 325
AM 544 4to (Hauksbók)   109, 132, 195, 324, 325
AM 551 a 4to   111, 326
AM 564 a 4to (Pseudo-
   Vatnshyrna)   96, 98, 103, 106, 109, 326
AM 575 4to   310, 325
AM 589 a–f 4to   108, 326
AM 622 4to   110, 326
AM 657 a–b 4to   108, 325
AM 604 a–h 4to
   (Staðarhólsbók)   103, 326
AM 604 g 4to (Staðarhólsbók rímna)   104, 326
AM 624 4to   247, 326
AM 666b 4to   307, 325
AM 748 1a 4to   68, 324, 325
AM 748 1b 4to   66, 326
AM 748 4to   194, 247, 326
AM Acc. 22   308, 326
Codex Guelferbytanus 42.7 Augusteus 4to   308, 326
Codex Upsaliensis DG 11   66, 324, 327
DG 4–7 fol.   307,
GKS 1005 fol. (Flateyjarbók)   95, 96, 99, 109, 147, 260–1, 265, 324, 326
GKS 1913 4to   110, 327
GKS 2365 4to (Codex Regius of the Poetic Edda)   57, 58, 68, 105, 194, 247, 324, 326
GKS 2367 4to (Codex Regius of the Prose Edda)   324
GKS 2845 4to   107, 326
ÍB 13 IV 8vo   255, 326
JS 8 fol.   6, 326
JS 27 fol.   5, 326
Lbs 1199 4to   255, 326
NRA 65   310, 326

*Ormsbók   102, 306, 325
Stockholm papp 4to nr 15   308, 326
Stockholm perg. 6 4to   102, 326
Stockholm perg. 7 4to   6, 326
Stockholm perg. 7 fol.   102, 307, 326
*Vatnshyrna   103, 106, 325
Már Jǫrundarson   278
*Märchensagas*   285, 290, 291
Margaret of Antioch, saint   292
Margareta I, queen   268, 324
Margrét Vigfúsdóttir   101, 124, 324
*Margrétar saga*   290, 292, 315
Marie de France   38–9, 222, 300, 314
   lais   38–9, 222, 301–03, 307, 313, 314
   'Bisclaret'   222
*Maríu saga*   201, 309
*Maríudrápa*   207
Marold, Edith   199–200
marriage   116, 122, 177, 180, 184–7, 189–91, 293
Mary, Virgin   110, 207, 209, 309, 320
*Maxims, Exeter* and *Cotton*   257
McKinnell, John   196
Melabók   132, 133, 271, 325
memory   10, 64, 82, 83, 146, 161–75, 217, 220, 224,
   cultural   3, 10, 161–75
   fictions of   165–7
*Merlínusspá*   195, 281, 319: see also *Prophetiae Merlini* under Geoffrey of Monmouth
metre   55, 66–70, 175, 199, 204, 216, 234, 250, 315, 317–21: see also eddic, skaldic *under* poetry
   dróttkvætt   63, 78, 79, 85, 206–7, 234, 246, 257
   fornyrðislag   195, 246, 247, 256
   hrynhent   207
   kviðuháttr   317
   ljóðaháttr   86, 216, 220, 246, 247, 250, 257, 319
   málaháttr   247
   rúnhenda   79
   stýfð rúnhenda   79
Meulengracht Sørensen, Preben   3, 121
Michael, saint   224
Middle English   7, 45, 315
Miðgarðsormr   200

## Index

Miller, Carolyn  20
Miller, Willian Ian  178
*Minnereden*  316
miracles  203, 292, 295–6, 316
*Mírmanns saga*  43, 304, 307
Mittell, Jason  287, 297
mnemonics  163–4, 167, 174
mockery  229
mode  45, 161, 167, 213, 253, 271, 284, 300
  and saga-writing  37–8; *see also under* sagas
  as *háttr*  6-7, 55, 70
  comic  174, 296, 310
  eddic  11, 57, 314, 317–9; *see also under* poetry
  emotion as  31; *see also* emotion
  heroic  174, 257
    epic  202
    ideology  117–9, 122
    legends  269
    poetry  151, 246, 264
    romance  300–5
    sagas  52
    *þættir*  261
  skaldic  34, 205, 206, 209, 229–33, 237, 244, 319; *see also under* poetry
Möðruvallabók; *see under* manuscript
Möðruvellir  101, 124, 134, 324
modality  32, 34–41, 42–4
multimodality  23, 34–41, 42–4
*Morkinskinna*  116, 117, 259, 263 265, 314, 315, 323, 327
*Möttuls saga*  303, 308, 321
mythology: *see also under* poetry
  and eddic poetry  194–201, 116, 214–6, 246; *see also under* poetry
  and kennings  103, 246
  and Snorri Sturluson  52, 67–8,
  and wisdom  221, 238, 250, 255–7: *see also under* poetry
mythography  52, 204–5, 210

Nicodemus  201
*níð*; *see* curse
Niðaróss  116, 117
*Niðrstígninga saga*  201
Níels Jónsson  310
Nítíða  138–42
*Nítíða saga*  138–42, 143

*Norna-Gests þáttr*  262, 264, 315
North Atlantic  132, 140, 147, 150, 154, 157, 230, 243
Norway
  Icelanders' adventures in  158, 188, 191, 263
  literary tradition in  38, 201, 220, 301, 302
  manuscript export to  91
  migration from  129, 130, 132, 134, 137, 154, 272
  politics of  115–9, 204, 230, 242
  relationship with Iceland  121, 124, 129, 168
  royal court of  157
O'Connor, Ralph  33, 36, 266, 267–9, 303, 307, 310, 314, 323, 324
Oddi  82, 85
Óðinn, deity  135, 196–9, 209, 215, 218, 223, 240, 254
Oddr Snorrason  202
Oddr Unason  272, 279
*Oddrúnargrátr*  318; *see also* lament
Óláfr Haraldsson (inn helgi), King and saint  64, 95, 152, 154, 202, 205, 209, 262, 265, 316, 323
Óláfr Hildisson  79, 87
Óláfr 'pái' Hǫskuldarson  183, 187–8, 201
Óláfr Tryggvason, King  62, 77, 152, 154, 202, 222, 261, 262, 264, 323
Óláfr Þórðarson, hvítaskáld  68–70, 316
*Óláfs ríma Haraldssonar*  324
*Óláfs saga Tryggvasonar*  95, 96, 261, 265
*Óláfs saga Tryggvasonar en mesta*  261
Ólöf geisli  186, 190,
Old Danish  2
Old English  247, 249, 257
Old French  7, 38, 299, 301, 303, 313, 314; *see also* Anglo–Norman; French
Old High German  222, 247
Old Icelandic  4, 25, 70, 71, 151, 202, 285
Old Saxon  247
Old Swedish  2, 7, 119, 301, 303, 304, 310, 314, 324
orality  73–88, 163

*Orkneyinga saga* 152, 203, 230–1, 234–5, 239–43
*Orkneyinga þáttr* 315
Ormr Barreyjarskáld 62–3, 77
*\*Orms saga* 65, 77
*Orms þáttr Stórólfssonar* 107, 263, 264
*\*Ormsbók; see under* manuscript
Orning, Hans Jacob 10
Örvar-Oddr 92, 107, 318
*Örvar-Odds saga* 107, 314, 318
Óttarr svarti 319
Óttarr Þorvaldsson 279

*Páls leizla* 317
*Pamphilus* 307
panegyric 27; *see also* praise–poetry
parataxis 61, 188, 246
*Parcevals saga* 303, 307
parhomoeon 68–9; *see also* rhetoric
paronomasia 68–9; *see also* rhetoric
*Partalópa saga* 303, 307
*Passio Olavi* 117
Paul, saint 253, 280, 317
performativity 10, 88
*Perus saga meistara* 108
*Petrsdrápa* 207
Petrus Alphonsi 307
*Piers Plowman* 269
Phelpstead, Carl 36, 148–9, 154, 156, 203
*Physiologus* 219–20, 315
place 10, 127–44
Plácitus (Placitus, later St Eustace), saint 246
*Plácitusdrápa* 246
Plato 16, 18
*Poetic Edda* 57, 173, 197, 212, 324, 326
poetry; *see also* metre
 advice 86, 197, 215 217–8, 249, 252, 261, 265–9, 305, 317–21
 battle 11, 229–44, 319, 320
 eddic 9, 52, 67, 68, 103, 109, 116, 156, 175, 215, 245–258, 305
  and manuscripts 103
  definition of 318-19
  elegies 179
 love 185, 229, 316, 320
 memorialising 82, 232, 235, 244, 318, 320

 mythological 11, 27, 68, 116, 194–201, 209, 214, 216, 222–3, 246, 257: *see also* mythology; mythography
 praise 73, 75, 82, 86, 182, 193–4, 198–9, 201, 204, 205–6, 229, 245, 319, 320
 skaldic 40, 52, 63, 68–70, 75, 182–3, 219, 224, 229–44, 245, 246, 305
  and mythology 198–201, 204
  as mode 2, 7, 10, 34, 53, 66, 206, 209, 229–30, 315, 317, 319
  description of 67, 319–20
  development of 27–8, 205, 265
  historicity of 115–6, 117, 151, 175
  wisdom 196–7, 206, 212, 214–9, 221, 247–52, 254, 255, 256–7, 319
politics 115–25, 154
polyphony 154, 203
polysystem theory 24–26. 149, 154, 156, 245, 263; *see also* Even-Zohar, Itamar
Poole, Russell 11, 239–41
*Precepts* 249, 257
Priscianus 316
prophecy 195, 277, 281, 295, 319
*Prose Edda* 66, 68, 70, 121, 136, 166, 171 175, 195–9, 204–5, 317; *see also* Snorri Sturluson
 and poetic modes 6–7, 55
 generic affiliation of 109, 152
 manuscripts of 66, 196, 205, 324
prosimetrum 73–88, 194, 196, 203, 205, 212, 215, 238, 247, 261, 265, 270, 276
 and form 61-6
 and skaldic poetry 242–4; *see also under* poetry
 generic classification of 7, 40, 284, 318, 319
proverbs 211, 213–4, 219, 220, 280
Pseudo-Vatnshyrna; *see under* manuscript
Pugh, Tison 34

Quinn, Judy 10

Ráðný 251, 257
Rafn, Carl Christian 36, 107, 150

*ragna rǫk*   195, 196, 204
*Ragnarsdrápa*   200
*Rannveigar leizla*   253
*Reginsmál*   215
*Rémundar saga*   304, 307
revenge
  in eddic poetry   319; *see also under* poetry
  in the legendary sagas   156; *see also under* sagas
  in the sagas of Icelanders   42, 180–3, 187–8, 191, 272, 279, 280; *see also under* sagas
  in skaldic poetry   230–2, 235–8, 240–4; *see also under* poetry
Reykjahólar   61, 77, 81, 267, 323
  wedding at   61–5, 77–83, 267, 323
*Rezeptionsästhetik*   55; *see also* Jauss, Hans Robert
rhetoric
  as generic marker   35, 214–16, 316
  classical   49, 67–70
  use of   18, 174
rhyme   82, 224; *see also* rímur
  as form   68, 70, 175, 234, 320
*riddarasögur* (chivalric sagas); *see under* romance
riddle   197, 211, 213, 216, 249, 255, 319
  elements of   84, 199, 233, 254, 256
*Rígsþula*   195, 197
*rímur* (rhymed verse)   4, 37, 52, 91, 305, 308, 309–11; *see also* ballad
  description of   320–1
  development of   27–8. 302–3
  in manuscripts   102–4
*Rímur af Flóres og Blanzeflor*   310
Rǫgnvaldr, Earl of Mœrr   230–1, 235, 242
Rohrbach, Lena   149–50, 157
Rök stone   193
Roland, Frankish warrior   156; *see also chansons de geste*
*Roman de la Rose, Le*   269
romance   9, 11, 275, 299–311; *see also* literature, courtly
  as term   17, 299–301
  bridal-quest   41, 250, 256
  maiden king (*meykónga sögur*)   41, 43, 108, 138–43, 311, 314
  translations of   26, 38–9, 118–19, 151, 155, 183–4, 299–302; *see also* translation
*riddarasögur*
  and emotion   178, 183–6
  and geography   127–30, 138–44
  and hybridity   37, 43–4
  as generic term   1, 6, 52–4, 285, 301, 308–9
  chronotope of   151–2, 155–6
  definition of   314
  development of   4, 26, 28, 38–9, 118–19, 123, 299–305
  generic features of   35, 41, 43–4, 53, 127–30, 300–7, 311
  indigenous   5, 26, 61, 99, 102, 123, 183, 267, 307, 311, 314
  manuscripts of   5, 50, 99, 101–2, 107–9, 111, 124–5, 307–9
  translated   61, 99, 102, 183, 307, 311, 314
*Rómverja saga*   316
Rösli, Lukas   6, 9
Rothman, Joshua   283, 286, 297
Rowe, Elizabeth Ashman   11, 36, 172
runes   214, 250, 254
*Rúnzivals þáttr*   156; *see also chansons de geste*
Russia   35, 136, 147

Sæmundr inn suðreyski   277, 279, 280
Sævaldi   257
*Saga of Saint Óláfr*   154
sagas; *see also* entries for individual sagas
  chivalric; *see* romance
  classical   44, 103, 107, 177, 178, 191, 288
  contemporary (*samtíðarsögur*)   52, 210, 283, 285, 303
    as term   52, 150
    description of   313
    generic features of   288, 290–1
    historical context of   120–3, 132, 149–50, 153, 156
    relation to other genres   152, 263, 283, 303

heroic 52
kings' (*konungasögur*) 129, 210, 291
  as term 1, 6, 52–3, 54
  description of 313
  development of 27, 117, 121, 151–5, 203
  generic features of 35, 37, 53, 61, 163, 168
  manuscripts of 102, 124
  relation to other genres 148, 203, 270, 303, 305, 315
legendary (*fornaldarsögur*) 24, 34, 41, 151, 168, 259
  and form 61, 63, 205, 212, 247
  and geography 129, 135–7
  as term 9, 56
  description of 314
  development of 26, 122–3, 155–6, 173
  generic feature of 35–8, 127–9, 152, 170, 209–10
  manuscripts of 6, 50, 99, 101, 107, 109, 124–5
  relation to other genres 4, 41, 43, 106–7, 111, 261, 266–7, 269–70, 303, 305, 318
of bishops (*byskupasögur*) 11, 154, 163, 283–97, 303
  classification of 37, 109, 152, 283–5
  description of 314
  generic features of 290, 293–7
of Icelanders (*Íslendingasögur*) 9, 11, 73, 177, 210, 251, 271–81, 291
  and emotion 178–91
  and form 61, 212
  and geography 127–34, 137–8, 142–4, 157–8
  and literary history 4, 26–8
  as term 7, 52–3, 275
  chronotope of 128, 147–8, 152, 155, 157–8
  description of 315
  development of 163, 168–73, 203–4
  generic features of 35–7, 41–3, 53, 127–9, 271–6
  historical context of 120–4, 156, 303

hybridity of 24, 44–5, 111, 271, 281, 305
manuscripts of 5, 50, 91–9, 102, 103–7, 109, 125, 202
relation to *þættir* 264–5, 270, 281, 315
post–classical 44, 106, 107, 177, 185, 191
*Sálus saga ok Nikanors* 304
Sámr, dog 222, 224
*samtíðarsögur; see under* sagas
saints' lives 11, 283–97: *see also* hagiography
  as poetry 206–7, 320
  as term 303
  definition of 283–4, 288–90, 315
  development of 202–4, 245–6, 257
  generic features of 155, 202, 290, 292
  manuscript of 102, 109, 202
  relation to other genres 148, 149–52, 156–7, 201, 285, 303, 316
satire 219, 269, 284
Sävborg, Daniel 179, 180, 184
Saxo Grammaticus
  *Historia Danorum* 37
Scandinavia 48, 107, 109, 127, 193, 306
  development of literature in 2, 11, 27, 35, 212, 301–3
  history of 115–25, 232–4
  as place 135, 137
Schaeffer, Jean–Marie 32
Schier, Kurt 284–5, 291, 303
Schlauch, Margaret 305
Schnall, Jens Eike 221, 224
Schorn, Brittany 10, 55, 195, 196, 250
script, emotive 42, 179–83, 186–91
See, Klaus von 329
Seidel, Katharina 307
*senna* 196, 197, 236, 318
*Separate Saga of Saint Óláfr* 61, 203
sermon 71, 210, 245, 263, 315, 317
settlement; *see also landnám*
  and *Íslendingasögur* 35, 36, 129, 130, 134, 144, 278, 315; *see also under* sagas
  historical 63, 106, 131–2, 147–8, 151–5, 157

literary depiction of 82, 131, 133, 136, 190
Sif Rikhardsdottir 9, 56, 179–80
Sighvatr Sturluson 296
Sighvatr Þórðarson 320
Sigrdrífa, valkyrie 194, 209
*Sigrdrífumál* 194, 215 216, 218, 256
*Sigrgarðs saga frækna* 143, 304
*Sigurðar saga fóts* 307
*Sigurðar saga turnara* 307
*Sigurðar saga þǫgla* 41, 43 304, 311
Sigurðr konungsson 137–8
Sigurðr Fáfnisbani 194, 195, 212, 215, 264
Sigurðr þǫgli 311
Sigurður Nordal 21, 150, 151
skáld (poet) 67, 78, 115–16, 121, 182, 185, 190–1, 200, 264, 269, 317
*Skáldatal* 199
*Skáldskaparmál* 63, 66, 68, 136, 199, 204–5, 217, 317
Skálholt, bishop's see 168, 283, 293, 295, 296, 314, 323
Skalla-Grímr Kveldúlfsson 131, 133, 154, 158
*Skikkjurímur* 308, 321
*Skírnismál* 116, 318
*Skjöldunga saga* 314
Skúli Bárðarson, Duke 66, 122, 204
Snorri goði Þorgrímsson 107
Snorri Sturluson 67–8, 109, 121–2, 136–7, 154, 198, 204–5, 208, 217, 240–2, 295, 317, 323
*Sólarljóð* 206, 216, 245–58
*Snorra Edda*; see *Prose Edda*
Sobchack, Thomas 286, 289, 297
*Solomon and Saturn* II 249, 257
*Sonatorrek* 41, 182, 188, 199
*Sörla saga sterka* 268
sorrow 177, 181–3, 187–8: see also emotion
space 10, 129, 130–3, 135, 137, 139, 144, 145–59, 197, 200
 as generic marker 35, 146–7, 150–2, 161, 166
 private 181–7, 191
 public 180–89
*speculum principis* (mirror of princes) 316–17; see also *Konungs skuggsjá*
spell 191, 214, 215, 256, 257, 296
Steingerðr Þorkelsdóttir 185, 191, 320
Steinsland, Gro 116
Stevens, David 133
*Stjórn* 5
*Stjörnu-Odda draumr* 11, 259–70
Stjörnu-Oddi 266, 269
Stranda-Hneitir 82
*Strengleikar* 222, 303, 307, 313, 314
Sturla Þórðarson 119, 121–2, 133, 149, 271, 314
*Sturlubók* 132, 133, 276
*Sturlunga saga* 109, 120–3, 148, 152, 153, 283, 284–5, 313
Sturlungaöld (Age of Sturlungs) 168, 323
Sturlungs (Sturlungar) 27, 133, 168, 313, 323
Styrmir Kárason 265
*Svarfdœla saga* 124
Sverrir Sigurðarson, King 62, 65, 77, 117, 152, 323
Sverrir Jakobsson 166
Sverrir Tómasson 203
*Sverris saga* 117, 124, 153, 265
*Svipdagsmál* 255, 256, 257
Svipdagr 256
Sweden 3, 119, 135, 139, 140, 242, 268, 301, 324

taxonomy 1, 11, 35, 47, 49, 61, 70, 313–21
terminology 6, 9, 17, 28, 47–60, 212, 203, 308, 309
textuality 10, 73–88
textualisation 58–9, 74–7, 133, 142
*Theogony* 193
*Third Grammatical Treatise* 68–70, 86; see also treatise
Thomas Becket 202, 207
*Thómas saga erkibyskups* 309, 201–2; see also Thomas Becket
time 10, 35–6, 53, 61, 63, 146–8, 150–6, 161, 166, 197
Todorov, Tzvetan 34

*Tóka þáttr* 262
Torf–Einarr Rǫgnvaldsson of Orkney 10, 11, 230–44
Torfi H. Tulinius 10, 168
translation 2, 7, 38–9, 61, 118–19, 151, 155–6, 183, 201–3, 247, 289, 299, 301–2; see also under romance
treatise 49, 67–70, 75, 86, 101, 108–10, 198, 204–5, 208, 210, 312, 315, 316, 317; see also *Konungs skuggsjá*
  grammatical 109, 316: see also Third Grammatical Treatise
  poetic 75, 204–5, 208, 317; see also *Poetics* under Aristotle
Tristan and Iseult, story of 204–5, 208, 317
*Tristrams saga ok Ísöndar* 185, 303
*Trójumanna saga* 307, 316
Troy 136, 205
Tucker, John 223
Turville-Petre, Gabriel 203
Tynjanov, Yuri 24

Úlfljótr 166
*Úlfhams rímur* 321
Úlfr Uggason 200, 201
Unnr djúpúðga 133, 183

Vafþrúðnir, giant 196, 218
*Vafþrúðnismál* 196, 216, 218, 319
*Valla-Ljóts saga* 169
Vatnsdalr 272, 281
*Vatnsdœla saga* 11, 271–82
*Vatnshyrna; see under* manuscript
Venantius Fortunatus 206
*Veraldar saga* 166, 171, 316
vernacular 2, 17, 90, 201, 299
Vésteinn Ólason 277
Víðarr, deity 136
Víga–Glúmr 92
*Víglundar saga* 24, 111, 185, 186, 188, 189–91, 305
Víglundr Þorgrímsson 186, 190
*Víkarsbálkr* 318
*Viktors saga ok Blávus* 43, 307, 308
*Vilhjálms saga* 304
*Vilmundar saga viðutan* 304
*vísa* (stanza) 63–4, 77, 240, 247, 318, 319

*Visio Thurkilli* 254
*Visio Tnugdali* 253, 317
vision 139–43, 206, 210, 247–8, 249, 253–55, 257, 266–9, 292, 295, 317
  dream 249, 266–9, 317
*Vision of the Monk of Wenlock* 254
*Vǫlsunga saga* 107, 156, 314
*Vǫlundarkviða* 194
*Vǫluspá* 195, 256, 319, 324
*Vǫluspá in skamma* 197
Vries, Jan de 276, 278

Wanner, Kevin 11
Wellendorf, Jonas 203–4, 258
Werronen, Sheryl McDonald 138
Whetter, Kevin 229, 244, 247, 255, 257, 275
William, Duke of Normandy and Conqueror of England 242–4
wisdom 10, 193, 196–7, 209, 211–26, 246–7, 249–52, 254–7, 307, 319; see also knowledge; wisdom *under* poetry
Wittgenstein, Ludwig 263–4
Wolfram von Eschenbach 300

*ýkjusögur* (exaggerating sagas) 309
*Ynglinga saga* 129–30, 134–7, 140, 155
*Yngvars saga víðfǫrla* 36, 148, 313

Zeus, deity 193

*þáttr, þættir* 11, 40, 52, 61, 95–6, 102, 106 168, 210, 259–70, 315
  skald 261, 263–5, 269–70
*Þiðreks saga* 308
Þingeyri, monastery 281, 323
Þjazi, giant 196, 200, 204
Þjóðólfr ór Hvínir 200
*Þórðar saga hreðu* 98, 99
*Þórðar saga kakala* 121
Þórdís the seeress 277
Þórdís Súrsdóttir 214
Þórðr Rúfeyjarskáld 87
Þórðr Þorvaldsson 78–81, 84
*Þorgeirsdrápa* 320
Þorgils Oddason 76–86
*Þorgils saga ok Hafliða* 61–4, 66–7, 77–88, 323

Þorgrímr prúði Eiríksson   186, 190
Þórir hafrsþió Ingimundarson
    ins gamla   273, 278
Þorkell krafla Þorgrímsson   272,
    276–7, 278
*Þorláks saga helga*   154, 290, 293, 314
Þorlákr Þórhallsson of Skálholt   293,
    294
*Þorleifs þáttr jarlsskálds*   265
Þorleifur Björnsson   99
Þorleifur Hauksson   293
Þórmóðr Bersason
    Kólbrúnarskáld   320
Þórólfr sleggja   274, 277
Þórr, deity   193, 196, 197, 199–201, 273

*Þórsdrápa*   199, 206, 209, 320
Þorsteinn bæjarmagn   263
Þorsteinn drómundur   102, 158
Þorsteinn Ingimundarson ins
    gamla   272, 273, 276–80
Þorsteinn Ketilsson   272, 276–8
Þorsteinn Þorvarðsson   266
*Þorsteins draumr Síðu–Hallssonar*   265,
    270
*Þorsteins þáttr uxafóts*   261, 264
*Þorvalds þáttr víðförla*   281
Þráinn the berserkr   62, 77
Þrymr, giant   197

# Studies in Old Norse Literature

1  EMOTION IN OLD NORSE LITERATURE
   Translations, Voices, Contexts
   Sif Rikhardsdottir

2  THE SAINT AND THE SAGA HERO
   Hagiography and Early Icelandic Literature
   Siân E. Grønlie

3  DAMNATION AND SALVATION IN OLD NORSE LITERATURE
   Haki Antonsson

4  MASCULINITIES IN OLD NORSE LITERATURE
   Edited by Gareth Lloyd Evans and Jessica Clare Hancock

5  A CRITICAL COMPANION TO OLD NORSE LITERARY GENRE
   Edited by Massimiliano Bampi, Carolyne Larrington and Sif Rikhardsdottir

6  THE MAPPAE MUNDI OF MEDIEVAL ICELAND
   Dale Kedwards

7  FRENCH ROMANCE, MEDIEVAL SWEDEN AND THE
      EUROPEANISATION OF CULTURE
   Sofia Loden

8  DISCOURSE IN OLD NORSE LITERATURE
   Eric Shane Bryan

9  SAINTS AND THEIR LEGACIES IN MEDIEVAL ICELAND
   Edited by Dario Bullitta and Kirsten Wolf

10 KINSHIP IN OLD NORSE MYTH AND LEGEND
   Katherine Marie Olley

11 POETRY IN SAGAS OF ICELANDERS
   Margaret Clunies Ross

12  THE OLD TESTAMENT IN MEDIEVAL ICELANDIC TEXTS
    Translation, Exegesis and Storytelling
    Siân Elizabeth Grønlie

13  STORY, WORLD AND CHARACTER IN THE LATE
        ÍSLENDINGASÖGUR
    Rogue Sagas
    Rebecca Merkelbach

14  THE PAGANESQUE AND THE TALE OF VǪLSI
    Merrill Kaplan

15  THE LIVES AND DEATHS OF THE NORSE GODS
    Jonas Wellendorf

16  SKALDIC POETRY AS CHRISTIAN PROPAGANDA HONOURING
        BISHOP GUÐMUNDR ARASON IN FOURTEENTH-CENTURY
        ICELAND
    Margaret Clunies Ross

www.ingramcontent.com/pod-product-compliance
Lightning Source LLC
Chambersburg PA
CBHW050526300426
44113CB00012B/1973